Master Drawings from the Yale University Art Gallery

Master Drawings from the Yale University Art Gallery

Suzanne Boorsch and John Marciari

WITH CONTRIBUTIONS BY

Nicole Bensoussan, Alvin L. Clark, Jr., Susan Greenberg,

Margaret E. Hadley, Elisabeth Hodermarsky, Rena Hoisington,

Jan Leja, and Edgar Munhall

Yale University Art Gallery, New Haven

IN ASSOCIATION WITH

Yale University Press, New Haven and London

First published in 2006 by
Yale University Art Gallery
P.O. Box 208271
New Haven, CT 06520-8271
www.artgallery.yale.edu

in association with
Yale University Press
P.O. Box 209040
New Haven, CT 06520-9040
www.yalebooks.com

Published in conjunction with the exhibition *Master Drawings from the Yale University Art Gallery*, organized by the Yale University Art Gallery.

The John and Mable Ringling Museum of Art
Sarasota, Florida
19 October 2006–7 January 2007

The Blanton Museum of Art
Austin, Texas
1 June–12 August 2007

Yale University Art Gallery
New Haven, Connecticut
12 February–8 June 2008

This exhibition and publication are made possible by the Florence B. Selden Fund and the Samuel H. Kress Foundation, with additional support provided by Mr. and Mrs. Bruce B. Dayton, B.A. 1940, and Dr. and Mrs. Edmund P. Pillsbury, B.A. 1965.

Copyright © 2006 by Yale University. All rights reserved. This book may not be reproduced, in whole or in part, including illustrations, in any form (beyond that copying permitted by Sections 107 and 108 of the U.S. Copyright Law and except by reviewers for the public press), without written permission from the publishers.

Editor: Tiffany Sprague
Content Editor: Monica Rumsey

Designed by Leslie Fitch
Set in Filosofia type by Leslie Fitch
Printed and bound in Singapore by
   CS Graphics
Prepress by Professional Graphics,
   USA

Library of Congress Cataloging-in-Publication Data
Yale University. Art Gallery.
Master drawings from the Yale University Art Gallery / Suzanne Boorsch and John Marciari ; with contributions from Nicole Bensoussan . . . [et al.].
    p. cm.
Catalog of an exhibition organized by the Yale University Art Gallery, to be held at the John and Mable Ringling Museum of Art, Sarasota, Florida, Oct. 19, 2006–Jan. 7, 2007, at the Blanton Museum of Art, Austin, Texas, June 1–Aug. 12, 2007, and at the Yale University Art Gallery, New Haven, Connecticut, Feb. 12–June 8, 2008.
Includes bibliographical references and index.
ISBN-13: 978-0-300-11433-1 (hardcover : alk. paper)
ISBN-10: 0-300-11433-8 (hardcover : alk. paper)
ISBN-13: 978-0-89467-962-9 (pbk : alk. paper)
ISBN-10: 0-89467-962-7 (pbk : alk. paper)
1. Drawing, European—Exhibitions.
   2. Drawing—Connecticut—New Haven—Exhibitions. 3. Yale University. Art Gallery—Exhibitions. I. Boorsch, Suzanne. II. Marciari, John. III. John and Mable Ringling Museum of Art. IV. Blanton Museum of Art. V. Title.
NC225.Y35 2006
741.94074′7468—dc22   2005036101

10 9 8 7 6 5 4 3 2 1

Cover illustrations: (front) detail of cat. no. 43; (back) cat. no. 52

Frontispiece: detail of cat. no. 48

Pages x–xi (left to right): details of cat. nos. 12 recto, (top) 64, (bottom) 47, 45, and 24

Pages 34–35 (left to right): details of cat. nos. 36, (top) 25 recto, (bottom) 46, 20, (top) 44, (bottom) 38, 71, and 31

Contents

VI Director's Foreword

VIII Acknowledgments

1 Introduction

37 Note on the Catalogue

38 CATALOGUE

247 Watermarks

255 Bibliography

281 Index

291 Artists in the Catalogue

293 Photography Credits

Director's Foreword

A propitious group of circumstances came together to bring about this traveling exhibition of old master European drawings from the collection of the Yale University Art Gallery. First, a long-planned restoration of the Art Gallery's Louis I. Kahn building meant that there would be no space available for special exhibitions of prints, drawings, or photographs during the time of our landmark's renovation. It thus occurred to Suzanne Boorsch—who, in 2000, had taken the position of Curator of Prints, Drawings, and Photographs at the Art Gallery, and whose particular interest is in the art of the European Renaissance—that the period of Kahn renovation would be an opportune moment to organize a tour of a selection of drawings from the collection, to be seen in different parts of the country, and then to be shown in the renovated Art Gallery upon their return. John Marciari, now the Nina and Lee Griggs Associate Curator of Early European Art, joined the staff in the summer of 2002 as the Florence B. Selden Fellow, with the express aim of working on the project. John had recently received his Ph.D. from Yale with a specialty in sixteenth-century Italian art and had already worked extensively with the drawing collection in the course of his graduate studies. The resulting exhibition, *Master Drawings from the Yale University Art Gallery*, is one of three collections-based exhibitions planned for national travel between 2006 and 2009. The other two exhibitions will focus on Yale's famed Société Anonyme Collection of modernist works and highlights from Yale's unparalleled collection of American art.

The Art Gallery had a strong collection of drawings at the time this exhibition was conceived, but once the exhibition was scheduled to take place, Suzanne and John put special effort into seeking out drawings that would broaden its range and did so with singular success: of the eighty-four works in the exhibition, eighteen have been acquired since 2000. Many American collections have a dearth of German drawings, and Yale's is no exception, so the addition of the *Circe* by Jörg Breu the Elder, the dramatic *Crucifixion* attributed to Johann Kellerthaler II, and *The Entombment of Christ* by Hermann Weyer have made a significant difference in this area. Drawings from Spain have also been underrepresented in the collection, so the large *Last Supper* by Diego López de Escuriaz begins to fill that gap. The collection has far fewer drawings from seventeenth- and eighteenth-century Italy and France than from the Netherlands, but the *Study of a Seated Old Man* by Domenichino and the *Medea* by

Pierre Monier begin to redress that balance, while Jean-Honoré Fragonard's spirited illustration of a scene from Ariosto's *Orlando Furioso* epitomizes all that is delightful about the French Rococo. Coincidentally, the first and last drawings in the catalogue—which is organized chronologically—are recent gifts to the Art Gallery by Yale alumni. The *Lion*, by an anonymous Venetian artist of the fifteenth century, was donated by Edmund P. (Ted) Pillsbury, B.A. 1965, and *Notre Dame of Paris Seen from the Quai de la Tournelle*, made by Johan Barthold Jongkind in 1863, was a gift from Bruce Dayton, B.A. 1940, and his wife, Ruth. We greatly appreciate the kind patronage and continued support of both of these distinguished alumni. Ted, who once served as the Art Gallery's Curator of European Art, and then as Director of the Yale Center for British Art, and Bruce, who strongly sustained the Art Gallery as a member of its Governing Board and a major benefactor, are helping to make this presentation of Yale's master drawings possible, something all of my colleagues and I are very pleased and proud to acknowledge.

It is also a source of great pleasure to me that this exhibition will be shown in institutions with collections that admirably complement the works in the exhibition. The John and Mable Ringling Museum in Sarasota, Florida, which has long been known for its outstanding collection of Renaissance and Baroque paintings, also holds a lesser-known collection of old master drawings. The Blanton Museum of Art in Austin, Texas, has recently acquired major collections of old master paintings, sculpture, drawings, and prints and now ranks as one of the prime repositories of such works in the American Southwest. Both of these museums, like the Yale University Art Gallery, are also teaching institutions, with ties, respectively, to Florida State University and the University of Texas.

I thus wish to express my enthusiastic thanks to John Wetenhall, Director of the Ringling Museum, and Jessie Otto Hite, Director of the Blanton Museum, both good friends, for collaborating with the Art Gallery to bring *Master Drawings from the Yale University Art Gallery* to their campus and public audiences.

Jock Reynolds
The Henry J. Heinz II Director
Yale University Art Gallery

Acknowledgments

In preparing a catalogue with such disparate material as is found here, with artists who represent four centuries and five or more countries, the authors inevitably rely on the resources and suggestions of colleagues around the world. We would therefore like to acknowledge our professional debts and offer sincere thanks to: Morton Abromson, Maryan Ainsworth, Christiane Andersson, Allan Appel, Carmen Bambach, Stephen Bann, David Becker, Sylvie Béguin, Eric Bertin, David Bindman, Rhea Blok, Jean Boorsch, Sylvie Brame, Julian Brooks, Hugo Chapman, Miles Chappell, Randolf Coleman, Dominique Cordellier, Elaine Evans Dee, Mario Di Giampaolo, Toni Dorfman, Marie-Anne Dupuy-Vachey, Molly Faries, Richard Field, Jan Piet Filedt Kok, Jay Fisher, Jeffrey Fontana, Peter Fuhring, Aprile Gallant, James Ganz, Walter Gibson, Laura Giles, Michael Goodison, Florian Härb, Jonathan Harrison, Egbert Haverkamp-Begemann, Mary Elizabeth Hellyer, Alona Horn, Linda Jansen, W. McAllister Johnson, Thomas DaCosta Kaufmann, Richard Kendall, Wouter Kloek, Shelley Langdale, Anne-Marie Logan, Peter Lukehart, Julia Marciari Alexander, Natalya Markova, Thomas McGrath, Jamie Montgomery, Jane Munro, Nancy Ward Neilson, Mary Newcome Schleier, Joan Nissman, Patrick Noon, Nadine Orenstein, Elizabeth Pilliod, Madeleine Pinault Sørensen, Michiel Plomp, Pavel Preiss, Sue Welsh Reed, Anne Röver-Kann, Martin Royalton-Kisch, Sagan Sanderson, Jane Sargent, Dorit Schäfer, David Scrase, Ann Sievers, Marten Snickäre, Nancy Sojka, Bent Sørensen, Perrin Stein, David Stone, Annette Strech, Gary Tinterow, Jane Turner, Ian Verstegen, Mia Weiner, Dennis Weller, Catherine Whistler, and Jon Whiteley.

We would also like to recognize the contributions of our curatorial colleagues at the Yale University Art Gallery, including Laurence Kanter, Susan Matheson, and William Metcalf, in addition to Susan Greenberg and Elisabeth Hodermarsky, who contributed entries to the catalogue. Anna Hammond, Deputy Director for Education, Programs, and Public Affairs, has overseen the project with great solicitude, and we especially want to express our appreciation for the encouragement and support of our director, Jock Reynolds, throughout the several years the exhibition and catalogue have been in preparation.

Others on staff at the Art Gallery have provided assistance of various sorts. All of the drawings in the exhibition have been examined by Theresa Fairbanks Harris and her staff at the paper conservation lab: Abigail Armistead, Amanda Gould, Dong-eun Kim, and especially Heather Hendry, who deserves particular thanks for her work in photographing the watermarks. Diana Brownell rematted and framed all of the drawings in the exhibition. Mark Aronson and Zelda Roland did conservation work on the frames. Susan Cole, John ffrench, and Janet Zullo Sullivan have been responsible for the new digital photography of the drawings. In the print room of the Art Gallery, Mimi Cole, Suzanne Greenawalt, and Russell Lord provided invaluable administrative assistance, and a number of graduate student interns—Eva Allan, Nicole Bensoussan, Margaret E. Hadley, Suzanne Karr Schmidt, and Vanessa Wolf—helped with the research on the drawings; two of them are also authors of catalogue entries herein. Allison Peil and Linsey LaFrenier in the Department of Early European Art also provided assistance on many matters, including the task of organizing the photographs used in the publication. The Art Gallery's archivist, Elise K. Kenney, has been a constant resource. Registrars Lynne Addison and the late Jennifer Bossman helped both with the research on the history of the collection for the catalogue and with the organization of the traveling exhibition.

We are especially grateful to Joanna Weber at the John and Mable Ringling Museum of Art, Sarasota, Florida, and Jonathan Bober and Cheryl Snay at the Blanton Museum of Art, Austin, Texas, for their enthusiastic assistance in bringing this exhibition to their museums.

Finally, this book is a far better product for the editorial and production assistance of Tiffany Sprague, at the Art Gallery; Patricia Fidler, Mary Mayer, and Kate Zanzucchi, at Yale University Press; copyeditors Claudia DePalma and Monica S. Rumsey; and for Leslie Fitch's design. Our sincere thanks to all the above, and our apologies to anyone we may have unintentionally omitted.

Suzanne Boorsch
Curator of Prints, Drawings, and Photographs

John Marciari
The Nina and Lee Griggs Associate Curator of Early European Art

Introduction

John Marciari and *Suzanne Boorsch*

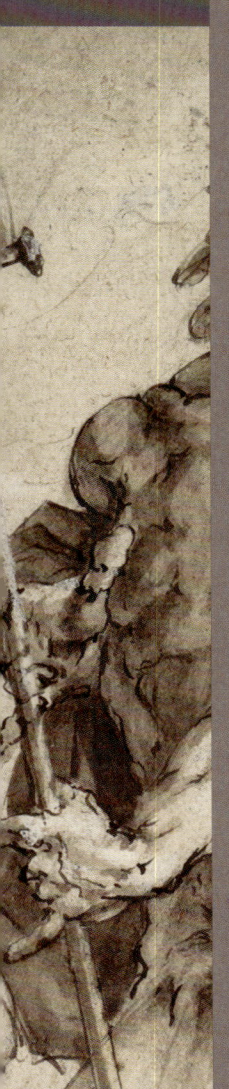

Master Drawings from the Yale University Art Gallery is the first general study of the old master drawings in the Yale University Art Gallery since the publication in 1970 of Egbert Haverkamp-Begemann and Anne-Marie Logan's *European Drawings and Watercolors in the Yale University Art Gallery 1500–1900*.[1] There have, of course, been many exhibitions drawn from the collection in the intervening thirty-six years, to say nothing of the discussion of individual drawings in books, articles, and the catalogues of exhibitions held elsewhere, but this will be the first exploration of the breadth and depth of Yale's collection of earlier European drawings since 1970. This group, including nearly 1,500 sheets, is still one of the least well known among the Art Gallery's holdings, and it has received far less scholarly or public attention than have Yale's justifiably famous collections of European modernism and of American paintings, drawings, and decorative arts. For this reason, above all, we have chosen to limit this exhibition and catalogue to "pre-Impressionist" or "pre-modern" European drawings.[2]

Because the examples featured in this exhibition catalogue represent only slightly more than five percent of this group of 1,500 drawings, the present volume can make no claim to be a complete revision of the 1970 catalogue. The drawings selected for exhibition and discussed at length here, however, do provide a representative sample, both of key acquisitions since 1970 and of important drawings that have long been in New Haven. The exhibition does not include merely the most finished or most impressive of Yale's drawings (although many finished and impressive drawings are to be found here), but rather a group that reflects the collection as a whole. The selection thus has drawings from all stages of the creative process and drawings for a wide variety of purposes—works preparatory for prints, stained glass, tapestries, and embroideries, as well as the more commonly expected studies for paintings. Some drawings are finished works in themselves, and as such reflect the rise of drawing as an independent art form, one to be collected; indeed, many comments on the history of collecting and on the means by which drawings come down to us can be found in the catalogue entries.

While Yale still lacks drawings by some of the key figures in the history of European draftsmanship—Leonardo da Vinci, Michelangelo, Albrecht Dürer, Raphael, Titian, and Rembrandt come immediately to mind—there are drawings in this exhibition and in the collection at large that reflect closely the exemplars those figures presented to their contemporaries. Those interested in Raphael, for instance, might look to numerous works by his close followers, including Polidoro da Caravaggio, Giulio Romano, and Perino del Vaga (cat. nos. 3, 9, and 12), and a student of Rembrandt is directed to our drawing attributed to Ferdinand Bol (cat. no. 50). On the other hand, in certain areas—the French eighteenth and nineteenth centuries, for example—the collection boasts works by an unbroken succession of major figures—Jean-Antoine Watteau, François Boucher, Jean-Baptiste Greuze, Jean-Honoré Fragonard, Théodore Géricault, Jean-Auguste-Dominique Ingres, Eugène Delacroix, Edgar Degas, and Honoré Daumier (cat. nos. 62, 63, 69, 72, 76, 77, 79, 82, and 83). It is hoped that this exhibition and catalogue will serve not only as an enticement to scholars, but also, for a broader public, as an introduction to the field of master drawings.

The Haverkamp-Begemann and Logan catalogue of 1970, long out of print, remains the primary reference for Yale's drawing collection and the source of much that follows.[3] This introduction seeks to review the history of the collection and to demonstrate how the progress of scholarship leads continually to the revision of any catalogue, even one as magisterial as the 1970 publication. The final section of this introduction aims to provide an overview of the exhibition by casting the

1 | School of Rembrandt (Govaert Flinck?), *Woman with a Tray*, early 1640s.

works in a narrative that examines some of the central themes and trends in the history of European draftsmanship.

In 1832, the same year that the Yale University Art Gallery was founded, it also received its first drawing, a *Self-Portrait* by Major John André, made in 1780, on the eve of his execution as a British spy. That work was given mainly as a historical document; it was not until 1890, at the prompting of John Ferguson Weir, the first director of the Yale School of the Fine Arts, that Yale would acquire a group of European drawings for their art-historical significance.[4] That first set of drawings came from the collection of Weir's recently deceased father, Robert Walter Weir, who had taught drawing at West Point from 1832 to 1876.[5] However estimable the intentions behind that purchase, few of the drawings lived up to the lofty attributions they had been given. A drawing said to be one of Michelangelo's studies for the Sistine *Last Judgment*, for example, is instead a workshop copy of one of Federico Zuccaro's studies for his *Last Judgment* in the cupola of the Duomo at Florence.[6] Yet a drawing of *Phaeton* (cat. no. 57), which Weir catalogued not entirely implausibly as by Charles Le Brun, has been shown to be by Jean Jouvenet, a pupil of Le Brun whose career was nearly as distinguished as that of his master. The Weir "Correggio," although once accepted as the work of the master by Corrado Ricci, was rejected by A. E. Popham and subsequent scholars; the drawing remains, nonetheless, typical of the quintessential Renaissance approach to designing compositions through the act of sketching.[7] Similarly, Weir's "Rembrandt" (fig. 1) is not by the master but by a close follower, perhaps Govaert Flinck, and is entirely typical of drawings from Rembrandt's school.[8] Other admirable drawings from the Weir purchase include a *Destruction of Sodom* originally attributed to Pietro Testa but later attributed by Pierre Rosenberg to Jean-Baptiste Corneille (fig. 2).[9]

In 1904, another work attributed to Correggio entered the collection, a large cartoon of the *Virgin and Child with Saint John the Baptist* (fig. 3).[10] Originally lent to the Art Gallery in 1875, the drawing also had Weir connections, as it came from the

2 | Jean-Baptiste Corneille, *Destruction of Sodom*, late seventeenth century.

collection of Captain and Mrs. Bradford R. Alden, who were, respectively, the godfather and the principal patron of Julian Alden Weir, John Ferguson Weir's half-brother.[11] Correspondence in the Art Gallery's archive reveals that there was some competition between the Weir brothers for the cartoon, which Julian Alden Weir wanted for the National Academy of Design.[12] The attribution to Correggio is, of course, unsustainable, and with this recognition in the 1940s, the drawing, which had hung in the main gallery of Italian paintings at the opening of Egerton Swartwout's new building in 1928, was removed to storage and forgotten. "Rediscovered" in 2002, the drawing is here published perhaps for the first time.[13] A rare and fascinating object, the cartoon also remains a scholarly and connoisseurial puzzle: suggested dates for the work, for example, have ranged from the mid-sixteenth to the mid-eighteenth century[14]—but the efforts taken to ensure its acquisition in 1904 reflect the ambitious plans that John Ferguson Weir established for the Art Gallery.

Gifts from Yale alumni constitute the next group of important acquisitions. In 1930, Warren H. Lowenhaupt, B.A. 1914, presented the fifty-three drawings (and eighty-two prints) collected by Frederick Benjamin Kaye, M.A. 1916. The quality of Kaye's collection was uneven, as was the case with most early American collections of European drawings. Many of the works remain anonymous, but the gift did include an interesting small group of drawings by French artists of the later seventeenth and eighteenth centuries, including Antoine Dieu, Noel-Nicolas Coypel, and Philippe-

3 | Anonymous Italian artist, *Virgin and Child with Saint John the Baptist*, last quarter of the sixteenth century(?).

4 | Philippe-Louis Parizeau, *The Blind Belisarius*, ca. 1780–85(?).

Louis Parizeau (fig. 4).[15] A strong group of British drawings came as part of the Kaye gift, as well as with the Edwin Austin Abbey Memorial Collection that arrived in 1937; all of the Art Gallery's British drawings, however, were transferred to the Yale Center for British Art upon its opening in 1977.[16]

Robert Lehman, B.A. 1913, the large part of whose collection was donated to the Metropolitan Museum of Art in 1975, had in 1941 presented to the Art Gallery fourteen drawings by Giovanni Battista Tiepolo (fig. 5),[17] along with sheets by Giovanni Battista's sons Domenico and Lorenzo (cat. no. 67), Luca Cambiaso, Bernard van Orley (cat. no. 4), and others. In 1945, Mrs. John Hill Morgan donated the collection of drawings owned by her late husband, who until shortly before his death in 1945 had been the Curator of American Painting at the Art Gallery. Alongside important American art, the Morgan gift brought Dutch sheets ranging from the seventeenth to the nineteenth centuries.[18] More Dutch drawings, mainly of military or marine subjects, came to the Art Gallery with the transfer from Yale's Sterling Library of a gift from Mrs. Cornelius Vanderbilt.

Between 1929 and 1957, Edward B. Greene, B.A. 1900, presented Yale with works from his extraordinary collection of portrait prints and drawings.[19] In addition to the works by Joseph Vivien and Hyacinthe Rigaud in this exhibition (cat. nos. 58, 59), other notable portrait drawings from Greene are by Cornelius Visscher[20] and Ottavio Leoni.[21] Another Leoni (fig. 6)[22] was a gift in 1952 from John S. Thacher, B.A.

5 | Giovanni Battista Tiepolo, *Standing Male Seen from Below*, 1740s.

6 | Ottavio Leoni, *"La Damigella d'Angiò,"* 1616.

1927, who also gave a lively watercolor by Antoine-Louis Barye, a watercolor by Manet after his painting (also at Yale) of *A Woman in Spanish Costume*, and the double-sided sheet by Henry Fuseli exhibited here (cat. no. 73).

Edith Malvina K. Wetmore, best known as a patron of the arts in connection with Chateau-sur-Mer, her house in Newport, Rhode Island, presented three drawings by Constantin Guys (cat. no. 81) in 1945, the first of many brilliant works especially by nineteenth-century French artists that would come to Yale from her collection; her bequest in 1966 also included the drawings by Ingres and Daumier in this exhibition (cat. nos. 77, 83), as well as drawings by Georges Seurat, Gustave Caillebotte, Auguste Rodin, and other artists working later than the scope of this catalogue. Other French drawings of the early and mid-nineteenth century came from Frank Altschul, B.A. 1908, who presented the gallery with nineteen drawings by Paul Gavarni, a complement to his gift of more than three thousand prints by that artist,[23] and from J. Watson Webb, B.A. 1907, and Electra Havemeyer Webb, who in 1942 gave three pastels by Jean-François Millet.

The core of the Art Gallery's collection of European drawings, however, arrived in 1961, when the drawings originally assembled in the early eighteenth century by John Percival, 1st Earl of Egmont (1683–1748), were transferred from the Yale Library, which had received them in 1957 from an anonymous donor.[24] Consisting of 543 drawings bound in six folio volumes arranged alphabetically according to

INTRODUCTION 7

7 | Jan Brueghel the Elder, *Village Meeting Place under Two Trees*, ca. 1612.

attribution, the gift immediately established the Yale print room as one of the foremost university collections in America, with something approaching a universal survey of European drawings.[25] This is not to say that every work in the Egmont Albums was a masterpiece. Where there was no old signature or inscription with an attribution, one had been added—and as might be expected, many of the Egmont attributions are best described as optimistic[26]—but the volumes nonetheless contain a remarkable wealth of material. Eighteen drawings in this exhibition are Egmont works, including the masterpiece by Bellange (cat. no. 34) that is surely one of the rarest and most valuable of the drawings in Yale's collection. The collection is particularly strong in Flemish drawings of the seventeenth century, with sheets by Jan Brueghel (fig. 7)[27] and Abraham Bloemaert (fig. 8),[28] among others. Works such as these were interleaved with sheets of far less quality, but the depth of the collection provides examples by which students might study the differences between an original drawing, a workshop version, and a later copy, as, for example, when they see juxtaposed the Egmont *Crucifixion* attributed to Hendrick de Clerck and a second version of the drawing acquired in 1978.[29]

8 | Abraham Bloemaert, *The Annunciation*, 1610.

The Egmont collection seems to have been assembled in the first two or three decades of the eighteenth century. Some drawings bear the collection stamps of Prosper Henry Lankrink (1628–1692) and were thus probably acquired in London, either directly from his posthumous sales in 1693 and 1694 or else soon after; at least one drawing (cat. no. 49) has the marks of the physician and collector Peter Sylvester, who died in London in 1718.[30] For the great majority of sheets, however, there is no indication whatsoever of their provenance. During his Grand Tour of Italy in 1705–07, Egmont purchased paintings, drawings, bronzes, medals, casts, and books with the intention of founding an academy of painters in Ireland, but French privateers confiscated this material on its way to Ireland.[31] Egmont's lifelong friend Bishop George Berkeley helped to console Egmont for this loss by acting as his agent in the acquisition of art during Berkeley's own Grand Tour of 1716–21.[32] Egmont's finest Italian drawings might, in fact, be those acquired by Berkeley. A broad look at the material in the albums suggests that Egmont himself bought from sales in Britain or the Low Countries, but there is no way to prove this speculation. He may have been aware that many of his drawings were copies, but, on reflection, this would seem unlikely. At a time when a thorough connoisseurship of drawings was a lengthy and hard-won process, collectors like Egmont are at least as much to be admired for the strength and range of their enthusiasm as to be faulted for lacunae in their knowledge. The dealers or agents from whom Egmont acquired drawings may not have been much more knowledgeable, although there is also the possibility that he was deliberately duped by a dealer or agent, for some of the copies in the albums seem to have been produced close to the time when he acquired the drawings. A sheet attributed by the Egmont hand to Michelangelo, for example, is a copy of a drawing at Chatsworth that was acquired by the 2nd Duke of Devonshire around the year 1700.[33] Faint black chalk framing lines on the Yale drawing correspond to the trimmed dimensions of the Chatsworth sheet, suggesting that the Yale copy might have been produced in the eighteenth century, presumably shortly before the original drawing was sold to Devonshire.

Attributions and copies aside, another aspect of the Egmont drawings that must be noted here, as it was by Haverkamp-Begemann and Logan, is that a number of the sheets were "embellished" by a later (and unskilled) hand that strengthened shadows and the occasional detail. Frequently, these embellishments are in the same gray or brownish wash as the framing lines on the drawings' mounts, making the task of identifying the later retouching easier. Two examples, also singled out in the 1970 catalogue, are the otherwise handsome *Vertumnus and Pomona* by Gerbrand van den Eeckhout (fig. 9) and *Hagar and the Angel* by Pieter Lastman, both of which have been somewhat disfigured by patches of flat gray wash.[34]

Gifts of drawings continue to add to the collection. Prof. and Mrs. Robert L. Herbert presented ten drawings by Jean-François Millet in 1970, supplementing the thirteen drawings by that artist already in the collection.[35] Ten Italian drawings came in 1975 from the Chase family of Waterbury, including the fine sheet by Baccio Bandinelli (cat. no. 2), while a number of eighteenth- and nineteenth-century

9 | Gerbrand van den Eeckhout, *Vertumnus and Pomona*, 1640–45.

French drawings were among the many works of art given by George Dix, B.A. 1934, M.A. 1942, during the 1970s and '80s. Similarly, the gifts to the Art Gallery by Mary C. and James W. Fosburgh, B.A. 1933, consisted mainly of American drawings, many of them by Fosburgh, but also brought an endowment, the funds from which helped secure for Yale the magnificent drawing by Claude Lorrain (cat. no. 48). The final drawing in this exhibition, a watercolor view of Notre Dame in Paris by Johan Barthold Jongkind (cat. no. 84), is a gift from Ruth and Bruce Dayton, B.A. 1940, whose generous support of the Art Gallery has concentrated on other areas of the collection, especially Asian and modern art. Other gifts are notable not for their quantity, but for the quality of a single given work; the 1981 gift of a sheet from Domenico Tiepolo's Punchinello series (cat. no. 74), from Mrs. Paul Wick and her children, in honor of Paul Wick, B.A. 1912, is a prime example.

As much as the Art Gallery has relied on generous donations from alumni and from other patrons, any collection based on gifts, however generous, would inevitably include a rather haphazard selection of works. Purchases can extend the collection, fill in gaps, or build upon randomly acquired strengths; other drawings might be bought simply because their particular rarity, quality, and interest are self-evident, regardless of their relationship to works already in the collection. Fortunately, the Art Gallery has been well endowed with purchase funds to make acquisitions of all types possible. The funds of the Griggs, Hanna, and Stoddard families, while not limited to the purchase of drawings, have been used to buy nine of the works in the exhibition. The Frederick M. Clapp, B.A. 1901, M.A. 1911, Fund, established in 1985, is dedicated to the purchase of Italian drawings from the fifteenth to eighteenth centuries; four of the drawings catalogued here (cat. nos. 3, 12, 39, and 70) were purchased with this fund.[36]

The greatest legacy to the print room, rivaling or even surpassing the gift of the Egmont Albums, is that of Everett V. Meeks, B.A. 1901, who served as professor and dean of the Yale School of the Fine Arts from 1920 to 1947. Upon his death in 1956, Meeks provided an endowment for the purchase of works on paper, with the sole stipulation that the works must have been created at least fifty years before the date of their acquisition. Occasional purchases of drawings had been made up to the 1950s, but most of the drawings to enter the collection were anonymous sheets of mainly academic interest. The Meeks Fund, however, enabled acquisitions on a grander scale and was put to immediate use: seven drawings, including Raymond Lafage's *Moses Receiving the Tablets of the Law* (cat. no. 56), were purchased in 1956, followed soon

10 | Jacob Matham, *Mercury with the Heads of an Old and Young Man*, 1599.

after with sheets by Gillot (cat. no 61), Géricault, Delacroix, Millet (cat. no. 80), and other artists of similar renown. Indeed, thirty-nine of the drawings in this exhibition, and scores of additional drawings in the collection (as well as hundreds of prints and photographs), were purchased with funds from the Meeks endowment, which remains one of the greatest and most constructive gifts in the Art Gallery's history.

Purchases also inevitably reflect the preferences and specializations of the curators responsible for them. In 1960, Egbert Haverkamp-Begemann, formerly the curator of drawings at the Boijmans Van Beuningen Museum in Rotterdam, was named the Art Gallery's Curator of Drawings and Prints.[37] In addition to his catalogue of the collection, Haverkamp-Begemann was responsible for buying a remarkable series of drawings between 1960 and 1968. These include fifteen sheets selected for this exhibition, a testament to his discerning eye. Alan Shestack, another specialist in European art, was the next Curator of Drawings and Prints and with Anne-Marie Logan, who remained on as Assistant Curator, continued the work that Haverkamp-Begemann had begun, through both exhibitions and the acquisition of drawings by Jacob Matham (fig. 10),[38] Jacques Callot (cat. no. 37), François Boucher (cat. no. 63), and others.

Following Shestack's appointment as Director of the Art Gallery in 1971, James Burke was named Curator of Drawings and Prints.[39] He purchased the sheet attributed to Bol in this exhibition (cat. no. 50) and other drawings by a range of artists including Charles-Joseph Natoire, Anne-Louis Girodet de Roucy-Trioson, Charles Meryon, Jean-Léon Gérôme, and Jean-Baptiste Carpeaux (fig. 11).[40] Furthermore, during Burke's tenure in the Print Room, the Art Gallery's collection of Italian drawings grew significantly through purchases proposed by Edmund P. Pillsbury, B.A. 1965, a specialist in Italian drawings who served first as Curator of European Painting at the Art Gallery and then as Director of the Yale Center for British Art. Since leaving the Yale museums, Pillsbury has continued to enrich the collection through gifts, including three works in this exhibition (cat. nos. 1, 18, and 43). Anne-Marie Logan, whose curatorial expertise also contributed much to the collection, has likewise

INTRODUCTION 13

11 | Jean-Baptiste Carpeaux, *Allegory of France, Study for France Enlightening the World and Protecting Agriculture and Science*, 1863.

presented a number of drawings in recent years, including the two studies by Theodoor van Thulden exhibited here (cat. no. 44).[41] The acquisitions made by Richard S. Field, Curator of Prints, Drawings, and Photographs from 1979 until 2000, concentrated on old master prints, photographs, and contemporary art—collections that have continued to grow through significant gifts as well as purchases. Nonetheless, he was responsible for acquiring the drawings by Perino del Vaga, Federico Zuccaro, Claude Lorrain, Ubaldo Gandolfi, and Bartolomeo Pinelli in this exhibition (cat. nos. 12, 19, 48, 70, and 75).

With Suzanne Boorsch's appointment as Curator in 2000, the drawings collection began to receive increased attention once again as the present exhibition was conceived. John Marciari, a specialist in Italian paintings and drawings, returned to the Art Gallery to work on the project, first as the Florence B. Selden Fellow in the Department of Prints, Drawings, and Photographs, and then as the Associate Curator of Early European Art. Just as Haverkamp-Begemann and Logan's cataloguing project led to acquisitions, so too this exhibition has engendered an acquisitive period for the field of old master drawings at Yale, and sixteen of the drawings presented here have been purchased in the past five years.

Yale's collection continues to be enriched, one might say, not only by new acquisitions, but also by new scholarship that elucidates the attribution, function, or context of works already in the collection. When Haverkamp-Begemann and Logan wrote in the latter half of the 1960s, many of the artists whose drawings they catalogued had not yet been the subjects of scholarly monographs. In light of the state of research at that time, the accomplishment of their catalogue cannot be overstated. Of the 543 drawings in the Egmont Collection, for example, 361 were reattributed by Haverkamp-Begemann and Logan, while still others were de-attributed and classified as anonymous. The 1970 catalogue, as noted above, remains a model for a collection catalogue and the primary reference for any work on Yale's collection. Nonetheless, with the scholarship of the past thirty-five years—to say nothing of the thousands of photographs and the search engines available on the Internet—there is much that might be added to the information provided in the older catalogue. A full account of all those revisions is beyond the scope of the present work, but a sampling of them might demonstrate the ways in which Yale's collection, like indeed all collections, continues to evolve though new research.

Not least significant among the new information available is evidence to reconsider questions of attribution. Thus, for example, the removal of the backing sheet from *The Mocking of Christ* by the so-called Master of 1527 (cat. no. 5), making it possible to see the long inscription there in Dutch and French, has both confirmed a probable link with two drawings in the Ashmolean Museum in Oxford and at the same time reinforced doubt about the attribution to the same hand, made in 1939, of another large group of drawings, in a similar but nonetheless distinct style.[42] Likewise, information uncovered in the course of writing an entry for this catalogue on the drawings by Theodoor van Thulden (cat. no. 44), made it clear that another drawing in the collection, long attributed to van Thulden, is actually the work of Abraham van Diepenbeeck.[43] An *Ornamental Design* previously attributed, albeit with reservations, to Jean Berain was recognized by Elaine Evans Dee as the work of Gilles-Marie Oppenord (cat. no. 60).

Many other attributions and re-attributions might be cited for drawings not included in this exhibition. A *David and Saint Cecilia* purchased and catalogued as the work of Frans Floris was later recognized by Julius Held and Carl Van de Velde as the work of Crispin van den Broeck.[44] An elegant, informal study of a *Standing Young Man* (fig. 12),[45] attributed by the Egmont hand to Antonio Tempesta, is another example. Reascribed to Jacopo da Empoli by Haverkamp-Begemann and Logan, this drawing was the subject of some discussion by the Florentine specialists who visited the Art Gallery in 1994 on the occasion of the exhibition *Vasari's Florence*. Though Alessandro Cecchi's suggested attribution to Jacopo Zucchi was not accepted by all, it can now be confirmed, for the drawing is here identified as a preparatory study for the figure of Saint Ansanus in Zucchi's altarpiece for the church of San Francesco, Siena.[46]

Besides the scholars mentioned above, the contributions of many pre- or post-doctoral interns and fellows working in the Print Room should also be noted. John Caldwell assisted Edmund Pillsbury with the 1974 exhibition *Sixteenth Century Italian Drawings* and the accompanying catalogue, and in the following year, Peter Sutton and Otto Naumann prepared the exhibition *Dutch Religious Art of the Seventeenth Century*, a project that developed from a museum training course taught by Alan Shestack. A selection of the French drawings acquired after the publication of the 1970 catalogue was exhibited in 1984, and the accompanying catalogue was written largely by graduate students and by curatorial interns and fellows, including Daniel Rosenfeld, Christine Poggi, Ann Temkin, and Stephen Goddard, then the National Museum Act Intern at the Gallery. Lyle Williams, the National Endowment for the Arts Intern in 1991, concentrated on the Dutch drawings, and Alvin L. Clark, Jr., who has contributed a number of entries to the present catalogue, first began work on Yale's French drawings during his time as a graduate student and as the NEA Intern.[47] John Marciari likewise began recataloguing Yale's collection of Italian drawings while a graduate student in New Haven when he was the Mellon Fellow in the department. Following in this tradition, an essential element of any teaching museum, a number of Yale graduate students have been involved with the present exhibition: Eva Allan, Nicole Bensoussan, Margaret E. Hadley, Suzanne Karr Schmidt, and Vanessa Wolf.

There is much more to the study of drawings than the basic questions of attribution, of course, and cataloguing efforts and discussion of the collection with other

12 | Jacopo Zucchi, *Standing Young Man (Saint Ansanus)*, ca. 1580.

scholars has yielded information and insights of many kinds, a sample of which might be provided here. A new look at the drawing by Giulio Romano in this exhibition (cat. no. 9) sheds light on the ways in which Giulio developed his compositions; it also helps clarify the iconography of the corresponding fresco, which has been misidentified in recent discussions. Neither in Yale's 1970 catalogue, nor when it was exhibited in 1974 and 1991, could Alessandro Allori's *Noli me Tangere* (fig. 13) be connected to any of his known work, but Simona Lecchini Giovannoni has since demonstrated that the drawing is a preparatory study for the tapestries that Allori designed for the Palazzo Vecchio.[48] Elizabeth Pilliod has also recently informed us that the inscription on the verso of this drawing is Allori's own signature, which suggests that this drawing might have been attached to the contract for the tapestries. A drawing acquired in 1975 as the work of Hendrick Goltzius (fig. 14) was only later recognized to be part of a set of more than sixty-five drawings by Sebastian Vrancx illustrating Virgil's *Aeneid*. The inscription on the lower part of the sheet, describing the banquet of Dido in Book 1, is not taken from any published translation of the epic and must be the work of Vrancx or one of his colleagues in the Antwerp Chamber of Rhetoric (the Rederijkers). Because this set of drawings was the largest scheme for illustrating the *Aeneid* in more than a century, it is also therefore significant for the creation of a new iconography based on the author's close reading of the text.[49] The attribution of Yale's portrait drawing by Bernini (cat. no. 55) has long been the subject of debate, but recent discoveries by Tommaso Montanari not only confirm the attribution but also identify the sitter as Sforza Pallavicino and demonstrate the friendly exchange behind the creation of the work. Similarly, Edgar Peters Bowron identified a drawing by Benedetto Luti (fig. 15), previously thought to depict an Evangelist, as the artist's study for his oval canvas of

13 | Alessandro Allori, *Noli me Tangere*, ca. 1595–98.

14 | Sebastian Vrancx, *The Banquet of Dido*, ca. 1615.

Isaiah in the nave of San Giovanni in Laterano, Rome; Bowron also explained that the unusual inscription on the verso ("Executed in crayons, this Single Figure, as Large as Life, at one End of the Geography Gallery in the Belvedere, Vatican") relates to the series of *modelli* that the patrons of the project required.[50] Examination and discussion often raise further questions. For example, there seems to be a scholarly consensus that the attribution to Pierre Subleyras of a large *Stoning of Saint Stephen* (fig. 16) can no longer be sustained, but no suggested reattribution has met with broad approval.[51]

These examples of ongoing scholarship, of which many similar cases might be cited, demonstrate some of the ways, in addition to outright acquisition, in which the collection continues to evolve. The full scope of the Art Gallery's acquisitions is published annually in the *Yale University Art Gallery Bulletin*. With new technology,

however, information about additions to the collection, as well as new information about drawings already owned by the Gallery, can now be made accessible quickly and widely, and much of the drawings collection is already available on the Gallery's website (http://artgallery.yale.edu). Information about provenance, published references, related works, and other relevant notes will continue to be added to keep the records up to date.

As mentioned above, Yale's collection in general, and even the specific works in this exhibition, might serve as an introduction to the history of European drawing for a more general readership, and it is to that discussion that we now turn.[52]

Very few drawings made prior to the fifteenth century survive today. There are, of course, many manuscript illuminations from earlier periods, but studies made in preparation for other works, or drawings made as independent, finished objects, remain rare survivals from before the fifteenth century. To some degree, this has to do with the fugitive nature of any work on paper, but there are also both practical and theoretical explanations that shed more light on the rate of survival. While paper had been known in Europe since the eleventh or twelfth century, the European papermaking industry only expanded during the fifteenth century. Gutenberg's invention of movable type in the 1450s, which may have been spurred by the greater availability of paper, in turn created a manifold increase in demand for it. The printed page supplanted the manuscript as the standard carrier of word and image, and the paper industry developed alongside the publishers. Paper quickly became much more widely available and affordable, and artists began to make sketches on paper where previously they had used wax tablets or slates.

As we look at artists of the fifteenth and sixteenth centuries, however, we can trace a theoretical approach to drawing that also helps account for the ever-increasing numbers of surviving drawings. Up to that time, artists often prepared or inherited model-books, sets of drawings of figures, animals, or compositions of common subjects. Often highly finished, these books were usually made on durable but expensive parchment; the drawings in them were meant to serve as models for an artist's entire career, if not also for his descendants or heirs as the books were passed down from generation to generation. Because of the long duration of their use, relatively few model-books survive today.[53] In the fifteenth century, however, especially in Italy, a new premium was placed on the creative act. Where it had once been enough to follow the paintings and model-book of one's master, now artists began to be judged on the basis of their own ability to develop figures and compositions.

15 | Benedetto Luti, *Isaiah*, 1716–17.

16 | Anonymous French artist (formerly attributed to Pierre Subleyras), *The Stoning of Saint Stephen*, second half of the eighteenth century.

Leonardo da Vinci, in particular, is associated with the rise of the sketch, the drawing with which the artist sought ideal form on the paper; the attempt to distill three-dimensional nature—as well as one's imagination—into a two-dimensional image was an act associated equally with the eye, the hand, and the mind. Even before Leonardo, though, the act of drawing had become theorized, and drawing came to be recognized as independent of painting, even if related to it.[54] Such ideas contributed to the creation of more drawings, and the same ideas also led to the earliest collections of drawings. Where before, an artist would for the most part be judged only by his finished works, now there was a new interest in the act of creation itself, the process by which an artist arrived at the finished work—or even, as especially in the case of Leonardo, in a process that need not necessarily arrive at completion. Thus, not only were more drawings made from the latter half of the fifteenth century onward, but also, more drawings are apt to have survived, for even a casual sketch, a working drawing, was now perceived as an indicator of an artist's genius, a prized artifact to be preserved.

It should also be mentioned that, concurrently with the increased appreciation for an artist's *virtù*, his creative originality, there was another factor of equal, if not even greater, importance in bringing about the demise of the model-book: the printed image. The production of what William Ivins famously described as the "exactly repeatable pictorial statement,"[55] a woodcut or engraved image that could be multiplied indefinitely, increased exponentially during the second half of the fifteenth century, paralleling the development of the printed book; with this infinite multiplication of available imagery, the model-book's inherent function disappeared. The rise of the papermaking industry, the development of printing (both of books and of single-sheet prints), and the evolution of artistic theory relevant to this story all happened, however, concurrently, and any attempt to privilege one over the other explanations risks oversimplification. The fact remains, though, that the "master drawing" is, essentially, the creation of the fifteenth century.

This exhibition opens with a single fifteenth-century drawing, a *Lion* by an unknown Venetian artist of the last third of the century (cat. no. 1). This drawing is fully a part of the model-book tradition, in which models often derived from previous works of art rather than from the direct study of nature. In this particular case, as noted in the entry below, there is little evidence that the artist ever looked closely at a lion; he seems rather only to have known how earlier generations of artists had drawn one. While this drawing is in pen and ink on paper, the delicate touch also derives from the earlier model-book tradition, for many drawings in model-books had been made with the thin lines of a metalpoint on the prepared surface of parchment (see fig. 1A, below). In contrast to such elegant precision, one might look to the bold lines in the sheet of sketches by Bandinelli (cat. no. 2). For Bandinelli, who worked in Florence in the generation following Leonardo, sketching was an independent act, something that every artist ought to do for hours every day, without necessarily any end product in mind. The strong lines of his drawing reflect decades of such practice, and the casual nature of the study is entirely at odds with that of the *Lion* of perhaps forty years earlier.

While the sculptor Bandinelli is associated with hundreds of drawings made with no apparent purpose other than the act of sketching itself, the notion that there was a proper sequence of preparatory studies for a painting (or for some other large work, such as a tapestry) is another of the legacies of Leonardo, one fully developed in the workshop of Raphael. Following this sequence, a project began with sketches to establish a composition, after which a clean drawing might be made to fix the organization of figures in a scene. Next, a series of figure studies would carefully examine the anatomy, as well as details of drapery or costume, for the main figures. A large finished *modello*, reflecting both the compositional sketches and the figure studies, would then be made, and from that, especially in the case of a fresco, a cartoon would bring the *modello* to the full scale of the finished work.

Although the standard pattern of compositional study, figure studies, *modello*, and cartoon was followed neither for every work nor by every artist, the basic practice was widespread, especially through the sixteenth and seventeenth centuries, and the present exhibition includes examples of all of these types of drawings. The *Marriage Procession of Psyche* by Raphael's assistant and follower Perino del Vaga (cat. no. 12) is an example of an artist's first compositional sketches, although in this case Perino seems to have been following the example of an earlier engraving (see fig. 12A, below), rather than creating an entirely new composition. The drawings by Cigoli, Caracciolo, Crespi, Bol, Castello, and Troppa (cat. nos. 25, 38, 40, 50, 51, and 53) are all also examples of such sketches. The *Seated Old Man* by Polidoro da Caravaggio (cat. no. 3) is typical of the figure studies in red chalk to come from the school of Raphael, and this exhibition and catalogue include similarly conceived figure studies in the drawings by Beccafumi, Domenichino, Vouet, and Jordaens (cat. nos. 11, 31, 42, and 52). For minor parts of fresco schemes, it is likely that the figure-study stage was omitted, as in the case of Giulio Romano's drawing for the small garden apartment at the Palazzo Te (cat. no. 9). This compositional study is not the artist's original sketch, but rather a clean copy and thus the second stage of the design process, something approaching a *modello*. There are no known figure studies for this or for any of the other parts of the corresponding ceiling, and given the relatively small scale of the fresco, it may well be that Giulio's assistants worked from little more than the sheet at hand. The drawings by Monier and Jouvenet (cat. nos. 54, 57) are more typical examples of the finished *modello*.

Cartoons, because of their size and because of the punching or incising used to transfer their design to the painting, are relatively rare survivals, especially for large fresco projects, in which the scale of the finished work often dictated that the finished cartoon would be cut into pieces corresponding to the *giornate*, the sections that would be painted in a single day. When a tapestry, a stained-glass window, or some similar object was to be produced by a craftsman other than the artist who conceived the composition, the original artist would also often produce a full-scale cartoon; because these cartoons for decorative arts are often smaller than the fresco cartoons, they seem to survive in a greater number. Van Orley's *Resurrection* (cat. no. 4), for example, represents a relatively advanced stage in the process of preparing a series of designs for stained glass; the composition for this subject would have been worked out at a smaller scale and then transferred to the three large joined sheets of the Yale drawing; this (as well as the dozen other drawings known in this series) was then squared in red chalk to guide the glassmaker in transferring the design in production of the actual window. The *Last Supper* by Diego López (cat. no. 23), likewise, was the cartoon for one of the richly embroidered vestments produced for the Escorial. In this case, and often by the later sixteenth century, steps were taken to preserve the cartoon itself. López's drawing, for instance, is pricked for transfer, but a second sheet of paper was placed behind the drawing when its outlines were pricked. This second sheet (pricked but undrawn) would have been pounced to transfer the design, so that the chalk dust used in pouncing would not deface the cartoon itself. Like all drawings, cartoons became desirable collectors' objects. The strategy employed at the Escorial was one way of preserving a cartoon by producing a functioning substitute; for a different type of substitute cartoon, a "cartoon-like" drawing made to satisfy collectors (but a drawing that did not actually function as a cartoon), see the work by Lanino (cat. no. 13).

There is often some correspondence between the ideas behind a drawing and the techniques used to create it. As mentioned above, the delicate precision of metalpoint suited the model-book, while the use of a thick pen, wet ink, and coarse paper were appropriate for the quick sketching of Bandinelli. Leonardo da Vinci pioneered the use of natural red chalks, which combine the precision of the metalpoint with the facility of the pen or charcoal. Just as Andrea del Sarto and Raphael followed Leonardo's conceptual model for drawing, so too they adopted his techniques and made extensive use of red chalk. Both the conceptual model and the technique can then be traced in the works by their own artistic descendants: Polidoro in the case of Raphael (cat. no. 3) and Naldini (cat. no. 18) (by way of Pontormo) in the case of Andrea del Sarto. The eclectic artists of the later sixteenth century, in turn—Federico Zuccaro (see cat. no. 19) and Cherubino Alberti (cat. no. 28), for example—combined red and black chalks for different, and often highly self-conscious, effects. Pen and ink and red chalk were particularly suited to the Florentine artists and their emphasis on *disegno*. The use of black and white chalks on blue paper, with the paper serving as a neutral ground while the chalks indicate shadows and highlights, is generally considered the legacy of Titian and his Venetian contemporaries; the pictorial or painterly, rather than purely linear, manner of such drawings seems to parallel the Venetian artists' use of oil paints and dark grounds on canvas supports.[56] Licinio's *Woman Holding a Vase* (cat. no. 8) reflects the new Venetian pictorialism.

On the one hand, Licinio's *Woman Holding a Vase* is conceptually somewhat old-fashioned, for Licinio treated his subject in the spirit of the model-book; he used this drawing as his model for the Virgin and Child in painting after painting. On the other hand, the drawing is clearly made from a model in the studio, and as such corresponds to the interest in naturalism that developed around the year 1500. The traditional art-historical framework that traces a progression from the High Renaissance to Mannerism, and then to the Baroque era during the course of the sixteenth century, is an oversimplification of a much more complex pattern of artistic development, but there is some truth to these style-categories.[57] Thus, for example, the rather straightforward interest in the natural world represented by Licinio's drawing had already begun to change by the time Polidoro da Caravaggio drew his *Seated Old Man*. Even if the latter drawing was taken from a live model in the studio, Polidoro has already begun to distort anatomy, hinting at the type of elongated Mannerist figures that can be seen fully developed in the drawings presented here by Salviati, Muller, Spranger, and Bellange (cat. nos. 14, 24, 29, and 34). In turn, the movement away from self-conscious, contrived, highly artificial figures of this type—the return to naturalism that was a characteristic of seventeenth-century Baroque—is evident in studies like those by Domenichino and de Gheyn (cat. nos. 31, 32). Moreover, just as Leonardo, one of the artists responsible for the scrutiny of nature that we associate with the High Renaissance, had drawn hundreds of caricatures, so too the artists who rediscovered naturalism in the early seventeenth century experimented with the genre; a fine example is the drawing by Guercino (cat. no. 43), who, like Domenichino, was a product of the Carracci family academy in Bologna.

The depiction of landscape parallels the broad strokes of artistic development that are evident in figure drawings. Thus, for example, we see the fantastic, idealized landscapes of Lodewijk Toeput or Hermann Weyer (cat. nos. 22, 35) give way in Northern art to those of Esaias van de Velde and Cornelis Vroom (cat. nos. 36, 47). The apparently (if not always actually) factual image of the countryside reflects the interest in characteristically Dutch subjects that is one of the hallmarks of Dutch art of the seventeenth century. The *Portrait of Two Gentlemen from Dordrecht* by Jacob Gerritsz. Cuyp (cat. no. 41), with a view of the artist's native city in the background, typifies this interest; attention to the ordinary is also evident in a work like that by Pieter Jansz. Quast (cat. no. 46). Conversely, the focus on the quotidian failed, for the most part, to take hold in France and Italy, as evidenced by the idealization of Claude's *Pastoral Landscape* (cat. no. 48); even a much later drawing like Hubert Robert's *Scola di Virgilio* (cat. no. 66), for all its topographical detail and anecdotal content, retains a sense of the *all'antica* ideal. Yet, at more or less the same moment, in a drawing like Boucher's *Dilapidated Farmhouse* (cat. no. 63), we see an attempt to combine the Netherlandish view of the world with the light, decorative touch of the French Rococo. Still later, the watercolor views by Théodore Rousseau and Johan Barthold Jongkind (cat. nos. 78, 84) manifest the immediacy and spontaneity that characterize the plein-air sketch, which would become a benchmark of Impressionism.

Some Renaissance artists used watercolors, but the medium did not become a standard studio technique until the eighteenth century, and its popularity ran parallel to the first interest in plein-air sketching. The French Academy seems to have placed a revived emphasis on classical draftsmanship, which might well account for the multitude of expressive and accomplished red chalk drawings from the eighteenth century, such as those by Watteau, Hubert Robert, and Greuze (cat. nos. 62, 66, and 69).[58] Other media and techniques developed for different reasons. The earliest pastel drawings date to the sixteenth century,[59] although the first artists who made much use of them—Leonardo da Vinci, Jacopo Bassano, and Federico Barocci (cat. no. 20)[60]— are not known to have had any direct contact with each other and seem to have developed the technique independently, each using the medium in rather different ways and for different pictorial purposes. Nor did the example of these artists have an influence beyond their immediate followers. Few, if any, artists in the early or mid-seventeenth century made significant use of pastels, but the medium found new life in France later in the century, as Joseph Vivien (cat. no. 58) and others recognized its possibilities, particularly for portraiture; Vivien was the first to exhibit a pastel portrait among the oil paintings in the French Salon, and his work prepared the way for the great portraitists of the eighteenth century: Rosalba Carriera, Jean-Étienne Liotard, and Maurice-Quentin de La Tour.

While some media are particularly associated with specific moments in the history of art, few techniques were entirely forgotten. Metalpoint drawings on prepared paper, for example, reappeared periodically throughout the sixteenth century, usually conceived as some sort of precious object,[61] and Degas's delicate pencil drawing of his young cousin (cat. no. 82), showing the sitter in the strict profile of fifteenth-century portraits, seems likewise deliberately to have evoked the appearance, if not the actual technique, of the earliest drawings in metalpoint.

Drawings served many purposes. Some stages of their use in a standard sequence, preparatory for paintings or decorative arts, are outlined above. This exhibition, like Yale's collection as a whole, also contains a relatively high number of sheets made in preparation for prints: even excluding sheets like those by Toeput, Muller, Boscoli, and perhaps Palko (cat. nos. 22, 24, 27, and 65), which seem to be drawings for prints that were never executed, there are at least nine drawings in the exhibition related to printmaking practice, and a brief look at some of these gives a further idea of the rich variety of means by which artists conveyed information that the printmakers would translate into engravings, etchings, wood engravings, or lithographs.[62]

In some cases, the sheet by Bellange for example (cat. no. 34), we see the artist working to clarify a composition that he would etch himself, as each of the several layers of media—black chalk, pen lines, brown washes, and stylus indentations—refined the original loose sketch. There were many other artists, however, such as Luca Penni, Maarten van Heemskerck, Maarten de Vos, and Bartolomaeus Spranger, whose oeuvre consisted in large part of drawings meant to be made into prints not by themselves but by professional etchers or engravers. For the works of Penni and de Vos in this exhibition (cat. nos. 10, 21), no print seems to have existed, but in *Mars, the Choleric Temperament*, by Heemskerck (cat. no. 15), for example, we find a drawing for which the engraving is known, and which the engraver was meant to—and did—copy essentially line for line. In the later sixteenth century, however, a new practice developed, in which an artist would draw in red chalk or in ink washes a composition to be engraved. Where earlier the reproductive engraver's mandate was mimesis, the exact replication of the original design, he now became an interpreter, a full collaborator with the original artist in the production of a new image. Chalk lines and ink washes, that is, could not be copied directly onto the engraving plate, and the printmaker was forced—or, more accurately, enabled—to devise his own systems of hatched lines to convey the shading and contours of the preparatory drawing. Printmaking thus became an act of invention analogous to the act of drawing itself. This transition, which might be traced to the work of the Netherlandish engraver Cornelis Cort, reached its fullest height in the work of Hendrick Goltzius and his circle.[63] An example of a preparatory drawing of this type is that by Spranger (cat. no. 29), for a print engraved by Muller. Moreover, the elaborate systems of swelling lines and curved cross-hatching developed by Cort, Goltzius, and other engravers in time became models for drawing practice, as a new generation of Netherlandish draftsmen came of age using the prints as their models. The sheets by Jacques de Gheyn and attributed to Gerrit Pietersz. (cat. nos. 32, 33) demonstrate this remarkable turnabout. The comparison of Gillot's chalk drawing of *The Feast of Pan* (cat. no. 61) and the corresponding print (fig. 61A), shown beside it in the exhibition, provides a further example of the ways in which engraved lines are an interpretation of a chalk sketch and highlights the particular strengths of each medium. Guys's pen and wash drawing of French veterans (cat. no. 81), intended to be rendered as a wood engraving in the *Illustrated London News* (although never actually published), harks back to the media used by Spranger: the wood engraver was to translate the artist's fluid image into linear terms as he saw fit. New printing media engendered further different styles of preparatory drawings, as for example in Millet's richly worked chalk study (cat. no. 80) for the then-new printmaking technique of lithography.

Finally, we should mention that a few of the drawings in the exhibition were without any doubt made as ends in themselves—although even these divide into different categories. A drawn portrait, although sometimes developed into a painted version, was usually the final product, as was certainly the case with the works by Vivien and Ingres here (cat. nos. 58, 77). The red chalk *Head of a Young Man* from the circle of Schmutzer (cat. no. 71) is a classic example of the academic study, ultimately deriving from sixteenth-century studio practice, overlaid with Charles Le Brun's studies of human expression in the seventeenth century, and becoming codified in the eighteenth. Unusually for artists of the seventeenth century, Weyer, Bramer, and Lafage all made large numbers of drawings as ends in themselves, Bramer's in distinct series (see cat. nos. 35, 45, and 56). Toward the end of the eighteenth century, such sequences of drawings had become more frequent, and the examples in the exhibition by Fragonard and Domenico Tiepolo (cat. nos. 72, 74) are from some of the most exuberant and delightful of such series ever to have been made.

The examples described above demonstrate how self-conscious the act of drawing became in European art, and indeed it is fair to say that nearly every sheet in this exhibition was probably made with at least some awareness on the part of the artist that any drawing, even a quick sketch, might be collected. Every stroke of the pen or chalk might thus be deemed to have significance, not only for its preparatory function but also as an artist's characteristic gesture. This awareness—perhaps even fear—that any drawing might become a collector's object and thereby something on which the artist's talents might be judged, seems to have led to the practice among certain artists, Primaticcio and Luca Penni (cat. no. 10) for example, of using a stylus to transfer the designs of their sketches so as to make clean copies of the drawings. Once the design was transferred, the looser original drawings, in which the artist's (perhaps laborious) search for the ideal form might more easily be seen, were apparently destroyed.[64] Inherent in this practice is the notion that drawings—and individual marks in them, rather than simply the final product in the broad view—offer us the most intimate glimpse of an artist's personality or talents; that notion is perhaps the ideal place to end this introduction and to turn to the drawings themselves.

1. Hereafter referred to throughout this catalogue as H-B and L.
2. Although the dividing line between "old master" and "modern" is a purely academic construct, we follow the general convention of placing it around 1860, or by using an artist's birth date of 1830 as a cutoff, although even these parameters have been loosely followed, as in the case of the early and traditionally conceived portrait drawing by Degas included in the exhibition (cat. no. 82). In fact, the year 1863, although it does not end conveniently in a "0" or a "5," seems to us perhaps the most judicious moment to situate this break, as it was marked by three key events in modern art: the death of the great Romantic painter Eugène Delacroix, the creation of Manet's *Déjeuner sur l'herbe*, and the first of the Salons des Refusés. The last drawing in the catalogue was made in this year.
3. In addition to the Introduction to the H-B and L catalogue, the section of this essay dedicated to the history of the collection owes much to Matheson 2001, a history of the Art Gallery, and especially to information supplied by Elise K. Kenney, Archivist of the Art Gallery, to whom we are particularly grateful.
4. This new phase of acquisition corresponded, not coincidentally, to the era when Weir called for the creation of an art gallery or museum as part of Yale College and distinct from the Art School.
5. Weir had lived in Italy in the 1820s, but it is not clear when he formed his collection of drawings, which contained works from all the European schools.
6. The drawing, inv. no. 1890.44 (H-B and L, no. A114), is related to the southeastern face of the cupola. The original drawing is probably that in the Albertina (Acidini Luchinat 1999, 2:95 and fig. 56), and there is a further copy in the British Museum (inv. no. 1862-10-11-186; Gere and Pouncey 1983, no. 302). The numerous copies and versions of all of Zuccaro's drawings for the cupola project presumably resulted from the complexity of the enormous project and the activity of many artists working under Zuccaro. For one of Zuccaro's own, highly finished studies for the project, see cat. no. 19.
7. Inv. no. 1890.28; H-B and L, no. 282. Recently proposed attributions of the drawing are to Correggio's Parmese follower Giorgio Gandini (by John Marciari and Mario di Giampaolo) and to the Veronese artist Bernardino India (by Florian Härb).
8. Inv. no. 1890.33, reed pen and brown ink, 16.5 × 12.8 cm. For the attribution to Flinck, see Sumowski 1967 and Sumowski 1979–92, 4:2092, no. 954x; H-B and L, no. 401, catalogued the drawing as "School of Rembrandt."
9. Inv. no. 1890.37, pen and brown ink and brown and gray wash, 13.8 × 19.8 cm. Rosenberg first tentatively advanced the attribution in his brief review of H-B and L (Rosenberg 1971, 133) and then repeated it in the following year (Toronto et al. 1972, 146), while also noting that drawings by Jean-Baptiste Corneille are "as scarce as those of his elder brother Michel Corneille the Younger are widely distributed."
10. Inv. no. 1904.1, black chalk and red, blue, and yellow washes, on twenty-nine pieces of joined paper, laid down and varnished, 213 × 132 cm; much of the drawing was "reinforced" in the nineteenth century with a waxy black crayon. "Cartoon," it might be noted for nonspecialists, derives from the Italian word *cartone*, which translates literally as a large piece of paper (*carta*). The term is used to refer to preparatory drawings made at the full scale of a finished work, which often (as in this case) required that many pieces of paper be joined together. For other examples and further discussion, see cat. nos. 4, 7, 13, and 23.
11. The drawing was a gift to the Gallery from Sarah Alden Derby, the daughter of Bradford R. and Anne C. Alden.
12. A search through the Art Gallery archives, as well as in the correspondence between the Weir brothers now preserved in the archive at the Weir Farm National Historic Site in Wilton, Connecticut, has not revealed any further information about the provenance of this work or of any of Robert Weir's drawings. There is, however, some discussion in the correspondence regarding the sale of the Zuccaro workshop drawing mentioned above, which the brothers believed to be by Michelangelo.
13. Removed to a paintings storeroom because of its size, the work seems to have escaped the attention of Haverkamp-Begemann and Logan. It came to light around 1980, but the files do not indicate that any research was then done on it, and it was not unearthed again until the inventory undertaken in 2002, prior to the renovation of the Art Gallery's Louis Kahn building. To our knowledge, it and the pastel by Vivien (cat. no. 58), which also hung in a storeroom until brought to light in the inventory of 2002, were the only two early European drawings then in the collection not included in the 1970 catalogue.
14. While much work remains to be done on this drawing, it might be noted here that it does have some stylistic and typological similarities to paintings and drawings, including cartoons, by the Cremonese artist Bernadino Campi and his followers.
15. The Parizeau is inv. no. 1930.221, pen and brown ink and wash, 37.6 × 47.1 cm. Of the aforementioned drawings by Dieu and Coypel, the first is included in Pierre Rosenberg's summary of the artist's drawings (Rosenberg 1979, 167), but Rosenberg has suggested, according to correspondence in the curatorial file, that the drawings attributed to Coypel are perhaps instead by Claude-Guy Hallé. See also, from the Kaye collection, the drawing by Benedetto Luti discussed below (fig. 15).
16. Also worthy of note are the hundreds of drawings by George Romney, now at the Yale Center for British Art, which were presented

to the Art Gallery between 1962 and 1964 by Mr. and Mrs. J. Richardson Dilworth, B.A. 1938.

17. Inv. no. 1941.289, pen and brown ink and brown wash over black chalk, 21.4 × 16.3 cm.

18. A charming scene of young boys chasing a girl, by Esaias van de Velde (inv. no. 1945.253.25; H-B and L, no. 431), is one of the highlights of this group.

19. See Wolf 1942.

20. Inv. no. 1937.338; H-B and L, no. 440.

21. Inv. nos. 1929.43 and 1937.331; H-B and L, nos. 292 and 294. The former, a 1616 *Portrait of a Cardinal*, has been identified by Robbin 1990, no. 52, as probably a portrait of a member of the Mignanelli family; the latter, a portrait of *Tommaso Neri* catalogued in 1970 as "Circle of Leoni," might well be by Leoni himself, although it is not part of his numbered sequence of drawings. Similarly, a badly damaged *Self-Portrait* of Guido Reni from the Greene collection (inv. no. 1937.333; H-B and L, no. A139), catalogued by Wolf and H-B and L as a copy, has since been reconsidered to be Reni's original (see, for example, Regina–Montreal 1970, no. 36). Not all of Greene's gifts were portraits; Tiepolo's *Industry Triumphing over Idleness* (inv. no. 1929.4; H-B and L, no. 307) is a notable exception.

22. Inv. no. 1952.12.5, black chalk, heightened with white, on blue paper, 22.4 × 16.5 cm. The drawing is dated December 1616 and inscribed on the verso, "La Damigella d'Angiò." While it would seem possible to identify the sitter, for there cannot have been many young female members of the house of Anjou in Rome in 1616, she has remained a mystery.

23. The collection, originally formed by J. Armelhaut and E. Bocher, the authors of Gavarni's catalogue raisonné, represents the most comprehensive holdings of his work outside of the Bibliothèque Nationale de France.

24. On the gift, see Eisler 1958 as well as the Introduction to H-B and L.

25. For reasons of treatment, preservation, study, and display, the Egmont drawings were in the 1960s removed from the albums and mounted separately. The acquisition numbers, consisting of three parts, correlate to the drawings' placement in the albums. All of the Egmont drawing numbers begin with 1961, the year of their acquisition, but the second numbers in the sequence, 61 through 66, refer to the volumes (1 through 6), and the third to the number of the drawing in the alphabetical sequence of its album. Thus, for example, inv. no. 1961.63.4 is the fourth drawing in the third volume; according to the original system under which the drawings were catalogued at Yale, drawing 1961.63.4 would have been Egmont III.4.

26. Apart from old signatures and inscriptions, attributions seem to have been added to the drawings in two different campaigns (it is unknown whether this was by the Earl himself or by his agent or librarian). The first "Egmont hand" added inscriptions in brown ink, such as those on cat. nos. 22 and 26, for example, while a second set of inscriptions are in graphite, like those on cat. nos. 6, 8, and 16, among others.

27. Inv. no. 1961.62.25, pen and brown ink and watercolor, 28 × 40.9 cm; see Anne-Marie Logan's entry in Wellesley–Cleveland 1993–94, no. 5, for a full discussion.

28. Inv. no. 1961.61.81, pen and brown ink and brown and red wash, heightened with white, 19.3 × 15.1 cm. The drawing is preparatory for an engraving by Jacob Matham (Hollstein DF, 11:28, no. 28).

29. The Egmont version is inv. no. 1961.63.69, H-B and L, no. 549. The other version is inv. no. 1978.38.

30. For Lankrink, see L. 2090 as well as Lankrink 1945; for further discussion of Sylvester, see L. 2108, 2110, and 2875–2877 and cat. no. 49 below.

31. Rand 1914, 57; also mentioned in Ingamells 1997, 757–758.

32. Rand 1914, 173–177. While there is no epistolary evidence that Berkeley purchased art for Egmont on the former's first Grand Tour in 1713–14, it would hardly be surprising for him to have done so, given the evidence from Berkeley's second tour. On Egmont, see also Egmont 1920–23. Egmont's diaries include a wealth of information on Parliament, the founding of Georgia colony, and music, but frustratingly little on art. It is clear that Egmont knew the great collectors of his day, and the few tantalizing references to art reveal his knowledge and appreciation of it (*cf.* his notes on the Raphael tapestry cartoons, Egmont 1920–23, 1:218–219), but there is nothing on the means by which his own collection was formed.

33. The Yale drawing is inv. no. 1961.61.3; H-B and L, no. A161. The Chatsworth sheet is inv. no. 160; see Jaffé 1994, 1: no. 82, where it is attributed to Beccafumi. The Chatsworth sheet bears an early-eighteenth-century attribution to Perino del Vaga, which is no closer to correct than is the Egmont attribution to Michelangelo; nor is the attribution to Beccafumi entirely convincing, although no satisfactory alternative has yet been suggested.

34. The Eeckhout is inv. no. 1961.63.47, pen and brown ink and two colors of gray wash, 18.4 × 15.6 cm. The Lastman is inv. no. 1961.64.6; H-B and L, no. 390. See H-B and L, 1:xii–xiii, for a full list of drawings apparently reinforced by the "Egmont hand." Retouching of this type was hardly limited to the Egmont collection, of course, and examples might be found in many print rooms.

35. Inv. nos. 1970.25.1–10.

36. Frederick Mortimer Clapp was the founding director of the Frick Collection in New York, and is best known to art historians for his 1916 monograph on Pontormo, which can be credited with reviving interest in the artist.

37. When first appointed in 1960, Haverkamp-Begemann held the title of Curator of Prints, which was changed to Curator of Drawings and Prints in 1963. There had not been a Curator of Drawings since James W. Barney, who held the post from 1930 through 1941.

38. Inv. no. 1971.97, red and black chalk with traces of white heightening, 14 × 11.7 cm.

39. In 1977, Burke's curatorial title, like the name of the department, was changed to "Prints, Drawings, and Photographs," in recognition of the increasing acquisitions of photography that characterized the department's agenda during his tenure.

40. Inv. no. 1976.42.3, black and white chalk on gray paper, 27 × 20.3 cm.

41. Anne-Marie Logan served as Assistant Curator from 1967 to 1971 and as Curator of Drawings and Prints from 1971 to 1972.

42. We are enormously grateful to Theresa Fairbanks Harris, Chief Conservator for works on paper at the Yale art galleries, and her staff, not just for making it possible to examine this particular sheet, but for providing a complete range of conservation work for all the drawings in the exhibition over the several years this catalogue has been in preparation. Their expertise has been invaluable, and their generosity with their time and knowledge is immensely appreciated.

43. Inv. no. 1961.65.5; H-B and L, no. 620 (as van Thulden).

44. Inv. no. 1967.48.3; H-B and L, no. 492 (as Floris); Held 1972, 45; Velde 1975, 90; and Washington–New York 1986–87, no. 21.

45. Inv. no. 1961.66.7, pen and brown ink and brown wash over red chalk, with traces of black chalk, 21.2 × 12.4 cm.

46. For the Zucchi altarpiece, see Avignon 1992, 269, no. 114. The painting (oil on canvas, 340 × 190 cm) was the altarpiece of the Patrizi chapel in San Francesco, Siena. The paintings in that chapel are attributed to Zucchi by Mancini and others. No date has hitherto been proposed for the work, but it seems to be from ca. 1580, based on stylistic comparisons with Zucchi's paintings in Santo Spirito and San Giovanni Decollato, Rome; more-

over, a trip to Siena in 1580 would account for what is otherwise a gap in Zucchi's known chronology. For another attribution resulting from the 1994 visits, see Scorza 1995–96.

47 For the exhibitions mentioned above, see New Haven 1974, New Haven 1975, New Haven 1984, and New Haven 1992. See also the two exhibitions organized by Clark, New Haven 1987 and New Haven 1991a.

48 Inv. no. 1961.61.1, pen and brown ink and brown wash over black chalk, heightened with white, squared in black chalk, on brown paper. See Lecchini Giovannoni 1991, 289–90 (under no. 152). See also New Haven 1974, no. 27; Oberlin–Brunswick–Hanover 1991, no. 3; New Haven 1991a, no. 3.

49 Inv. no. 1975.89. See Ruby 1990 and, for additional comments, Reznicek 1993, 274.

50 Inv. no. 1930.209, black, red, and white chalk, with white heightening (partly oxidized), 38.7 × 28.9 cm. See Bowron 1979, 208, n. 98; see also Philadelphia–Houston 2000, under no. 243.

51 Inv. no. 1964.9.7, pen and brown ink and wash, over black chalk, heightened with white, 40 × 22 cm.

52 What follows is a summary, based on the drawings in the exhibition, of a complex history. Those wishing for a general history of European drawings and a discussion of some of the key issues in the study of that material should also look to De Tolnay 1943, James et al. 1997, and Rosand 2002.

53 On the model-book tradition, see especially Elen 1995.

54 For further discussion of this point, see especially Rosand 2002, Chapter 2.

55 Ivins 1953, 2 and passim.

56 Earlier artists, those working in southern Germany during the late fifteenth century, for example, had used the richly colored grounds of prepared papers as a middle tone, to which they added black line and white highlights, but the Venetians' use of chalks distinguishes their drawings from the earlier examples.

57 The categories are useful for describing general trends, but the problem with them occurs when the categories take on a life of their own, as, for example, when Mannerist style has been equated with spiritual crisis. The categories also tend to emphasize the differences and, accordingly, to disregard the equally important continuities from one generation to the next, a point echoed in Chappell 2005.

58 The drawing by Schmutzer or a member of his immediate circle (cat. no. 71) is a further reflection of this trend, for although this drawing was probably created in Vienna, Schmutzer had links to the French Academy through having studied with Johann Georg Wille in Paris.

59 Pastels, technically speaking, are manufactured crayons, in which ground pigment is suspended in a waxy medium; see James et al. 1997, 72–74, for further discussion. The chalks used in the Renaissance are naturally occurring substances. On pastels in the Renaissance, see McGrath 1998.

60 Leonardo is said to have used pastels, but most of the colored drawings known by him are actually in red, black, and yellow chalks.

61 The metalpoint portraits by Hendrick Goltzius (see Amsterdam–New York–Toledo 2003–04, 57–77) are a good example.

62 For the most part, Yale's collection of drawings for prints has come together by accident, with many of the sheets arriving in the Egmont Albums. The number of print-related sheets there is probably the result of Egmont's having purchased a substantial part of his collection in the Netherlands, where cities like Antwerp had long been centers for print production. In addition to the drawings in the exhibition, notable other examples include: the drawing by Bloemaert illustrated above (fig. 8); a series of scenes from the life of Saint Philip Neri by Jacques Stella (inv. nos. 1961.65.75–83; H-B and L, nos. 16–24); two studies by Jacques de Gheyn for the *Exercise of Arms* manual of 1607 (inv. nos. 1959.38.25–26; H-B and L, nos. 375–376); a drawing by Lucas Franchoys the Younger (inv. no. 1961.63.61; H-B and L, no. 569) for a print of *Salome Receiving the Head of Saint John the Baptist* by Adriaen Lommelin (Hollstein DF, 11:95, no. 3); and a study by Philip Fruytiers for the *Distribution of Franciscan Cords* (inv. no. 1961.63.63; H-B and L, no. 573) that was printed by Jacobus Neefs (Hollstein DF, 14:137, no. 14, there identified as *Saint Bernard Distributing Girdles to the Pious Brothers*).

63 For further discussion of this development in reproductive printmaking, especially with regard to Cort's collaboration with Girolamo Muziano, see Marciari 2000, 174ff.

64 We do not, to our knowledge, have any documentary evidence for this practice (which has received little, if any, critical comment), but even allowing for the various circumstances through which only a small percentage of Renaissance drawings survive, a survey of the known drawings of a Primaticcio or a Penni, such as was possible in the large monographic exhibition on Primaticcio held in 2004–2005 (Paris 2004–05), provides ample support for the hypothesis.

Catalogue

Note on the Catalogue

ARRANGEMENT OF ENTRIES

Catalogue entries are arranged chronologically by date of drawing.

MEDIUM

The principal instrument and medium are given first, followed by other media in order of importance. Paper is noted only when other than white or off-white antique laid paper.

SIZE

Measurements are of the sheet, height before width. Dimensions are given in both centimeters and inches. If the drawing is shaped irregularly, maximum measurements are given.

WATERMARKS

Watermarks, when present, are described in each entry, with reference to standard watermark dictionaries where possible. For reproductions of the watermarks, see the Watermarks appendix. The majority of the watermarks have been captured using an Associated X-Ray Corporation 255 HOTSHOT low energy, long wavelength x-ray ("Soft" or Grenz radiography) system on Kodak Industrex® M100 film. Digital infrared images have been captured (for cat. nos. 28, 29, 30, 48, 53, and 72) using an Artist® multi-spectral imaging camera and accompanying Artist® PC and PanaVue ImageAssembler software. The remaining watermarks (cat. nos. 47, 54) were captured with a simple digital photograph taken with transmitted light. All of the reproductions have been digitally modified to increase contrast and improve legibility.

INSCRIPTIONS

Inscriptions are assumed to be in a hand other than the artist's unless so indicated. The location and medium of the inscriptions are described.

PROVENANCE

The provenance is given chronologically; each owner is separated from the next by a semicolon. Collector's marks are noted, when possible, with reference to Frits Lugt's *Les marques de collections de dessins et d'estampes*, Amsterdam, 1921, and supplement, The Hague, 1956.

REFERENCES

The References section at the beginning of each entry includes all published references to the drawing in books, articles, and exhibition catalogues; when these references give an attribution different from that now assigned, the alternate attribution is noted in parentheses. Dealer and auction catalogues are listed in the References section only when the catalogues included a substantial entry on the drawing, or if the attribution was different from that now given. All bibliographic citations are given in shortened form; full citations are found in the Bibliography at the back of this volume.

ILLUSTRATIONS

No drawing is reproduced larger than actual size.

AUTHORS

NB	Nicole Bensoussan
SB	Suzanne Boorsch
ALC	Alvin L. Clark, Jr.
SG	Susan Greenberg
MEH	Margaret E. Hadley
EH	Elisabeth Hodermarsky
RH	Rena Hoisington
JLL	Jan Leja
JJM	John Marciari
EM	Edgar Munhall

1 Anonymous Artist

Venetian, last third of the fifteenth century

A Lion, ca. 1480

Pen and brown ink over leadpoint or black chalk, 14.5 × 23 cm (5 11/16 × 9 1/16 in.)

PROVENANCE: private collection, Switzerland; Sotheby's, New York, 14 January 1987, lot 14; Edmund P. Pillsbury

REFERENCES: Zurich 1973, no. 171; Pfäffikon–Geneva 1978, no. 46; Durand 1983, 26 and 31; *YUAG Bulletin* (2002): 144

Tercentennial gift of Edmund P. Pillsbury, B.A. 1965. 2001.75.2

The fifteenth century witnessed the development of new drawing practices in Italy. As the rise of the printing press led to the growth of the paper industry, paper increasingly replaced parchment in the artist's studio. Parchment was a costly material, and drawings on it were generally limited to formal, finished works, often executed in the delicate, precise, and labor-intensive medium of silverpoint, which required the application of a carefully prepared ground to the drawing surface. In contrast, paper was affordable enough to be used with some abandon, and early drawings on paper include quick sketches, experiments to solve pictorial problems, as well as more finished drawings; the more flexible pen and ink thus became the favored drawing medium. All these early drawings were, however, utilitarian objects and were so often consulted in the studio context that their use over time tended to destroy them. Drawings in metalpoint were apt to fade; iron-gall ink often ate through the paper on which it was used. Finally, the culture of collecting drawings only developed in the decades after 1500. In short, despite the importance of fifteenth-century drawings in the history of Renaissance art, the odds were against their survival and sheets like the present one are rare.[1]

Although it serves as a testimony of the new practices, the *Lion* is equally characteristic of an early mode of draftsmanship, for it derives from the drawing-book or model-book tradition rather than from life studies. That is, while lions were kept in an enclosure at the Ducal Palace in Venice,[2] it is clear that the artist who drew this one barely studied the animals. Instead, working in a studio tradition that stretched back to the Middle Ages, he would have made his lion by consulting or copying an older drawing. Every studio had drawing-books for this purpose. They functioned as a studio's pictorial archive and contained the stock images an artist might need to reproduce: various flora and fauna, architectural motifs, drapery and figure studies, and other such designs.[3] Lions like the one in this drawing were particularly useful for a Venetian artist, for the lion was the symbol of Saint Mark, patron saint of Venice, so that the lion itself became one of the city's emblems. The lion also appeared in a range of religious and mythological subjects—Saint Jerome, Daniel, Samson, and Hercules for example—as well as in allegorical and courtly imagery.[4] In other words, every fifteenth-century Venetian artist would have had to paint lions, and when called on to do so, would refer to the images in his model-books. The present sheet, carefully drawn first in leadpoint or black chalk and then reinforced with brown ink, is almost certainly from one such book; the stains on the drawing are likely to be from the transfer of iron-gall ink from adjacent pages.[5] Rather than a casual or experimental sketch, a careful drawing like this would have been created to serve as a model for other works.

Drawing-books were either passed from master to assistant, or were copied by an artist leaving one studio to set up a studio of his own. The images in such books might be updated or improved from one book to the next, but they were still remarkably consistent within one milieu. This drawing can, accordingly, be compared closely with those in a number of other Venetian drawing-books, including the two by Jacopo Bellini, the most beautiful and famous fifteenth-century examples (fig. A).[6] Bellini's book now in Paris is drawn partly on the parchment leaves of an older drawing-book of the late fourteenth century, perhaps one bequeathed to him by his master, Gentile da Fabriano. In most cases, Bellini applied a new ground layer over the old drawings and reworked them, using the older images (barely visible through the new ground) as a guide.[7] In one case, however, the older page was not reworked, and we can see how closely Bellini's images of circa 1430–50 were modeled on the older drawings.[8] Another Venetian model-book with drawings by several artists of the Pisanello and Bellini circles, the so-called Codex Vallardi, also contains several pages with lions and further demonstrates how consistently the basic image of the beasts passed from studio to studio and from artist to artist.[9] Given the consistency of the lion imagery in all these Venetian drawing-books, we can conclude with some certainty that the Yale drawing comes from the same Venetian milieu but probably from the later end of the tradition. The drawing is farther removed from nature than are some of the earlier studies—despite the lively rendering of the mane, for example, this animal actually looks less like a lion than do many of the earlier drawings. The artist seems, moreover, to have been specifically aware of Jacopo Bellini's drawing-books. He used the same media that Bellini did in his drawing-book now in London (pen and ink over leadpoint on paper) and, like Bellini, attempted to create an elegant, finely finished image rather than merely an outline.[10] Even if it never attains the levels

FIGURE 1A | Jacopo Bellini, *Lions*, ca. 1430–50. Paris, Musée du Louvre.

of Bellini's drawings, the *Lion* is nonetheless a rare and important example of Venetian draftsmanship from the second half of the Quattrocento.

JJM

1. On early drawing practice, see especially Ames-Lewis 2000 and Nottingham–London 1983. Ames-Lewis 2000, viii, also comments on the particular rarity today of quattrocento drawings by Venetian and Northern Italian artists, which are outnumbered by extant Central Italian drawings "in the order of seven to one."
2. Eisler 1989, 154, citing Hodgson 1910, 347.
3. On the drawing-books, see Elen 1995. On the most famous drawing-books to survive from the period, those of Jacopo Bellini, see Eisler 1989.
4. Lions could also be used, for example, in images such as the engraving of a *Lion, Dragon, and Fox Quarreling*, probably a political allegory, or on playing cards, as in the *Fortitude* of the Tarocchi. See Hind 1938–48, 1:255 and pl. 405, and 1:238 and pl. 355, respectively. Other roughly contemporary examples of lion imagery include the bold circa 1490 engraving simply of a standing lion (Hind 1938–48, 1:266 and pl. 437); the lion being taught by Cupid to sing, on the reverse of Pisanello's 1444 medal of Leonello d'Este; and, most famous of all, Carpaccio's 1516 painting of *The Lion of Saint Mark* (Venice, Palazzo Ducale).
5. Leadpoint, an alloy of lead and tin, is similar to silverpoint except that it can be used on unprepared paper, in contrast to the ground preparation required by silverpoint. Because the underdrawing has been largely rubbed away, it is difficult to be certain whether it was actually in leadpoint (the more likely given the period and milieu in which this drawing was made as well as the fineness of the lines) or very fine black chalk.
6. Bellini's drawing-book on parchment is Paris, Louvre, inv. no. RF 1475-1556 and RF 425, 427, 428. His drawing-book on paper is London, British Museum, inv. no. 1855-8-11-1/98 (these henceforth referred to as Bellini's "Louvre book" and "London book"). See Eiser 1989 for the most complete scholarly account of them, for earlier bibliography, and particularly for the facsimile images.
7. See, for example, Louvre book, folio 78v (fig. A), where the new ground does not cover the old page at lower left, and has lifted away in several other areas.
8. Louvre book, folio 77v.
9. For the Codex Vallardi, see Elen 1995, no. 14, with further bibliography. For the lion pages, which might be attributed to the Bellini studio, see Eisler 1989, 140–141 and figs. 5–6. In view of the tradition of lion imagery, attempts to link the present drawing to a particular painting have proved inconclusive.
10. There is some debate over the question of whether Jacopo Bellini or his sons added the ink strengthening to these designs and, if the latter, whether they did so under their father's direction. Regardless of the hand, the point here is that the Yale drawing seems to follow the Bellini book.

2 Baccio Bandinelli
Gaiole in Chianti 1488–1560 Florence

Sheet of Studies, ca. 1519–22

Pen and brown ink on beige paper, laid down
28.8 × 20.7 cm (11 5/16 × 8 1/8 in.)

INSCRIPTIONS: recto, upper right, in brown ink: *R*; recto, lower center, in brown ink: *187*, or perhaps *L87*; verso, in black chalk: *121*, circled; verso, in graphite: *B33402*

PROVENANCE: Charles Sackville Bale (L. 640), stamp on verso; probably the drawing sold in Bale's sale, Christie, Manson, and Woods, London, 9–14 June 1881, lot 2247, "Anatomical Studies" by Bandinelli (sold to "Knowles"); Edith Chase; Mrs. Rodney Chase

REFERENCES: *YUAG Bulletin* 36.1 (1976): 37; Ward 1982, no. 255

Gift in memory of Henry S. Chase, class of 1877, and Rodney Chase, class of 1920. 1975.101.10

Although primarily a sculptor, Baccio Bandinelli was a prolific and accomplished draftsman. For Bandinelli, as indeed for most artists of the Florentine Renaissance, *disegno* was the foundation for all art, and the act of drawing was the process by which an artist would exercise his creative genius and define himself. Bandinelli would accordingly have spent hours each day producing drawings: some in preparation for sculpture, others as finished presentation sheets or designs for engraving, and still others as creative exercises or simply for his own pleasure. The depiction of Bandinelli's "Academy" in engravings by Agostino de' Musi and Enea Vico reveals the artist's theoretical as well as practical approach to the art of design, even if there is little evidence to suggest that such an Academy did exist. Despite the critical failure of Bandinelli's sculpture, his drawings were enthusiastically praised, even by his political rival Vasari, through whose writing Bandinelli's reputation otherwise suffered.[1]

This sheet, in the bold graphic style that is Bandinelli's trademark, is one of several hundred to survive from his hand. It is probably to be counted among those that the sculptor made as graphic exercises, sketches done either for their own sake or else as experimental motifs that might be incorporated into a more careful design. The broad pen and coarse paper are the combination of medium and support that Bandinelli generally used for such studies, presumably because the paper's porous surface absorbed the wide lines of fluid ink that facilitated rapid execution of these sketches.[2] The juxtaposition of overlapping heads, turned at various angles, seems to have been a sort of "graphic problem" that Bandinelli often posed for himself, to judge from a number of similar sheets.[3] Some of these drawings of heads are clearly portraits or copies of sculpture, but those in the Yale drawing, of a type found everywhere in Bandinelli's work, are much more likely to have been created from the artist's imagination. The hands, feet, and legs sketched here are of the same stamp; although perhaps inspired by fragments of antique sculpture or by modern paintings (the hand at lower left is reminiscent of Adam's in Michelangelo's Sistine chapel *Animation of Adam*), they are probably recollections drawn freely in the artist's studio rather than careful copies from these models. These motifs nonetheless offer some grounds for suggesting that the drawing dates from Bandinelli's time in Rome around 1519–22. The heads, hands, and feet of the Yale drawing can also be compared to some of the artist's more finished works from that period, including the *Slaughter of the Innocents* at Chatsworth, the preparatory drawing for an engraving executed by Marco Dente in 1520–21.[4] Bandinelli, however, surely kept drawings like the Yale *Studies* in his studio and referred to them from time to time, and any dating of a particular sheet is speculative as one can find similar motifs appearing in multiple works. Furthermore, he would have made numerous drawings of this type, quickly capturing or perfecting ideas, even as he worked on more careful compositional sketches.

Finally, these sheets would have served as models for the many young artists who studied with Bandinelli. A drawing in the Musée des Beaux-Arts, Lille, generally attributed to the workshop of Bandinelli, would seem to be one such example, as it includes profile heads, a leg and a foot, and a hand study very similar to those in the Yale drawing.[5] In sum, while the exact function or origin of a drawing like the Yale sheet is impossible to determine, the work is probably best appreciated as a pure graphic act in its own right, the sort of bold drawing that made Bandinelli a model for so many young Florentine artists.

JJM

1. Vasari (Milanesi) 6:190. After criticizing much of Bandinelli's sculpture, Vasari admitted toward the end of his biography of the artist that he had collected many of the latter's drawings for his own Book of Drawings, and that "one can surely do no better" than them.
2. Ward 1982, 70–71. Ward (68) also notes that this drawing is probably trimmed down from the full 45 × 31.5 cm sheets that Bandinelli usually used for these studies but is otherwise in the best possible condition. The coarse paper may also have been simply a cost-saving measure for an artist who drew as prolifically as did Bandinelli.
3. Ward 1993 also comments on Bandinelli's tendency to make such drawings. Other examples include: the *Three Heads*, New York, Metropolitan Museum of Art, inv. no. 63.125, pen and brown ink, 32.1 × 20.8 cm; and the *Male Heads in Two Rows*, Stockholm, Nationalmuseum, inv. no. 128, pen and brown ink, 35.3 × 27.2 cm. More finely drawn and carefully finished studies of this type are also found, such as the *Two Studies of the Head of a Boy*, Cracow, National Museum, Czartoryski Collection, inv. no. XV-Rr. 1959, pen and brown ink, 19.6 × 21.3 cm; and the *Two Studies of a Head of a Youth*, Chicago, Art Institute, inv. no. 1996.606, pen and brown ink, 23.8 × 25.4 cm. For an example in sculpture, see Bandinelli's *Deposition* of 1528 in the Louvre.
4. Chatsworth, Devonshire Collection, inv. no. 24, pen and brown ink and wash over red chalk, 38.8 × 56.6 cm; see Mantua–Vienna 1999, no. 200. There are also echoes of the Yale sketches in the drawing of *The Eternal Appearing to Adam and Eve*, Paris, École des Beaux-Arts, inv. no. 27, pen and brown ink, 43.6 × 29 cm. The *Study of Two Men*, Los Angeles, Getty Museum, inv. no. 85.GB.277, pen and brown ink, 21 × 34 cm, dated ca. 1525, is also stylistically similar.
5. Lille, Musée des Beaux-Arts, inv. no. Pl. 12, black chalk and pen and brown ink, 34.5 × 24.5 cm.

3 Polidoro Caldara, called Polidoro da Caravaggio

Caravaggio ca. 1499–ca. 1543 Messina

Figure Study of a Seated Old Man (recto), ca. 1519–22; *Unknown artist after Perino del Vaga, Study for the Castel Sant'Angelo* (verso), ca. 1545

Red chalk (recto); pen and brown ink and brown wash over black chalk, with oxidized white heightening (verso), 24.1 × 16.8 cm (9½ × 6⅝ in.)

INSCRIPTIONS: recto, upper left, in black chalk: *93*

PROVENANCE: Holtkott collection, Cologne; acquired from Mia Weiner, Norfolk, Conn.

REFERENCES: New York 1985, no. 10 (as Salviati); Dacos 1987, 381 (as Pedro Campaña [recto] and as Jeremias van Winghe after Josse van Winghe [verso]); *YUAG Bulletin* (2004): 161

Frederick M. Clapp, B.A. 1901, M.A. 1911, Fund. 2003.63.1

RECTO

Polidoro da Caravaggio was one of the most innovative members of Raphael's workshop, and the frescoes with which he covered the facades of many Roman palaces were among the most often copied paintings of the early sixteenth century. In the words of the sixteenth-century theorist Giovanni Battista Armenini, these frescoes served as a veritable "Institute of the Arts" for young painters of the following generation. Yet, as Sydney Freedberg has noted, "time has dealt more drastically with the accomplishment of Polidoro da Caravaggio than with that of any other major artist of [the early 16th century]"[1] and very few of Polidoro's Roman paintings survive. The *Figure Study of a Seated Old Man*, however, a work of Polidoro's Roman period, demonstrates both the artist's legacy from Raphael and the innovative qualities so admired by the following generation.

Polidoro Caldara was born around 1499 in the town of Caravaggio near Bergamo and arrived in Rome sometime around 1515–16. According to Vasari, Polidoro first found work as a manual laborer, hauling buckets of plaster for the fresco painters working under Raphael and Giovanni da Udine in the Vatican Loggia. He quickly demonstrated his considerable talents as a draftsman, however, and began working alongside the painters, especially Perino del Vaga, who had also recently arrived in Rome. In most documents of the late 1510s, Polidoro and Perino del Vaga are named together, and they worked essentially side by side at this early phase of their careers. Yet, already by the last stages of the Loggia project, the unquiet or dramatic aspect of Polidoro's figures could be distinguished from Perino's more elegant forms. Similarly, the proportions of the *Seated Old Man* depart somewhat from the most classical aspects of Raphael's art and hint instead at the mannered style that would develop fully in Roman and Florentine art of the next decade.

At this early stage in his career, nonetheless, Polidoro adhered to the rationalistic approach to drawing that was characteristic of Raphael's workshop, in which a series of sketches—compositional drawings (*modelli*) as well as more detailed studies of figures—was preparatory to essentially all paintings, even for relatively small works; conversely, most drawings from the workshop were made with a specific project in mind. In this particular case, the *Seated Old Man* can perhaps be linked to the scene sometimes (but unconvincingly) identified as *The Death of Socrates* in a painted frieze at the Palazzo Baldassini in Rome (fig. A), dated to the early 1520s.[2] The *Seated Old Man* appears to be a figure study for the man at the lower right edge of the bed, although the connection between painted figure and drawing is not immediately apparent. Reconstruction of the design process helps to show that link. The *modello* for this painting has also survived and is today in the National Gallery of Art in Washington (fig. B).[3] Although the Washington *modello* and the present figure study are different types of drawings, the similarity of the old man's pose (seated on a block and seen three-quarters from the back), his notably elongated head, and the consistent fall of light, argue in favor of their relationship. The positions of the man's arms and legs are unresolved in the figure study, although some vague lines above the man's lap might be read as indicating the book that the figure holds in the *modello*, if not in the final painting, where his arms are crossed. Given the changes between the Washington drawing and the final work, it is hardly surprising to see changes from the figure study to the finished painting. The Yale drawing served as a study not of arms or legs, but rather of the fall of light on the slumping and twisted torso, the one consistent element from *modello* to figure study to painting. Similarly, the verso of the Washington drawing has a study generally thought to be an alternate idea for the woman at the lower left edge of the bed in the compositional drawing, a figure entirely changed in the finished work.[4] In sum, the coordinating *modello* and figure drawings demonstrate the characteristic working process of an artist trained in Raphael's workshop, and even if some doubt may remain about the connection between the Yale sheet and the Palazzo Baldassini drawings, the former still stands as a paradigmatic example of Roman figure drawing in the 1520s.[5]

The verso of the drawing was not made until some twenty-five years later, and by a different artist. While Polidoro had painted at the Palazzo Baldassini, his companion Perino del Vaga was at work in the adjacent salone of the palace.[6] It seems likely that Polidoro's and Perino's drawings were simply gathered

VERSO

POLIDORO DA CARAVAGGIO 43

FIGURE 3A | Polidoro da Caravaggio, *Deathbed Scene (Death of Socrates?)*, ca. 1519–22. Rome, Palazzo Baldassini.

FIGURE 3C | Perino del Vaga, *Study for the Castel Sant'Angelo*, ca. 1545–47. Florence, Galleria degli Uffizi.

FIGURE 3B | Polidoro da Caravaggio, *Deathbed Scene*, ca. 1519–22. Washington, D.C., National Gallery of Art.

together when work was complete, or, alternatively, when Polidoro fled Rome during the Sack of 1527, as the city was being plundered by troops of Charles V, Holy Roman Emperor and King of Spain. Perino, who remained in the city, may have taken possession of his associate's drawings, for Perino surely still had the *Seated Old Man* twenty years later, in 1545–47, when he was working at the Castel Sant'Angelo. The drawing on the verso of the sheet is a copy of one of Perino's own studies for the Sala Paolina (fig. C),[7] a copy that must have been made by one of Perino's assistants in the 1540s rather than from the fresco: the cherubs at the bottom of the sheet appear only in Perino's drawings; there is actually a door in that space in the Sala Paolina. A hypothetical situation can easily be imagined: One of Perino's assistants, asked by the master to make a copy of the Sala Paolina sketch (perhaps as an educational exercise), came across a twenty-five-year-old scrap of paper in Perino's studio. Anyone in that studio would have realized that the drawing was not one of Perino's own, but it is unlikely that one of Perino's fifteen- or twenty-year-old assistants could have recognized the *Seated Old Man* as the work of Polidoro, who had gone to Naples twenty years earlier. The assistant would simply have made use of an otherwise mysterious old sketch when he drew on the back of the sheet. The juxtaposition of the two sketches, however, provides a fascinating glimpse of workshop practice and the processes, or accidents, by which Renaissance drawings have come down to us.[8]

The *Seated Old Man* was previously attributed to Salviati and later to Pedro Campaña, but was recognized as the work of Polidoro by Nicholas Turner, an attribution confirmed by Alessandro Nova and about which there can be no doubt.[9] Apart from the drawing's connection to the Palazzo Baldassini project, the drawing sits easily alongside other figure studies by Polidoro, including the *Saint Jerome* formerly in the collection of Jak Katalan,[10] the *Seated Figure with Raised Arms* at the Getty,[11] and the *Figure Studies, possibly for a Triton* in Stockholm.[12]

JJM

1. Freedberg 1993, 200.
2. On the fresco, see Ravelli 1988.
3. Inv. no. 1991.9.1, red chalk, 21 × 29 cm. The drawing has been published several times, with the fullest description by J. A. Gere in New York 1987, no. 82.
4. The verso drawing has been published often. See, for example, Leone di Castris 2001, 76.
5. A closer look at the frieze reveals that Polidoro's skill as a painter did not yet match his ability as a draftsman; indeed, the painting lacks the elegance both of the *modello* in Washington and of the *Seated Old Man*. It might be noted, though, that the stumpy characteristics of the figures in the frieze are shared by the figures in many of Perino's paintings at the time, but not Perino's drawings. One wonders whether this was not a conscious decision, perhaps guided by a then-current understanding of classical art derived from sarcophagi or from the Column of Trajan. For a further example, compare the *Meeting of Janus and Saturn* from the Villa Lante, Rome, now in the Bibliotheca Hertziana, with the preparatory drawing in the Louvre (inv. no. 6078), illustrated in Leone di Castris 2001, 93, figs. 23 and 24. The Louvre drawing, furthermore, provides a stylistic comparison with the Yale drawing.
6. On Perino's work in the palace, see Wolk-Simon 2002, 11–21, and Parma Armani 1986, 255–257.
7. Florence, Uffizi, inv. no. 66 Orn., pen and brown ink and brown and gray washes, heightened with white, squared in black chalk, 35.4 × 30.4 cm.
8. Armenini notes that Perino's daughter had a large cache of his drawings, which she sold to the dealer Jacopo Strada. Other sheets, perhaps including this one, must have passed into the workshops of the artists who finished Perino's Castel Sant'Angelo project after his death. Wolk-Simon 2003, 57, n. 5, has recently made the interesting suggestion that the large group of drawings in Budapest might be those that went to Strada.
9. The sheet was originally offered for sale by Mia Weiner with an attribution to Salviati, and was later attributed to Peter de Kempeneer/Pedro Campana by Dacos 1987.
10. The drawing, red chalk, 20.8 × 13.4 cm, was sold at Sotheby's, London, 10 July 2002, lot 1; see New York 1994, no. 62, and Leone di Castris 2001, no. D181.
11. Los Angeles, Getty Museum, inv. no. 84.6.B.31, red chalk, 20.7 × 18.5 cm; Leone di Castris 2001, no. D165.
12. Stockholm, Nationalmuseum, inv. nos. 377–378/1863, red chalk, 27.5 × 18.6 cm; Bjurström and Magnusson 1998, no. 512, and Leone di Castris 2001, no. D252. The aforementioned *Meeting of Janus and Saturn* of ca. 1524 (Paris, Louvre, inv. no. 6078, red chalk, 19.8 × 28.5 cm), although a *modello* rather than a figure study, provides a further close comparison.

4 Bernard van Orley
Brussels 1488–1541 Brussels

The Resurrection, ca. 1525–30

Black chalk, with white heightening, squared in red chalk, on three sheets joined together, 88.6 × 47.9 cm (34⅞ × 18⅞ in.)

INSCRIPTIONS: recto, lower right, in pen and brown ink: *XX*

PROVENANCE: Robert Lehman, New York (by 1925)

REFERENCES: De Tolnay 1943, 132, no. 162; Cambridge 1967b, unnumbered cat.; H-B and L, no. 502; Paris–Florence 1980–81, 165; Farmer 1981, 302; Washington–New York 1986–87, no. 92; *Handbook*, 201

Gift of Robert Lehman, B.A. 1913. 1941.302

Bernard van Orley, the most important artist in Brussels in his day, was a prolific painter and designer of tapestries and stained glass. In 1518 he was appointed court painter to Margaret of Austria, sister of the Holy Roman Emperor Charles V and Regent of the Netherlands, and following her death in 1530 he worked for her successor, Mary of Hungary. Until about 1525 his work was primarily as a painter, but after that date he seems to have given more attention to creating designs for tapestries and stained glass.[1] Yale's drawing is one of a series of Passion scenes designed by van Orley almost certainly for stained glass, of which thirteen are known today. Besides the one at Yale, three are in the Musées Royaux d'Art et Histoire in Brussels[2] and three in the Kupferstichkabinett in Berlin;[3] two at the École des Beaux-Arts, Paris;[4] and one each at the Institut Néerlandais, Paris;[5] the Metropolitan Museum of Art, New York;[6] the Fogg Museum, Cambridge, Mass.;[7] and in a private collection.[8] All are in black chalk, squared for transfer in red chalk. They are all drawn on a support consisting of two or more sheets of paper fastened together, and all are relatively close in height; widths vary from 47 to 67 cm. At least four are rounded at the top, and three others have lines that might indicate that the top of the composition was intended to fit an arched field. Six of the thirteen drawings bear Roman numerals; *The Descent of the Holy Spirit (The Pentecost)*, at the Fogg, is marked "XX—" (the part of the paper bearing the third digit

has been torn off), so it would seem there were at least twenty-one in the series. There is no readily apparent pattern to these numbers; they do not correlate with the biblical order of the subjects.[9]

The drawings would seem all to have been part of the same campaign for the decoration of a set of windows in a church, and they all represent the same, fairly advanced, stage in the highly organized and multifaceted enterprise of creating a narrative set of stained-glass windows. The church for which they were designed, however, is not known, and no window following any of these designs survives. There is a window extant, in the church of Saint Peter in Solre le Château, France, depicting *Pilate Washing His Hands*,[10] the same subject as the drawing now in the Metropolitan Museum in the series of which Yale's drawing is part. The Solre le Château windows are documented as having been made by 1532. The composition, however, is significantly different from the one in the present series, and for this reason and also because the Saint Peter's window has completely different proportions—slightly wider than it is tall, with a decorative architectural frame across the top and on the sides—it seems likely that it would have been generated from a drawing that was part of a different series.

Max J. Friedländer was the first to attribute some of the drawings to van Orley, and Jean Helbig, Charles de Tolnay, and Ludwig Baldass, discussing different drawings in the series, concurred,[11] but Julius Held saw a close relationship between the Berlin drawings and the artist who painted *Scenes from the Lives of Saint Catherine and Saint Roch*.[12] Since then, opinions have varied considerably, both regarding the series as a whole and individual drawings within it. In 1970 Haverkamp-Begemann and Logan published Yale's drawing as "a product of the van Orley workshop." John David Farmer in 1981 brought together a group of works, including the Yale drawing, that he thought were by a hand he called the "Master of the Raleigh *Ascension* and *Pentecost*," referring to two paintings in the North Carolina Museum of Art, Raleigh.[13] Emmanuelle Brugerolles, in 1985, wrote of the two drawings in the École des Beaux-Arts that they were "probably" by van Orley;[14] in 1986, John Hand, writing about Yale's drawing, followed Farmer's suggestion that the artist was the same as the person who did the paintings in Raleigh.[15] Karel Boon in 1992, however, rejected Farmer's suggestion, writing that the series must be by the same designer as the *Scenes from the Lives of Saint Catherine and Saint Roch*, in the Musées Royaux des Beaux-Arts de Belgique;[16] Maryan Ainsworth in 1996 went back to Farmer's idea, writing that the drawings are "more probably by the so-called Master of the Raleigh *Ascension* and *Pentecost*."[17]

There is no doubt that this series of drawings is a product of the van Orley workshop, probably dating from around the second half of the 1520s, but since most undisputed drawings by van Orley are designs for tapestries, in pen and wash, with a much more delicate effect than the bold black chalk of this and the other drawings of the series, it is difficult to be categorical about the authorship of this group. Recently, however, Michiel Plomp asserted his conviction that *Pilate Washing His Hands*, acquired in 2003 by the Metropolitan Museum, is indeed by van Orley.[18] Maryan Ainsworth agrees with this conclusion.[19] Yale's drawing is so similar in handling to the one in the Metropolitan that both seem almost certainly to have been done by the same hand.

As every writer about these drawings has noted, the compositions hark back to some extent to Albrecht Dürer's three printed *Passion* series, especially the so-called small woodcut *Passion*. Dürer's influence, already great in the Netherlands through the dissemination of his prints, was reinforced by his travels there in 1520 and 1521, and van Orley himself was Dürer's host for a dinner in Brussels in late August or early September 1520.[20] For the subject of the *Resurrection*, however, the general compositional scheme—with the risen Christ in the center and the several soldiers assigned to guard the tomb in positions of fright or awe—had become conventional by this period. The drawing does have in common with Dürer's small woodcut *Passion* composition the placement of figures in the distance with a fence behind, visible beneath Christ's right hand, and a steep hill rising on the other side. The figure of the risen Christ recalls some in van Orley's paintings, for example the main figure in *Job Receiving Ill Tidings* on the interior of the right shutter of the Job Altarpiece (*The Virtue of Patience*) of 1521 in the Musées Royaux des Beaux-Arts de Belgique in Brussels.[21]

SB

1 New York 2002b, 287–339, while focusing on van Orley as a designer for tapestry, provides an overview of his oeuvre and his artistic importance.
2 See Helbig 1943, figs. 114–116; H-B and L, 268–271, figs. 52–54.
3 Inv. nos. 13607–09; Bock and Rosenberg 1930, 1:45; Baldass 1944, figs 150–152.
4 Paris–Hamburg 1985–86, nos. 43–44.
5 Boon 1992, no. 156.
6 Plomp 2003.
7 Harvard 2003, 27–28.
8 P. Ruys-Raquez in Brussels 1983, no. 10.
9 The thirteen drawings, in the Biblical order, are *Christ Washing the Feet of the Disciples* (Brussels, 91.5 x 67 cm, marked "IX"); *Christ Taking Leave of His Mother* (Berlin, 86 × 48.5 cm, top arched); *The Betrayal of Christ* (Institut Néerlandais, Paris, 76.2 × 52.4 cm); *Christ Before Caiaphas* (private collection, Brussels, 84 × 62 cm); *Christ before Pilate* (Berlin, 86.7 × 63.6 cm, marked "II"); *Christ before Herod* (Brussels, 91.5 × 67 cm, marked "III"); *Pilate Washing His Hands* (Metropolitan Museum of Art, New York, 92 × 61.5 cm, top arched); *Christ Nailed to the Cross* (École des Beaux-Arts, Paris, 80.4 × 49.7 cm, indication for arched top?); *The Raising of the Cross* (École des Beaux-Arts, Paris, 82.4 × 47 cm, indication for arched top?); *The Crucifixion* (Berlin, 87.5 × 62.4 cm); *The Resurrection* (Yale, marked "XX"); *Christ Appearing to His Disciples* (Brussels, 91.5 × 67 cm, marked "X," arched top?); *The Descent of the Holy Spirit (The Pentecost)* (Fogg Art Museum, Cambridge, Mass., marked XX–[torn off], indication for arched top).
10 Grodecki, Perrot, and Taralon 1978, 246–247 and pl. 32.
11 Friedländer 1922, pl. 11; Friedländer 1967, 8:133; Helbig 1943, figs. 114–116; De Tolnay 1943, no. 162; Baldass 1944, 177.
12 Held 1931, 108–109.
13 Farmer 1981, 253–258, 301–302.
14 Paris–Hamburg 1985–86, nos. 43–44.
15 Washington–New York 1986–87, no. 92.
16 Boon 1992, no. 156.
17 *Grove Dictionary* 23:526.
18 Plomp 2003.
19 Oral communication, 16 July 2003.
20 Dürer 1971, 65.
21 Inv. no. 1822; Friedländer 1967, 8, no. 85, pls. 78–81.

5 The Master of 1527
Dutch, active ca. 1527

The Mocking of Christ, ca. 1525–30

Pen and brown ink with gray wash, over black chalk, 26 × 19.8 cm (10¼ × 7¾ in.)

INSCRIPTIONS: a long inscription, much of it indecipherable, on verso (see fig. A)

PROVENANCE: acquired from H. M. Calmann, London

REFERENCES: Bruyn 1960, 113, no. 7 (as Aertgen van Leyden); London 1960, no. 18 (as Aertgen van Leyden); *YUAG Bulletin* 30 (1964): 13 and 50 (as Master of the Miracles of the Apostles); H-B and L, no. 330; Washington–New York 1986–87, no. 2 (as Aertgen van Leyden)

Everett V. Meeks, B.A. 1901, Fund. 1963.9.29

The identity of the artist of this drawing is still far from certain. A small group of sheets in a style close to the distinctive one of Yale's drawing were first grouped by Paul Wescher, who called the artist "the Master of 1527," because of a drawing in the Louvre, *Suffer the Little Children to Come unto Me*, which is dated 1527.[1] In the same article he gathered another group of drawings under the name of "Master of the Apostles' Miracles," based on another drawing in the Louvre, the *Story of Ananias*, and a *Healing of the Lame* in Berlin.[2] In 1939 I. Q. van Regteren Altena fused these two groups, identifying the artist of all of these drawings as Aertgen van Leyden, proposing a list of 144 works—fifty-seven paintings, eighty-one drawings, two prints, and four paintings on glass—some known, others only listed in documents.[3] In 1960 Josua Bruyn added twenty-eight drawings to this list, including the sheet now at Yale, at that time with the dealer H. M. Calmann.[4] In 2001 two drawings from this large group were sold at auction, both attributed to Aertgen van Leyden. *The Pool at Bethesda* is one of the drawings originally given to the Master of 1527, while *The Adoration of the Shepherds* was among the group given to the Master of the Apostles' Miracles.[5]

Haverkamp-Begemann and Logan, in the catalogue of 1970, still preferred to retain the name "Master of 1527," and in 1980 K. G. Boon warned that "the attribution of the entire group to a single painter or draftsman becomes a hazardous enterprise."[6] David Becker, writing about a drawing of *King David Praying* in Bowdoin in 1985, and Martin Schapelhouman, cataloguing two drawings in the Ashmolean in *Kunst voor de beeldenstorm* (1986), both kept the name Master of 1527; in the same publication Schapelhouman catalogued another Ashmolean drawing as by the Master of the Apostles' Miracles.[7] Even though the attribution of *The Mocking of Christ* to Aertgen van Leyden was endorsed by J. Richard Judson in the catalogue of the exhibition *The Age of Bruegel*,[8] the earlier division still seems sound. Jan-Piet Filedt Kok, another of the authors of *Kunst voor de beeldenstorm*, recently stated that he, too, is "still inclined to go back to the Master of 1527 for [Yale's] drawing and the Master of the Apostles' Miracles for the other group."[9]

Besides the Paris drawing *Suffer the Little Children*, a core group that, although extremely limited, would seem definitely to be by the same hand as Yale's drawing, includes a *Scene from the Story of Absalom* in Berlin,[10] *King David Praying* at Bowdoin, a *Circumcision* in Dusseldorf,[11] the two Ashmolean drawings, and *Achan Buries the Treasure Plundered from Jericho in His Tent*.[12] A thorough reexamination of all the drawings that have been associated with Aertgen van Leyden, beginning with this core group, could result in a considerably clearer definition of the oeuvre of the artist of Yale's drawing and that of perhaps several others.

The extensive inscription on the verso of this drawing (fig. A) in Dutch and French, in a sixteenth-century hand (or perhaps two hands), is comparable to those on the *Allegory of Justice and Wisdom* and *The Unrighteous*

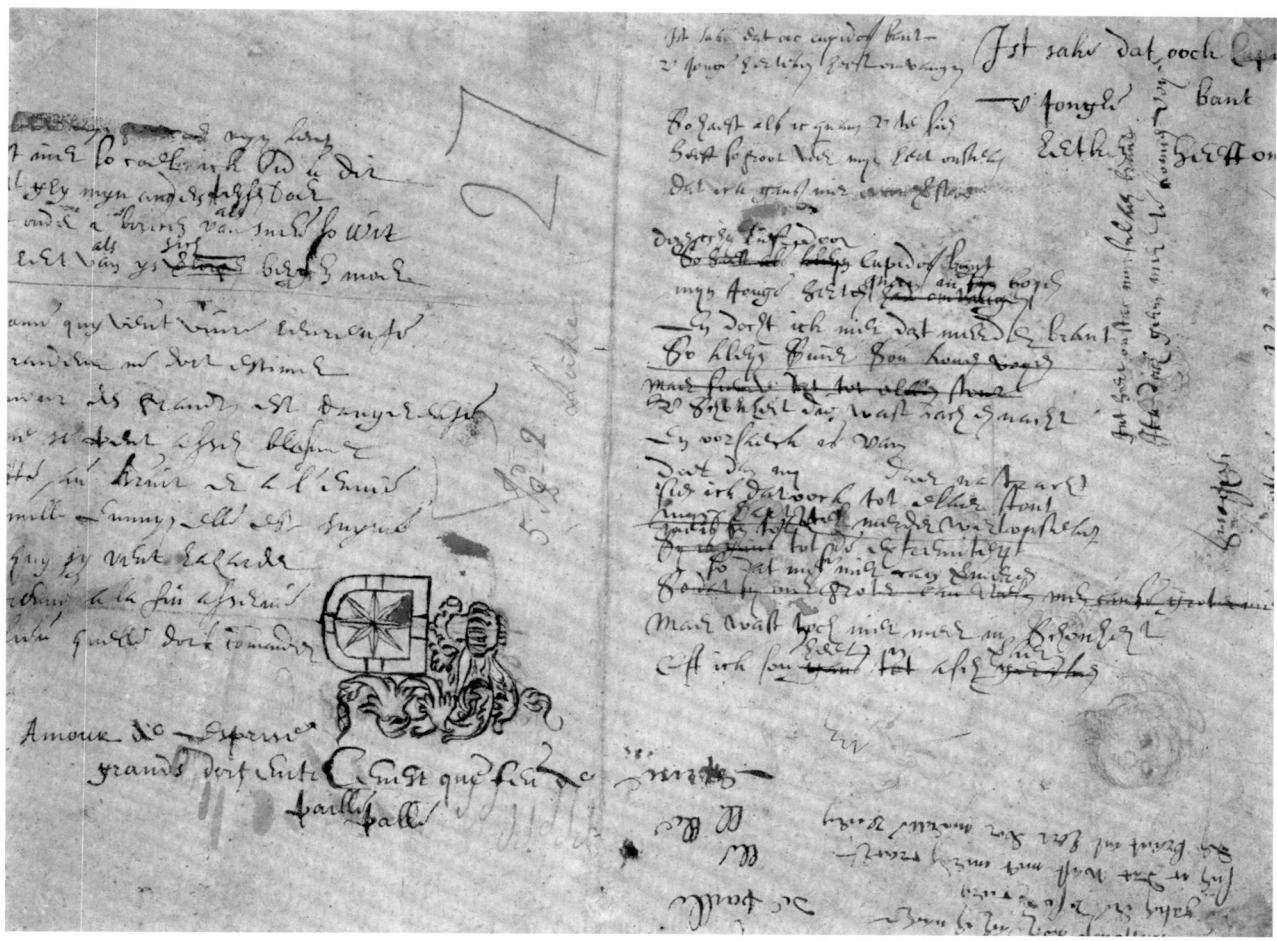

FIGURE 5A | Verso of cat. no. 5

Judge in the Ashmolean.[13] The drawn coat of arms on the Yale sheet, in the same ink, has not yet been identified.

SB

1. Inv. no. 20893; Lugt 1968, no. 99; Wescher 1928, 251 and 253, fig. 7.
2. Paris, Louvre, inv. no. 18899; Wescher 1928, 249, fig. 4. Berlin, Kupferstichkabinett, inv. no. 11993; Bock and Rosenberg 1930, 1:42.
3. Regteren Altena 1939.
4. Bruyn 1960, additional drawings in Appendix II, 112–114.
5. Christie's, New York, 24 January 2001, lots 150 (private collection), 151 (now Metropolitan Museum of Art, inv. no. 2001.110); see also Prybram-Gladona 1969, nos. 91, 92.
6. Florence–Paris 1980–81, 145–146.
7. Brunswick et al. 1985–86, no. 1; Amsterdam 1986, no. 51, *Allegory of Justice and Wisdom*, 1946.305; no. 52, *The Unrighteous Judge*, 1946.358; and no. 54, *The Angel Departing from the Family of Tobias*, 1863.139. I wish to thank Jane Turner for providing additional information about the Ashmolean drawings.
8. Washington–New York 1986–87, no. 2.
9. By electronic communication, 25 September 2003.
10. Inv. no. 24607; Berlin 1973, no. 24.
11. Regteren Altena 1939, 130, fig. 2.
12. Bruyn 1960, 111, fig. 44, ex coll. Milford, on Basel art market in 1952.
13. Those two drawings at the Ashmolean also came through the dealer H. M. Calmann, London.

6 Jan Swart van Groningen
Groningen ca. 1500–at least 1562 Gouda?

The Beheading of Saint Barbara, ca. 1525–30

Pen and brown ink and brown wash, squared in black chalk, 32.5 × 25.8 cm (12 13/16 × 10 3/8 in.)

WATERMARK: on backing sheet, large fleur de lys (not illustrated)

INSCRIPTIONS: recto, lower right, in pencil: *De Vos*

PROVENANCE: John Percival, 1st Earl of Egmont (1683–1748); John T. Graves; Robert Hoe (sale, New York, Anderson Auction Company, 15–19 April 1912, Library of Robert Hoe, Part III, A–K, no. 949); Yale University Library (anonymous donor, 1957)

REFERENCES: H-B and L, no. 332

Egmont Collection, Yale Library Transfer. 1961.66.38

Jan Swart, born in Groningen and active in Gouda and Antwerp, was a painter and designer of stained glass and prints—both woodcuts and etchings.[1] He was the head of an active and prolific workshop, producing mainly designs for glass. It is possible that the *Beheading of Saint Barbara* was meant to be carried out in stained glass; in any case the light squaring, in black chalk, is an indication that the drawing was a model for a work in some other medium. Van Mander wrote that Swart went to Italy, and although there is no certain evidence to corroborate this statement, it seems likely that he went to Constantinople, which he would almost certainly have reached by sailing from Venice. One of Swart's best-known woodcuts, thought to be from the first half of the 1520s, is *Jesus Preaching from a Ship*, in which three of the four men in the central group of listeners are wearing turbans. He also made a *Procession of Turkish Riders*, in five sheets, dated 1526.[2] Thus if he did make such a trip to Italy and the Near East, it would most likely have preceded that date. Swart is thought to have lived in Antwerp from 1524 to 1528. He produced sixty-nine designs, plus two title pages, for the Vorsterman Bible, published in Antwerp in 1528–29.[3] Earlier scholars have proposed that he may have died during the 1550s, but it has recently been shown that he painted an altarpiece in 1562.[4]

The Beheading of Saint Barbara shows several episodes in the life of the third-century saint. Barbara converted to Christianity against the wishes of her father, so he punished her by imprisoning her in a tower; some versions have it that she was imprisoned first, and converted subsequently. She escaped while her father was on a journey. In the middle ground, at the left, the saint stands alone, meditating; farther back she is seen instructing workmen to put a third window in the tower, to symbolize the Trinity. At midground right is the episode where Barbara's father meets two shepherds and asks them for news of her; when one of them speaks about Barbara's Christian deeds, the father turns that shepherd's sheep into grasshoppers—several grasshoppers are visible between the saint and her father. In the foreground Barbara's father, dressed in a robe secured by a rope slung low around his waist and wearing a Turkish turban, is about to behead his daughter, who kneels on the ground in front of him, her hands together in prayer. Once he has killed her, a thunderbolt descends and kills the father, who is seen at the top being carried off by a devil. Because of the episodes of the grasshoppers and the thunderbolt, Saint Barbara has traditionally been venerated as a protector against plague and lightning.

Over Swart's long working life, his style changed from a late Gothic one, with a nervous line and somewhat disjointed figures, to a more Italianate manner, with a smoother line and more full-bodied figures. This drawing was probably made relatively early, perhaps in the later 1520s. Another drawing of a female saint, *Saint Catherine of Alexandria Refusing to Renounce Her Faith*, is relatively close in size to Yale's drawing, but that one is on prepared paper, with white heightening. Ludwig Baldass and Frits Lugt saw that one as likely dating from later in Swart's career, so the two are probably not related.[5] The style of Yale's drawing is similar to that of the two well-known woodcuts mentioned above, *Jesus Preaching from a Ship* and the *Procession of Turkish Riders*.

SB

1. There is no monograph on Swart. See Dodgson 1910; Beets 1914; Baldass 1918; Washington–Boston 1983, 314–317; Boon 1992, 1:360–365; Amsterdam 1986, 1:78–79, 2:175–177, 245–250; New York 1995, 166–174. For Swart's activity in prints, see Hollstein DF 29:107–125.
2. Van Mander (Miedema) 1:169; Hollstein DF 29:110, no. 5 and 29:112–113, nos. 8–12.
3. Hollstein DF 29:115–120, nos. 21–91; see also Beets 1915 and Washington–Boston 1983, no. 94.
4. Savelsberg 1989.
5. Paris, Louvre, inv. no. 19004, pen and ink and gray wash, heightened with white, on paper prepared with a greenish-yellow wash, 28 × 20.7 cm; Baldass 1918, no. 62; Lugt 1968, no. 116.

7 Jörg Breu the Elder and Workshop
Augsburg 1475/80–1537 Augsburg

Circe Transforming the Men of Ulysses into Animals, ca. 1525–35

Pen and brown ink, reworked in black ink, paper roughly trimmed to edge of design and laid down. Roughly circular, diameter 24.3 cm (9 9/16 in.)

PROVENANCE: private collection, France; acquired from Monroe Warshaw, New York

REFERENCES: *YUAG Bulletin* (2004): 158

Everett V. Meeks, B.A. 1901, Fund. 2003.30.1

Jörg Breu the Elder, along with Hans Holbein the Elder and Hans Burgkmair, formed a triumvirate of leading artists in Augsburg in the early sixteenth century. Like them, and like their contemporary Albrecht Dürer, Breu combined the distinctly German style of the Danube School with a classicism more often associated with Italian art. Under the influence of his sophisticated Augsburg patrons, Breu created a range of works, including altarpieces, manuscript illuminations, history paintings, and secular fresco decorations, as well as designs for woodcuts, book illustrations, and stained glass.

The majority of Breu's surviving drawings, including the present sheet, are related to the production of stained glass. Most have secular subjects—from mythology, history, or the courtly tradition—and were presumably made for the homes of Augsburg merchants and humanists. Breu designed, for example, a series of roundels with hunts and battles for the Imperial Hunting Lodge of Emperor Maximilian at Lermoos, Tyrol; another more or less complete series showing the labors of the months was commissioned by a member of the Hoechstetter family of Augsburg, and a set of tournament scenes is also well known.[1] Another group of roundel designs, all representing characters from Greek and Roman legend and history, seems to make up a set with which the *Circe* should perhaps be included. Other examples from this group include the *Ulysses and Telemachus Slaying the Suitors* and *Titus Manlius Torquatus Killing the Gaul* in the British Museum, the *Death of Marcus Curtius* and *Lucretia* in Berlin, the *Cleopatra* in Stuttgart, and the *Death of Agamemnon* in the Morgan Library, New York.[2] The subjects of these roundels would seem to fit together, although rather than from a single literary source they apparently derive from a range of texts including Plutarch's *Lives*, the *Gesta Romanorum*, Boccaccio's *Famous Women* (*De mulieribus claris*), and Petrarch's unfinished *De viris illustribus*.

Boccaccio's *Famous Women* is almost certainly the source for the *Circe* image seen here, rather than Homer's *Odyssey*, from which the story is best known today. The latter was only translated into German later in the sixteenth century, whereas Boccaccio's text was an early "best-seller," printed in German at least four times before 1500. In Homer's version of the Circe story, all the men are transformed into pigs, while in Boccaccio's, they simply become "various animals," corresponding more closely to the scene shown by Breu. Finally, Breu was himself responsible for a set of woodcut illustrations to an edition of Boccaccio's text.[3] These were not published until after the artist's death, and were probably designed later in his career than the stained-glass design. Nonetheless, his woodcut illustration to the book (fig. A) is clearly based on the woodcut found in the 1473 and 1479 editions of the text (fig. B),[4] so it is not difficult to imagine that Breu had the earlier text and image in front of him when he set out to draw this roundel. There are very obvious similarities in the manner of showing the transformed men as humans in courtier clothing, with the heads of animals.[5]

The textual source might explain, furthermore, some of the iconographical oddities of this depiction. The chapter heading in the German editions of Boccaccio's *Famous Women* refers to Circe, "the daughter of the Sun." Monroe Warshaw has suggested that this might account for the halo of light around her head. Circe holds a book in her left hand and points with her right, a combination of attribute and gesture often used to indicate the casting of spells. Indeed, Circe seems generally to have been treated as a witch in contemporary imagery. A woodcut in the *Nuremberg Chronicle* of 1493, for example, shows her offering the men of Ulysses a potion, and in the German-text edition of the *Chronicle*, she is described as a "Schwartzkünstlerein," a practitioner of the black arts.

FIGURE 7A | Jörg Breu the Elder, *Circe*, from Boccaccio, *Ein schöne Cronica, oder, Hystoribüch, von den fürnämlichsten Weybern*, Augsburg, 1541. Cambridge, Mass., Harvard University, Houghton Library.

Moreover, in the *Chronicle* woodcut, she is attended by a woman, but in the Yale drawing, that assistant has been transformed into a little demon, perhaps to emphasize that Circe "exercised her sorcery by means of demonic delusion," as related in Ulrich Molitor's *On Female Witches and Seers*, perhaps the most popular contemporary book on witches, to judge from its publication in nineteen editions between 1489 and 1500.[6] Circe's wings, however, remain an unsolved iconographical problem. Popular legend held that witches could fly, but never, in the many images of witches and Circe, is she or any other witch shown with wings.[7]

Regarding the attributions of the many surviving drawings produced by Breu and his workshop for the glass painters, the line between Breu's originals and the workshop copies is unclear. Sixty sheets survive, for example, for the roundel designs of the twelve months. In attempting to clarify the types, functions, and attributions of these drawings, Andrew Morrall has outlined three broad categories: 1) the original autograph designs, most of which are more linear than would be convenient for the glass painters to follow; 2) copies by Breu and his workshop in pen, ink, and wash, probably versions of the designs given to the glass painters, who could more easily translate the areas of wash into the painted shades of glass; and 3) simple outline copies.[8] The present drawing, however, does not fit easily into any of these categories. It was first drawn in pen and gray-brown ink, but with less detail and verve than is found in the best, surely autograph, drawings by Breu. Many of the contours were then strengthened, and shading added by hatching, in a thicker pen and black ink. These black lines do seem to be in Breu's hand, for they have a vitality absent from the original gray-brown drawing. Moreover, most of the parallel hatching lines run from upper left to lower right, a slightly unusual practice but one consistent with that in many of the drawings considered to be Breu's own. Presumably, Breu made an original (now lost) drawing for the composition, and had a member of his studio make a clean copy of the design. Breu would then have completed the drawing by adding the strong hatching to indicate shadows. A subsequent version of the composition, probably made mainly by the workshop, would have replaced the hatching with wash, thereby preparing the design to go to the glass painters. The earlier version (i.e., the present sheet) would have either remained in the workshop or might have been sent to the patron for approval. When a design was accepted, the drawing sometimes became the possession of the patron; otherwise, a drawing such

FIGURE 7B | Artist unknown, *Circe*, from Bocaccio, *Buch von den hochgeruemten Frauen*, Ulm, 1473. Cambridge, Mass., Harvard University, Houghton Library.

as the present work may have served as a *vidimus*, a sort of legal "certified copy" establishing what the patron had seen and the artists would produce.[9]

JJM

1. On Breu and his designs for painted glass, see especially Morrall 2001, and Los Angeles–St. Louis 2000, 202–232.
2. Respectively, London, British Museum, inv. nos. 1949-4-11-109, pen and black ink, 24.4 cm diameter, and 1912-12-20-1, pen and black ink, 24 cm diameter; Berlin, Kupferstichkabinett, KdZ inv. nos. 17665 and 4406; Stuttgart, Staatsgalerie, Graphische Sammlung, inv. no. 7; and New York, Pierpont Morgan Library, inv. no. 1966.1. See Rowlands 1993, 1:41–43, for further discussion of the group.
3. Hollstein G 5:182, nos. 528–608: illustrations to Boccaccio 1541.
4. Boccaccio 1473, reprinted in facsimile as Boccaccio 1924.
5. It has also been suggested that the depiction derives from Boethius's *Consolation of Philosophy*, in which the Ulysses and Circe story is also related. Boethius, however, writes that "no part of [Ulysses' men] remained unchanged—they lost both voice and body . . . " and accordingly this text seems less likely to have been the source.
6. The most complete discussion of Circe imagery, on which the preceding paragraph has been based, is in Zika 2002, which contains a summary of previous research.
7. On contemporary images of witches, see Sullivan 2002 and Davidson 1987. Another possible identification of the woman in this drawing, although less likely because the text was far less known in Breu's milieu than was Boccaccio's, is that she represents Melissa, the good witch from Ariosto's *Orlando Furioso*, who transformed men back to their own forms, as seen in Dosso Dossi's painting now in the Borghese Gallery, Rome. But even as Melissa, there would be no reason for her to have wings.
8. Morrall 2001, 58. See also van Treek 2000.
9. On the *vidimus*, see Morrall 2001, 58–59 and Wayment 1979. On glass production and preliminary designs, see also Los Angeles–St. Louis 2000, and Husband 1998.

8 Bernardino Licinio

Venice ca. 1489–ca. 1549/65 Venice

Woman Holding a Vase, ca. 1530

Black chalk, heightened with white, on blue-gray paper. 21.4 × 14.7 cm (8 7/16 × 5 13/16 in.)

INSCRIPTIONS: recto, lower left, in graphite: *A del. Sarto*

PROVENANCE: John Percival, 1st Earl of Egmont (1683–1748); John T. Graves; Robert Hoe (sale, New York, Anderson Auction Company, 15–19 April 1912, Library of Robert Hoe, Part III, A–K, no. 949); Yale University Library (anonymous donor, 1957)

REFERENCES: Rearick 1967, 382–383; H-B and L, no. 273; New Haven 1974, no. 5; Vertova 1975, 381, 441, and 452; London 1983–84, no. D20; New Haven 1991a, no. 11; *Handbook,* 200; Rearick 2001, 46–47

Egmont Collection, Yale Library Transfer. 1961.65.46

While much less innovative than either Giorgione or Titian, Bernardino Licinio is perhaps more typical of the artists working in Venice during the first half of the sixteenth century. Like Palma Vecchio and Giovanni Cariani, to whom he might best be compared, Licinio came from a Bergamesque family but spent most of his career in Venice. He was trained in the circle of Giovanni Bellini, perhaps even in Bellini's own workshop, and had a successful career producing traditionally styled portraits, altarpieces, and small devotional paintings for Venice and other cities in Northern Italy. Although essentially a conservative artist, Licinio was aware of Giorgione and Titian, and his works show some reflection of their developments; a number of Licinio's early paintings from the 1510s and '20s have at times even been mistakenly attributed to Giorgione. Licinio never, however, embraced the more dramatic aspects of Titian's style, preferring instead solid, symmetrical, and quiet compositions.[1]

The *Woman Holding a Vase* is entirely typical of Licinio's art. On the one hand, the use of black and white chalk on blue paper was a new practice devised by Venetian artists in the years around 1510 and suggests that Licinio may have seen drawings by Titian or one of his early followers, such as Paris Bordon. On the other hand, this new technique is used to create a drawing that adheres to the late medieval model-book tradition.[2] Reflecting other practices that became standard in Venice only in the early sixteenth century, the study is drawn from life and pays attention to volume, which is depicted with strong chiaroscuro; yet, the study fixed the image of the seated woman for Licinio and he never strayed far from this pose. Substituting an infant for the vase and making small changes to the drapery, head, or hands, Licinio used this woman—identified by her ample figure, centrally parted hair, low-necked but high-waisted dress, tilted head, and slightly parted legs—for the figure of the Virgin Mary in at least ten paintings. These include the *Enthroned Madonna,* formerly in San Vito, Ferrara, signed and dated 1530; the 1532 *Madonna and Child with Saints Nicholas, Francis, and Louis of Toulouse,* from the Chichester-Constable collection in England; and the 1535 *Enthroned Madonna and Ten Saints* in Santa Maria dei Frari, Venice (fig. A), which was probably Licinio's most important

FIGURE 8A | Bernardino Licinio, *Enthroned Madonna and Ten Saints*, 1535. Venice, Santa Maria Gloriosa dei Frari.

paintings. Rearick also compared the *Woman Holding a Vase* to two drawings that appear in Licinio's painted group portrait, *An Artist with Five Pupils*, at Alnwick Castle. The Yale sheet remains, however, the only surviving drawing whose attribution to Licinio has been universally accepted.[6]

JJM

1 Vertova 1975 is the most complete survey of the artist's life and works, but for good brief introductions, see also Rearick 1967, and *Grove Dictionary* 19:330. Vasari confused Licinio with his contemporary Pordenone, and only in the twentieth century has Licinio's personality come to be understood on its own. As Rearick 1967, 382, notes, "the drawings previously attributed to Bernardino Licinio have accrued to his *oeuvre* through imaginary associations with paintings and the vague image of him as a 'housebroken' Pordenone."
2 On the model-book or pattern-book tradition, see cat. no. 1, above, on the *Lion* drawn by a Venetian artist of the previous generation.
3 On the Split painting, see Prijateli 1980, 151–153. For reproductions of the other paintings mentioned above, see Vertova 1975. Another example, not included in either of those sources, is the *Madonna and Child with Saints*, sold Sotheby's, London, 8 April 1987, lot 154.
4 David Scrase in London 1983–84, 258.
5 Rearick chose instead to date the drawing closer to 1520, the date which he would give to some of the undated related paintings, but Vertova argued convincingly for placing those paintings and the Yale drawing much closer to 1530.
6 For a discussion of the other drawings that have been attributed to Licinio, see Rearick 1967, 382–383, n. 1, and Vertova 1975, 440–441.

commission. Licinio occasionally reversed the pose, as seen in his 1532 *Sacra Conversazione*, in the Musée des Beaux-Arts, Grenoble, and his *Madonna and Child with Saints Joseph and Catherine*, in a private collection in Split, among others.[3] The back of the canvas at Split has a drawing that is clearly based on the Yale model, and the practice of tracing it through the canvas in order to reverse the pose reveals what has been described as "the literal-minded simplicity of spirit that pervades all Licinio's work."[4] All the dated paintings related to the Yale drawing come from the 1530s and, accordingly, it seems likely that the drawing was made right around 1530, when Licinio completed the Ferrara altarpiece that is the earliest of the set.[5]

The Yale drawing was first attributed to Licinio by Rearick, who recognized the connections between the drawing and Licinio's

9 Giulio Romano (Giulio Pippi)
Rome 1492/99–1546 Mantua

Gaius Marcius Coriolanus Discovered among the Volscians, ca. 1530–34

Pen and brown ink over traces of black chalk or charcoal, 26.8 × 33.5 cm (10%⁄16 × 13³⁄16 in.)

INSCRIPTIONS: verso, on old (nineteenth-century?) backing sheet, in graphite: *Caius Marius discovered amongst the Volscians*

PROVENANCE: Sir Peter Lely (L. 2092); Sir Thomas Lawrence (L. 2445); Samuel Woodburn, London, 1836; Lord Francis Egerton, 1st Earl of Ellesmere (L. 2710b), and by descent to the Duke of Sutherland; Sotheby's, London, 5 December 1972, lot 35; acquired from Shickman Gallery, New York

REFERENCES: Ellesmere 1898, no. 149; Hartt 1958, 1:142 and no. 180; London 1972, no. 35; Cooper 1976; Verheyen 1977, 34, 65 n.107, 131; *YUAG Bulletin* 36.2 (1977): 38 and 44; Mantua 1989, 362; Vienna 1989, 146; New Haven 1991a, no. 38; Bazzotti 1996, 92–93; Belluzzi 1998, 1:476; Taylor in New York 1999a, no. 28

Maitland F. Griggs, B.A. 1896, and Everett V. Meeks, B.A. 1901, Funds. 1976.91

Although this drawing has long been recognized as a study for a fresco in the Camera di Attilio Regolo in the Appartamento del Giardino Segreto of the Palazzo Te in Mantua (fig. A), the identification of the scene has been, and continues to be, the subject of much debate. The two most convincing arguments are those of Verheyen, who, in agreement with the old inscription on the backing of the drawing, identified the scene as Gaius Marcius Coriolanus discovered among the Volscians, and of Ugo Bazzotti, who more recently argued that the scene depicts the Clemency of Alexander the Great.[1]

The basis for Bazzotti's reassessment of the subject is that the scene in the fresco is depicted out of doors, whereas the discovery of Gaius Marcius took place inside of the house of Tullus Amfidius; Bazzotti proposes instead that the scene is *The Clemency of Alexander the Great,* as related in the *Historiae Alexandri Magni* by Quintus Curtius Rufus, published in many editions in both Latin and Italian during the Renaissance. In that account, one reads that a storm scattered Alexander's army, and as one common soldier returned to camp, senseless and numb with cold, Alexander offered the man his own seat by the fire. Having recovered from the cold and realizing where he was sitting, the soldier was alarmed, but Alexander calmed him, explaining that while to have sat in the royal throne would have been a capital offense among the Persians, it was salvation among the Macedonians.

FIGURE 9A | Giulio Romano and workshop, *Coriolanus Discovered Among the Volscians*, ca. 1530–34. Mantua, Palazzo Te.

This identification would fit into the decorative project of the room as a whole. The vault of the Camera di Attilio Regolo, that is, is divided into nine sections: a large central scene with an *Allegory of the Virtues of Federico Gonzaga*, four narrative scenes in the corners, and four allegorical figures depicting the cardinal virtues. Each of the narratives relates to the virtue to its left: the scene of *Horatius Coclitis on the Ponte Sublicio* is flanked by *Fortitude*, the *Judgment of Zaleuch* is flanked by *Justice*, and the *Death of Attilius Regulus* is flanked by *Wisdom* or *Prudence*. The remaining allegorical figure is *Charity*, to which the scene of *The Clemency of Alexander the Great* would clearly relate. Bazzotti noted, furthermore, that this subject would have been familiar to Giulio, for it had previously been painted on a house facade in Mantua. Taylor and Belluzzi have agreed with Bazzotti's arguments in their subsequent publications on the drawing and the fresco.

Based on a close observation of the preparatory drawing, however, a return to the previous identification of the scene as *Gaius Marcius Coriolanus Discovered among the Volscians* is here proposed. The bottom corner of the pentagonal fresco might depict a rocky ledge, but the fire sits on a much more regular, apparently man-made platform. Furthermore, in the drawing, which represents Giulio's first thoughts about the details of the subject, the bottom edge of the scene shows a set of steps that suggests an interior setting. At the very least, the setting is sufficiently ambiguous that it should not be used as grounds for identification. The expressions on the faces of the figures in the drawing, however, are much better suited to the Coriolanus story. After leading a successful campaign against the Volscians, the Roman general Coriolanus returned home. He became a politician, but, for his refusal to submit to the desires of the plebeians, he was exiled from Rome. Vowing revenge, he found his way into Antium, the city of the Volscians, and went in disguise, heavily cloaked, to the house of his old rival general Tullus Amfidius and sat before the hearth fire there.[2]

Returning to the drawing, we see that the central standing figure is angry, whereas Alexander the Great, at the appropriate moment of the story proposed by Bazzotti, should be conciliatory. In contrast, anger is the apt expression for the moment when the Volscian general Tullus Amfidius discovers his old enemy Coriolanus seated at his hearth fire. The mixed expressions of anger and confusion among the other soldiers are likewise suitable. The seated figure does not wear soldier's costume, as would be the case in the Alexander the Great story; instead, the only notable element of his clothing (even more clearly visible in the finished fresco) is the cloak that the standing man is lifting from his head, again following the Coriolanus legend.

The setting and expressions are far less clear in the fresco than in the preparatory drawing, but we might prejudice the latter in attempting to clarify the iconography. Giulio had many assistants at the Palazzo Te and seems not to have painted many of the frescoes himself, especially in the latter stages of decoration, including the secret garden apartment, and it is not difficult to imagine that an assistant could have misinterpreted an unfamiliar story.[3] The frescoes have also been affected by restorations over the centuries, such that the expressions are less legible than those of the drawing. We might also recall Vasari's statement that "Giulio always expressed his ideas better in drawings than in finished work or in paintings, displaying (in the drawings) more vivacity, boldness, and expression."⁴ Finally, as noted by Verheyen, who alone among modern scholars identifies the scene as the Coriolanus story, all four of the narratives on the vault are included in the *Memorabilium exempla* of Valerius Maximus, a copy of which was in Federigo Gonzaga's private library, and the stories are linked to the virtues with which they are associated in Giulio's frescoed vault.⁵

Subject aside, this sheet is typical of Giulio's draftsmanship. In drawings done earlier in his career, Giulio's style is often difficult to distinguish from Raphael's and, like Raphael, he worked according to the classic procedure of *primo pensiero*, *studio*, and *modello* as described by Vasari. In Mantua, however, Giulio developed the abbreviated design practice described in detail by Armenini. He began with quick sketches, usually in chalk or charcoal but sometimes in ink, which established the basic positions of figures in the composition. He would rub the back of this first sketch with charcoal, creating a sort of carbon paper, and then transfer the outlines by tracing them with a stylus. He would fix the outlines of the new drawing in ink, beat a handkerchief against the sheet in order to remove most of the charcoal tracings, and then finish the drawing by refining contours and adding hatching in ink and wash.⁶

The present sheet is a perfect example of this second stage of Giulio's Mantuan design process. The faint black chalk or charcoal lines that remain have a flatness indicating that they are transferred rather than drawn by hand directly on the sheet; moreover, the white paper has a bluish cast that results from having been rubbed lightly by the charcoal used in the transfer process.⁷ One can see that Giulio traced some of the contours lightly in ink before wiping away the charcoal, but then changed his mind as he refined the drawing. The process is most clearly visible in the "extra" leg between the legs of Tullus Amfidius, drawn tentatively in simple strokes rather than the darker, reworked pen lines of most of the drawing. The expressions and details, however, have no underdrawing; it was in this drawing that Giulio first added these elements to the composition.

Later drawings, and perhaps also a cartoon, presumably followed this drawing.⁸ The fresco is simplified, eliminating three of the figures in the background of the drawing. It is in this sheet, however, and in others like it, that one can see the essence of Giulio's design process. As it combines expressive poses and emphatic details (many of which are derived from antique prototypes) and refines the contours with a visible graphic intensity, this drawing makes us witness to the moment in which Giulio gave the composition its essential form.

JJM

1. Other identifications include: Quintus Cincinnatus and the Ordeal by Fire (Hartt); Gaius Mucius Scaevola thrusting his hand into the fire (Cooper); and Cincinnatus called into the service of the state (Oberhuber). For discussion of other drawings relating to this room at the Palazzo Te, see New York 1999a, 98–105 (with references to previous bibliography). The composition is also recorded, in reverse, in an anonymous print perhaps by an artist of the Fontainebleau school (cf. *TIB* 33:361, no. 86). The etching, which is drawn to the same scale as the Yale drawing, omits the steps or rocks at the bottom but adds four figures to the crowd in the background.
2. Coriolanus, so called for having previously captured the Volscian city of Corioli, went on to fight for the Volscians, leading their army in a series of battles that brought them right to the gates of Rome. At that moment, however, the women of Rome, led by Gaius Marcius's wife and his mother, appealed to the general, who agreed not to attack his native city. Returning to Antium, he was put to death by the Volscians.
3. By the 1530s, it was reported that Giulio "did not have time to follow his assistants' work 'except to give it a glance each day.'" (J. Cox-Rearick in New York 1999a, 23, quoting a letter of Aurelio Recordati to Duke Federico Gonzaga, 23 May 1538, published in Ferrari 1992, 2:764.)
4. Vasari (Milanesi) 5:528.
5. For example, Horatius Cocles and Fortitude, Coriolanus and Charity, Zaleucus and Justice, and Atilio Regulus and Prudence or Wisdom. See Verheyen 1977, 34 and 65 n. 107. William Shakespeare's *Coriolanus* is further testament to the legend's popularity in the Renaissance.
6. Armenini 1977, 147–148.
7. Taylor, by contrast, declared this to be Giulio's *primo pensiero*, but did not account for the flat lines of the underdrawing.
8. For an example of a drawing representing a later stage of the design process, see the Fitzwilliam Museum *modello* for *Regulus in the Barrel*, one of the other pendentives in the Camera di Attilio Regolo (New York 1976, no. 17); another drawing for that fresco (sold Sotheby's, London, 15 May 1983, lot 13) is earlier and closer to the Yale drawing. Furthermore, a drawing in the Getty (inv. no. 84.GA.648, pen and brown ink over black chalk, heightened with white, 24.9 × 31.8 cm) for the *Allegory of the Virtues of Federico II Gonzaga* in the center of the ceiling of the same room compares to the Yale drawing (and like it comes from Peter Lely's collection), but a sheet in the British Museum (inv. no. 1895-9-15-642, pen and brown ink over black and red chalk, 22 × 29.4 cm) appears to be still earlier in the design process and gives a further idea of Giulio's working practice. A small-scale and quickly executed fresco such as this one might not have required a full cartoon.

10 Luca Penni

Florence ca. 1505–1556/57 Paris

Jupiter and Semele, ca. 1540–45

Pen and brown ink and brown wash, incised with stylus, 21.6 × 20.3 cm (8½ × 8 in.) (corners clipped)

WATERMARK: The paper shows no watermark, but the chain lines about 22–23 mm apart are typical of paper used at Fontainebleau during the reign of Francis I.

INSCRIPTIONS: recto, lower center, in brown ink, *Rosso Fiorentino*; verso, in graphite, center: *W1303*; lower center: *77* (circled); lower left: *28 / 146*

PROVENANCE: acquired from Monroe Warshaw, New York

REFERENCES: *YUAG Bulletin* (2004): 160

Everett V. Meeks, B.A. 1901, Fund. 2003.93.1

Luca Penni was born in Florence about 1505 and worked with his older brother Gianfrancesco, an assistant to Raphael in the Vatican. Luca was probably the youngest of the artists who can be deemed direct inheritors of Raphael, Giulio Romano being the prime one, and Polidoro da Caravaggio and Perino del Vaga (see cat. nos. 3, 9, and 12) closely following. After Raphael's death in 1520 and the Sack of Rome in 1527, Luca is said to have worked in Genoa during the early 1530s with Perino, who was his brother-in-law, on the decoration of the palace of Andrea Doria, Emperor Charles V's naval commander. Penni may also have spent some time in Mantua, where Giulio had gone in 1524. Penni subsequently proceeded to France, perhaps at the invitation of his compatriot Rosso Fiorentino, who between 1530 and 1540 was the chief artist at the court of Francis I at Fontainebleau.

Penni is first documented at Fontainebleau in 1537.[1] In his first years there, he was among the best paid of the artists, and his career seemed assured. But after Rosso committed suicide in 1540, the Bolognese artist Francesco Primaticcio took over as artistic impresario; apparently a rivalry developed, and thereafter Penni remained in Primaticcio's shadow. Because the biographer Giorgio Vasari got much of his information from Primaticcio, he gave little prominence in his *Lives of the Artists* to Penni.

Nonetheless, Penni's oeuvre can be reconstituted. Well over a hundred of his compositions survive, the majority in prints, of which many are etchings by Jean Mignon and Léon Davent; there are also engravings by Giorgio Ghisi and René Boyvin.[2] For some of these prints a corresponding drawing exists; in addition, a fair number of drawings are known that have no corresponding print. Since 1972 a handful of paintings have been identified as by Penni, and his designs were also used for enamels, stained glass, silver, marble, and even floor tiles.[3]

The drawing depicts Jupiter and Semele, a story from Ovid's *Metamorphoses* (3:259–315) and the kind of erotic scene in classical dress generally associated with Fontainebleau. Semele was the daughter of Cadmus, and a suite of episodes recounting his story can be reconstituted from extant Fontainebleau drawings and prints, although it is not known where, or even if, this suite was painted in the château.[4]

Here, Semele, one of many attractive mortal women whom Jupiter seduced, is stretched out in a pose reminiscent of that in the well-known antique statue of Sleeping Ariadne, otherwise known as the "Vatican Cleopatra."[5] Because Semele had become pregnant by Jupiter, his jealous wife, Juno, persuaded Semele to ask Jupiter to make love to her in his full glory. Semele, having got Jupiter's vow to grant her any wish, made her fateful demand, and he could not go back on his word. Here, Jupiter hovers in the air above Semele, thunderbolts in each hand, and accompanied by his eagle. Juno is shown in the distance, in the upper left. Four heads of putti and three adult heads—some perhaps signifying the winds—all with distraught expressions, are witness to the disaster about to happen: for the power of Jupiter's thunderbolts would reduce Semele to ashes. The unborn baby—who was rescued, sewn into Jupiter's thigh, and eventually born—was Bacchus.[6]

The famous Gallery of Francis I at Fontainebleau originally was to have two small, enclosed *cabinets* (small antechambers) at the central point of the length of the Gallery, one on each side, appended as it were to the outer walls. The one on the south side was apparently never built, but the one on the north, the *cabinet* of Semele, existed until 1786,

when the width of the wing was doubled. The exact shape, function, and decoration of this *cabinet* are unclear, but an image by Primaticcio of Jupiter and Semele, recorded in an etching by Léon Davent, almost certainly shows the composition painted there (fig. A).[7] In this context Semele was described by Sylvie Béguin as "consumed by Jupiter's fire, that is to say, purified by love" and "the very image of (carnal) knowledge and union."[8]

Penni's design is not known in any other medium, although in a raking light incisions along the main lines of the drawing can be discerned, as though a print had been contemplated. It is also possible that the incisions preceded the drawn lines—in other words, that an earlier drawing was put over the paper when it was blank, the main lines were incised strongly enough so the marks would transfer to this sheet, and then the artist redrew the composition onto this sheet. This method is consistent with the practice of the artists of the Raphael School and also that of Primaticcio and other artists working at Fontainebleau.

The inscription, in an old hand, ascribes the drawing to Rosso, but its style is unmistakably Penni's. More normative and classicizing than that of Rosso, Penni's style clearly derives from Raphael, although the figures

FIGURE 10A | Léon Davent, *Jupiter and Semele*, early 1540s. Paris, Bibliothèque Nationale de France.

are somewhat more elongated and mannered, more formal, than Raphael's. Penni's compositions are always balanced and harmonious; even for a subject like that of the present drawing, with its sensual content and catastrophic ending, Penni has created a composition of exquisite elegance.

SB

1 Laborde 1877, 1:135, 409. Mentions of Penni between 1540 and 1550: 191, 195, 198.
2 Albricci 1982 lists ninety prints after Penni, although about seventeen of these should be disattributed, and at least some twenty more should be added.
3 No monograph exists on Penni. Information on him can be found in Paris 1972–73 (with previous bibliography), 127–330, 315–321, and elsewhere; Béguin 1975; Béguin 1982, 53; Cordellier in Paris 1983–84, 159–160; Béguin 1987; Grodecki 1987; Béguin 1991; Boorsch in Los Angeles–New York–Paris 1994–95, 87–93, 267–282, and Acton (ibid.), 325–335; Wilson-Chevalier 1996; Zerner 1996, 131–136.
4 For a suite of ten images depicting episodes in the story of Cadmus, and a hypothesis concerning their location at Fontainebleau, see Jenkins in Paris 2004–05, 241–246.
5 In 1540, Primaticcio was in Rome making plaster casts of the ancient sculpture in the Vatican Belvedere, from which bronze copies were to be executed in the foundry at Fontainebleau. The Ariadne was among this set, and Primaticcio's cast or bronze (made sometime between 1540 and 1547), rather than the Vatican original, probably served as Penni's model. In support of this argument, which also indicates a date of 1540 or later for Penni's drawing, it might be noted that Penni's Semele is nearly supine, like Primaticcio's Ariadne, in contrast to the more upright position of the Vatican sculpture.
6 A painting by Giulio Romano in the J. Paul Getty Museum, *The Birth of Bacchus* (inv. no. 69.PB.7), depicts a slightly different version of the story, in which Bacchus was born before Semele was consumed by flames; see Mantua 1989, 440–441; Jaffé 1997, 54. A drawing by Giulio of the same subject (although showing a very different composition from the painting) is also in the Getty (inv. no. 95.GA.27); see New York 1999a, no. 39. These works by Giulio seem to have been the earliest renditions of the subject of Semele. A drawing of *Jupiter and Semele*, probably by Jean Cousin the Younger, is in London, British Museum, inv. no. 1935-3-9-1; see New York–London 2005–06, no. 8.
7 See, most recently, Paris 2004–05, 98–99. The Davent print is Zerner 1969, LD 11; another etching by Davent after Primaticcio of the same subject is LD 68.
8 Béguin et al. 1972, 167: "consumée par le feu de Jupiter, c'est-à-dire purifiée par l'amour," and "l'image même de la connaissance et de l'union." See also Zerner 1996, 85.

11 Domenico Beccafumi
Cortine in Valdibiana Montaperti 1484–1551 Siena

Kneeling Man, ca. 1544

Red chalk with a few stylus indentations; original sheet of paper trimmed to edge of figure and laid down. Backing sheet 25.4 × 17.5 cm (10 × 6⅞ in.); figure approximately 19 × 16.5 cm (7½ × 6½ in.)

INSCRIPTIONS: recto, in pen and brown ink, lower center: *macarino da Siena*; just above right foot of figure: *m*

PROVENANCE: acquired from Eugene V. Thaw and Co., New York

REFERENCES: *YUAG Bulletin* 34 (1973): 56; New Haven 1974, no. 3; Gordley 1988, 436 and no. 33x (as Neroni); Torriti 1998, 341, no. D176

Maitland F. Griggs, B.A. 1896, Fund. 1972.37

Domenico Beccafumi, the leading painter in Siena during the first half of the sixteenth century, was one of the more distinctive and innovative artists of his time. Although clearly aware of contemporary trends in Roman and Florentine art, he rarely left Siena and developed a manner characteristically his own. Serpentine bodies are such a signature element of his work, for example, that Beccafumi is often seen as one of the early Tuscan Mannerists, but he alternately embraced massive anatomies that rival those of Michelangelo's figures.[1] Primarily a painter, Beccafumi was also "probably the most imaginative, daring, and versatile printmaker of the Italian Renaissance."[2] His woodblock prints are particularly notable for their bold style; these chiaroscuro woodcuts, moreover, helped Beccafumi find formal solutions for one of his largest and longest commissions, the designs for the inlaid marble pavement of the cathedral in Siena.

The pavement designs occupied Beccafumi through nearly his entire career, but the *Sacrifice of Melchizedek* just to the right of the high altar (fig. A), for which the *Kneeling Man* is probably a preliminary study, was one of the last parts of the pavement to have been executed.[3] While there are changes from the drawing to the pavement figure, they are not more than are often found between preparatory drawings and finished works, especially between a small drawing and a large-scale figure like that in the pavement. The reversed position of the highlight and shadow on the figure's left leg is one such example. Moreover, the two- or three-color scheme of the cut marble floor limited the amount of detail possible in the finished work and necessitated the simplification of the elaborately folded drapery seen in the chalk drawing. In short, Beccafumi would have made small figure studies like this early in the design process of the pavement, but there were probably several stages of that process between this drawing and the creation of the cartoons that he ultimately supplied to the marble workers.[4] Nonetheless, details like the prominent shadow line defining the figure's back and spine, his extraordinary beard, the tilt of his head, and his unusual pose (a combination of profile and three-quarters view from behind), argue in favor of a link between drawing and pavement.[5] This drawing is typical, furthermore, of the monumental mode that the artist developed later in his career, a style also seen in his circa 1547 woodcuts of the *Apostles*.

This is one of many surviving drawings linked to the pavement project, but one of only a few in red chalk, for Beccafumi more often worked in media whose chiaroscuro effects matched more closely those of the cut marble pavement.[6] Indeed, as has often been noted, the task of designing the chiaroscuro pavement was, along with Beccafumi's chiaroscuro woodcuts, one of the impulses that led to the artist's bold planar drawing style. His uses of various drawing media, that is, are as innovative as are his exercises in printmaking. He worked in a broad range of media including pen and ink, wash, black chalk, red chalk, and grisaille brush drawings in oil and tempera paint on paper. When Beccafumi did draw in red chalk later in his career, he tended to eschew the gradations of tone that the medium allowed, instead using a sort of three-tone system with the white paper left bare for highlights, chalk hatching used for a medium value, and firmly traced lines defining essential contours. He often used a stylus to create the design, so that there would be no contour lines between the white paper and the hatched areas.[7] The left thigh of the figure in the present drawing, for example, has a stylus indentation rather than a line separating the chalk hatching from the bare paper highlight.[8] It is not difficult to see this technique as one that would have been developed with the marble pavement in mind, and it might be argued that Beccafumi is here using a single piece of chalk as an expedient substitute for the pen, ink, and wash that he used for the final cartoons, with the cross-hatched and shaded areas of chalk standing in for the wash that indicated the darker marble, and the firmly pressed and reinforced contours replacing the pen lines that indicated pitch-filled contour lines to be cut into the marble. The effect in the drawing is of chiaroscuro rather than the sfumato found in the chalk drawings by many of Beccafumi's Tuscan contemporaries, and even in some of the artist's own drawings.[9]

The subsequent history of this drawing also merits some comment. The original sheet was trimmed around the edges of the figure and laid down, a practice used by Vasari and other early collectors to divide sheets of studies into multiple drawings. In the case of the present sheet, this "silhouetting" was probably done by an early collector, for the inscription along the bottom edge of the mounting sheet is in a handwriting typical of the sixteenth or seventeenth century and identifies the artist as "Macarino," a variant on the name that Beccafumi used to sign his prints and by which he was generally known to his contemporaries. A number of other drawings by Beccafumi bear inscriptions with variations on the artist's nickname and have been similarly cut around the figure.[10] Some of these latter sheets have the blind stamp of an unidentified collector, a mark of six small circles arranged in a hexagonal pattern, but it is not clear whether that collector was responsible for cutting the drawings.

JJM

1 On Beccafumi, see especially Siena 1990, Landau and Parshall 1994, Torriti 1998, and Lincoln 2000.
2 Landau 1991, 450.
3 Only the *Sacrifice of Abraham* in front of the altar is later. For documents and discussion relating to the pavement, see Sanminiatelli 1967, 50 n. 27 and 62 n. 101, as well as Collareta in Siena 1990, 652–676.
4 A number of these cartoons survive and are today in the Pinacoteca at Siena. See Torriti 1998, nos. D48 and D75 or Siena 1990, nos.

FIGURE 11A | After Domenico Beccafumi, *Sacrifice of Melchizedek*, ca. 1544. Siena, Duomo.

175–177. Further comments on Beccafumi's cartoons are found in Bambach 1999, 290–293.

5   Pillsbury and Caldwell in New Haven 1974, no. 3, argue that "the connection of the drawn figure with any of those [in the pavement] is not close enough to warrant a positive identification," but Torriti 1998, 341, also identifies the figure as a study for Melchizedek. The figure just to the right of Moses in the ca. 1525 *Moses Striking Water from the Rock* is similar, but it seems to me more likely that the earlier design inspired this drawing than the other way about. Beccafumi seems often to have looked to his earlier works for figures, and his woodcut of the *Four Evangelists* (Torriti 1998, D153 and 154) follows this pattern by adapting the *Melchizedek* to another solution. A drawing at the National Gallery of Art, Washington (inv. no. 1971.61.1; Torriti 1998, no. D177) shows this evolution.

6   Drawings like Florence, Uffizi, inv. nos. 1250 and 1254, and Paris, Louvre, inv. no. 258, all in pen, ink, and wash, are more typical of his studies for the pavement and demonstrate his interest in strong chiaroscuro.

7   Lincoln 2000, 96, similarly notes, in a discussion of Beccafumi's red chalk drawing of *Mucius Scaevola* in the Morgan Library (inv. no. 1964.7), "evidently . . . , Beccafumi preferred not to show the contours, progressively removing them in favor of strongly shaped areas of shadow, expressing the placement and solidity of figures and objects uncompromisingly in terms of shadow."

8   This indentation is visible only under raking light, and on the whole, there are few such stylus marks in this drawing, although the process of laying the original sheet down—and the pull of the underlying paste over time—may have flattened some other indentations. Other indentations might have been lost when the original sheet was trimmed around the figure's silhouette. Beccafumi seems often to have used the stylus, although not always for the same purpose. For other examples, see Siena 1990, nos. 120, 121, 123, 127, 128–130, 147, 151, and 155.

9   For an example of the latter, see his *Study for the Head of Saint Michael*, Paris, Louvre, inv. no. 9177 (Torriti 1998, no. D51), or *Two Nude Men*, Chatsworth, Devonshire Collection, inv. no. 6. Landau and Parshall 1994, 273, in discussing the latter drawing and Beccafumi's related engraving, note that Beccafumi, at this earlier moment of his career (ca. 1520–25) had problems transitioning from one medium to another. By the time he made the Yale drawing, however, Beccafumi had carried out many more experiments with chiaroscuro prints and seems to have shifted his red chalk style to that described above. For a drawing with similar red chalk technique, see Florence, Uffizi, inv. no. 10773F.

10 For example, see "macherino" on Florence, Uffizi, inv. no. 1259F, or "mecarino" on Uffizi inv. no. 10748F. Beccafumi signed his *Two Nude Men* print "Micarino." Trimmed drawings include Uffizi inv. nos. 17137F, 17138F, and 17402F. *Pace* Pillsbury and Caldwell in New Haven 1974, who write that "the drawing at Yale is the only Beccafumi drawing known to have been similarly treated."

RECTO

12 Perino Buonaccorsi, called Perino del Vaga

Florence 1501–1547 Rome

The Marriage Procession of Psyche, study for the Sala di Psiche in the Castel Sant'Angelo, Rome (recto); *Frieze of Heavily Draped Figures* (verso), 1545–46

Pen and brown ink and brown wash (recto); pen and brown ink (verso), 12 × 25 cm (4¾ × 9¹³⁄₁₆ in.)

WATERMARK: shield with crossed arrows, surmounted by a crescent (not in Briquet, Heawood, or Piccard)

INSCRIPTIONS: verso, at left, in pen and brown ink: partial and illegible list and a column of sums

PROVENANCE: Sotheby's, New York, 13 January 1993, lot 27; acquired from Michael Miller/Lucy Vivante Fine Arts Inc., New York

REFERENCES: *YUAG Bulletin* (1997–98): 100–101; Parma 2000, 217 n. 1 (where the drawing is incorrectly identified as YUAG inv. no. 95.5.1); Mantua 2001, 313–315 (incorrectly identified as YUAG inv. no. 1996.5.15); Miller 2002, 98–105

Everett V. Meeks, B.A. 1901, and Frederick M. Clapp, B.A. 1901, M.A. 1911, Funds. 1996.5.1a, b

Perino del Vaga was born in Florence but moved to Rome around 1515–16 and came of age in Raphael's workshop. Like Giulio Romano and Polidoro da Caravaggio, he assisted in Raphael's Roman decorative projects and had much to do with the development of the Mannerist style out of Raphael's later work. Perino left Rome following the Sack in 1527 and, like his former colleagues, was one of the key figures in the spread of the new style to Northern Italy and beyond.[1] He returned to Rome in 1537 and became the principal artist to Pope Paul III, who attempted to revive the grand patronage of his predecessors Julius II and Leo X. Perino thus completed the decoration of the Stanza della Segnatura and the Sistine Chapel, the two principal sites of the Roman High Renaissance, and then spent the final years of his life decorating the papal apartment in the Castel Sant'Angelo in conscious emulation of Raphael's decorative schemes.[2] The *Marriage Procession* is a preparatory drawing for a fresco (fig. A) in the Sala di Psiche (the Room of Psyche) there.

Derived from Apuleius's *Metamorphoses*, the tale of Cupid and Psyche was popular throughout the Renaissance.[3] Psyche was a mortal girl so beautiful that she aroused the jealousy of Venus. Fearing divine retribution, her father went to the oracle of Apollo at Miletus, but the oracle informed him that he ought to conduct Psyche to a mountaintop for "deadly nuptial rites," as she had no hope of a mortal spouse. The oracle had to be obeyed, and the Yale drawing shows the resulting grim procession, considered by Psyche's family to be both her wedding and her funeral. Psyche, however, was whisked away from the mountaintop and then underwent a series of trials before eventually marrying the immortal Cupid and becoming immortal herself. At the least, the story was an amusing tale of love that celebrated the ennoblement of Psyche through her union with a god. The depiction of divine banquets appealed to the Renaissance love of courtly magnificence, which surely contributed to the story's constant reappearance in Renaissance painting. Thus, for example, Raphael's Psyche frescoes at the Villa Farnesina in Rome are usually considered to relate to the marriage of his patron, the famously wealthy Agostino Chigi, to a woman of a lower social class, while Giulio Romano's Room of Psyche at the Palazzo Te in Mantua is thought to reflect the desire of Federico Gonzaga to marry Isabella Boschetta.[4] Furthermore, over a decade before Perino executed the Castel Sant'Angelo frescoes, he had painted a version of the story at Palazzo Doria, Genoa, to celebrate the marriage of Andrea Doria and Peretta Usodimare.[5]

VERSO

Beyond its connotations of love, the story of Psyche also came to be interpreted as an allegory of the trials and triumph of humanity and the movement toward divinity. It is surely in this latter sense that it was understood in the Papal Apartments, for during his long career in the church, Alessandro Farnese had endured many trials, including the Sack of Rome and the Protestant schism.[6]

Perino thus had numerous visual sources from which to draw, but foremost among them in 1545 was still another version of the story, the series of prints designed by Michiel Coxcie and engraved in the mid-1530s by the Master of the Die and Agostino Veneziano (Agostino de Musi). A set of thirty-three scenes with verse inscriptions, these prints provided a far more literal translation of the story into images than did any of the earlier frescoes.[7] A comparison of the *Marriage Procession* drawing with the corresponding print (fig. B) demonstrates at once how Perino derived the basic composition from the print while creating a narrative that was in every way artistically superior. The trumpet players of the drawing are far more dramatic, and the plodding, heavily hooded figures of Psyche's family, at left, convey the complex emotional tone of the scene—a ceremony both nuptial and funereal—in a way that the print fails altogether to do. Throughout the frieze, fur-

FIGURE 12A | Perino del Vaga and workshop, *Marriage Procession of Psyche*, 1545–46. Rome, Castel Sant'Angelo.

thermore, Perino transforms the cherubic Cupid of the prints into a far more convincingly desirable young man. The added drama of the narratives, the elongated, graceful figures, and the richer range of details are all typical of Perino's art and, more broadly, of the culture of imitation-with-improvement that was the benchmark of the *bella maniera*.

The rediscovered account-book for the Castel Sant'Angelo project allows the painted Psyche frieze, and presumably also the related drawings, to be precisely dated between August 1545 and May 1546. As Raphael had done before, Perino employed a large workshop of artists, and the artist responsible for the execution of any given painting at the Castel Sant'Angelo is accordingly a matter of debate, although the ruinous, much-repainted state of the frescoes probably prohibits any certain conclusions.[8] Regardless of the final

FIGURE 12B | The Master of the Die, *Marriage Procession of Psyche*, mid-1530s. New York, Metropolitan Museum of Art.

painting, Perino was surely responsible for the design of the frescoes, and there is no question about the attribution to him of Yale's drawing, which contains all his characteristic mannerisms. Similar compositional studies have been identified for two others of the nine narrative scenes in the room.[9]

The verso of the *Marriage Procession* shows a series of the small-headed, heavily draped figures that are commonly found in Perino's late drawings. The figures cannot be linked to any of the other paintings in the Room of Psyche or the contemporary Room of Perseus at the Castel Sant'Angelo, but they do fit among a group of drawings that show similarly massive figures.[10] One of these drawings, at the Fitzwilliam Museum, has what appears to be a procession on the verso; Elena Parma links it to the Room of Psyche *Marriage Processsion*,[11] but the hats worn by the men in the Fitzwilliam and the Getty drawings are inconsistent with the classical draperies worn by the figures of that project. The drawings probably represent instead elements of an additional frieze project that was never executed, perhaps because of Perino's untimely death in 1547.

JJM

1 For further discussion of Raphael's workshop, the beginnings of Mannerism, and the spread of that style, see the drawings elsewhere in this catalogue by Polidoro da Caravaggio (cat. no. 3), Giulio Romano (cat. no. 9), and Luca Penni (cat. no. 10).

2 For comments on Perino, Paul III, and the revival of High Renaissance patronage and style, see Wolk-Simon 1989, 515–523. Despite an interest in earlier projects, Perino was also responsible for the increasing emphasis on decorative frames and ornaments that would characterize decorative painting in the following generation.

3 The story was also related by Fulgentius and Boccaccio, but from the time it was rediscovered around 1350, Apuleius's version became the standard, from which subsequent Renaissance retellings took their start.

4 See, for example, Oberhuber 2000, 173–180; Gonzaga spent his youth in Rome and surely knew the Farnesina frescoes.

5 On Perino's Genoa cycle, see Parma Armani 1986, Chapter 6, and Parma 2000.

6 On the interpretations and depictions of the tale in the Renaissance, see Cavicchioli 2002, which also includes a complete retelling of the story as related by Apuleius; the entire issue of *Fontes* 3 (2000); and Jong 1998. Parma 2000 makes the related observation that the adjacent Room of Perseus might be interpreted with Luther in mind.

7 For the prints, see *TIB* 29:195–227, nos. 39–71. Three of the prints are signed by Agostino Veneziano, while the rest are by the Master of the Die. The attribution of the designs to Coxcie comes from Vasari (Milanesi) 5:435–436. The most complete account of them is Cavicchioli 2000, 189–204, which includes a summary of previous scholarship as well as some of Coxcie's preparatory drawings including that for the *Marriage Procession*. The date of the prints remains uncertain, although they must have been done during Coxcie's time in Italy, circa 1531–39. They are often said to have been the source for Perino's Psyche frescoes in Genoa, but those frescoes, which must be before 1533, probably predate the print series and almost certainly derive directly from the woodcut illustrations in Matteo Maria Boiardo's Italian edition of the *Metamorphoses* (published 1518 and in many editions thereafter), which were also the models for Coxcie.

8 On the organization of Perino's workshop at the Castel Sant'Angelo, with comments on the account-book and on the restoration of the frescoes, see Rome 1981. The general opinion seems to be that Perino painted the narratives, while assistants painted the decorative surrounds, but I would argue instead that the relative awkwardness of the figures in the frescoes suggests that Perino had little to do with their execution. The best published photographs of the Psyche frieze, which show the extent of modern retouching, are in Cavicchioli 2002. For another drawing related to Perino's workshop, see the verso of Polidoro da Caravaggio's *Seated Old Man* (cat. no. 3, above).

9 The two other compositional studies are Vienna, Albertina, inv. nos. 13560 and 13561, both pen and brown ink and gray-brown wash, 12.4 × 25.1 cm and 12.2 × 24.7 cm. For a complete discussion see Mantua 2001, nos. 178–179. The discussion there also includes two further drawings, Albertina inv. no. 465 and British Museum inv. 1952-2-29-10, that have been linked to the project. The lower left section of Albertina inv. 465 is often described as a study for the hooded figures of Yale's drawing. See also Parma Armani 1986, Chapter 9. Paris, Louvre, inv. no. 10435, also linked to the project and sometimes considered Perino's own, seems to me to be a copy.

10 New York, Metropolitan Museum of Art, inv. no. 61.180; Cambridge, Fitzwilliam Museum, inv. no. 33.1998; Oxford, Ashmolean Museum, inv. no. P.II 229 verso; Cambridge, Mass., Harvard University Art Museum, inv. no. 2002.95.51; Los Angeles, J. Paul Getty Museum, inv. no. 88.GG.132. See Mantua 2001, 296–300.

11 Mantua 2001, 299.

13 Bernardino Lanino
Vercelli ca. 1512–1581 Vercelli

Two Apostles, Study for the Last Supper, 1546–48

Black and white chalk, with stumping, on blue paper; laid down, 53.5 × 38.4 cm (21 × 15⅛ in.)

PROVENANCE: acquired from H. M. Calmann, London

REFERENCES: *YUAG Bulletin* 28 (1962): 30; H-B and L, no. 271; New Haven 1974, no. 15; Coleman 1988, 234, 264, and 646–647; New Haven 1991a, no 23

Everett V. Meeks, B.A. 1901, Fund. 1961.9.53

A native of Vercelli and long active there, Bernardino Lanino was among the most important painters working in the Piedmont region of northwestern Italy during the middle of the sixteenth century. He received his early training with the local painter Baldassare de Cadighis, but by 1530 was associated with Gaudenzio Ferrari, who worked throughout Piedmont and Lombardy. Lanino followed his master to Milan, where both immediately fell under the influence of Leonardo da Vinci and his followers. Leonardo's *Last Supper* essentially defined painting in mid-century Milan, such that the subject was repeatedly taken up by other artists in the city. Gaudenzio Ferrari painted a version for the church of Santa Maria della Passione, an altarpiece which then became the model for Lanino's own *Last Supper*, painted for San Nazzaro Maggiore around 1546–48 (fig. A).[1] The Yale drawing is clearly related to the latter painting, which, like Leonardo's, placed emphasis on a range of facial types and expressions. The two apostles are Saint Peter at left, asking for the name of Christ's betrayer, and Saint John at right, who leans on the shoulder of Christ, otherwise not seen in the drawing.

Matching the figures in Lanino's painting in size and in most details, the *Two Apostles* seems at first glance to be a fragment of a cartoon, a full-scale drawing for the altarpiece. The drawing lacks, however, the punched holes or indented outlines that one would expect if the sheet had been used to transfer the full-scale design to the panel for painting; moreover, the high degree of finish and especially the gradual sfumato shading from light to dark are unnecessary—even impractical—for a cartoon intended mainly to transfer the design. Instead, the *Two Apostles* represents a different type of drawing, the so-called *ben finito cartone*. Over the course of the sixteenth century, sophisticated collectors came to prize not only finished paintings, but also artists' working drawings. Cartoons, seen as the culmination of the design process, were particularly desirable for collectors but had rarely survived because the traditional methods of transferring the design from the drawing to a panel or fresco weakened the paper (with punched holes or with sharp stylus incisions along the outlines) or even blotted out the drawing (with pouncing dust). In light of the new interest in these drawings as collectible objects in their own right, artists took measures to preserve cartoons. Instead of punching and pouncing, the *calco* method served for panel paintings: the back of the cartoon was rubbed with charcoal, which would serve as a kind of carbon paper, to transfer the design to the prepared panel when the outlines were lightly traced on the front of the drawing. Alternately, or additionally, artists began to make substitute

FIGURE 13A | Bernardino Lanino, *Last Supper*, ca. 1546–48. Milan, San Nazzaro Maggiore.

cartoons. The original cartoon, that is, would be used to produce one or more additional large drawings; one version—either the original or one of the copies—would be used in the production of the painting, but the other version or versions could be worked up to a higher degree of finish, and this *ben finito cartone* could then be saved or presented to a patron.[2]

Leonardo had created a taste for the *ben finito cartone* in Milan, but Gaudenzio, Lanino, and their associates became the most active proponents of the tradition, and nearly sixty full cartoons from these artists survive in the Accademia Albertina in Turin.[3] Most of the cartoons in Turin, although worked up with a sfumato chalk technique that was the legacy of Leonardo, have incisions along the outlines and actually seem to have been used for the production of paintings. The Yale *Two Apostles*, however, bears no such evidence and seems, rather, to be a substitute cartoon, a drawing produced from the original cartoon, and not a fragment of a larger work. Filling an entire sheet of paper, the drawing includes the upper arm of Christ in addition to the two central figures, but the apostle who sits on the nearer side of the table in the painting, whose head should overlap Saint John's arm at the lower left corner of the drawing, is not present, as he would be if this were a true cartoon. A pair of faint, curving lines on Saint John's right shoulder trace the contour of the missing head. These curving lines, so light as to be almost invisible in photographs of the drawing, might well be left over from the first stages of the drawing, when the original cartoon was transferred, probably by the *calco* method, onto this sheet: they have the flat, uninflected quality characteristic of such transferred drawings.[4] While it was necessary to include the disembodied arm of Christ in order for the figure of Saint John to make sense, the back of a head at lower left would only be a distraction in this drawing, and Lanino has omitted it. Looking further at the drawing, with the idea that it was a substitute cartoon, one can see a number of places where Lanino reinforced these transferred outlines or used them as guidelines for his shaded and stumped areas of chalk. In sum, the *Two Apostles* seems to be an elegant fiction; pretending to be a fragment of a cartoon, it is instead a substitute almost surely created with a collector in mind.[5]

Origins aside, the drawing is typical of Lanino's style, a somewhat sentimentalized and melancholy take on Leonardo's work, with little of the self-conscious mannerisms that we find in contemporary drawings by Central Italian artists. Similarly, the use of black and white chalk on blue paper in this soft manner reveals an interest in volumes and shadow that is characteristic of drawings by Northern Italian artists, in contrast to the greater emphasis placed on contour in Central Italy. Many of Lanino's compositional drawings seem relatively timid, with their fine details carefully drawn in white heightening, but a cartoon like the *Two Apostles* shows the artist at his finest.

JJM

1 Coleman 1988, 406–408, notes that the altarpiece (oil on panel, 314 × 225 cm), today hanging in the crossing of the church, was until World War II in the Corpus Domini chapel. Lanino is documented as working on the Saint Catherine chapel in San Nazzaro Maggiore in 1546–48, and the *Last Supper* has always been thought to date from the same moment. For Gaudenzio's painting, see Viale 1969, 73 and fig. 96, and Agosti 1996, fig. 1.
2 For a discussion of the *ben finito cartone*, substitute cartoons, and the related practices, see Bambach 1999, especially chapters 7 and 8.
3 For the most complete record of the cartoons, see Turin 1982; for further discussion of Lanino's cartoons see Vercelli 1985.
4 See the discussion of similar lines in the drawing by Giulio Romano discussed above (cat. no. 9).
5 Coleman 1988, 14–15, suggests that drawings like the *Two Apostles* were auxiliary or preliminary cartoons used to work out the details of a key figure or two. There is little evidence, however, that Lanino was still experimenting with the figures in the Yale drawing. Lanino's *Madonna and Child* in the Biblioteca Reale, Turin, inv. no. 16159 D.C., also seems to bear traces of *calco* transfer at the contours and might be considered a parallel case for the Yale drawing, and one that can be studied more carefully because both the finished painting (*Madonna and Child with Saints*, London, National Gallery, inv. no. 700, signed and dated 1543) and a large cartoon fragment (Birmingham, Barber Institute) also survive. See Vercelli 1985, no. 11.

14 Francesco de' Rossi, called Salviati
Florence 1510–1563 Rome

Prophet, ca. 1550–55

Pen and brown ink and brown wash with white heightening, over black chalk, on buff paper, 27.1 × 19.8 cm (10 11/16 × 7 13/16 in.)

INSCRIPTIONS: verso, lower left, in brown ink: *di Fr.co salviati*

PROVENANCE: Nicholas Lanier (L. 2908); Peter Lely (L. 2092); Sotheby's, London, 26 November 1974, lot 19; acquired from Paul Drey Gallery, New York

REFERENCES: *YUAG Bulletin* 36.1 (1976): 46; "La Chronique des Arts," in *Supplement to the Gazette des Beaux-Arts* (March 1976): 38, ill. 144; Mortari 1982, no. 397; New Haven 1991a, no. 1; New Haven 1994, no. 21

Maitland F. Griggs, B.A. 1896, Fund. 1975.78

The *Prophet* is one of a number of similar drawings Salviati made of single figures in pen, ink, and wash on buff or light brown paper. The group also includes the *Roman Soldier* in the Hermitage Museum, Saint Petersburg (fig. A), the drawings of *Jason* and the *Roman Soldier* in the British Museum, the *Running Soldier* in the Louvre, the *Seated Soldier* in the Ambrosiana in Milan, and a *Standing Soldier* in a British private collection.[1] For a few years after Salviati returned to Rome in 1548, he abandoned the highly ornamental manner of his early drawings and experimented instead with inflated, expressive figures that show a clear response to Michelangelo's *Last Judgment* and Pauline Chapel paintings. The *Prophet* and similar drawings demonstrate this figure canon and can be dated to the years around 1550.

All of these sheets are brought to a fairly high level of finish, yet only the London *Soldier* truly corresponds to one of Salviati's paintings of the time,[2] which suggests that these drawings formed some project of their own. It has been proposed that they were for chiaroscuro woodcuts,[3] but most of the figures do not have clear attributes that would identify them; nor do they seem to form a set, as might be expected if intended for prints. Another possibility is that they might have been intended as gifts to potential patrons.[4] Alessandro Nova has shown, however, that Salviati probably kept these drawings in the studio, for he used the poses as is, or slightly modified, in multiple paintings.[5] The *Prophet* and similar works might thus be seen as Salviati's attempt to define the new type of monumental figures to which he then attained. The drawings are highly contrived and highly finished works, clearly something more than casual experimental sketches for the artist and his workshop. Salviati appears instead to have created a set of finished reference works, an artistic practice more associated with the model-book tradition of the Middle Ages and the early Renaissance than with artists working in the later sixteenth century, whom we generally imagine working in the creation-via-sketching manner of Leonardo and Michelangelo.

Salviati might have been inspired to make drawings of this type as a means of facilitating the execution of the large decorative schemes

FIGURE 14A | Francesco Salviati, *Roman Soldier*, ca. 1550–55. Saint Petersburg, State Hermitage Museum.

that were his main concern, and indeed, we find multiple "echoes" of these drawings in Salviati's Roman paintings. The Yale *Prophet*, for example, has much in common with the *Saint Bartholomew* and especially the *Saint Andrew* that Salviati painted on the altar wall of the Oratory of San Giovanni Decollato in 1550. The *Roman Soldiers* in London and Saint Petersburg, in turn, resemble figures at the margins of Salviati's Palazzo Sacchetti frescoes of 1552–54 and, as noted above, the London *Soldier* appears in the Cancelleria *Martyrdom of Saint Lawrence*. As Nova has observed, these Roman projects have an "abstract" or even pastiche-like quality that resulted from the working process documented by these drawings: "the decorative impact of the painting was more important than its compositional structure."[6] Thus, while drawings like the Yale *Prophet* are the quintessential expression of Salviati's late style, and of mid-century Mannerism more generally, they also betray some of the qualities against which artists of the next generation would react so strongly.

JJM

1 Saint Petersburg, Hermitage, inv. no. 4654, pen and brown ink and gray and brown wash, heightened with white, on light brown paper, 27.5 × 20.7 cm; London, British Museum, inv. nos. 1946-7-13-53 (*Jason*), and 1946-7-13-54 verso (*Warrior*), both pen and brown ink and brown wash, heightened with white, 28.6 × 21.7 cm and 28.4 × 21.3 cm, respectively; Paris, Louvre, inv. no. 778, pen and brown ink and brown wash, heightened with white, over black chalk, on ochre paper, 26.5 × 21.2 cm; Milan, Ambrosiana, Cod. F.262 Inf. N. 39, pen and brown ink and brown wash, heightened with white, over black chalk, 42.2 × 27.2 cm. The private collection *Standing Soldier* is published in Rome–Paris 1998, no. 61, and as noted there, another version of the drawing is in the collection of Jeffrey Horvitz, Boston. Other examples of this type of drawing include a *Seated Woman* (Paris, Louvre, inv. no. 21078) and the *Creation of the Animals* (Florence, Uffizi, inv. no. 14351). A *Standing Woman*, London, British Museum, inv. no. 1946-7-13-518 seems to be a copy of another.

2 The figure corresponds to that at the far right in the *Martyrdom of Saint Lawrence* in the Cappella del Palio at the Palazzo della Cancelleria, Rome.

3 Michael Hirst's suggestion is cited in New York 1998, no. 17.

4 Indeed, upon returning to Rome, Salviati would have been well aware of Michelangelo's gift-drawings for Tommaso de' Cavalieri and Vittoria Colonna, for those were being reproduced by Vico, Beatrizet, and others in the mid- and late 1540s.

5 This idea was first put forth by Nova in an entry on the Ambrosiana *Seated Soldier*, in Washington et al. 1984, no. 53, and then developed fully in Nova 1992.

6 Nova 1992, 99.

15 Maarten van Heemskerck
Heemskerck 1498–1574 Haarlem

Mars, the Choleric Temperament,
1565

Pen and brown ink, incised for transfer, 21 × 24 cm (8¼ × 9⁷⁄₁₆ in.)

INSCRIPTIONS: recto, in pen and brown ink, lower center: *Heemskerck*; lower right: *1565*; lower left: *2*

PROVENANCE: William Stirling (later Sir William Stirling-Maxwell); by descent to Lt.-Col. William Stirling of Keir (sale, London, Sotheby's, 21 October 1963, lot 36 [with *Luna, the Phlegmatic Temperament*]); acquired from Schaeffer Galleries, New York

REFERENCES: *YUAG Bulletin* 30.2 (1965): 12 and 38; H-B and L, no. 328; New Haven 1986, no. 53; Amherst 1990, no. 4; New Haven 1992, no. 3; New Hollstein DF, *Maarten van Heemskerck*, Part 2, under no. 543; New Hollstein DF, *Muller Dynasty*, Part 1, under no. 102

Everett V. Meeks, B.A. 1901, Fund. 1964.9.4

Born in the small town of Heemskerck, near Haarlem, Maarten van Heemskerck trained in Haarlem and Delft, joining the workshop of Jan van Scorel in Haarlem in the late 1520s. Scorel had been among the first artists from the northern Netherlands to visit Italy, and his return to Utrecht in 1524 and subsequent dissemination of the Italian style is regarded as a major turning point in the history of art of the Netherlands. Van

FIGURE 15A | Harmen Jansz. Muller after Maarten van Heemskerck, *Mars, the Choleric Temperament*, 1566. New York Public Library.

Heemskerck followed Scorel's example, traveling to Italy in 1532 and remaining there for four or five years. This visit profoundly affected his style, and because van Heemskerck was one of the most prolific suppliers of drawings created expressly to be made into prints—producing nearly six hundred of them between 1537 and his death in 1574—he in turn played an enormous part in bringing the high Mannerist style of Michelangelo and Giulio Romano to the North.

Mars, the Choleric Temperament is one of a set of four images representing the four temperaments, a concept ultimately originating in classical antiquity. The temperaments were thought to derive from four kinds of fluids, or humors—blood, choler, black bile, and phlegm—present in all humans, and the preponderance of one fluid was believed to govern the behavior of each individual, resulting in a sanguine, choleric, melancholic, or phlegmatic temperament. In this elaborate system of belief, carried through the medieval period and right up to the seventeenth century, the temperaments also were thought to correspond with the four seasons, the elements, the ages of man, and even the winds. Thus the sanguine temperament corresponded with spring, air, childhood, and the south wind; the choleric with summer, fire, youth, and the east wind; the melancholic with autumn, earth, maturity, and the north wind; and the phlegmatic with winter, water, old age, and the west wind.[1] Van Heemskerck, somewhat unusually, showed each temperament under the reign of a planet. Images of the planets and their "children," i.e., those over whom they had influence, had been common since the fifteenth century, and van Heemskerck fused this tradition with that of images of the temperaments.

Mars, the god of war, was the obvious choice to symbolize the choleric temperament. He is shown seated on a cloud surrounded by fire, while on Earth below him are manifestations of war. In the foreground to the left a smith is forging arms; the armored man near the center holds both a sword and a gun while the two men farther to the right duel with swords. In the mid-ground, cannons and warriors seem about to attack cities, and a farmstead is burning. In the sky above are three signs of the zodiac: Sagittarius the archer, Leo the lion, and Aries the ram—reversed from their chronological order in the drawing so they will be the right way around in the print. Aries, Leo, and Sagittarius, the first, fifth, and ninth signs of the zodiac, all correspond to the element of fire.

The drawing is incised for transfer to an engraving plate; the set of four prints, of which this is the second (fig. A), was engraved, in reverse, by Harmen Jansz. Muller, and published probably by Philips Galle.[2] The first engraving is *Jupiter and Venus, the Sanguine Temperament*, the third *Saturn, the Melancholic Temperament*, and the last *Luna, the Phlegmatic Temperament*; this is dated 1566. The drawing for *Luna, the Phlegmatic Temperament*, also signed and dated Heemskerck 1565, is in the collection of the Pierpont Morgan Library, New York (fig. B).[3]

The engraving of *Mars, the Choleric Temperament* is inscribed: *Armorum rabies, incendia, praelia, strages / Luctiferum agnoscunt*

FIGURE 15B | Maarten van Heemskerck, *Luna, the Phlegmatic Temperament*, 1565. New York, Pierpont Morgan Library.

Martem, dominumq[ue] cruentum (the madness of arms, fires, battles, and slaughter acknowledge Mars, the bearer of strife and cruel lord). These verses, and those on the other prints, were written by Adrian de Jonghe, a philologist, botanist, and the town physician of Haarlem, who latinized his name to Hadrianus Junius, and who in his lifetime was considered to be the most erudite man after Erasmus. Junius wrote the verses for numerous series by van Heemskerck, most of them in the 1560s. Junius wrote his texts after the images existed, with the aim of elucidating their meaning.[4]

SB

1 See Veldman 1980, with earlier bibliography.
2 See New Hollstein DF, *Maarten van Heemskerck*, Part 2: no. 543; also Hollstein DF 8:246, no. 439; 14:103, no. 112, and New Hollstein DF, *The Muller Dynasty*, Part 1:203, no. 102.
3 Inv. no. 1986.7, pen and brown ink over black chalk, 21 × 24 cm; see Stampfle 1991, no. 73, where it is noted that "the sheet may in the past have been washed, and this would account for the faintness of the ink in certain areas and for the absence of stylus marks present on the companion sheet in New Haven."
4 See Veldman 1974; reprinted in Veldman 1977, 97–112.

16 Anonymous (probably French)

Three Scenes from the Life of John the Baptist: John the Baptist Preaching, Baptism of Christ, Beheading of John the Baptist, 1572

Pen and brown ink, brush and blue ink, blue wash, squared in black chalk, 25.7 × 42.9 cm (10 1/16 × 16 7/8 in.)

INSCRIPTIONS: on mount, recto, lower right, in pencil: *de Vos*

PROVENANCE: John Percival, 1st Earl of Egmont (1683–1748); John T. Graves; Robert Hoe (sale, New York, Anderson Auction Company, 15–19 April 1912, Library of Robert Hoe, Part III, A–K, no. 949); Yale University Library (anonymous donor, 1957)

REFERENCES: H-B and L, no. 513 (as School of Louvain)

Egmont Collection, Yale Library Transfer. 1961.66.39

Three narratives encapsulate the function of John the Baptist as herald and forerunner of the Messiah. In the central scene, John baptizes Christ and witnesses a manifestation of the Trinity.[1] At left, John preaches repentance to crowds who came to hear him in the wilderness. As a result of John's bold teaching, Herod imprisoned him. When Salome, the daughter of Herod's sister-in-law and mistress Herodias, danced for Herod on his birthday, he promised to give Salome whatever she wanted. Herodias advised that she ask for John the Baptist's head on a platter. Salome followed her counsel, and Herod ordered the execution. The panel at the right shows the executioner putting John's severed head on the platter that Salome extends toward him.[2]

The anonymous artist of Yale's drawing generally conformed to traditional iconography, although one detail is unusual. God the Father, seen in the sky at Christ's baptism, wears a papal tiara. Depicting the tiara on God the Father's head could not have been merely a neutral statement of status or divine priesthood at this place and time; instead, it asserts a pro-Roman-Catholic agenda. The year 1572 marked the height of anti-Protestant sentiment in France, epitomized by widespread persecution in the wake of the Saint Bartholomew's Day Massacre. During this incident, several dozen French Huguenots—who had come to Paris for the wedding of the Protestant Henry of Navarre to Margaret of Valois (Queen Catherine de Medici's youngest daughter)—were killed by Catholic nobles and citizens on the night of 24 August. The queen had instigated the massacre. Several months of mass persecution then began throughout France, and tens of thousands of Huguenots died. The newly elected pope, Gregory XIII, praised the zeal of the French Catholics in combating heresy.

Haverkamp-Begemann and Logan hypothesized that this drawing was a study for a tapestry. Indeed, it is reminiscent of the drawings for the renowned tapestry series of the *History of Artemisia*, based on a poem written by Nicholas Houel around 1560, making the parallel between the ancient queen, widow of Mausolus, who carried on a strong rule after his death, and Catherine de Medici, who in 1551 became the widow of Henry II.[3] There is another French drawing in tripartite form from this period, also assumed to be for a tapestry, depicting episodes from the life of Saint Nicholas of Myra—with borders similar to those of Yale's drawing (fig. A).[4] This comparison suggests that Yale's drawing could have been made for a series of tapestries devoted to saints, but until the possibility can be more thoroughly investigated, this suggestion must remain a hypothesis.

The biblical subject and pro-Catholic bias also suggest that the drawing could have been a study for a print—the most common medium for propaganda. During the Wars of Religion (1562–98, also called the Huguenot Wars), hundreds of propagandistic prints were made in the quarter of rue Montorgueil in Paris and elsewhere.[5] God the Father is shown wearing the papal tiara in three Montorgueil prints of a series of the *Apocalypse* preserved in an album at the Bibliothèque Nationale, Paris.[6] He also wears it in an image of *The Triumph of the Trinity*, the sixth and last in a series of the *Triumphs* of Petrarch.[7]

To date, no existing print corresponding to Yale's drawing has been identified. Both the framing devices and the compositions of the three scenes in the Yale drawing are generally reminiscent of the Montorgueil group. More than 250 Montorgueil prints from the second half of the sixteenth century survive, if only in single impressions in the album in Paris where the above-mentioned Apocalypse prints are kept. Many more of these must have existed, which are now completely lost.

Various features of this drawing derive from the first School of Fontainebleau—the Italianate columns, as well as the putti and the garlands along the upper frame—an influence that persisted in French art through the sixteenth century. The figures with slightly elongated limbs and small heads are fairly close to the work of Antoine Caron, whose artistic beginnings were at Fontainebleau in the 1540s, and whose designs were reproduced

FIGURE 16A | Artist unknown, French, *Three Scenes from the Life of Saint Nicholas of Myra*, 1570s. Paris, Bibliothèque Nationale de France.

in prints from the rue Montorgueil.[8] Some of the figures are closer in style to the heavier, more classicizing images of Henri Lerambert, active in Paris in the last decades of the sixteenth century and well-known as a designer of tapestries.[9] Although the drawing has not been convincingly attributed to a particular artist, its pro-Catholic iconography and general style seem to indicate a French, probably Parisian, origin.

MEH

1 "And Jesus being baptized, forthwith came out of the water: and lo, the heavens were opened to him: and he saw the Spirit of God descending as a dove, and coming upon him. And behold a voice from heaven, saying: This is my beloved Son, in whom I am well pleased," Matthew 3:16–17.
2 Mark 6:21–28.
3 Guiffrey 1920; Minneapolis 1993; Denis 1999.
4 Paris, Bibliothèque Nationale, inv. no. B5 rés f. 2, pen and blue-gray ink and wash, 37.1 × 52.9 cm.
5 See Adhémar 1954; Benedict in Los Angeles–New York–Paris 1994–95, 108–137.
6 Paris, Bibliothèque Nationale, Est. Ed 5g Rés, fols. 100–102 and Courboin 1900–1901, 72–73, nos. 686–691. These six prints have identical format and borders; the last one has the address "A Paris par Guillaume Saulier, à l'Espinette, & Jacques Laloüette, rue Montorgueil." Of the five images showing God the Father; two of them, *Christ with the Seven Candlesticks and Other Scenes* and *Angels Holding the Four Winds and Other Scenes* (fols. 100, 100v, Courboin nos. 686–687) do not show him with the papal tiara; but he does wear it in *The Apocalyptic Woman and Other Scenes*, *The Whore of Babylon and Other Scenes*, and *The Angel with the Key to the Bottomless Pit and Other Scenes* (fols. 101v, 102, 102v, Courboin nos. 689–691).
7 Paris, Bibliothèque Nationale, Est. Ed 5g Rés, fol. 132v, Courboin 1900–1901, 77, no. 20. This print has the address "A Paris par Charles le Vigoureux, Rue Montorgueil, à l'Image St. Pierre."
8 For example *Bigthan and Teresh Plotting the Death of Ahasuerus*, Paris, Bibliothèque Nationale, Est. Ed 5g Rés, fol. 46, Courboin 1900–1901, 12, no. 134; Caron's drawing is Munich, Staatliche Graphische Sammlung, inv. no. 19528.
9 Denis 1999.

17 Frans Pourbus the Elder
Bruges 1545/46–1581 Antwerp

It Is All Hay, 1575

Pen and brown ink and brown wash over black chalk, with circle outline in red chalk, 25.9 × 23.6 cm (10³⁄₁₆ × 9⁵⁄₁₆ in.)

WATERMARK: on backing sheet, shield with a Strasburg lily or fleur-de-lys, topped with a crown, similar to Heawood nos. 1785, 1793, and 1809; see also the watermark on a drawing by Paul Sandby, in Sievers, Muehlig, and Rich 2000, no. 22. This is one of several different watermarks found in the mounting pages of the Egmont Albums.

INSCRIPTIONS: recto, in pen and brown ink, lower right: *on tal 1575*; on robe of priest: *vlvte apostata*; at top left: *francisco pourbus / fecit in antwen / 1575*; at lower right edge: *10 . . .*

PROVENANCE: John Percival, 1st Earl of Egmont (1683–1748); John T. Graves; Robert Hoe (sale, New York, Anderson Auction Company, 15–19 April 1912, Library of Robert Hoe, Part III, A–K, no. 949); Yale University Library (anonymous donor, 1957)

REFERENCES: Haverkamp-Begemann 1969, 65–66; H-B and L, no. 503; Vandenbroeck 1987, 126; Gibson 1992, 76

Egmont Collection, Yale Library Transfer. 1961.65.9

Frans Pourbus the Elder has been known primarily as a portrait painter, although recent scholarship has added considerably to our knowledge of his oeuvre of subject paintings made in the years between 1569–70, when he became a free master in the Antwerp painters' guild, and his early death barely more than a decade later.[1] Pourbus was first a student of his father, Pieter Pourbus, in his native Bruges, and then of Frans Floris, in Antwerp, by 1564. The robust, somewhat stiff figures in Pourbus's paintings are strongly reminiscent of Floris's work, and Pourbus's paintings helped to spread Floris's italianizing style throughout the Netherlands.

Yale's drawing is one of an extremely limited number known by Pourbus, and the only one that is both signed and dated. A drawing in the British Museum, *The Flood*, is signed; this work is also in a circular format, slightly larger than Yale's drawing.[2] Thus the sheet at Yale is a benchmark for attribution of others, although at present it would seem that extraordinarily few have survived. It is also possible, however—as has been the case with Pourbus's paintings—that a number of drawings exist that are currently misattributed to other artists. The style of this drawing is considerably freer than that of Pourbus's paintings, revealing an artist able to render the human figure in action with ease and naturalism, within a composition that sits comfortably on the sheet.

Yale's drawing illustrates a well-known proverbial phrase, *Al Hoy* ([It Is] All Hay). Proverbs were enormously popular in the Netherlands of the sixteenth century, following the publication of the *Adagia* by Desiderius Erasmus, first in Paris in 1500, then in an enlarged and annotated version from the famous Aldine Press in Venice in 1508, and with innumerable subsequent editions. Gibson reported that five different books of proverbs were published in Antwerp alone in the 1550s and '60s, in Latin and vernacular languages.[3]

Pourbus has depicted a fool in the center handing hay to a cardinal and a soldier, who lean forward eagerly to receive it; another fool in the background proffers hay on a pitchfork to a young woman. Other figures are grabbing at the haystack. The proverb reflected the common understanding in the Netherlands of this time that hay represented something trivial, or worthless.[4] The composition is thus to be interpreted as a *vanitas*, an allusion to mankind's folly in striving for transient earthly gains and pleasures, essentially carrying the same meaning as Hieronymus Bosch's *Hay Wain* (versions at Madrid, Prado, and El Escorial, Monasterio de San Lorenzo). The first documented commentary on that painting is by Ambrosio de Morales, who described the *Hay Wain* as a representation "of the whole of our miserable life and the fierce delight we take in its vanities. . . . It is in the form of a hay wagon, in Flemish, which, in Castilian, amounts to 'wagon of worthless things.' This hay wagon, is thus truly a 'trash cart' and its name matches its meaning."[5] An etching of 1559 thought to be by Frans Hogenberg titled *Al Hoy* (All Hay), published by Bartholomeus de Momper (fig. A), shows that the symbolic meaning of hay in Bosch's painting was still current in Antwerp at that date.[6] This etching may well have been the inspiration for one of the floats in the *Ommegang*, the religious procession in Antwerp at the Feast of the Assumption in 1563, which consisted of a hay wagon ridden by a devil and followed by unsavory characters trying to pluck the hay. The printed program for the procession specified the meaning, "So long as the hay wain is loaded, None shall have their fill of pulling."[7] Another drawing of the same subject by a Netherlandish artist, also in circular format, is known, attributed to Adriaen Pietersz. Crabeth.[8]

Fools were often part of public spectacles in the Netherlands in the fifteenth and sixteenth centuries—dramatic presentations, or processions such as the *Ommegangen*. In 1561 Antwerp was the site of a *Landjuweel*, a drama competition, and the procession was led by the private fool of the dean of the Chamber of Rhetoric *De Violeren*, organizer of the event; the Chamber's own fool rode on horseback.[9] During this period, the attitude toward fools ranged from their being seen as innocent simpletons to being associated with sin,[10] but their function—to point out humanity's weaknesses—was constant, and writers put into the mouths of fools things they would not otherwise have dared to say. In Yale's drawing the fool, actively distributing worthless, frivolous material, is definitely a promoter of vice.

The circular format of the drawing must have been determined by its intended use. Compositions to be painted on glass were often round, and very possibly this image was intended for glass; the diameter of the circle outlined in red chalk, about 26.8 cm (10½ in.), was a size common for glass roundels (see cat. no. 7).[11] Conceivably, also, it might have been destined to be one of several small tondi in a larger work illustrating men's follies, or sins. This sort of subject in a round format was part of a long tradition in the Netherlands—one of the best-known examples of which was the tabletop depicting the seven deadly sins painted by Bosch, with scenes of the *Four Last Things* (Death, Last Judgment, Heaven, and Hell) in roundels in the corners.[12] Roundels epitomizing the sins themselves are depicted in the four corners of each etching in the series of seven on this subject by Léon Davent, after designs by Luca Penni (see cat. no. 10), made in France in the mid-1550s.[13] Whatever the specific purpose of Yale's drawing, it seems most likely that

FIGURE 17A | Probably Frans Hogenberg, *Al Hoy* (*All Hay*), 1559. Brussels, Bibliothèque Royale de Belgique.

the image was preparatory for some sort of ensemble, rather than being a single independent work.

1. See Velde 1979–80 and Velde 1994.
2. Haverkamp-Begemann 1969, 65–66, discusses three drawings previously given to Frans Pourbus the Elder, adding the Yale drawing and also attributing a *Merry Company at Table in a Landscape* in the Lugt Collection to the artist, for a total of five, but then subtracting a *Saint George* in Vienna, leaving four. Boon in Florence–Paris 1980–81, no. 129, and Boon 1992, no. 186, however, attributes the *Merry Company* to Jan Snellinck the Elder.
3. Gibson 1992, 75.
4. The fundamental article on the significance of hay is Lebeer and Grauls 1938; see also Keyser 1939–40, and, more recently, Einem 1976 and Vandenbroeck 1984 and 1987, and Gibson 1992. Further writings on the subject can be found in Mieder and Sobieski 1999. See also Sullivan 1991, in which she argues persuasively that the humanistic perspective, as well as the folkloristic one, should be brought to bear in interpretation of proverb subjects by Bruegel and other sixteenth-century Netherlandish artists.
5. "... todo nuestra vivir miserable, y el grande embebecimiento que en sus vanidades traemos.... Y hase entender cómo carro de heno, en flamenco, tanto quiere decir como carro de nonada, en Castilla. Assi, aquel carro siendo de heno, es verdaderamente carro de nonada, y assi tiene su nombre al propio de lo que significa." Quoted in Salazar 1955, 124–125.
6. The etching is not in Hollstein DF.
7. Keyser 1939–40, 134; Gibson 1981, 438; Vandenbroeck 1987, 111–112.
8. Vienna, Albertina, inv. no. 7848, pen and olive-brown ink and wash, diam. 26 cm; Benesch 1928, no. 108. See also Vandenbroeck 1987, 126–127, and Gibson 1992, 75–76.
9. Brussels 1994, 29, and no. 17.
10. See Hüsken 1996, 115.
11. Popham 1932, 176, Pourbus, no. 1, describes *The Flood* as "presumably a design for glass."
12. Madrid, Prado; see Marijnissen 1987, 329–345.
13. Zerner 1969, LD, nos. 86–92.

18 Giovanni Battista Naldini
Fiesole 1535–1591 Florence

Study of a Seated Youth, ca. 1575

Red chalk and red wash with thin white heightening, 22.6 × 20.3 cm (8⅞ × 8 in.)

INSCRIPTIONS: verso, lower left, in graphite: *In* (?) *8635*

PROVENANCE: C. G. Boerner, Dusseldorf, 1971, no. 137 (as Pontormo); Edmund P. Pillsbury

REFERENCES: *YUAG Bulletin* 34 (1973): 57; New Haven 1974, no. 32; New Haven 1991a, no. 4; Oberlin–Brunswick–Hanover 1991, no. 31; New Haven 1994, no. 54

Gift of Edmund P. Pillsbury, B.A. 1965. 1972.38

Giovanni Battista Naldini spent much of his career working under Giorgio Vasari on some of the most important artistic projects commissioned by the Medici Dukes in Florence: the 1565 wedding of Francesco I, the Sala del Cinquecento and the Studiolo in the Palazzo Vecchio, and the renovations of Santa Maria Novella and Santa Croce. Naldini's paintings reflect the influence of Agnolo Bronzino, Alessandro Allori, and Giorgio Vasari, the leading artists of the day, but Naldini had received his initial training from Jacopo Pontormo, the greatest artist of the previous generation, and his drawing style always remained close to the model of Pontormo, to whom this drawing was once attributed. More than a mere stylistic resemblance, Naldini's drawings continued the essential design practices of his master. He was, furthermore, among the founders of the Accademia del Disegno and was responsible as much as any artist for the revival of Andrea del Sarto and Pontormo as models for young artists in the later part of the century.[1] It is often said that Naldini's drawings most resemble Pontormo's figure studies of the early 1520s, sketches made over a decade before Naldini's birth;[2] a plausible explanation is that Naldini inherited this group of his master's drawings and used them as touchstones throughout his career. Naldini may also have allowed this set of Pontormo drawings to be studied at the Accademia del Disegno, which might account for the numerous copies of them by Florentine artists of the late Cinquecento.[3]

Like Pontormo, Naldini was an obsessive draftsman, with a rigorous and disciplined approach to design. He developed compositions through the traditional series of *primi pensieri* followed by figure studies followed by *modelli* and cartoons.[4] Like most artists active in Florence in the second half of the sixteenth century, Naldini often quoted figures from paintings by artists of the previous generation; indeed, the pose of the *Seated Youth* resembles many of the foreground figures that, without any narrative function, act instead as decorative and framing elements in cinquecento Florentine painting.[5] Even for these quotations, however, and certainly for new poses, Naldini made figure studies. These were ideally drawn directly from live models in the studio, but while Naldini's paintings included figures of all ages and sizes, the most readily available models were the *garzoni*, the artist's young male assistants.

We thus find scores of studies by Naldini like the present drawing, of youths taking up poses that, in the finished work, would be given either to men or women, both old and young, and to lithe angels or chubby cherubs. One of the many examples that might be cited is the British Museum's *Youth Seated on the Ground Holding a Large Open Book*, which is actually a figure study for the old woman seated in the middle ground of his *Presentation in the Temple* in Santa Maria Novella, Florence.[6] Another is a large *Seated Youth* in the Uffizi, which is surely a study for the woman in the foreground of the Santa Croce *Entombment*.[7] Most of these drawings are careful analytical studies, regardless of their casual appearance; like Pontormo, Naldini seems generally to have had a specific reason for undertaking any given drawing.[8]

Despite the appearance of figures in similar poses throughout Naldini's work, none seems to match the *Seated Youth* exactly, so that the drawing cannot be linked absolutely to any of his known paintings. There are similar figures in the foregrounds of his *Collecting Ambergris* for the studiolo in the Palazzo Vecchio, his *Entombment of Christ* in Santa Croce, and his *Visitation* on the vault of the Altoviti chapel in Santissima Trinità dei Monti, Rome. The closest match might be the *putto* to the left of the altar in the crypt of the chapel of Saint Antoninus in San Marco, Florence.[9] There is also a putto in a similar pose in the foreground of Naldini's *modello* for the *Presentation in the Temple* altarpiece in Santa Maria Novella, although the figure does not appear in the finished altarpiece.[10] As that picture demonstrates, Naldini sometimes made changes to his composition late in the design process, even after the *modello* was painted, so it is possible that the figure to which the Yale *Seated Youth* corresponded might have been subsequently modified or entirely omitted from the final work. A number of drawings with youths in similar positions could possibly even represent such refinements of the pose.[11] Finally, all of the aforementioned paintings date to the 1570s, and comparison of the *Seated Youth* to the other drawings for those paintings further suggests a date of circa 1575 for the Yale sheet.

Regardless of its connection to any painting, the *Seated Youth* bears all the benchmarks of Naldini's drawings in red chalk and includes his characteristic shorthand mannerisms of jagged fingers and "lobster-claw" feet. The rapidly drawn but forcefully strengthened contours are typical of the artist and show him at his best. For this drawing, Naldini experimented with the use of a dilute red wash for shading, but he more often used cross-hatching in chalk. The use of a brush with thin, almost pigmentless watercolor to clean or correct areas of the drawing, or even as a sort of "stopping-out" agent as seen here, is an unusual technique among Florentine artists, but one that Naldini used with some frequency.[12] Such inventiveness, as well as the attention paid to drawings that would have led Naldini to develop this technique, are entirely typical of Naldini's art. In Bernard Berenson's apt summation, "drawings by Naldini are numerous, and so full of spirit, so pictorial, so lively in execution that an hour spent looking over his albums at the Uffizi must count among the pleasures of the student of cinquecento Florentine draughtsmanship."[13]

JJM

1 The most complete account of Naldini's life and career remains Barocchi 1965. For a summary of the traditions of Florentine design, the Pontormo revival, and Vasari's attempt to diminish Pontormo's reputation, see Feinberg 1991.
2 Naldini's date of birth, traditionally given as circa 1537, is actually 3 May 1535 according to a document discovered and published by Elizabeth Pilliod; see Pilliod 2001, 77.
3 Whether the Accademia del Disegno fulfilled its teaching mission or was instead a more functionary organization was long a subject of debate, but recent studies have made clear that it did instruct artists. See Feinberg 1991 and, for a more recent summary, Barzman 2000.
4 Like Pontormo's drawn *modelli*, Naldini's tend not to be of the highly finished variety, but are still energetic sketches, albeit ones that incorporate the various figure studies. Naldini also made a number of painted *modelli* (see Hall 1979 for examples) that served the role that highly finished drawings might alternately have done.
5 It recalls without exactly matching, for example, the nude boy in the foreground of Pontormo's *Visitation* in Santissima Annunziata, Florence.
6 London, British Museum, inv. no. 1893-7-31-16, red chalk, heightened with white, with additional work in black chalk, 25.2 × 30.8 cm; London 1986, no. 160.
7 Florence, Uffizi, inv. no. 657S, red chalk, 29 × 42.5 cm; Barocchi 1965, 263–264 and figs.108c and 110a.
8 It should be noted that Naldini was not the only artist to use *garzoni* for studies of very different kinds of figures, although he did so more often than did most of his contemporaries. Pontormo made many such studies; the boy on the steps of the Santissima Annunziata *Visitation*, for example, likewise began as an older youth before being transformed into a boy. See Cox-Rearick 1964, no. 12.
9 These putti may have been painted by Naldini's young assistant Giovanni Balducci, but according to Naldini's designs. See Barocchi 1965, 262–263.
10 The *modello* and the altarpiece are reproduced in Hall 1979, figs. 62 and 66. The *modello* is there identified as being in a private collection but it is now at Chapel Hill, Ackland Art Museum, inv. no. 77.41.1.
11 See, for example, Florence, Uffizi, inv. no. 7493, red chalk, 21.4 × 20 cm (identified by Schaefer 1982, 128 and pl. 21, as a study for *Collecting Ambergris*); also, Uffizi inv. no. 657S, noted above.
12 Other examples include the aforementioned British Museum *Youth with a Book*, where the technique is more readily visible because the paper has darkened, as well as Paris, Louvre, inv. nos. 9551 and 12415. The technique also appears in drawings by Francesco Curradi, Naldini's pupil.
13 Berenson 1938, 1:321.

19 Federico Zuccaro
Sant'Angelo in Vado 1540/42–1609 Ancona

Redeemed Souls and Allegorical Figures: Study for the Last Judgment in the Cupola of the Duomo, Florence, 1575–76

Pen and brown ink and brown wash, 41.9 × 55.5 cm (16½ × 21⅞ in.)

PROVENANCE: Galleria W. Apolloni, Rome; William H. Schab Gallery, New York; Sabatino Abate, Jr., Boston; Christie's, New York, 19 April 1988, lot 43; acquired from Hill-Stone, Inc., New York

REFERENCES: Rome 1978, no. 9; Gere and Pouncey 1983, 194–195 (under no. 308); *YUAG Bulletin* (1989): 91; Milwaukee–New York 1989–90, no. 68; New Haven 1991a, no. 39; New Haven 1994, no. 61; Acidini Luchinat 1999, 2:86 and 116 n. 41

Everett V. Meeks, B.A. 1901, and Leonard C. Hanna, Jr., B.A. 1913, Funds. 1989.61.1

Filippo Brunelleschi's great dome of the Florence cathedral had been the foremost symbol of that city from the moment of its completion, but the dome's inner face remained undecorated for nearly 150 years until Vincenzo Borghini, the humanist prior of the Ospedale degli Innocenti, and Giorgio Vasari began designing a program of frescoes under the patronage of Duke Cosimo I de' Medici.[1] They saw the project as an undertaking equivalent to the Sistine Chapel, not least of all because the cupola was to have a Last Judgment. Duke Cosimo granted the official commission in August of 1571, and by 1573, Vasari had made drawings for the entire scheme.[2] Vasari and Borghini devised a program that relied heavily on Michelangelo's fresco, on the mosaics in the Florence baptistry, and on the *Comedy* of the great Florentine poet Dante Alighieri. The octagonal dome was to have the Elders of the Apocalypse in the uppermost register, with angels bearing the instruments of the Passion and a heavenly tribunal below, followed by a series of allegorical figures representing the Beatitudes, the Gifts of the Holy Spirit, and the Virtues; the damned in Hell would appear in the lower register. At Vasari's death in June of 1574, however, two-thirds of the fresco was yet to be painted.[3]

A year passed before the commission was given to Federico Zuccaro. Born in the Marches near Urbino, Zuccaro had worked in Rome, Venice, the Netherlands, and England before arriving in Florence in 1575. Despite his varied experience, he was hardly an obvious choice to complete the project and met with much hostility from Florentine artists. He nonetheless took up the project in

November 1575, began painting the following August, and completed work in August 1579.⁴ A large body of drawings survives for the cupola and includes sketches from all stages of the design process as well as multiple versions or copies of the more finished *modelli*. Some of these multiples must have been used to organize work in Zuccaro's large studio; others were probably produced to show to the patrons and supervisors of the Opera del Duomo for approval, for Zuccaro was still relatively unfamiliar to the Florentines, and it is inconceivable that he would have been allowed to execute so prominent (and so complicated) a project without close supervision.⁵ Some drawings are in nearly pristine condition, suggesting that they were clean copies for presentation, while others including the Yale drawing have creases and splattered ink suggesting that they may have remained in the workshop.

The large drawing at Yale is a *modello* for the middle registers of the cupola's west face (fig. A). The allegorical figures in the lower half represent, according to Borghini's description, the first of the eight biblical beatitudes from Jesus' Sermon on the Mount: "Blessed are the Poor in Spirit, for theirs is the Kingdom of Heaven" (Matthew 5:3) at center, with "Fear of God" at left and "Humility" at right. The upper part of the drawing, representing a section of the heavenly court, depicts "all the rest of the Christian people: the married and widowed, poor and rich, the leisured and the workers—in short, every age, sex, and quality," as described by Borghini. As elsewhere in the project, Zuccaro's drawing loosely followed the basic arrangement of figures from Vasari's preparatory studies, but the substitution of more "ordinary" figures in static, frontal poses (rather than Vasari's twisting figures) is typical of Zuccaro's departure from Vasari's models and of his preference for clarity over aesthetic complexity.⁶ The man carrying a shovel, at left, and the pilgrims with staffs at left and right, for example, are nowhere in Vasari's drawings.

The Yale drawing comes from fairly late in the design process, after Zuccaro had made both compositional studies for the full cupola sections and studies for figures or groups, but before some final changes that appear in the final fresco.⁷ The next stage of the process is represented by a version of the drawing, now in the British Museum, which matches the Yale study in nearly all details but in a slightly stiff manner that reveals it to be a copy, albeit one by Zuccaro or a close workshop assistant. The British Museum drawing, however, has the addition of a few sketches in chalk at the upper corners almost certainly by Zuccaro himself.⁸ In the final fresco, that is, a number of the figures in the upper register of the Yale and the British Museum *modelli* are replaced with portraits of Zuccaro, his family, other artists (including Vasari and Giambologna), and other individuals associated with the project (Vincenzo Borghini, Bernardo Vecchietti, et al.).⁹ A number of additional drawings that are studies for these portraits survive and were presumably made after the Yale and the London *modelli*.¹⁰ Finally, Zuccaro labeled his self-portrait in the fresco with an inscription that also gives the date 1576; thus the west octant must have been among the first sections that he painted, and the Yale drawing can be securely dated to 1575–76.

JJM

1 Vasari mentions drawings for the cathedral in a list of projects on the back of a letter he received in September 1568 (Frey 1982, 2:407). The recent restorations of the dome revealed that Brunelleschi himself envisioned fresco or mosaic decoration and provided scaffolding anchorages for such work, as noted by Acidini Luchinat 1998, 238.

2 Borghini's own description of the program survives and was published by Guasti 1857, 132–140. Vasari noted in a letter of 1573 (quoted in Turner et al. 1997, 133) that he had prepared all of the drawings, so that any experienced painter would be able to complete the work.

3 On Vasari's work for the dome, see especially Monbeig Goguel 1972, 177–195, for the drawings, and Acidini Luchinat 1998 for the frescoes. Other summaries of the project are New Haven 1994, 45–51, and Acidini Luchinat 1994.

4 For a summary of Zuccaro's work on the cupola, see Heikamp 1967, and, more recently with good illustrations and updated bibliography, Acidini Luchinat 1999, Chapter 13.

5 Mundy, in Milwaukee–New York 1989–90, 218, suggests further that some of the large finished drawings may have been applied to

FIGURE 19A | Federico Zuccaro, Detail of the *Last Judgment*, 1575–79. Florence, Duomo.

the model of the cupola seen in a drawing (Florence, Uffizi, inv. no. 11043F) and a painting (Rome, Bibliotheca Hertziana) by Zuccaro.

6 Zuccaro began work by studying Vasari's drawings, as indicated in a letter of 1575 from his advocate Bernardo Vecchietti to Duke Cosimo; see Smith 1978, 27–28. Vasari's preparatory drawings for this section of the dome are Paris, Louvre, inv. nos. 2122b and 2138; Acidini Luchinat 1999, 2:78, figs. 15 and 16. The different styles of Vasari's and Zuccaro's frescoes are immediately apparent even when looking at the dome from far below on the floor of the church.

7 New York, Metropolitan Museum of Art, inv. no. 1961.53 (Milwaukee–New York 1989–90, no. 66) is an example of a study for the entire southwest octant of the cupola; the drawing for the entire west octant seems not to survive. For figure studies preliminary to the Yale drawing, see Rome, Istituto Nazionale per la Grafica, inv. no. FC.130634 for Humility and the adjacent angel; and Florence, Uffizi, inv. nos. 10987F and 11052F for the trumpeting angels and the beatitude figure, respectively. Also worth noting is Cambridge, Harvard University Art Museums, inv. no. 1987.3, a study for the southwest octant; this sheet was in the same collections as the Yale drawing until 1988 and represents a parallel stage of the design process; for further discussion see Milwaukee–New York 1989–90, no. 67 (although it is there identified as being for the west octant, and the Yale drawing for the southwest).

8 London, British Museum, inv. no. 1863-5-9-630, pen and brown ink and brown wash, with some purple wash at the upper edge, and with black and red chalk used for the heads in the upper corners, 44.1 × 57.2 cm; see Gere and Pouncey 1983, no. 307, and London 1986, no. 168 (with color reproduction). Jacks, in New Haven 1994, 50, is alone in thinking the British Museum drawing is preparatory to Yale's. The British Museum has other "second versions": see Gere and Pouncey 1983, nos. 302–309. The Fogg drawing mentioned above is similarly replicated by Vienna, Albertina, inv. no. 14330 (Acidini Luchinat 1999, 2:82, fig. 28); this and other drawings in the Albertina, and also a study for the Angels of the west octant, Ann Arbor, University of Michigan Museum of Art, inv. no. 1973/2.81, all with purple-pink wash, seem to be from the same set of copies as these British Museum drawings.

9 Heikamp 1967, 49–50, catalogues the portraits, including a number not identified by Zuccaro with inscriptions.

10 See, for example, Zuccaro's portrait of Aniello di Mariotto del Buonis, one of the plasterers who worked with Zuccaro on the cupola: Palermo, Museo Nazionale, inv. no. 15484/43, red and black chalk, 28.2 × 21 cm; see Palermo 1995–96, no. 38. Mundy, in Milwaukee–New York, 1989–90, no. 68, gives references for additional portrait drawings related to this octant; these are part of an enormous body of portraits and life studies in black and red chalk that Zuccaro made during his years in Florence. One such portrait drawing in the Yale University Art Gallery, a *Head of a Boy*, inv. no. 1976.37, black and red chalk, 9.2 × 7 cm, bears mentioning here, although it is not related to the cupola. Formerly attributed to Barocci (for example, Cleveland–New Haven 1978, no. 34), the drawing is instead probably by Zuccaro and sits easily among his many portraits in red and black chalk; Paris, Louvre, inv. nos. 4593, 4594, 4597, 4599, 4612, and 4635 are among the many close comparisons.

20 Federico Barocci
Urbino 1535–1612 Urbino

Head of a Girl, Study for the Madonna del Popolo Altarpiece, ca. 1575–79

Black and red chalk, heightened with white chalk, with touches of yellow pastel, on faded blue paper, 25.2 × 19.1 cm (9 15/16 × 7 1/2 in.)

INSCRIPTIONS: recto, lower right, in pen and brown ink: *162*; verso, center, in black chalk: *Di Fedrico Varogio*

PROVENANCE: D. D. Campbell; Sotheby's, London, 26 November 1970, lot 27; acquired from William H. Schab Gallery, New York

REFERENCES: New Haven 1974, no. 28; *YUAG Bulletin* 35 (1974): 61; Cleveland–New Haven 1978, no. 37; *Handbook*, 199; Sievers, Muehlig, and Rich 2000, 48

Maitland F. Griggs, B.A. 1896, Fund. 1973.141

Federico Barocci received his first artistic training in his native Urbino from the Venetian artist Battista Franco; he then traveled to Rome in the early 1550s, still a young man, and studied the works of Michelangelo, Raphael, Polidoro da Caravaggio, and others, before returning to Urbino via Pesaro, where he also studied the paintings by Titian in the Delle Rovere collection. Barocci went back to Rome in 1560 and began to enjoy some success there, but when struck by a serious illness (rumored to have been the result of poisoning by jealous rivals), he returned home to Urbino, where he was based for the rest of his career. Despite residence in that relatively remote city, Barocci's varied experience led him—like other contemporary painters who had similar eclectic training—to investigate aspects of naturalism, theatricality, and narrative structures that would move painting away from Mannerism and toward the beginnings of Baroque style. His innovations were much admired, and Barocci's success was unparalleled among his contemporaries; he sent paintings to satisfy commissions from the pope, the emperor, the king of Spain, and the Grand Duke of Tuscany. Artists of the following generation learned much from his work, and Barocci was an essential model for the innovations of the Carracci, Rubens, and others.[1]

In Urbino, Barocci developed an individual and complex manner of working out compositions. He began with rough sketches, as did all of his contemporaries, but then seems to have moved rather quickly to a full *modello* and cartoon before he began making many of his detailed studies of head, hands, and other key elements. Where most of his contemporaries would have studied such details at an earlier stage of the design process, Barocci seems to have waited at least until the cartoon was complete or, perhaps more likely, until the painting was underway, for he drew the head and hand studies (as well as feet and even heads of animals) at the size that the elements would actually appear in the paintings (see fig. B).[2] In his biography of Barocci, the seventeenth-century theorist Bellori argued that Barocci would place these studies on the canvas and trace the contours with a stylus. Neither Yale's *Head of a Girl*, however, nor most similar pastel studies by the artist, show evidence of having been so treated, and it seems instead that Barocci relied on an innate sense of scale, rather than some mechanical means, to transfer the drawings to the painting. These remarkable large-scale heads and hands have few parallels among sixteenth-century drawings. More than simply an unusual convention of an artist outside a major artistic center, the studies also signify a shift in artistic theory. Where artists of the previous generation were praised for qualities like *sprezzatura*, an apparently effortless creation of graceful figures, Barocci was instead consistently praised for his *diligenza*, his diligence, and his perceived perfection of nature through arduous study. To some degree, this shift in attitude might be linked to a seriousness related to the Counter-Reformation.[3]

Barocci employed traditional pen, ink, wash, and chalk for his *primi pensieri*, and his cartoons are generally in black and white chalk on beige or blue paper, but for the detailed studies of heads and hands he chose the far less common techniques of oil paint on paper or, like the present work, pastel; he is among the first sixteenth-century draftsmen to make use of the latter material. In contrast to black, red, and white chalk, which are naturally occurring substances, pastels were manufactured by combining ground pigment with gum arabic or some other binder.[4] Generally used on blue paper, pastels enabled Barocci to study color in addition to form and tone. The *Head of a Girl* was drawn relatively early in Barocci's career, not long after he began to use pastels, which are limited here to a few spare touches of ochre in the hair and perhaps some pink in the cheeks. Yet, even these touches, when combined with black, white, and red chalk, hint at the full chromatic range that Barocci would use in his finished paintings.[5] In his life of Barocci, Bellori states that the artist learned the technique by studying some large pastel drawings by Correggio, but no such studies survive and there is some reason to doubt whether they ever existed.[6] Leonardo da Vinci is also said to have used pastel studies for the heads of the Apostles in the *Last Supper*, but it is doubtful that Barocci could have seen such drawings.[7] Instead, Barocci probably adopted the use of color in drawings from artists who had worked in the circle of Raphael at Rome.[8] An alternate, but not mutually exclusive hypothesis, is that Barocci developed his pastel technique because of the illness he suffered for the last fifty years of his life, which limited him to only a few hours of painting each day before the fumes of the oil media would become problematic for him; pastels could be made from the same pigments that would have been used in the oil paint.[9]

FIGURE 20A | Federico Barocci, *The Madonna del Popolo*, 1576–79. Florence, Galleria degli Uffizi.

The *Head of a Girl* is a study for Barocci's *Madonna del Popolo* altarpiece now in the Uffizi (fig. A), which was painted for the chapel of the Fraternity of Holy Mary of the Misericordia in the church of Santa Maria della Pieve at Arezzo. Giorgio Vasari originally held the commission, and upon Vasari's death in 1574, the Fraternity wrote to Florence for advice on the selection of a new painter. That Barocci was eventually chosen, rather than one of Vasari's Florentine colleagues, is surprising, for Barocci was still a relative unknown; presumably, he won the commission based on the quickly spreading fame of the *Deposition* in Perugia, his only major work before that date. Barocci traveled to Arezzo in the spring of 1575 to sign the contract and to inspect the chapel but executed the painting back home in Urbino. A series of letters between Barocci and the Fraternity allows us to track the history of the commission and the delays in the completion of the painting, which was finally finished in 1579 and delivered to the church in June of that year.[10]

The early letters between Barocci and the rectors of the Fraternity indicate that the original idea was for the altarpiece of the *mistero della Misericordia* ("the mystery of the Merciful Heart"), but Barocci explained to the rectors that it did not "seem to be a subject likely to make a beautiful altarpiece" and suggested the more common scenes of Annuciation, Assumption, or Visitation. As eventually stipulated in the contract, the altarpiece was to depict "the Virgin interceding and praying to Her Son on behalf of the populace, shown with the particular qualities and conditions appropriate to each individual figure." Both the complexity of the unusual subject matter and the importance of the commission led the artist to create a remarkable range of drawings, and Barocci designed a composition of far more intricacy than the contract required.[11] He included portraits of the Fraternity's rectors at the right edge of the canvas and decided to merge the image of the Virgin-intercessor at the top of the canvas with images evoking the charitable mission of the Fraternity in the lower part of the altarpiece.

The *Head of a Girl* relates to a relatively

minor figure in the painting, the young girl at lower left who looks across her mother's body toward her younger brother at the bottom of the scene. This figure is barely indicated in the *modello* for the painting,[12] but began to be developed further in a drawing in the Uffizi.[13] The Yale study, drawn to the same scale as the final painting (fig. B), established the correct angle for the head and helped Barocci determine the difficult alignment of the girl's downward and sideward gaze. Minor details like the position of the eyes play a key role in the painting, as the gazes of the various figures beckon the spectator, highlight acts of mercy, or lead the viewer to the divine intercession at the top of the scene. The importance of drawings like the present work in the creation of such early Baroque theatricality is self-evident.

JJM

FIGURE 20B | Photomontage juxtaposing cat. no. 20 at full scale with corresponding figure in Barocci's *Madonna del Popolo*.

1 The main source for the life of Barocci is Bellori 1672, 169–196, which has been many times republished. An English translation is in Cleveland–New Haven 1978, 11–24. For the most complete discussions of Barocci's work, see Cleveland–New Haven 1978 as well as Olsen 1962 and Emiliani 1985. For a more recent study with good illustrations, see Turner 2000.

2 Pillsbury was the first to argue this point (in Cleveland–New Haven 1978, 9), which the current discussion seeks to confirm, although his hypothesis was not generally followed by Emiliani or Turner. Ian Verstegen and I presented a further elaboration of these arguments in a paper delivered at the College Art Association's annual meeting in 2005 and are working on an article that will discuss Barocci's drawing practice in greater detail; this entry relies on our collaborative work. Even if many of the head and hand studies were made after the cartoon was complete, this was not always the case, as indicated by drawings like the *Study of the Chest and Right Arm of a Nude Male* at Princeton (inv. no. 48-595), at a much smaller scale than the Senigallia *Entombment*, to which it relates. The most highly finished oils and pastels, however, generally seem to be at full scale and probably follow the completion of the cartoon.

3 On this point, see Lingo 1998, Chapter 4. An emphasis on diligent study is a common trope in the biographies of artists of Barocci's generation; for another example, see the biography of Girolamo Muziano, Procacci 1954. Bellori's praise for Barocci's working method, however, is not directly related to Counter-Reformation concerns, but instead arose from Bellori's perception of Barocci, who mediated between the excess fantasy represented by Mannerism and the excess naturalism represented by Caravaggio, as a model for Baroque classicism.

4 For the making of pastels, see James et al. 1997, 72–74. For the history of the medium, see especially McGrath 1998, 3–9.

5 Aronberg Lavin 1956, 435–439.

6 Skepticism about the Correggio pastels was first advanced by Pillsbury in Cleveland–New Haven 1978, 8, and echoed by McGrath 1998, 3 and 7, n. 3.

7 G. P. Lomazzo, *Trattato della Pittura* (1584), in Ciardi 1974, 2:170. Leonardo probably did use pastels, to judge from drawings by his Milanese followers, for which see New York 2003.

8 McGrath 1998, 4–5.

9 McCullagh 1991, 59, and McGrath 1998, 6 and 9, n. 44.

10 A complete transcription of the contract is in Cleveland–New Haven 1978, 25–37. Emiliani 1985, 129–134, includes a more complete sequence of the letters.

11 *The Madonna del Popolo* is the painting by Barocci for which the greatest number of drawings survive, and probably also one of those for which the greatest number of preparatory sketches were done. Olsen linked seventy-five surviving sheets to the painting, and Emiliani sixty-nine, but neither included the Yale *Head of a Girl*. See Pillsbury 1976, 62, for further details. On the iconography, see also Lingo 1998, 326ff.

12 Long in the Devonshire collection at Chatsworth, the drawing was later at Christie's, New York, 28 January 1999, lot 56. It has been illustrated many times, including Emiliani 1985, 130, and Cleveland–New Haven 1978, 58.

13 Florence, Uffizi, inv. no. 812E, black and red chalk and pastel, 28 × 41.7 cm; Emiliani 1985, 149, fig. 292.

21 Maarten de Vos

Antwerp 1532–1603 Antwerp

Jonah Thrown Overboard, 1580s

Pen and brown ink and brown wash over black chalk, heightened with white, 28 × 22.3 cm (11 × 8 13/16 in.)

INSCRIPTIONS: recto, bottom left, in pencil: *Sadeler*

PROVENANCE: John Percival, 1st Earl of Egmont (1683–1748); John T. Graves; Robert Hoe (sale, New York, Anderson Auction Company, 15–19 April 1912, Library of Robert Hoe, Part III, A–K, no. 949); Yale University Library (anonymous donor, 1957)

REFERENCES: Judson 1969, passim; H-B and L, no. 510; Amherst 1990, no. 12; *Handbook*, 201; Hollstein DF 44: under no. 144

Egmont Collection, Yale Library Transfer. 1961.65.51

Maarten de Vos is thought to have traveled to Italy during the 1550s, spending some time in Rome and Florence, and in Venice reportedly working in the studio of Tintoretto, although there is still no certain evidence on this question.[1] In 1558 he was enrolled as a master in the Guild of Saint Luke in Antwerp, and despite pro-Reformation sympathies at an early stage he remained in Catholic Antwerp throughout his life.[2] He was among the most sought-after painters there, providing numerous altarpieces to replace those destroyed in the iconoclastic riots of 1558 and 1566. The fact that Antwerp was the leading city for print production in the second half of the sixteenth century was probably a factor in de Vos's remaining there, for he was the most prolific designer for prints of his generation. He produced about 1,600 designs, which were engraved by Adriaen and Hans II Collaert, Hendrick Goltzius, Pieter de Jode I, Crispijn de Passe I and II, the Wierix brothers, and many members of the Sadeler family: Aegidius, Jan I, Jan II, Raphael I, and Raphael II.[3] In all, more than 500 of de Vos's drawings exist today, most of which were preparatory for prints.[4]

The biblical story illustrated here is among the earliest subjects to appear in Christian imagery: Jonah is cast overboard to calm the raging tempest that Jehovah created when Jonah disobeyed him (see *Book of Jonah*, chapter 1). Jonah is swallowed by a "great fish" (the specific words of the Bible; only later was the creature called a whale), and then, after three days, is disgorged unharmed. This narrative, understood by Christian scholars as a prefiguration of Christ's death and resurrection, was a common subject in Northern Europe during the sixteenth century. Artists rendered it in stained glass, paintings, and prints; Maarten van Heemskerck (see cat. no. 15), Dirck Barendsz., and others made series of drawings for prints.[5] Yale's spirited drawing is one of six known renditions of this subject by de Vos. By his time, the basic elements in the drawing had become standard for the subject: the fish with gaping mouth in the foreground, sailors trying to control a boat in a raging sea, and other sailors heaving Jonah overboard. To the left, above the sailors' heads, de Vos has also depicted Jonah safely deposited on dry land.

A second extant drawing of this subject by de Vos, in a round format and dated 1585, was preparatory for a print by Crispijn de Passe I, published by Philips Galle; the print was one of a series of six illustrating the story of Jonah.[6] De Vos made three other designs for prints of this subject, each also part of a Jonah series—another by Crispijn de Passe I, one by Anton Wierix II, and one by Anton II and Hieronymus Wierix; the last is also datable to around 1585.[7] Finally, de Vos made at least one painting (fig. A), dated 1589, formerly in Berlin but destroyed in the Second World War.[8]

Yale's drawing has been described as specifically preparatory for the painting of

FIGURE 21A | Maarten de Vos, *Jonah Thrown Overboard*, 1589. Formerly Berlin, Staatliche Museen (destroyed).

FIGURE 21B | Crispijn de Passe I after Maarten de Vos, *Jonah Thrown Overboard*, ca. 1585. New York, Metropolitan Museum of Art.

FIGURE 21C | Anton Wierix II after Maarten de Vos, *Jonah Thrown Overboard*, 1580s. Brussels, Bibliothèque Royale de Belgique.

FIGURE 21D | Anton II and Hieronymus Wierix after Maarten de Vos, *Jonah Thrown Overboard*, ca. 1585. New York, Metropolitan Museum of Art.

1589,[9] and Christiaan Schuckman, who compiled the Hollstein volumes on de Vos, specified that the drawing is to be related to one of the prints by Crispijn de Passe I (fig. B).[10] The drawing, however, seems no less close to the above-mentioned prints by Anton Wierix II and Anton II and Hieronymus Wierix (figs. C and D), and it may make more sense simply to consider them all as variations on a theme. Judson worked out what seemed to him a logical progression for the works, beginning with the small roundel dated 1585, for one of the engraved series by Crispijn de Passe I,[11] and ending with the painting. Again, however, this proposed chronology is not compelling, and it seems sufficient to assume that the three undated works—Yale's drawing, one of the prints by de Passe, and the one by Anton Wierix II—were all made in the same decade, the 1580s.

As long ago as 1952 it was pointed out that Rembrandt's painting *Christ in the Storm on the Sea of Galilee* (stolen from the Isabella Stewart Gardner Museum, Boston, in 1990) looked back to an engraving of the same subject after de Vos, by Adriaen Collaert.[12] Another engraving of this subject after de Vos, by Cornelis Galle I, seems perhaps an even closer prototype for the painting, and it is also more than likely that Rembrandt, in devising the composition of his only sea painting, also looked at the prints after de Vos of *Jonah Overboard*, since the two subjects share almost all their compositional elements, with the exception that in *Christ in the Storm*, no one is being thrown out of the boat.[13]

SB

1 See Meijer in Aikema and Brown 2000, 133–143, esp. 137–138. See also Brussels–Rome 1995, 397–399. Carlo Ridolfi first reported that Vos worked with Tintoretto: Ridolfi 1648, 2:75.
2 Bert W. Meijer, in Brussels–Rome 1995, 397, writes that de Vos converted to Catholicism.
3 See Hollstein DF 44–46, and Amsterdam 1996a, 15–19.
4 Reinsch 1967 listed 372 drawings but did not know of Yale's. Hulst 1968, 505, wrote that about 500 drawings were known, but that many more must have once existed.
5 See Steffen 2000, especially 10–12, and Amsterdam 1996a, no. 38.
6 The drawing is Antwerp, Plantin-Moretus House, inv. no. 734, reproduced in Judson 1969, 293, fig. 3; Delen 1938, no. 101; Reinsch 1967, no. 13, 2. The engraved series is Hollstein DF 44: nos. 148–153 (*Jonah Thrown Overboard*, no. 149), also 15:131, nos. 25–30 (*Jonah Overboard*, no. 26).
7 The three other series are: 1) Hollstein DF 44: nos. 142–147 (*Jonah Thrown Overboard*, no. 144) and 15:131–132, nos. 31–36 (*Jonah Overboard*, no. 33); 2) Hollstein DF 44: nos. 154–157 (*Jonah Overboard*, no. 154), and 59: nos. 49–52 (*Jonah Overboard*, no. 49); and 3) Hollstein DF 44: nos. 158–161 (*Jonah Overboard*, no. 159) and 59: nos. 53–56 (*Jonah Overboard*, no. 54).
8 Staatliche Museen, inv. 709; Zweite 1980, no. 75, fig. 90.
9 See H-B and L, no. 510.
10 Hollstein DF 44: no. 144.
11 Hollstein DF 44: nos. 148–153 and 15:131, nos. 25–30.
12 See Lugt 1952; Walsh 1985, 8–9. The print by Adriaen Collaert is Hollstein DF 44: no. 333.
13 The engraving of *Christ in the Storm on the Sea of Galilee* by Galle is Hollstein DF 44: no. 293, and 7:64, no. 24.

22 Lodewijk Toeput, called Ludovico Pozzoserrato

Mechelen ca. 1550–1604/05 Treviso

(A) *Allegory of Winter* and (B) *Allegory of Spring*, ca. 1585–90

Pen and gray-black ink and blue and gray-brown wash over traces of black chalk,
(A) 27.4 × 41.5 cm (10¾ × 16⅜ in.);
(B) 27.3 × 41.6 cm (10¾ × 16⅜ in.)

INSCRIPTIONS: (A) recto, lower left, in brown ink: *Sebastian Vranks*; (B) recto, lower left, in brown ink: *Sebastian Francks*

PROVENANCE: John Percival, 1st Earl of Egmont (1683–1748); John T. Graves; Robert Hoe (sale, New York, Anderson Auction Company, 15–19 April 1912, Library of Robert Hoe, Part 3, A–K, no. 949); Yale University Library (anonymous donor, 1957)

REFERENCES: Providence 1968, no. III, 3; H-B and L, nos. 507–508; London 1975, 170–171; Katritzky 1987, 83–85; Mason Rinaldi and Luciani 1988, 95, 116, 121; Amherst 1990, nos. 19–20; Boon 1992, 1:46; Gerszi 1992, 388; Omaha–Little Rock–Sarasota 1997–98, no. 16; Gerszi 1999, 91

Egmont Collection, Yale Library Transfer. 1961.63.65 and 1961.63.67

Born in Mechelen and first trained in Antwerp (perhaps by Maarten de Vos [see cat. no. 21]), Lodewijk Toeput traveled to Italy as a young man, like so many Flemish artists who were his contemporaries. He was in Venice by the mid-1570s and seems to have spent some time in Tintoretto's workshop but, after a trip to Florence and Rome in the latter part of that decade, settled in Treviso, near Venice. Based in that small city for the rest of his life, Toeput nonetheless followed recent developments in the art both of Northern Europe and of Italy, especially with respect to landscape painting. His paintings and drawings of small hermit saints in broad landscapes and his secular cycles of the seasons or months might be compared equally to those of Pieter Bruegel and Jan Brueghel and to the landscapes and genre scenes of Jacopo Bassano; they anticipate the works of Paul Bril, Joos de Momper the Younger, Sebastian Vrancx, and others.[1]

The present drawings, attributed to Vrancx by the compiler of the Egmont Albums,[2] were reattributed to Toeput by Haverkamp-Begemann, who also identified the scenes as allegories of the months of January and May. While the attribution of the drawings has never been questioned, it might now be proposed that these drawings represent, rather than two of the twelve months, two of the four seasons. The old identifications were based on the very similar depictions of the months in a print series by Adriaen Collaert, for which the preparatory drawings by Joos de Momper the Younger are in the Rijksmuseum.[3] De Momper surely made his designs with Toeput's drawings in mind—and probably

with Toeput's drawings literally in front of him—so that elements of the Yale *Spring* are found in de Momper's *May* and elements of the Yale *Winter*, such as the bull-baiting in the street or the *commedia dell'arte* troop, are found in de Momper's *January*,[4] but there is evidence to suggest that de Momper was expanding Toeput's cycle. There is relatively little difference, for example, between de Momper's images of *April* and *May*, as both rely on the Yale drawing of *Spring* by Toeput. Furthermore, the two Yale drawings can be connected to two other drawings of the same size, media, and finish (figs. A and B); together the four drawings, at Yale, the National Gallery in Washington, and the Fitzwilliam, seem to constitute a complete set of the four seasons.[5] The drawings lack the zodiacal signs usually associated with images of the months. Even more tellingly, the drawings' foreground figures of Janus, Venus, Ceres, and Bacchus often signify the four seasons (and do so elsewhere in Toeput's work), but that set of gods cannot readily be expanded to gods representing the twelve months.

While the *Four Seasons* drawings are highly finished and could have been a completed work on their own, Toeput might alternately have planned them as studies for a print series, for they compare in some ways to his preparatory drawings illustrating a series of Aesop's fables.[6] Series of the *Four Seasons* or *Months* were one of Toeput's specialties, and he painted several sets of these subjects: one now in a Venetian private collection,[7] for example, and another in the Villa Chiericati-Mugna outside of Vicenza.[8] The Yale drawings and their companions are not preparatory for these paintings, but they do bear some relationship to a third set, of which there are parts in Providence and elsewhere, although those panels might, in fact, be by a later artist who had access to Toeput's drawings.[9] Several canvases, now in scattered collections, seem to relate even more closely to the drawings of the *Four Seasons*. A *Summer* that appeared at Phillips, London, in 1997, for example, is clearly based on the Washington drawing,[10] and an *Autumn*, a canvas of roughly the same size as the Phillips *Summer*, appeared at auction in 2002.[11] The *Autumn* does not match the Fitzwilliam drawing as closely as the Phillips painting relates to the Washington *Summer* and, moreover, the two canvases have foreground figures of very different scales, so that the two pictures probably did not constitute half of a single set of *Four Seasons*. Whatever the case, Toeput and his followers produced several series of paintings that relate to the drawings discussed here.[12]

There was, of course, a long history of depictions of the seasons and months in manuscript painting, printmaking, and elsewhere. Toeput relied on traditional motifs such as the herdsmen of *Winter* (which recall, for example, the *Return of the Herd* from Bruegel's series), but he also added elements that were characteristically his own.[13] The garden of *Spring*, for example, is found throughout

LODEWIJK TOEPUT 93

FIGURE 22A | Lodewijk Toeput, *Summer*, ca. 1585–90. Washington, D.C., National Gallery of Art.

FIGURE 22B | Lodewijk Toeput, *Autumn*, ca. 1585–90. Cambridge, Fitzwilliam Museum.

Toeput's works (in his *Open Air Concert* in the Museo Civico, Treviso, for example), but it probably represents an idealized garden rather than something in Treviso or elsewhere in the Veneto; similarly, the villa at right, with a temple-inspired portico, adopts the language of Palladio, but does not seem to depict a particular building.[14] Toeput's landscapes, likewise, are neither clearly representations of Italy nor of his native Netherlands: the broad, flat landscape to the right side of the *Winter* seems northern, but the walled city to the left might represent Treviso, while the ruined archway seems to allude to the antiquities of Rome. For all his anecdotal naturalism and the secular subject matter of his landscapes, Toeput's landscapes have an idealization and abstraction that compare to those of his sixteenth-century contemporaries but do not approach the depictions of the world found in the work of Netherlandish artists in the following generations.[15]

Dating of Toeput's work has often proven difficult, but the present series almost certainly dates to the later 1580s. The large drawn landscapes of the *Four Seasons* are more complex than those in the Venetian private collection *Seasons*, which derive from various sources, but they do compare to those of the Villa Chiericati-Mugna, which are dated to circa 1590.[16] Toeput may have been inspired by Adriaen Collaert's 1585 series of months after designs by Hans Bol, or by Maarten de Vos's *Four Seasons* of 1588, which were also engraved by Collaert; at the least, it seems that his drawings are of the same general moment.[17] Joos de Momper's visit to Italy, during which he saw the Toeput drawings that would be the basis of his own series of the months, provides one final bit of evidence for dating Toeput's drawings, for de Momper's visit probably took place before his marriage in Antwerp in September of 1590, providing a *terminus ante quem* for Toeput's own series.

JJM

1 On Toeput, in addition to the works cited above, see Menegazzi 1957, Menegazzi 1961, and Aikema and Brown 2000, in which Mason's essay also explores the connections between Toeput and Bassano. Toeput's work might also be compared to Veronese's landscape frescoes in the Villa Barbaro at Maser, which were even once attributed to Toeput. Many of the later Northern travelers to Italy, including de Momper and Vrancx, seem to have stopped in Treviso and studied Toeput's works.
2 On the Egmont Albums, see the Introduction to this volume.
3 The prints are Hollstein DF 4:207, nos. 559–570. For the drawings, see Boon 1978, nos. 361–372.
4 As H-B and L noted long ago, the similarity supports the old tradition that de Momper studied with Toeput. A *Carnival Scene* (Cambridge, Fitzwilliam Museum, inv. no. PD.741-1963, pen and brown ink and blue wash, 22.2 × 34.7 cm), formerly attributed to Toeput and now attributed by the museum to de Momper, is a variation on the Yale *Winter* but does not fit into the de Momper series. Katritzky 1987, 95, attributes the drawing to Louis de Caulery, who was a pupil of de Momper.
5 Washington, D.C., National Gallery of Art, inv. no. 1980.2.1, pen and black ink with blue and gray wash, over black chalk, 27 × 42.5 cm, hitherto identified as *Harvest Scene*; Cambridge, Fitzwilliam, inv. no. PD.741-1963, pen and gray-black ink with blue and gray-brown wash, over black chalk, 27.5 × 42.2 cm, hitherto identified as *September*. While the similarity of these drawings to the Yale sheets is noted by Gerszi 1992, they have never before been considered a complete set.
6 See Menegazzi 1957, 199–200, and Menegazzi 1988, 67.

7   Larcher Crosato 1985.
8   Crosato 1962, 127–130.
9   See Menegazzi 1961, figs. 146–147, for the Providence *Winter* and *Summer* (actually probably *Spring* or a spring month), which are both now in the museum at the Rhode Island School of Design. Meijer 1988, 121, publishes another painting of the set, a work that suggests that there were originally six or twelve months in the series, rather than simply the four seasons. Another painting at Kinross House, Scotland, is very similar to the aforementioned panels but is from still another set, one surely by an artist working in the Netherlands. The attribution of all these panels has occasionally been questioned, and they might indeed all be by a Northern follower who made use of Toeput's drawings and/or de Momper's related works (the Kinross House panel has recently been attributed to David Vinckboons). The use of a panel support would be unusual for an artist based in the Veneto in the later Cinquecento, and nearly all of the easel paintings securely attributed to Toeput are on canvas. A drawing of *March* (New York, Metropolitan Museum of Art, inv. no. 1975.131.193, pen and brown ink and gray wash over black chalk, 16.2 × 27.1 cm) might indicate still another set of drawings or paintings by Toeput.
10 Phillips, London, 2 December 1997, lot 199, incorrectly identified as *Autumn*. This is probably the same painting that was sold at the Dorotheum, Vienna, 10 June 1997, lot 200, and might be the same painting that was sold at Christie's, London, 4 April 1986, lot 133, which Gerszi 1992, 378, linked to the drawing.
11 Franco Semenzato, Venice, 9 February 2002, lot 168.
12 Another oval panel related to the Yale *Winter*, formerly on the London art market (see Katritzky 1987, fig. 8), lacks Janus or any other figure in the foreground and would thus seem to be the remnant of still another set of pictures at a smaller scale than those mentioned above. This panel, like some of the drawn variants, seems to be by a Northern artist rather than by one of Toeput's followers in Treviso, and accordingly supports the notion that de Momper carried the drawings home with him to Antwerp.
13 There is extensive literature on depictions of the months and the seasons, but for an essay treating Toeput's immediate milieu, see Mason 2000.
14 The triple-arched front is similar to Palladio's Villa Pisani, Bagnolo, although the building's plan does not match that of the building in the drawing. Toeput's *View of an Italian Villa* in the National Museum, Warsaw (see Gerszi 1992, fig. 28), seems to depict the same (imaginary) building. On the villa theme, see also Larcher Crosato 1988.
15 For examples of the later trend, see the landscapes by van de Velde and Vroom (cat. nos. 36 and 47).
16 Menegazzi 1961, 124, based on the research later published by Crosato 1962; the villa was struck by lightning in 1587, and the frescoes date from the campaign of renovation carried out between 1587 and 1590.
17 Collaert's engravings of Bol's twelve landscapes with zodiacal signs and the life of Christ are Hollstein DF 4:205, nos. 511–522; another undated series of the months, by Collaert after Bol, is Hollstein DF 4:206, nos. 523–534. Collaert's prints of de Vos's series of the Seasons are Hollstein DF 4:204, nos. 457–460. Neither Bol nor de Vos seems to have been in Italy at the time, but Toeput may well have seen the prints.

23 Diego López de Escuriaz

Spanish, active at the Escorial ca. 1587–1597

The Last Supper: Design for the Hood of a Liturgical Cope, probably 1589

Pen and brown ink and brown wash, heightened with white, on blue paper; pricked for transfer, 50.8 × 41.6 cm (20 × 16 3/8 in.)

PROVENANCE: probably from one of several albums of embroidery designs formerly in the library at the Escorial but dispersed in the nineteenth century; Sotheby's, New York, 13–14 January 1989, lot 275; acquired from Mia Weiner, Norfolk, Conn.

REFERENCES: *YUAG Bulletin* (2005): 163

Everett V. Meeks, B.A. 1901, Fund. 2004.82.1

Little is known about Diego López de Escuriaz, who is documented as working at the Escorial from 1587 to 1597.[1] He was one of a number of native Spaniards employed by King Philip II in the Escorial workshops but, like most of those artists, he worked in the shadow of the Italian masters Federico Zuccaro (see cat. no. 19), Pellegrino Tibaldi, and Luca Cambiaso. Even if not directly trained by one of the Italians, López created works that demonstrate their influence in both style and technique. The combination of bold chiaroscuro, white heightening, and blue paper used in this drawing of the *Last Supper*, for example, recalls works by Tibaldi and Zuccaro, and by Zuccaro's Italian followers, including Trometta and Raffaellino da Reggio. The composition and figure style of this, and of all López's works, are similarly Italianate.

Richly embroidered vestments had a long tradition in Spain and were often represented in paintings—Alonso Sanchez Coello's *Saint Stephen and Saint Lawrence* (Escorial) or El Greco's *Burial of Count Orgaz* (Toledo, Santo Tomé) are familiar contemporary examples—but they played a particularly important part in the liturgical life at King Philip II's monastery, where the high altar and two reliquary altars of the Basilica of San Lorenzo each had fifty different sets of vestments and altar coverings that were changed according to the liturgical seasons and feast days.[2] Most of these vestments were executed in the 1580s and '90s by embroidery workshops established in the monastery, and the designs were created by a team of Spanish artists led by the painters Miguel Barroso and Diego López de Escuriaz.[3] With its outlines completely pricked for transferring the design, this *Last Supper* is identifiable by its size and shape as a cartoon for the hood of a liturgical cope. It matches two other hood cartoons now in the Musée des Beaux-Arts at Orléans;[4] together, the drawings are likely to be the set of three cope hood designs for which López was paid on 4 July 1589.[5] It remains to be discovered whether the corresponding garments survive among the collection of sixteenth-century vestments at the Escorial, which includes many executed to López's designs.[6]

Although it has been pricked, there is no evidence that this cartoon was ever pounced. Instead, the Escorial workshops seem to have employed a system of substitute cartoons in which the original drawings were backed with a second piece of paper, so that the pricking went through both; this second sheet, pricked but without any drawing, was then pounced, transferring the design to the fabric to be embroidered. A number of these substitute cartoons survive in bound volumes at the Escorial.[7] The original drawings were also stored in the Escorial library, where many remain today, but some volumes seem to have been removed in the nineteenth century and were later broken up. The Yale drawing, like most of the other Escorial embroidery designs to come on the market in recent decades, probably came from those latter volumes.[8]

Philip II acquired a collection of prints for the Escorial artists to use when creating their designs,[9] and it is clear that López made use of that resource. There is much that is familiar in his rendition of the Last Supper: the general composition evokes Dürer's version of the subject in his *Large Passion*, and figures like the three foreground Apostles are repeatedly found in later sixteenth-century engravings of the subject. Of those prints surely in the early collection at the Escorial, the closest precedent for López's composition is probably the woodcut by Virgil Solis in his *Biblische Figuren* series of 1565 (fig. A).[10] While López's composition is thus, frankly, somewhat derivative, it is entirely representative of the tendency for artists at the Escorial and more broadly in Renaissance Spain to emulate their famous counterparts in Italy and in Northern Europe.

López's *Last Supper* is one of the first early Spanish drawings to enter Yale's collection,[11] but serves as an ideal starting place for a discussion of art in Renaissance and Baroque Spain. The *bordados*, the designs for the embroidery workshops, represent one of the largest groups of extant Spanish drawings from the period and have been described as "important documents of the period . . . indispensable for our understanding of the functioning of a specialized workshop in the unique social and cultural milieu at the Escorial."[12]

JJM

FIGURE 23A | Virgil Solis, *Last Supper*, 1565. London, British Museum.

1 The most extensive survey of López's work is Angulo and Peréz-Sánchez 1975; other discussions include Paris 1991, no. 12, and Boubli 1999, 355–356.
2 Mulcahy 1994, 28–33; see also Siqüenza 1963, 357–365.
3 On the vestments at the Escorial, see especially Junquera de Vega 1963.
4 *Adoration of the Shepherds* and *Circumcision*, inv. nos. 1980A and 1980C, pen and brown ink with white heightening, on blue-gray paper, 48.8 × 40.3 and 48.7 × 40.1 cm; see Angulo and Peréz-Sánchez 1975, nos. 186 and 191.
5 Zarco Cuevas 1931, 148; Angulo and Peréz-Sánchez 1975, no. 186, citing this, mistakenly give the date as 4 July 1597, which has often been repeated in later discussions.
6 Others of the vestments embroidered after López's designs are published in Junquera de Vega 1963 and, with color reproductions, in *El Escorial* 1987, figs. 181, 199, and 202.
7 Bambach 1999, 289–290 and Appendix 3.
8 Paris 1991, 62 (under no. 12). Other sheets from the volume probably include three sheets in the National Library at Madrid and one in Edinburgh, at the National Gallery of Scotland. López's *Adoration of the Magi*, acquired by the Louvre in 1991 (inv. no. RF 42750), and *Four Prophets* (attributed to the Master D, who worked with López), which the Louvre acquired in 1995 (inv. no. RF 44337), probably also come from the set.
9 For the collection, with commentary, see González de Zárate 1992–96.
10 *TIB* 19:346, no. 1.124.
11 Yale's collection includes significant works by Picasso, Gris, and Miró, but of earlier Spanish drawings, the only other notable example is a *Portrait of Velazquez*, inv. no. 1980.103, black chalk, 12.8 × 8.9 cm. When given to the museum, this drawing was considered to be a self-portrait by Velazquez, as argued by Benesch 1979, 39–40, but the attribution was later questioned by McKim-Smith 1980, no. 17.
12 Boubli 1999, 355–356.

24 Jan Harmensz. Muller
Amsterdam 1571–1628 Amsterdam

Neptune, ca. 1589–90

Pen and dark brown ink and brown wash, heightened with white, over black chalk on light tan paper, 42.1 × 29.1 cm (16¾ × 11½ in.)

WATERMARK: small sun in a shield, like the central element of Briquet nos. 13981 and 13982 (eastern France, 1580s); this watermark not among those noted by Filedt Kok in New Hollstein DF, *Muller Dynasty,* Part 2:261–329

INSCRIPTIONS: recto, in pen and brown ink, lower left: *muller op*; upper right: *Muller*; verso, in pen and brown ink, lower left: *o / ab / 346*; also: *Muller,* with *Goltzius* superimposed (in pencil); right of center, near bottom: *aab*

PROVENANCE: acquired from Peter Claas, London

REFERENCES: *YUAG Bulletin* 30 (1964): 14 and 51; H-B and L, no. 396; Reznicek 1980, 119 and no. 13; Roberts 1986, 82, under no. 55; Amherst 1990, no. 24; *Handbook,* 200

Everett B. Meeks, B.A. 1901, Fund. 1963.9.7

Jan Muller is better known today for his roughly one hundred engravings—after designs by Hendrik Goltzius, Cornelis Cornelisz. van Haarlem, Abraham Bloemaert, and especially the Rudolfine artists Bartholomaeus Spranger (see cat. no. 29) and Adriaen de Vries—than for his drawings, but his oeuvre of sixty or so establishes him as a draftsman of the first rank.[1] In his early years he was one of the prime practitioners of Northern Mannerism, influenced especially by Goltzius and Spranger. Later, his style became more subdued and naturalistic, but he never totally abandoned Mannerism, even though the prevailing taste turned sharply away from it, beginning early in the seventeenth century. He spent most of his life in his native Amsterdam, where his father Harmen was a prominent book printer and publisher and also an engraver and woodcutter, with 136 prints in the most recent catalogue (Harmen Jansz. Muller made the engraving after Yale's drawing by Maarten van Heemskerck, cat. no. 15).[2]

Neptune is one of a series of similar drawings of gods—shown full-length, nude, in the same media and commensurate size—four of which, depicting Mars, Jupiter, Vulcan, and Pluto, are at Windsor Castle (figs. A–D).[3] E. K. J. Reznicek has also associated a drawing of Hercules, now at Leiden, with this group, although it is not as finished as the others, and it is only roughly half their size.[4] Leo van Puyvelde attributed the Windsor drawings to Bartholomaeus Spranger,[5] and A. Welcker to Hendrik Goltzius,[6] but Reznicek correctly identified them as works by Muller.[7] The erroneous attributions confirm the strong influence that these artists of the previous generation exerted on Muller.

The drawings in this series may have originally been intended as models for prints. Just as Neptune's trident is in his left hand, so is Vulcan's hammer, and while Jupiter holds thunderbolts in both hands, it is his left arm that is raised as though he is about to hurl one. (Whether or not the Hercules was intended for the same series, he is also shown

FIGURE 24A | Jan Harmensz. Muller, *Mars*, ca. 1589–90. Windsor, Royal Library.

FIGURE 24C | Jan Harmensz. Muller, *Vulcan*, ca. 1589–90. Windsor, Royal Library.

FIGURE 24B | Jan Harmensz. Muller, *Jupiter*, ca. 1589–90. Windsor, Royal Library.

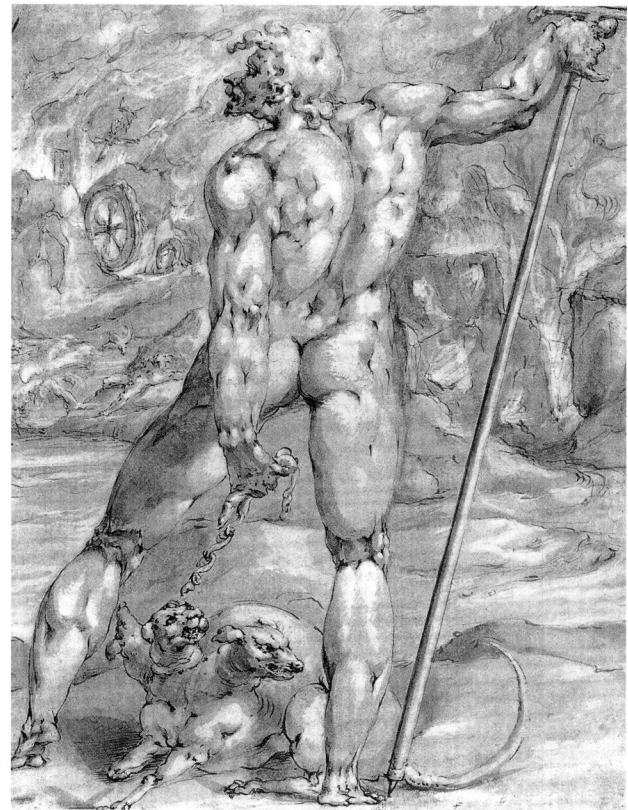

FIGURE 24D | Jan Harmensz. Muller, *Pluto*, ca. 1589–90. Windsor, Royal Library.

holding his club in his left hand.) But if there was an idea for a print series, it apparently was abandoned; there is no indentation on Yale's drawing to indicate a transfer of the design, and no such print series is known.

Scholars agree that the drawing was made early in Muller's career, around 1590, before a traditionally presumed trip to Italy.[8] Reznicek wrote of the drawings in the years he designated as "the Spranger period"— between 1588 and "ca. 1594," the time he supposed Muller departed for Italy—as a "wild manneristic group."[9] This muscular figure of the god of the sea seen from slightly below, standing in a commanding pose on a rocky shore with a triton, two hippocamps, and a dolphin in the water behind him—his strong features in a fierce expression, his hair and beard flying wildly, and claw-like hands with several fingers outstretched— epitomizes that description.

SB

in the back matter (p. 327) indicates at the very least that such a trip might have taken place in the mid-1590s: there is just one print listed in 1594, the *Last Supper* after Gillis Congnet; in 1595 there is no certain print at all, and the only one that Filedt Kok infers to have been done in that year is Muller's engraving after Ligozzi, *The Dead Christ Lamented by an Angel*. This is Muller's only print after an Italian model. Ligozzi was working for the Medici in Florence, and although he traveled to Verona, Mantua, and Ferrara in the early 1590s, he did not leave Italy. Filedt Kok wrote that "given its small format, the model could well have been sent to, and engraved in, Amsterdam" (Filedt Kok 1994, 241), but without a prior connection between Ligozzi and Muller, this hypothetical sole instance of a drawing being sent by Ligozzi to be engraved by Muller in Amsterdam seems on the whole less likely than an encounter between the two artists in Italy. Until definite evidence one way or the other is produced, however, the question must remain open.

9 Reznicek 1980, 120.

1 For his prints, see New Hollstein DF, *The Muller Dynasty*, Part 2; for the drawings, see Reznicek 1956 and Reznicek 1980.
2 New Hollstein DF, *The Muller Dynasty*, Part 1: 67–244; the engraving after Heemskerck is no. 102.
3 Windsor, Royal Collection, inv. no. 12965, *Mars*, 41 × 30 cm; inv. no. 12966, *Jupiter*, 42 × 27.5 cm; inv. no. 12967, *Pluto*, 40 × 29.5 cm; inv. no. 12968, *Vulcan*, 41.2 × 27.5 cm; all pen and dark brown ink and wash, over traces of black chalk, heightened with white; see Reznicek 1956, 118, nos. 37–40, *Vulcan* illustrated 76, fig. 7; see also Roberts 1986, nos. 55, 56.
4 Reznicek 1956, no. 9, illustrated 76, fig. 8. Roberts 1986, 82, listed a *Tityus* in Brussels (Reznicek 1956, no. 14) as possibly part of this series, but that drawing is a copy of one by Cornelis van Haarlem in the Albertina, Vienna, its dimensions are not close to those of the other sheets, and, furthermore, Tityus was not a god, so the suggestion seems implausible.
5 Puyvelde 1942, nos. 133, 133a, 134, 134a, all illustrated.
6 Welcker 1950.
7 See note 3.
8 Jan Piet Filedt Kok is skeptical on the question of a possible trip to Italy, stating that the evidence traditionally adduced does not support such a presumption (Filedt Kok 1994, 236, 241, and New Hollstein DF, *The Muller Dynasty*, Part 2:16, 19). In *Muller Dynasty*, Part 2, Filedt Kok's own thorough catalogue of Muller's engravings, however, the chronological table

25 Ludovico Cardi, called Il Cigoli
Castelvecchio di Cigoli 1559–1613 Rome

Resurrection, 1590–91

Pen and brown ink and reddish-brown wash (recto); pen and brown ink (verso), 27.2 × 19.2 cm (10 11/16 × 7 9/16 in.)

INSCRIPTIONS: recto, in pen and black ink, upper left: *Cardi detto il Cigoli 1590*; lower right: *10*; lower right, in graphite: *20*; verso, upper left, in graphite: *No. 113*

PROVENANCE: unidentified owner (partial stamp on recto, at upper edge, center); Conte Giulio Litta-Visconti-Arese, Milan; Christie's, London, 25 March 1969, lot 78; acquired from Shickman Gallery, New York

REFERENCES: *Apollo* 39 (March 1969): 21 (reproduced in advertisement); "Acquisitions," *Art Journal* 33.1 (1973): 62; Chappell 1974, 470, 472; New Haven 1974, no. 42; Palm Beach 1974, no. 12; *YUAG Bulletin* 35 (1974): 61; Joachim and McCullagh 1979, 47; Matteoli 1980, 168; Faranda 1986, no. 6a; Chappell 1990, 54–55; New Haven 1991a, no. 8; Oberlin–Brunswick–Hanover 1991, no. 15; Florence 1992, 18–19, under no. 10; McCullagh and Giles 1997, 89; Sievers, Muehlig, and Rich 2000, 61; Chappell in Chicago–Detroit 2002, 156

Maitland F. Griggs, B.A. 1896, Fund. 1973.67

RECTO

When this sheet of studies for a *Resurrection* came to light in the 1960s, it was associated with Cigoli's painting of the subject now in the Pinacoteca Comunale, Arezzo. That painting had traditionally been identified as the altarpiece commissioned in 1590 by Don Giovanni and Duke Ferdinando de' Medici for the Cappella dei Forestieri in the Pitti Palace, Florence. In 1974, however, Miles Chappell identified another painting, then in the storerooms of the Pitti, as the 1590 altarpiece (fig. A).[1] Because the Pitti altarpiece dates to 1590, a year earlier than the Arezzo picture (which is signed and dated 1591), the Yale drawing has since been associated with the earlier work, presumably because studies of this type seemed more likely to relate to the artist's first version of a subject. The Pitti altarpiece was the most important commission to that point in Cigoli's career, and he surely made many preparatory sketches, but it is here proposed that the Yale drawing might relate instead to Cigoli's second version of the *Resurrection*, the painting now in Arezzo (fig. B).[2]

As has often been noted, Cigoli must have begun his design for the Pitti altarpiece with a look at the highly esteemed *Resurrection* of about 1574 by Santi di Tito, with whom he had studied; it was probably at this moment, in fact, that Cigoli made his finished drawing after Santi's painting.[3] In contrast to the greater number of figures in Santi's altarpiece, Cigoli simplified the subject, a change that might be attributed to the differences in temperament between the two artists but which probably had also to do with the smaller size of the Pitti altar. Cigoli's nephew and biographer Giovanni Battista Cardi noted that a number of accomplished masters were asked to submit designs for the commission, but the drawings submitted by the other masters could not be made to work in an altarpiece as confined as that of the Cappella dei Forestieri.[4] Recently discovered

VERSO

with alternate positions for the figure of Christ. In addition to Santi's *Resurrection*, Cigoli seems also to have studied other Florentine treatments of the subject from the previous generation. In particular, the foreshortened figures for the lower part of the composition seem to derive from Vasari's *Resurrection* in Santa Maria Novella and Bronzino's in Santissima Annunziata.[7]

The frame drawn around the central composition shows, however, that these sketches were perhaps not for the Pitti altarpiece, but rather for the second version of the subject. Cigoli started the drawing by lightly sketching a tall rectangle in light brown ink. He then added figures, some of which crossed over the edge of the frame. A second frame, in darker, thicker ink, makes allowances for the figures, and must have been added after them, while the figures that crossed the earlier frame lines indicate that the frame was drawn before them. That is, Cigoli began by setting out a tall, thin rectangular frame, and then worked to fit his figures into that space, but the Pitti altarpiece is of a different shape entirely. Given what we know of the history of the Cappella dei Forestieri commission, in which the size (and unusual proportions) of the altarpiece were an issue, it seems unlikely that Cigoli would have begun by drawing a frame so different from the necessary proportions. In contrast, though, the frame in the Yale drawing matches almost exactly the 1:1.59 width-to-height ratio of the Arezzo altarpiece, and probably represents Cigoli's first thoughts as to how he might adapt the composition he had painted in 1590 to the larger, taller altarpiece he completed in the following year.[8]

Cigoli's first compositional idea in the drawing uses the more or less symmetrical composition of the Pitti altarpiece. In the marginal sketches, we see him shift the jumble of soldiers to the left edge of the frame, and then, in the sketches on the verso— especially the one drawn at the center of the sheet—to develop the more upright, serpentine figure of Christ used in the asymmetrical design of the much narrower Arezzo painting. Other drawings must surely have followed this one, which never shows the full composition as painted. The motif of the angel greeting the women at the tomb is hinted at in the upper right of the framed sketch on the recto, for example, but the idea was far from resolved

documents indicate, furthermore, that Andrea Boscoli, another of Santi di Tito's pupils, actually won the competition and painted an altarpiece, but his painting was then judged unsatisfactory and returned.[5] Cigoli surely had these issues in mind as he began to experiment with the arrangement of figures; by paring down their number, he was able to devise a composition that suggested the grandeur that his Medici patrons desired even in the smaller altarpiece.[6]

The looseness of its pen lines and its marginal variations suggest that the Yale drawing must have been among Cigoli's first sketches for a new altarpiece, if not the first drawing itself. He began with the composition at center on the recto and then, in the margins, experimented with alternate poses and positions for the soldiers in the foreground. The shield-bearer is seen to twist in the sketches at right and then to turn completely in the uppermost and lowest sketches, a position that would have moved him from the right to the left side of the composition. On the verso of the sheet, Cigoli experimented with alternate groups of soldiers for the left edge and

FIGURE 25A | Cigoli, *Resurrection*, 1590. Florence, Palazzo Pitti.

FIGURE 25B | Cigoli, *Resurrection*, 1591. Arezzo, Pinacoteca Comunale.

at this stage; yet by moving the angel to the upper margin, Cigoli began to separate the scene from that of the sprawling soldiers, which overlaps it in the Pitti painting. There was still much work to be done on the composition, but this drawing provides an interesting glimpse into the working process of a professional artist who had been asked to replicate his most important painting to date.

JJM

1 See Chappell 1974, and, for the newly restored Pitti altarpiece, Chicago–Detroit 2002, no. 20. Chappell is surely correct in identifying the Galleria Palatina painting as the altarpiece of the Pitti chapel, for both its size (148 × 118 cm) and its canvas support agree with the payment records for a canvas altarpiece approximately two Florentine *braccia* (roughly 160 cm) tall; the Arezzo painting is on panel and is nearly twice as tall (270 × 170 cm).

2 I would like to note that although Miles Chappell disagrees with a number of my arguments about this drawing, especially with the proposal that it relates to the second *Resurrection*, this entry has been much enriched by our detailed discussions of the sheet. See the references cited above for other, later drawings associated with the Pitti altarpiece.

3 Florence, Uffizi, inv. no. 764F; Florence 1985, no. 94.

4 Cardi 1913, 20, referring to the *Resurrection* altarpiece: "fu data commissione di farne il disegno a più d'un maestro de' più pratici, i quali fatti i loro schizzi, furono interrogati se le figure verrebbero nell'opera grande secondo una certo lor terminata misura; questi rispondendosi di no, dissero che in cosi angusto luogo era impossibile il poterlo consequire."

5 Bellesi 1998, 49–68, and Padovani 2000, 45–53.

6 Cardi 1913, 20: [Cigoli] " . . . facendo il suo disegni e scherzando con l'attitudini per la scarsità del luogo, andò in maniera disponendolo e scorciando le figure che credette venissero grandi conforme che ne era stato richiesto, e mostratolo, affermò che nell'opera sarebbero secondo il lor desiderio . . . "

7 I would like to thank Jeffrey Fontana for this observation. He also notes that the foreshortened poses used by Bronzino and Vasari themselves derive from Rosso Fiorentino's *Moses Defending the Daughters of Jethro* and that Cigoli's use of sources is part of a larger trend of interest at the end of the century in the generation of Andrea del Sarto, Rosso, and Pontormo.

8 See Sievers, Muehlig, and Rich 2000, no. 11, for a similar example of Cigoli's use of frames.

26 The Master of the Egmont Albums

Flemish(?), active in Italy and probably also in Cologne, late 16th century

(A) *Battle of the Tritons* and (B) *Battle of Horsemen*, ca. 1590–95

Pen and brown ink over black chalk, (A) 27.3 × 36.4 cm (10¾ × 14⁵⁄₁₆ in.); (B) 27.4 × 36 cm (10¹³⁄₁₆ × 14³⁄₁₆ in.)

WATERMARK: (A) Dragon over a house, like Briquet no. 1383, a type produced in Basel (1585), Cologne (1595), Geneva (1598), and elsewhere, ca. 1585–1607; (B) on backing sheet, "IHS" surmounted by a cross, with "Ivilledary" below. This mark, produced in many variants in eighteenth-century England (for example, Heawood nos. 71, 1793, 1809, and 2971), is on the page from the Egmont Album on which the drawing was mounted

INSCRIPTIONS: (A) recto, lower right, in brown ink: *Hans Van Accken*; (B) recto, lower right, in brown ink: *Hans van Aken f.*

PROVENANCE: John Percival, 1st Earl of Egmont (1683–1748); John T. Graves; Robert Hoe (sale, New York, Anderson Auction Company, 15–19 April 1912, Library of Robert Hoe, Part III, A–K, no. 949); Yale University Library (anonymous donor, 1957)

REFERENCES: H-B and L, nos. 498–499; Palm Beach 1974, no. 46; Boon 1978, no. 516; Paris–Florence 1980–81, 21–23; Robels 1983, 38; Amsterdam 1986, nos. 325–326; "New Acquisitions: Drawings," *The J. Paul Getty Museum Journal* 16 (1988): 162; Starcky 1988, no. 92; Munich 1989–90, nos. 41–42; Dacos 1990, 49–68; Boon 1992, 1:422–426; Goldner and Hendrix 1992, no. 100; Rome–Brussels 1995, no. 252; Dittrich 1997, 60; van der Sman 1997, 7–10; van der Sman 1999, 45–65; Caracciolo 2001, 667–689

Egmont Collection, Yale Library Transfer. 1961.61.8 and 1961.61.9

In 1958, when Philip Pouncey saw the group of drawings at Yale by this then-unknown artist, he was struck by the bold, distinctive style of the works, which he connected to several sheets in London. Pouncey dubbed the artist the "Master of the Egmont Albums," a name derived from the albums compiled by John Percival, 1st Earl of Egmont, in which the four drawings had come to Yale.[1] Since then, many additional sheets have been

attributed to the artist, who must be one of the most often-discussed anonymous Renaissance draftsmen. His accepted corpus of drawings now numbers at least thirty and, according to some scholars, as many as fifty sheets,[2] with former attributions ranging from Hans von Aachen and Frans Francken to Peter Paul Rubens, Francesco Salviati, and Pordenone. This range of former attributions is indicative of the artist's eclecticism. It is generally assumed that he was trained in the Netherlands, perhaps in the Antwerp circle of Frans Francken, but he might alternately have been born or trained in Germany, for he was also well aware of the work of Albrecht Dürer and perhaps lived in Cologne.[3] Whatever his origins, the artist surely spent much time both in Venice and in Central Italy, for his sources include Raphael, Polidoro da Caravaggio, Giulio Romano, Titian, and Domenico Campagnola. In Nicole Dacos's fundamental study of the artist, she convincingly argued that the draftsman had assimilated aspects of Roman drawing style from the later sixteenth century, but Dacos's identification of the artist as Teodoro d'Errico, a Dutch painter active in Rome and Naples from 1574 to 1610, whom Dacos further identified as Dirck Hendricksz. Centen has not been readily accepted, and the artist remains anonymous.[4] It seems certain, nonetheless, that he was active in Italy in the later sixteenth century, although much of his career might have been in Northern Europe.

The two drawings exhibited here are the basis of the artist's reconstructed personality and show all of his characteristic mannerisms. He worked out compositions of dizzying complexity in black chalk, over which he then applied strong pen lines, often in two different shades of brown ink, juxtaposing dark, hatched shadows alongside areas of untouched white paper. The fantastic subject matter seen here is also typical of the artist, although he also treated more common religious themes. The *Battle of Horsemen*, for example, takes up one of the artist's favorite subjects,[5] but the bizarre costumes can hardly be explained even if one considers the crescent moons on the standards as an indication that the army depicted is Turkish or Islamic. The drawing might be a response to the conflict between the Christians and the Ottoman Empire in the years leading up to the Battle of Lepanto in 1571; similarly, a number of other battle scenes by the artist include soldiers firing arquebuses, which must set the scenes in the later sixteenth century.

Whatever their source or meaning, most of the battle scenes that have been attributed to the Master of the Egmont Albums are essentially the same size as the two Yale drawings and might have been conceived as a set, perhaps for a print series similar to the contemporary one by Antonio Tempesta, as Maria Theresa Caracciolo has suggested.[6] There is no indication, however, that prints were ever executed after these drawings, although Starcky and van der Sman both cite examples of other prints made in Cologne apparently after other drawings by the Master.[7] The watermark on one of the Yale drawings, furthermore, is found in paper produced in Cologne during the 1590s; while neither the watermark nor the prints provide absolute evidence that the artist worked in Cologne, this coincidence suggests a possible place and likely date for the works at hand. One of the prints, engraved by Crispijn de Passe I, is inscribed *Quinten d. M. invent*, which must be a reference to Quinten Massys the Younger, who died in Frankfurt. It is tempting to suggest that the Egmont Master might be Massys the Younger, but the latter's works are not well-enough known; there is nothing in the signed and dated "Sieve Portrait" of Queen Elizabeth I (Siena, Pinacoteca Nazionale) to connect him to the drawings in question.[8] In sum, the Master of the Egmont Albums continues to resist identification, but with a graphic production ranging from the awkward and derivative to the strikingly original, he remains a fascinating mystery, and there is still much to be learned about his unusual and well-traveled career.[9]

JJM

1 In addition to the drawings exhibited here, two depictions of the *Nativity* at Yale, inv. nos. 1961.61.11 and 1961.61.12, have been universally accepted as the work of the Master of the Egmont Albums. Two additional sheets, inv. nos. 1961.63.86 and 1961.63.87, for which Haverkamp-Begemann and Logan rejected the attribution, have been accepted by some scholars. On the Egmont Albums, see the Introduction to this catalogue.

2 For a broad definition of the artist's style, see Starcky 1988. While there are still single sheets that might be questioned, the inclusion in the corpus of the looser drawings with broad use of wash, no matter how different they might appear from the pen-and-ink drawings, seems to be justified, as explained also by van der Sman 1999, 45–46.

3 Nicole Dacos first drew connections between Dürer and the Master of the Egmont Albums; see Dacos 1990. It might also be noted that the *Battle of the Titans* reprises the subject of Dürer's well-known drawing in the Albertina, although the similarity there is more of subject than of style. The Cologne connection is discussed below.

4 The artist has also been identified as Anthonie Blocklandt, Domenico Beccafumi (see cat. no. 11), Domenico Puligo, Claudius Cock, and a "Northern follower of Salviati and Naldini," although none of these suggestions has found wide acceptance.

5 On the artist's interest in scenes of battle, see especially Caracciolo 2001.

6 Caracciolo 2001, 683. Other battle scenes include: Lyon, Musée des Beaux-Arts, inv. no. 1962-716; Munich, Staatliche Graphische Sammlung, inv. no. 1987:22; Cologne, Wallraf-Richartz Museum, inv. no. 1913-90; and a set of drawings recently sold: Sotheby's, Amsterdam, 2 November 1987, lot 17; Sotheby's, London, 23 March 1972, lot 91, now New York, The Phillips Family Collection; Montpellier 1988, lot 34; London 1999, lot 9.

7 Starcky 1988, 91, discovered that Crispijn de Passe I engraved one of the drawings in the Louvre that had sometimes been attributed to the Master of the Egmont Albums (Hollstein DF 15:138, no. 88). As Boon (1992, 1:423) also notes, de Passe probably found the drawing during his time in Cologne between 1594 and 1610. Van der Sman (1997, 10) suggests that a *Crucifixion* (Hollstein G 27:29, no. 2A) and series of female martyrs (Schöller 1992, 148–150) by Raphael de Mey are also after drawings by the Master of the Egmont Albums; little is known about de Mey, but he also worked in Cologne ca. 1590.

8 For the portrait by Quinten Massys the Younger, who was the son of Jan Massys and the grandson of Quinten Massys, see Torriti 1990, no. 454.

9 While the old attribution of the Yale drawings to Hans von Aachen has never been taken seriously because the drawings are clearly in another hand, Hans von Aachen was born in Cologne (his name derives from the place of his father's birth) and returned there several times; it is tempting to wonder if the Master of the Egmont Albums was in some way associated with von Aachen. The drawings also bear some resemblance to those of one of von Aachen's Roman associates, Hans Speeckaert, although he died in Rome and cannot be the artist in question.

27 Andrea Boscoli
Florence ca. 1560–1608 Rome

The Road to Calvary, ca. 1600

Pen and brown ink and brown wash over black chalk, laid down, 23.3 × 30.6 cm (9 3/16 × 12 1/16 in.)

WATERMARK: on backing sheet, partial Whatman watermark (not reproduced)

INSCRIPTIONS: verso, in graphite, upper left: *53*; center: *15*; lower right, in pen and brown ink: *Roubiliac*

PROVENANCE: Roubiliac Collection, perhaps Louis François Roubiliac (1702–1762); Robert Udney (1755–1802) monogram on mount, lower right, L. 2248; Walter von Wenz (1898–1963), Kasteel Heyen; acquired from R. M. Light and Co., Boston

REFERENCES: *YUAG Bulletin* 30 (1965): 13 and 37; Kingston 1966, no. 21; H–B and L, no. 265; Regina–Montreal 1970, no. 28; New Haven 1974, no. 38; Thiem 1977, 297; Florence–Rome 1983–84, 50; New Haven 1991a, no. 9; Oberlin–Brunswick–Hanover 1991, no. 8; *Handbook*, 199; Brooks 1999, 281–285; Tuyll van Serooskerken 2000, 84

Everett V. Meeks, B.A. 1901, Fund. 1964.9.48

Given its frequent inclusion in exhibitions over the past forty years, this drawing is today among the best-known works by the prolific draftsman Andrea Boscoli. The neatness of the composition hints at the artist's training in the studio of the Florentine painter, architect, and draftsman Santi di Tito, but this sheet is accented by the broad shading and pretty calligraphy that are the benchmarks of Boscoli's style. Even if not as dramatically individualistic as some of Boscoli's almost "cubist" figure studies, the Yale drawing is still entirely typical of his work.

It has often been suggested that this drawing might have been a preparatory design for a print project. The style of the work is similar to other prints after Boscoli, and the size and rectangular format would be appropriate for a print. Moreover, the work seems to derive from a study of prints by Dürer, Martin Schongauer, and other Northern masters, and as such seems to fit into a broader trend of Florentine artists of the later sixteenth century looking back to art of the beginning of the century, both by Florentine and by Northern artists.[1]

In 1984, Bert Meijer connected this drawing to Boscoli's set of six similar drawings now in the Teyler Museum, Haarlem; more recently, Julian Brooks has expanded that idea, connected the Yale and the Haarlem drawings to another in Berlin (figs. A–B), and suggested that the set was probably designed with the intention of creating a set of prints depicting the Passion of Christ or the Life of Christ.[2] Boscoli had earlier designed a Passion series, which was engraved by the

FIGURE 27A | Andrea Boscoli, *Ecce Homo*, ca. 1600. Berlin, Kupferstichkabinett.

FIGURE 27B | Andrea Boscoli, *Flagellation*, ca. 1600. Haarlem, Teyler Museum.

Flemish draftsman, engraver, and publisher Pieter de Jode I around 1598. The Yale drawing and the related sheets are larger than this first series, and of substantially more intricate design, which suggests that they are later than the de Jode Passion. Likewise, Boscoli's later works tend, as does this composition, to include naturalistic touches that seem to be inspired by the examples of Cigoli, Barocci, and Barocci's Sienese followers, thus also arguing for a date in the last decade of Boscoli's life.

The second Passion or Life of Christ series, however, was never executed in print. De Jode had returned to Antwerp soon after making the first Passion, and Boscoli might have had difficulty in finding an engraver to assist with the second project. Despite the success of other print series—those by Boscoli's Florentine contemporary Antonio Tempesta, for example, or the Saint Catherine series, also engraved by de Jode after designs by Francesco Vanni—the complexity of Boscoli's large designs, with deep recessions into space and many figures of varying scale, could have been a dissuading factor for many prospective printmakers, given the time it would have taken to engrave such prints. To judge from the gaps in the sequence, Boscoli might even have abandoned the enterprise before finishing the entire series, perhaps when he left Florence around 1600, although the missing drawings could simply have been lost over the centuries. Still another possibility is that these were drawings executed for their own sake, without prints in mind. In any case, the drawings sit alongside Boscoli's scenes from Tasso's *Gerusalemme Liberata* and from Ovid's *Metamorphoses*, other late series of uncertain function.[3] Whatever its purpose, the *Road to Calvary* remains a typical example of the narrative style characteristic of Boscoli and so many other Florentine artists at the end of the sixteenth century.

JJM

1 For further discussion of this point, see Feinberg in Oberlin–Brunswick–Hanover 1991. Other parallels can be drawn between the present work and a drawing of the same subject by Fra Bartolomeo, Florence, Uffizi, inv. no. 1236E; the study of Fra Bartolomeo's drawings would likewise have been an unsurprising practice for a member of the Florentine Accademia del Disegno.

2 Brooks calls this series a Passion of Christ, but the set of drawings that he identifies includes a broader range of scenes and might be better termed a Life of Christ. The drawings that Brooks connects to the Yale drawing, all roughly 23 × 31 cm and in media like that of the Yale sheet, include: Haarlem, Teyler Museum, inv. nos. C56 (*Massacre of the Innocents*), C60 (*Christ Washing the Feet of the Apostles*), C61 (*Agony in the Garden*, for which see also Uffizi, inv. no. 8206F), C57 (*Christ before Pilate*), C58 (*Flagellation*), and C59 (*Crucifixion*), all of which are illustrated and discussed in Tuyll van Serooskerken 2000, and Berlin, Kupferstichkabinett, inv. no. 15805 (*Ecce Homo*).

3 See Brooks 2000.

28 Cherubino Alberti

Borgo San Sepolcro 1553–1615 Rome

Study for a Resurrection of Lazarus, ca. 1600

Black and red chalk, outlines incised for transfer; laid down, 34.4 × 25.2 cm (13⁹⁄₁₆ × 9¹⁵⁄₁₆ in.)

WATERMARK: crown with six-pointed star above, similar to Briquet nos. 4834, 4854, and Heawood no. 1118, a type produced in Italy in the latter half of the sixteenth century. (Note: the reproduction shows an extra chain line to the left of the crown, which is from the backing sheet.)

PROVENANCE: acquired from Richard Day, London

REFERENCES: *YUAG Bulletin* 36.1 (1976): 37 (as Follower of Michelangelo)

Everett V. Meeks, B.A. 1901, Fund. 1975.42.1

This highly finished Michelangelo-inspired study for a Resurrection of Lazarus is one of the more enticing mysteries in Yale's collection of Italian drawings, both regarding its attribution and its function. Attributions to Agnolo Bronzino, Alessandro Allori, Giovanni Battista Naldini, and Francesco Salviati have all been suggested, but none has met with much acceptance. It is here proposed that the drawing is by Cherubino Alberti, a native of Borgo San Sepolcro who enjoyed a successful career in Rome as both a printmaker and a painter.[1] Alberti made a close study of Michelangelo's works (he produced a series of engravings of the Sistine Chapel, for example) and often used the combination of red and black chalk seen here. Perhaps resulting from his work as a reproductive engraver, he seems to have been highly conscious of graphic style, and his drawings, like the present sheet, often include figures in such different manners that at first glance they seem to have been drawn by two different hands. Comparisons for the handling of media, the derivation from eclectic sources, and the treatment of anatomy—as well as for the very nature of the Yale drawing—can all be found among the many drawings from the Alberti Album in the Istituto Nazionale per la Grafica at the Farnesina, Rome.[2] Among the scattered single sheets by the artist, close parallels might be drawn as well to a sheet of studies last seen at Sotheby's in 1990, the present whereabouts of which are unknown.[3]

The drawing is a fascinating record of the emulation not only of the style of Michelangelo's figures but also of the very manner in which Michelangelo drew them. Michelangelo was notoriously unwilling to take studio apprentices or assistants and had few pupils in the traditional sense, but a number of his drawings were nonetheless available to artists—in most cases because Michelangelo had presented them as gifts—and were eagerly studied. The finely hatched black chalk seen in the *Lazarus* particularly resembles the way Michelangelo handled the medium in his drawings of *The Punishment of Tityus*, *The Rape of Ganymede*, and *The Fall of Phaeton*. These drawings, presented as gifts to the young Roman nobleman Tommaso de' Cavalieri, were among the most famous and most copied of Michelangelo's graphic works.[4]

The Yale drawing is a study of the Resurrection of Lazarus. The central figure is Lazarus, who is shown being lifted from the grave by the men sketched in red chalk; he is brought back to life by Christ, who is represented only by the outline of an uplifted arm and flowing robe at the far left of the sheet. A drawing of this type would usually be preparatory for a painting, but neither a painting nor a print of the subject by Alberti is known. Moreover, the outlines of the figures in this drawing were transferred to this sheet by tracing them with a stylus (parts of Lazarus's right hand, for example, are only indicated by these stylus lines), which implies that the figures were fully worked out on another sheet even before this drawing was begun, despite the sketchy appearance of the red chalk. In sum, its careful execution and the changes in drawing manner, from the highly finished, Michelangelesque black chalk, to the freely drawn red chalk for the secondary figures, to the sketchy outline of Christ, perhaps indicate that this was not a true preparatory study; it might be hypothesized that the drawing is instead a complex fiction, a work that pretends to be a preparatory figure study but that was instead made for its own sake, as an artist's curiosity or a presentation piece for a sophisticated collector, like the Michelangelo drawings that were its ultimate source.

JJM

1 For the fullest treatment of Alberti's career, see Witcombe 1981; Abromson 1978; and Rome 1983–84. See also Gere and Pouncey 1983, 20–23. The attribution of the present sheet to Alberti was also suggested, independently, by Florian Härb.
2 See Rome 1983–84. Unfortunately, neither the black-and-white reproductions in that catalogue, nor any that might have been printed here, can convincingly convey the parallels between the handling of media in the Yale sheet and the drawings in Rome. For a similar treatment of anatomy, see, for example, Cherubino's studies of the Belvedere torso, inv. nos. F.N. 2957, 3038, 3039, 3040; nos. 93–97 in Rome 1983–84.
3 Sotheby's, New York, 12 January 1990, lot 8; previously in the Michel Gaud collection sold at Sotheby's, Monaco, 20 June 1987, lot 85. The looping, loose red chalk might also be compared to drawings like the *Prudence*, Washington, National Gallery of Art, inv. no. 1991.150.1, red chalk, 28.7 × 17.7 cm.
4 For further discussion of the copies after Michelangelo, especially of the Tommaso de' Cavalieri drawings, see Washington et al. 1996–98. For further discussion of the Michelangelo gift-drawings and the style in which they were made, see Nagel 1997; Nagel 2000; and Rosand 2002, Chapter 6.

29 Bartholomaeus Spranger
Antwerp 1546–1611 Prague

Venus and Mercury, ca. 1600

Pen and brown ink and gray wash, heightened with white, 37 × 25.3 cm (14½ × 10 in.)

WATERMARK: double eagle with a crown above, similar to Briquet nos. 256, 276, and 278, found on German paper of the 1570s and 1580s; on backing sheet, fleur-de-lys in a double circle, similar to Heawood no. 1591 (Venice, 1691)

PROVENANCE: John Gaskin (a letter from Anthony Blunt in the curatorial files clarifies that Gaskin had been the owner, and not Blunt, who had been listed in the Colnaghi sale catalogue); acquired from P. and D. Colnaghi and Co., London

REFERENCES: London 1974, no. 27; *YUAG Bulletin* 35.3 (1975): 42–43, 50; Amherst 1990, no. 23; Strech 1996, no. 40A; New Hollstein DF, *The Muller Dynasty*, Part 2: under no. 68; Sievers, Muehlig, and Rich 2000, 60

Enoch Vine Stoddard, B.A. 1905, Fund. 1974.38

The Holy Roman Emperor Rudolf II attracted a glittering array of international artists to his imperial court in Prague—the Flemish painter and printmaker Bartholomaeus Spranger, the German painter Hans von Aachen, the Swiss painter and architect Joseph Heintz the Elder, and the Dutch sculptor Adriaen de Vries were the foremost of those working there, establishing the elegant and extravagant style that came to be known as Northern Mannerism. Trained in his native Antwerp, Spranger traveled briefly to France in 1565 and then spent ten years in Italy, first in Milan and Parma—where the work of Correggio and Parmigianino influenced him profoundly—and later in and near Rome, alongside Federico Zuccaro (see cat. no. 19), producing works for Cardinal Alessandro Farnese and Pope Pius V. In 1575 Spranger went to Vienna in the service of the Holy Roman Emperor Maximilian II, and in 1576 he began to work for Maximilian's successor Rudolf, the patron with whom he is most closely associated. He was named court painter in January 1581, joined the painters' guild there in 1584, and in 1588 was granted a title of nobility.

Spranger had an enormous influence on the following generation, especially in the Netherlands, at least partly through the prints after his compositions, the first of which was made by Cornelis Cort in 1573, while Spranger was in Italy (this was Cort's only print after Spranger).[1] Once Hendrick Goltzius was introduced to Spranger's work, he strove to become the prime engraver of the latter's designs. Goltzius made his first print after Spranger in 1585, and six more before 1590.[2] Well before the time Spranger made *Venus and Mercury*, he and other artists (such as Maarten de Vos, see cat. no. 21) had departed from the traditional method of detailed line drawings to be followed by an engraver, like the one made by Heemskerck in 1565 (cat. no. 15), providing instead looser ink and wash sketches like this one, which allowed the engraver freedom to use linear means of his own choosing to replicate the design. Jan Harmensz. Muller (see cat. no. 24) never went to Prague, but he began engraving Spranger's designs in Amsterdam around 1590, presumably having inherited, so to speak, the position of engraver of Spranger's work from Goltzius when the latter departed for Italy that same year. Muller engraved thirteen plates after Spranger, including two large allegorical pieces glorifying Rudolf II, *Apotheosis of the Arts* of 1597, and *Bellona Leading the Imperial Armies against the Turks*, dated 1600.[3] The engraving of *Venus and Mercury* (fig. A) is also thought to have been made around 1600, and thus Spranger probably made his drawing in or not long before that year.[4]

This drawing does not show incisions or evidence of any other method of transfer, and numerous differences between it and the finished print suggest that a subsequent version was more likely the one from which Muller worked to make the engraving. In the engraving—which is in reverse from the drawing, as would have been normal and foreseen by Spranger—the putto standing next to Mercury holds the god's caduceus, whereas in the drawing a simple line goes upward at more or less the same angle. The arrow held by the putto near Venus likewise is only summarily indicated in the drawing. The two doves in the foreground of the print, and the bow they seem to be examining, are not indicated at all in the drawing.

Spranger is known to have made duplicate drawings, as well as close variants of his own compositions; for instance, two versions of *Mars and Venus*, one in Frankfurt dated 1596, and one at Smith College dated 1597, are both deemed autograph.[5] The composition of these drawings, in turn, is close to—but clearly a variant of—that of a print by Goltzius dated 1588, for which no drawing is extant.[6]

The erotic quality of this composition is typical of Spranger's images, and in fact of Rudolfine art in general. Although there is no episode in ancient mythological sources in which Venus and Mercury are lovers, Spranger made several compositions showing this subject: a drawing, now in Basel,[7] was rendered in engraving by Pieter de Jode (fig. B), probably in the early 1590s.[8] Another drawing, in Karlsruhe, probably a copy of an original by Spranger, is a variant of this composition.[9] A painting, probably made after 1595, is closer compositionally to Yale's drawing and the Muller engraving than to those earlier drawings: Venus stands in profile, one arm reaching to Mercury, the other touching a putto standing close behind her; another putto is beyond the figure of Mercury; and drapery hangs in the background. The painting has been interpreted as an allegory in which Venus rewards Mercury for his eloquence, which sustains love; Konrad Oberhuber plausibly suggested that the idea for the allegory may have come from the discussion of Venus and Mercury in Vincenzo Cartari's *Imagini de i dei de gli antichi*, first published in Venice in 1556 and republished several times before the end of the century.[10] The pertinent text reads, "Plutarch wrote that the ancients used to put the statue of Mercury with that of Venus, and in so doing made it understood that lovers thus conjoined need smooth and gentle diversions and pleasing words between them, because these often bring into being, and maintain, love between people."[11] In the painting, Venus holds out a crown of laurel to be placed on Mercury's head, whereas in Yale's drawing (and in the Muller engraving), Venus's arm is around Mercury's neck and the spread index and middle fingers of her hand indicate his mouth—the source of his eloquence; this gesture would seem to confirm the emphasis on Mercury's smooth tongue.

The Latin text in the lower margin of the engraving further corroborates this idea. It reads: *Ad Veneris furtum faciunt ut pocula Bacchi, / Sic facit et plectro lingua diserta suo. /*

FIGURE 29A | Jan Harmensz. Muller after Bartholomaeus Spranger, *Venus and Mercury*, ca. 1600. New York, Metropolitan Museum of Art.

FIGURE 29B | Pieter de Jode I after Bartholomaeus Spranger, *Venus and Mercury*, ca. 1590–95. New York, Metropolitan Museum of Art.

Exemplum est huius cursor Cyllenius artis, / Ut novit vivis Ida perennis aquis. (As the cups of Bacchus defraud Venus, so does an eloquent tongue with its lyre. An example of this art is the runner Cyllenius [Mercury], as he refreshes himself by the constantly running waters of Ida.) It is not known who supplied the inscription.

The composition, clearly deriving from Muller's print, was reproduced on a round Dutch faience dish of the early seventeenth century.[12]

SB

1 New Hollstein DF, *Cornelis Cort*, no. 106.
2 See Filedt Kok 1993, 170; Amsterdam–New York–Toledo 2003–04, 81ff.
3 See New Hollstein DF, *The Muller Dynasty*, Part 2.
4 Filedt Kok 1994, 250.
5 See Princeton–Washington–Pittsburgh 1982–83, no. 49, and Sievers, Muehlig, and Rich 2000, no. 10.
6 Hollstein DF 8:110, no. 321; Amsterdam–New York–Toledo 2003–04, no. 32.
7 Basel, Kunstmuseum, Kupferstichkabinett, inv. no. U.I 214, O.Z. 6. See Niederstein 1931, 8, fig. 2; Oberhuber 1958, 92 and 245, Z. 6; Strech 1996, no. 24.
8 Oberhuber 1958, 287, no. 63; Hollstein DF 9:204, no. 97; Strech 1996, no. 24.
9 Karlsruhe, Kunsthalle, Kupferstichkabinett, Brentel Klebeband K, fol. 14v; Oberhuber 1958, 261, Z. 82.
10 Vienna, Kunsthistoriches Museum, inv. no. 1100; see Kaufmann 1988, no. 20.42, and Essen–Vienna 1988, no. 580, for the painting. Oberhuber 1958, 122, first related the painting to Cartari. Cartari's book, published by Francesco Marcolini in Venice in 1556, was republished by Vincenzo Valgrisi, also in Venice, in 1571, with eighty-one etchings by Bolognino Zaltieri, and then again with these same plates in Venice in 1580. The book quickly became enormously popular; besides other editions published in Venice, there were French and Latin editions published in Lyon in 1581, and an English edition published in London in 1599.
11 Cartari 1976, 541: " . . . scrive Plutarco, che solevano gli antichi mettere con la statua di Venere quella di Mercurio anchora, volendo in questa guisa dare ad intendere, che gli amorosi congiungimenti hanno bisogno di trattenimenti dolci e soavi, e di parole piacevoli, perche queste fanno spesso nascere, e conservano Amore fra le persone."
12 Sèvres, Musée National de Céramique, inv. no. 22412, high-temperature polychrome faience, diam. 45 cm; see Fourest 1980, 11.

30 Attributed to Johann Kellerthaler II
Dresden 1560/62–1611 Dresden

Crucifixion, ca. 1600–1610

Pen and brown and black ink and brown wash, with white heightening, on two joined sheets of light brown paper, 31 × 41.5 cm (12 3/16 × 16 5/16 in.)

WATERMARK: gothic letter "P" with a crown (?) above (the watermark is cut by the edge of the sheet), akin to Briquet nos. 8798, 8827, and 8880 (all German/Austrian, last quarter of sixteenth century)

INSCRIPTIONS: a long letter covers the left half of the verso (see text below for more details)

PROVENANCE: private collection, New York; Christie's, London, 4 July 2000, lot 221; acquired from Hill-Stone, Inc., New York

REFERENCES: *YUAG Bulletin* (2003): 155

Everett V. Meeks, B.A. 1901, Fund. 2002.87.1

Although the question of its authorship presents some problems, this dramatic and accomplished work demonstrates the quintessential qualities of Central European draftsmanship around the year 1600. Drawn by a follower of Hans von Aachen and Bartholomaeus Spranger (cat. no. 29), the sheet embodies the suave grace of international Mannerism as well as the strong, angular lines more typical of German art. As a depiction of the Crucifixion, it is a tour de force that combines a host of motifs, ranging from the pathos of the Virgin and John the Evangelist (to the right) to the almost comic scene of soldiers gambling for the robes of Christ (in the middle distance at left). Other depictions of the Crucifixion produced in this medium—Hans von Aachen's painting and related drawing of 1602,[1] and Aegidius Sadeler's 1590 print after Christoph Schwartz,[2] for example—include many of the same motifs, but few have quite the same degree of movement through space or of combined anguish and grace as the present work.

The most probable attribution of the drawing is to Johann Kellerthaler II, who worked as a painter, sculptor, and engraver but is best known as a goldsmith. His commissions seem to have come mainly from the Saxon court in his native Dresden, but he was well aware of artistic movements beyond the walls of his native city. His drawing style is so strongly influenced by Hans von Aachen, for example, that he must have had some contact with the latter, either from a visit to Rudolf II's court at Prague or else during von Aachen's 1602 visit to Dresden. The present sheet has the crowded compositions, elegant figures, and bold cross-hatching found in other drawings by Kellerthaler, and also agrees with them in minor details and characteristic shorthands such as the triangular eyes, small mouths, and blocky fingers.[3] If this *Crucifixion* is by Kellerthaler, it may have been a preparatory design for a painting or for a silver relief comparable to those that he made for a *hausaltar* of Christian II, Elector of Saxony.[4] The relief sculptures on that altar, especially the central scene of the *Resurrection*, display the same lively approach to their religious subject matter that is seen in the *Crucifixion* drawing. Alternately, given its high finish and variety of media, this drawing might have been a collector's piece in its own right.

An alternate attribution to the little-known goldsmith Hans Petzelt of Frankfurt an den Oder has also been proposed. Petzelt's known graphic oeuvre consists of a single drawing in Nuremberg, a work that is attributed to him because he is named in an inscription on the sheet.[5] There are some obvious connections between the draftsmanship of the *Crucifixion* and that of the *Baptism of Christ* attributed to Petzelt. It might be suggested, however, that the inscription on the latter refers not to the author of the drawing but rather to Petzelt as the artist who would translate the design into a work of decorative art. Moreover, the Nuremberg drawing is remarkably similar to Kellerthaler's work, and another drawing in the same collection, of the same subject matter, in the same media, and on the same size sheet, is signed by Kellerthaler.[6] In short, the sheet Geissler attributed to Petzelt might be by Kellerthaler; even if not, the connection between the *Crucifixion* and the drawing attributed to Petzelt is less convincing than are the comparisons between the drawing and Kellerthaler's works.[7]

Regardless of the attribution, the work is a first-rate example of Central European art around the year 1600. Showing the influence of Italian Mannerism in the art of distant cities such as Dresden and Prague, it documents the international character of art at the turn of the seventeenth century, while also demonstrating the strong graphic style that was the legacy of the German Renaissance.

A long, undated letter from Dorathea Brunsterin to a Herr Miller covers the left half of the verso; stains and faded ink make a full transcription impossible, as does the irregular orthography: the author even closes the letter with a postscript, "May my lord not be exasperated with my incomprehensible writing." Nothing is known about Brunsterin or Miller, but it is clear that the letter, which deals with domestic issues, does not relate to the drawing on the recto and was instead probably written decades later, to judge from what seems to be seventeenth- or eighteenth-century handwriting. By that time, surprisingly, this impressive sheet must have been considered little more than scrap paper, to be turned over, folded in half, and reused.[8]

JJM

1. Vignau-Wilberg 1988, 302–305. For a related drawing and commentary, see also Turner et al. 1997, 152–153.
2. *TIB* 72, Part 1:87, 055.
3. The Yale drawing compares especially to the *Judgment of Paris* (Cologne, Wallraf-Richartz-Museum, inv. no. Z 242, pen and brown ink and wash, 26.5 × 17.9 cm) and the *Banquet of Achelous* (Munich, Staatliche Graphische Sammlung, inv. no. 1044, pen and black ink and gray wash, 18.4 × 14.7 cm), recently published in Bodnár 2005, figs. 2 and 3. Bodnár 2005, 186, notes that only sixteen drawings have been linked to the artist. The most complete illustration of Kellerthaler's work as a draftsman, discussing thirteen of the sheets, is Schade 1969, 64–73. Bodnár 2005, 186, also notes that the set of drawings discussed as anonymous by Baker 2003 are by Kellerthaler.
4. The altar is now in the Grünes Gewölbe, Dresden. See Dresden 1986, 370. None of Kellerthaler's drawings has been connected to a finished work, but so few of his drawings survive that this is hardly surprising.
5. Nuremberg, Germanisches Nationalmuseum, inv. no. Hz. 25; Stuttgart 1979–80, 2:150.
6. Nuremberg, Germanisches Nationalmuseum, inv. no. Hz. 20; Stuttgart 1979–80, 2:100–101.
7. One other possible attribution of the *Crucifixion* is to Jacob Schwender, whose *Preaching of the Baptist* in the Städtischen Kunstsammlungen, Regensburg (inv. no. 1961-1) has the same combination of Mannerist grace and faceted forms; the quickly sketched faces of the crowd in both drawings are also very similar. Unfortunately, too little is known about Schwender (and for that matter, Kellerthaler) to be certain of the differences between their graphic styles.
8. I am indebted to Margaret E. Hadley for deciphering, transcribing, and translating the legible parts of the letter.

31 Domenico Zampieri, called Domenichino
Bologna 1581–1641 Naples

Study of a Seated Old Man, ca. 1604

Black chalk with white heightening on blue paper, 30.6 × 23.3 cm (12 1/16 × 9 3/16 in.)

INSCRIPTIONS: verso, at center, in pencil: *174.88a*

PROVENANCE: probably the drawing described as "old man, sitting on ground, with left hand lifted, black chalk, with touches of white, on blue paper" by Domenichino, sold Gutekunst und Klipstein, Bern, 21–22 June 1949, lot 573; private collection, New Jersey; acquired from Mia Weiner, Norfolk, Conn.

REFERENCES: Spear 2002, 162; *YUAG Bulletin* (2004): 158

Everett V. Meeks, B.A. 1901, Fund. 2003.103

Domenichino was among the most influential artists in the development of the Baroque style in Bologna, Rome, and Naples during the early seventeenth century. He received his first training in the studio of the late Mannerist artist Denys Calvaert but left that studio—and joined the Accademia degli Incamminati led by the Carracci family of artists—after a conflict that occurred when Calvaert caught the young Domenichino copying a Carracci drawing. Annibale Carracci had already left Bologna, but Domenichino made a careful study of his works and in 1602 followed him to Rome. The two artists became closely associated, and their works from this period are remarkably similar.

The *Seated Old Man*, a figure study from a live model, reflects the new approach to painting that Domenichino would have learned from the Carracci. Whereas many artists of the previous generation distorted figures according to a sophisticated aesthetic of mannered grace and ideal beauty, the Carracci academy's emphasis on the close study of nature meant, in practical terms, that figures were to be based on life. A drawing like Domenichino's *Old Man* might thus be considered the very paradigm of the new Baroque art.

For all the ideology behind drawings like this sheet, however, the figure studies by Domenichino were fundamentally practical works, intended as preparatory sketches in the production of paintings rather than as finished works in themselves. In this case, the drawing was for the figure of Saint Peter in a *Liberation of Saint Peter from Prison* that Domenichino painted in 1604 (the original, formerly Potsdam-Sanssouci, is lost; fig. A is a copy that replaced the original in the sacristy at San Pietro in Vincoli, Rome).[1] In this study, we see the artist attempt to resolve the tense, twisting pose that would convey the saint's astonishment at the moment the angel appeared, in the middle of the night, to liberate him from prison. Domenichino has also included the arm of the angel reaching down from the top of the sheet, as if to serve as a constant reminder that Peter's pose was in reaction to the angel's startling appearance. This juxtaposition of the angel's hand and Peter's upraised arm evidently caused Domenichino some problems, however, and in the final painting, Peter's left arm was lowered. A related figure study, for the sleeping soldier at far right in the painting, survives among the large group of Domenichino's drawings at Windsor Castle (fig. B).[2] In the Windsor drawing, the soldier's right arm rests on the ground, but it is raised up behind his head in the painting, suggesting that Domenichino felt that something was necessary to counterbalance the changed position of Peter's arm. In the drawing for Saint Peter, Domenichino used both black and white chalk to record the fall of light across the saint's

FIGURE 31A | After Domenichino, *Liberation of Saint Peter from Prison*. Rome, San Pietro in Vincoli.

FIGURE 31B | Domenichino, *Study of a Sleeping Man*, 1604. Windsor, Royal Library.

shoulders, arms, chest, and legs, but his lower torso and genitals are barely indicated. This, too, is consistent with the drawing's function as a preparatory sketch, for the saint would never have been shown nude in the final painting.

With regard to the drawing's role as a preparatory sketch rather than a finished work in itself, a word might be said about its condition. The creases across the center of the sheet are rope marks that resulted from the papermaking process (paper was draped over a rope as it dried), rather than later damage; they indicate that this was not a particularly fine piece of paper, but given the number of preparatory drawings that artists like Domenichino and Annibale Carracci made in developing a composition, it is not surprising that they used rough, less expensive papers in the workshop.[3] Similarly, the green and white oil paint stains at upper right, and the oil stains at upper and lower left, are not uncommon on figure drawings by these artists and serve as a reminder that these studies were very close at hand as the artists worked on the paintings.

The painted *Liberation* was one of Domenichino's first independent works. He is said to have been encouraged to paint it by Monsignor Giovanni Battista Agucchi, who would go on to become one of the more important theorists behind the classical strain of Baroque art.[4] Agucchi and Annibale Carracci had encouraged Domenichino to make a close study of Raphael's works in Rome, and the *Liberation* was surely created with Raphael's fresco in the Vatican in mind. In contrast to Raphael's classical but essentially static approach to the subject, Domenichino's composition is infused with the new muscular, animated style of both Annibale Carracci—his *Resurrection* of 1593 (Paris, Louvre), for example—and Caravaggio. In his later works, Domenichino would develop a highly classical style closer to Raphael's model than to Caravaggio's, but his 1604 drawing for the *Liberation of Saint Peter* is in every way a document of the development of Baroque art in Rome around the year 1600.

JJM

1. For discussion of the painting, see especially Spear 1982, 133–134. The picture was lost in the Second World War but is known through old photographs and several copies.
2. Windsor, Royal Library, inv. no. 1006r, black and white chalk on blue paper, contours of the recto incised for transfer, 29.4 × 23.8 cm; see Pope-Hennessy 1948, 89. The drawing is illustrated and more completely discussed in Spear 1967, 53–54, and again by Spear 1982, 133–134. When Domenichino died in Naples in 1641, the drawings in his studio were kept together and eventually passed en masse into the British Royal Collection. There are nearly 2,000 drawings by Domenichino at Windsor, an extraordinary rate of survival for the works of a seventeenth-century artist (compare, for example, the 300 or so drawings that survive from the long-lived Bernini).
3. While some blue paper was finely prepared for writing or printing, artists often instead chose the coarser blue paper intended for use as a wrapping, especially for wrapping sugar (hence the Italian description of a medium grayish blue as "carta da zucchero"); see Bruckle 1993 for further discussion of blue paper.
4. On Agucchi, see Spear 1982, Chapters 2 and 3, and Ginzburg Carignani in Rome 1996–97, 121–138. The classic discussion of Agucchi's influence is, of course, Mahon 1947.

RECTO

32 Jacques de Gheyn II

Antwerp 1565–1629 The Hague

A Youth Seated at a Table (recto); *Head of a Child with Curly Hair* (verso), ca. 1604

Pen and brown ink on brownish paper, 13.5 × 10.3 cm (5 5/16 × 4 1/16 in.)

INSCRIPTIONS: recto, in pen and brown ink, upper right: *DGheyn* ("D" and "G" as monogram); lower right: *Jac. de Gheyn*

PROVENANCE: John Percival, 1st Earl of Egmont (1683–1748); John T. Graves; Robert Hoe (sale, New York, Anderson Auction Company, 15–19 April 1912, Library of Robert Hoe, Part III, A–K, no. 949); Yale University Library (anonymous donor, 1957)

REFERENCES: Eisler 1958, 87; H-B and L, no. 379; Poughkeepsie 1970, no. 42; Judson 1973, 19, 20, pl. 86; Washington–Denver–Fort Worth 1977, no. 6; Sarasota 1980–81, no. 77; Regteren Altena 1983, no. 731; *Handbook*, 204

Egmont Collection, Yale Library Transfer. 1961.63.79

Jacques de Gheyn II was the most eminent of the three artists with the same name, who spanned three generations. His father, Jacques I, was a glass-painter and miniaturist working in Antwerp; eight etchings are now attributed to him, though the rest of his work has largely disappeared.[1] Jacques II's son, Jacques III, who worked in The Hague and Utrecht, is known primarily for his twenty-four idiosyncratic etchings, many of which depict unusual subjects, with highly dramatic lighting and a certain bizarre feeling. Eight paintings and more than 100 drawings are also given to Jacques III.[2]

In 1983 I. Q. van Regteren Altena catalogued 1,052 designs as by Jacques II; most are drawings, but some are compositions known only through prints; he also listed forty-seven paintings.[3] Recent scholarship ascribes 457 prints to Jacques II (with perhaps a few to be added from the "attributed" list), almost all of them done before 1600.[4] Many of Jacques II's designs depict the customary repertory of biblical and allegorical subjects, portraits, landscapes, and drawings from live models; more unusual are a few of his drawings that can be described as early examples of genre scenes. An album of parchment leaves has detailed studies in watercolor, in the tradition of natural history illustrations, depicting mostly flowers, with some insects and other animals.[5] Most idiosyncratic among his drawings are some twenty compositions categorized by Regteren Altena as "monsters, ghosts, and witches," the meaning of many of which remains mysterious to this day.[6] Finally, the most novel in subject are the 123 drawings for the *Wapenhandelingen*, a book on the exercise of arms, commissioned from de Gheyn in 1597 by Jan van Nassau-Siegen, a nephew of Maurice (then Count of Nassau, later Prince of Orange). The book, with engravings by members of the de Gheyn workshop made after the drawings, was authorized for publication in 1606 and was finally published in 1608.[7]

It has been suggested that *A Youth Seated at a Table* represents de Gheyn himself, or his son, but neither of these identifications can be sustained. The sitter is probably a young artist in the studio; the correlation of facial features and hair makes it virtually certain that the model is identical to one of the two figures—the one with longer hair—shown in *Six Studies of Heads*, as Haverkamp-Begemann and Logan have already remarked.[8] That drawing cannot be dated precisely, but was probably made between 1603 and 1605. De Gheyn's early works betray a debt to Hendrick Goltzius, but once the younger artist achieved his mature style, there was a long period with little change. Haverkamp-Begemann and Logan reported that Regteren Altena had suggested in the 1960s (by oral communication) a date of around 1610–12 for

VERSO

this drawing, probably because he thought it represented the artist's son, Jacques III, born about 1596. But by the time Regteren Altena put together his catalogue raisonné, he clearly had revised his thinking: in the plates, which are organized roughly chronologically, he put this drawing after several others securely dated in 1604 and before one dated 1605.[9] If the sitter is indeed the same as the one in *Six Studies* (Regteren Altena's no. 774), these two drawings should probably be placed somewhat closer together chronologically than they appear in Regteren Altena's catalogue—*Six Studies* is pl. 227, among the drawings securely dated in 1603.

The *Head of a Child* on the verso cannot be definitively associated with an image of a child in other drawings. Naturally, it is tempting to suggest an identification of the child as the artist's son, and this certainly seems a possibility, as the features and round cheeks are similar to those of a child in a drawing generally thought to represent Jacques III that Regteren Altena dates to around 1603.[10]

The iconography of the drawing has always been read as having moralizing overtones, the candle referring to the brevity of life, the writing implements connoting the vanity of earthly endeavors. These meanings are in keeping with de Gheyn's industrious outlook and may well have been implicit in the image, although given de Gheyn's many other drawings that simply depict individual figures, or studies of heads or limbs, it is perhaps unnecessary to insist too strongly on symbolic content in the drawing.

SB

1. See Regteren Altena 1983, 2:9–11; New Hollstein DF, *De Gheyn Family*, Part 1:11–25.
2. Regteren Altena 1983, 2:162–177; New Hollstein DF, *De Gheyn Family*, Part 2:239–280.
3. Regteren Altena 1983, 2:12–161. A large *Vanitas* still-life painting by Jacques de Gheyn II is also at Yale, inv. no. 1957.36, oil on panel, 118 × 165 cm.
4. New Hollstein DF, *De Gheyn Family*, Part 1:27–254; Part 2:3–238.
5. Regteren Altena 1983, 2:141–143; Paris 1985a, no. 9.
6. Regteren Altena 1983, 2:83–87.
7. See Gheyn 1971; the drawings are Regteren Altena 1983, nos. 342–464, pls. 85–155; the engravings are New Hollstein DF, *De Gheyn Family*, Part 2: nos. 341–457; Gheyn 1999; see also Krefeld–Oranienburg–Apeldoorn 1999–2000, no. 4/14. Some scholars (Regteren Altena 1983, 2:65; Filedt Kok 1990, 277) have suggested that the book was not authorized for publication until a truce in the war against Spain was close, and there seemed no danger the enemy could benefit from knowing how the Dutch drilled. Kist, however, thought that the delay could have been simply because Maurice and his nephew William Louis of Nassau were skeptical about its value (Gheyn 1971, 15; Gheyn 1999, vii). The Yale University Art Gallery has two of these drawings, inv. nos. 1959.38.25 and .26; H-B and L, nos. 375, 376; Regteren Altena 1983, nos. 352 and 402, pls. 90, 120.
8. Regteren Altena 1983, no. 774, pl. 227.
9. Regteren Altena 1983, pls. 272, 273, 282a, nos. 522, 523, 773, plus three drawings in the watercolor album, pls. 172, 192, 193, nos. 909, 929, 930, are all dated 1604; pl. 313, no. 131, is dated 1605. *Youth Seated at a Table* is pl. 310.
10. Regteren Altena 1983, no. 673. This identification would reinforce the dating of Yale's drawing to that year.

33 Attributed to Gerrit Pietersz. (erroneously called Sweelinck)
Amsterdam 1566–before 1612 Amsterdam

The Satyr and the Peasant, ca. 1610?

Pen and brown ink and brown wash over traces of black chalk, 29.5 × 30.7 cm (11⅝ × 12 1/16 in.)

WATERMARK: lion with crown and sword, with "Honig" below; see Churchill no. 160 (undated)

INSCRIPTIONS: verso, center, in graphite: *98*; verso, lower right, in graphite (erased): *Spranger 1600*

PROVENANCE: Daniel Katz, London; acquired from Hill-Stone, Inc., New York

REFERENCES: *YUAG Bulletin* (2004): 161

Everett V. Meeks, B.A. 1901, Fund. 2003.97.1

Gerrit Pietersz. studied in Amsterdam with the glass-painter Jacob Lenartz., and with Cornelis Cornelisz. van Haarlem. He lived in Antwerp around 1594–95 and then traveled to Rome, returning to Amsterdam in or shortly before 1600.[1] There he became the teacher of Pieter Lastman, who in turn taught Rembrandt. A painter and draftsman, Pietersz. also made a half-dozen etchings, five of which bear the date 1593. These remain within the prevailing Northern Mannerist style, but they have an entirely original flavor, with bold, undulating lines similar to those in *The Satyr and the Peasant*, and they rank him as the first significant figure in the tradition of Dutch etchers before Rembrandt.[2] Pietersz. was the brother of the famous composer and Amsterdam city organist Jan Pietersz. Sweelinck, and thus Gerrit is sometimes incorrectly also called by the surname "Sweelinck." When Pieter J. J. van Thiel wrote on Pietersz. in 1987, the artist's known oeuvre comprised only twenty-six works—twelve paintings, eight drawings, and the six etchings; four engravings after his designs are also known.[3] Yale's drawing was unknown to van Thiel; the attribution to Pietersz. was proposed by Martin Royalton-Kisch. The subjects of Pietersz.'s works are mostly religious, with a few taken from classical mythology or history; there is one portrait, that of his brother Jan.[4] Even for an artist who died relatively young, this output is small, and it seems highly likely that more works—particularly drawings—exist, either unknown or misattributed to better-known artists such as Abraham Bloemaert, whose early work is similar to that of Pietersz.

The story depicted in this assured and sprightly design is one of Aesop's fables. Subjects from fables and proverbs were an important part of Northern European—especially Dutch—art production in the sixteenth and seventeenth centuries, although no other composition by Pietersz. treating any of Aesop's fables, in any medium, is known. The story told in the drawing is that of a satyr who invited a traveling peasant to a meal, but when the peasant first blew on his cold hands to warm them, and subsequently on his hot soup to cool it, the satyr sent him away, saying he didn't want a guest who blew both hot and cold. Aesop's fables were illustrated in books both in Italy and in Northern Europe from the fifteenth century onward, with either woodcuts or engravings, but no book containing this image as an illustration has been identified. The drawing could also have been a preliminary study for a painted series of moralizing tales—by Aesop or some other author—which is unknown today.

SB

1. See Washington–New York 1986–87, 244–247; Amsterdam 1993–94, 313 and nos. 37–39; Schuckman, in *Grove Dictionary* 24:777–778.
2. Hollstein DF 17:107–113; Boston–St. Louis 1980–81, 18–20.
3. The fundamental article on Pietersz. is Bauch 1938; van Thiel 1987 brings this work up to date.
4. Van Thiel 1987, 367, lists all the work given to Pietersz. as of the date of that publication.

34 Jacques Bellange
active Nancy 1602–1616 Nancy

Holy Family with Saints Anne and Mary Magdalene, ca. 1611–12

Pen and brown ink and brown wash over black chalk, incised for transfer, on paper toned with yellow ochre pastel, 34 × 25.5 cm (13 5/16 × 10 in.)

WATERMARK: shield with "4SM," Briquet no. 9838 (Lorraine, 1587)

INSCRIPTIONS: recto, lower right, in pen and brown ink: *Bellange*

PROVENANCE: John Percival, 1st Earl of Egmont (1683–1748); John T. Graves; Robert Hoe (sale, New York, Anderson Auction Company, 15–19 April 1912, Library of Robert Hoe, Part III, A–K, no. 949); Yale University Library (anonymous donor, 1957)

REFERENCES: Eisler 1963; Oberhuber 1967, 254; Providence 1968, no. 16; H-B and L, no. 3; Walch 1971, 106, 214–216; Des Moines–Boston–New York 1985–86, no. 22; Cleveland–Cambridge–Ottawa 1989–90, no. 5; New Haven 1991b, 8–9; *Handbook*, 202; Thuillier 1992, 154; Los Angeles–New York–Paris 1994–95, no. 182a; Griffiths and Hartley 1997, 32, 54–56; Rennes 2001, no. 25

Egmont Collection, Yale Library Transfer. 1961.61.37

Jacques Bellange spent his entire documented career as a court artist in Nancy, the capital of the staunchly Catholic independent duchy of Lorraine.[1] Although he executed mural paintings, festival decorations, costume designs, and easel paintings for the Dukes of Lorraine, prints and drawings constitute most of his surviving oeuvre. This highly finished drawing is remarkable because it is one of the artist's few surviving preparatory studies for prints and allows us to see the simplification of the composition as Bellange worked from the drawing to his etching of the *Holy Family with Saints Anne and Mary Magdalene* (fig. A).[2] It depicts a *sacra conversazione* of the Virgin and Child surrounded by Saints Anne, Joseph, Mary Magdalene, and angels. The curtain held up by Saint Joseph and the presence of angels as background spectators create the dramatic effect of a "play-within-a-play."[3] The close placement of the figures in a diagonal composition around the central figure of the Christ child lends a certain intimacy and stability to the scene. The child exchanges a loving glance with his mother, who holds him on her lap with both hands. Mary Magdalene, crouching before them, leans forward to kiss the baby's foot, which she grasps gently in her left hand; her gesture, recalling her attitude in scenes of the Crucifixion or Entombment, alludes to the child's future sacrifice. These themes are in keeping with the Counter-Reformation religious iconography that one finds frequently in Bellange, as well as in the work of other native Lorraine artists of his time, such as Jacques Callot and Georges Lallemant.

FIGURE 34A | Jacques Bellange, *Holy Family with Saints Anne and Mary Magdalene*, ca. 1611–12. New Haven, Yale University Art Gallery.

While the subject matter was common for Bellange's milieu, the elongated limbs, small oval faces, spider-like fingers, and frothy, "soap-suds curls"[4] visible here demonstrate Bellange's intensely personal late Mannerist style. These elements betray a variety of influences: the Italian tradition originating with Parmigianino, the School of Fontainebleau (itself strongly influenced by Parmigianino), and Netherlandish Mannerism. Many of the stylistic features and motifs of this drawing are echoed in other works by Bellange. The curtain as a framing device appears in all of Bellange's etchings of the *Virgin and Child*, as well as in his *Death of Portia* etching. The lower portion of a fluted column, in the upper corner of the composition, is found in two different versions of the *Adoration of the Magi*.[5] The bonnet and facial features of Saint

Anne closely resemble a red chalk drawing of a martyr saint.[6] The Virgin's profile face, elegant upswept hairdo, and courtly attire are repeated in a later etching of the *Virgin and Child at the Crib*, which depicts the Virgin daintily embracing the child.[7] In the Yale drawing, Mary Magdalene is depicted with her traditional attributes of ointment jar and long hair, but similar attributes are conspicuously absent from Anne and Joseph; indeed, the rendering of saints without attributes occurs several times in Bellange's work.[8]

The Yale sheet, heavily worked in several media, shows the effects of its having been a working drawing for Bellange's print production. Bellange apparently began the drawing in black chalk, but as he refined his sketch, he strengthened the five main figures with ink and wash and obliterated the background angels with a thick layer of wash. Thus, the decision to omit the angels from the composition in order to correct the overcrowding was made at this early stage in the drawing process. Bellange then used a stylus to transfer the ink outlines, continuing to make alterations such as reworking Mary Magdalene's lower hand and omitting the drum on which the Virgin is seated.[9] All of these changes are visible in the resulting etching, which is the same size as the drawing and can accordingly be judged as resulting directly from this sheet.[10] The evidence of these changes, even after the completion of the drawing, testifies to Bellange's hand in the production of the etching and dispels any doubts raised by Walch and other historians about the attribution of the print to Bellange.[11]

Because of the interrelationship between the two works, the etching thereby provides clues to the dating of the drawing. That is, Walch proposed that Bellange's first etching attempt is found in the 1610–11 funeral book for Duke Charles III, where Bellange inserted a self-portrait on horseback into a small space in an etching by Friedrich Brentel of the procession escorting the new duke, Henri II.[12] Following this chronological benchmark, a date a year or two later would seem appropriate for the etching after the Yale drawing. This early dating is supported by the lack of technical sophistication in this etching when compared to later work. Griffiths and Hartley assert that its uniformity of gray tones is due to its plate having been etched with a single bite in the acid bath, as opposed to the creation of a tonal, layered effect through multiple bites. Moreover, the foul biting in the space above the Christ child is an accident that is unexpected in the work of a more experienced printmaker. Finally, the careful stippling often seen in the faces of figures in Bellange's etchings is not yet employed in this early phase of his experimentation with the medium.[13] The date of the drawing thus falls logically within the time frame of 1611–12, which was for Bellange an early stage of printmaking yet a very mature stage of draftsmanship.

NB

1 His activity dates from 1602–1616. He is recorded as having taken an apprentice in 1595, but there is a large gap in the biographical documentation between 1595 and 1602. Thuillier 1992, 92.
2 RD 5:87, no. 10; Rennes 2001, no. 25. Other drawings by Bellange that have been linked to specific prints include an *Adoration of the Magi* (Vienna, Albertina, inv. no. 11754; Rennes 2001, no. 8) that was engraved by Crispijn de Passe; and a drawing in Paris (Louvre, inv. no. 23712), which depicts only one figure group in the upper left of Bellange's *Resurrection of Lazarus* (RD 5:85, no. 6; Rennes 2001, no. 71).
3 Eisler 1963, 35.
4 Griffiths and Hartley 1997, 56.
5 See Rennes 2001, nos. 8 and 53.
6 Paris, Bibliothèque Nationale; Rennes 2001, no. 4.
7 RD 5:85, no. 5; Rennes 2001, no. 58.
8 Another example is the etching of *Three Female Saints* (RD 5:88, no. 13; Rennes 2001, no. 70), two of whom lack any attribute while the third carries simply a martyr's palm frond. These refined women, like the figures in the Yale drawing and many of Bellange's representations of the Virgin, have the appearance of pious aristocrats.
9 Bellange's above-mentioned drawing in the Albertina for an *Adoration of the Magi* also represents the Virgin seated on the drum of a column, a symbol of triumph over paganism.
10 The etching underwent three states; Yale's impression is of the second state and bears a "grapes" watermark as illustrated in Griffiths and Hartley 1997, 125–132, no. 2.
11 Walch (1971, 214–215) first questioned the attribution to Bellange; her reattribution of the print to the "Circle of Bellange" is followed by Elisabeth Hodermarsky in New Haven 1991b, 9. The prevailing opinion, however, always seems to have been in favor of the original attribution of the print to Bellange himself.
12 Walch 1971, 62–63, no. 1. Although Thuillier recently rejected the attribution of the portrait to Bellange, Griffiths and Hartley have embraced it. We agree that the hand of Bellange is readily apparent and provides a striking contrast to the rather static style employed in the rest of the print.
13 See Los Angeles–New York–Paris 1994–95, 445, and Griffiths and Hartley 1997, 32 and 56.

RECTO

35 Hermann Weyer
Coburg 1596–after 1621 (1672?) Coburg?

The Entombment of Christ (recto); *Landscape with a City on a River* (verso), ca. 1615

Pen and black ink and two colors of brown wash, with white heightening, on paper coated with yellow wash (recto); pen and brown ink (verso), 15.1 × 19.8 cm (5 15/16 × 7 13/16 in.)

PROVENANCE: Oskar Wichtendahl, Hannover, 19th century (painter in Hannover, ca. 1900; his stamp at lower left, not in Lugt), and by descent in the family; acquired from Martin Moeller, Hamburg

REFERENCES: *YUAG Bulletin* (2004): 162

Everett V. Meeks, B.A. 1901, Fund. 2003.33.1

Hermann Weyer came from a family of artists in Coburg, Germany. His father and his brother, both named Hans, were painters, and the family may have been related to the better-known Nuremberg artist Gabriel Weyer. Hermann Weyer's career remains, on the whole, mysterious. Several of his drawings are inscribed with dates between 1607 and 1621, but he may have lived long into the seventeenth century.[1] He probably received his first training from his father, but there are so many reflections of Netherlandish art in his drawings that he might have spent some time in a center like Antwerp; at the very least, he made a careful study of Netherlandish prints. He has the landscape sensitivity of a Danube School artist, but also the suave sophistication associated with the International Mannerists and the Prague School.[2]

The majority of Weyer's known drawings are, like the present sheet, two-sided works with a figural composition on one side and a landscape on the other.[3] Because of their relatively small size and the fact that they are double-sided, and also because many are, like the present sheet, trimmed around the edges, Heinrich Geissler concluded that many of Weyer's works must have come from a sketchbook. Even if this is the case, the complex combination of media and the relatively high finish of the works indicate that these were final, finished works, creations in their own right, rather than preparatory sketches. *The Entombment of Christ* on the recto of this sheet is at first glance coolly elegant, but on further study demonstrates a sort of nervous energy. Strong chiaroscuro is used to convey the somber mood of the scene, but such touches as the white heightening to indicate the

VERSO

delicate flames of the torches are a testament to Weyer's self-conscious technique. Chiaroscuro woodcutting developed as a way for printmaking to reproduce the appearance of wash drawings, but it might be suggested that the tables had turned by Weyer's generation, for drawings like this *Entombment* seem to be based on the finished appearance of the chiaroscuro woodcuts produced around 1600 by Hendrick Goltzius and Abraham Bloemaert. Drawn first in brush and brown ink on a yellow-washed paper, then worked up with two colors of brown wash, black ink pen lines, and finally, white heightening, the *Entombment* is a virtuoso performance.

The landscape drawing on the verso of this sheet is informal by comparison but still fits into a tradition of landscape drawings of the later sixteenth century, for which there were many models, ranging from Bruegel to Goltzius. This landscape, it might be said, is falsely naïve, appearing at first to be drawn from life but upon closer examination seeming more like a rustic fantasy; it is not hard to imagine the increasingly sophisticated collectors of the seventeenth century appreciating such ambivalent qualities. In fact, while a number of Weyer's drawings survive, only a handful of paintings are even attributed to him, and he presumably made a career as a graphic artist by producing sheets like this one. Such drawings are likely to have been made for the same audience that collected the prints that had been Weyer's models.

JJM

1 A dissertation begun by Christine Wolff in 2001, as reported in *Kunstchronik* 2001, is entitled *Studien zum zeichnerischen Werk des Hermann Weyer (1596–1672?)*. This study has not yet been published, and efforts to contact the author have failed, but the dissertation's title suggests that she has uncovered some evidence for giving these dates (i.e., "1596–1672?") for the artist, rather than the "1596–after 1621" that is otherwise universally used.

2 The most complete account of the artist's work to date remains Mayer 1931–32. See also Geissler in Stuttgart 1979–80, 1:230–232; Princeton–Washington–Pittsburgh 1982–83, 80–81; Starcky 1985; and Germann-Bauer 1996.

3 Examples include the *Rest on the Flight* (recto)/*Landscape with a Man leading a Cow* (verso) in the Herzog Anton Ulrich-Museum, Braunschweig, inv. no. Z 391, and another *Resurrection of Lazarus* (recto)/*Landscape with a Bridge* (verso) sheet sold at Sotheby's, Amsterdam, 5 November 2002, lot 15. Others were on the New York art market in 2003–04.

36 Esaias van de Velde
Amsterdam 1587–1630 The Hague

Farm to the Right of a Frozen River, 1616

Black chalk, 13.2 × 25.4 cm (5 3/16 × 10 in.)

INSCRIPTIONS: recto, bottom center, in black chalk: *e. v. velde 1616*

PROVENANCE: acquired from C. G. Boerner, Düsseldorf

REFERENCES: *YUAG Bulletin* 32 (1968): 48; H-B and L, no. 430 (as *Winter Landscape*); Poughkeepsie 1976, no. 6; Keyes 1984, no. D77; *Handbook*, 206

Everett V. Meeks, B.A. 1901, Fund. 1967.39

Esaias van de Velde was a member of a family of artists working in the northern Netherlands in the late sixteenth and early seventeenth centuries. His father, Hans, was a painter and art dealer; his cousin Jan van de Velde I was famous as a calligrapher; Jan's son Jan II was a prolific printmaker; his grandson Jan III a painter; and Esaias's nephew was the painter Jan Martens. Born in Amsterdam, Esaias moved to Haarlem in 1609 after the death of his father and joined the Guild of Saint Luke in 1612. In 1618 he moved to The Hague, where that same year he was inscribed in the Guild of Saint Luke; he remained in The Hague for the rest of his life. Besides close to two hundred paintings he made on his own, Esaias collaborated with several contemporaries to provide staffage for their paintings. Landscape is the largest category among his paintings, but he also produced genre and allegorical scenes and biblical subjects. George Keyes catalogued 215 drawings as by Esaias and listed forty-three more for which he was not certain of the attribution. Esaias also made about forty etchings, mostly in the years 1614 to 1618, when he lived in Haarlem. As with Esaias's paintings, the great majority of his drawings and etchings are landscapes.[1]

Most of Esaias van de Velde's surviving early drawings are in pen and brown ink and washes, but his use of chalk for Yale's drawing is evidence of his mastery by 1616 of this medium, which he used increasingly during subsequent years. Here, Esaias has varied his touch with the chalk, using just a few strong lines on figures, buildings, and trees. He has darkened the right foreground with horizontal strokes on the mass of trees, and used rounded strokes to follow the form of the largest trunk. The building and trees in the distance are delineated more lightly. The various postures of the figures are described with just a few lines, which convincingly convey their balance and their weight.

Yale's drawing typifies the kind of naturalistic depiction of the Dutch landscape that came to the fore in the second decade of the seventeenth century, in the work of Claes Jansz. Visscher in Amsterdam, and that of Esaias and Jan van de Velde II, and Willem Buytewech in Haarlem. Esaias played a leading role in the move toward naturalism, away from the artificial conventions for rendering landscape prevalent in the sixteenth century.[2] The innovative low horizontal format epitomizes the wide flatness of the Dutch terrain itself—a format that Rembrandt would return to in his etchings of several decades later— and the width seems all the greater because of the low viewpoint, that of an ordinary observer on the ground. In this unassuming scene the human elements—the skaters and the buildings—are in perfect equilibrium with the natural ones—the frozen river, the trees, the birds, and the sky. The emergence of realism in Dutch landscape at this time can be seen as a celebration of the newly emerged United Provinces—the Protestant territories that had successfully resisted the efforts of the Spanish to take them over— a paean to both the topography and the unostentatious, hardworking people of these artists' native land.

SB

1. Keyes 1984, the standard reference for Esaias van de Velde, includes a fully illustrated catalogue raisonné of the paintings, drawings, and prints. See also Amsterdam–Boston– Philadelphia 1987–88, 497–503. For etchings by and after Esaias, see Hollstein DF 32:241– 299; etchings by Esaias are in Boston–St. Louis 1980–81, nos. 27–29, 39–41, 58, 59.
2. See Stechow 1947 and Stechow 1966, 19–22, 51–54, 86–87 and elsewhere, as well as the references above.

RECTO

37 Jacques Callot
Nancy 1592–1635 Nancy

Figure Studies (recto); *A Stage Set* (verso), ca. 1616–17

Red chalk, 23.7 × 17.5 cm (9 5/16 × 6 7/8 in.)

INSCRIPTIONS: recto, lower center, in pen and brown ink: *OOO*.

PROVENANCE: H. M. Calmann, London (sale catalogue 1958, no. 27); acquired from Schaeffer Galleries, Inc., New York

REFERENCES: *YUAG Bulletin* 33 (1971): 18; Toronto et al. 1972, no. 21; New York 1975, 32; Washington 1975, no. 62; New Haven 1984, no. 12; Nancy 1992, no. 59; Ternois 1993, 361–362; Ternois 1999a, no. S.1467

Everett V. Meeks, B.A. 1901, Fund. 1970.2.5

Beginning in 1614, the French artist Jacques Callot was lodged at the Uffizi palace in Florence and received a regular pension from the Medici family, who had hired him to create prints documenting the festivals that played an important role in the life of the Florentine ducal court.[1] This drawing of comic figures, musicians, dancers, a falling man, a cavalier, and two wrestlers would seem to relate to that practice, and its close relationship with the prints executed by Callot during his stay in Florence provides a convenient means of dating and interpreting the drawing within its cultural context. Yet, as Diane Russell asserts, the Yale drawing is not a straightforward preparatory study for an etching; unlike the contemporary drawings used as true preparatory studies for the *Balli di Sfessania*,[2] for example, there is no direct correlation of these figures with any particular print. Instead, the visual affinity of this drawing with representations of the performers that animate prints like the *Guerra d'Amore* of 1616 suggests that Callot employed these chalk sketches as a repertoire of types to be used as inspiration for the figures in his large-scale, heavily populated etchings. The cavalier and the two fighting men in the drawing, for example, resemble figures in the foreground of one of the infantry battles from the *Guerra d'Amore*; other figures in the sheet evoke Callot's *Gobbi* series of 1616 and the *Balli di Sfessania* of 1618–20. Rather than a document of a particular performance, that is, studies like this seem to have been used by Callot as a storehouse of theatrical figures for multiple prints.

The figures appear to have been drawn freely from life, and the three needle holes along the short edge suggest that the sheet was once part of a portable sketchbook that Callot would have used while observing performances. Two sheets in the Pierpont Morgan Library also have these holes and sketches that are apparently related.[3] The man at the lower left of the Yale sheet drinks from a raised wine jug, a motif that also appears on one of the Morgan sheets, while the second Morgan sheet contains dancing dwarves and fiddlers, also similar to those on the Yale drawing. In all these drawings, each figure or figural grouping exists independently of the others. The lack of physical context indicates that Callot was interested in capturing figures in extremely varied kinds of motion rather than creating a unified composition.

Some of the figures—the fiddler at the lower center, for example—seem to wear *commedia dell'arte* masks. These freely executed studies reveal Callot's fascination with the improvisational aspect of court spectacle, particularly with the popular theatrical mode of the *commedia dell'arte*. Often incorporated into Medici festivities, the *commedia dell'arte* featured stock characters who typically improvised their roles. The figures in Callot's drawings maintain this air of spontaneity, although their depictions in prints of Giulio Parigi's theatrical designs have a choreo-

VERSO

graphed pomp that is entirely absent from the whimsical figure sketches. This difference between the drawings and the prints sheds light on Callot's creative process. One might view the drawing as a one-of-a-kind virtuoso performance, akin to the *commedia dell'arte*: it is impossible to replicate exactly, but Callot still succeeds in adapting these colorful characters as source material for his prints.

The verso of this drawing features a lightly rendered theater design that probably depicts one of the temporary stages that were erected for outdoor performances in Florence.[4] This sketch also replicates basic compositional elements that reappear in many of Callot's contemporary prints, such as the large *repoussoir* figures on the side gesturing into an open, receding, theatrical space.

A curious inscription of three circles and a dot appears in pen on the bottom of the drawing of figural sketches. Rosenberg was the first to call attention to this marking and observe its presence on three other drawings by Callot of comic figures, as well as on a drawing by Stefano della Bella of a horseman and a nymph.[5] The presence of the marking on the drawing by Stefano della Bella negates the possibility that the drawings with this inscription all came from a single sketchbook belonging to Callot and suggests that it is instead probably the mark of an early collector.[6]

NB

1 Ternois 1962, 52–53. These festivals usually commemorated important occasions such as weddings, the arrival of a foreign dignitary, or carnival. They tended to include three phases of performance: triumphal entries, mock battles or ballets, and theatrical *intermezzi*; for more on the festivals, see Blumenthal 1980 and Saslow 1996. Callot remained in Florence until the death of Cosimo de' Medici II in 1621.
2 Nancy 1992, nos. 137–170.
3 New York, Pierpont Morgan Library, inv. nos. 1972.14 and 1972.15; see New York 1975, nos. 12–13. A fourth drawing, Chicago, Art Institute, inv. no. 1940.59 (see Washington 1975, no. 63) is also apparently from the same sketchbook.
4 Washington 1975, 101.
5 The drawing by della Bella, formerly in the Baranowicz collection, was at Wildenstein when noted in New York 1975, 32.
6 Rosenberg, in Toronto et al. 1972, 142, speculated that the marking may be a collector's mark of Medici origin, but this remains uncertain. The three other Callot drawings probably from the same sketchbook (i.e., the above-mentioned two in the Morgan Library and the one in Chicago) also have these marks. Rosenberg also noticed a numbering system, possibly indicative of a common collector: the New York drawings by Callot have the numbers 114 and 116 marked on them in graphite, while the Chicago sheet has the number 107. Rhea Blok, curator of the forthcoming new edition of Lugt's *Marques de collections* has informed us (by electronic communication to John Marciari, 3 February 2003) that markings like the "OOO." are on two additional drawings: a Roman School *Fall of Phaeton*, sold Christie's, Paris, 27 November 2002, lot 26; and a drawing by Stefano della Bella with a dealer in Paris. Dr. Blok suggests that the marks might be the price codes of an early Florentine art dealer.

38 Giovanni Battista Caracciolo, called Il Battistello

Naples 1578–1635 Naples

Compositional Study, ca. 1616–20

Black and white chalk, with touches of red chalk, on blue paper, 35.7 × 31.2 cm (14 × 12¼ in.)

PROVENANCE: acquired from Hill-Stone, Inc., New York

REFERENCES: unpublished

Everett V. Meeks, B.A. 1901, Fund. 2005.128.1

The Neapolitan artist Giovanni Battista Caracciolo was probably trained by Belisario Corenzio, but with the arrival of Caravaggio in Naples, became the latter's first and most faithful Neapolitan disciple and, subsequently, one of the city's leading painters. He adopted Caravaggio's naturalism and tenebrism but executed both canvases and (unlike Caravaggio and most of his immediate followers) large fresco cycles, having learned the latter technique as a young artist. Similarly, where Caravaggio is notable for having made minimal use of drawings, Caracciolo remained faithful to the active drawing practice that he inherited from Corenzio. The present work, a new addition to Caracciolo's known corpus, is thus interesting as an example of "Caravaggesque" draftsmanship, in the sense that we here see the sort of pictorial problems that a Caravaggesque artist sought to resolve on paper. At the same time, this sheet demonstrates the quirky anatomy, elaborate draperies, and technically brilliant foreshortening that are characteristically Caracciolo's own.[1]

Drawings by Caracciolo remain rare finds, and fewer than 120 sheets have been convincingly connected to the artist.[2] Yet, comparison with those sheets, and particularly with the large group of drawings now in Stockholm,[3] dispels any doubt about the attribution of the present work. Every aspect of the sheet is consistent with those drawings. The elaborately folded or gathered draperies, which might be considered a holdover from his training under the Mannerist Corenzio, compare to those of the *Kneeling Gentlewoman*, *Madonna and Child*, and several *Drapery Studies* in Stockholm.[4] The slashes that indicate eyes and mouth with brilliantly minimalist gestures (one might note, especially, the two faces—one of them indicated only by the hints of eyes, nose, and mouth—to the right of the bearded figure's left elbow) are likewise found throughout the Stockholm drawings. Even the oddly small head of the figure at far right, loosely connected to his neck, compares to that of the *Kneeling Gentlewoman*, while the "disjointed" limbs recall, for example, those of the so-called *Three Lazzaroni* in the Louvre.[5] Above all, the drama of the sheet, in which the viewer senses the artist's attempt to capture the emotion of the scene as he tried out the group's overlapping poses and twisting positions while paying relatively little attention to their anatomy, is consistent with the very spirit of Caracciolo's art.

This compositional study cannot be definitively linked to any of Caracciolo's extant works. It could be an early preparatory study for the fresco of *The Miracle of Saint Simon Stock* in the vault of the Saint Simon Stock chapel in Santa Teresa agli Studi in Naples, which Caracciolo painted in 1616–17.[6] The drawing and fresco both include a group of figures at right reaching or leaning down toward a fallen figure at left; the drawing also compares very closely in materials and technique to the studies for the project now in Stockholm.[7] If not for the fresco in Santa Teresa, the work might instead be an early idea for Caracciolo's canvas of the *Miracle of Saint Anthony* in San Girolamo dei Genovesi, also painted in around 1620.[8] In neither of those works, however, nor in any other extant painting, do figures reach down for such a dramatically foreshortened figure as is indicated at lower left here, in Caracciolo's typical shorthand.[9] In sum, there is too little evidence to draw a firm conclusion about the function of this drawing, and it could simply be for a project that never advanced to completion. Regardless of its link to any painting, however, the sheet remains a dramatic demonstration of the artist's working process and a key new addition to Caracciolo's work.

JJM

1 On Caracciolo, see especially Causa 2000, Naples 1991, Prohaska 1978, and Stoughton 1973. Important insights are also found in London–Washington 1982–83.

2 On Caracciolo's drawings, see Causa 2000, 153–174, as well as Causa Picone 1993 and Moir 1970.

3 Moir 1970 remains the most complete discussion of these sheets, but see also, more recently, Bjurström and Magnusson 1998, nos. 845–871.

4 Stockholm, Nationalmuseum, inv. nos. NM 1749/1863, NM 1689/1863, NM 1709/1863, NM 1710/1863, and NM 1711/1863; Bjurström and Magnusson 1998, nos. 849, 851, and 865–867. These are just a selection of many sheets that might be compared.

5 Paris, Louvre, inv. no. 9605; Causa 2000, no. G33 (fig. 133).

6 Causa 2000, no. A47.

7 See especially the preparatory drawing for that fallen figure, Stockholm, Nationalmuseum, inv. no. NM 1752/1863; Bjurström and Magnusson 1998, no. 846.

8 Causa 2000, no. A63.

9 Caracciolo's abbreviated notations of form make it difficult to determine whether we have two figures, or one figure and an alternate sketch for the position of the head, at lower left.

39 Francesco Curradi
Florence 1570–1661 Florence

Half-Length Female Figure (recto); *Seated Soldier* (verso), ca. 1620–25

Black and white chalk on buff paper, 27.2 × 22.4 cm (10 11/16 × 8 13/16 in.)

INSCRIPTIONS: recto, at right, in pen and brown ink: *A Maggiori comprò in Roma nel 1816*

PROVENANCE: Alessandro Maggiori (L. 3005b); Pier Giulio Breschi (L. 2079b); Claudio Argentieri (L. 486b); mark "JGE" (perhaps J. C. Gentry, Lugano); acquired from Nissman, Abromson, Brookline, Mass.

REFERENCES: *YUAG Bulletin* (2004): 158

Frederick M. Clapp, B.A. 1901, M.A. 1911, Fund. 2003.96.2

Despite a long and successful career working for the Medici, Francesco Curradi—like most Florentine artists of the seventeenth century—is little known today.[1] He received his early training in the studio of Giovanni Battista Naldini (see cat. no. 18) and matriculated in the Accademia del Disegno at the age of twenty. Like most of his contemporaries, Curradi was a prolific draftsman and he developed an individual manner of drawing, particularly in soft chalks on rough paper, as seen in the present work. Most of his paintings, like those of his slightly older and better-known contemporaries Passignano (Domenico Cresti) and Jacopo da Empoli, show the rich pageantry, joined with pictorial simplicity, that represent the equal influences of the Medici court and of the Counter-Reformation.

The recto drawing of a half-length woman, perhaps an image of the goddess Flora or some other allegorical figure, cannot be linked to any of Curradi's paintings but, like other drawings of female heads by Curradi, might have begun as an experiment in facial expressions and bodily gestures.[2] Indeed, the figure evokes the melancholy sentimentality that would become increasingly characteristic of Florentine art later in the seventeenth century in the work of such artists as Carlo Dolci and Cesare Dandini, who studied with Curradi. Similar figures and formats were often used by Dolci and Dandini for historiated portraits, but given the absence of any identifiable likeness and the heavy working

RECTO

FIGURE 39A | Francesco Curradi, *Rinaldo and Armida*, ca. 1620–25. Florence, private collection.

VERSO

of this sheet, it might be more easily considered a drawing simply for the sake of drawing than as a study to clarify a figure for a painting. In any case, with a minimum of detail despite the layers of chalk, it is a masterwork by an artist fully in command of his media. The figure emerges from a soft sfumato haze as Curradi allows the texture of the paper, as much as the pressure of his hand, to draw marks from his chalk.

The verso of this sheet has been identified by Roberto Contini as a preparatory sketch for Curradi's painting of *Rinaldo and Armida* (fig. A).[3] Curradi painted a series of mythological and literary subjects in the early 1620s, including many for Carlo de' Medici,[4] and the similarity of the painting to those documented works allows this sheet to be securely dated to the same period. The drawing is a characteristic preparatory figure study by Curradi, similar to many of the nearly two hundred sheets by the artist in the Uffizi. As was typical of his figure studies of this type, the drawing matches the finished painting almost exactly, with only a few minor changes to Rinaldo's armor.[5]

The early history of this sheet is unknown, but its provenance since the early nineteenth century is fully documented. As recorded in his inscription on the verso, the famous collector Alessandro Maggiori purchased this drawing in Rome in 1816. Like most of Maggiori's collection, this sheet then passed to Pier Giulio Breschi, whose collection was then acquired *en bloc* by Claudio Argentieri. It remained in the Argentieri family until the collection was dispersed in the late 1950s.[6] This sheet was probably then acquired by J. C. Gentry of Lugano (the "JGE" mark at lower right is thought to be his), whose drawings have been sold over the past few years.

JJM

1 Curradi has not been the subject of an extended study; the most complete notes on his works are McCorquodale's entries in London–Cambridge 1979, 30–34; Cantelli 1983, 53–55; and Contini 1989.
2 For example, Paris, Louvre, inv. no. 31, black chalk, with touches of white, on tan paper partially prepared with gray wash, 24.5 × 18.9 cm; see Paris 1982a, no. 43.
3 For the painting, see Sacchetti 1989, 29 and 31.
4 See Chiarini 1999.
5 On Curradi's preparatory studies, see especially Contini 1989.
6 The Yale University Art Gallery's study by Barocci of *Saint Francis* (inv. no. 1975.31) was also in the Maggiori, Breschi, and Argentieri collections. On Maggiori, see Dania 1995.

40 Daniele Crespi
?Milan ca. 1597/99–1630 Milan

The Mocking of Christ, ca. 1630

Black chalk, 21 × 24.5 cm (8¼ × 9⅝ in.)

PROVENANCE: private collection, Cleveland; private collection, New York; acquired from Monroe Warshaw, New York

REFERENCES: *YUAG Bulletin* (2003): 154

Everett V. Meeks, B.A. 1901, Fund. 2002.6.1

Despite a brief career that lasted little more than a decade, Daniele Crespi was, before his untimely death around age thirty, one of the foremost painters in Milan.[1] His first training was probably with Guglielmo Caccia, il Moncalvo, and he later studied the works of Giovanni Battista Crespi, il Cerano, and Giulio Cesare Procaccini, the leading Milanese painters of the previous generation. Around the year 1623, however, Daniele Crespi broke from the model of these masters, a shift that is probably related to his additional study of Emilian, Tuscan, and Genoese art. By the later 1620s, Crespi seems also to have absorbed the influence of Caravaggio and the Carracci,[2] and he is seen today as one of the key figures in moving Lombard art away from the Mannerist style of the later Cinquecento and toward the clear, monumental Baroque.

The Mocking of Christ has all the characteristics of Crespi's art. The intense emotion seen especially in the kneeling foreground figures is a benchmark of the Lombard Seicento, and the energetic, crowded composition similarly recalls Crespi's roots in the work of Cerano, Morazzone, Procaccini, and other Milanese artists of the first decades of the seventeenth century. The monumental figure of Christ, in turn, hints at Crespi's departure from those models. Another certain precedent for the composition is Titian's *Mocking of Christ* (Paris, Louvre), then in the church of Santa Maria delle Grazie, Milan.[3]

Crespi spent the final years of his life at work on two large cycles for the Carthusian

FIGURE 40A | Daniele Crespi, *The Mocking of Christ*, ca. 1630. Pavia, Certosa.

monasteries at Garegnano and Pavia. A *Mocking of Christ* or *Crowning with Thorns* in the small cloister at the Certosa di Pavia (fig. A) is the only known painting of the subject by Crespi, and the present drawing is probably related to that fresco. There are evident differences between the two compositions, but the drawing is in the style of Crespi's *primi pensieri*, and there are often significant changes from these first sketches to the final paintings in his late work; the general trend of these changes is toward a painting that is simpler and calmer than the energetic drawings, a pattern also seen in this case.[4] Moreover, the wall in the cloister allotted to *The Mocking of Christ* is only half as wide as the walls for the other Passion scenes, but it might be presumed that Crespi had not foreseen this at the early stage when he made the Yale sketch, the proportions of which are more like the wider scenes. The arrangement of figures and the dimensions of the space in this drawing do indeed fit well alongside the other, wider cloister frescoes. Crespi's changes to the composition, making it narrower and reducing the number of figures, would probably have been made in a subsequent drawing,[5] but no other drawings for *The Mocking of Christ* or any of the other scenes in the cloister are known today.

Crespi also used pen and ink for his *primi pensieri* and generally used pen lines to reinforce and fix the contours of drawings begun with black chalk. Those pen lines are absent here, but the drawing shows the typical abbreviations Crespi used for heads and hands, and there can be no question about its attribution. The absence of pen lines might have to do with its being a preparatory study for a relatively unimportant part of the large fresco cycle in Pavia, a work done more quickly than the prominent frescoes in the choir of the church. The cloister frescoes, moreover, are among the last of Crespi's works and may have been executed with even greater rapidity than the rest of the cycle, and perhaps wholly by assistants, because as Crespi was completing work in 1630, plague broke out in Milan.[6] Crespi rushed home, leaving Pavia on 21 June, but by 19 July he was dead, as were his mother, his wife, and their two sons. With Crespi's death—and with the broader devastation of the city by the plague—the great age of Milanese art begun by Carlo and Federico Borromeo came to a close.[7]

JJM

1. On Crespi, see especially Neilson 1996, as well as Neilson's entry on the painter in *Grove Dictionary* 8:147–149. More recently, see also Bora 2003.
2. On Crespi's formation, see Neilson 1996, Introduction, especially 7–11, and Frangi 1996. Gregori 1973 also proposes a trip to Rome as a factor in Crespi's stylistic evolution.
3. Titian's painting, which remained in Milan until carried to Paris by Napoleon's troops, was a model for many important Milanese paintings of the early seventeenth century. For further examples and discussion, see Bober 1985, 63ff.
4. Neilson 1973, 385, writes of another Crespi composition that "this change from drawing to painting, from Lombard technique and emotion to the calm and considered final work is typical of Daniele." For further examples, compare Crespi's drawing of the *Adoration of the Magi* (New York, Pierpont Morgan Library, inv. no. 1981.41, pen and brown ink and wash over charcoal; Neilson 1996, fig. 82A) to the final fresco in the choir of the Certosa di Pavia (Neilson 1996, fig. 56F), or the *Raymond Diocrès* (Milan, Ambrosiana, Cod. F. 271 inf. n. 3, pen and black chalk and brown wash on prepared paper, 21.1 × 31.1 cm) and the related fresco in the Certosa di Garegnano.
5. Such a *modello* would presumably have been in a style and technique like that of the *Saint Ugo Blessing the Certosa outside Grenoble* (Milan, Ambrosiana, Cod. F. 266 inf. n. 37, pen and brown ink and wash, over black chalk, with white heightening, on prepared paper, 26.7 × 34.3 cm; see Neilson 1996, fig. 73) for a fresco in the Certosa di Garegnano (Neilson 1996, fig. 40B). Similarly, compare the *primo pensiero* for the *Adoration of the Shepherds* in the choir of the Certosa di Pavia (Paris, private collection, pen and brown ink and wash, 25.5 × 19 cm; Neilson 1996, fig. 83) with the *modello* for the same scene (Stockholm, Nationalmuseum, inv. no. NMH 1086/1863, pen and brown ink and wash over black chalk, with white heightening, on gray paper; Neilson 1996, fig. 82B).
6. The ruinous condition of the cloister frescoes, even after the restorations of 1986–87 (fig. A, taken in 2002), makes accurate attribution impossible, but Neilson 1996, 53–54, no. 48, has suggested that they may have been executed mainly or wholly by Crespi's assistants, possibly even after his death. This may also account for some of the changes in the compositions.
7. New York 2002a, 11. As Neilson 1973, 385, notes, the plague of 1630 is the one made famous in Alessandro Mazzoni's *I Promessi Sposi*.

41 Jacob Gerritsz. Cuyp
Dordrecht 1594–1652 Dordrecht

Portrait of Two Gentlemen from Dordrecht, ca. 1630

Black chalk heightened with white, with a few touches of black ink, on buff paper, 16.8 × 27.9 cm (7 5/16 × 11 in.)

INSCRIPTIONS: recto, bottom left, in black chalk: *JG* [monogram] *CVÿP F*; on mount, lower left, in graphite: *J. G. Cuyp*

PROVENANCE: John Percival, 1st Earl of Egmont (1683–1748); John T. Graves; Robert Hoe (sale, New York, Anderson Auction Company, 15–19 April 1912, Library of Robert Hoe, Part III. A–K, no. 949); Yale University Library (anonymous donor, 1957)

REFERENCES: Eisler 1958, 87; H-B and L, no. 368; Dordrecht 1977–78, 104, n. 1; New York–Paris 1977–78, 45, n. 4; Nagasaki 1993–94, 64; Athens 2002, 138, no. 2; Dordrecht 2002, 75–77 and no. d5

Egmont Collection, Yale Library Transfer. 1961.63.20

Jacob Gerritsz. Cuyp was the son of a glass painter, Gerrit Gerritsz. Cuyp, and the father of the best-known artist of the family, Aelbert Cuyp. Jacob's younger half-brother, Benjamin Gerritsz. Cuyp, was also a painter. Jacob entered the Guild of Saint Luke in Dordrecht in 1617. The largest part of Jacob's painted oeuvre are portraits, but he also painted subjects from the Bible, allegories, genre scenes, still lifes, and animals: a set of twelve engravings by Reinier van Persyn, *Diversa Animalia Quadrupedia ad vivum delineate . . .*, published in Antwerp in 1641, shows his facility for animal studies. Although perhaps about 120 paintings by Jacob—or by himself and his son Aelbert—have survived, his drawn oeuvre is much more limited. Some fifteen drawings are now thought to be by his hand, plus two made in conjunction with his son—and several of these attributions are still tentative.[1] Only two drawings, including *Portrait of Two Gentlemen of Dordrecht*, are signed. Further drawings by Jacob Cuyp may well exist, wrongly attributed to other artists. According to Houbraken he studied with Abraham Bloemaert in Utrecht,[2] but Jacob spent most of his life in Dordrecht and was the major artist there in the first half of the seventeenth century.

Although the two men in Yale's drawing may appear somewhat self-consciously posed, they do seem to relate comfortably to each other, and the scene has considerable natural charm. The man at the left looks straight at the viewer with an expression that is difficult to characterize, seeming perhaps as though about to speak. The second man, shown in profile, is looking at the first. Although both are individualized and probably represent specific persons, their identity has not come down to us. Haverkamp-Begemann suggested that the drawing might be an independent work, and that, in any case,

FIGURE 41A | Jacob Gerritsz. Cuyp, *Boy Catching a Goat*, 1630s(?). New Haven, Yale University Art Gallery.

the two men, with their elegant costumes and accompanied by playful hunting dogs, represent the upper social classes of the town of Dordrecht.[3] The clothes the men are wearing were in fashion around the year 1630. Dordrecht itself, in a view from the south, is seen in the distance.[4]

The assured and lively handling of the black chalk is evidence of Cuyp's self-confidence in this medium, which is that of most of his extant drawings. Another drawing by Cuyp in Yale's collection (fig. A) is similar in feeling and indeed in composition to *Two Gentlemen*, with a boy catching a goat on a rise in the foreground, plants in the lower right corner, and considerable detail in the middle- and background, in this case several other figures chasing goats, and ships at sea in the distance.[5] Another drawing, in red and black chalk, with similar confident yet sensitive handling as the two drawings at Yale is the *Portrait of a Nineteen-Year-Old Man* in the Institut Néerlandais, Paris, dated 1630.[6] Yet another drawing similar to this group is *Seated Shepherdess*, preparatory for a painting of 1628. Since very few of Cuyp's drawings are related to known paintings, comparison of the *Seated Shepherdess* and the painting is useful in showing how some of the freedom and natural quality of Cuyp's drawings tended to be lost when the figure was combined with others and translated into the more formal medium of paint.[7]

SB

1 See Dordrecht 2002, passim; for the drawings, 75–81, 194–199; for prints after Jacob Cuyp, 198–199, and Hollstein DF 5:103; for the Persyn prints, Hollstein DF 17:73–74, nos. 11–23.
2 Houbraken 1718–21, 1:238; Houbraken 1976, 1:238.
3 Dordrecht 2002, 75.
4 See H-B and L, and Dordrecht 2002.
5 Inv. no. 1961.61.71, black chalk, 15.3 × 21.1 cm; H-B and L, no. 369; Dordrecht 2002, no. d8.
6 Inv. no. 3864; New York–Paris 1977–78, no. 28; Dordrecht 2002, no. d3.
7 Painting in Amsterdam, Rijksmuseum, inv. no. A1793; drawing in Darmstadt, Hessisches Landesmuseum, inv. AE 649; see Dordrecht 2002, nos. 7 (cat. rais. 13), d6. According to Haverkamp-Begemann, the models in *Seated Shepherdess* were probably the painter's wife and son (Dordrecht 2002, 77).

42 Simon Vouet
Paris 1590–1649 Paris

Two Women, ca. 1630–35

Black and white chalk on tan paper, laid down, 39.9 × 24.8 cm (15 11/16 × 9 3/4 in.)

INSCRIPTIONS: recto, lower right, in pen and brown ink: *Simon Vouet / 5.1* (illegible)

PROVENANCE: John Percival, 1st Earl of Egmont (1683–1748); John T. Graves; Robert Hoe (sale, New York, Anderson Auction Company, 15–19 April 1912, Library of Robert Hoe, Part 3, A–K, no. 949); Yale University Library (anonymous donor, 1957)

REFERENCES: Crelly 1962, 230, no. 157C; H-B and L, no. 28; Toronto et al. 1972, 224, under no. 150; Brejon de Lavergnée 1987, 67–68, no. 47; Cleveland–Cambridge–Ottawa 1989–90, no. 57; *Handbook*, 206

Egmont Collection, Yale Library Transfer. 1961.66.34

As founder of the early modern school of French painting, Simon Vouet's importance to the history of French art cannot be overstated. By blending the latest trends in Romano-Bolognese art with aspects of earlier French traditions, like the Mannerism of Fontainebleau, Vouet became unsurpassed in Paris for a mode of grand decorative painting where figures in swirling draperies glide effortlessly across the surface of his canvases in slow, measured rhythms. As the second non-Italian *principe* of the Accademia di San Luca in Rome during his long sojourn in Italy, and later as first painter to Louis XIII upon his return to France in 1627, Vouet introduced many of the Italianate principles that were later used by his students and their contemporaries as part of the ideological foundation for the fledgling French Académie Royale de Peinture et de Sculpture. Beginning with Charles Le Brun—his most celebrated pupil, who became first painter to Louis XIV and founding director of the Académie—the majority of the leaders of French art for the next two centuries were part of a direct line of teachers and students whose artistic parentage can be traced back to Vouet.

The present drawing depicts a young woman in deep thought standing in near profile, with a subsidiary study of the head and torso of another woman, at slightly larger scale.[1] These two women resemble the figures of Pharaoh's daughter and her ladies in a tapestry cartoon illustrating the *Finding of Moses*, one of a series of eight Old Testament subjects commissioned by Louis XIII soon after Vouet returned from Italy, but the connection is not a direct one.[2] The fact that the exact purpose of the Yale sheet remains unknown is not unusual. There are many extant figure drawings by Vouet, but for reasons that remain unclear, most of his composition sketches are lost. This often makes it difficult to know the commissions to which some of his numerous figure studies relate.

FIGURE 42A | Simon Vouet, *Woman Rushing Forward*, ca. 1630–35. Paris, École des Beaux-Arts.

FIGURE 42B | Simon Vouet, *Woman Leaning Forward with Subsidiary Study of a Hand Holding a Staff*, ca. 1630–35. Paris, Musée du Louvre.

Yale's *Two Women* is close to other drawings of the early 1630s, such as the *Woman Rushing Forward* in the École des Beaux-Arts in Paris (fig. A),[3] the *Woman Leaning Forward with Subsidiary Study of a Hand Holding a Staff* in the Musée du Louvre in Paris (fig. B),[4] and further studies in Amsterdam and New York.[5] Drawn rapidly with black and white chalk on tan paper, they all reveal Vouet's mastery of both the human form and drapery. Searching and often reworked contours render the figures three-dimensional and, when necessary, sets them in motion. Details of faces and anatomical extremities, such as hands and feet, are frequently omitted unless a specific emotion or gesture is being studied. Often, these kinds of details and their variations are examined with additional studies on the same sheet, resulting in an extremely elegant *mise-en-page*. As Barbara Brejon de Lavergnée has noted, in the 1630s Vouet's draperies are executed with a nervous, busy line and strong contrasts of light and dark.[6] The chiaroscuro, often realized with short, tightly spaced parallel hatching, endows the draperies with volume. The nervousness of the line animates his already well-conceived figures and, when needed, heightens their motion. Studies like the Yale Vouet serve as an eloquent reminder of the artist's insistence on the importance of drawing after the posed model throughout his career.

ALC

1 Curiously, William Crelly once doubted the attribution to Vouet (oral communication), but since then, Pierre Rosenberg, Barbara Brejon de Lavergnée, and Hilliard Goldfarb have all correctly returned it to his oeuvre. See Goldfarb in Cleveland–Cambridge–Ottawa 1989–90, 119.
2 First noted in 1964 by Pierre Rosenberg in the draft of a text on the French drawings at Yale in the curatorial files of the Department of Prints, Drawings, and Photographs at the Art Gallery.
3 Simon Vouet, *Woman Rushing Forward*, black and white chalk on tan paper, 38.9 × 21.7 cm, Paris, École Nationale Supérieure des Beaux-Arts, inv. no. M1282; see Brejon de Lavergnée 1987, 88, no. 42; and Emmanuelle Brugerolles and David Guillet in Paris–Geneva–New York 2001, 58–62, no. 14. It should be noted that my comparison is for the recto only, as someone in Vouet's studio probably executed the verso of this drawing.
4 Simon Vouet, *Woman Leaning Forward with Subsidiary Study of a Hand Holding a Staff*, black and white chalk on tan paper, 23 × 20.9 cm, Paris, Louvre, inv. no. RF 28228; see Brejon de Lavergnée 1987, 67–68, no. 37.
5 For these two sheets in the Rijksprentenkabinett, Amsterdam, and the Metropolitan Museum of Art, New York, see Brejon de Lavergnée 1987, 67–68, no. 46, and Bean and Turčić 1986, 289, no. 325, respectively.
6 Brejon de Lavergnée 1987, 24–30.

43 Giovanni Francesco Barbieri, called Guercino
Cento 1591–1666 Florence

Caricature of a Man Wearing a Large Hat, ca. 1630–40

Pen and brown ink, 30.4 × 23 cm (11¹⁵⁄₁₆ × 9¹⁄₁₆ in.)

INSCRIPTIONS: recto, lower right, in graphite: *305/230/1/c*

PROVENANCE: partly illegible collector's stamp on recto, lower left, possibly L.106, Alfonso IV d'Este (1634–1662); Sotheby's, London, 20 May 1985, lot 484 (as Bolognese 17th century); Mia Weiner, New York; Edmund P. Pillsbury

REFERENCES: Cambridge–Ottawa–Cleveland 1991, 209, under no. 92; *YUAG Bulletin* (1991): 104–105

Gift of Edmund P. Pillsbury, B.A. 1965. 1991.39.2

As David Stone notes in his discussion of similar works by Guercino, the word "caricature" (Italian *caricatura*) derives from *ritratti carichi*, "loaded portraits."[1] Leonardo da Vinci's grotesque heads were precedents for drawings of this type, but the genre was only fully developed in the early seventeenth century, particularly by the Carracci and the artists trained in their academy. Guercino, who had trained under the Carracci, became one of the foremost caricaturists of the seventeenth century, along with Annibale Carracci, Gian Lorenzo Bernini (see cat. no. 55), and Pier Francesco Mola (1612–1666).[2] Caricatures were an amusing drawing exercise, but the genre had serious roots grounded in the Carracci reform of painting. Figure studies like Yale's drawing by Domenichino (cat. no. 31) were the most obvious aspect of the Carracci reform, but a caricature's distortion or overemphasis of the appearance of a particular feature of a person required equally careful study of the subject's actual appearance. That is, both the figure drawings and the caricatures were "from life" or "from nature" and might be seen as a fundamental part of the Carracci project of turning away from the Neoplatonic ideals that characterize much of later sixteenth-century Italian art, in which beauty was thought to reside in the mind, rather than in nature. Moreover, the caricature's effectiveness lay in its ugliness, and the idea of truth revealed though gross distortion was the type of *concetto*, or conceit, that was endlessly fascinating to early Baroque artists.[3] This sheet is one of scores of caricatures by Guercino, but it is among the largest, most forceful, and most humorous of those drawings.[4] A sketch of similar size and subject matter—an emaciated man in a large hat—is in the Philadelphia Museum of Art,[5] and there are numerous sheets among the many caricatures in the Royal Library at Windsor that might be compared to this one.[6]

Dating of Guercino's caricatures has proven notoriously difficult. One of the drawings at Windsor that is closest in style to the Yale sheet was done on the back of a letter dated 1635.[7] Guercino often reused paper in his workshop, so this letter cannot be used to establish the date of the Windsor drawing, much less the Yale drawing, with any certainty. Nonetheless, rough parallels might be drawn between the pen work of a caricature like Yale's and other types of pen drawings made by Guercino in the 1630s,[8] so that the 1635 letter gives at least an approximate date.

Guercino resided in his native Cento for most of the 1630s, but by that point his fame had spread so widely that requests for his paintings came from as far away as England. He often worked in nearby Bologna, of course, and in 1632–33 was summoned to Modena to paint portraits for the young Duke Francesco I d'Este. The Yale caricature might have been drawn during that trip, for the smudged collector's stamp in the lower left corner seems to be that of Alfonso IV d'Este, Francesco I's son. It is not difficult to imagine that Guercino drew caricatures while engaged in painting portraits at the Este court, and a caricature made for Francesco I could well have passed into his son's collection.

The subsequent provenance of the drawing remains unknown until its appearance at auction in 1985, where it was catalogued simply as "Bolognese, 17th century." Mia Weiner recognized the drawing as the work of Guercino, an attribution subsequently confirmed by Diane de Grazia and David Stone.[9]

JJM

1 Stone in Cambridge–Ottawa–Cleveland 1991, 194.

2 The Yale Art Gallery also owns a typical caricature by Mola (inv. no. 1975.42.2, pen and brown ink and brown and gray washes, 12.3 × 19.4 cm), which has only recently been published, by Boorsch and Marciari in Costamagna, Härb, and Prosperi Valenti Rodinò 2005, no. 121.

3 On caricature in seventeenth-century Italy, see especially Princeton–Cleveland–Los Angeles 1981–82, 25–52; reprinted as Lavin 1990, 19–50.

4 Large groups of Guercino's caricatures survive at the Princeton Art Museum and the Royal Library at Windsor. For the most complete discussion of them, see Mahon and Turner 1989, 117–121, and Cambridge–Ottawa–Cleveland 1991, 192–209.

5 Philadelphia Museum of Art, inv. no. 1984-77-1, pen and brown ink and brown wash, 29.2 × 20.8 cm; see Stone in Cambridge–Ottawa–Cleveland 1991, no. 92.

6 See especially Mahon and Turner 1989, nos. 327 and 328.

7 Mahon and Turner 1989, no. 327.

8 For comparative examples, see the studies for Guercino's *Martyrdom of Saint Bartholomew* of 1635–36 (Cambridge–Ottawa–Cleveland 1991, nos. 32–35) or the *Bearded Man with a Celestial Globe* at Princeton (Cambridge–Ottawa–Cleveland 1991, no. 36).

9 See Cambridge–Ottawa–Cleveland 1991, 209.

44 Theodoor van Thulden
's-Hertogenbosch 1606–
1669 's-Hertogenbosch

(A) *The Companions of Ulysses Open the Bag of Winds* and (B) *Ulysses Receives the Homage of the Loyal Serving Women while Eurycleia Informs Penelope of Ulysses' Return*, ca. 1632

Black chalk, (A) 21.5 × 33 cm (8½ × 13 in.); (B) 17.8 × 30.5 cm (7 × 13¾ in.)

WATERMARK: (A) foolscap, similar to Churchill nos. 337–339, a type used in Dutch and French papers of the seventeenth century

INSCRIPTIONS: (A) recto, lower right, in black chalk: *16*; verso, upper edge, in pen and brown ink: *Ulisse aborde en Eolie, & s'y r'affrechit durant quelque temps, apres le quel Eolie / Roy de cette isle le remet, du son(?) vent(?). Siet(?) page 13;* (B) recto, in pen and brown ink, along right side of sheet: *Euriclee nourrice d'Ulysse, advertit Penelope du retour du prince son Maistre, les domestiques duquel le viennent tous saluer, & nous apprennent par leur exemple; que le contentement des vrays serviteurs d'une maison ne s'entretient que par la presence de leur maistre*; lower right: *44*.

PROVENANCE: Herbert Feist, New York; Phillips, New York, 8 June 1983, lot 50; Anne-Marie Logan

REFERENCES: Béguin, Guillaume, and Roy 1985, 235, 297; Wood 1990, 3–53; *YUAG Bulletin* (1997–98): 105

Gift of Anne-Marie Logan. 1997.45.2.1–2

Theodoor van Thulden spent his early career in Antwerp where, from 1621 to 1622, he trained under the portrait painter Abraham van Blyenberch; by 1626 van Thulden was listed as a master in the painter's guild. His early works are strikingly Mannerist in style, a tendency that was reinforced by his trip to France from 1631 to 1633, where he made drawings after the sixteenth-century frescoes in the Château de Fontainebleau. While van Thulden is commonly described as a pupil of Peter Paul Rubens, the influence of Rubens is detectable in van Thulden's work only after his return from France in 1634, when he collaborated with Rubens on designs for the Triumphal Entry of Ferdinand of Spain into Antwerp, and not in drawings like the two described here.[1]

Van Thulden's early fascination with the School of Fontainebleau, and with the decorations of the Galerie d'Ulysse in particular, was shared by other Northern artists of his time including Rubens, Abraham van Diepenbeeck, and the brothers Louis and Mathieu Le Nain, who borrowed and reused motifs from the frescoes in this room on multiple occasions.[2] The two Yale drawings are copies after Primaticcio's frescoes in the Galerie d'Ulysse and are preparatory designs for van Thulden's series of prints entitled *Les travaux d'Ulysse*, which was issued in multiple editions by various publishers between 1633 and 1640 (figs. A and B).[3] The prints, which reproduced the fifty-eight sequential episodes from Homer's *Odyssey* that Primaticcio painted in the gallery between 1541 and 1559, are the best remaining record of the decoration, which has since been destroyed.[4]

The first Yale drawing depicts the ill fortune that befell Ulysses and his crew during their homeward journey. They were almost

FIGURE 44A | Theodoor van Thulden, *The Companions of Ulysses Open the Bag of Winds*, from *Les travaux d'Ulysse*, Paris, 1640. New Haven, Yale University, Beinecke Rare Book and Manuscript Library.

FIGURE 44B | Theodoor van Thulden, *Ulysses Receives the Homage of the Loyal Serving Women*, from *Les travaux d'Ulysse*, Paris, 1640. New Haven, Yale University, Beinecke Rare Book and Manuscript Library.

home, within view of the shore, when Ulysses decided to sleep after nine restless days of navigating the ship. His companions, overcome with greed and curiosity, opened the mysterious bag containing storm winds that Aeolus, the god of winds, had given Ulysses as a means of ensuring his speedy return. Once opened, the bag released adverse winds that blew the ships far from their destination. In the drawing, Ulysses is shown in a sleeping posture, with his arm slung over his head, at the right edge of the boat as chaos erupts around him. The drawing, like Primaticcio's original, emphasizes the confusion of the moment: the contours of the ships are lost amid flailing limbs, windblown sails, and figures struggling to stay aboard. The composition is arranged around the central figure shown from behind, who still holds the bag of Aeolus. Faces personifying the escaped winds appear at the upper edge.

The second drawing presents a more complex narrative in its conflation of three closely related episodes from the *Odyssey*: the punishment of Melanthios, the joyful greeting Ulysses receives from his serving women, and Eurycleia rushing up the stairs to notify Penelope of her husband's long-awaited return. In contrast to the other drawing, which emphasizes the helplessness of Ulysses, this drawing portrays him in an appropriately heroic light. Ulysses stands triumphantly over Melanthios, the goatherder who had provided the enemy suitors with arms and suffered the punishment of having his hands, feet, ears, and genitals severed. The goatherder's detached hand and ears can be seen in the left foreground. The women embrace Ulysses warmly, while in the background, Eurycleia eagerly approaches the seated figure of Penelope. The juxtaposition of brutality, tenderness, and revelation imparts a heightened sense of emotion to this scene.

The attribution of these drawings hinges on their relationship to two albums of drawings in the Albertina in Vienna and the Bibliothèque Royale in Brussels. The Albertina album comprises fifty-five drawings in black and red chalk copied after the Galerie d'Ulysse, and the Brussels album includes drawings in a similar technique and medium, apparently by the same hand as the Vienna album, after other Fontainebleau works.[5] The graphic style of these two albums is very different from van Thulden's prints, and we agree with Jeremy Wood's reattribution of the albums to Abraham van Diepenbeeck instead of to van Thulden. As Wood notes, the album drawings compare in style to drawings securely attributed to van Diepenbeeck.[6] The albums might thus be those that, according to an annotation by Padre Sebastiano Resta, van Diepenbeeck made when he was sent to France by Rubens.[7] The authors of the latest catalogue of works by Theodoor van Thulden questioned Wood's hypothesis by arguing that Padre Resta is not a credible source and that there is no other proof of van Diepenbeeck's activity in France.[8] As Wood suggests, however, the likelihood that van Diepenbeeck made his own copies after the Galerie d'Ulysse and was intimately familiar with its frescoes is reinforced by the fact that he plagiarized the frescoes in his illustrations for several French books, including the *Temple des Muses* of 1655, to say nothing of Rubens's borrowings from the Galerie d'Ulysse, which were reliant on van Diepenbeeck's copies.[9]

The Yale drawings, by contrast, are among those that Wood convincingly argues are van Thulden's own drawings after Primaticcio.[10] They agree in style with van Thulden's prints and even have the same dimensions as the printed plates but are clearly not copies after the finished works. Indeed, van Thulden's drawings are far less detailed than are van Diepenbeeck's, presumably because the former were mainly aids to the production of the prints, rather than finished copies in their own right. Thus, Yale's van Thulden drawings are—like Yale's drawings by Bellange (cat. no. 34), Callot (cat. no. 37), and others—an interesting and important record of a printmaker's preparatory sketches.[11]

NB

1. Boston–Toledo 1993, 361.
2. Wood 2000, 156.
3. Hollstein DF 30:111–121, nos. 32–96. The inscription on the drawing of *Ulysses and the Serving Women* corresponds to the caption that accompanies the printed image. These captions describe the narrative and include a moral lesson in italics. The inscription for the *Bag of Winds* print, which does not appear on the Yale drawing, reads: "Deplorables effets de la tourmente, advenuë par l'imprudence des compagnons d'Ulysse, qui durant qu'il dormoit furent si mal avisez que d'ouvrir le sac de cuir ou estoient enfermez les vents; Bel exemple, ce me semble, pour confirmer la verité de ce commun dire; qu'il se faut tenir au bien que l'on a, sans s'opposer aux conseils de ceux qui nous l'ont fait, & qu'une trop grande curiosité tourne toujours à la ruine de ceux qui en sont les autheurs." The prints are signed with the monogram TvT and are numbered 1–58. These numbers also correspond to the numbers 16 and 44 that appear in the lower right corner of the Yale drawings. The prints reproduced here are from the edition published by François L'Anglois, Paris, 1640.
4. The Galerie d'Ulysse was on the second floor of the building situated between the main courtyard (the Cour du Cheval Blanc) and the Jardin des Pins at Fontainebleau. This building was demolished in 1738–39 and was replaced by the current brick-and-stone structure, the Louis XV wing. For a full treatment of the decoration, see Béguin, Guillaume, and Roy 1985, and Paris 1972–73, 480–481.
5. 's-Hertogenbosch–Strasbourg 1991, 117–126.
6. The attribution of the albums to van Thulden originated with the late-eighteenth-century collector François-Jean-Joseph Mols, who owned a large number of these drawings. Dimier 1900, 421, proposed that the drawings in the Vienna album should be attributed to van Diepenbeeck on stylistic grounds, but this attribution was subsequently ignored until Jeremy Wood's 1990 article. As Wood 1992, 328, explains: "The Fontainebleau copies [in Vienna and Brussels] show a heavy but broken use of outline, a somewhat grainy texture to the chalk, and considerable internal modeling—hatched and cross-hatched, or applied more smoothly—all of which are characteristic of securely attributed drawings by Van Diepenbeeck." On the other hand, drawings by van Thulden, including the Yale drawings, employ more curved contours and display much less tonal modeling.
7. This annotation appears on a drawing by van Diepenbeeck, which is a copy after Niccolo dell'Abbate's *Pietà* from Fleury-en-Bière, now in the Biblioteca Ambrosiana in Milan. Wood 1990, 9, Appendix 3.
8. Roy in 's-Hertogenbosch–Strasbourg 1991, 99–100 and 116.
9. Wood 2000, 166.
10. See Wood 1990, n. 82 in Appendix 3, for a list of these drawings that should be grouped as van Thuldens alongside the Yale drawings.
11. Following from Wood's clarification of the drawing styles of van Thulden and van Diepenbeeck, the reattribution of one other drawing at Yale should be noted. Inv. no. 1961.65.5, red chalk, 22 × 34.9 cm, a drawing after Rosso's *Twins of Catania* fresco in the Galerie François I at Fontainebleau, was formerly attributed to van Thulden (H-B and L, no. 620), but this red chalk study is so close to the style of the Vienna and Brussels albums that it should also be reattributed to van Diepenbeeck instead, as indicated by Wood 1990, n. 41 in Appendix 3.

45 Leonaert Bramer
Delft 1596–1674 Delft

Dead Christ Mourned by Angels, 1630s

Pen and black ink and gray wash on brown paper, 18.4 × 27.1 cm (7¼ × 10¹¹⁄₁₆ in.)

INSCRIPTIONS: recto, lower right, in pen and brown ink: *Leonard Bramer*

PROVENANCE: John Percival, 1st Earl of Egmont (1683–1748); John T. Graves; Robert Hoe (sale, New York, Anderson Auction Company, 15–19 April 1912, Library of Robert Hoe, Part 3, A–K, no. 949); Yale University Library (anonymous donor, 1957)

REFERENCES: H-B and L, no. 357; Milwaukee 1992, no. 27

Egmont Collection, Yale Library Transfer. 1961.62.2

Leonaert Bramer was unusual among his Dutch contemporaries in having spent the first fourteen years of his artistic career away from Holland. At the age of eighteen he left his native Delft and traveled through France to Italy, eventually living for more than ten years in Rome. He was a member of the *Bentvueghels* (Birds of a Feather) group of Netherlandish artists in Rome, which included Wouter Crabeth II and Cornelis van Poelenburch, and in Italy he enjoyed the patronage of Mario Farnese, Prince of Parma, and Cardinal Desiderio Scaglia. Bramer returned to Delft in 1628 and joined the Guild of Saint Luke in 1629; there he received commissions for palace decorations from the Stadtholder Frederick Henry and his nephew, Prince John Maurice of Nassau, and also from the Delft civic guard. These works, carried out in fresco, a most unusual medium for the Netherlands, are now destroyed, but an *Ascension* that Bramer painted on the ceiling of the Prinsenhof in Delft survives.[1] Influenced by Caravaggio, Bramer is known as a painter of night scenes, and he in turn was an influence on Rembrandt.

Bramer was prolific both as a painter and as a draftsman, and some 160 paintings and 1,300 drawings survive.[2] Although *Dead Christ Mourned by Angels* is monochromatic, many of Bramer's drawings were brightly colored, in an idiosyncratic technique and style that make them easily recognizable. The majority of Bramer's extant drawings were made in series, most of which were ends in themselves, although it has recently been shown that some of Bramer's sets of drawings were made as designs for the ceramic ware that was a sought-after product of Delft.[3] Although making images in series had been a common practice for prints since the fifteenth century, it was unusual to do so with drawings. Only a few of Bramer's contemporaries made similar series of drawings (other than as models for prints), and those were on religious subjects; Bramer's series illustrating classical or recent literary works were even more unusual.[4]

Other drawings by Bramer, including *Dead Christ Mourned by Angels*, have not been identified as part of any set. The technique of Yale's drawing, with its nervous calligraphy and strong contrasts of lights and darks, is typical of Bramer's work in the 1630s.[5] In fact, it is similar to a *Betrayal of Christ* signed and dated 1637,[6] and although Yale's drawing is less high and slightly less wide than that drawing, the *Dead Christ* appears to have been trimmed slightly at the top and right, and thus the two sheets might originally have been closer in size. The drawings, of course, may have been preparatory for paintings, and a number of paintings of the *Betrayal of Christ* exist or are documented,[7] but there seems to be no existing or documented painting that relates to Yale's drawing.

Yale's drawing was called *Dead Abel Mourned by Angels* by Haverkamp-Begemann and Logan, but in 1992 Frima Fox Hofrichter suggested that the subject was more probably *Dead Christ Mourned by Angels*, which seems likely.[8] As Hofrichter pointed out, the dead Abel is a rare subject, and when it is depicted the mourners are Adam and Eve, Abel's parents, rather than angels; there seems to be no example in art of the theme of the dead Abel mourned by angels. Although some of the texts that Bramer illustrated are unusual choices, these were probably commissions and thus not selected by the artist, and while he was tremendously inventive in creating compositions, Bramer, who was Catholic, is not known for inventing new iconographical types for biblical subjects. Two other images of the *Dead Christ Mourned by Angels* by Bramer are on the recto and verso of a sheet at Bowdoin College.[9] In these, Christ is shown lying on a slab, one drawing with the head in the foreground and the other with the feet, both strongly foreshortened as in the painting by Mantegna that surely provided Bramer's inspiration. According to Michiel Plomp, the Bowdoin sheet is part of a series.[10]

SB

1. Documents on Bramer are listed in Paul Huys Janssen, "Leonaert Bramer, His Biography as told by Documents," in Delft 1994, 13–34. Besides the article on documents, that exhibition catalogue includes thorough information on Bramer's work, as well as an essay on his patrons in Delft. The fundamental book for Bramer's paintings is Wichmann 1923; a summary catalogue of the paintings, based on Wichmann but with rejections and additions, is in Delft 1994, 277–309.
2. Delft 1994 also has an essay by Michiel C. Plomp, "Leonaert Bramer the Draughtsman," 182–208, which gives an overview of Bramer's activity in drawing, its place in his career, and its relation to the art of his time; 209–275 catalogues the drawings in the exhibition; a list of drawing sets is 310–320.
3. Plomp 1999.
4. Delft 1994, 203.
5. I wish to thank Michiel Plomp for sharing his ideas concerning the dating and other aspects of this drawing (electronic communication, 5 February 2005).
6. Milwaukee 1992, no. 23 (New York, private collection), also not identified as part of any set.
7. Wichmann 1923, nos. 126a, 127–129, and four additional ones listed in Delft 1994, 290.
8. Milwaukee 1992, no. 27.
9. Brunswick et al. 1985–86, no. 16; Milwaukee 1992, no. 28.
10. See Delft 1994, 314, set no. 19.

46 Pieter Jansz. Quast

Amsterdam 1605/06–1647 Amsterdam

Old Peasant Couple Seated, 1637

Red chalk on parchment, 13.3 × 14.3 cm (5¼ × 5⁹⁄₁₆ in.)

INSCRIPTIONS: recto, lower right, in red chalk: *PQuast / 1637*; in pen and black ink: *Pet. Quast Engraver / 1637* (date partially obscuring date in red chalk); verso: illegible inscription obscured by backing sheet

PROVENANCE: John Percival, 1st Earl of Egmont (1683–1748); John T. Graves; Robert Hoe (sale, New York, Anderson Auction Company, 15–19 April 1912, Library of Robert Hoe, Part 3, A–K, no. 949); Yale University Library (anonymous donor, 1957)

REFERENCES: H–B and L, no. 399

Egmont Collection, Yale Library Transfer. 1961.65.12

Pieter Quast, born in Amsterdam but spending from 1634 to 1644—about half of his relatively short working life—in The Hague, was among the earliest of the Netherlandish, and especially Dutch, group of artists whose primary subject matter was low-life characters—peasants, beggars, soldiers, street performers—in taverns or out-of-doors. In this he paralleled his contemporary Adriaen Brouwer, who moved early from Amsterdam to Antwerp, and the slightly younger Adriaen van Ostade, who worked all his life in Haarlem. Quast was probably also influenced by the grisaille paintings that combined words and images, often with didactic, moralizing messages, made by Adriaen van de Venne, who lived in The Hague from 1625 to 1662.[1] Rembrandt van Rijn, born in 1606 and thus a contemporary of Quast's, also made drawings and prints (although not paintings) of beggars, but Rembrandt's beggars are sympathetic renditions of individuals as opposed to Quast's more equivocal images; Rembrandt's oeuvre also includes a wider range of religious subjects, portraits, and landscapes than Quast's. That Quast did not necessarily view beggars sympathetically is suggested by the subtitle on his series of twenty-six etchings of beggars and peasants. The main title is *Tis al verwart gaeren* (literally, It Is All Confused Yarn, or It Is All a Tangle), but the subtitle is *Vermomde Bedelaaren en andere Gespuis* (Disguised Beggars and Other Scum). The view that beggars might be feigning disability in order to live without working was widespread in the Holland of his time, although that view coexisted with a genuinely charitable attitude toward the deserving poor.[2] But the cynicism expressed in the subtitle may be that of the publisher rather than Quast, since the first edition of the print series, in 1638, simply had the main title printed underneath the first image. A full title page—with the added subtitle—was apparently not associated with the series until its second edition, published by Claes Jansz. Visscher in 1640.[3]

Quast was influenced by the prints of Jacques Callot (for a sheet of figure studies by Callot, relating to some of his prints, see cat. no. 37), particularly the series of extravagant couples, the *Balli di Sfessania*, and the *Gobbi* (hunchbacked dwarves), both published about 1622, as well as the *Gueux* (beggars) of around 1622–23.[4] Quast was even sometimes called the "Dutch Callot." He seems also to have had a particular interest in the theater,[5] and these influences fused in the presentation of figures in drawings such as the one at Yale. There is a certain ambiguity in the image; the energy and tension in the figures hint that they could be *representations* of peasants—that is, theatrical, or invented, peasants, rather than real ones. The couple is shown as though on a shallow stage, with the man's right leg crossed over his left one at a jaunty angle, his head leaning on his right hand; his hat sports a curled feather similar to those in the Callot prints, and there is a suggestion—in the gestures and glances—of a narrative. If there is a narrative, however, it is not self-evident, and the peasant couple remains intriguing, leaving the viewer to wonder what the two are looking at, why the woman is pointing, and what, if anything, their expressions are meant to signify.

Some seventy engravings by Quast or by others after his designs are known,[6] and the numerous copies after these attest to their enormous popularity. The fact that many of Quast's drawings are on parchment—over fifty of these, mostly landscapes, are in the Louvre[7]—would also seem to be evidence of a widespread vogue for his work, as the luxurious support suggests they would have been destined for collectors. The contrast between the humble subjects and the costly material on which they were drawn may have added piquancy to their appeal. It has been suggested that the Dutch painter Paulus Potter followed Quast's lead in the use of parchment,[8] and Nadine Orenstein has observed that, besides Potter, Hendrick Hondius I and Gerrit de Heer, also working in The Hague in the 1630s and '40s, made drawings on parchment, so the practice may have had some particular raison d'être in that city.[9] In any case, despite the popularity of Quast's subjects, his work was apparently not sufficient to sustain him financially, and a few years after his return to Amsterdam he died destitute.

SB

1 No general study of Quast has been done since Bredius 1902, and Bredius 1915–22, 1:273–274. For van de Venne, see Bol 1989, especially 93–111.
2 These conflicting attitudes and the works of art reflecting them are thoroughly and perceptively discussed in Reinold 1981.
3 Hollstein DF 17:243, no. 7; Orenstein 1996, 204–205, nos. 483–509. For the title page, see Hoop Scheffer 1974, fig. 1.
4 Lieure 1924–29, nos. 279; 379–402; 407–426; and 479–503.
5 Stanton-Hirst 1982.
6 Hollstein DF 17:242–246.
7 Paris, Louvre, inv. nos. 22836–22872.
8 The Hague 1994–95, 40, and see 39, fig. 2; 42, fig. 7; 49, fig. 13; and nos. 32, 33, 36, 38.
9 By oral communication, 12 May 2005. I am grateful to Nadine Orenstein for sharing this observation with me; she hopes to find time to investigate this phenomenon more thoroughly. For Hondius, see Orenstein 1996.

47 Cornelis Vroom the Younger

Haarlem ca. 1591–1661 Haarlem

Panorama with a Country House before an Inland Sea, ca. 1638–40

Pen and brown ink, 29.2 × 44.8 cm (11½ × 17⅝ in.)

WATERMARK: arms of Burgundy and Austria, similar to Churchill nos. 264, 266, 269, and to Heawood no. 481

INSCRIPTIONS: recto, lower left, in brown ink: *cvroom* [CVR in monogram] *16_ _* [cut at bottom and indecipherable]; on old mount, lower left, in pencil: *Meyrhinge*

PROVENANCE: John Percival, 1st Earl of Egmont (1683–1748); John T. Graves; Robert Hoe (sale, New York, Anderson Auction Company, 15–19 April 1912, Library of Robert Hoe, Part III, A–K, no. 949); Yale University Library (anonymous donor, 1957)

REFERENCES: Paris et al. 1968, 175–176; H-B and L, no. 441; Keyes 1975, 83–84 and no. D26; Poughkeepsie 1976, 19; New York–Paris 1977–78, 184; Rutgers 1983, no. 131; Amsterdam–Boston–Philadelphia 1987–88, 519; Cambridge–Montreal 1988, no. 103; New Haven 1992, no. 13; *Grove Dictionary* 32:735

Egmont Collection, Yale Library Transfer. 1961.64.56

Cornelis Vroom received his first training from his father, the marine painting specialist Hendrick Cornelisz. Vroom, but abandoned marine painting to concentrate on other aspects of landscape painting and drawing. By his associations with other Haarlem artists, including Pieter Jansz. Saenredam, and through the influence of prints after the works of Adam Elsheimer and other Northerners who had lived in Italy, Vroom devised a lyrical, refined view of landscape, often taking high panoramic viewpoints that removed the bustle of everyday life from his scenes and replaced it with the deep calm seen here.[1] The present work, one of only thirty or forty surviving drawings by Vroom, has the meticulous, delicate pen work—at times becoming a stipple-drawing—that seems a deliberate counterpoint to the broad views of his compositions.[2]

This large sheet shows one of Vroom's characteristic panoramas, with bands of dark trees and the shadow of the dunes in the foreground leading the eye back into the landscape. There are two small figures near the wagon in the middle distance and some ships on the inland sea or estuary; the roof of a substantial country house peaks above the trees at left. Nonetheless, the drawing is a celebration of the landscape rather than of any human presence. The dark foreground creates a rather conventional *repoussoir*, something Vroom would have learned from Italianate models, but in contrast to the drawing by Claude in this exhibition (cat. no. 48), the view is not obviously mediated through a filter of classical literature and might instead be considered deliberately modern.

A few Netherlandish artists, including Hendrick Goltzius and Esaias van de Velde (see cat. no. 36) had experimented with the panoramic viewpoint earlier in the century,[3] but Vroom and other artists of the 1630s—Jan van Goyen and Pieter Jansz. Post among them—began an era with a new commitment to broad, naturalistic views. The detail of

FIGURE 47A | Cornelis Vroom the Younger, *Panorama with a Country House*, ca. 1638–40. Paris, Institut Néerlandais.

Vroom's precise pen work might be considered a figment of such conscious realism. As celebrations of the characteristic Dutch landscape, such scenes were necessarily straightforward and set in the present, although we know that artists often took liberties with topographical details and that Vroom and his contemporaries surely created these prospects with a rich set of moralizing or nationalistic associations in mind. In thus readapting a classical reading of the landscape to a modern Dutch vernacular, Vroom may have been influenced by Constantijn Huygens I, a courtier and diplomat at the court of Prince Frederick Henry, one of Vroom's principal patrons.[4]

A smaller version of this composition is in the Fondation Custodia at the Institut Néerlandais, Paris (fig. A).[5] As Haverkamp-Begemann and Logan have explained, the Paris drawing is executed in ink over a sketch in black chalk and would seem to be the earlier of the two versions.[6] No one has ever questioned the attribution, however, of the darker and more detailed Yale sheet, which seems to be Vroom's own more elaborate version. Haverkamp-Begemann and Logan read the inscribed date, which is buried in the pen work at lower left and would be indistinct even if not cut at the bottom edge, as 164 and suggested a date of 1649, but Keyes and others have argued that the style is that of the late 1630s.[7] The absence of trees framing the composition in a traditional way, which are seen in Vroom's earlier dated panoramas,[8] might be cited as evidence in favor of a date in the late 1630s or after 1640. Dating aside, Keyes's hypothesis that the Yale drawing is some sort of presentation *modello* based on the smaller Paris sheet has not met universal approval but seems plausible.[9] If the supposition is correct, it is likely that Vroom planned to paint a landscape for the owner of the property in the picture, but no corresponding painting is known. Attempts have also been made to identify the large house in the distance at left, but without any convincing conclusions.[10] Whatever its precise purpose, this drawing is one of Vroom's largest and most ambitious, and a key example of the sort of new landscape art that he and other Haarlem painters helped to create, a genre that received its fullest expression later in the century in the work of his younger contemporaries, Rembrandt and Jacob van Ruisdael.

JJM

1. Vroom scholarship starts with Rosenberg 1928, and Keyes 1975 is the only monograph, to which is added Keyes 1982. See also Biesboer 1978–79.
2. Keyes has attributed forty drawings to Vroom, of which ten or fifteen have been put into question by Biesboer 1978–79 and others. Robinson (Amsterdam et al. 1991–92, no. 30) notes that Vroom's technique "owes something to the drawings of Buytewech and of Esias and Jan van de Velde . . . " but "identification of the sources of Vroom's technique in no way detracts from the originality of his achievement."
3. Sutton in Amsterdam–Boston–Philadelphia 1987–88.
4. The bibliography on Dutch landscape is ever-expanding. The classic study is Stechow 1966, but for a summary of trends since then, see Amsterdam–Boston–Philadelphia 1987–88, especially the introductory essays by Sutton and Schama. More recently, see also Gibson 2000. On the theme of naturalism and Dutch landscape, see also the drawing by Esaias van de Velde in this exhibition (cat. no. 36).
5. Inv. no. I6984, pen and brown ink over black chalk, 10 × 31.5 cm.
6. H-B and L, no. 441.
7. Keyes 1975, 137 n. 47, has a careful transcription of the inscription and insightful commentary. See also New York–Paris 1977–78, 184–185. The question of dating style is complicated by the existence of two versions of the composition. Duparc (Cambridge–Montreal 1988, 230) notes that "the possibility of a considerable lapse of time between the two [versions] should not be ruled out"; there is, however, no parallel case to view as evidence.
8. Boston, Abrams Collection, pen and brown ink, 19.2 × 25.3 cm, signed and dated 1631; London, Victoria and Albert Museum, inv. no. Dalton 977-900.
9. New York–Paris 1977–78, 184–185, notes in apparent disagreement that "there is at present no proof of Keyes's suggestion." In contrast, Sutton and Chong (Amsterdam–Boston–Philadelphia 1987–88, 519) echo Keyes's thought.
10. Keyes 1975, 227; New York–Paris 1977–78, 185. Traditionally called at Yale *View near Haarlem,* the alternate title given here seems preferable in light of Keyes's explanation that the landscape appears to be that of an area further south, near Lisse. Keyes also notes that the house is of the sort built by Jacob van Campen in the 1630s and that van Campen built a house near Lisse for Johann Dedel, for which, unfortunately, no documentation exists.

48 Claude Lorrain
Chamagne, Lorraine 1604/05–1682 Rome

Pastoral Landscape, 1639

Pen and brown ink and wash over black chalk, with white heightening, 23 × 30 cm (9 1/16 × 13 in.)

WATERMARK: shield with saint or pilgrim akin to those in Washington–Paris 1982–83, 446–447, nos. 20, 21

INSCRIPTIONS: verso, lower center, in pen and brown ink: *Claud IV / fecit 1639*

PROVENANCE: from the so-called "Wildenstein Album," probably assembled by Claude's heirs. This either passed from Claude's studio into the collection of Queen Christina of Sweden (1626–1689) and thence to Cardinal Decio Azzolini (d. 1689), whose nephew Marchese Pompeo Azzolino sold that collection in 1696 to Prince Livio Odescalchi, or else, was sold directly by Claude's heirs to Odescalchi, in whose collection it was noted in 1713; by descent in the Odescalchi family until 1845; Polish collection until 1939; Swiss collection until 1960; Georges Wildenstein, 1960–68; Norton Simon, Pasadena, Calif., 1968–80 (the album was disassembled in 1970 and the sheets were sold individually in 1980–81); acquired from Eugene V. Thaw and Co., New York

REFERENCES: Roethlisberger 1962, no. 46; Roethlisberger 1968, no. 624; Roethlisberger 1971, no. 16; *YUAG Bulletin* 38.3 (1983): 38 and 58; New Haven 1984, no. 41; Cleveland–Cambridge–Ottawa 1989–90, no. 29; *Handbook*, 204

James W. Fosburgh, B.A. 1933, and Mary C. Fosburgh Collection Fund. 1981.108

Claude Gellée, called Claude Lorrain after the duchy where he was born, arrived in Rome when he was only twelve or thirteen years old and remained there for nearly his entire life. He received his early training while an assistant to the landscape artists Goffredo Wals and Agostino Tassi and remained a specialist in that genre for the rest of his career. His painted and drawn prospects combine a close study of nature and light with classical subject matter and literary themes. These "ideal landscapes," more ordered than nature itself, found an eager clientele in the educated elite of Rome and elsewhere. By the end of his life, Claude was esteemed as Europe's greatest landscape painter, a reputation he held for centuries after his death. He was equally adept as a draftsman, and his masterful landscape drawings were also prized, but because Claude was reluctant to part with them, most were still in his studio at his death.[1]

The Yale *Pastoral Landscape*, although clearly laid out in black chalk, is brought to life by the various and masterful use of brush and wash, which is used to indicate both the different textures of foliage and the light and shadow around and beneath the leaves. Bold planes of light and dark shadows create space and structure in a way rarely before seen in nature studies. The technique seems to blur the line between painting and drawing. This type of "painterly drawing" can be considered consistent with all of Claude's work and also with broader trends in artistic practice in seventeenth-century Rome, as seen on the one hand in the increasing interest in plein air sketching and, on the other hand, in the practice of painting directly from life to the canvas by Caravaggio and his followers. Claude was among the most active practitioners of plein-air drawing, often sketching along the Tiber River outside the Porta del Popolo to the north of Rome or else on excursions to Tivoli and the Campagna. Yet, just as Caravaggio's aggressive naturalism was filtered through his sophisticated conception of image-making, and as the Carracci had adapted their life drawings to an abstracted classical style, so too, Claude's larger and more finished landscape drawings adapt his study of nature to an idealized pastoral mode. Indeed, for all its mastery of nature, this *Pastoral Landscape* was probably drawn in the studio, for the framing lines and the *repoussoir* elements of shepherd and tree at left suggest deliberation on the part of the artist.[2] Claude's landscapes were highly esteemed, not least of all because they thus appealed to devotees of both the naturalistic and the classical strains of Roman Baroque painting.[3]

As in most of his works, Claude here includes a human presence that animates the landscape. A shepherd and his flock sit under the trees in the foreground, empty boats rest along the far shore in the middle distance, and several figures, perhaps a hunting party, can be seen on the right, moving into the distance; in addition to this group of figures drawn in wash above and to the right of the boats, two small standing figures, delineated only in black chalk, are just visible under the trees near the center of the drawing. There is, of course, no clear narrative to be drawn from such elements. The point is a more lyrical, abstracted impression of nature as influenced by literary modes such as the pastoral.[4]

The drawing is signed and dated on the verso: *Claud IV fecit 1639*.[5] Pastoral views of this type were the mainstay of Claude's work in the 1630s, in contrast to the biblical and mythological subjects of his later career. The composition is likewise entirely consistent with other works of the later 1630s, both in terms of its general style and for motifs such as the tree branch slanting obliquely (and masterfully) back into depth at the left side of the drawing. The "IV" of the inscription stands for *in urbe* (in the city), which is to say that the drawing was made in Rome, but comparisons might also be made with a number of sheets related to the trips Claude undertook in 1638–39 to draw Civitavecchia, Castel Gandolfo, and San Marinella for Pope Urban VIII. Examples include the *Pastoral Landscape with Castel Gandolfo*, the *Landscape with a Hunting Party*, and the *Herdsman with Seated Peasants* in the British Museum, all from the *Liber Veritatis*, and the *View of Santa Marinella* in a private collection.[6] The *View of Santa Marinella* seems to be preparatory for a painting and as such is somewhat unusual among Claude's drawings before the 1650s.[7] In the case of the Yale drawing, there is no corresponding painting, and the drawing can instead be considered a completed work in its own right, with the puddles and smeared areas of ink and white heightening perhaps to be imagined as an inherent part of the drawing act. The framing lines likewise suggest that Claude conceived of the composition as a finished work. As noted above, however, Claude refused to part with his drawings, so that one must imagine a composition like the present sheet not as a work intended for sale, but rather, as a deeply personal investigation into the possibilities of landscape.[8]

After Claude's death, his heirs combined many of his best drawings, both loose and from sketchbooks, in albums that were then offered to prominent collectors. The Yale drawing was part of one such collection, the so-called "Wildenstein Album" that is first

recorded in the collection of Prince Livio Odescalchi (the nephew of Pope Innocent XI) in 1713. As Marcel Roethlisberger has noted, the Wildenstein Album was "the most authentic and comprehensive anthology of Claude's drawings" and "almost every sheet is one of the finest of its kind, or a specimen without peer."[9] Not only distinguished because of their high quality, the Wildenstein drawings, because kept in the album until relatively recently, are among the best preserved of Claude's works. The present drawing is no exception.[10]

JJM

1. Roethlisberger 1971, 6. Nearly 1,300 of Claude's drawings, in a wide variety of style and finish, survive. There is a vast bibliography on Claude's landscapes, but in addition to Roethlisberger's catalogues of paintings and drawings (Roethlisberger 1961 and 1968), notable studies of the drawings include Fry 1907, Kitson 1961 and 1978, Washington–Paris 1982–83, and Whiteley 1998. One other drawing by Claude is at Yale, a late *Tree Study*, inv. no. 1971.5, from the so-called Animal Album (Roethlisberger 1968, no. 1011).
2. It should also be noted that the outlines of the landscape's middle planes are traced in black chalk on the verso of this drawing, which might have something to do with practice in the studio. Kitson 1978, 23–24, notes that several sheets of the *Liber Veritatis* have similar tracings on the verso.
3. On the issues of Claude's subject matter, literary themes, and contemporary artistic theory, see Wine 1994.
4. Wine 1994, 29, notes, ". . . it would be wrong to assume that because a painting by Claude had no subject derived from an identifiable literary source, it was therefore without meaning." Many others have made similar observations. On the issue more broadly, see Gilbert 1952.
5. The inscription was only revealed in 1970 when the album was disassembled; this and other inscriptions on the Wildenstein Album versos forced a reconsideration of the basic chronology of Claude's drawings as set out in Roethlisberger 1968 (where, for example, this drawing was dated 1645–50).
6. London, British Museum, inv. nos. 1957-12-14-41, 1957-12-14-42, and 1957-12-14-43; see Whiteley 1998, nos. 31–33 and page 78, where the private collection drawing is also illustrated. The *Liber Veritatis* was Claude's record of his completed paintings, but as Kitson 1978, nos. 36–37, notes, the *Landscape with a Hunting Party* and the *Herdsman with Seated Peasants* are atypical—and problematic—because they relate, with some variations, to two sides of a single painting, the *Landscape with a Country Dance* in the Louvre, which was painted for Urban VIII around 1637, although the placement of the drawings in the *Liber* suggests that the drawings were made in 1639. Urban may have commissioned a variant version of the painting in 1639.
7. Whiteley 1998, 32.
8. Similarly, Michael Kitson, in a discussion of Claude's possible motives behind the creation of the *Liber Veritatis* (Kitson 1978, 24), wonders "what type of mind can have produced such a work, the beauty and elaborateness of which go far beyond any utilitarian purpose it may have had?"
9. Roethlisberger 1971, 6–7. On the album, see Roethlisberger 1962 and 1971 and Washington–Paris 1982–83, no. D29; on Odescalchi's collection, see also Roethlisberger 1985–86. An old tradition held that this album was initially sold to Queen Christina of Sweden, whose collections passed upon her death in 1689 to Cardinal Decio Azzolino before being acquired *en bloc* by Livio Odescalchi. The Odescalchi collection, however, included thousands of drawings acquired elsewhere, and there is no evidence to suggest whether or not the Wildenstein Album came from Christina.
10. The *Pastoral Landscape* has much in common—size, style, subject, and date—with drawings from Claude's disassembled "Tivoli Book" (see Roethlisberger 1968, 62–63), other sheets from which were bound into the Wildenstein Album. The connection between the Yale drawing and the Tivoli Book has not been previously noted, presumably because the drawing lacks the numbering found on other sheets, but those numbers have been rubbed on others and could similarly have been removed here.

49 Nicolaes Berchem
Haarlem 1620–1683 Amsterdam

The Calling of Matthew, ca. 1639

Black and white chalk on blue paper, laid down, 19.8 × 26.4 cm (7¾ × 10⅜ in.)

INSCRIPTIONS: recto, lower left, in brown ink: *Berchem / apres son maitre Moyart*

PROVENANCE: Peter Sylvester (L. 2108, 2877); John Percival, 1st Earl of Egmont (1683–1748); John T. Graves; Robert Hoe (sale New York, Anderson Auction Company, 15–19 April 1912, Library of Robert Hoe, Part III, A–K, no. 949); Yale University Library (anonymous donor, 1957)

REFERENCES: H-B and L, no. 341; Schatborn 1974, 6–8; Tümpel 1974, 31–34, 107, 139, and no. 114; New Haven 1975, 11 and no. 21; New York 1988, no. 26; *Grove Dictionary* 3:757; Stefes 1997, 367–369

Egmont Collection, Yale Library Transfer. 1961.64.77

Nicolaes Berchem was a notably prolific artist, responsible for hundreds of paintings and more than fifty etchings, but the present drawing is thought to be among his earliest surviving works. According to the biographer Arnold Houbraken, Berchem trained first with his father, Pieter Claesz, and then subsequently with Jan van Goyen, Claes Cornelisz. Moeyaert, Pieter de Grebber, Jan Wils, and Jan Baptist Weenix. Such a sequence of masters is indeed unusual, and Houbraken's account has been questioned. (Weenix, for example, was a year younger than Berchem and was more likely a contemporary collaborator than a master.) The Yale drawing, a copy after Moeyaert as suggested by the inscription,[1] is perhaps the best "documentary" evidence to support Houbraken.

Berchem has extracted this group from the middle ground of Moeyaert's *Calling of Matthew* (fig. A),[2] so that the subject of the scene is not immediately apparent. We do not see Christ but only the tax collector Matthew and his associates, shown in contemporary dress, as is often the case in paintings of this subject. The decision to copy only one element of a model was relatively common among seventeenth-century artists: Rubens's drawings are one example that comes to mind. Moreover, the isolation of the key figures to create a focus on human drama and the secularization of traditional religious subjects are, as Sutton and Naumann have noted, typical of Berchem's milieu.[3] In any case, the purpose of the drawing was probably not as a preparatory study for a painting, but rather, as a drawing exercise. Moeyaert's painting was done in 1639, and the logical assumption is that Berchem, then eighteen or nineteen years old, would have made the drawing while training under Moeyaert at that time. Berchem later took up the *Calling of Matthew* in his circa 1655–57 panel (Mauritshuis, The Hague), painted in collaboration with

FIGURE 49A | Claes Cornelisz. Moeyaert, *The Calling of Matthew*, 1639. Braunschweig, Herzog Anton Ulrich-Museum.

Weenix, but that composition is neither closely related to this drawing nor to Moeyaert's model.[4]

Stylistically, this sheet fits with a group of similar studies in chalk on blue paper from Berchem's earlier years, but interestingly, it has little to do with Moeyaert's drawings. The precedent is instead likely to be the work of Pieter van Laer, "il Bamboccio," who returned from Italy in 1639 and remained in Haarlem until 1642, just when Berchem would have drawn this sheet. Berchem's *Calling of Matthew* is in a tighter, more meticulous technique than are the looser black and white chalk drawings of van Laer, but that tightness could be due either to the fact that Berchem was making a copy or to this being one of his first essays with these media. His slightly later drawings with chalks on blue paper—the group in the Kunsthalle, Hamburg, identified by Schatborn, for example[5]—are even closer to van Laer's model, and as Haverkamp-Begemann and others have noted, the figure at right in *The Calling of Matthew* is more loosely sketched than the rest of the drawing and already seems to prefigure Berchem's later, more lively style.

JJM

1 This inscription (in French, on a Dutch drawing that was in England by the early eighteenth century) is perhaps in the hand of the French-born Peter Sylvester (the stamps at lower left are his). Sylvester lived in Holland and was associated with the court of William III, where he might have acquired the drawing in the 7 December 1683 sale of Berchem's estate, before moving to London, where he died in 1718. The Egmont Albums are thought to have been assembled in the first decades of the eighteenth century, so the drawing was likely to have been bought or received by Egmont directly from Sylvester; it is one of relatively few Egmont drawings for which an earlier provenance is known. Because of this earlier inscription, the "Egmont hand" has not added an inscription or attribution like those on most sheets in the albums.

2 Braunschweig, Herzog Anton Ulrich-Museum, inv. no. 228.

3 New Haven 1975, 11.

4 For the painting, see Duparc 1980. The only real comparison is that the man behind the table in both compositions strikes a similar pose, but this is not enough to suppose that Berchem even had this earlier drawing in mind.

5 Schatborn 1974.

50 Attributed to Ferdinand Bol
Dordrecht 1616–1680 Amsterdam

King Ahasuerus and Queen Esther Acknowledging Mordecai's Role in Saving the Jews, ca. 1645–52

Pen and brown ink and brown wash, 20.5 × 29.8 cm (8 1/16 × 11 3/4 in.)

WATERMARK: shield with stylized horn and crown above

INSCRIPTIONS: verso, in graphite, upper right: *Rembrant*; left, just below center: *L / A8307*; bottom center: *Rembrand*[t?]

PROVENANCE: Galliera, Paris, 18 June 1965, lot 133 (as School of Rembrandt); Sotheby's, London, 9 July 1968, lot 43 (as Attributed to Gerbrand van den Eeckhout); Gallery Alfred Brod, London; acquired from Herman Shickman Gallery, New York

REFERENCES: *YUAG Bulletin* 36.1 (1976): 40 and 43 (as Eeckhout); Sumowski 1979–92, 1: no. 157 (as Bol); New Haven 1992, no. 24 (as Bol)

Everett V. Meeks, B.A. 1901, Fund. 1975.81

This scene was correctly identified by Werner Sumowski in 1979 as Mordecai kneeling before Queen Esther and King Ahasuerus.[1] The subject is drawn from the Book of Esther, an Old Testament source commonly used by seventeenth-century Netherlandish artists who portrayed the queen as a heroine who saved her people, the Jews, from the destruction plotted against them by Haman, one of the king's chief counselors. In her attempts to convince Ahasuerus of Haman's deceit, Esther was aided by her uncle, Mordecai, seen here kneeling as he accepts an expression of the king's gratitude. During the first half of the seventeenth century, the salvation of the Jews became a popular subject in large part because many of the inhabitants of the Netherlands saw parallels between their domination by the Spaniards and the plight endured by the Jews.

Dutch artists of the highest stature, such as Rembrandt; his teacher, Pieter Lastman; his noted contemporary, Jan Lievens; and many of Rembrandt's pupils drew upon the Book of Esther as a source for paintings, prints, and drawings.[2] Lastman's paintings of Old Testament themes, many depicting subjects that had previously appeared only in prints, played a vital role in the dissemination of biblical imagery in the northern Netherlands because they provided painted prototypes for the work of many later artists. This is particularly true of his *Esther's Feast* of about 1618 (also called *The Wrath of Ahasuerus*; Warsaw, National Museum) and *The Triumph of Mordecai*, dated 1624 (Amsterdam, Museum het Rembrandthuis). Rembrandt's etching of about 1641, *The Triumph of Mordecai* (B. 40), was derived from Lastman's composition, and many drawings by Rembrandt's pupils refer directly or indirectly to Lastman's *Esther's Feast*.[3]

Careful examination of this drawing helps clarify the narrative because it reveals that the artist varied the emphasis he placed on each of the figures. The principal actors are not the royal couple, as one might expect, but the king and Mordecai, whose gestures effectively tell the story. Ahasuerus, whose status is clearly defined by his clothing—long, regal robes adorned with a wide ermine collar and a conspicuously large crown—raises his hand in a benevolent gesture toward Mordecai, who, with head bent slightly forward, displays his acceptance of the king's gratitude by folding his hands across his chest. The draftsman cast Esther as a mere observer, a passive role defined by her hands, clasped and calmly folded just below her waist.

The details of the setting, although summarily drawn, suggest the throne room of Ahasuerus's palace in Shushan. The king and queen have just descended a pair of steps over which the king's robes still trail, and a canopy, indicated by thin, wavy pen lines and a single broad stroke of a brush, extends over them. They gaze upon Mordecai, who kneels before them. The small figures to the far left, visible through the arch, are members of the palace guard, and the long, thin lines seen rising above their heads represent the weapons—lances or halberds—they often carried on the palace grounds. In introducing guardsmen as staffage, the artist may have been influenced by the work of the sixteenth-century draftsman Maarten van Heemskerck (see cat. no. 15), whose designs for a well-known series of eight prints narrating the life of Esther also included tiny, ubiquitous armed figures of this kind.[4]

The drawing illustrates an obscure episode from among the many more popular ones, like those van Heemskerck represented, that comprised the story of Esther's eventful life. The artist's selection of a little-known episode strongly suggests that he reviewed the biblical text before selecting it because the conflict played out between the protagonists (Ahasuerus and Mordecai), and the principal antagonist, Haman had already been resolved by the time this scene—the royal acknowledgment of Mordecai's loyalty to the crown and to the Jewish nation—took place. It is worth noting that at least one other artist in Rembrandt's immediate circle, Philips Koninck, also represented this event in a drawing formerly in the collection of the Warsaw University Library. Koninck's *Mordecai before Esther and Ahasuerus*, signed and dated 1664, however, differs from the present sheet in

FIGURE 50A | Rembrandt, *The Repentant Judas*, 1629. Great Britain, private collection.

important ways: it contains more figures; the royal couple is shown seated, not standing; and Mordecai is shown standing, not kneeling.[5] These differences support the opinion offered above regarding the artist's use of sources—namely that Koninck, like the author of the present drawing, created *Mordecai before Esther and Ahasuerus* based on his own interpretation of the literary source, not on a visual prototype.

Among the figures represented in the present sheet, only the figure of Mordecai offers insight into how the artist derived his pose. Given Mordecai's kneeling position and the tilt of his head to the left, it seems likely that the artist knew Rembrandt's painting *The Repentant Judas* of 1629 (fig. A), where he found a prototype for Mordecai in the figure of Christ's infamous betrayer.[6] Rembrandt's *Judas* had become a well-known pathos formula by the mid-1630s thanks in part to Jan van Vliet's bust-length etching of it, dated 1634.[7]

Identifying with certainty the artist who created *King Ahasuerus and Queen Esther Acknowledging Mordecai's Role in Saving the Jews* is not an easy task. Sumowski identified the draftsman as Bol, an attribution that is not without merit because, in general terms,

this work was executed by an extremely competent hand, like Bol's, and because, in more specific terms, the presence of thin, freely drawn, wavy lines of the type seen above and to the right of the royal couple have often been associated with Bol's style. Nevertheless, the work displays characteristics that make it difficult to place it securely in his oeuvre. First and most important, the pronounced application of wash to define the background of the throne room and create shadows, like that cast by Mordecai's upper body on Esther's dress and traditionally understood to be a practice characteristic of Bol, has recently been reassessed and found to be inconsistent with his use of the medium.[8] Second, Ahasuerus's small, detailed facial features are drawn in a way that is uncharacteristic of the artist; and finally, the thin pen lines that define the figure of Esther are too tentative to be seen unequivocally as Bol's work. At this time the drawing may be best classified as "attributed to Bol" rather than placed without reservation in his drawn oeuvre.

An approximate date for this sheet may be derived by comparing it to one of Bol's drawings in the Hamburger Kunsthalle, *Joseph Interpreting the Prisoners' Dreams*.[9] In that work, dated to the mid- to late 1640s,

Bol used the Judas prototype to create one of the prisoners.[10] As noted above, this was the same model used by the artist of the present sheet to fashion the figure of Mordecai. Bol's inventive transformation of the Rembrandt model suggests that *Joseph Interpreting the Prisoners' Dreams* predated the present drawing, in which the adaptation of the model was carried out in a more straightforward way, and allows one to place the creation of the present work in the late 1640s or early 1650s.

JLL

1 Sumowski 1979–92, 1: no. 157.
2 The following list of works by Rembrandt, Lastman, Lievens, and pupils of Rembrandt demonstrates the extreme popularity of themes related to Esther's life.

   Works by Rembrandt: *Esther* (or *Bathsheba*?), ca. 1633, painting, Ottawa, National Gallery of Canada; *Esther* (*The Great Jewish Bride*), ca. 1635, drawing, Stockholm, Nationalmuseum (Benesch 1954–57, no. 292); *Esther* (*The Great Jewish Bride*), 1635, etching, B. 340; *Ahasuerus on His Throne*, late 1630s, drawing, Amsterdam, Rijksprentenkabinet (Benesch 1954–57, no. 85); *Triumph of Mordecai*, ca. 1641, etching, B. 40; and *Esther's Feast*, 1660, painting, Moscow, Pushkin Museum.

   Works by Lastman: *Esther's Feast*, ca. 1618, painting, Warsaw, National Museum, and *Triumph of Mordecai*, 1624, painting, Amsterdam, Rembrandthuis.

   Works by Lievens: *Esther's Feast*, ca. 1625, painting, Raleigh, North Carolina Museum of Art, and *Esther's Feast*, ca. 1628, drawing, Dresden, Kupferstich-Kabinett.

   Although numerous Rembrandt pupils used the Book of Esther as a source for their work, three of them in particular, Willem de Poorter, Jan Victors, and Aert de Gelder, repeatedly used it as a source for their paintings. For de Poorter, see Sumowski 1983–94, 4: nos. 1627, 1628, 1631, and 1632; for Victors, see Sumowski 1983–94, 4: nos. 1724, 1727, and 1729; for De Gelder, see Dordrecht–Cologne 1998–99, nos. 15, 16, 20, 23, and 24. A partial list of drawings of Esther's Feast by pupils includes the following: Gerbrand van den Eeckhout: Munich, Staatliche Graphische Sammlung (Sumowski 1979–92, no. 757), and The Hague, private collection (Sum. 761); Aert de Gelder: Budapest, Szépmüvészeti Múzeum (Sum. 1074); Samuel van Hoogstraten: Vienna, Albertina (Sum. 1241); and Jan Victors: unknown location (Sum. 2330), formerly Bremen, Kunsthalle (Sum. 2336), formerly Düsseldorf, C. G. Boerner (Sum. 2339), Amsterdam, Rijksprentenkabinet (Sum. 2342), and Moscow, Pushkin Museum (Sum. 2343).
3 See above, note 2, for pupils' drawings.
4 Van Heemskerck's designs were engraved by Philips Galle in 1564; see New Hollstein DF, *Maarten Van Heemskerck*, Part 1: 132–138, nos. 151–158.
5 Pen and brown ink and brown wash, 13.1 × 17.6 cm; see Sumowski 1979–92, 6: no. 1344.
6 Great Britain, private collection, oil on panel, 79 × 102.3 cm.
7 For reproduction of van Vliet's etching, see Amsterdam 1996b, no. 9.
8 The generous and uneven use of wash seen here is also found in *The Holy Family in a Room* (Darmstadt, Hessisches Landesmuseum, inv. no. AE 592, pen and brown ink and brown washes, 18 × 27.2 cm), until recently considered one of Bol's more important autograph drawings. Leja 2004, 1:91–97, however, has argued that the uneven application of wash in the Darmstadt sheet is one reason to place it outside Bol's oeuvre.
9 Hamburg, Kunsthalle, inv. no. 22412, pen and brush and brown ink, 16.5 × 22.8 cm; see Hamburg 1994–95, 31, no. 19.
10 For dating of the Hamburg sheet, see Leja 2004, 1:160–161; for Bol's use of Rembrandt's *Judas*, see Leja 2004, 1:163–164, 2: pls. 206, 207.

51 Valerio Castello
Genoa 1624–1659 Genoa

The Perdono of Saint Francis,
ca. 1645–55

Pen and brown ink and gray-brown wash over red chalk, 32.2 × 25.2 cm (12 11/16 × 9 15/16 in.)

INSCRIPTIONS: recto, in pen and brown ink, upper left: *1759*; lower right: *Parmesan*

PROVENANCE: acquired from C. G. Boerner, Düsseldorf

REFERENCES: New Haven 1974, no. 51 (as North Italian, circa 1600); Palm Beach 1974, no. 79 (as Bertoia); Olszewski 1981, no. 86 (as Attributed to Bertoia); De Grazia 1991, no. D/R 46 (as Lombard, perhaps around Moncalvo); New Haven 1991a, no. 25 (as Lombard, close to Giulio Cesare Procaccini)

Maitland F. Griggs, B.A. 1896, Fund. 1972.92

The present drawing, a lively, accomplished Baroque study, has often been exhibited because of its high quality, despite doubts over its attribution and subject matter. The composition has hitherto been catalogued generically either as *A Vision of Saint Francis* or *Christ and the Virgin Appearing to Saint Francis*. The kneeling figure at lower right, with halo, monastic habit, and the stigmata, is surely Saint Francis of Assisi, while the figures at upper left are probably Christ and the Virgin Mary. The most commonly depicted visions of Saint Francis are the scenes of the stigmatization and of Saint Francis consoled by musical angels, but neither of those would include an angel presenting a bouquet of flowers. What we see here is, rather, a representation of the Perdono of Saint Francis, otherwise known as the Portiuncula (or Porziuncula) Indulgence, a late and controversial addition to the standard accounts of the life of the saint. In that story, Francis was praying in his chapel at Portiuncula near Assisi and had a vision in which Christ appeared to him and granted a plenary indulgence to all who would visit the chapel in the future.

The most familiar representation of the scene is Federico Barocci's painting of 1576 and related etching of 1581. That composition simply shows Francis praying in the chapel, with Christ, the Virgin, and Saint Nicholas (the name-saint of Nicolò Ventura, the painting's patron) and a few cherubs above. In the early 1590s, however, an earlier moment of the story also began to be included in images of the Perdono; some versions of the Franciscan legend relate that earlier in the evening of his vision, Francis experienced some temptation and by way of resisting threw himself into a bramble bush near the chapel, only to have roses spring from the places where his blood hit the bush. The flowers borne by the angel at lower left refer to that miracle. This iconography appeared more or less simultaneously in Francesco Vanni's altarpiece of about 1592 for the church of San Francesco in Pisa and Giovanni Battista della Rovere's fresco in Sant'Angelo, Milan. It was widely disseminated through Francesco Villamena's *Vita di San Francesco* of 1594 and continued to be represented throughout the seventeenth century.[1] Vanni's altarpiece included a figure of Saint John the Evangelist, whose presence might have had something to do with the patron, as had been the case with Barocci's Saint Nicholas; similarly, the two female figures behind Saint Francis, to the right in this drawing, although difficult to identify—the dish held by one would presumably become a clearer iconographic attribute in the final painting—are probably female saints who would relate to the patron or the dedication of the church or chapel for which a related painting was intended.

The attribution of this drawing has long been problematic. As indicated by the old inscription at lower right, it was at some point thought to be by Parmigianino, and when acquired by Yale in 1972, it was attributed to Jacopo Bertoia, one of Parmigianino's followers in Parma. It was later suggested that the drawing is by a Lombard artist of around 1600, and specifically someone in the circle of Giulio Cesare Procaccini, whose drawing style was much influenced by the earlier works of the Parmesan artists. More recently, a new attribution to the Genoese artist Valerio Castello was proposed independently by Nancy Ward Neilson, Florian Härb, and the present writer. Mary Newcome Schleier has confirmed the attribution to Castello and will publish the drawing in a forthcoming article.[2]

Castello's short career is not well documented, and the limits of his oeuvre remain problematic. Relatively few drawings have been attributed to him, and not many of those are linked to surviving paintings. Nonetheless, the bold technique of the present drawing has much in common with Castello's work, not only his drawings but also with the lively brushwork and dramatic compositions of his paintings. The catalogue of Castello's drawings includes works in an apparent variety of styles,[3] but of those drawings generally accepted as Castello's, this sheet compares to several, including the *Finding of Moses* in the Louvre[4] and the *Martyrdom of Saint Lawrence* recently with Jean-Luc Baroni.[5] These drawings share the Parmigianesque profiles and figures set off by parallel hatching like that in the Yale sheet.[6] The old suggested attribution to the circle of Giulio Cesare Procaccini was not far off, for Castello studied the older artist's works both in Genoa and during a trip to Milan and Parma in the early 1640s. While dating of Castello's drawings has proved difficult, the present sheet's influences from Parmigianino and Procaccini might suggest a date in the 1640s; as further—if still inconclusive—evidence for that date it might be noted that in that decade, Domenico Fiasella, Castello's master, produced a similar representation of the Perdono for San Francesco d'Albaro in Genoa.[7] Indeed, the linear style of the Yale drawing does resemble Fiasella's, which might also point to an earlier date for its creation. Finally, Fiasella's workshop produced a variant on that painting for San Francesco, Ventimiglia (destroyed in 1944 and known only in a poor photograph), with two saints added beside Christ and the Virgin.[8] It is tempting to wonder whether Castello's drawing might have related to that commission, not the least of all because no other similar compositions have been linked to the artist. Regardless of its original function, however, the *Perdono* stands as a representative of Castello's dazzling draftsmanship and, more broadly, of the dramatic yet elegant style characteristic of mid-seventeenth-century Genoese art.

JJM

1 On the versions by Vanni and Villamena, see Rome 1982–83, nos. 68 and 112. The precise circumstances and date of Vanni's commission are not known. Della Rovere's version was discussed by Thomas McGrath in a paper delivered at the College Art Association's annual meeting in 2005; McGrath also made the compelling argument that the rose imagery was in some ways a Franciscan response to the popular Dominican *Madonna of the Rosary* imagery. For a discussion of the Perdono and Franciscan concerns of the Cinquecento, see especially Lingo 1998, 338ff.

2 I would like to thank Mary Newcome Schleier, with whom I have discussed this drawing at some length, for sharing her thoughts on the drawing. Her own discussion will be published in *Studi di storia dell'arte* in 2006.

3 The standard monograph on Castello is Manzitti 1972 (new edition 2004), but there is much in the book that has been disputed; for his drawings, see also Newcome 1975, Newcome Schleier 1981, Royalton Kisch 1982, Paris 1985b, and Florence 1989.

4 Paris, Louvre, inv. no. 9199, pen and brown ink and wash over red chalk, heightened with white, on paper prepared with a pink wash, 16.8 × 21 cm; see Paris 1985b, no. 56. This connection was noted by Mary Newcome Schleier in a letter to the author; she notes further that another, better version of the drawing was recently with Didier Aaron.

5 New York–London 2004, no. 33, pen and brown ink and wash over black chalk, heightened with white, squared in red chalk, 20.9 × 20.7 cm. As explained in the catalogue entry, Newcome Schleier confirmed the attribution of that drawing and noted another autograph version of the composition in the Statens Museum fur Kunst, Copenhagen.

6 Another similar drawing, although one itself of a disputed attribution that might be worth reconsidering in light of the Yale drawing and the others mentioned above, is the *Adoration of the Shepherds* in the Christ Church gallery at Oxford, inv. no. 0403, pen and brown ink and wash over red chalk, heightened with white, on brownish-toned paper, 17.3 × 13 cm; see Byam Shaw 1976, no. 1102. David Acton in Boston 1989, no. 12, following Byam Shaw 1976 and Popham 1968, maintains that the drawing is by Vincenzo Caccianemici; I am inclined to agree with Newcome Schleier's attribution of it, and the related print, to Castello, for which see Newcome Schleier 1981. The drawing was not in Manzitti's 1972 edition but is included as no. D13 in the 2004 edition.

7 Newcome Schleier draws the connection between Castello's *Perdono* and Fiasella's in her forthcoming article; for Fiasella's *Perdono*, see the entry by Massimo Bartoletti in Genoa 1990, no. 30.

8 Genoa 1990, under no. 30.

52 Jacob Jordaens
Antwerp 1593–1678 Antwerp

A Goat, ca. 1657

Red, black, and yellow chalk, with touches of red and brown wash, heightened with white, 25.4 × 19.9 cm (9 15/16 × 7 7/8 in.)

PROVENANCE: acquired from Henri Baderou, Paris

REFERENCES: *YUAG Bulletin* 30.1 (1964): 18 and 50; Antwerp–Rotterdam 1966–67, no. 64; Jaffé 1966, 629; Cambridge 1967b, unnumbered cat.; Held 1967, 96; Ottawa 1968–69, no. 254; H-B and L, no. 578; Hulst 1974, no. A321; *Handbook*, 204; Hulst 1982, 313; Wellesley–Cleveland 1993–94, no. 30

Everett V. Meeks, B.A. 1901, Fund. 1963.9.3

Jordaens—along with Peter Paul Rubens and Anthony van Dyck—was one of the great triumvirate of Baroque painters in Antwerp. After the death of both of those—van Dyck, in any case, had been in England since 1632—Jordaens became the chief artist of the city, at the head of a large and productive workshop. He was a pupil of Adam van Noort and in 1616 married Catharina, van Noort's eldest daughter. He entered the Guild of Saint Luke in 1615, registered as a *waterscilder* (watercolor painter), and agreed to be head of the Guild in 1621. Jordaens is perhaps best known for his exuberant portrayals of Flemish domestic life, such as the feast at Twelfth Night (*The King Drinks*) or the proverb *As the Old Sang, so the Young Pipe*.[1] His numerous paintings and tapestries also include portraits and biblical, mythological, and historical scenes, all imbued with a robust, earthy realism. Jordaens enjoyed honors and fame throughout his long life. He received commissions from Queen Christina of Sweden; Amalia van Solms, widow of Frederick Henry, Prince of Orange; the town fathers of Amsterdam; and even a somewhat mysterious one from the king of England.[2] His sympathy for the Dutch Reformed faith, which he formally embraced late in life, may have contributed to his being chosen for some of these commissions.

More than 450 drawings by Jordaens are known.[3] This deft life study of a goat was certainly the drawing used for an *Adoration of the Shepherds* (fig. A), signed and dated 1657, now in the North Carolina Museum of Art, as Michael Jaffé was the first to point out.[4] The viewpoint and the stance of the goat are the same, except that the goat's head is turned to the left in the painting; the distinctive coloring of the animal's hair is identical. Anne-Marie Logan suggested that the same sketch might have served for the goat in the tapestry *Natura Paucis Contenta* (Nature Is Content with Little) in the series of *Proverbs* commissioned in 1644;[5] if this were true, the date of the drawing would be more than a decade earlier than the *Adoration of the Shepherds* altarpiece. The suggestion is somewhat implausible, however, as there is considerably stronger correspondence between the drawing and the North Carolina painting than between the drawing and the tapestry: the goat in the tapestry is at a slightly different angle—its left foreleg is seen to the left of the two hind legs, rather than between them (the image provided by Jordaens would have shown the right foreleg to the right of the hind legs, as the tapestry would have reversed the original direction), and the distribution of lights and darks in the goat's hair is notably different.[6] It seems unlikely that Jordaens would have used a drawing recently made in the 1640s for the tapestry, but with significant changes, and then pulled the same drawing out again more than a dozen years later and reused it, with a much closer correspondence, for the *Adoration*.

FIGURE 52A | Jacob Jordaens, *Adoration of the Shepherds*, 1657. Raleigh, North Carolina Museum of Art.

Animals are perhaps more abundant in history compositions by Jordaens than in those of any other artist—the North Carolina *Adoration* includes, besides the goat and the requisite ox and ass, a sheep, a dog, and a (dead) duck. Goats are plentiful in his oeuvre, as in *The Infant Jupiter Fed by the Goat Amalthea*,[7] *Satyr Playing the Flute*,[8] or *Pan Punished by Nymphs*.[9] At least one other religious painting, a *Presentation in the Temple*,[10] shows a goat, also from the rear and also with a child nearby. Although few drawings specifically of animals have come down to us—this is the only one showing a goat—it seems likely that Jordaens would have made hundreds of studies of the animals that appear in his works—horses, dogs, cats, cows, sheep, goats, pigs, monkeys, fowl—and that only a small fraction of these drawings has survived.[11]

SB

1 Versions of *The King Drinks* are in Brussels, Musées Royaux des Beaux-Arts de Belgique, inv. no. 3545; Kassel, Gemäldegalerie, inv. no. GK, 108; Paris, Louvre, inv. no. 2014; Vienna, Kunsthistorisches Museum, inv. no. 786. Depictions of *As the Old Sang, so the Young Pipe* are in Antwerp, Koninklijke Museum voor Schone Kunsten, inv. no. 677; Berlin, Schloss Charlottenberg, inv. no. 1.3849; Ottawa, National Gallery of Canada, inv. no. 15790; Paris, Louvre, on deposit at Valenciennes, Musée des Beaux-Arts, inv. no. 1407-MR794; and a French private collection.
2 See Hulst 1982, 26.
3 See Hulst 1974, 1980, and 1990.
4 Inv. no. 55.7.1, see North Carolina Museum of Art 1998, 95; Ottawa 1968–69, no. 254.
5 Wellesley–Cleveland 1993–94, no. 30.
6 Nelson 1998, no. 32, does not list Yale's drawing in relation to this tapestry.
7 Paris, Louvre, inv. no. 1405; Kassel, Gemäldegalerie, inv. no. 103; and see Antwerp 1993, no. A45, for discussion of Jordaens's treatment of this subject.
8 Amsterdam, Rijksmuseum, inv. no. A198.
9 Amsterdam, Rijksmuseum, inv. no. A601 (on loan to The Hague, Mauritshuis, inv. no. 849).
10 Antwerp, Rubenshuis.
11 Hulst 1974, 653–654, lists only ten authentic studies by Jordaens solely of animals (as opposed to compositional studies in which animals are included), one doubtful, and four copies; Hulst 1980 adds one copy, and Hulst 1990 four more authentic ones.

RECTO

53 Girolamo Troppa
Rocchetta in Sabina 1630–after 1710 Rome?

Jupiter, Juno, and Io (recto);
Animal Studies (verso), ca. 1665

Pen and brown ink and brown wash, with white heightening, partly oxidized (recto); pen and brown ink and brown wash over red chalk (verso), on blue paper, 20 × 25 cm (7⅞ × 9 13/16 in.)

WATERMARK: fleur-de-lys in a circle, topped by a crown, similar to Heawood no. 1632 (Roman, seventeenth century)

INSCRIPTIONS: verso, lower center, in pen and brown ink, probably in the hand of the artist: *Troppa*

PROVENANCE: unknown collector (small stamp in brown ink on mount: a crown in a circle; not in Lugt); Van Horn Estate, Pasadena, Calif.; private collection, Pasadena, Calif.; acquired from Monroe Warshaw, New York

REFERENCES: *YUAG Bulletin* (2003): 156–157

Everett V. Meeks, B.A. 1901, Fund. 2002.6.2

Girolamo Troppa was a contemporary of Pier Francesco Mola, Giovanni Battista Gaulli, and Carlo Maratti in later seventeenth-century Rome, and although he was highly enough esteemed in his day to be awarded a knighthood, he is little known today.[1] He was something of a chameleon, whose paintings and drawings often bear close resemblance to those of his more famous contemporaries. Many of his works have, in fact, been misattributed to those artists mentioned above, and also to a more diverse group including Giovanni Lanfranco, Giovanni Benedetto Castiglione, Giacinto Brandi, Gaspare Diziani, and others.

Troppa's habit of signing his paintings has proved useful in clarifying a number of attributions and, similarly, a large percentage of his drawings, including the present sheet, are inscribed "Troppa" in a consistent script that seems to be the artist's signature,[2] also providing a core group of works that are the basis for further attributions. This drawing is a new addition to Troppa's oeuvre and has not hitherto been noted in studies on the artist. Signature aside, this double-sided sheet, in

VERSO

which animated pen work is combined with multiple layers of wash, is typical of his work.

When acquired, the recto of this drawing was identified as *Juno Calling upon Aeolus to Destroy the Trojan Fleet*, a common subject in seicento Rome.[3] While the identification of Juno with her peacock is unmistakable, all versions of the Aeolus story include either a view of the fleet in the distance or else show Aeolus holding a bag of winds; the Yale drawing has neither. Instead of Aeolus, the seated male figure in the Yale drawing should probably instead be identified as Jupiter, for his left hand seems to grasp the bundle of thunderbolts that were his primary iconographic attribute (see, for example, cat. no. 10). In the distance, furthermore, instead of Aeneas's ships, we see the hindquarters of an animal; a putto above Juno's head points the viewer's attention toward the disappearing beast, which, by comparison with Troppa's animal studies on the verso, is surely a cow. The drawing must thus depict the popular story of Jupiter and Io, in which Jupiter disguised his lover Io as a cow to protect her from the wrath of his wife, Juno. No painting of this subject by Troppa is known today, but such a scene could fit well alongside his extant mythological paintings, such as the *Mercury and Argus* and *Apollo and Marsyas* in Copenhagen.[4]

There is no documentary evidence for dating the Copenhagen mythologies,[5] but they have generally been placed in the later 1660s, when Troppa's style was closest to Mola's. Indeed, just as the Copenhagen mythologies have been compared to the works of Mola, so too the Yale drawing has something in common with drawings by Mola and his closest followers, including Giovanni Battista Pace.[6] Relatively few of Troppa's known drawings can be dated by connecting them with securely dated paintings, but it seems plausible to suggest that the Yale drawing might represent Troppa's style in the earlier part of his career, in the mid- to late 1660s, before he worked with Gaulli, who seems to have influenced Troppa's style in drawing as well as painting.[7]

The drawing on the verso, showing cows, sheep, and goats, is in the same romantic pastoral mode as the recto, but it cannot be linked to any specific painting. The animals might either have been a study for the background elements of a painting or could otherwise have been an unconnected drawing exercise, perhaps inspired by the Io story on the recto; either way, similar beasts are found in other paintings by Troppa.

The blue paper and white heightening used in this drawing are rare for Troppa, but they are found in the drawings of both Mola and Giovanni Batttista Pace, which constitute further evidence for placing the Yale sheet in the earlier part of Troppa's career.[8] Furthermore, based on general stylistic similarities as well as a comparable handling of media, one further drawing can here be attributed to Troppa, a *Phaeton Kneeling before Helios, Asking to Drive the Chariot of the Sun*, among the anonymous drawings in the British Museum (fig. A).[9] The London sheet is clearly a design for a ceiling fresco, but while we know that Troppa did work in that medium (at Santa Marta and Sant'Agata in Rome, for example), we have no record of a secular project to which the drawing might be connected. Nonetheless, the technique of the London drawing is so much like that of the Yale drawing, and likewise shares the Yale sheet's low viewpoint, so that it is possible that both might have been combined, perhaps with other (missing or unidentified) compositions, in one ceiling, but this remains mere speculation. For now, it is hoped that the addition of the Yale and London drawings to the Troppa corpus might lead to further attributions in the attempt to reconstruct the artist's career.

JJM

1. The first reconstructions of Troppa's career are by Rudolph 1977, Busiri Vici 1980, and Schleier 1990 and 1993, but the artist still lacks a full-length critical study.
2. Schleier 1990, 24–25.
3. Versions were painted in the Pamphili palaces in Rome (by Pietro da Cortona in 1651–54; see Briganti 1982, no. 117) and Valmontone (painted initially by Mola in 1657–58 and replaced in 1661 by Mattia Preti; see Cocke 1968 and Montalto 1955). Another version of the subject was planned by Maratti for the Villa Falconieri at Frascati; see Rudolph 1986 and Turner 1999. Still another version is in a drawing by Giacinto Calandrucci, Düsseldorf, Kunstmuseum, inv. no. FP 2219; see Graf 1986, no. 612.
4. There is a record in the 1699 inventory of the dealer Pellegrino Peri of a painting by Troppa with "Jupiter and other figures" (Lorizzo 2003, 172) that might be related to this drawing. This picture is described as being 5 × 7 palmi, which would be something like 110 × 154 cm based on a standard of 22 cm/palm; the Copenhagen paintings are slightly smaller, at 96 × 132 cm, but the proportions are the same and the measurements in inventories are often approximations.
5. According to Busiri Vici 1980, 24, these two pictures were not among the set acquired by Lambert van Haven in 1668 for the Danish royal collection, but rather, passed from the collection of Herman van Swoll (on whom see Montias 1987, 73–74) into an Amsterdam auction in 1699 and were only acquired for Copenhagen in 1763, so that, unlike the other Copenhagen paintings, there is no easy way of dating them.
6. Schleier 1990, 24, takes issue with the comparison of Mola and Troppa, writing that the similarity is only in "a generic resemblance in the liberal use of wash and pen." While Troppa's pen work is quicker and more nervous than Mola's, similarities to Mola's drawings (those for Valmontone, for example) are nonetheless evident. On Pace, see Cocke 1991.
7. On Troppa's work with Gaulli at Santa Marta al Collegio Romano, Rome, see Dunn 1988.
8. See, for example, Mola's *Christ Carrying the Cross* in Düsseldorf, Kunstmuseum, inv. no. FP 8111 (Lugano–Rome 1989–90, no. III.61) and the *Rebecca and Eliezer*, Vienna, Albertina, inv. no. B281 (Koschatzky, Oberhuber, and Knab 1971, no. 80), which has been variously attributed to Mola and Pace (see Cocke 1991, 374, no. 6). Harris 1992, 219, notes that Cocke's discussion leaves "the character of a Pace drawing difficult to grasp"; it is tempting to wonder whether some of Troppa's early works might not be mixed among these others, adding to the confusion.
9. London, British Museum, inv. no. 1872-10-12-3303, pen and brown ink and brown wash, heightened with white, over black chalk, on blue paper, 21 × 37.7 cm; see Turner 1999, no. 336. Like many of Troppa's drawings, the London sheet has been alternately attributed to a range of seicento Roman artists including Passeri, a "Gaulli follower," and a "Maratti follower."

FIGURE 53A | Here attributed to Girolamo Troppa, *Phaeton Kneeling before Helios*, ca. 1665. London, British Museum.

54 Pierre Monier (or Mosnier)
Blois 1641–1703 Paris

Medea Slaying Her Children,
ca. 1665–66

Pen and brown ink and brown and gray wash, over black chalk with traces of red chalk, heightened with white, 55.9 × 40.6 cm (22 × 16 in.)

WATERMARK: Saint (Annunciatory Angel) in shield; see below for further discussion

INSCRIPTIONS: recto, lower left, in pen and brown ink: *Monsieur Mosnier francese*

PROVENANCE: acquired from Christopher Bishop, Milford, Conn.

REFERENCES: unpublished

Everett V. Meeks, B.A. 1901, Fund. 2005.127.1

Pierre Monier[1] was the son of Jean Mosnier and received his first artistic training from his father, who had been one of the principal painters to Marie de' Medici. He traveled to Paris following his father's death and entered the studio of Sébastien Bourdon, to whom he remained an assistant at least until 1663, when he worked for Bourdon at the Hôtel de Bretonvilliers. In the following year, Monier's *Jason Capturing the Golden Fleece* (Paris, École des Beaux-Arts)[2] won the first of the competitions for the Prix Royal (later known as the Prix de Rome). He was in Rome by mid-1665 and, with a letter of introduction from Bourdon, was among the last French artists to have studied with Poussin before his death; Monier was also among the first *pensionnaires* at the newly created French Academy in Rome. He returned to Paris by 1674, when he was accepted into the Académie de France. The Académie named him professor in 1686, and his lectures were published in 1698 as a *Histoire des arts qui ont rapport au dessin*. Although Monier executed a number of prominent commissions for paintings, frescoes, and tapestries, most seem not to have survived and he is not well known today.[3] The present drawing is thus an important addition to his small known oeuvre.[4]

Inscriptions on drawings are often misleading, but the "Monsieur Mosnier francese" here is so improbable, one might say, that it must be genuine. Consistent with the Italian description of the artist as "francese," everything about the drawing fits with what is known of Monier's work at the time he was in Italy. The basic style and use of media resemble Bourdon's drawings, and the study of ancient sculpture that the drawing conveys is a reflection of what we know to have been Monier's primary interest in Italy. In an address delivered to the Académie in July of 1670, that is, Bourdon explained that he had asked Monier to contact Poussin in Rome, to learn the master's method of measuring sculptures, and to make a new set of drawings for use by Bourdon and the rest of the Académie back in Paris.[5] The present drawing reflects that study in Rome, with an image (in reverse) of the Belvedere Cleopatra (now known as the Sleeping Ariadne) appearing in relief in the distance at right; the figure of Medea at center also resembles that of the Chiaramonti Niobid. Furthermore, the drawing echoes Poussin's own version of the subject, a composition later described by Bellori although it may have existed only in drawings.[6] The paper is also Italian and, perhaps not coincidentally, one that Poussin used while in Rome.[7] Considering further influences that might be detected in Monier's drawing, one might cite the works of Raphael and Giulio Romano, who were already established as the ideal models (with Poussin) for artists in the French Academy.[8]

Monier's prize-winning painting of 1664 had depicted the story of the Golden Fleece and surely took its theme from Pierre Corneille's play *Le conquête de la toison d'or*, which was performed in Paris throughout the early 1660s.[9] The title page of the first edition of Corneille's play suggests that it is to be read as a commemoration of the marriage of King Louis XIV and his new queen, Marie-Thérèse, but whether the allusion was quite so straightforward has been debated.[10] In any case, there was some iconographic tie between Jason and Medea and Louis XIV, and the present drawing was certainly created with some similar royal allusion in mind.

With her dragon-drawn chariot at lower right, the central figure of this drawing must be Medea, in the act of murdering her children, after which she would escape in the chariot, which belonged to her grandfather, Helios. There is, however, some difficulty in sorting out several iconographical oddities in the composition. The man atop the loggia is surely Jason, who looks on in horror while Medea slaughters their children, but he is accompanied by two figures that might be identified as Creusa, for whom Jason had deserted Medea, and Creusa's father Creon. In the textual sources for the story, Medea had killed Creusa and Creon before she murdered her children, but Monier was perhaps following the above-mentioned drawing by Poussin, in which Creusa is similarly shown on a loggia with Jason.[11] More difficult to explain are the three children in this composition: one dead or dying on the ground behind Medea and beneath the wailing nurse, another (apparently dead) child held by the woman at left, and a still-living infant held between Medea and the winged figures arriving at center. Jason and Medea had two children, and this third child remains a mystery. Moreover, the winged figures that usually appear in depictions of the Medea story are the Furies,[12] but the furies are female, and the figures here, one male and one female, must be something else. The winged gods Hypnos (Sleep) and Thanatos (Death), sometimes shown lifting a corpse to carry it to the underworld, would not be inappropriate here, but both of those gods are male. Nonetheless, the gestures of the woman holding an infant behind Medea and of the female winged figure might indicate that the "third child" is the soul of the dead infant, in which case the two figures here might be Thanatos (a bearded male) and Iris or one of the Furies. In sum, the full meaning of Monier's composition is still to be discovered, but there is ample precedent for complex narrative in French art of the later seventeenth century; the arriving deities and the still-living child are perhaps to be read as allegories or emblems rather than literal figures in the narrative.[13] Along the same lines, for example, the Cleopatra in the distance is probably no mere marker of antiquity but rather a commentary on the character of Medea: in the preface to his *Rodegune*, Corneille describes Cleopatra as a "second Medea." The great number of auxiliary figures and the highly theatrical setting—reminiscent of the "machines" that Corneille's *Toison d'or* and other works had newly introduced in French playhouses[14]—are likewise consistent with the other known works by Monier in particular, and, more broadly, with the art of his contemporaries including Charles Le

Brun, Charles de La Fosse, Jean-Baptiste Corneille (who accompanied Monier to Rome),[15] Jean Jouvenet (see cat. no. 57), and others.

The complexity of the subject and the high finish of the drawing suggest that Monier might have intended to make a large painting of the composition, perhaps for presentation to the Académie or the king himself, but no related work is known. Regardless of its intended function, Monier's *Medea* is a tour de force, and beyond helping to reconstruct the career of the little-known artist, the drawing, in showing a new facet of his draftsmanship, may help sort out other problems of attribution in the sheets attributed to Bourdon and his pupils.[16] Still more broadly, with its demonstrated study of ancient and modern Roman art, and with its complex iconography and sophisticated literary allusions, the *Medea* is a striking illustration of the art connected with the Académie de France and the French Academy in Rome.

JJM

1. The artist is variously described by his contemporaries as Mosnier, Monier, and Monnier. His name was originally Mosnier, but it is given as Monier on the title page of his 1698 *Histoire des arts qui ont rapport au dessin*. Chennevières-Pointel 1847–62, 2:190, writes that the artist changed the spelling to follow the then-new mode of orthography.
2. See Goldstein 1967, and, more recently, New York–Princeton 2005, 263–265 and 305.
3. On Monier's life and works, see especially Chennevières-Pointel 1847–62, 2:190–198; Rosenberg 1985; Thierry Bajou's entry in the *Grove Dictionary* 22:190–191; and Thuillier 2000, 68. Christopher Bishop, from whom the drawing was acquired, is responsible for recognizing it as Monier's (it had been misattributed to Pieter Molyn) and for first explaining its significance to me; this entry relies heavily on his research and insights.
4. The attribution to Monier of the drawing of *A Rustic Concert* in Angers (Musée des Beaux-Arts, inv. no. MTC 78), accepted as Monier's since published in London et al. 1977–78, no. 72, and hitherto one of the benchmarks for his drawing style, has itself been questioned; see Paris 1993, no. 141.
5. Mérot 1996, 249.
6. The drawing is Windsor, Royal Collection, inv. no. RL 11893; see Clayton 1995, no. 62. Blunt 1945, no. 264, questioned the attribution of this sheet, but it has been accepted as Poussin's by Clayton, Rosenberg, Prat, and other recent scholars. In any case, Creusa is also included in the related drawing (Windsor, Royal Collection, inv. no. RL 11892; Clayton 1995, no. 61), the attribution of which to Poussin has not been questioned. Bellori 1672, 449, includes a description of Poussin's composition in his life of the artist, but no painting of this subject is known and, as Clayton suggests, his account may have been based on the drawing. The drawing likely to have been seen by Bellori and Monier (Windsor, Royal Collection, inv. no. RL 11893) was part of a volume probably assembled by Cassiano del Pozzo (1588–1657), which after Cassiano's death passed into the collection of his brother, Carlo Antonio.
7. See Clayton 1995, 203, figs. 16 and 25. Similar watermarks appear on Windsor, Royal Collection, inv. no. RL 11979, a study for Poussin's *Dance before a Herm of Pan* of ca. 1631–32 (London, National Gallery), and on Windsor, Royal Collection, inv. no. RL 11980, a study dated to ca. 1625–27 and loosely linked to the painting of *A Nymph and a Drinking Satyr* (Moscow, Puskin Museum). On the former, see also Roberts 1986, 191, no. 72.
8. Monier is even documented as drawing from Raphael and Giulio Romano's frescoes in the Vatican Palace; see Bertolotti 1886, 141. Monier's (and the Académie's) interest in Giulio Romano would continue, for Monier was one of a team of artists charged with producing a series of tapestry cartoons after drawings by Raphael and Giulio Romano; see London et al. 1977–78, no. 72.
9. Monier might also have known of the similar spectacle, designed by Ménestrier and with sets by Thomas Blanchet, which was performed in Lyon in 1658 on the occasion of the king's visit there, for which see Galactéros-DeBoissier 1991, 205–210.
10. See Goldstein 1967 and Wygant 1994. Confusing the issue further, the later elements of the Medea story, those represented in the present drawing, do not appear in Corneille's *Toison d'or* but are found in his *Médée*, first performed in the 1630s, during the reign of Louis XIII. Both Jason and Medea had, nonetheless, become part of Louis XIV's iconography. In addition to the examples discussed by Goldstein, a set of ca. 1668 fountain designs for Versailles includes a (never-executed) Medea fountain: Paris, Louvre, inv. no. 29825, attributed to Charles Le Brun; see Beauvais 2000, 2: no. 2468.
11. Clayton calls the inclusion of Creusa "a rare narrative slip by Poussin." The prominent statue of Athena in Poussin's drawings would suggest a probable identification for the statue below the loggia in Monier's drawing.
12. See, for example, the large South Italian krater of ca. 400 B.C. in the Cleveland Museum of Art, inv. no. 1991.1; Neils and Oakley 2003, no. 17.
13. See Montagu 1968 and Goldstein 1967 (which relies on Montagu's then-still-unpublished text), which discuss comparably complicated readings of Monier's *Jason Capturing the Golden Fleece*. Christopher Bishop has also suggested that the figures before Medea might represent war and peace, or concord and discord, who are similarly paired in the Prologue to Corneille's play.
14. An engraving in the 1664–66 edition of Corneille's *Théâtre* (see Corneille 1998, 43) shows a dragon-borne Medea in an aerial battle with Zethes and Calais (the twin sons of Boreas), who accompanied Jason and the Argonauts. The print illustrates the spectacular conclusion to Corneille's *Toison d'or*, and although it does not relate directly to the later parts of the Medea story, there is perhaps a relationship between its depiction of the winged Zethes and Calais and Monier's inclusion of the similar figures in the present drawing.
15. Jean-Baptiste Corneille is not a well-documented artist, and only a few drawings have been attributed to him, but for one, see the Introduction, fig. 2.
16. Rosenberg 1985 begins with the statement that "the least explored area of old master drawings remains . . . that of seventeenth-century France" and ends with the suggestion that several drawings attributed to Bourdon and others might instead be by Monier. Thuillier 2000 likewise laments the confused state of drawings around Bourdon; a similar sheet formerly attributed to Bourdon, recently with W. M. Brady, New York, was able to be reattributed to Jacques-Claude Friquet only when it was removed from an old backing and a contemporary inscription was revealed.

55 Gian Lorenzo Bernini
Naples 1598–1680 Rome

Portrait of Cardinal Sforza Pallavicino, 1665–66

Red chalk on buff paper, 37.9 × 22.2 cm (14^{15}⁄₁₆ × 8¾ in.)

INSCRIPTIONS: recto, lower center, in pen and brown ink, in an old hand: *Del Cavaliere Bernini*

PROVENANCE: Hugues de Lionne (1611–1671); John Percival, 1st Earl of Egmont (1683–1748); John T. Graves; Robert Hoe (sale, New York, Anderson Auction Company, 15–19 April 1912, Library of Robert Hoe, Part III, A–K, no. 949); Yale University Library (anonymous donor, 1957)

REFERENCES: H-B and L, no. 285 (as Bernini?); Regina–Montreal 1970, no. 37; Held 1972, 42; Bloomington–Pittsburgh–Oberlin 1983, no. 27 (as Unidentified Bernini Follower); Harris 1985–86, 98 (as a student's copy after a lost original by Gaulli); New Haven 1991a, no 42; *Handbook*, 203 (as Attributed to Bernini); Montanari 1997, 42–68; Montanari 1998, 344–345; Siena 2000, no. 242

Egmont Collection, Yale Library Transfer. 1961.61.36

FIGURE 55A | Artist unknown, *Portrait of Cardinal Sforza Pallavicino*, ca. 1666–70. Rome, Sant'Andrea al Quirinale.

Although long associated with Bernini, and with a very old inscription attributing it to the artist, this drawing has been the subject of many questions over the years. It has been variously catalogued as an original by Bernini, a copy after him, a copy after Giovanni Battista Gaulli, and an original by an unidentified follower of Bernini. The subject of the portrait, moreover, has been identified as Bernini himself, as Pope Clement IX, or as some other, unidentified, sitter.[1] The obviously poor condition of the drawing surely lies behind many of these questions: the chalk is faded, the paper damaged, and the eyes retouched. In a recent article and exhibition, however, Tomaso Montanari has finally provided a convincing account of the drawing, securing the attribution to Bernini and identifying the sitter as Cardinal Sforza Pallavicino (1607–1667).[2]

Sforza Pallavicino was at the very center of the literary and artistic circles in seventeenth-century Rome. Although the first-born son of his noble family, he entered the priesthood and received doctorates of philosophy and theology. He joined the Jesuits in 1637 and was soon thereafter appointed professor of philosophy, and later theology, at the Collegium Romanorum. He was the author of poems, plays, theological lectures, and a monumental history of the Council of Trent. Although Pallavicino has not been the subject of much attention from modern art historians, he also played an important role in the Roman art world. He may have been responsible for the program of Andrea Sacchi's *Divine Wisdom* ceiling in the Palazzo Barberini,[3] and he has been linked to the development of Baroque aesthetic language and to the administration of Jesuit patronage in the second half of the century. A nearly lifelong friend of Pope Alexander VII, Pallavicino was a major figure at the papal court and has been described as "the official interpreter of Roman culture and its neo-humanistic compromise between scholasticism and naturalism, elegance and clarity, and fantasy and reason."[4]

Given the cardinal's position and interests, it is hardly surprising to find that he and Bernini were closely associated. Pallavicino played a key role in the negotiations that led to Bernini's trip to France in 1665, because Hugues de Lionne, former minister of Louis XIV at the papal court, wrote to Pallavicino and requested his assistance in the matter. It is clear that Lionne had known Pallavicino,

and perhaps also Bernini, even before the artist's trip to France, and the correspondence concerning that journey seems to have renewed the friendship of the minister and the cardinal. In December of 1665, shortly after Bernini's return, Lionne requested that the cardinal send him a portrait of himself, ideally by the great Bernini. Pallavicino initially deferred, and it was long uncertain whether the portrait was ever made. Montanari's discovery of a manuscript biography of the cardinal in the archive of the Gregorian University in Rome, however, reveals not only that the portrait was executed, but also that it was a drawing, rather than a painting, as had usually been presumed. From this starting point, Montanari was able to identify the portrait as the Yale drawing, confirming the identity of the sitter by comparison with a painted portrait of the cardinal in Sant'Andrea al Quirinale, Rome (fig. A).[5]

The red chalk and rough brown-flecked buff paper used for this drawing are similar to those in many of Bernini's portraits. As noted above, however, the red chalk of the Yale sheet has faded, apparently from long exposure to light, and at some point, the eyes of the figure were reinforced, probably by the same hand that reworked various other drawings in the Egmont Albums.[6] Yet, even the drawing's condition might be said to support Montanari's identification of the portrait. Like the other drawings in the Egmont collection, the portrait was bound into an album sometime not long after 1700; most of the fading must thus have occurred in the first thirty or forty years of the drawing's life.[7] The old inscription at the bottom of the drawing must likewise date to those years, for it is clearly in a seventeenth-century script and not in the prosaic hand that annotated so many other drawings in the albums. While not proving the case, the evidence of the early history of the drawing is certainly consistent with the proposal that it was a precious gift, solicited from the leading artist of the day and given by the sitter to an important acquaintance, who would logically have hung it for all the same reasons that painted portraits were made, given, and exhibited: to show important connections. Finally, the spare touch seen here compares to that in Bernini's famous late *Self-Portrait* at Windsor, the *Portrait of Cardinal Scipione Borghese* in the Morgan Library, and the *Portrait of Clement X* in Leipzig.[8] Like those works, the *Sforza Pallavicino* was an intimate psychological portrait rather than an imposing "official" image, befitting its function as a testament to the relationships between Bernini, Pallavicino, and Lionne.

JJM

1. For full citations, see the references listed above. In addition to the published references, the Gallery's curatorial files include letters from both Rudolf Wittkower and Walter Vitzthum indicating that both intended to publish the drawing as by Bernini himself, although neither scholar did so before his death.
2. Montanari 1997. This and Montanari's other discussions, cited above, must be credited for most of the following discussion.
3. Harris 1977, 12–13.
4. Raimondi 1966.
5. The cardinal is also said by his biographer to have kept a copy of the drawing for himself; Montanari identifies a sheet in Darmstadt, attributed to Gaulli, as that copy (Darmstadt, Hessisches Museum, inv. no. AE1557). Kept in Pallavicino's palace, the latter drawing was likely to have been the model for the painted portrait in Sant'Andrea al Quirinale.
6. For further comments on the Egmont Albums and their retouching, see the Introduction to this catalogue, as well as H-B and L, 1:xii–xiii.
7. The dark areas around the margins of the drawing result from the glue used to attach it to the backing paper, probably by Egmont in the early eighteenth century; the entire surface of the drawing, however, is badly faded.
8. For these and other examples of Bernini's portrait drawings, and for the most recent discussion of Bernini as a portraitist, see Edinburgh 1998, 47–62.

56 Raymond Lafage
Lisle sur Tarn 1656–1684 Lyon

Moses Receiving the Tablets of the Law, ca. 1680?

Pen and brown ink over black chalk, 23.5 × 35.8 cm (9 5/16 × 14 1/8 in.)

INSCRIPTIONS: recto, lower right, in pen and brown ink: *Lafage fecit.*; on mount, lower center, in pencil: *No. 8*; in pen and brown ink: *Moïse recevant les tables de la loi;* verso, lower center, in blue pencil: *Donnadieu;* lower right, in graphite: *K* over *J*

PROVENANCE: Alcide Donnadieu (ca. 1791–1861), stamp on verso, L. 98; acquired from Durlacher Bros., New York

REFERENCES: H-B and L, no. 7

Everett V. Meeks, B.A. 1901, Fund. 1956.9.66

Raymond Lafage was something of an anomaly in his day, because his oeuvre consists for the most part of drawings, plus some thirty prints. He never learned to paint, although it seems probable he intended to do so. In 1678, at the age of twenty-two, Lafage went from Toulouse, near his birthplace, to Paris, and in 1679 to Rome, where he shared a first prize for drawing at the Academy of Saint Luke. In Rome, besides being exposed to the grandiloquent forms of the Roman Baroque, he was evidently impressed by the forms and compositions of Michelangelo. He also is said to have learned to draw by copying prints after subjects by Francesco Primaticcio, an influence that is clearly evident in his work. In 1680 Lafage returned to France, first to Aix-en-Provence and then to Paris. In 1682 he went to Antwerp with the engraver and publisher Jean van der Bruggen, who published an album of some fifty prints by five engravers, first in Paris in 1689 and later in Amsterdam.[1] Lafage's early death at age twenty-eight followed a fall from a donkey when he was in Lyon; reportedly he was on his way back to Italy because he wanted to see the work of Correggio.[2]

Lafage's known oeuvre today consists of well over three hundred drawings in pen and ink, some with added blue-gray wash, most in the same loose, energetic style as the Yale drawing, as well as the thirty etchings.[3] Although his oeuvre has received scholarly attention in the second half of the twentieth century, it still awaits a thorough study, which would almost certainly locate additional drawings now unknown. The enormous appeal of Lafage's work after his death is attested to by the existence of some 125 prints reproducing his drawings published in the seventeenth century and more than 100 in the eighteenth.[4] His drawings were owned by most of the eminent eighteenth-century collectors, including the greatest of these, Pierre Crozat. Lafage was not listed at all in the first edition of Pellegrino Antonio Orlandi's *Abecedario pittorico* of 1704, but in the second edition, which was dedicated to Crozat and amplified by information supplied by him and other collectors, Orlandi asserted that "Lafage stupefied Rome with his extraordinary style of drawing, with few strokes and pure contours, with such ferocity that he seems to make a mockery of Michelangelo, Giulio Romano, and Annibale Carracci."[5]

Subjects of Lafage's compositions fall into two broad categories—bacchanals and religious subjects drawn from both the Old and New Testaments. All of Lafage's own prints depict bacchanalian subjects. The large number of compositions depicting episodes from the story of Moses—close to thirty are known—might seem to suggest that Lafage had a cohesive scheme in mind, but no evidence of such a scheme exists, whether in the form of a commission, or of a series of prints. Within the prints, it is only in the works of other printmakers that the Moses subjects appear, and these are not a group by a single individual but rather the work of a number of different printmakers.[6]

In Yale's drawing, Moses is depicted essentially as in Lafage's other compositions: he is an old man with a head of curly hair and a full beard, dressed in a tunic and drapery; his feet are bare. Moses kneels, holding the Tablets of the Law, while God, above and behind the tablets, seems to be indicating a line of the text; two cherubs support God in the air, while three others blow trumpets. Moses is depicted with rays emanating from the top of his head; the biblical text says "the skin of his face shone" after his encounter with God (Exodus 34:29–30, 35). In the lower left the Israelites are seen dancing around the Golden Calf, which Aaron had fashioned for them from the gold ornaments he had gathered. When Moses came down from Mount Sinai and saw his people worshipping the Golden Calf, he smashed the tablets on the ground.

There are far fewer depictions in the history of art of *Moses Receiving the Tablets of the Law* than of other Moses subjects, although Lafage made at least one other drawing of this subject, now in the British Museum, London (fig. A).[7] This drawing, considerably larger than Yale's, encompasses a broader view. Two figures at the left—one on ground almost as high as that on which Moses kneels, the other somewhat lower—make gestures of amazement, while on the plain below can be seen the tents of the Israelites, a group of worshippers in front of the Golden Calf, and a rocky outcropping in the distance. Although Yale's drawing also shows the worship of the Golden Calf, it focuses more closely on the encounter of Moses with God. The seemingly explosive force emanating from God and the Tablets of the Law, and the humbler position of Moses, with his knees more completely bent and his torso closer to the ground, impart an emotional intensity to Yale's drawing lacking in the example in the British Museum.

A drawing with this subject was sold at the Silvestre sale in 1810, but there is no way of knowing whether that is the one that eventually came to Yale.[8]

SB

1. Lafage 1689. See Arvengas 1965, 75.
2. The principal modern sources for Lafage's life and work are Toulouse 1962; Whitman 1963; Arvengas 1965; and Lisle sur Tarn 1990. See also, concerning a sketchbook made by Lafage in Rome, Fusconi 1996, Sproti 1996, Pomponi 1996, and Buonocore et al. 1996, 246ff., plates 1–72.
3. In Toulouse 1962, Robert Mesuret catalogued 320 drawings, plus another 133 compositions known only in prints, and 59 otherwise described. He also listed 143 rejected drawings. Lafage's prints are catalogued in RD 2: 147–159, nos. 1–21; *IFF XVIIe siècle* 6:35–46, nos. 1–31.
4. The prints after designs by Lafage are catalogued most completely in Arvengas 1965, 75–99.
5. See Orlandi 1719, 379: ". . .fece stupire Roma per il terribile modo del disegnare a pochi tratti, e puri contorni, con tale feracità, che pareva si burlasse del Buonaroti, di Giulio Romano, e di Annibale Carracci. . . . "
6. For compositions of Moses subjects by Lafage, see Toulouse 1962, nos. 12–19, 190–199, 345–351, 459–460; Arvengas 1965, 77, 79–80, 91, 95, 98 (some of these prints may reproduce drawings listed, but not illustrated, in Toulouse 1962); Lisle sur Tarn 1990, no. 22.
7. London, British Museum, inv. no. Oo, 3-2, pen and brown ink and wash, 42.6 × 62.9 cm.
8. Toulouse 1962, under no. 196: Mireur 1911–12, 4:134. Medium and dimensions are not listed.

FIGURE 56A | Raymond Lafage, *Moses Receiving the Tablets of the Law*, ca. 1680. London, British Museum.

57 Jean Jouvenet
Rouen 1644–1717 Paris

Phaeton Driving the Chariot of Apollo,
ca. 1680

Pen and brown ink with gray and black wash over black chalk, heightened with white, on gray-brown paper, laid down, 46.8 × 34.8 cm (18 7/16 × 13 11/16 in.)

INSCRIPTIONS: on backing sheet, verso, upper left, in pen and brown ink: *no. 6 / no. 6 LeBrun*

PROVENANCE: Robert W. Weir, West Point

REFERENCES: *YUAG Bulletin* 5 (1931): 39; Rosenberg 1966b, no. 25; Rouen 1966, 136–137; Schnapper 1967, 135–143; H-B and L, no. 6; Thuillier and Foucart 1970, 54; Toronto et al. 1972, 166–167; Schnapper 1974, 40–41, no. 10; Providence 1975, no. 27; Los Angeles 1976, no. 146; Brejon de Lavergnée 1979, 86; *Handbook*, 205; Malgouyres 2000, 51, under no. 42

Purchased from the estate of Robert W. Weir. 1890.17

In the last quarter of the seventeenth century, Jean Jouvenet, along with Charles de La Fosse, Antoine Coypel, and the brothers Bon de Boullogne and Louis de Boullogne, were the most eminent protégés of Charles Le Brun, who was then at the pinnacle of his career as first painter to Louis XIV and director of the Académie Royale de Peinture et de Sculpture. Like each of his accomplished young colleagues, Jouvenet went on to lead a highly distinguished career of his own with innumerable royal, religious, and private commissions. For Antoine Schnapper, Jouvenet's contribution to French art was "his ability to revitalize the French tradition by the realism of his inspiration and the breadth of his execution."[1] To this encomium, one might add the rigorous structure of his compositions, his impressive blend of the lessons learned from both Poussin and Rubens, his capacity to work on a grand scale, and the incredible plasticity of his forms.

The subject of the Yale drawing is taken from Ovid's *Metamorphoses*.[2] Phaeton was the son of Clymene, Queen of Ethiopia, and of Apollo, in his guise as Helios, god of the sun. While visiting the heavenly palace of Helios, Phaeton asks to drive his father's famous golden chariot across the sky to announce a new day in fulfillment of a previously granted wish. Helios regrets the open nature of the granted wish, but after his son persists, he feels forced to concede. The Yale drawing depicts the beginning of the ill-fated journey, when members of the court of Helios such as his sister Aurora, goddess of the dawn, throws open her gates and the four winged horses are yoked and led by the Horae, also known as the Four Seasons. Later, after an optimistic start, the youthful and half-human Phaeton loses control of the chariot and begins to scorch the Earth, so that Jupiter, king of the gods, is forced to destroy both Phaeton and the chariot in order to prevent the destruction of the planet.

The Yale drawing relates to *The Departure of Phaeton* in the Musée des Beaux-Arts, Rouen (fig. A).[3] This canvas of about 1680 bears the arms of the Longueil family, and was probably commissioned by Jean de Longueil for his family's celebrated residence in the country just outside Paris, the Château de Maisons, where it was placed over the mantel in a room on the *piano nobile*. Compositionally, the drawing is more successful than the painting. Although the Rouen canvas is cut down and in poor condition, one can see that the division between the darkness of night and the light of the coming day is so forced that the space reads poorly. Moreover, one of the Horae, just left of center, seems to obstruct the advance of the chariot. By contrast, the Yale study is animated by strong patches of light and shade that flicker across richer cloud formations, and the design remains open, so that the full forward force of the heavenly chariot under the tremendous arc of the Zodiac can be appreciated. Two other thematically related and roughly contemporary compositions by the artist survive, which have often been connected or confused with the Longueil commission: *Dawn* in the Kunstbibliothek, Berlin (fig. B),[4] and *Dawn* in the Kunsthaus Heylshof, Worms (fig. C).[5]

The Yale Jouvenet, a relatively early work, reveals that the key to the artist's many gifts was his talent as a draftsman. Even though the well-known eighteenth-century collector and historian Antoine-Joseph Dézallier d'Argenville, in one of his longest biographies, criticized Jouvenet for occasionally generating compositions that were a bit too dense and active, he also praised the artist's astonishing gifts of invention and his energetic draftsmanship.[6] Each of the figures in the present study is meticulously rendered, and each of their emphatic gestures intensifies the impact of the design. Dézallier d'Argenville also noted that Jouvenet's highly finished compositions completed with gouache, like the Yale drawing, were particularly admired and rare.[7] This sheet is a perfect example of how Jouvenet utilizes dark paper as the middle tone, delineates his basic structure with pen and ink, begins his contrasts with dark wash, and completes the composition with white gouache in order to endow his forms with volume and to perfect the chiaroscuro.

History has not been kind to artists working in France at the end of the Grand Siècle. Their work has often been decried as too academic, dry, or uninspired. Fortunately, myths like these are dispelled by masterworks like the Yale Jouvenet.

ALC

1 Schnapper 1974, 93.
2 Book 2:150–327. See also the *Imagines* of Philostratus, Book 1:11.
3 Dépôt de l'Etat, Rouen, Musée des Beaux-Arts, inv. no. D-819-3, oil on canvas, 250 × 196 cm. The painting was not in the death inventory of René de Longueil in 1677, so it is more likely to have been commissioned by his son, Jean. It was still at Maisons when the comte d'Artois took possession of the property in 1782. See the discussion in Malgouyres 2000, cat. 42.
4 Berlin, Kunstbibliothek, inv. no. Hdz 6630, red chalk with pen and black ink and brush with black ink wash, heightened with gouache, on grayish tan paper, 33.5 × 25 cm; see Schnapper 1974, 225, no. 151, fig. 168.
5 Worms, Kunsthaus Heylshof, inv. no. W59, pen and black ink and brush with black ink wash, heightened with gouache, on grayish tan paper, 25.7 × 41.7 cm; see Brejon de Lavergnée 1979, 86, fig. 4.
6 Dézallier d'Argenville 1762, 4:209 and 213.
7 Dézallier d'Argenville 1762, 4:213.

FIGURE 57A | Jean Jouvenet, *The Departure of Phaeton*, ca. 1680. Rouen, Musée des Beaux-Arts.

FIGURE 57B | Jean Jouvenet, *Dawn*, ca. 1680. Berlin, Kunstbibliothek.

FIGURE 57C | Jean Jouvenet, *Dawn*, ca. 1680. Worms, Kunsthaus Heylshof.

58 Joseph Vivien
Lyon 1657–1734 Bonn

Portrait of a Man, ca. 1680–1695

Pastel on blue-gray paper, mounted on wood panel, 76.2 × 63.5 cm (30 × 25 in.)

INSCRIPTIONS: label on verso, in pen and brown ink, in an eighteenth- or nineteenth-century hand: *[J]oseph Vivien / Lyon (Rhône) en 1657 / [B]onn, près Cologne en 1735*

PROVENANCE: Adolphe le Goupy, Paris (early 20th century); Edward B. Greene, Cleveland

REFERENCES: unpublished

Gift of Edward B. Greene, B.A. 1900, in memory of Emerson Tuttle, B.A. 1914, M.A. (Hon.) 1930. 1946.110

Exhibited at Yale University Art Gallery only

The recent rediscovery of the pastel *Portrait of a Man* in storage at the Yale University Art Gallery was an exciting one, because there are few works by Joseph Vivien in American collections. Vivien should be credited as the first significant artist to create large-scale pastel portraits that imitated the appearance of oil paintings, works that were intended to be placed under glass—to protect their friable surfaces—framed, and displayed.

Little is known about the beginning of Vivien's career.[1] All his early works are either lost or cannot be attributed to him with any certainty. The first extant document puts him in Paris in 1672 as a student of the history painter François Bonnemer, and in 1678 the Académie Royale de Peinture et de Sculpture awarded him second prize for his painting depicting Adam and Eve (now lost). By the 1680s—and perhaps following the advice of Charles Le Brun, director of the Académie Royale—Vivien had turned to the lucrative and competitive business of portraiture. Given the growing interest in pastels in the second half of the seventeenth century, specializing in the medium was a shrewd way for Vivien to distinguish himself in the Parisian portrait market. By the turn of the century, his unprecedented ability to translate the effects of oil painting into pastel would bring him international recognition, even before he became a full member of the Académie Royale in 1701 with the submission of his two assigned reception pieces—pastel portraits of the architect Robert de Cotte and the sculptor François Girardon (Paris, Louvre).[2] Vivien had been asked to send a self-portrait (dated 1699) to the Uffizi in Florence for the collection of artists' self-portraits owned by Cosimo III de' Medici, Grand Duke of Tuscany,[3] and in 1700 Vivien was commissioned to portray the Dauphin, Louis de France, as well as his three sons.[4] His contemporary Florent Le Comte lauded the artist as "le Vandick du siecle pour le Pastel."[5] And in the Salon of 1704, the artist exhibited no fewer than twenty pastel portraits. Vivien's work became widely known through numerous reproductive engravings after his portraits.

One of Vivien's most notable accomplishments was his appointment as court painter to Maximilian II Emanuel, Elector of Bavaria—for whom the artist began working in the 1690s—and then subsequently to Maximilian's brother Joseph Clemens, the Elector-Archbishop of Cologne. Upon the death of the latter, Vivien also served as court painter to his successor and nephew Clemens August. In the eighteenth century, Vivien was one of many French artists employed by foreign monarchs seeking to emulate French taste. The financial compensation was certainly an incentive to work for such rulers, as was the prestige of being associated with a royal court, and, in Vivien's case, for patrons linked to the French royal family through marriage. The sister of Maximilian II Emanuel and Joseph Clemens, Maria Anna Christine Victoria, had been the wife of the Dauphin. Vivien spent decades fashioning an imposing series of oil and pastel portraits of the Electors' families. So many official commissions, of course, necessitated several trips abroad, and the artist spent considerable time away from Paris to visit Maximilian II Emanuel's courts in Brussels and Munich, as well as Joseph Clemens's court in Bonn. From 1715 to 1733, Vivien increasingly devoted his time to painting the most ambitious work of his career: *Allegory of the Reunion of Maximilian II Emanuel, Elector of Bavaria, with his Family* (Munich, Bayerische Staatsgemäldesammlungen).[6] The artist, in fact, died in Bonn in 1734 at the age of seventy-seven while transporting this monumental group portrait to Munich.

Although the identity of the sitter in the Yale pastel is unknown, the multiple ribbon bows behind his lace cravat enable us to date the portrait to the 1680s or early 1690s.[7] *Portrait of a Man* may very well be the artist's earliest extant work.[8] The palette and technique adumbrate the formal tendencies of Vivien's later pastels. Here we see the artist's preference for vivid jewel tones, such as the raspberry-colored bows and the pink-red lining of the cape—these rich hues enliven the otherwise muted palette of gray, brown, black, and white, drawing attention to the sitter's face. The shades of raspberry and pink are picked up in the sitter's left cheek. In certain areas, such as those of the flesh, Vivien carefully blended his strokes, whereas in other passages he left his fine strokes visible, whether to distinguish individual strands of hair in the voluminous brown wig, to delineate the crisp details of the lace pattern in the cravat, or to define the sitter's nose and blue eyes in his long face. Vivien's goal was verisimilitude, and the tactility of the pastel medium could not be better suited for rendering flesh and fabrics. *Portrait of a Man* reminds us why, by the eighteenth century, the medium was commonly referred to as *peinture au pastel*. It was Vivien who prepared the ground for that extraordinary flowering of the pastel that would culminate in the works of Rosalba Carriera, Jean-Étienne Liotard, and Maurice-Quentin de La Tour.

RH

1. The best source on Vivien is Börsch-Supan 1963. See also Ratouis de Limay 1946, 18–23, and Monnier 1972, nos. 14–20.
2. Börsch-Supan 1963, 167, no. 24, and 174, no. 35; Monnier 1972, nos. 15–16.
3. Börsch-Supan 1963, 189–190, no. 88; Rosenberg et al. 1977, 40–41, no. 8.
4. There are versions of these portraits in both Paris and Munich. Börsch-Supan 1963, 180–181, nos. 58–59; 186–187, no. 76; and 165–166, no. 18; Monnier 1972, nos. 18–20. The version of the Dauphin's portrait that was once in the collection of Louis XIV has disappeared.
5. Le Comte 1699–1700, 3:266; Le Comte 1972, 334.
6. Munich, Bayerische Staatsgemäldesammlungen; Börsch-Supan 1963, 191, no. 102.
7. See de Marly 1987, 83 and 88. I have given the portrait a date of ca. 1680–95, keeping in mind that changes in fashion—in this case, the wearing of a plain cravat in the 1690s—sometimes do not take full effect for a few years.
8. Börsch-Supan 1963, 164, no. 9, dates Vivien's first documented portrait, of Nicolas Barré (now lost), to ca. 1686, and 165, no. 17, dates Vivien's first firmly attributed extant pastel, of Jean de la Bruyère (private collection), to ca. 1695.

59 Hyacinthe Rigaud
Perpignan 1659–1743 Paris

Portrait of Edward Villiers, 1st Earl of Jersey, 1698–99

Black and white chalk, heightened with white, and lightly squared in black chalk, on blue paper; laid down, 37.5 × 28.6 cm (14¾ × 11 5/16 in.)

PROVENANCE: Edward B. Greene, Cleveland

REFERENCES: Wolf 1942, no. 10; Newark 1960, no. 42 (as Attributed to Rigaud, but noting George Gallenkamp's attribution to Viénot); H-B and L, no. 27 (as Attributed to Viénot); Toronto et al. 1972, 203; O'Neill 1984b, 186–194; Cambridge et al. 1998–2000, 156 (as Attributed to Charles Viennot); Meaux 2000, 42; Perreau 2004, 236, n. 299

Gift of Edward B. Greene, B.A. 1900. 1937.329

Hyacinthe Rigaud's state portraits, showing sitters in rich clothing and full wigs against backgrounds of columns or flying drapery, present the lasting image of late Baroque court culture, and especially of Louis XIV's Versailles. So great was Rigaud's reputation, especially after his 1701 portrait of Louis XIV (Paris, Louvre), that scores of important foreign visitors to Versailles commissioned portraits from the artist. This beautiful drawing, related to Rigaud's portrait of Edward Villiers, 1st Earl of Jersey (1656–1711), is one such case (fig. A). Villiers had accompanied Queen Mary of England to the Netherlands in 1677 for her marriage to William of Orange and, returning to England, was a favorite at the new court. In 1695–97 he served as William III's envoy-extraordinary to the United Provinces, for which he was created Earl of Jersey, and between September 1698 and May 1699 he was in Paris as ambassador-extraordinary to the court of King Louis XIV; Rigaud painted Jersey's portrait (and made this drawing) at that time. Throughout William III's reign, Jersey occupied various offices including that of Lord Chamberlain, but he fell from favor after the accession of Queen Anne in 1702.

The Yale drawing is one of many that carefully copy Rigaud's finished portraits. The faint squaring on these sheets was the last thing added to the drawing, indicating that it was not used in producing the drawings, but rather, would have been used to transfer the compositions to some other work. It is nonetheless universally believed that the drawings are records of, rather than preparatory to, the finished paintings, and that the squaring might have been used in making engravings of the pictures, or else functioned in cases when the pose or the setting of one composition would be replicated in a portrait for a later client.[1] Yet, the primary function of these sheets was probably to record Rigaud's achievements.[2] The drawings were kept in portfolios, and it is clear that Rigaud understood them as a set or series, for they are remarkably consistent in media, finish, and size.[3]

The attribution of these sheets has, however, been the subject of some debate, for a successful painter like Rigaud necessarily employed a substantial workshop of assistants,[4] and Rigaud's account books list payments to three different assistants for drawn copies of the master's portraits. The first group of these payments was made in 1700 to "Viénot," who has been identified as Charles Viennot, and includes an entry for "un dessein [sic] de milord Jersey."[5] George Gallenkamp argued that the Yale drawing was this copy by Viennot,[6] and subsequently, questions have been raised about many of the drawings related to Rigaud's portraits.[7] In contrast, Mary O'Neill reminds us that many of these sheets, rather than simple copies by pupils

FIGURE 59A | Hyacinthe Rigaud, *Portrait of Edward Villiers, 1st Earl of Jersey*, 1698–99. Cambridge, St. John's College.

and assistants, exhibit "a remarkable degree of characterization and spontaneity and insight . . . virtuoso execution and refined charm," and should instead be considered the work of Rigaud himself.[8] Indeed, there is little essential difference between the handling of media in the Yale sheet and that in other drawings whose attribution to Rigaud has never been questioned: the large *Samuel Bernard* in Kansas City, for example,[9] and the few surviving preparatory studies such as the *Studies of Hands* in San Francisco.[10]

The questions regarding authorship that arise from these drawings are not limited to Rigaud alone but are instead representative of a common problem in the study of seventeenth- and eighteenth-century portraiture. On the one hand, many seventeenth-century patrons accepted as the work of "van Dyck" a range of paintings that included works done wholly by him as well as those done largely by his studio but under his supervision. On the other hand, the writings of the eighteenth-century critic and collector Dézallier d'Argenville suggest that at least some connoisseurs made subtle distinctions between different copies by the master and those by his studio.[11] As O'Neill points out, drawings like *Lord Jersey* are copies in the sense that they follow earlier works, but they are nonetheless "second originals" by the master. While Viennot might have begun work on the sheet by laying out the composition, this drawing must have been worked up and finished by Rigaud himself.[12] There are no weak or wooden passages that reveal the hand of an assistant, and instead the bravura touches that convey so impressively the textures of silk, skin, and lace are entirely consistent with those in drawings surely by the master.[13] Even in its slightly rubbed condition, the Yale drawing helps one understand Mariette's enthusiasm for Rigaud: "for his treatment of drapery, I would dare to say that he surpassed all those who preceded him."[14]

JJM

1. For examples of drawings made for engravings, see O'Neill 1984a.
2. The Duke de Saint-Simon explains that Rigaud's usual practice was to keep a record of all his work (quoted in O'Neill 1984b, 192, n. 12).
3. Among the other drawings of similar finish, media, and size (38 or 39 × 28 or 29 cm), also with light squaring like the Yale sheet, are: Paris, Louvre, inv. nos. 32726 and 32725; Chicago, Art Institute, inv. no. 1922.310; Frankfurt, Städelsches Kunstinstitut und Städtische Galerie, inv. nos. 1068 and 1862; the *Portrait of a Lady* in the Horvitz Collection, Boston; and many others.
4. On Rigaud's workshop and assistants, see Perreau 2004, 85ff.
5. Roman 1919, 71.
6. Gallenkamp's attribution, with references to a forthcoming article on Viennot, is cited in Newark 1960, no. 42, and in Gallenkamp 1960, 228, n. 24, but the indicated article seems never to have been published.
7. In addition to the various published discussions of the attribution problem, the "School of Rigaud" or "Attributed to Rigaud" label under which many drawings are catalogued in museum and sale catalogues is often a reflection of the problem of the copyists rather than of the quality of the drawings.
8. O'Neill 1984b, 186. See Perreau 2004, 118–120 for similar arguments. There are more drawings after Rigaud's paintings than there are references to copies by Viennot and the other assistants, although as Margaret Morgan Grasselli notes (Cambridge et al. 1998–2000, 365, n. 2) "not all of Rigaud's account books have survived, making it impossible to know how many drawings were produced by members of his studio."
9. Kansas City, William Rockhill Nelson Gallery of Art, inv. no. 66.15; see O'Neill 1984a or Toronto et al. 1972, no. 122.
10. San Francisco, California Palace of the Legion of Honor/Achenbach Foundation, inv. no. 1953.34; see Toronto et al. 1972, no. 123.
11. Dézallier d'Argenville 1745, 1:xli–xlii, quoted in part by O'Neill 1984b, 186–187.
12. O'Neill 1984b, 186, cites a well-known passage in Rigaud's will that refers to "un portefeuille de Dessins dapres les portraits faits par le Sieur Testateur et qu'il a retouchés."
13. Another possible hypothesis regarding the matter of copies is that Viennot might have been responsible for making copies of Rigaud's drawings, rather than for the original drawn copies after the portraits. In support of this idea, one might cite a sheet in Darmstadt (Hessiches Landesmuseum, inv. no. Hz 2493) that is, as O'Neill notes (O'Neill 1984b, 187) "merely an accurate copy" of the drawing in Chicago (Art Institute, inv. no. 1922.310) that is connected with Rigaud's lost portrait of *Gédéon Berbier du Metz*. This is another of the portraits that Viennot was paid to copy, and one might speculate that the Darmstadt drawing, rather than the Chicago original, was Viennot's work. Carrying the idea further, it might also be suggested that the copies like that in Darmstadt could have been kept close at hand as Rigaud and his studio reused poses and props in later portraits, while the more carefully finished drawings like the *Lord Jersey* sheet remained safely in portfolios.
14. Mariette 1851–60, 4:1857–1858, quoted in Toronto et al. 1972, no. 123.

60 Gilles-Marie Oppenord
Paris 1672–1742 Paris

Ornamental Design with Father Time, ca. 1700

Pen and brown ink and gray wash, 41 × 28.7 cm (16 1/8 × 11 15/16 in.)

PROVENANCE: Maurice Delacre (d. 1938), Ghent; his sale, Gutekunst und Klipstein, Bern, 21–22 June 1949, lot 168 (as French School, eighteenth century); Edmond Fatio, Geneva, stamp lower right (not in Lugt); acquired from H. M. Calmann, London

REFERENCES: Viale Ferrero 1957, 379, fig. 19, and no. 91 (as Verain); London 1960, no. 23 (as Berain); H-B and L, no. 4 (as Berain); Dee 1990

Everett V. Meeks, B.A. 1901, Fund. 1961.9.38

Gilles-Marie Oppenord was the son of an *ébeniste du roi,* and thus grew up in the milieu of artists in the royal service, living with his family in an apartment in the Louvre between 1684 and 1692. In the latter year, as a protégé of Edouard Colbert, Superintendent of the Royal Buildings, he was sent to Rome to continue his studies of architecture and design, and it was Rome that was his prime teacher. He remained there for seven years, affiliated with the French Academy, filling numerous sketchbooks and albums with drawings of the significant Roman monuments, particularly the buildings of Gian Lorenzo Bernini and Francesco Borromini.[1] Following his return to Paris, Oppenord did not at first receive a royal position, but he enjoyed ecclesiastical and private patronage; he also made book illustrations, an activity he continued throughout his life. Eventually he became chief architect to the Duke of Orléans, who, upon the death of Louis XIV in 1715, became Regent for the five-year-old Louis XV. In 1722 Oppenord was granted a title of nobility, and he was chief architect for the Church of Saint-Sulpice from 1725 to 1731. He became Director of the Royal Manufactories, and then Director-General of Buildings and Gardens. Among Oppenord's private patrons was the greatest of the French collectors, Pierre Crozat; the artist lived the last decade of his life in a rented apartment in the Hotel Crozat.[2]

Although Haverkamp-Begemann and Logan published this inventive and exuberant drawing as by Jean Berain, they expressed some doubt about the attribution, and as early as 1976 Elaine Evans Dee stated her opinion that it is by Oppenord.[3] In 1990 she published the drawing, characterizing the "bold, sure, fluid pen line [and] the shading in gray wash within the outline" as comparable to the sketches Oppenord did in Rome.[4] Peter Fuhring had independently come to the same conclusion about the attribution of the drawing to Oppenord.[5] Dee proposed a date for Yale's drawing shortly after the artist's return from Rome, although she did not suggest any destination for the design.

The iconography of the drawing alludes to the passage of time, with a hint of a funerary theme. The decoration is divided into four tiers. The figure of Time, naked except for a cloak falling behind him, the handle of his scythe within the crook of his arm and holding a struggling infant, on the third tier, is the focus of the composition. Above this figure is a baldaquin hung with draperies, which have been colored with a gray wash; on top of this baldaquin sits a winged hourglass, symbolizing the fleeting nature of time. To right and left of Father Time are braziers atop filigree tripods. In the tier below, the base of which is the top of a console that constitutes the bottom tier, a small central panel shows two nymphs, one holding an arrow pointed downward—an emblem of death—dancing around a draped sculptural figure. Flanking this scene, female figures seated on sphinxes hold the leashes of two barking hounds who are shown standing on their hind legs at the outer sides of the console, on the level below. A male and a female term, bending forward to fit under the top surface of the console, hold curved horns that have puffs of smoke emerging from their ends.

Numerous other drawn works by Oppenord show similar figures of Time; some examples are a drawing at the Metropolitan Museum, some of the sketches in a printed book, the pages of which Oppenord used for his own designs, and a sketch at the École des Beaux-Arts, Paris.[6] Similar dogs can also be found, in, among others: a design for a panel with Diana, in Berlin; a study for a cartouche in the Metropolitan Museum; a design for a coach panel, also with Diana; and sketches in some of the pages of the printed book mentioned above.[7] The use of small dots to create a background, as in the scene below the figure of Time, is also seen in this book.[8]

Although but a small percentage of Oppenord's designs were actually built (and nothing of what was built survives), he was greatly admired, and his influence was widespread through three series of engravings of his designs published by Gabriel Huquier. They are familiarly called by names reflecting the size of the plates: *Recueil de dessins d'ornement,* with 72 plates, is called *Le moyen Oppenord* and brings together suites published separately in 1737 and 1738. *Livre de fragments d'architecture recueillis et dessinés à Rome d'après les plus beaux monuments (Le petit Oppenord),* with 168 plates, was published before 1748, and *Le grand Oppenord,* with 120 plates, between 1748 and 1751.

SB

1. Connors 1996.
2. There is no monograph on Oppenord. Peter Fuhring recently summarized his activity in Paris–Sydney–Ottawa 2003–06, 313, and see 302–314. See also Dee 1982; Fuhring 1989, nos. 56–59, 854; Dee in *Grove Dictionary* 23:457–459. Elaine Dee generously consulted with me about this drawing (by oral communication, 19 June 2005, and by electronic communication, 21 August 2005).
3. Manuscript note in curatorial file, Department of Prints, Drawings, and Photographs, dated 26 March 1976.
4. Dee 1990, 334.
5. Electronic communication, 31 March 2005. I am very grateful to Peter Fuhring for sharing his comments about this drawing with me.
6. See New York 1991–92, no. 84; Fuhring 1989, no. 58, 5 recto and 25 recto; and Paris–Sydney–Ottawa 2003–06, no. 79-18. The book catalogued as no. 58 in Fuhring 1989 is now at Montreal, Canadian Centre for Architecture.
7. See Fuhring 1989, no. 56 and no. 58, 54 verso; Dee 1990, fig. 3; New York 1991–92, no. 85.
8. Fuhring 1989, no. 58, 8 recto.

61 Claude Gillot
Langres 1673–1722 Paris

The Feast of Pan, 1707–08

Red chalk over graphite on light tan paper, laid down onto tan paper; left, right, and lower edges outlined with dark brown ink

Remounted in three sections: left, 15 × 10 cm (5 15/16 × 3 15/16 in.); right, 14.9 × 9.7 cm (5 7/8 × 3 13/16 in.); middle, 16.3 × 16.6 cm (6 7/16 × 6 9/16 in.)[1]

PROVENANCE: Edmond and Jules de Goncourt, Paris, after 1848 (L. 1089); sale, Paris, 15–17 February 1897, no. 105; acquired from Hector Brame, Paris

REFERENCES: E. de Goncourt, *Notes manuscrites concernant les achats des Goncourt*, MS, n.d., Paris, Institut Néerlandais, Collection Frits Lugt; Paris 1879, no. 467; Poley 1938, 49; Los Angeles 1961, no. 8; Munhall 1962, 22–35; H-B and L, no. 51; Launay 1991, no. 112; *Handbook*, 208; Raux 1995, no. 20; Stein 1997, 75; Choné 1999, 34–43; New York–Ottawa 1999–2000, no. 56

Everett V. Meeks, B.A. 1901, Fund. 1958.9.5a

Claude Gillot made this drawing as probably the final preparation for a print of the same subject that he executed, in the same direction, as one in a set of four prints, etchings with engraving, published by Pierre de Rochefort, circa 1708 (fig. A). These four prints represent *Bacchanales* or bacchanalian celebrations to the pagan gods Pan, Diana, Bacchus, and Faunus.[2] While the inscription on each of the four prints, "*Inventé, peint et gravé par C. Gillot*," suggests they were based on paintings executed earlier by the artist, no such works are known today (one relating to *The Feast of Bacchus* in the Musée d'Art et d'Histoire at Langres is only a crude copy after Gillot's print).[3] However, red chalk studies for the *Feast of Diana Interrupted by Satyrs* and *The Feast of Faunus, God of the Forests*, both in the same direction as the prints, do exist—the former in a European private collection (fig. B), the latter in the Harvard University Art Museums, Cambridge, Mass. (fig. C).[4] None is known relating to *The Feast of Bacchus*. The Musée des Beaux-Arts, Lille, possesses another drawing of *The Feast of Pan* by Gillot (fig. D), also in red chalk and of identical dimensions as the others mentioned above.[5] Its many compositional differences, however, suggest—as Perrin Stein has argued—that it "was made first, before a series was planned."[6]

The artist may have employed counterproofs of these drawings to transfer the compositions to his engraving plate. One such counterproof, of *The Feast of Faunus, God of the Forests*, was spotted by Alan Wintermute at a London sale of 3 April 1995, miscatalogued under lot 149 as a work by Charles-Nicolas Cochin.[7] The Yale drawing, however, shows no evidence of ever having been counterproofed.

The small stamp in black ink, "DE GONCOURT," in the lower right corner of this drawing, attests to its previous ownership by the distinguished collectors Edmond and Jules de Goncourt. Edmond's description of the two brothers' collections, *La maison d'un artiste*, provides an eloquent appraisal of Gillot's individual style as manifested in this *Feast of Pan*:

> the teacher of Watteau, a great talent, equally at ease with antique themes as with those of the contemporary Italian comedies, a draughtsman with an elegant

FIGURE 61A | Claude Gillot, *The Feast of Pan*, ca. 1708. New Haven, Yale University Art Gallery.

FIGURE 61B | Claude Gillot, *The Feast of Diana Interrupted by Satyrs*, ca. 1708. Private collection.

FIGURE 61C | Claude Gillot, *The Feast of Faunus, God of the Forests*, ca. 1708. Cambridge, Mass., Fogg Art Museum, Harvard University Art Museums.

FIGURE 61D | Claude Gillot, *The Feast of Pan*, ca. 1708. Lille, Musée des Beaux-Arts.

and intricate line, whose pen produced sketches full of fantasy, but who was never able, in his finished drawings, to rid himself of the dry manner of the print-maker. His pencil is rather like the point of an etching-needle which would cut into the paper, and viewed from a distance, his sanguine drawings look like counterproofs of delicate prints executed in red ink."[8]

Earlier, in the eighteenth century, the great connoisseur Pierre-Jean Mariette had called Gillot's *Bacchanales* "his greatest works."[9]

EM

1 Of the known studies for the *Bacchanales*, *The Feast of Pan* is the only one composed on three pieces of paper and the only one with a raised central section. Wintermute in New York– Ottawa 1999–2000, 202, suggested that Gillot "may have made a mistake, or changed his mind while composing the drawing and salvaged the sheet by 'patching' in the new section."

2 Populus 1930, 75–79.

3 Reproduced in Choné 1999, 43.

4 The private collection drawing, sold Christie's, London, 2 July 1991, no. 154, is in red chalk over graphite, 16.5 × 36.7 cm. The drawing at Harvard, inv. no. 1991.163, is red chalk over graphite, 16.1 × 36.2 cm. See Raux 1995, 90 n. 3, and Wintermute in New York–Ottawa 1999–2000, 202–203.

5 Inv. no. 1414, red chalk over graphite, 15 × 36 cm. De Goncourt MS (see references), 13, no. 133 ("*Bacchanale, sanguine, 20 francs*"); Poley 1938, 47, no. 55; Raux 1995, no. 20; Choné 1999, 43.

6 Stein 1997, 75.

7 Wintermute in New York–Ottawa 1999–2000, 203, n. 3.

8 Goncourt 1881, 1:83–84.

9 For the quotation "*ses meilleurs ouvrages,*" see Populus 1930, 75.

62 Jean-Antoine Watteau
Valenciennes 1684–1721 Nogent-sur-Marne

Two Recruits, ca. 1715

Red chalk, 16.1 × 15.6 cm (6 5/16 × 6 1/8 in.)

PROVENANCE: Jean-Pierre Norblin de La Gourdaine, Paris; Martin Norblin de La Gourdaine, Paris; Baronne de Conantré, Paris; her daughter, Baronne de Rublé, Paris; her daughter, Mme de Witte, Paris; her daughter, Marquise de Bryas, Orange; Galerie Cailleux, Paris

REFERENCES: Goncourt 1875, under no. 619; Cailleux 1959; YUAG Bulletin 28 (1962): 28 and 52; Mongan 1965, 45; Cambridge 1967b, unnumbered cat.; H-B and L, no. 70; Washington–Paris 1984–85, no. 37; Berlin 1985, no. 23; Handbook, 209; Rosenberg and Prat 1996, no. 277; New York–Ottawa 1999–2000, no. 11; Grasselli 2001, 314

Everett V. Meeks, B.A. 1901, Fund. 1961.9.39

The delicacy of his touch, the graceful movement of his figures, and the elegance of his *mise-en-page* have made Jean-Antoine Watteau one of the greatest and most admired draftsmen of the western tradition. His drawings were so esteemed during his own time that soon after his death a selection of them was engraved and assembled in what is known as the *Recueil Jullienne*.[1] Unlike his most distinguished colleagues, Watteau was not a student formed by the Académie Royale de Peinture et de Sculpture. Despite his incessant practice of drawing—an activity he preferred to painting—his formation was not based on the rigorous and systematic study of the nude required by the Académie, and his finished compositions were not prepared by what was then considered to be a standard series of preparatory studies. This may be one of the reasons for the seemingly complete or finished appearance of so many of his sheets. The vast majority of his drawn oeuvre consists of figure studies, to which he often returned for source material when contemplating a composition for a canvas. One of the most special and enigmatic aspects of Watteau's production is the mood of quiet reflection evoked in so many of his works. Although it is believed that most of his studies were drawn

FIGURE 62A | Jean-Antoine Watteau, *Three Studies of a Drummer*, ca. 1714. Cambridge, Mass., Fogg Art Museum, Harvard University Art Museums.

spontaneously after individuals he encountered during his daily activities, it often seems as if his images are floating before us from the interior world of his imagination.

A considerable portion of Watteau's early paintings is devoted to military subjects, a theme to which he returned frequently throughout most of his short career.[2] Executed in red chalk—the artist's preferred medium—his *Two Recruits* is a late and particularly refined example of the type of soldier drawing that Watteau utilized from his sketchbooks to produce his military compositions.[3] This sheet resurfaced only in the late 1950s, when it was discovered and published by Jean Cailleux, together with three other studies of soldiers that were all once part of the collection of the late-eighteenth-century painter Jean-Pierre Norblin de La Gourdaine.[4] Although roughly two dozen of Watteau's drawings of soldiers are known, there are no extant detail studies. Instead, each of these works depicts the full figure of each recruit.[5] In the Yale drawing, we intrude upon a private moment between two soldiers in the midday sun; one recruit stops to adjust his shoe, as his companion pauses with him and looks on, perhaps continuing the conversation they were having only moments before. Watteau's touch in this sheet is remarkably soft and atmospheric. He endowed each of these two figures with an exceptional ease of motion and, characteristically, extreme care was elaborated on the details of their hats, their coiffures, their uniforms, and their weaponry. Like most of his studies of soldiers, the two recruits in the present drawing are not found in any of Watteau's military paintings, although the kneeling recruit was engraved in the *Recueil Jullienne*.[6]

Historically, there are a number of different approaches to the dating of Watteau's studies of soldiers. The two most recent surveys of his corpus of nearly seven hundred drawings continue with this tradition. Margaret Morgan Grasselli prefers to see these soldier studies divided into several fairly distinct groups, dating from around 1708 to 1715, but the combined effort of Pierre Rosenberg and Louis-Antoine Prat proposes a more dispersed placement, with dates that range from 1709 to 1715. The Yale drawing is dated by Rosenberg and Prat to either 1712 or 1714/15, whereas Grasselli (with whom the present author agrees) considers only the latter date of 1715 as a possibility. It is closest in handling to soldier studies in the Louvre in Paris and the Musée Condé in Chantilly, which display the same thin, fluid line and a similar sensitivity to surface and atmospheric light.[7] Moreover, it depicts a detail of weaponry—both a sword and a knife held to their sides by a belt—that appears in only one other military scene by the artist, his lost *Departure of the Garrison*, which dates no earlier than 1715, and is known through an engraving by Simon-François Ravenet the Elder.[8]

The present drawing and its closest comparisons form one of at least three late groups of soldier studies. The second group includes the *Three Studies of a Drummer* of circa 1714 in the Fogg Art Museum, Cambridge (fig. A);[9] and the third group contains the *Three Soldiers Holding Rifles* of circa 1715 in the Institut Néerlandais in Paris (fig. B).[10] When compared to the Yale drawing, the soldiers in the slightly earlier Fogg sheet reveal a somewhat more rigid approach to form, as well as a greater tendency toward tonal consistency across the sheet, whereas those in the

FIGURE 62B | Jean-Antoine Watteau, *Three Soldiers Holding Rifles*, ca. 1715. Paris, Institut Néerlandais.

Institut Néerlandais drawing display livelier figures generated by a bolder use of chalk that results in a larger range of contrasts.

ALC

1. Jullienne 1726–28, no. 242 (engraved by Jean Audran).
2. For a selection of Watteau's earlier military pictures, see Pierre Rosenberg in Washington–Paris 1984–85, nos. P4–P6 and P15–P16.
3. For Watteau's technique as a draftsman, see Margaret Morgan Grasselli in Washington–Paris 1984–85, 53–59, and, most recently, the Introduction to Rosenberg and Prat 1996, 1:ix–xxxii.
4. The other three drawings are Rosenberg and Prat 1996, nos. 209, 210, and 278. See Cailleux 1959.
5. On the types of drawings depicting soldiers, see Margaret Morgan Grasselli in Washington–Paris 1984–85, 63–64, 88–89, 95–97, and 102–103.
6. Watteau's drawings of soldiers include Rosenberg and Prat 1996, nos. 25, 26, 57–61, 64–68, 94, 151–153, 176–180, 209–210, and 277–278.
7. *Two Soldiers, One Seated and One Standing*, Paris, Louvre, inv. no. 27544; Rosenberg and Prat 1996, no. 152. *Two Soldiers, One Seated and Drinking and One Walking Toward the Right*, Chantilly, Musée Condé, inv. no. A.I. 304bis/N.I. 448; Rosenberg and Prat 1996, no. 153.
8. For the first mention of this interesting detail, see Margaret Morgan Grasselli in Washington–Paris 1984–85, 103; for the engraving after the lost painting, see Dacier, Hérold, and Vuaflart 1921–29, no. 276.
9. Cambridge, Mass., Harvard University Art Museums, inv. no. 1964.14, red chalk, 15.3 × 19.3 cm; Rosenberg and Prat 1996, no. 210. This second group of three includes Rosenberg and Prat 1996, no. 206.
10. Paris, Institut Néerlandais, Collection Frits Lugt, inv. no. I.7208, red chalk, 15.1 × 19.9 cm; Rosenberg and Prat 1996, no. 209. Others in this last group include Rosenberg and Prat 1996, nos. 176–180 and 278.

63 François Boucher
Paris 1703–1770 Paris

The Dilapidated Farmhouse, ca. 1740

Black and white chalk, heightened with white, on blue paper, 34.6 × 48 cm (13⅝ × 18⅞ in.)

INSCRIPTIONS: recto, signed, lower left, in pen and brown ink: *f Boucher*; verso, in graphite, center: *41 1/2: 58*; lower right: *Kaur(?)*; lower center: *68*

PROVENANCE: Jean-Claude-Gaspard de Sireul (1720/30–1781), Paris; his sale, Paris, 3 December 1781, lot 101; Geheimrat A. Köster; his sale, C. G. Boerner, Leipzig, 13 November 1924, lot 89; Cafmeyer; Lucien Guiraud; sale, Paris, 15 March 1968, lot 7; Galerie Cailleux, Paris; Charles E. Slatkin, Inc. Galleries, New York

REFERENCES: Paris 1951, xx; Ananoff 1966, 163, no. 609; *YUAG Bulletin* 32.3 (1970): 31; Washington–Chicago 1973–74, no. 56; Eisler 1975, no. F.15; New York 1980, no. 54; Landau 1983, 372–373; New Haven 1984, no. 2; *Handbook*, 207; Paris 2003–04, 68 and 75

Everett V. Meeks, B.A. 1901, and Paul Mellon, B.A. 1929, Funds. 1969.16

"Boucher was one of those men who indicate the taste of a century, express, personify, embody it. In him, French eighteenth-century art was manifest in all the peculiarity of its character. Boucher was not only its painter but its chief witness, its chief representative, its very type."[1] The words of the distinguished late-nineteenth-century critics and connoisseurs Edmond and Jules de Goncourt still provide one of the most incisive understandings of Boucher's enormous contribution to the visual arts of his time. The artist's brilliant and prolific career—he boasted to have produced more than 10,000 drawings and 1,000 paintings—was punctuated by a steady series of achievements, from his student years in the atelier of François Le Moyne and his winning of the coveted Prix de Rome, to his eventual appointments as painter to Madame de Pompadour, director of the Académie Royale de Peinture et de Sculpture, and first painter to Louis XV.[2]

The Yale Boucher has an illustrious provenance, as it was once in the collection of Jean-Claude-Gaspard de Sireul, the artist's most avid contemporary devotee, who possessed more than two hundred of Boucher's paintings, drawings, and pastels.[3] The mixture of black and white chalk and gouache on blue paper seen here is one of the artist's most preferred techniques. In this work the contours are enlivened by the vigor of his strokes, his frequent but pointed use of white across the composition, and his active use of the blue of the sheet as the middle tone. The vitality of Boucher's hand in this drawing was even noted in the catalogue of Sireul's sale as *une touche spirituelle*. Although the media utilized to execute the present sheet is rather typical for Boucher, some seemingly atypical aspects of his draftsmanship and composition are also evident here. These include an unusually high level of finish, a notable compression of space into the foreground, and a lack of figures of any significant scale. These qualities serve as an important reminder of two important facets of Boucher's endeavors in the mid-1730s. The first is that the artist produced stage designs for operatic productions of the Académie Royale de Musique.[4] The atypical characteristics described above would be obligatory if the drawing was indeed created as a backdrop for a theatrical production. In which case, one cannot help but imagine that the actors are about to make their entrance on stage. Second, Boucher was also asked to submit designs for the Beauvais Tapestry Factory by its newly appointed director, Jean-Baptiste Oudry, sometime soon after 1734, and the venture was enormously successful. For this type of work, as Boucher ably demonstrates, large open areas must be avoided, but the staffage and other details should not detract from the primary protagonists that have not yet been drawn.[5]

One of Boucher's most important contributions to eighteenth-century art was his approach to the pastoral landscape.[6] Removed from the classical tradition of Claude (see cat. no. 48), the *fête galantes* of Watteau (see cat. no. 62) and his followers, and the realism of his own earlier, rustic landscapes—produced during Boucher's stay in Italy at the urging of Nicolas Vleughels, director of the French Academy in Rome—Boucher's paintings and drawings in this genre count among the most original works of his time. Oudry's contribution to landscape was one of the many influences that led to Boucher's mastery in this field. Indeed, Oudry's series of drawings in black and white chalk on blue paper depicting views in and around Arceuil, and works like his *Exterior of a Gardener's House* of 1740 in the Staatliches Museum, in Schwerin (fig. A), with a well and composition similar to Boucher's, suggest that the two artists often discussed and drew landscapes together.[7] Drawings like Boucher's later copy after a *Dilapidated Cottage* by Cornelis Gerritsz. Decker (fig. B),[8] also demonstrate that Boucher often looked to Northern masters. He considered this aspect of his research so significant that he often purchased and drew after Northern works in his own considerable collection.[9]

The Yale Boucher certainly dates after his return from Italy in 1731. Several scholars have noted that at some time during the mid-1730s, Boucher shifted from the simple rusticity of his earlier Italianate works to a new level of thematic and technical refinement.[10] In his most developed examples, sylvan landscapes provide the setting for simply attired, but courtly, shepherds and shepherdesses—often inspired by his work for the theatre—who are engaged in both everyday rustic tasks and amorous activities. The Beauvais Factory and the Opéra, two of Boucher's largest commissions during the second half of the 1730s, along with their related requirements and his increasing contact with Oudry, suggest a date for the Yale drawing somewhere between 1735 and 1745. Another work from this period, the *Landscape with a Tower near Beauvais* of circa 1742 in the Rijksprentenkabinet, Amsterdam, reveals the same use of black

FIGURE 63A | Jean-Baptiste Oudry, *Exterior of a Gardener's House*, 1740. Schwerin, Staatliches Museum.

FIGURE 63B | François Boucher after Cornelis Gerritsz. Decker, *Dilapidated Cottage*, ca. 1760. Paris, Musée du Louvre.

and white chalk and/or gouache on blue paper.[11] Although later dates for the present drawing have often been suggested, they seem unconvincing because, after the early to mid-1740s, Boucher's landscape drawings respond more directly to the subtlety and softness of Oudry's Arceuil drawings before returning to a new realism during the last decade of his life.[12]

ALC

1   Goncourt 1881, 55.
2   I offer my sincerest gratitude to Françoise Joulie for her assistance with my research on this drawing. See Laing in *Grove Dictionary* 4:511–519 for a recent summary of Boucher's life and work.
3   For more on Sireul, see Laing in New York–Fort Worth 2003, no. 65.
4   For Boucher's activity as a stage designer, see Landau 1983.
5   For more on Boucher and tapestry design, see Standen in New York–Detroit–Paris 1986, 325–344.
6   See Laing in New York–Detroit–Paris 1986, 325–344, where the discussion is focused on the artist's paintings. Many of the author's observations can also be applied to Boucher's finished composition drawings. One of the key indicators of Boucher's success with this genre is the large number of prints executed after his landscapes. For some of these, see Jean-Richard 1978, esp. nos. 956–961, 1135–1159.
7   Schwerin, Staatliche Museum, inv. no. 4574, pen and black ink and brush with black and brown wash, heightened with white gouache, over black chalk on brown paper, 35.4 × 46 cm; see Opperman in Paris 1982b, no. 125. For the Arceuil drawings, as well as others, see also Paris 1982b, nos. 22–25 and 129–138.
8   Paris, Louvre, inv. no. RF 14757, black chalk on tan paper, 40.5 × 29 cm.
9   See Joulie in Dijon–London 2004–05, where the author discusses and demonstrates this significant new aspect of the artist's work.
10 See Joulie in Dijon–London 2004–05, 59 and 64; and Méjanès in Paris 2003–04, 68.
11 Amsterdam, Rijksprentenkabinet, inv. no. RP-T-1959-32, black and white chalk and white heightening, with stumping, on blue paper, 23.4 × 35.9 cm; see Rijdt in Amsterdam–Paris 2003, 116–119.
12 For later datings of the Yale sheet, see Kenney in New Haven 1984, 16, and Shoolman Slatkin in Washington–Chicago 1973–74, 65–75, and for Boucher's later landscapes, see Méjanès in Paris 2003–04, 69–70.

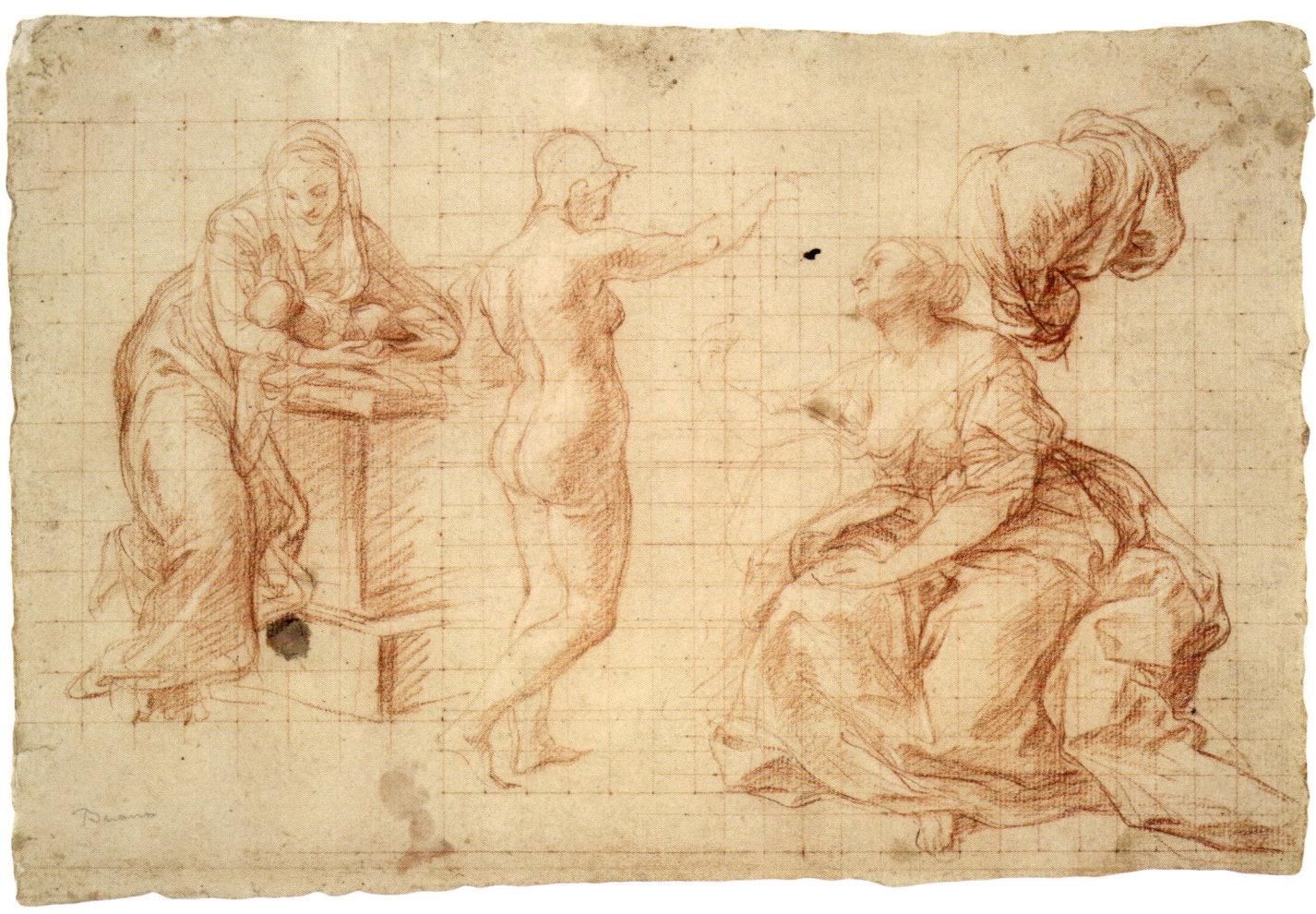

64 Pompeo Batoni
Lucca 1708–1787 Rome

Studies for the Nativity and the Choice of Hercules, ca. 1748

Red and white chalk on paper prepared with light brown wash, 24.1 × 35.7 cm (9½ × 14 1/16 in.)

INSCRIPTIONS: recto, lower left, in black chalk: *Buono*(?); verso, in graphite, center: *L2*; lower right: *? Batoni / J28301*

PROVENANCE: acquired from P. and D. Colnaghi and Co., London

REFERENCES: *YUAG Bulletin* 31 (1966): 21; H-B and L, no. 302; Clark and Bowron 1985, no. D141; New Haven 1991a, no. 47; *Handbook*, 207

Everett V. Meeks, B.A. 1901, Fund. 1965.9.16

During his lifetime, Pompeo Batoni was among the most famous artists in Europe, one whose works were sought by the nobility of courts across the Continent and especially by British and Irish Grand Tourists.[1] His portraits are well known today, but in the first part of his career, Batoni was most famous as a painter of mythological and religious narratives.[2] Profoundly interested in the highest classical style, he was an avid student of antiquity and of the work of Raphael, Domenichino, and Guido Reni. Like those artists, he adhered to the great tradition of *disegno*, in which compositions were carefully developed with compositional sketches followed by detailed figure studies drawn from live models.[3] The present sheet bears witness to that process and to Batoni's prodigious talents as a draftsman.

The drawing is a study for figures in two different compositions. The figure at left is for the Virgin in Batoni's small *Nativity* in the Galleria Nazionale d'Arte Antica at the Palazzo Corsini, Rome (fig. A).[4] This work, set in a dimly lit stable, is a variation on Correggio's *La Notte*, and like it, focuses on the intimacy between Madonna and child. The figure of the Virgin in the Yale sketch is inspired by Correggio, but Batoni seems to be trying to improve on his model; in the earlier painting, the Virgin's body is placed behind the manger, but here, she is shown full-length and her entire body curves forward to cradle the infant. The Rome painting has been dated to circa 1748 on the basis of stamps in its original silver frame, a dating consistent with the other drawings on the sheet, which relate to a commission of 1748.

The studies at center and right are preparatory for the figures of Minerva/Virtue and Venus/Vice in Batoni's *Choice of Hercules*. The subject—a moral tale in which Hercules is made to choose between the seductions of Venus and the hard road to Virtue and the Temple of Glory (indicated by Minerva)—was perennially popular with artists in Baroque Rome, and Batoni painted this subject several

FIGURE 64A | Pompeo Batoni, *Nativity*, ca. 1748. Rome, Palazzo Corsini, Galleria Nazionale d'Arte Antica.

times. The Yale drawing relates most closely to the version in the Liechtenstein Museum, Vienna, painted for Prince Joseph Wenzel von Liechtenstein in 1748 (fig. B).[5] The figure of Venus in this study is virtually identical to that in the painting; the figure of Minerva, although rendered as nude in the drawing but clothed in the painting, is also consistent. The drapery study at upper right relates to the clothing Minerva wears in the finished work.[6]

The nude study of Minerva, however, raises a few questions and suggests that the drawing is perhaps not as straightforwardly linked to the Liechtenstein painting as it might at first seem. In Batoni's 1742 version of the subject, now in the Palazzo Pitti, Florence (fig. C),[7] the pose of Minerva was essentially identical to this sketch. When Batoni changed the figure of Venus in the later painting, it was logical for him to have made new drawings,[8] but the differences between the Minerva figures in the Florence and Vienna versions are so slight (consisting mainly in shifts of her costume) that one might wonder why it would have been necessary to return all the way to the stage of studying a nude model. One possible explanation is that the nude Minerva in the Yale drawing predates the other sketches on the sheet and was made as early as 1742. In support of this idea, it can be noted that the drawing is on a buff-colored prepared paper very similar to that which Batoni used for the nude life study for the 1742 Venus;[9] yet, the chalks used for the three studies on the Yale sheet are so consistent as to argue against its being from two different dates. Another odd aspect of the Yale sheet is that the figures of Venus and Minerva are not drawn to the same scale: Venus is drawn larger in relation to Minerva than she is in the final paintings. Likewise, the carefully drawn squaring grids, used to transfer the studies to

FIGURE 64B | Pompeo Batoni, *The Choice of Hercules*, 1748. Vienna, Liechtenstein Museum.

FIGURE 64C | Pompeo Batoni, *The Choice of Hercules*, 1742. Florence, Palazzo Pitti.

the full-size painting, are not the same for the two figures (approximately 11.5 mm for Minerva and 10.5 mm for Venus).[10]

In the end, it might be impossible to resolve all the questions raised by the Yale drawing, but the complexity of the sheet, with multiple stages of figure studies and various systems to enlarge the figures to the size of the final painting, serves to demonstrate the sophistication of Batoni's working practice. Beyond all these complexities, however, we might end simply by admiring the drawing, an eloquent support for the argument that Batoni was the greatest draftsman in eighteenth-century Rome.

JJM

1. Batoni, so famous in his day, was practically forgotten in the nineteenth and earlier twentieth centuries. The restoration of his fame was due especially to Anthony M. Clark, whose magnum opus on Batoni, which appeared posthumously, was edited and prepared for publication by E. P. Bowron (Clark and Bowron 1985).
2. As noted by Bowron (Philadelphia–Houston 2000, 305–306), Batoni's interest in subject pictures waned after the critical failure of his *Fall of Simon Magus* altarpiece for Saint Peter's, on which Batoni had worked for nearly a decade, from 1746 to 1755.
3. For a précis of Batoni as a draftsman, see Clark and Bowron 1985, 34–39, and Bowron's entries in Philadelphia–Houston 2000, nos. 310–318, especially nos. 314–315.
4. Inv. no. 731; Clark and Bowron 1985, no. 120.
5. Inv. no. G 161; Clark and Bowron 1985, no. 123. This painting was in Vaduz until the recent opening of the Liechtenstein Museum in Vienna.
6. The poses of Minerva and Venus are very similar in the version at the Galleria Sabauda, Turin (inv. no. 471), dated to the early 1750s, except that Minerva's right arm, pointing to the temple at upper right in the drawing and in the Liechtenstein painting, is bent to point across her body to the temple at upper left in the Turin version (for which, see Clark and Bowron 1985, no. 173). There are no extant drawings connected with this slight modification.
7. Inv. no. 8547; Clark and Bowron 1985, no. 67.
8. Similarly, when Batoni modified Hercules in the Turin version, he made new studies for the figure; see Clark and Bowron 1985, nos. D108 and D150.
9. Berlin, Kupferstichkabinett, inv. no. KdZ 26446; Clark and Bowron 1985, no. D27. This drawing is not squared.
10. Nor, however, does the squaring grid match that on the Hercules for the Florence version (Philadelphia Museum of Art, inv. no. 1978-70-159; Clark and Bowron 1985, no. D165; Percy and Cazort 2004, no. 40).

65 Franz Karl Palko
Breslau (now Wroclaw) 1724–1767 Munich

The Astronomer Galileo (The Sense of Sight?), ca. 1750–60

Pen and brown ink over black chalk, 23.5 × 20 cm (9¼ × 8 in.)

INSCRIPTIONS: recto, lower edge, in pencil: *Galileo*; verso, center, in pencil: *319 % / Fontebasso Venitien 18me / Galileo / Col.: Andreossi* [sic]

PROVENANCE: General Count A. F. Andreossy (d. 1828), according to inscription on verso; E. Calando, stamp in purple ink, twice, verso (L. 837); acquired from Monroe Warshaw, New York

REFERENCES: Preiss 2005; *YUAG Bulletin* (2005): 165

Everett V. Meeks, B.A. 1901, Fund. 2004.3.1

Franz Karl Palko—son of the artist Anton Palko and brother of the portraitist Franz Anton Palko—was the most accomplished member of his family of artists working in Central Europe in the first two-thirds of the eighteenth century. Although Franz Karl has justly been described as "one of the greatest representatives of Central European Rococo,"[1] he has to a great extent been forgotten. After completing his studies at the Academy in Vienna, he worked with the great painter, architect, and stage designer Antonio Galli Bibiena. Palko went to Dresden in 1749 to decorate the palaces of Heinrich Graf von Brühl, and in 1752 became official court painter there. Palko created lavish and dramatic decorative programs in the grand Venetian manner of Veronese and Tiepolo, but much of his work in Dresden was lost with the deliberate destruction by Brühl's adversary, Frederick II, of the buildings Palko had decorated in fresco. During these years he also received commissions elsewhere, the most important among them being the decoration of the Jesuit Church of Saint Nicholas in Prague. In 1764, although already ill, he moved to Munich and again became court painter, but his production there was meager, and he died shortly thereafter. The great French connoisseur and collector Pierre Jean Mariette bought two of Palko's drawings for the Church of Saint Nicholas from the artist's widow, writing of them in his *Abecedario*, "they are in the grandest manner, and I do not at all regret the high price they cost me. I have few in my collection that give me as much satisfaction."[2]

Yale's engaging drawing shows a slender, bearded, elderly man, dressed in an elegant robe with a tie visible near his left shoulder, fitted trousers, sandals, and a skullcap. He is identifiable as the astronomer Galileo Galilei, because of the telescope in the left foreground of the drawing, an instrument he had perfected and which had virtually come to be his symbol.[3] He is seated comfortably in a chair at what appears to be the top of a tower, from which he can study the heavens, and his head is tilted slightly back so that he can look upward. A column with a spiral frieze, topped by a sculpture of a standing figure, is visible in the background beyond the low wall at the left, suggesting a location high off the ground. The astronomer's right arm rests on an armillary sphere, and in his left hand he holds a pair of dividers; a blank tablet leans against the wall supporting his left arm. On the wall above his right arm are indications of forms, the meaning of which is elusive—they might be fragments of letters or other symbols in relief, or perhaps other small instruments.

Pavel Preiss made the entirely plausible suggestion that this image may have been part of a series of the *Five Senses*, this one representing *Sight*. The telescope was used for an image of *Sight* as early as the 1610s, in a series made in Rome by Jusepe de Ribera, and this association had become relatively commonplace by the middle of the eighteenth century.[4] Preiss also surmised that the drawing was intended to be reproduced as a print, since Galileo holds the dividers in his left hand. This is certainly possible, but since one leg of the dividers might well be held in the left hand while the right hand manipulates the other, the argument is not conclusive. In any case, today there seems to be no trace of any printed series of *The Five Senses* designed by Palko.

The straightforward linear technique of this drawing is similar to several others among the fifty-one by Palko catalogued by Preiss,[5] although many of the known drawings are in chalk or have added wash. The drawings in pen alone closely resemble Palko's six known etchings, although, oddly perhaps, the only drawing that strictly corresponds to an etching was done in graphite with added washes and body color.[6]

SB

1 Preiss in *Grove Dictionary* 23:855. Preiss has devoted a large percentage of his professional work to Palko. The most recent book is Preiss 1999, with extensive previous bibliography (in Czech, with a summary in German, 322–342). Preiss did not know of *The Astronomer Galileo* at the time of that book, but in 2005 he not only confirmed the attribution but published an article about the drawing. Publications especially concerning Palko's drawings are Preiss 1975 and Salzburg 1989. See also Lille 2002–03, 204–205 and nos. 19, 28, 29.
2 Mariette 1851–60, 4:72: "ils sont de la plus grande manière, et je ne regrette point le haut prix qu'ils m'ont coûté. J'en ai peu dans ma collection qui me satisfassent autant." These drawings are now in the Louvre, inv. 18740, 18741; see Preiss 1999, K-24, K-25; Paris 1967, nos. 189, 190; Paris 1981, nos. 177a, b.
3 Preiss 2005, 117.
4 The Ribera painting is in Mexico City, Museo Franz Meyer; see Spinosa 2003, no. A31. In a painting of *The Sense of Sight* by Philip Mercier, made about 1744–47, now in the Yale Center for British Art, New Haven (inv. no. B1974.3.17), the telescope is one of several optical instruments used by the five people depicted.
5 Preiss 1999, K-11, 12, 14–16, 19, 20, 22, 23.
6 Preiss 1999, 54, *Christ and the Samaritan Woman*, K-4 and GL-1.

66 Hubert Robert
Paris 1733–1808 Paris

Ruins at the Sea near Naples: The "Scola di Virgilio," 1760

Red chalk, 33.5 × 45.6 cm (13 3/16 × 17 15/16 in.)

WATERMARK: shield with diagonal bar, with fleur-de-lys above, similar to Heawood nos. 60, 69, 86, 96, and others, a type generally produced in eighteenth-century France and England

INSCRIPTIONS: recto, lower center, in red chalk (in Robert's hand): *Roberti / 1760 / Scola di virgilio napoli*; on mount, in graphite, lower right: *Hubert Robert 1760*; upper center: *789 / II*

PROVENANCE: Pierre Decourcelle; his sale, Paris, Galerie G. Petit, 29–30 May 1911, lot 146; Madame Icard; acquired by Galerie Cailleux, Paris, 1962; acquired from Galerie Cailleux, 1963

REFERENCES: *YUAG Bulletin* 30 (1964): 19; H-B and L, no. 62; Washington 1978–79, no. 5; Montague Massengale 1979, 64 and 66; Detroit–Chicago 1981–82, no. 102; Cayeux and Boulot 1989, 63; Rome 1990–91, no. 46; *Handbook*, 208; Lamers 1995, 120; Rosenberg 2000, 110–111

Everett V. Meeks, B.A. 1901, Fund. 1963.9.72

When Hubert Robert arrived in Rome in 1754, he had received a classical education and had studied in Paris with the sculptor René-Michel (also called Michel-Ange) Slodtz. Nonetheless, it was the experience of Rome that made him an artist. Through the intercessions of his patron, the Comte de Stainville (later the Duc de Choiseul), Robert was accepted, and eventually made *pensionnaire*, at the French Academy, where his various associates and influences included Charles Joseph Natoire (then the Academy's director), Giovanni Paolo Panini (the professor of perspective, who also made a series of paintings for Choiseul), and Jean-Honoré Fragonard (see cat. no. 72). Surrounded by the city's ancient monuments, Robert quickly developed the fascination with ancient ruins that would last throughout his career.[1]

The practice of sketching Roman buildings and the landscapes of the Campagna had long been encouraged at the French Academy, but around 1760 both Fragonard and Robert developed a type of luminous red chalk drawing from nature, of which the present sheet is a brilliant example, that had few precedents in French art. As Colin Bailey has noted, 1760 was something of an *annus mirabilis* for both Robert and Fragonard, and

FIGURE 66A | Hubert Robert, *The Ponte di Caligula, Pozzuoli*, 1760. Boston, Horvitz Collection.

although recent work on the two artists has tended to downplay their actual interaction,[2] the similarity of their interests and stylistic development is remarkable. The most famous works of that year are probably the red chalk studies that Fragonard made at the Villa d'Este in Tivoli during a summer trip there with the Abbé de Saint-Non. Equally impressive, however, are the studies that Robert made on a trip to Naples earlier that year, drawings that further raise the question of whether Fragonard influenced Robert or whether the influence might have been the other way about.[3]

Setting off in April and returning in June, Robert and Saint-Non made a tour to the south of Italy. They traveled to Naples and the surrounding area, following the popular Grand Tour itineraries of other French, German, and British travelers, although they also visited the ancient Greek ruins at Paestum, which had only been rediscovered in the previous decade. Most of Robert's drawings from this trip seem to have been of landscapes and ruins like those seen in the present sheet, but he also made some drawings after paintings, similar to the ones Fragonard later made for Saint-Non when they traveled through Northern Italy on their return to France in 1761.[4] Even during the tour of Southern Italy, Saint-Non recognized where Robert's talents lay; as recounted in his diary, "I took Robert with me, a young painter of great promise and a first-rate talent in the genre of architecture and ruins."[5]

The Yale drawing depicts a series of ruins popularly known as the Scuola (or Scola) di Virgilio, found at the tip of the Posillipo peninsula, west of Naples. As was the case with the nearby "Tomb of Virgil," the so-called School of Virgil actually had little, if anything, to do with the ancient poet. Largely ruined but still visible under the water, the structure was perhaps part of a seaside bath attached to the so-called Imperial Villa on the site, a complex begun by Lucullus in the late Republic and expanded by Publius Vedius Pollio, who left it to Augustus.[6] In any case, Saint-Non and Robert probably visited the site out of interest in the impressive complex of ruins, which extend below the water for some distance, and not because of its literary associations, which Saint-Non recognized as little more than popular legend.[7]

Like many of Robert's drawings from that trip, like many of his Roman views, and like many of his later paintings, architectural or archeological accuracy was of relatively little importance. He chose a point of view that conveys a sense of the seaside atmosphere, one that might have related to the first impression of an arriving traveler, but which obscured the monument behind the rocks in the foreground. The figures, drawn in Robert's characteristic schematic shorthand, likewise emphasize the anecdotal: he includes the boys at left with their fishing poles and dog, and the boat beyond them, which seems to depict seated travelers listening to the gesturing local guides. In his evocative view of the ruins, Robert creates a Romantic contest between the works of humans and the actions of nature and time.

The precise itinerary of Robert and Saint-Non is not known, for in his diary for the trip, Saint-Non writes that, having commented on the sites in his diary during the trip of the previous year, he will not describe them again. The only certain evidence that Robert and Saint-Non visited a given site is the existence of one of Robert's drawings.[8] To the previously published drawings relating to the journey, we can add one further drawing, *The Ponte di Caligula* in the Horvitz Collection, Boston (fig. A).[9] Showing ruins and a rustic bridge at Pozzuoli, this site was close to the School of Virgil and the drawing was perhaps even made on the same day as the Yale sheet. Like the School of Virgil, the "Bridge of Caligula" also had a name that reflected popular legend rather than archeological fact: Caligula's famous bridge between Pozzuoli and Baiae had actually been a pontoon bridge,[10] and the ruins seen in the Horvitz drawing probably constituted part of the structure of the ancient port.

The Naples journey of 1760 (and an earlier trip in 1759) must have loomed large in Saint-Non's memory, for twenty years later he undertook the publication of his *Voyage pittoresque, ou description des royaumes de Naples et de Sicile*, which appeared in four folio volumes between 1781 and 1786.[11] The text of this work, it is now known, was largely written by Dominique-Vivant Denon, whom Saint-Non sent to Naples in 1777–78 along with the artists Louis-Jean Desprez, Claude-Louis Châtelet, and Jean-Augustin Renard. Most of the plates in the *Voyage pittoresque* were engraved after drawings by these latter artists, but nineteen of them were based on the drawings that Robert had made during the trip of 1760. The Yale drawing was not, however, among the drawings used for the engravings, and the School of Virgil site was represented instead with a broader view drawn by Châtelet.

JJM

1. On Robert in Rome, see especially Rome 1990–91 and Bailey 1992, Colin Bailey's review of the exhibition.
2. Rome 1990–91 cites only two instances where the artists are known to have made drawings side by side: as Bailey 1992, 599, notes, "Neither Fragonard nor Robert, it would appear, invited the other's close scrutiny: the Goncourts' image of the young men working side by side in the gardens of the Villa d'Este is one of their more invidious fictions, which this catalogue firmly lays to rest." It might be noted, however, that there is one drawing in the catalogue (26, fig. 7), and others cited by Bailey 1992, 600, and Montague Massengale 1979, 67, that seem to be joint efforts.
3. Bailey 1992, 600. See also Rosenberg 2000, 110. Contrary to what is sometimes stated, Fragonard did not accompany Robert and Saint-Non on their trip to Southern Italy.
4. Saint-Non's prints after the Robert and Fragonard drawings of famous paintings would appear as the *Fragmens des peintures et des tableaux les plus intéressants des palais et églises d'Italie*, 190 plates issued between 1770 and 1773, and the *Griffonis* of 1775–78. The Art Gallery has recently acquired two prints by Saint-Non (inv. nos. 2006.9.1 and 2006.9.2), after Fragonard's drawings of paintings by Ludovico Carracci and Polidoro da Caravaggio, which are part of that series.
5. Rosenberg and Brejon de Lavergnée 1986, 122–123.
6. Already ruined in the eighteenth century, most of the building is under water today, although other parts of the villa remain. See Günther 1913.
7. The often-quoted description in Saint-Non's *Voyage pittoresque* is worth citing again: " . . . ruins called the 'School of Virgil,' a name given, like so many others, by the Neapolitan people, without any reason except the most ignorant and unreasonable superstition in connecting a name long celebrated in the place. It is more natural to follow the opinion of those who think these are the ruins of the famous house of Lucullus . . . "
8. Rosenberg and Brejon de Lavergnée 1986, 122.
9. Boston, Horvitz Collection, inv. no. D-F-673, red chalk, 23.6 × 42.5 cm. I would like to thank Alvin L. Clark, Jr., for bringing the drawing to my attention. In addition to those drawings included or mentioned in Rome 1990–91, Robert's view of *Terracina* (Paris 1983, no. 47) also surely dates from his journey with Saint-Non.
10. Suetonius, *Gaius*, 19; Cassius Dio 59.17.1–11.
11. On the *Voyage pittoresque*, see especially Lamers 1995.

67 Lorenzo Baldissera Tiepolo
Venice 1736–1776 Madrid

Head of a Woman, ca. 1760

Black and red chalk, with stumping, 32.3 × 22.6 cm (12 11/16 × 8 7/8 in.)

WATERMARK: "AS" with a trefoil above and "C" below

INSCRIPTIONS: recto, lower right, in brown ink: *Tiepolo*; verso, in graphite, upper left: *47*; lower left: *12*

PROVENANCE: Luigi Grassi, Florence (L. 1171b); his sale, Sotheby's, London, 13 May 1924, lot 119; Robert Lehman, New York

REFERENCES: Cambridge 1970, no. 66; H-B and L, no. 323 (as Attributed to Lorenzo Tiepolo); *Handbook*, 209; Madrid 1999, 162

Gift of Robert Lehman, B.A. 1913. 1941.298

When writing about Lorenzo Tiepolo, it is difficult to resist repeating Giuseppe Fiocco's *bon mot* dismissal of the artist as a "little master who was heir to too great a name."[1] The simple fact is that Lorenzo never did match the achievements or fame of his father, Giambattista, nor even those of his older brother, Giovanni Domenico (see cat. no. 74), but putting aside the Tiepolo standard, Lorenzo was an artist of some talent, and his work has rightly been the subject of reconsideration in recent decades.[2] He received his training in the family workshop and began to emerge as a recognizable artist around 1750, when Giambattista was at work on the frescoes in the Residenz at Würzburg. He accompanied his father and brother to Madrid in 1762, where Giambattista died in 1770. Although his brother Domenico then returned to Venice, Lorenzo remained in Spain, trying unsuccessfully to be named court painter, until his own untimely death in 1776.

Lorenzo developed a recognizable style as a printmaker, mainly reproducing his father's work,[3] but he held little interest in the altarpieces and decorative frescoes that had been the mainstay of the Tiepolo workshop. He concentrated instead on portraits, genre scenes, and half-length studies of saints, allegorical figures, "philosophers," and similar expressive types, usually executed in oils or pastels. Most of the drawings attributed to him are head studies in chalk, like the present work.[4] These drawings take their point of departure from the works of Giambattista and Domenico, who also made head studies in chalk, but a core group of Lorenzo's work, initially identified by old inscriptions, has allowed some clarification of his oeuvre. Multicolored chalks (usually on white or buff paper rather than the blue paper preferred for such studies by Giambattista and Domenico), and the combination of stumping with superimposed thin lines to redefine contours and highlights (visible in the present drawing), are the benchmarks of Lorenzo's technique.[5] Close comparisons can be made to the *Head of a Young Man* in the Taubman Collection, the *Head of an Old Woman (perhaps Saint Anne)* in the Morgan Library, and the *Study after Vittoria's Bust of Palma Giovane* in the École des Beaux-Arts, Paris.[6] These studies partake of the technical virtuosity everywhere evident in drawings by the Tiepolo family, but it has also been suggested that Lorenzo's handling of chalk, like his subsequent preference for pastels, instead owes much to the example of his Venetian contemporary Rosalba Carriera.

Very few of Lorenzo's drawings have been connected to his finished works in oil or pastel. On the one hand, the head studies might simply be exercises in rendering expressions and emotions; Bernard Aikema has made the compelling suggestion that Lorenzo's studies could be a response to the statement by the critic Francesco Algarotti (a friend of the Tiepolo family) that the Venetian School lacked "subtlety in expression."[7] On the other hand, the unusual angle of the head and the way in which the drawing stops abruptly at the lower right corner suggest that Tiepolo intended to insert this head into a more elaborate composition, and it is not difficult to imagine it among the crowds of similar ones in his paintings and pastels. There is not, however, a head in any of Lorenzo's known finished works that corresponds to this drawing; this lack of correspondence has made the dating of his drawings a matter of conjecture. The head studies are usually placed in the earlier part of Lorenzo's career, before his departure for Spain in 1762. The Italian provenance of the Yale sheet (the large stamp at upper right is that of the Florentine Luigi Grassi) would likewise seem to suggest its creation in Italy around the year 1760.[8]

JJM

1 Fiocco 1925–26, 17, ". . . piccolo maestro, erede di un nome troppo grande."
2 The most recent and most complete attempts to reevaluate and catalogue Lorenzo's work are Madrid 1999, Venice Mestre 1997–98, Cambridge–New York 1996–97, and Thiem 1993 and 1994, all of which build upon earlier work by George Knox, Terisio Pignatti, and others.
3 See Boorsch 1996, as well as Marini in Venice Mestre 1997–98, 43–47.
4 The most complete catalogue of Lorenzo Tiepolo's drawings is that by Pieter Roelofs and Bernard Aikema in Madrid 1999, 147–179. There is also a group of pen, ink, and wash drawings by Lorenzo, but many of these are copies of earlier drawings by Giambattista. One such pen, ink, and wash drawing of a *Saint in Adoration of the Madonna and Child* at Yale, inv. no. 1941.296, was formerly attributed to Lorenzo before being given to Giambattista, but may be worth reconsideration.
5 Other attributions continue to be the subject of scholarly debate, including the groups of related head studies in Würzburg and at the Fogg, on which see Aikema's summary in Cambridge–New York 1996–97, no. 115.
6 Taubman Collection, black chalk and gray wash, with touches of red, green, brown chalk, 37.7 × 28.2 cm; Paris, École des Beaux-Arts, inv. no. 2341, red and black chalk, 38.5 × 26.2 cm; New York, Pierpont Morgan Library, Scholz collection, inv. no. 1983.64, black chalk with touches or red and blue chalk, 37.6 × 28.5 cm. See Madrid 1999, 155 fig. 59, and nos. 44 and 47, for these drawings, which are all at roughly the same scale as the Yale head, although the sheet of the latter has been trimmed.
7 Cambridge–New York 1996–97, 304.
8 The paper on which the Yale head is drawn also seems to be Italian; the watermark has not been definitively identified, but it is an Italian type: compare Heawood no. 3084. The Morgan Library *Head of an Old Woman* has a provenance descending from Domenico Bossi (also known as Johann Domenik Bossi), a pupil of Domenico Tiepolo who was perhaps part of the Bossi family of *stuccatori* that worked with the Tiepolo family at Wurzburg; this suggests that the Morgan drawing was also made before Lorenzo's departure for Spain. It should be noted, however, that the *Bust of Palma Giovane* is dated to the later 1760s in Madrid 1999.

68 Jean-Baptiste Le Prince
Metz 1734–1781 Saint Denis-du-Port

Seated Kalmuck Warrior, ca. 1760

Black chalk, 41.3 × 25.4 cm (16¼ × 10 in.)

INSCRIPTIONS: recto, lower right, in black chalk: *L. P. 176* (last digit cut off); backing sheet, verso, upper right, in pen and blue ink: *N° 35*; in pencil, lower left: *D757F*; lower center: *Kgb:ohszg*; right of center: *RSNTO*; at right: *eszg / V1020 / 15* (illegible)

PROVENANCE: anonymous sale, Hôtel Drouot, Paris, 16 May 1958, no. 29; Bernard Houthakker, 1964; acquired from H. Shickman Gallery, New York

REFERENCES: *YUAG Bulletin* 31.3 (1967–68): 27 and 57; H-B and L, no. 57

Everett V. Meeks, B.A. 1901, Fund. 1966.9.35

About 1750 Jean-Baptiste Le Prince went from his native Metz to Paris, where he studied with François Boucher (see cat. no. 63). In 1752 Le Prince made a disastrous marriage, and when that had dissolved, in 1757 he set out for Russia, where his brother François-Simon had been established in the service of the Empress Elizabeth since 1742. His sister Anne-Catherine-Louise and brother-in-law Jean-Baptiste-Jude Charpentier (who taught languages at the Academy of Sciences) were also in Saint Petersburg, and his half-brother, Jean-Robert, was in Moscow. Most of the artists who served the Russian imperial court were either Italian or French; other Frenchmen in Russia around that same time were the painter Louis Tocqué; Louis-Joseph Le Lorrain, invited in 1758 to be the first director of the Russian Academy of Fine Arts, and Jean-Michel Moreau, known as Moreau Le Jeune, accompanying him; Louis Lagrenée, who succeeded Le Lorrain as Director of the Russian Academy, along with his brother Jean-Jacques; and another artist from Metz, the sculptor Nicolas Gillet.[1]

Le Prince remained in Russia until September 1762, working for the Empress

FIGURE 68A | Jean-Baptiste Le Prince, *The Halt of the Kalmucks*, 1772. New York, Metropolitan Museum of Art.

Elizabeth and her successor Peter III, and traveling in areas where few western voyagers, and even fewer artists, had ventured before—making hundreds of sketches of people and costumes. The quantity and the range of dates of the work he did for Elizabeth and Peter in Saint Petersburg, however, indicate that he probably traveled less than had been assumed, and the previously held belief that he went as far as Siberia may not be true. It also seems likely that he did not meet Jean Chappe d'Auteroche, the author of the *Voyage en Sibérie*, until about 1763 or '64, when both were back in Paris, and that it was there that Le Prince was engaged to provide illustrations for this book. The book was published in 1768, with fifty-two etched and engraved plates, of which thirty-two followed designs by Le Prince. These drawings, made between 1764 and 1766, survive today in the Rosenbach Library in Philadelphia.[2]

Le Prince's return to Paris coincided with a growing French interest in Russia, kindled by the publication of *History of the Russian Empire under Peter the Great* by Voltaire, in two parts, in 1760 and 1763, and increased by the ascension to the imperial throne of Catherine II (the Great), in June 1762, through a coup d'état involving the murder of her husband, Peter III. Le Prince was in a prime position both to capitalize on and to augment this vogue, having brought back notebooks and individual drawings of Russian subjects—plus some actual costumes and other ethnographic material. The sketches he had made during his five years in Russia became the basis of his artistic production for most of the rest of his life. Le Prince was accepted as a member of the Academy of Painting in 1765 with a painting of a Russian subject, an Orthodox Baptism,[3] and at least twenty more paintings of such subjects by Le Prince are known.

Le Prince had made a few etchings before leaving for Russia, but between 1764 and 1768, after his return to Paris, he issued close to one hundred prints of Russian subjects (including scenes in the areas that are now Latvia and Estonia), in more than a dozen different suites. Around 1768 Le Prince began experimenting with the recently invented medium of aquatint, contributing significant refinements to the technique. Aquatint is a kind of etching, in which a textured ground is bitten into the plate, producing in the print the effect of wash. Le Prince made seventy-nine prints in this medium.[4]

According to Mary-Elizabeth Hellyer, at least thirty-two extant drawings by Le Prince were probably made in Russia. She stated that she knew of no drawings later than 1765 that were signed with initials and dated and that in her opinion, Yale's drawing was made in Russia—that is, by 1762.[5] Hellyer thought the subject was likely to have been a Kalmuck (Calmouk), a member of a nomadic tribe from southwestern Russia, and indeed Le Prince published an aquatint in 1771, showing a Kalmuck with the same distinctive type of hat as seen on the subject of Yale's drawing, and turned-down mustaches.[6] Another aquatint, called *The Halt of the Kalmucks* (fig. A), published in 1772, shows a man in the center of the composition also wearing the same kind of hat, and a man at the left whose posture and sword are similar to those of the figure in Yale's drawing (in reverse direction from the drawing).[7] Yale's *Seated Kalmuck Warrior* clearly was not a specific prototype for this print—a drawing in the Louvre shows its general composition, and two other drawings are related to the main figure—but the figure in Yale's drawing could well have been among those in Le Prince's mind as he prepared the print. No painting or print with Yale's seated warrior as its principal subject, however, is known.[8] A drawing of a *Kalmuck Archer*, similar in style and treatment of subject to Yale's drawing, and also in black chalk (with a few additional touches of brown), is also signed with initials, and is dated 1760 (fig. B).[9] This drawing, on a sheet somewhat larger than Yale's but with the figure itself drawn to the same scale, is also laid down, and its decorative mat is identical to Yale's. It is possible these two drawings were done at the same time, and that Yale's drawing would thus also date to 1760.

SB

FIGURE 68B | Jean-Baptiste Le Prince, *Kalmuck Archer*, 1760. Private collection.

1. Several recent publications have thorough, if concise, biographies of Le Prince: Marie-Liesse Pierre-Dulau in Poussou, Mézin, and Perret-Gentil 2004, 131–140; Madeleine Pinault Sørensen, "Le Prince et les dessinateurs et graveurs du *Voyage en Sibérie*," in Chappe d'Auteroche 2004, 1:125–144; and Diederik Bakhuÿs in Rouen 2004–05, 13–22. See also Metz 1988.
2. Specifically for Le Prince's travels, see Madeleine Pinault Sørensen in Poussou, Mézin, and Perret-Gentil 2004, 390–398. For the *Voyage en Sibérie*, see Philadelphia–Pittsburgh–New York 1986–87; Chappe d'Auteroche 2004; Rouen 2004–05.
3. Paris, Louvre, inv. no. 7331.
4. Le Prince's prints are catalogued in Hédou 1879; Portalis and Béraldi 1880–82, 2:667–677; and *IFF XVIIIe siècle* 14:435–482. See also Washington 2003–04, 29, and nos. 20, 21, and Rouen 2004–05, 19, 20. Le Prince's method is described in *Encyclopédie* 1782–1832, 47:622–625; this is reprinted in Hédou 1879, 179–188.
5. Hellyer 1982, no. 20. I have not seen this dissertation, but Mary-Elizabeth Hellyer has kindly provided me with information, by letter and electronic communication during March–April 2005, and I thank her for her generous help.
6. Hédou 1879, no. 131; Portalis and Béraldi 1880–82, 2:676, no. 38; *IFF XVIIIe siècle* 14:479, no. 168.
7. Hédou 1879, no. 141; Portalis and Béraldi 1880–82, 2:676, no. 27b; *IFF XVIIIe siècle* 14:479, no. 169, 24 × 18.6 cm. The print was exhibited in Rouen 2004–05, no. 41; Le Prince's drawing for this print is Paris, Louvre, inv. no. 30623, illustrated in Poussou, Mézin, and Perret-Gentil 2004, pl. XII.
8. I wish to thank Madeleine Pinault Sørensen for her kindness in looking through the Le Prince *"feuilles libres"* (single prints) at the Bibliothèque Nationale, Paris, on my behalf.
9. Sotheby's, New York, 23 January 2001, lot 306; with Didier Aaron, London, Paris, New York.

69 Jean-Baptiste Greuze
Tournus 1725–1805 Paris

Head of an Old Man, Study for A Marriage Contract, 1761

Red and black chalk and gray wash over graphite; laid down, 55.6 × 39.4 cm (21⅞ × 15½ in.)

INSCRIPTIONS: verso, upper right, in graphite: *10EE*

PROVENANCE: Captain A. Morrison, Basildon Park, 1914; Prince Merchersky, Paris; acquired from Mathias Komor, New York

REFERENCES: London 1914–15, no. 110; *YUAG Bulletin* 28 (1962): 29 and 51; Cambridge 1967b, unnumbered cat.; H-B and L, no. 53; Notre Dame 1972, no. 39; Toronto et al. 1972, 164; Hartford–San Francisco–Dijon 1976–77, no. 31; Paris 1984–85, 227; *Handbook*, 208; New York–Los Angeles 2002, 78, under no. 18; Paris 2002a, 84–86

Everett V. Meeks, B.A. 1901, Fund. 1961.9.1

Greuze copied this drawing from his nearly identical study for the head of the father of the bride in the painting *A Marriage Contract* (fig. A). The original drawing (fig. B), on white paper and slightly smaller, is the one Johann-Georg Wille recorded purchasing from the artist on 17 July 1761: "I have bought from M. Greuze a large head of an old man drawn in black and red chalks on white paper. It is the head of the father in the *Marriage Contract*, a picture he is now working on. It cost me three gold louis."[1] The boldness and fluid handling in this drawing contrast with the more precise technique of the copy. Having utilized the original as a model during the execution of his painting, and having then sold it to his friend Wille, Greuze—doubtless aware of its great quality—must then have executed this copy in order to sell it, too.

In contrast to the upright posture of the figure in these studies, in his painting *A Marriage Contract* Greuze positioned the old man's head tilted back, as though he were speaking more forcefully. In his description of this painting in his *Récapitulation* of the Salon exhibition of 1761, the critic Denis

FIGURE 69A | Jean-Baptiste Greuze, *A Marriage Contract*, 1761. Paris, Musée du Louvre.

FIGURE 69B | Jean-Baptiste Greuze, *Head of an Old Man, Study for A Marriage Contract*, 1761. Private collection.

Diderot referred to this father as "an old man of sixty years, with gray hair, a kerchief twisted around his neck; he has an air of simple good-heartedness that pleases."[2] Baron Grimm, Diderot's coauthor, wrote a bit more effusively of the same figure: "One cannot look at this old man of Greuze's without feeling tears coming to the eyes. What a good father! How surely deserving he is of the mellowness that he feels at this moment! . . . Certainly he must be saying to his son-in-law: My son, do not thank me for the money; it is for my daughter that you must thank me; she is more precious to me than all that I possess."[3]

EM

1   "J'ay acheté de M. Greuze une grande tête de vieillard dessinée sur paper blanc aux crayons noirs et rouge. C'est la tête du père de l'*Accord du mariage*, tableau qu'il fait actuellement. Elle m'a coûté trois louis d'or." Wille 1857, 1:173. The drawing, in a private collection, is in red and black chalk, stumped, over graphite, 47.6 × 33 cm.
2   As written, "un vieillard de soixante ans, en cheveux gris, un mouchoir tortillé autour de son cou; il a un air de bonhomie qui plaît." Diderot 1957, 1:142.
3   "On ne peut regarder ce vieillard de Greuze sans se sentir venir les larmes aux yeux. Quel bon père! Qu'il est bien digne de la douceur qu'il éprouve en ce moment! . . . Le père lui dit certainement: Mon fils, ne me remercie pas de l'argent; c'est de ma fille qu'il faut me remercier; elle m'est bien plus chère que tout ce que je possède." Diderot 1957, 1:144–145.

70 Ubaldo Gandolfi

San Matteo della Decima 1728–
1781 Ravenna

The Sacrifice of Isaac, ca. 1770

Pen and brown ink and brown wash over black chalk, 31.2 × 21.8 cm (12 5/16 × 8 9/16 in.)

PROVENANCE: acquired from Flavia Ormond, London

REFERENCES: *YUAG Bulletin* (1993): 106

Frederick M. Clapp, B.A. 1901, M.A. 1911, Fund. 1992.111

The Gandolfi family of painters—Ubaldo, his brother Gaetano, and Gaetano's son Mauro—have often been described as the "last followers of the Carracci," a backward-looking characterization that is, in some ways, damning praise, for it emphasizes the artists' indebtedness to an earlier generation without acknowledging their own lively, accomplished style.[1] There is some truth, nonetheless, in recognizing that the Gandolfi carried the Carracci interest in academic draftsmanship, especially in delineating the human figure, forward to the end of the eighteenth century, when they were the most important artists in Bologna and the surrounding region.

The Sacrifice of Isaac demonstrates the usual benchmarks of Gandolfi style: a whir of energy, dramatically posed figures (often highly foreshortened), and bold chiaroscuro. As so often in the family's work, much attention is paid to the figures, but the setting is indicated only summarily. In this case, the screen of trees at right is unconvincing, while the planes of wash that indicate the rocky foreground are as much a two-dimensional pattern as a convincing indication of three-dimensional space. As has often been noted, it is difficult to distinguish the styles of Ubaldo and Gaetano,[2] but pen lines ending in quick little hooks, often dropping a blob of ink as can be seen here, are one of Ubaldo's particular characteristics.[3] The attribution of the Yale sheet is complicated, however, by another version of the drawing, nearly identical in size, facture, and technique, in a Canadian private collection.[4] The main difference between the two drawings is that the Canadian sheet has red chalk underdrawing, where the Yale sheet has black chalk. Certain passages of the Canadian drawing, furthermore, seem ever so slightly more convincingly drawn, thus suggesting that it was the earlier work. Although both drawings have chalk underdrawing to indicate the basic forms, for example, there seems to be a more active searching for the final contours of the figures in pen lines of the Canadian sheet, presumably indicating a moment when the drawing's form was being decided; the Yale sheet, for all its liveliness, can perhaps be seen as having a better idea where each pen line would go. So similar is the general handling of the pen and wash, however, and so adept the hand of both drawings, that we are evidently not faced with a later copy by some anonymous artist, but rather, with a copy by the artist himself. There also exists a pair of virtually identical drawings apparently both by Gaetano Gandolfi for his *Saint Jerome Listening to the Angels' Trumpets*.[5] For whatever reason, the workshop seems to have made high quality duplicates of some drawings.

The Sacrifice of Isaac has not been connected with a known painting, although one additional drawing of the subject, a variant version of the composition, would seem to indicate that the artist had some project in mind.[6] Another possibility is that the notably prolific Ubaldo made the drawing for its own sake, for *The Sacrifice of Isaac* was a perennially popular subject, one with which Ubaldo may simply have wanted to experiment. The thematically different but compositionally similar paintings of the *Liberation of Peter* and *Saint Jerome Listening to the Angels' Trumpets* executed by Ubaldo and Gaetano might even be seen as inspiration for such experimentation. Whatever the function of the Yale sheet, dating of Gandolfi drawings has proved as difficult as the question of attribution, but by comparison with the above-mentioned works and with others that can be dated via documentary evidence, the *Isaac* seems to be of the late 1760s or around 1770.

JJM

1. For extended thoughts on the Gandolfi critical fortunes, see Cazort in Ottawa–Little Rock 1993, 11–12.
2. Difficulty in distinguishing between the brothers' work extends to their paintings as well as their drawings. Yale's painting of the *Liberation of Saint Peter* (inv. no. 1983.81, alternately attributed to Ubaldo and Gaetano), for example, has been described as a "paramount example of scholarly bemusement over the attribution of Gandolfi paintings" (Ottawa–Little Rock 1993, 15 and no. 36); the presence in Stuttgart of a second version (Cento 2002, no. 6) only complicates the matter. A preparatory drawing in Stuttgart for the painting has likewise been attributed to both artists.
3. Cazort Taylor 1976, 164.
4. Ottawa 1976, no. 26. Also Bagni 1992, no. 704.
5. Cazort Taylor 1976, 159. The drawings are: Venice, Cini Foundation, inv. no. 31.621, and Florence, Uffizi, inv. no. 20446. Similarly, see the three very close drawings (at the Metropolitan Museum, the Prado, and in a private collection) for Gaetano's *Beato Gioacchino Piccolomini*, Bagni 1992, nos. 210–212.
6. The additional drawing, in a private collection, is Bagni 1992, no. 705. Bagni includes the studies among his "studi per probabili dipinti." Gaetano painted a very late version of the subject (Bagni 1992, no. 395), but it is based on a print after a Johann Liss painting and is unrelated to the Yale composition.

71 Circle of Jakob Matthias Schmutzer
Vienna 1733–1811 Vienna

Head of a Young Man, 1780

Red chalk, 46 × 36 cm (18⅛ × 14 3/16 in.)

WATERMARKS: crowned coat of arms with half parts anchor and two-headed eagle, and countermark containing the initials S and B (not in Briquet, Heawood, or Piccard)

INSCRIPTIONS: recto, upper right, in red chalk: *Martin ___ (?) / in Wien 1780*; lower right, in graphite: *Martin . . . / S. 1783*; lower right, in red ink, crossed out in black ink: *S9 NM*

PROVENANCE: acquired from Hill-Stone, Inc., New York

REFERENCES: *YUAG Bulletin* (2004): 165

Everett V. Meeks, B.A. 1901, Fund. 2004.20.1

In the upper right corner of *Head of a Young Man* is an inscription, which may be a signature. The name Martin is clearly legible, but the second word, presumably the family name, cannot be read with certainty, and it has not been possible to match any plausible reading with a known artist. When this drawing was acquired by the Yale University Art Gallery, it had an attribution to the Austrian painter and printmaker Jakob Matthias Schmutzer, but it seems more likely that it was made by either a student or a member of his circle whose given name was Martin. Many works are known bearing Schmutzer's signature, and most of these are dated, suggesting that he habitually signed and usually dated his drawings;[1] hence, he probably did not make this work.

Although Schmutzer is no longer widely recognized, he built a long and successful career under imperial Habsburg patronage. In 1762, Schmutzer went to study with a leading engraver in Paris, Johann Georg Wille. Wille was an active artist, teacher, and collector who promoted awareness of German engraving. Schmutzer studied with Wille until 1766, when he was appointed director of the newly founded Viennese engraving academy; the following year, Empress Maria Theresa made Schmutzer her imperial engraver. He remained the engraving academy director throughout his career, even after it was amalgamated with the fine arts academy in 1772.[2]

Unlike Wille's other students, who specialized in landscapes, Schmutzer typically composed figural works. While still in Paris, Schmutzer hosted figure-drawing sessions in the evening for fellow students,[3] and it appears that he continued this practice throughout his career, both to be a role model for his pupils and to improve his own work. Schmutzer's instructional writing emphasized the importance of daily practice. He perpetually sought to improve his skills, so that others would not overtake or surpass him.[4] Head and figure studies by Schmutzer that date from the 1760s to 1805 show that he continued to render the figure throughout his working life. Among Schmutzer's works in the collections of the Kupferstichkabinett, Berlin; the Albertina, Vienna; the Narodni Gallery, Prague; the Metropolitan Museum of Art, New York; and those recently on the art market, a large proportion are such studies.

Yale's drawing is close in every respect to Schmutzer's signed drawings. One close comparison is Schmutzer's *Head of a Young Man* at the Metropolitan Museum of Art, signed in the center at the bottom, and dated 1774 (fig. A).[5] The subject, composition, shading, and medium are similar. Both drawings seem to have been made quickly, almost certainly from life. The watermark in the paper of Yale's *Head of a Young Man* is identical to that in the paper of two other drawings at the

FIGURE 71A | Jakob Matthias Schmutzer, *Head of a Young Man*, 1774. New York, Metropolitan Museum of Art.

FIGURE 71B | Circle of Jakob Matthias Schmutzer, *Head of a Man*, 1780. Boston, Horvitz Collection.

Metropolitan Museum—one signed, the other attributed to Schmutzer's circle.[6] Thus, it seems incontrovertible that Yale's drawing originated in Schmutzer's orbit.

A similar *Head of a Man*, in the Horvitz collection, is also inscribed at the top right "Martin ___" and dated 1780 (fig. B).[7] As with Yale's drawing, the second word is difficult to decipher. The handwriting is roughly similar to that on Yale's drawing, although with subtle differences of module and slant. Both drawings show a crisp rendering of the ruffled collar and varied articulation of the strands of hair. Furthermore, in both drawings the cross-hatchings on the face are somewhat more highly visible than in the drawings signed by Schmutzer, and both have the anatomical idiosyncrasy of placing the tip of the earlobe parallel to the lips, rather than to the bottom of the nose. Since the models in the two drawings are clearly not the same individual, the name "Martin" would not be a reference to the subject, so it seems highly likely that the two drawings were executed by the same artist.

The dramatic pose and theatrical costume of the figure in Yale's *Head of a Young Man*, as well as of those in other studies by Schmutzer and artists close to him, suggest that the works were probably not intended as portraits but rather as studies of expression. The drawing of expressive heads was a staple of academic training from the time of Charles Le Brun, whose pioneering work on basic expressions, *Conférence sur l'expression générale et particulière*, influenced generations of academic artists.[8] Schmutzer's works and those of his circle contain more subtle grades of emotion than are conveyed in Le Brun's work. In the case of Yale's *Head of a Young Man*, the expression reveals a skeptical curiosity or a moment of recognition. Jean-Baptiste Greuze (see cat. no. 69), eight years older than Schmutzer and a friend of Wille's, was inspired by the work of Le Brun and made numerous drawings of the passions. Pierre-Charles Ingouf engraved a series of Greuze's head studies as a gift for Wille in 1766, before Schmutzer returned to Vienna.[9] Thus, Schmutzer would have known these expression studies by Greuze, and he may have shared them with his students.

Jean-Honoré Fragonard (see cat. no. 72) painted a series of so-called *portraits de fantaisie*, seventeen of which are now known, beginning around the time Schmutzer left Paris. Most of these figures are in somewhat dramatic poses, and dressed in unusual costumes, often with ruffs such as those on many of the models in drawings by Schmutzer and his circle.[10] Like the drawings of the Schmutzer circle, these paintings combine the characteristics of portraits and expressive heads, ultimately defying classification, and it is tempting to suggest that Schmutzer had at least known of some of these extraordinary works as well.

MEH

1 Over fifty signed drawings by Schmutzer are listed as follows, and there surely are many more: Friedländer, Bock, and Rosenberg 1921–30, 1:329; Tietze et al. 1933, 4:185–186, and 5: nos. 2283–2290; Christie's, New York, 11 January 1989, lots 193–203; Preiss 1996, nos. 57–59. The Metropolitan Museum of Art has twelve unpublished drawings signed by Schmutzer and mostly dated, with dates ranging from 1774 to 1805, inv. nos. 53.228.1–12, plus three attributed to his circle, inv. nos. 53.228.13–15.

2 Nagler 1835–52, 17:367–372; Duplessis 1857, 2:211–212 and 317; Thieme-Becker 30:184–185; London 1994, 36–37.

3 Schulze Altcappenberg 1987, 71.

4 Specifically, " . . . selbst in der Kunst täglich weiter zu gehen, damit sie mich nicht einholen oder gar übertreffen," Vienna, Archiv der Akademie der Bildenden Künste, inv. no. VA 1766, f. 176, cited in Schulze Altcappenberg 1987, 27.

5 Inv. no. 58.228.3, red chalk, 59 × 45.3 cm.

6 *Head of a Woman* (inv. no. 53.228.1, signed and dated 1782) and *Two Male Heads* (inv. no. 53.228.14, attributed to the circle of Schmutzer, offprint worked up in red chalk, copy of Peter Paul Rubens's *Ambrose Receives Emperor Teodosio* in Vienna's Kunsthistorisches Museum) have the identical watermark; *Head of a Young Man* (fig. A) has a watermark from the same source but a different lot, measuring approximately one centimeter larger.

7 Boston, Horvitz Collection, inv. no. D-N-4, red chalk, 55.1 × 40.5 cm. I wish to thank Alvin L. Clark, Jr., for sharing information about this drawing.

8 Montagu 1994, 111–124, reprints the 1698 published version of this lecture.

9 *IFF XVIIIe siècle* 11:606–607, nos. 1–9; New York–Los Angeles 2002, 156–159, 232–233.

10 See Paris–New York 1987–88, 255–293.

72 Jean-Honoré Fragonard
Grasse 1732–1806 Paris

In Despair, Olympia Throws Herself on the Bed, probably 1780s

Black chalk, with brown and gray wash, 38.4 × 25.4 cm (15 1/8 × 10 in.)

WATERMARK: RM

PROVENANCE: Hippolyte Walferdin (believed to have acquired his important collection of Fragonard drawings, including 137 of the Ariosto series, from Fragonard's descendants); Louis Roederer, Reims; Louis Olry-Roederer; A. S. W. Rosenbach, Philadelphia; John Nicholas Brown; acquired from David Tunick, New York

REFERENCES: Mongan, Hofer, and Seznec 1945, pl. 57; Washington 1945, no. 49; Dupuy-Vachey 2003, no. 84; New York 2004, no. 3

Everett V. Meeks, B.A. 1901, Fund. 2004.22.1

Jean-Honoré Fragonard was immensely successful and honored while still relatively young. Briefly a pupil of Jean-Siméon Chardin, Fragonard began working in the studio of François Boucher (see cat. no. 63) in 1749. Fragonard won the Prix de Rome in 1752 and in 1756 traveled to Italy, where in 1758 he met his contemporary Hubert Robert (see cat. no. 66). When Fragonard returned to Paris, he quickly became famous and might well have received the highest official positions of first painter to the king and director of the Academy. Instead, he chose an independent path, producing few of the history subjects that were still the most prestigious in the hierarchy of painting categories, preferring instead to create virtuoso half-length portraits in an unprecedented sketchy manner, and delightful decorative ensembles celebrating the carefree joys of youth and love. Fragonard outlived his own popularity, however, and by about 1780, according to his grandson Théophile Fragonard, his work was out of fashion, eclipsed by the new neoclassicism.[1]

On the basis of style, it is thought that Fragonard's series of drawings illustrating Lodovico Ariosto's *Orlando Furioso* was done in the 1780s, and if indeed Fragonard's output of paintings had diminished by then, that is all the more reason to suppose he would have had time to work on this project. Furthermore, Théophile Fragonard indicated that it was after the moment when his grandfather's work had gone out of fashion—when he was approaching the age of fifty—that he made these drawings.[2] *Orlando Furioso* reached the height of its popularity in France around 1780. Although it seems likely that Fragonard read the poem in Italian,[3] two French translations—both in prose—appeared in Paris: one by Louis d'Ussieux, published between 1775 and 1783, and one by Louis-Élisabeth de La Vergne, Count of Tressan, in 1780; Niccolò Piccinni's opera *Roland*, derived from the poem, was composed and performed in Paris in 1778.[4] It has recently been suggested that Fragonard's project might not have been begun until the late 1780s, as a commission from Pierre Didot,[5] but this is unlikely—among other reasons because Fragonard's daughter, Rosalie, died in 1788, and the joie de vivre with which these drawings are infused seems inconceivable at a time when Fragonard had just suffered this tragic loss.

Ariosto's poem, recounting the exploits of Charlemagne's nephew Roland, was of truly heroic proportions. First published in Ferrara in 1516 (although revised over many years until a definitive edition was published in 1532), it consists of 46 cantos, the shortest having 72 verses and the longest 199, each verse being 8 lines long. Before turning to Ariosto, Fragonard had created several series inspired by great literature: one series, of paintings, illustrated Torquato Tasso's *Gerusalemme Liberata*; another consisted of twenty-six drawings for *Don Quixote* by Cervantes[6]; and another was a rich series of about forty drawings for *Contes et nouvelles* of Jean de La Fontaine.[7] The 177 known drawings illustrating *Orlando Furioso*, however, are probably the most admired of them all.[8]

Nonetheless, much is still obscure about the series: there is no certainty about the date, and why the drawings were made—whether there was a commission, whether Fragonard created them in the hope of generating a new edition of the epic, or whether he was making the drawings essentially for his own pleasure—is unknown. It would seem that, at a certain point, he abandoned the project, as the drawings illustrate scenes from only the first sixteen cantos of the poem. Marie-Anne Dupuy-Vachey does set forth a hypothesis—recognizing that, as of now, it cannot be proven: that the drawings were done not as preparation for prints, but simply for a collector as a unique suite to accompany the text. The freedom of the pen and washes in Fragonard's drawings would indeed be impossible to replicate in prints using line alone, although a talented practitioner adept in the new method of aquatint might have been able to capture much of their spirit and verve in that print medium.[9] Fragonard's friend the Abbé de Saint-Non was an innovator in aquatint, and Fragonard was also a friend of Jean-Baptiste Le Prince (see cat. no. 68), who made significant refinements to the technique. If Le Prince (who was two years younger than Fragonard and only forty-seven when he died in September 1781) had not made his last aquatints in 1774 and moved out of Paris because of illness in 1775, it would be tempting to think that Fragonard had hoped that Le Prince might translate his Ariosto drawings into prints.[10]

Dupuy-Vachey's suggestion was that the patron for the series might have been Pierre-Jacques-Onésyme Bergeret, the wealthy financier with whom Fragonard made his second trip to Italy, in 1774, and whose death in 1785 could have been the reason for the project's coming to a halt.[11] Although it is well known that after their return from Italy Fragonard and Bergeret had a serious disagreement over ownership of drawings that Fragonard had made during the trip, Fragonard continued to have good relations with the financier's son Pierre-Jacques, to the extent that Fragonard's daughter was staying on the property of the younger Bergeret at the time of her death, at age nineteen, in 1788.[12] The bulk of the Ariosto drawings seems to have been in Fragonard's possession at the time of his death in 1806.[13]

Yale's drawing portrays a character in one of the minor stories of the epic. Olympia, daughter of the Count of Holland, and her lover Bireno, Duke of Zeeland, had fallen asleep together, but during the night Bireno awoke and left her, setting sail on his ship. When she awoke, Olympia reached out for him but discovered that he was not there; she ran to the shore, climbed on a rock, and swooned when she realized his ship had gone. This drawing shows Olympia having returned to the bed and thrown herself on it in despair. Dupuy-Vachey singles out the suite of seven

drawings illustrating this sequence—which she characterizes as "breathless"—as manifesting a sort of exchange of roles between Ariosto and the artist: "The former tells the misadventure of the young woman in two lines, with a concision that underlines the brutality of the offense, whereas the artist wins the sympathy of the spectator by multiplying the images of the young princess of Holland in despair."[14] The thrust of Olympia's fall is conveyed by her flying hair, the lines of her dress, and the depression in the bed covers from her dive into them. Her emotional state is conveyed by the age-old gesture of arms flung upward. The canopy flowing downward from a tree branch, which the previous night had enveloped a scene of love, now suggests a cascade of tears. The work exemplifies Fragonard's extraordinary and seemingly effortless command of the unusual combination of black chalk and washes that he favored, and his boundless capacity for invention, in his full maturity.

The lines from *Orlando Furioso* illustrated here are from canto X, verse 27 (verse 26 is also cited to provide additional context):

Ma i venti, che portavano le vele
But the wind that carried far out to sea

Per l'alto mar di quel giovane infido,
The sails of this false young man,

Portavan anco i prieghi, e le querele
Also carried away the pleas and laments

De l'infelice Olimpia, e 'l pianto e 'l grido,
Of hapless Olympia, and her sobs and cries.

La qual tre volte, a se stessa crudele,
Three times, bent on her own destruction,

Per affogarsi si spiccò dal lido:
She made to drown herself; but finally

Pur al fin si levò da mirar l'acque,
She stopped gazing at the water, rose and

E ritornò, dove la notte giacque.
Returned to where she had passed the night.

E con la faccia in giù stesa su 'l letto,
She fell prone on the bed,

Bagnandolo di pianto, dice a lui:
Bathing it in tears, and thus addressed it:

Iersera desti insieme a dui ricetto:
Last night you gave welcome to two of us;

Perchè insieme al levar non siamo dui?
Why then were we not still two in the morning?

O perfido Bireno, o maladetto
O faithless Bireno! o cursed

Giorno, ch'al mondo generata fui!
Day that I was born!

Che debbo far? che poss'io far quì sola?
What shall I do? What can I do here alone?

Chi mi dà ajuto? (oimè) chi mi consola?
Who will help me? alas, who will comfort me?[15]

SB

1 See Valogne 1955, 9, or Rosenberg 1989, 12. The past several decades have seen an abundance of scholarly work on Fragonard; the exhibition catalogue Paris–New York 1987–88 gives a comprehensive view of the artist, and Cuzin 1988 catalogues 420 extant paintings, plus 212 lost ones. Rosenberg 1989 lists 451, including those known only by a replica, copy, or print. Ananoff 1961–70 lists over 2,700 drawings by Fragonard, although it excludes the 137 Ariosto drawings already published by Mongan, Hofer, and Seznec. Dupuy-Vachey 2003 is a comprehensive study of the Ariosto drawings, with thorough previous bibliography, and see also Seznec 1945; Washington–Cambridge 1978–79, 152–167; London 1978; Wakefield 1979; Philadelphia–Houston 1985.
2 Valogne 1955, 9, and Rosenberg 1989, 12–13.
3 See Seznec 1945, 30. An Italian edition was published in four volumes in Venice in 1772–73, and Fragonard was in Venice with Bergeret 19–31 July 1774; see L'isle-Adam–Grasse 2001–02, 50, and Bergeret de Grancourt 1895, 380–396. In his diary entry for 24 July (387), Bergeret remarked on the large number of booksellers in Venice.
4 Dupuy-Vachey 2003, 7.
5 Madrid 2003–04, 258.
6 See Paris–New York 1987–88, 508–509; Madrid 2003–04, 257–262.
7 Paris 1992–93, 191–274.
8 Dupuy-Vachey 2003 lists 176 drawings. Since the publication of her book, she has discovered, thanks to Marianne Roland-Michel, another one, probably an illustration for canto X (France, private collection). I am grateful to Marie-Anne Dupuy-Vachey for this information (by electronic communication, February 2005).
9 One print corresponding to one of these drawings is known to have been made, by Jean-Philippe-Guy le Gentil, Count of Paroy, of the subject *Demons Help the Old Hermit Catch Up to Angelica* (Dupuy-Vachey 2003, no. 64), exhibited at the Salon of 1787, although no impression of it is known today, and it is not listed in Portalis and Béraldi 1880–82, 3:273–277. The print could well have been an aquatint, as the two small portraits by Paroy listed in Portalis and Béraldi are in that medium. The drawing is in a private collection. See Dupuy-Vachey 2003, 24.
10 See Rouen 2004–05, 19, 20. Le Prince's method is described in *Encyclopédie* 1782–1832, 47:622–625; this is reprinted in Hédou 1879, 179–188; for use of aquatint by Saint-Non and Le Prince, see Washington 2003–04, 29, and nos. 10, 20, 21.
11 Dupuy-Vachey 2003, 23–24. She suggests (24 n. 1), not implausibly, that Bergeret is evoked, through the costume and the two accompanying dogs, in the depiction of Ippolito d'Este, to whom Ariosto is shown dedicating the poem in the first drawing of the series (Dupuy-Vachey 2003, no. 1, Paris, Louvre, inv. no. RF 24319). The suggestion that Bergeret might have been Fragonard's patron had in fact been made by Portalis 1880, 318.
12 See Dupuy-Vachey 2003, 24; L'isle-Adam–Grasse 2001–02, 22, 93.
13 For the history of the drawings as a group, see Dupuy-Vachey 2003, 21 n. 3.
14 Dupuy-Vachey 2003, 13. "Le premier raconte la mésaventure de la jeune femme en deux strophes, concision qui souligne la brutalité de l'offense, tandis que l'artiste entraîne la compassion du spectateur en multipliant les images montrant la jeune princesse de Hollande au désespoir."
15 The Italian is from Ariosto 1772–73, an edition that Fragonard might well have read, especially since he traveled in Italy in 1774; the translation is adapted from Ariosto 1973 and Ariosto 1998.

73 Henry Fuseli
Zurich 1741–1825 London

Male Nude and Seated Hermit (recto);
Male Nude (verso), ca. 1790–1800

Pen and brown ink, 31.8 × 19.5 cm
(12½ × 7¹¹⁄₁₆ in.)

WATERMARK: Large Garden of Holland / Maid of Delft with "Pro Patria," similar to Churchill no. 128 and many other examples, but no exact match has been identified. The watermark is a type common in paper of the late eighteenth century

INSCRIPTIONS: recto, vertically along left edge, in brown ink: *Perch' I Pisan' Lucca veder non ponno*

PROVENANCE: John S. Thacher, Washington, D.C.

REFERENCES: Schiff 1959, 126; Minneapolis–New York 1962, no. 42; H-B and L, no. 201; Schiff 1973, no. 869; Palm Beach 1974, no. 23; Williamstown 1980, no. 9

Gift of John S. Thacher, B.A. 1927. 1952.12.4.a–b

Although the son of the Swiss painter Johann Caspar Füssli, Henry Fuseli had little formal training as an artist and instead received a thorough education in theology, classical literature, and epic poetry. Forced to leave Zurich in 1762 after writing a pamphlet against a corrupt official, Fuseli traveled through Germany and England. He eventually abandoned his interests in theology and philosophy and, deciding to pursue a career as an artist, traveled to Italy. Fuseli spent eight years in Rome. He made a careful study of ancient art but rejected the rigid classicism espoused by Johann Joachim Winckelmann and other contemporary critics. Instead, relying on a range of influences that included Michelangelo and his contemporaries, Fuseli developed a dramatic, individual style. Keyed to explore human psychology, especially in the face of violence or tragedy, his art is among the earliest manifestations of the Romantic movement that would become the dominant trend in European art of the early nineteenth century.[1]

In 1779, Fuseli returned to England, where he spent the rest of his life. He dedicated himself to history painting, sometimes devising fantastic subjects of his own (as in his famous *Nightmare* of 1781) but more often

RECTO

VERSO

taking motifs from Shakespeare, Milton, the Nordic Poets, and Dante.[2] The inscription on the present sheet is from the thirty-third canto of Dante's *Inferno*, from a passage in which Count Ugolino della Gherardesca sees his old adversary Ruggiero degli Ubaldini hunting on Monte San Giuliano between Pisa and Lucca (*per che i Pisani veder Lucca non ponno*; literally, "because of which the Pisans cannot see Lucca"). Of all the lines from the gruesome story of Ugolino, this is surely one of the least significant, and its interest to Fuseli and its relationship to his drawing have long been a mystery. Fuseli's own depictions of the Ugolino story have nothing to do with the figures drawn here.[3]

Fuseli's mind, however, was a storehouse of literary and art-historical quotations, and it is here proposed that the connections between the drawing and text on this sheet might be explained as resulting from that coincidence of miscellaneous source material. The nude is adapted from the central figure of Michelangelo's *Battle of Cascina*, which depicted a battle between the Florentine and Pisan armies on the plains outside of Pisa—in other words, on the plains just below the hills described in the line from Dante. It is not difficult to imagine the complexly erudite Fuseli making a drawing after the *Battle of Cascina* and then having the line from Dante come to mind, explaining its appearance here.

The figure seems to have been first drawn on the verso of this sheet, to judge from the sketchier outlines of this version and because the orientation of the drawing on the verso matches Fuseli's source. He then traced through to the recto, making a clean copy and thereby reversing the figure. Both studies have the left-handed cross-hatching found throughout Fuseli's work. Michelangelo's original cartoon had, of course, been destroyed long before Fuseli's time, and the source for this drawing was one of the later copies, most likely the painted copy by Bastiano (Aristotile) da Sangallo at Holkham Hall, Norfolk, or possibly an undated engraving after that painting published in London, sometime around 1800, by Luigi Schiavonetti, who moved in the same circles as Fuseli (both were associated with William Blake, and Schiavonetti later engraved some of Fuseli's paintings).[4] The figure of the seated hermit does not seem to relate to the heroic nude, nor to the stories of Ugolino or the Battle of Cascina, and its function here—if indeed the drawings on this sheet can be considered to have any function at all—remains unclear.[5] Some comparison can be made between the juxtaposition of equally different types in this sheet and in Fuseli's similar double-sided drawing of *A Woman before the Laocoon* (fig. A).[6]

Fuseli's drawings are often difficult to ascribe to a particular date. The artist returned to Dante and Michelangelo throughout his career, so neither source offers chronological assistance in this case. Gert Schiff suggests a date of circa 1790 on the basis of style. Comparisons can be made between this sheet and several dated drawings including a *Classical*

FIGURE 73A | Henry Fuseli, *A Woman before the Laocoon*, ca. 1801–05. Zurich, Kunsthaus.

Scene in the Ashmolean dated 1790[7] and two drawings after Spenser's *Faerie Queen* dated 1794 and 1796;[8] the possible connection between this drawing and Schiavonetti's print, as well as the similarity to *A Woman before the Laocoon* might favor a date in the latter part of the 1790s or even just after 1800.

JJM

1   The most comprehensive treatments of Fuseli's life and art are Schiff 1973 and Hamburg–London 1974–75. Powell 1951 is a good short introduction to Fuseli's drawings, and Knowles 1831 remains a valuable reference for Fuseli's writings and the earliest bibliography; see also Weinglass 1982 for biographical material.

2   In Sacheverell Sitwell's memorable phrasing, Fuseli was a man who "liked to write about painting and to paint about literature" (quoted in Powell 1951, 29).

3   Fuseli illustrated the Ugolino story twice, first in a drawing of around 1790 (Zurich, collection of Dr. Conrad Ulrich; Schiff 1973, no. 427) and later in a painting exhibited at the Royal Academy in 1806 (now lost).

4   Michelangelo's well-known preparatory drawing of this figure, now in the British Museum, London (inv. no. 1887-5-2-116; Wilde 1953, no. 6), has sometimes been suggested as a source (Minneapolis–New York 1962; H-B and L), but the man's left arm in that drawing is hidden, and his torso is at a slightly different angle, whereas the figure as recorded by Sangallo and Schiavonetti matches that drawn by Fuseli. Tomory 1972, fig. 97, illustrates another drawing after a figure in the Cascina cartoon (Auckland, Art Gallery, inv. no. 1965/45, pen and brown ink with mauve wash, 23.4 × 18.7 cm, which he dates to ca. 1790–91; Schiff 1973, no. 1785, dates it ca. 1791–92.

5   Given the old man's position on the sheet, his beard, and his pose, he might be imagined as Fuseli's joking variation on the old man at lower right in the copies after the Cascina cartoon, but the variant is so far from its source that the idea can remain only speculation.

6   Zurich, Kunsthaus, inv. no. 1913/7, pen and black ink over black chalk, 32 × 40.4 cm; see Schiff 1973, no. 1072. Schiff dates the drawing ca. 1801–05.

7   Oxford, Ashmolean Museum, pen and brown ink, 35 × 33.5 cm; see Schiff 1973, no. 1042 or Powell 1951, no. 28.

8   Zurich, Kunsthaus, inv. no. 1914/24, pen and brown ink, 22.5 × 22.6 cm (Schiff 1973, no. 1005), and Oberhofen, Kt. Bern, Frau Beatrice Ganz, pen and ink with wash, 51.5 × 62.5 cm (Schiff 1973, no. 1006).

74 Giovanni Domenico Tiepolo
Venice 1727–1804 Venice

Punchinello Feeding the Peacocks, ca. 1800

Pen and brown ink and brown wash over black chalk, 29.4 × 40.8 cm (11 9/16 × 16 1/16 in.)

WATERMARK: "GAF" in a twisted heart

INSCRIPTIONS: recto, lower right, in brown ink, probably in the artist's hand: *Domo. Tiepolo f.*; upper left, in both pencil and light brown ink, superimposed: *69*

PROVENANCE: possibly in the collection of Michelangelo Guggenheim, Venice; part of the set sold at Sotheby's, London, 6 July 1920, lot 41; P. and D. Colnaghi and Co., London; Richard Owen, Paris (1920–21); Philip Hofer, Cambridge, Mass.; Mr. and Mrs. Paul Wick, Youngstown, Ohio

REFERENCES: Chicago 1938, no. 103; Cambridge 1940, no. 37; Byam Shaw 1962, 52 n. 3; Bloomington–Stanford 1979, no. S43; Knox 1983, 145, no. 69; *YUAG Bulletin* 38 (1983): 35 and 89; Gealt 1986, no. 65; New Haven 1991a, no. 21; *Handbook*, 209; Udine–Bloomington 1996–97, 246

Gift of Mrs. Paul Wick and her children, Paul M. Wick, B.A. 1939, William A. Wick, B.A. 1941, Peter A. Wick, B.A. 1943, and Mrs. Osborne Howes, in honor of Paul Wick, B.A. 1912. 1981.32

A stock character in the *commedia dell' arte*, Punchinello was everywhere in eighteenth-century Venice but seems to have assumed a particular significance for Domenico Tiepolo. He made Punchinello the primary subject of the frescoes in the family villa at Zianigo[1] and of the drawn series *Divertimento per li regazzi*, from which the present sheet comes. Yet, Domenico's Punchinello is not the vulgar, lecherous glutton of the Punch and Judy shows but instead, a humanized—if not fully human—doppelganger of the artist and his audience. Punchinello was Domenico's "Everyman," and where Apollo or some other empyrean god might be seen as the signature motif of his father Giambattista Tiepolo's art, the last glimmer of the Baroque, it is the Punchinello series that sums up Domenico's work.[2]

While the 104 drawings that make up the *Divertimento per li regazzi* can be read as a rough narrative of Punchinello's life, the subjects of the individual scenes are so strange and various that it is impossible to read them in any logical progression. Using the numbers recorded in the upper left margins of the sheets, which seem perhaps to have been Tiepolo's own notations, James Byam Shaw

FIGURE 74A | Giovanni Domenico Tiepolo, *Feeding Turkeys in a Farmyard*, 1791. New Haven, Yale University Art Gallery.

suggests that the scenes may be grouped into five "chapters": the ancestry and childhood of Punchinello; his various trades and occupations; his adventures in strange countries; his social and official life; and his last illness and death.[3] Numbered 69, the *Punchinello Feeding the Peacocks* clearly fits into the third of these categories. Apart from the obvious decorative qualities and exotic connotations of the peacocks, the birds might be variations on the theme of Punchinello's own avian origins and physiognomy. Punchinello's name and birdlike profile are generally understood as relating to his association with chickens, and in the first narrative scene of the *Divertimento* series, we find Punchinello hatched from an enormous egg atop which nests a turkey-hen. The eccentric anatomy of the peacocks can likewise be compared to Punchinello's own. Finally, Tiepolo seems to be playing with Punchinello's courtship through the juxtaposition of Punchinello and his accompanying lady with the pairs of peacocks and peahens. Stylistically, like so many of Tiepolo's works, the drawing is a technical tour de force with the space defined only by subtle tints of wash.

It has often been observed that, as he began to draw the Punchinello series, Tiepolo apparently had a great stock of his own drawings as well as those of his father close at hand, together with prints by Callot, della Bella, Castiglione, and others, for a daunting range of source material has been traced in the series. In the case of *Punchinello Feeding the Peacocks,* one such source is a drawing of *Feeding Turkeys in a Farmyard* from Tiepolo's "contemporary life" series of the previous decade (fig. A), a sheet that is—purely by coincidence—also at Yale.[4] The act of feeding birds and the ways in which pairs of birds face each other in the two sheets seem to confirm that the earlier composition was in the artist's mind, and while the turkeys are part of the elaborate Punchinello iconography that Tiepolo created for himself, it is impossible to derive any clear meaning through the juxtaposition of the sheets.[5]

Indeed, the meaning of Tiepolo's quotations, and the artist's intentions in creating the series, have been the subject of widely varying interpretation. Byam Shaw dismisses the quotations as the work of an "old and tired" artist whose "visual imagination was failing."[6] Gealt likewise seems, as John Spike notices, almost embarrassed by the obvious use of source material, while Spike emphasizes the range of "impious jokes" for "the amusement of the cognoscenti."[7] Whichever interpretation one chooses, it bears noting that Tiepolo's quotations are surely to be understood as functioning like those found throughout sixteenth- and seventeenth-century art, and not the result of some modern sense of impoverished imagination.[8] This author, at least, is inclined to understand the series as only falsely naïve and to read the title page, in Philip Fehl's felicitous phrase, as "a clown's apology."[9] The Punchinello dedication to children is thus similar in tone to Callot's dedication of his *Capricci* to "girls studying drawing," as Adriano Mariuz has also observed.[10] In such a view, the series is both simple narrative and complex *capriccio*, and the universal history of Punchinello might take its place among the masterpieces of eighteenth-century art, alongside the works of Chardin, Goya, and others who have been so much more praised for their sophistication by modern scholars.

While they represented something like Domenico Tiepolo's artistic will and testament, the Punchinello drawings remained essentially unknown to scholars until their appearance at a Sotheby's sale in 1920.[11] They were already loose sheets by this point,[12] although they had surely been in an album before that time. After being bought by Richard Owen in 1920, the entire set was exhibited together for the last time in 1921 in Paris at the Musée des Arts Decoratifs, after which Owen broke up the set and sold the sheets to various collectors.

JJM

1 See Pedrocco 1988. Executed in the 1790s, most of the frescoes were later detached from the walls and are now in the Ca' Rezzonico, Venice.

2 There is a large bibliography—and a range of interpretation—for the Punchinello series. In addition to the works cited among the "References" above, see also Fehl 1979 and the many reviews of Gealt 1986 including those by John Spike, Brinsley Ford, Ronald Paulson, and Adriano Mariuz.

3 Byam Shaw 1962, 55–57. He notes, however, that even if the numbers are Tiepolo's own, "that numbering was careless, and does not represent the proper sequence."

4 Yale University Art Gallery, inv. no. 1971.93, pen and brown ink and brown wash over black chalk, 28.5 × 41.0 cm. Gealt 1986, 28 n. 2, links this drawing to the Punchinello series, if not to the peacock scene.

5 It is tempting to compare Tiepolo's non-logical Punchinello iconography to the art of twentieth-century masters such as Jasper Johns or Jim Dine, who evolved similar personal iconography. Though anachronistic, the comparison to the well-known Pop Art model does perhaps help evoke some of the ways in which Tiepolo used his stock of motifs.

6 Byam Shaw 1962, 57.

7 Spike 1980, 285. See also, of course, Bloomington–Stanford 1979, and Gealt 1986. For documentary evidence of Domenico's collections, see Byam Shaw 1962, 18, on the Tiepolo sale of 1845, which probably consisted mainly of works that had passed down from him. There is certainly something of a learned joke to the whole enterprise. As Knox 1984, notes, Giambattista Tiepolo may have been inspired to take up the Punchinello story on the basis of the Venerdì Gnoccolare during Carnival in Verona, and that the Veronese intellectual Scipione Maffei might have been the recipient of the earliest drawings of the subject.

8 Moreover, from Domenico's own works, one should draw parallels to his *Flight into Egypt* series, on which see Byam Shaw 1962, 31, as well as Middletown–New Haven 1988.

9 Fehl 1979, 784. Fehl's is, for this author at least, the most compelling discussion of the series.

10 Mariuz 1971, 87.

11 The drawings were said by Morassi 1941, 282, n. 16, to have come from the collection of Michelangelo Guggenheim, Venice. Because they were not in Guggenheim's posthumous 1913 auction, Byam Shaw was disinclined to believe this record, but as Jaynie Anderson notes (Anderson 1988, 568), Guggenheim was the greatest dealer of his generation in Venice and may well have sold the drawings before his death.

12 Byam Shaw 1962, 52, citing Sacheverell Sitwell, who saw the drawings at the sale.

75 Bartolomeo Pinelli
Rome 1781–1835 Rome

Achilles Swears an Oath to Avenge the Dead Patroclus, Killed by Hector, 1808

Pen and black ink with brown and gray washes over graphite, 41.3 × 54.6 cm (16¼ × 21½ in.)

INSCRIPTIONS: verso, in pen and ink, in the artist's hand: *Pinelli Inventò e fece Roma 1808 / abita No.90. vicino il Caffè degli / Inglesi Piazza di Spagna*; lower right, in graphite: *D 337 / Achille giura di vendicare il corpo di patroclo, ucciso da Ettore*

PROVENANCE: Hans Freiherr von und zu Aufsess (1801–1872), Aufsess (Bavaria) and Nuremberg (L. 2479); private collection, New York; acquired from W. M. Brady and Co., New York

REFERENCES: New York 1999b, no. 26; *YUAG Bulletin* (2000): 144–145

Everett V. Meeks, B.A. 1901, Fund. 1999.24.1

One of the most prominent and prolific artists of the early Ottocento, Bartolomeo Pinelli was part of a group of painters—along with Giuseppe Cades, Felice Giani, Henry Fuseli (see cat. no. 73), Luigi Sabatelli, and Pelagio Palagi—that represented a bridge between Neoclassicism and Romanticism. Pinelli's varied and prodigious output catered heavily to the tourist trade and included countless drawings in a wide range of media, sculptures in terracotta, and several print series—primarily in etching, and, after 1830, in lithography. Today Pinelli is relatively unknown outside of Rome but during his lifetime was terrifically popular and recognized throughout Europe. A number of distinguished French Romantic contemporaries—including Chateaubriand, Delacroix, Géricault, and Baudelaire—mention him in their writings.

Bartolomeo Pinelli was born in Rome and received his academic training as both draftsman and sculptor, first in Bologna at the Accademia di Belle Arti, and later at the Accademia di San Luca in Rome. He also studied at the Scuola di Nudo on the Capitoline Hill in Rome, where he won two first prizes, in drawing (1807) and in sculpture (1809). Pinelli painted few oils,[1] preferring watercolor and graphic media. Though known today for his Roman genre subjects and costume studies, Pinelli's oeuvre was actually highly diverse and included landscape views, portraits, drawings of antiquities, and classical and mythological subjects—all of which found a welcome reception with Italophiles eager for souvenirs of their Grand Tour experience. Apparently Pinelli was well aware of the popularity of his subjects and, as Roberta J. M. Olson has noted, very likely chose his studio because of its strategic proximity to the section of Rome most trafficked by tourists.[2] Indeed, by 1808 (the date of Yale's drawing) Pinelli was often adding his address to his signature, as is the case with the present sheet (see above).

FIGURE 75A | Bartolomeo Pinelli, *Achilles Drags the Body of Hector before the Walls of Troy*, 1808. New York, private collection.

Yale's drawing illustrates the scene in Homer's *Iliad* in which the Greek hero Achilles mourns the death of his dearest friend, Patroclus—slain by the Trojan hero Hector—and swears to seek vengeance: "I will not bury you till I bring to this place the armour / and the head of Hektor. . . . " Achilles directs his attendants to wash the clotted blood from the wounds of Patroclus, and to lay him on a bier, until his death be avenged: " . . . they washed the body and anointed it softly with olive oil / and stopped the gashes in his body with stored-up unguents / and laid him on a bed, and shrouded him in a thin sheet . . . "[3] In his illustration, Pinelli has dramatically positioned the central figures of Achilles and Patroclus in a V-shaped coupling in which their lower torsos strategically overlap, while their upper torsos diverge. The figures' opposing arms reach outward as though from a single body and, in a dramatic flourish, Achilles' right hand gestures upward in active resolve, while that of Patroclus hangs down, limp and lifeless. The pose recalls many Renaissance depictions of the Lamentation; the three female figures at the right foreground, tending to the wounds, suggest the three Marys.

There is a pendant to Yale's drawing (fig. A) that illustrates a subsequent episode in Homer's *Iliad* (Book XXII, 395–515), in which Achilles (again the central subject) rides victoriously on his chariot, dragging the slain Hector, with the walls of Troy visible in the distance.[4]

The high finish of the present work and its pendant suggests that the drawings were intended for a series illustrating Homer's *Iliad*, a project that was apparently never completed. The precise execution of the pair fits well with descriptions of Pinelli's working method for his finished designs: the artist began with quick studies in graphite, often in sketchbooks, then worked these up, eventually creating meticulous drawings in graphite, pen and ink with watercolor, or pen and ink with wash.[5] These two studies are closely related not only by subject, but also by size, medium, and inscription,[6] and work superbly well as pendant images, creating compelling juxtapositions: interior vs. exterior, female vs. male; rest vs. action; defeat vs. victory.

Stylistically, Yale's drawing and its pair are grounded in the academic tradition in which Pinelli trained, particularly in the artist's impeccable attention to details of anatomy and textual accuracy, which not only recalls the heroic style of Jacques-Louis David but also reveals Pinelli's own penchant for the illustrative. Pinelli's close attention to the musculature of Achilles' torso reflects his close study of sculpted classical nudes—and, indeed, his own proficiency as a sculptor.[7] Yale's drawing is also related to an 1809 drawing that Pinelli used for *Venus before Jupiter in the Presence of the Gods*, a print from his series illustrating Virgil's *Aeneid*, published in Rome in 1811.[8] There also exists a related series of twelve large pen-and-ink drawings illustrating François Fénélon's *Adventures of Telemachus*, which, like the Yale drawing, were made in 1808.[9]

Though there are few documents that record Pinelli's personal life, it is known that in Rome he lived with and probably married Mariangela Gatti, with whom he had two children. Intriguingly, Pinelli named the elder of the two (born in 1809, the year after he made Yale's drawing) Achille.

EH

1 Falconieri 1835, 70, lists just seven paintings (though according to Roberta Olson, this number has recently been disputed). See also Olson 1980, 75.
2 Olson 1980, 75.
3 Homer 1951, 18:334–335; 350–352.
4 Homer 1951, 22:395–400. "[Achilles] spoke, and now thought of shameful treatment for glorious Hektor. / In both of his feet at the back he made holes by the tendons / in the space between ankle and heel, and drew thongs of ox-hide through them, / and fastened them to the chariot so as to let the head drag, / and mounted the chariot, and lifted the glorious armour inside it, / then whipped the horses to a run, and they winged their way unreluctant."
5 Olson 1980, 77.
6 The pendant drawing to Yale's bears the inscription: *Pinelli Fece 1808 Roma / abita no. 90 Piazza di Spagna*; and below, in a different hand: *il corpo di Ettore dietro il Suo Carro / averlo uccido*.
7 Interestingly, Pinelli made a terracotta sculpture of *Achilles Dragging the Body of Hector*, which is signed and dated 1833 and is now in the Museo del Palazzo Venezia. Baltimore–Worcester–Pittsburgh 1992, 115.
8 Ottawa, National Gallery of Canada, inv. no. 41261, pen and brown ink, with brown and gray wash, on wove paper, 44.3 × 59.9 cm.
9 The *Telemachus* drawings are in the Art Institute of Chicago, inv. nos. 1963.559–1963.570; see Joachim 1980, 67–71. Another similar, if later, series of drawings by Pinelli is the set made for the *Mythology Illustrated* of 1826 (*Mitologia Illustrata*, Rome, Galleria Nazionale d'Arte Moderna).

76 Théodore Géricault
Rouen 1791–1824 Paris

The Rescue of the Survivors of the Raft of the Medusa, 1818

Pen and brown ink over graphite, 18.9 × 28 cm (7 7/16 × 11 in.)

INSCRIPTIONS: verso, lower right, in graphite: *D.3252*

PROVENANCE: William Bateson; L. G. Duke; M. de Beer; P. and D. Colnaghi and Co., London; Paul Mellon, Upperville, Va. (stamp, verso, in blue ink); Yale Center for British Art

REFERENCES: Eitner 1983, 165; New Haven 1984, no. 10; New York–San Diego–Houston 1985–86, no. 66; San Francisco 1989, no. 35

Transfer from the Yale Center for British Art, Paul Mellon Collection. 2005.56.1

Géricault's *Raft of the Medusa* (fig. A) remains one of the key monuments both of Romanticism and of the movement toward Realism and the painting of modern subjects in nineteenth-century France. As is well known, the painting caused a sensation when it was exhibited at the Salon of 1819, the result less of the painting itself than of the political controversy associated with the historical event it depicts. When the government-owned frigate *Medusa*, carrying French soldiers and settlers to Senegal, ran aground off the African coast in July 1816, 150 passengers and crew were left on a crude raft while the captain and officers rowed away in lifeboats. Mutiny and other fighting were followed by cannibalism; only fifteen survivors remained when the raft was rescued after thirteen days. The horrible event, barely reported by the Ministry of the Navy, was soon exposed in French and foreign newspapers and quickly became the means by which the opposition attacked the favoritism and incompetence of the Bourbon government.

Early in 1818, following a visit to Italy, Géricault returned to Paris and began considering subjects for the Salon of the following year.[1] He gravitated to the events of modern history and settled on the *Medusa*, which had been resurrected in public debate following the November 1817 publication of a detailed account of the events by two survivors, Alexandre Corréard and Henri Savigny. Géricault experimented with compositions depicting various moments of the story—the mutiny, cannibalism, and rescue—before settling on the moment of highest tension, when the survivors spotted the rescue craft and tried to attract its attention.

The present drawing is one of a small number of early studies that focus on the final rescue.[2] All of these are fairly loose sketches,

THÉODORE GÉRICAULT 223

FIGURE 76A | Théodore Géricault, *The Raft of the Medusa*, 1818–19. Paris, Musée du Louvre.

but as Eitner notes, Géricault's habit of building compositions by successive additions and transformations, as well as his habit of clinging to motifs once he had invented them, allows a reconstruction of the drawings' sequence.[3] The Yale sheet, the most elaborate of those depicting the rescue, is thus probably the latest of the known sketches for this episode of the story. Where the other sketches for the rescue are drawn quickly in pen and ink, parts of the Yale sheet were first laid out in graphite, as if copied from an earlier sketch. Géricault still appears to have abandoned this scheme after the Yale drawing, to judge from the lack of any additional studies that develop its figures. Yet, these early ideas for the project, which seem to indicate plans for a rather matter-of-fact reporting of the incident, might be considered a more radical artistic solution than the final painting, as they hint at the Realism that would be developed by the next generation.[4] Géricault's finished work, in contrast, is cast as a more timeless depiction of human drama, one conceptually and stylistically closer to the example of seventeenth-century Baroque painting. This transformation took place through a series of preparatory sketches made over the course of many months, a practice likewise adopted from old traditions, but once Géricault transferred the design to his monumental canvas, he painted the individual figures directly from live models posed in the studio, following a modern practice he inherited from Jacques-Louis David through Pierre Guérin.[5]

Differing so greatly from Géricault's final composition, this drawing long went unrecognized.[6] It was acquired by Paul Mellon as the work of James Barry, but when it arrived at the Yale Center for British Art in 1977, Andrew Wilton recatalogued it as "anonymous." In 1980, David Bindman recognized the sheet as Géricault's, an attribution confirmed soon afterward, and later published, by Lorenz Eitner. With the change of attribution, the drawing was transferred from the Yale Center for British Art to the Yale University Art Gallery.[7]

JJM

1 Rosenthal 1980 reveals that the enormous canvas was purchased on 24 February 1818, by which time Géricault had already decided to work on a monumental scale.

2 The other compositional drawings depicting the rescue are: a drawing in the Art Institute of Chicago, formerly in the Dubaut Collection, Paris (Eitner 1972, no. 2); Malzeville, Charles Cournault Collection (Johnson 1978, 256); Dijon, Musée des Beaux-Arts (Eitner 1972, no. 1). Eitner 1972, 140, nos. 3–4, notes that two sketches of the abandoned raft, while never likely to have been a plan for the finished painting, also date to this moment of the composition's evolution.

3 Bayonne, Musée Bonnat, inv. no. NU 699, seems to elaborate the figure of a man lifting one of his fellow sailors, apparently documenting the transformation of the figures at back left in the Chicago drawing into the figures at left in the Yale sheet: see Grunchec in New York–San Diego–Houston 1985–86, fig. 66b.

4 When considering Géricault's approach to the subject, Eitner 1983, 165, also makes the shrewd observation that the artist seems not to have experimented with the treachery of the Medusa's captain or with the moment in which the raft was cast adrift, the two most politically scandalous moments of the story.

5 For a thoughtful discussion of the artist's careful development of the composition, see Eitner 1972 and especially Eitner 1983, 171–185.

6 The drawing's "lost identity" makes its provenance harder to trace, but it is tempting to wonder whether it might have come to the English collector William Bateson from one of the five posthumous sales in London of the collection of Horace His de la Salle, who owned one of the related drawings of the rescue, the above-mentioned drawing now Dijon, Musée des Beaux-Arts (Eitner 1972, no. 1).

7 The old inventory number at the Yale Center for British Art was B1977.14.5204.

77 Jean-Auguste-Dominique Ingres
Montauban 1780–1867 Paris

Portrait of Marie Marcotte at the Age of Sixteen Months, 1830

Graphite on cream-colored wove paper, 29.7 × 24.2 cm (11 1/16 × 9 1/2 in.); design area: 24.5 × 19 cm (9 5/8 × 7 1/2 in.)

WATERMARK: "F D'ANGOUMOIS" on original backing sheet

INSCRIPTIONS: recto, lower right, in graphite: *Ingres à PaPa et à maman*; verso of old mount, in pen and black ink: *Ma fille Marie / à l'âge de 15 mois / Mariée au bon Alexandre Legentil / au mois d'octobre 1846 / Marcotte*

PROVENANCE: Marcotte family until 1934; Jacques Seligman, New York; Edith Malvina K. Wetmore

REFERENCES: Blanc 1870, 238; Delaborde 1870, no. 368; Lapauze 1903, no. 67; Lapauze 1911, 286; Christoffel 1940, 139; Naef 1958, 342; Cambridge 1967a, no. 65; *YUAG Bulletin* 31.3 (1967–68): 25 and 57; Cohn 1969, 17, 19, 21, 22; H-B and L, no. 133; Naef 1977–80, no. 325; *Handbook*, 212; Ternois 1999b, 24; Ternois 2001, 184

Bequest of Edith Malvina K. Wetmore, 1966.80.7

Although Ingres painted numerous frescoes and canvases depicting religious, mythological, allegorical, and history subjects, he is best known for his renditions of coolly sensual nude women, so-called *Odalisques*, and his classicizing portraits. The latter exist in large numbers, close to one hundred paintings and at least 460 drawings.[1] Ingres attended art school in Toulouse, and was later a pupil of Jacques-Louis David in Paris. He received the Prix de Rome in 1801 but remained in Paris for lack of travel funds. Disappointed in the reception of his paintings exhibited in the Salon of 1806, however, Ingres finally departed for Rome and became a *pensionnaire* at the French Academy there. In 1810 he met Charles Marcotte, called Marcotte d'Argenteuil, who held the post of Inspector of Forests and Waterways in the occupying French government, the Papal States having been annexed to France in 1809. Marcotte was to become Ingres's first patron and lifelong friend, and Ingres made no fewer than twenty-one portrait drawings of fourteen members of the Marcotte family.[2]

In a letter of 10 May 1830 to his friend the artist Léopold Robert, Marcotte wrote, "Our good Ingres made a couple of weeks ago a pretty little sketch of this little girl,"[3] thus seeming to date the drawing fairly precisely to some time in April. Since Marie, the first of Marcotte's three children, was born in late November 1828, she would then actually have been sixteen months old, rather than fifteen, as indicated by the inscription written by her father on the back of the mount. This inscription, however, was obviously written many years later—her wedding to Alexandre Legentil in October 1846 is also noted—so the error is understandable. Ingres's letters show that he was particularly fond of Marie,[4] and he drew another portrait of her in 1846, and also one of Legentil, shortly before the couple's wedding.[5]

Yale's drawing is one of a pair that are virtually identical; the other drawing (fig. A), distinguishable by an additional inscription at lower left, *oh! que J'aime grand maman!* (Oh! how I love Grandmother!)—possibly in the hand of the little girl's maternal grandmother, to whom the other version presumably was given—is in a private collection.[6] At least ten other such pairs or groups (since there are sometimes more than two) exist among Ingres's drawn portraits; two of the

FIGURE 77A | Jean-Auguste-Dominique Ingres, *Portrait of Marie Marcotte at the Age of Sixteen Months*, 1830. Paris, private collection.

other pairs also show members of the Marcotte family—Marcotte himself, and his mother at eighty-four years old.[7]

The correspondence of virtually every line in the drawings of Marie Marcotte—even the signature, inscription, and date at lower right in Yale's drawing and its twin have the same formation and placement—suggests that at least one was created using some mechanical means, such as tracing, which Ingres used relatively often, or an optical apparatus. Neither version, however, is on tracing paper, and the fact that both drawings were made on a commercially available prepared tablet—that is, a piece of paper already fastened around a cardboard backing—precludes any possibility that one version was traced from the other.[8]

No study has yet focused on the aggregate of the pairs of Ingres drawings to try to ascertain how they were made or if the method seems to be consistent throughout the group, but Marjorie Cohn did make a close study of the two more or less identical profile portraits, both signed and dated 1811, of Guillaume Guillon Lethière—one in the Fogg Museum, Cambridge, the other in the Musée Bonnat, Bayonne. She established that the Bayonne sheet has a stylus imprint under the eye. As part of the same study, she also established that a group portrait in the Museum of Fine Arts, Boston, of Alexandre Lethière (son of Guillaume), his wife, and their daughter, made in Rome in 1815, also has underdrawing in stylus underneath the pencil. In this case, she noted that the underdrawing covers a more extensive area than in the Guillaume Lethière portrait, and that this stylus underdrawing matches indentations on another version of the group portrait, in the Musée Ingres in Montauban.[9]

Yale's drawing also has some discernible stylus indentations: in the eyes, the cap, and the skirt.[10] It has not been possible to establish whether or not the one in Paris has such indentations, but in any case, what seems most probable is that at least one of the drawings was made with the help of some device, perhaps mechanical but more likely optical. The camera lucida, a device that allows an artist to see a three-dimensional image as though it were flat, was invented by William Hyde Wollaston early in the nineteenth century,[11] and at least one artist in relation to Ingres in Rome is known to have used this device.[12] David Hockney has suggested that Ingres used it for many of the portraits he made of visitors to Rome during the years he was there, from 1806 to 1820,[13] and it also seems possible that he used it for some parts of this portrait; the lines of the dress and the chair have the swiftness and the look of not having been "groped for," in Hockney's phrase, characteristic of works made using this device.[14] The camera lucida was also used to produce copies of existing flat works of art.[15]

SB

1. Over ninety painted portraits are catalogued in Wildenstein 1956, and 456 drawings in Naef 1977–80, plus fifteen in Bertin 2001. Forty-two paintings and 101 drawings were included in London–Washington–New York 1999–2000.
2. Ternois 1999b, 29; Naef 1958; Naef 1977–80, 2:503–533.
3. "Le brave Ingres a fait il y a une 15e de jours un joli petit croquis de cette petite fille." Ternois 2001, 184. Robert himself made a drawing of Marie when she was about six years old (Paris, private collection); see Paris 2001a, no. 31.
4. Ternois 1999b, 24 and 27, n. 74.
5. Naef 1977–80, nos. 403, 404.
6. Naef 1977–80, no. 326; Paris 2001b, no. 23. Marcotte's mother had died in January 1830: see Naef 1977–80, 2:526, and Paris 2001b, no. 20.
7. See Naef 1977–80, no. 64, Marcotte (the second version is a tracing, Musée Ingres, Montauban); and nos. 295, 296, his mother. Among other pairs or groups are nos. 33–35; 69, 70; 85, 86; 91, 92; 102–105; 113, 114; 135, 136; 272, 273.
8. The cream wove drawing paper was stretched taut around a sheet of cardboard approximately .5 cm (⅛ in.) thick, with its edges glued around the sides and at the back. A piece of pale gray-blue laid paper was also stretched around the cardboard, between it and the white sheet. For more discussion of this and similar tablets, and the large number of drawings that Ingres made on them, see Cohn in Cambridge 1967a, 240–243; Cohn 1969. See also Ternois 1999b, 77 and 78, n. 10. The portrait of Marie Marcotte in Paris was also drawn on such a prepared tablet. I am grateful to the owner of this drawing for graciously allowing me to see it, and to Eric Bertin for facilitating this visit.
9. Cohn 1968. The Guillaume Lethière portraits are Naef 1977–80, nos. 69, 70; for the Alexandre Lethière group portrait, see no. 140 and 1:412–413.
10. I am most grateful to Theresa Fairbanks Harris for her interest and help in examining the drawing.
11. He invented and patented the camera lucida in 1806 and published a description in 1807; see Wollaston 1807. See also Hammond and Austin 1987, 6–7; Kemp 1990, 200, 321; Hockney 2001, 203–204, 215–216.
12. This artist is the so-called Master of the Little Dots. See Tinterow, Hale, and Bertin 2000, 195; Georges Vigne in London–Washington–New York 1999–2000, 527–528.
13. Hockney 2001, 229, 285, and elsewhere. It was the exhibition of Ingres portraits in London–Washington–New York 1999–2000 that inspired Hockney to pull together and bring to public attention the thoughts that had long been in his mind about Western artists' use of optical devices; see also Weschler 2000.
14. Hockney 2001, 23, 25.
15. Wollaston's patent, British patent no. 2993, is for "An instrument whereby any person may draw in perspective, or may copy or reduce any print or drawing." Hammond and Austin 1987, 18, n. 6.

78 Pierre-Étienne-Théodore Rousseau

Paris 1812–1867 Barbizon

The Stone Bridge, ca. 1830

Watercolor on tan paper, laid down, 15.8 × 22.8 cm (6¼ × 9 in.)

PROVENANCE: studio of the artist (estate stamp in black ink, *TH-R*, L. 2436); P.-A. Cheramy, Paris (sale, Paris, 5–7 May 1908, lot 406); Mrs. Walter Feilchenfeldt, Zurich, from whom acquired

REFERENCES: Paris 1944, no. 237; *YUAG Bulletin* 30.1 (1964): 24 and 51; Cambridge 1967b, un-numbered cat.; Schurr 1969, 34; H-B and L, no. 164; *Handbook*, 214; Munich 1996, no. C80; Schulman 1997–99, 1: no. 56

Everett V. Meeks, B.A. 1901, Fund. 1963.9.74

While it is impossible to identify the exact site painted in this spirited watercolor by Théodore Rousseau, its immediacy and spontaneity suggest that it was executed outdoors, rather than in the studio.[1] Rousseau seldom inscribed dates on his drawings, so they are typically dated to the year in which he is known to have visited a particular site (his well-documented sketching tours of the Auvergne, which he visited in 1830, or Normandy in 1831 and 1832, and the Jura region in 1834, are the primary examples).[2] When a drawing is not of an identifiable locale, dating is more difficult. Certain elements, however, characterize this watercolor as an early work, such as the attention given to the trees' foliage rather than to their trunks and limbs, or the technique of scratching through the paper to bring out white highlights, visible in the foreground along the muddy road.[3] This latter method indicates Rousseau's interest in British landscape watercolor and the work of John Constable and Richard Parkes Bonington, which greatly influenced French naturalistic landscape painting during the Restoration and early July Monarchy.[4] Rousseau's familiarity with British art and his sketching tours in France complemented his earlier academic training in the studios of historical landscape painter Jean Charles Joseph Rémond and history painter Guillaume Guillon Lethière.[5]

What is certain, however, is that the watercolor inspired two later paintings by Rousseau (figs. A, B). These works, dated by Schulman to 1843–47, are now in private collections.[6] Upon first glance, there appears to be little significant difference between the watercolor

FIGURE 78A | Pierre-Étienne-Théodore Rousseau, *The Small Stone Bridge*, 1843–47. Private collection.

FIGURE 78B | Pierre-Étienne-Théodore Rousseau, *The Small Stone Bridge*, 1843–47. Private collection.

and the paintings of some ten years later. Rousseau retains the watercolor's basic composition of a muddy country road that leads to a small stone bridge, which then curves into the verdant landscape toward two small houses in the distance. The linear, mostly horizontal, path of the road and bridge contrasts effectively with the striking verticality of the tall, thin trees, which structures the watercolor along a solid horizontal/vertical axis, a strategy that Cézanne would later use to considerable effect in his landscapes. In the paintings, Rousseau also firmed up the trees, and better articulated their trunks and branches, as one would expect in the move from outdoor sketch to studio painting. More intriguing is his metamorphosis of the figures in relation to the landscape. In the watercolor, the figures appear to be elegant travelers being driven in a horse-drawn carriage, as Rousseau carefully articulates two heavy-set seated men, their backs to us, clad in black with top hats; facing them (and the viewer) is a woman holding a red parasol (a small spot of red that serves as a focal point, as in much Barbizon painting). The several horses are presumably driven by coachmen, who are not visible, though the tall, lean form of a footman is evident to the right of the group. In the later paintings, this varied group is simplified and rusticated, to become a pair of featureless men seated in a cart that is pulled by a small horse or donkey. They have now become local folk for whom the bridge merely provides a means of travel from point A to point B, a neutral element of their daily routine, as opposed to the watercolor's urbanites, who venture to the country for a day trip to view those same elements—a picturesque stone bridge from days gone by, or the lush green of sylvan forests, like the trees that rise elegantly beside them, their loose, dancing forms glistening with sea-green highlights. Rousseau accents these changes in content with slight alterations in composition. In the watercolor, a gentle U-shape, comprised of the riverbank and the trees to its left and right, cradles the landscape and evokes the slow, rocking motion of a comfortable moving carriage. In the later paintings, this rococo undulation has been leveled, as if deemed an unnecessary flourish in what is now the depiction of daily routine.

The removal in the later paintings of the watercolor's elitist subject matter, its traditional narrative of picturesque travel, as well as its differentiation between traveler/spectator and the landscape, all convey Rousseau's response to shifting conceptions of naturalism and landscape art during this key transitional period in French art and society. Central to artists and critics of Rousseau's day was the question of how "truth" could be conveyed in landscape painting, as a means to convey its modernity, in contrast to the art of the past. This "truth" depended largely upon who populated the landscape—who "belonged" to the land, and who did not.

SG

1. I am grateful to Michel Schulman, author of the artist's recent and much-needed catalogue raisonné, for generously responding to my inquiries and for suggesting that Yale's watercolor is a plein-air drawing. I thank him also for kindly providing illustrations of the comparative paintings.
2. The definitive source for Rousseau's biography and travel is Sensier 1872.
3. For a helpful study of dating Rousseau's early work, see Wisdom [n.d.].
4. H-B and L, 98–99, emphasize the ties between Rousseau's watercolor and British art, and deem the watercolor Rousseau's "eloquent tribute" to the British art of watercolor. Patrick Noon's recent exhibition catalogue on the subject of Anglo-French Romanticism secures the connection between British watercolor and French naturalism. See London–Minneapolis–New York 2003–04.
5. Rousseau's academic training led him to pursue, unsuccessfully, the Rome Prize for historical landscape in 1829. The Rome Prize for historical landscape had been established by the French Academy in 1817.
6. The two works, both dated to 1843–47, are in oil on panel and are, respectively, 33 × 49 cm and 24.8 × 31.7 cm; see Schulman 1997–99, 2: nos. 290 and 291.

79 Eugène Delacroix

Charenton-Saint-Maurice 1798–1863 Paris

Studies for the Personifications of Industry, Agriculture, War, and Justice for the Salon of the Palais Bourbon, Paris, 1833–36

Pen and brown ink, 25 × 37 cm (9 13/16 × 14 9/16 in.)

PROVENANCE: studio of the artist (estate stamp, L. 838a); sale, Paris, Hôtel Drouot, 16–29 February 1864; Fix-Masson (sale, Paris, Hôtel Drouot, 4 June 1937, lot 25); John Rewald, New York; acquired from Thomas Agnew and Sons, Ltd., London

REFERENCES: Robaut 1885, no. 1659; New York 1944, no. 72; *YUAG Bulletin* 28 (1962): 34 and 50; H-B and L, no. 95; *Handbook*, 211

Leonard C. Hanna, Jr., B.A. 1913, Fund. 1961.9.26

When the thirty-five-year-old Eugène Delacroix received the commission from the French government to decorate the Salon du Roi (the main meeting room) and the Library of the Palais Bourbon, now the National Assembly, he was already a famous and somewhat controversial figure. In 1822, the first painting he submitted to the Paris Salon, *Dante and Virgil*, had been acclaimed and was immediately bought by the government; nine years later, his *Liberty Leading the People*, shown at the Salon of 1831 and also bought by the French state, put him among the premier artists of France in his day. He traveled to North Africa and Spain during six months in 1832, and this trip, besides exposing him to light and color unlike any in France, deeply impressed him with its echoes of antique culture. Delacroix is considered the quintessential Romantic, and yet he aspired to paint in the grand tradition of Michelangelo, Rubens, and Poussin, and to carry out elaborate decorative schemes like those of the Venetian masters.

Delacroix is generally better known for his individual paintings than for his decorative ensembles, but during a good half of his working life he was occupied with providing images for large public spaces. The Salon du Roi was the first; the Library of the same building followed, from 1838 to 1842; the Library of the Palais du Luxembourg, 1840–46; the ceiling of the Galerie d'Apollon in the Louvre, 1849–51; the Salon de la Paix in the Hôtel de Ville, 1851–52 (destroyed in 1871); and finally the Chapel of the Holy Angels in the Church of Saint-Sulpice, which Delacroix worked on between 1850 and 1861—all provided scope for the grandeur and fertility of his imagination.

The Palais Bourbon had been reconstructed in 1829 by the architect Jules de Joly, and

Delacroix was chosen to decorate the Salon in 1833.[1] This room was eleven meters square, with three doors or windows on each wall. Delacroix himself described the room as "badly disposed for painting."[2] The largest spaces to be decorated were four coffers in the ceiling, nearly three times as wide as they were high, and a frieze at the top of each wall, broken by the arches of the windows and doors. Also to be painted were four square coffers in the corners of the ceiling and two vertical panels on each wall between the windows.

Delacroix chose the iconography for the room in consultation with his friend Frédéric Villot.[3] The images represent, in Delacroix's words, the "life-forces of the State."[4] Each of the four large coffers, and the wall below it, is devoted to one of these "forces." In his account, Delacroix wrote that "Agriculture and Commerce furnish the elements of life, in material produced or exchanged; Justice conserves the security of relations among the individuals in a State. War is the means of protection from attacks from outside."[5]

The first subject seen upon entering the room is *Justice*, above and behind the throne, on the west wall; *Agriculture* and *Industry* are at left and right; and *War* is behind. *Justice*, the figure at upper right in the drawing, represents, in Delacroix's words, "the attribute of supreme power and the principal bond of human society."[6] In the painting, the figure's left arm rests on two large books, and she extends her scepter over a woman hugging a baby; an old man at the other end of the canvas is also under her protection. The lower figure at the left of the drawing is a study for *Agriculture*, shown in the painting with a child at her breast and other children nearby; at the left a laborer is sowing seeds, and piles of fruits and vegetables, as well as ten birds in the air, represent the joys of abundance. In the drawing, the study for *Industry* is at top left. That figure, as painted, holds an olive branch in her left hand. Since *Industry* is closely allied with *Commerce*, marine commerce is depicted by an anchor in the lower right corner and a putto with a trident, while a putto holding a caduceus stands for the "rapidity of transactions."[7] *War* is the figure in the foreground of the drawing; in the painting she wears a small breastplate and a helmet adorned with laurel leaves, and she supports three flagpoles in the crook of her arm. Two women in black look, for one last time, at "the features of the father or husband, fallen to defend his country."[8]

Delacroix's earliest sketches for the large coffers manifested considerable agitation and movement,[9] but eventually he rejected these in favor of relatively sedate single female allegorical figures—perhaps, as Johnson suggested, the authorities may have required such a change.[10] Since Yale's drawing shows all of the figures in poses close to their final form, it seems likely that, with the four fairly well developed, Delacroix drew them together on one sheet as a means of focusing on a comparison of their poses and attitudes.

Justice, arguably the most important figure in the ensemble, is the most dynamic, actively leaning toward the right, to extend her protection over the vulnerable; the figure in the drawing is essentially carried over into the painting. *Industry*, or *Commerce* (at top left), also leans toward the right in the drawing, if less markedly; this figure, too, is more or less carried over into the painting, although there her posture is more upright. The position of *Agriculture* (lower left) is changed in the painting so that she leans farther backward; her knees are lowered, and her legs are crossed at the ankles. *War*, the most developed figure in the drawing, has been given the more active legs of *Agriculture* in the painting, although reversed, and *War* looks not straight ahead but toward the left. In the drawing, *War* is differentiated by being positioned in the opposite direction from the other three, and this difference persists in the final decoration of the Salon.

SB

1 For the Salon, see Robaut 1885, 136–144 and nos. 512–542 and additions, 487; Moreau-Nélaton 1916, 1:165–180; Paris 1963, 195–203; Sérullaz 1963, 27–47; Johnson 1981–89, 5:1–31; Sérullaz et al. 1984, 1:118–133, and nos. 170–214; Paris 1995, passim, esp. 19–35 and nos. 1–9; Jobert 1997, 177–190.
2 ". . . mal disposée pour la peinture"; Moreau-Nélaton 1916, 1:170. This and other citations from Delacroix are from an account he wrote in 1848, first published in *L'art*, 16 July 1878. It is quoted in full in Moreau-Nélaton 1916, 1: 170–175; and almost completely in Sérullaz 1963, 43–44. Robaut 1885, 136–144; Johnson 1981–89, nos. 507–510; and Jobert 1997, 182–185, also cite considerable parts of this text.
3 Johnson 1981–89, 5:3; Jobert 1997, 182.
4 "Les forces vives de l'État."
5 "L'Agriculture et le Commerce fournissent les éléments de la vie dans les matières produites ou échangées; la Justice conserve la sécurité des relations entre les particuliers d'un état. La guerre est le moyen de protection contre les attaques du dehors."
6 ". . . l'attribut de la puissance suprême et le lien principal de la société humaine."
7 ". . . la rapidité des transactions."
8 ". . . les traits du père ou du mari qui est tombé pour défendre le pays."
9 The sale after Delacroix's death included 248 sheets of studies in relation to the Salon du Roi; Paris 1995, 175. Some of the studies for the coffers are Paris 1963, nos. 259–262; Sérullaz et al. 1984, nos. 171–182; New York 1991, nos. 31, 33; Paris 1995, nos. 1–9.
10 Johnson 1981–89, 5:3.

80 Jean-François Millet
Gréville 1814–1875 Barbizon

The Rescue of the Daughters of Daniel Boone and Richard Callaway, 1851

Charcoal and brown chalk, 44.1 × 57.7 cm (17 3/8 × 22 11/16 in.)

WATERMARK: partial mark (cut by margin) of "J. What[man] / Turkey [Mill]"

INSCRIPTIONS: recto, lower left, in charcoal: *J. F. Millet*

PROVENANCE: Karl Bodmer; anonymous owner (sale, Paris, Galerie Petit, 21 May 1879, lot 38); Henri Rouart, Paris (sale, Paris, Galerie Manzi-Joyant, 16–18 December 1912, lot 239); acquired from Durlacher Brothers, New York

REFERENCES: Soullié 1900, 136; Smith 1910, 78–85; Moreau-Nélaton 1921, 1:96–98; Draper 1943, 108–110; *YUAG Bulletin* 25 (1960): 26 and 55; H-B and L, no. 145; London 1976, 112–113, no. 61

Everett V. Meeks, B.A. 1901, Fund. 1959.9.11a

Intent on escaping the stresses of city life and immersing himself in the struggles of the common man, thirty-five-year-old Jean-François Millet—still somewhat of an unknown in avant-garde art circles—moved from Paris to the small artists' colony in the village of Barbizon in June 1849.[1] By November of that year, he was joined by Swiss artist Karl Bodmer who, like Millet, longed to leave "hateful" Paris, and devote himself once again "body and soul" to nature and to art.[2]

Seventeen years earlier, Bodmer had established a reputation as one of the first artists to depict American Plains Indians, following an extended trip to the U.S. territories in 1832–34, as the official artist-illustrator in the entourage of Prince Maximilian of Wied-Neuwied. By 1851, two years after his arrival in Barbizon, Bodmer was commissioned by the engraving and lithography firm of Goupil, Vibert and Company to create a series of large-folio lithographs that would serve as an extensive illustrative account of pioneer life in America.[3] The account would be published as the *Annals of the U.S. Illustrated—The Pioneers*. Bodmer accepted the Goupil commission, but because he was busy with other projects, he asked his friend Millet to assist with the venture. Millet had never visited America, nor seen an American Indian himself, but he was apparently interested in Indian subjects and had, in the early 1840s, read James Fenimore

VERSO

Cooper's *The Last of the Mohicans* (1826).[4] The primitive and naturalistic subject matter of the commission also may have interested Millet for its affinities to his own peasant themes. In 1852, after just four lithographs were produced in a modest edition,[5] the venture was abruptly terminated when Goupil discovered that Bodmer had "farmed out" the commission, at least in part, to the young unknown Millet.[6] Yale's drawing, preparatory for the second of the four realized lithographs (fig. A),[7] illustrates the rescue of Daniel Boone's daughter, Jemima, and her friends Betsey and Frances Callaway, who were kidnapped by Cherokees outside Fort Boonesborough, Kentucky, in July 1776, and taken forty miles over rough terrain.[8] This print and its companion image, *The Capture,* are based on Cooper's somewhat loose interpretation of the Boone-Callaway tale, which he incorporated into chapters 10–12 of *The Last of the Mohicans*.

Millet was apparently working on the preparatory drawings for the print series in the summer of 1851, writing to his friend Marolle on 19 July, "I am making drawings of savages . . . the drawings in question must be very well put together, because they are to be made into prints. But that's not all: moreover, they have to be as clearly articulated as possible."[9] Without question, this preparatory drawing does have a certain "pommadé," or "fancied up," quality, which, of course, was altogether appropriate for an illustration. Yet despite Millet's description, this resulting preparatory drawing, with its rapid strokes of black chalk, can hardly be described as "ficelé," or tightly drawn, despite the fact that it was preparatory for a lithograph, and thus should have been more precisely rendered.

The sketchy, rushed quality of the drawing, however, is successful in enhancing a sense of movement and drama in the scene—especially when Millet combines this nervous mode of depiction with additional devices of shadowy foreground, bright internal lighting, and bold composition, to evoke a mood of terror and mayhem. First, he vertically bisects the drawing, hinging it upon the three central frontiersmen, their backs to the viewer, arranged in a dramatic downward cascade away from the central tree trunk, their positions ranging from standing to squatting to nearly prone. These figures form a dark band that separates the composition's light-filled upper left from its murky right half. Each man directs his rifle (and thus the viewer's attention) toward the action at the left. In a clever and evocative reversal of normal associations of good versus evil, Millet places the Cherokee kidnappers and their prey in the bright, firelit left half of the composition, while the noble frontiersmen, led by Boone and Callaway, are hooded in virtual darkness at the right. Thus, in this image, light represents danger, fear, and chaos; while darkness offers safety, bravery, calm.

More can be learned about Millet's development of the composition by comparing this relatively finished drawing to an earlier version, on this sheet's verso. In the earlier drawing Millet has already worked out the two principal figure groups: the embracing figures of Jemima Boone and her father, Daniel, at center right, as well as those of Betsey and Frances Callaway frantically gesturing to their rescuers at center left. Yet, in this earlier sketch, Millet has not yet worked out the dramatic "pommadé" of the compositional layout. Here, the two tree trunks that form a central "V" appear on the same plane, with no suggestion of spatial recession; in the final drawing, the left branch of the "V," rendered more lightly, appears recessed into the woods, as do the gesturing girls, and, indeed, the entire left half of the drawing.

While there is no question that Millet was solely responsible for this and the other extant preparatory drawings for the series, there has been some controversy over the authorship of the final prints. In 1906, Loys Delteil credited Millet with two of the four lithographs—this one of *The Rescue*, as well as *The American Mazeppa*. More recently, however, Robert L. Herbert claimed that it is unlikely that Millet transferred the designs to the stones himself and instead that Bodmer was responsible for all four of the lithographs, since Millet's concurrent effort in lithography, a version of his painting of *The Sower* (1851), was technically clumsy in comparison to these beautifully rendered prints.[10]

Though Yale's preparatory drawing is unquestionably by Millet's hand, it is nonetheless somewhat atypical for the artist—not only in its sketchiness (Millet usually employed a much more precise drawing style), but also in its evocation of both movement and sound. Here, Millet conveys a sense not only of the physical chaos, but also of the cacophony of the scene: the cries of the terrified girls, the shots of the Kentucky rifles—qualities that one rarely associates with this painter of the quiet, the pastoral, the contemplative.

EH

1 According to Herbert, the Revolution of 1848, which signaled the triumph of the common man over governmental tyranny, marked something of a "cleavage" in Millet's career, and moved him to focus on peasant subjects. Herbert 1966, 33.
2 Letters from Karl Bodmer to Prince Maximilian, 25 March 1845 and 10 September 1848; see Bodmer 1984, 364.
3 The print series was to be marketed simultaneously to Goupil's readers in both New York and Paris; the lithographs carry inscriptions in both languages.
4 Millet's interest in American Indians and in the writings of James Fenimore Cooper was noted by his first biographer, Alfred Sensier. See also Smith 1910, 83, who notes that Millet exhibited some twenty or more Indian subjects at the Beaux-Arts galleries in 1887.
5 The four realized prints in the series include: *The Capture of the Daughters of Daniel Boone and Richard Callaway*, *The Rescue of the Daughters of Daniel Boone and Richard Callaway* (fig. A), *The Leap of Major McCullough*, and *Simon Kenton alias Butler Tortured by the Indians* (or *The American Mazeppa*). See London 1976, 113. Four preparatory drawings by Millet's hand exist for this series. In addition to Yale's drawing, the others are: *Simon Butler, the American Mazeppa* (Cherbourg, Musée Thomas Henry); *The Leap of Major McCullough* (Cherbourg, Musée Thomas Henry); and *The Fortress* (Budapest, Szépművészeti Múzeum). These four images were reunited for the first and only time since Millet's death in the 1976 exhibition at the Hayward Gallery, London; see London 1976, nos. 61–64.
6 Apparently Bodmer showed at least one of Millet's drawings to Goupil, who found it unsatisfactory as an illustration suitable for transfer into print—"malheureusement . . . un objet d'art." See Moreau-Nélaton 1921, 1:96, quoted in London 1976, 113.
7 The impression of Bodmer's hand-colored lithograph reproduced and exhibited here is Yale University Art Gallery, inv. no. 2005.2.2, 35.6 × 53 cm.
8 By the early 1820s, when James Fenimore Cooper was beginning to write some of the first adventure stories of the American West, Daniel Boone had become a full-fledged semi-mythical hero. See Philadelphia 1985, no. 24.
9 "Je fais des dessins de sauvages . . . les dessins en question doivent être très ficelés, puisque c'est pour la gravure. Mais, ce n'est pas tout: il faut qu'en outre, ils soient d'un style aussi pommadé que possible . . . " See London 1976, 113, and H-B and L, no. 145.
10 Delteil 1: nos. 25–26. Though Bodmer did not credit Millet for any of the prints in the series, in 1889 he added a notation to the set of four prints that he sold to G. A. Lucas (New York Public Library, Avery Collection) indicating that Millet had done the figures. Clearly, this drawing and the other preparatory drawings for the series provide evidence that Millet was responsible for the entire compositions, not just the figures. See letter from Robert Herbert, 29 July 1965, Yale Art Gallery curatorial file, and London 1976, 113. It should further be noted that Bodmer was a skilled printmaker: from age thirteen to age twenty-three, he was apprenticed to Johann Jakob Meier (a prominent Zurich engraver and his maternal uncle). H-B and L, no. 145, attributed the print to Millet, rather than to Bodmer.

FIGURE 80A | Karl Bodmer, *The Rescue of the Daughters of Daniel Boone and Richard Callaway*, 1851. New Haven, Yale University Art Gallery.

81 Constantin Guys

Flushing 1802–1892 Paris

Old Soldiers of the Empire, ca. 1856

Pen and brush and brown ink with brown, blue, gray, yellow and red watercolors, 24.8 × 37.7 cm (9¾ × 14¹¹⁄₁₆ in.)

WATERMARK: J. WHATMAN / TURKEY MILL / 1855

INSCRIPTIONS: recto, upper right, in pen and brown ink: *2369*

PROVENANCE: Bruce Ingram, London; P. and D. Colnaghi and Co., London; Kraushaar Galleries, New York; Edith Malvina K. Wetmore

REFERENCES: New York 1931, no. 51 (as *Veterans of the Empire depositing their offerings of crowns of imortelles* [sic] *and garlands of flowers on the Napoleon Column in the Place Vendome* [sic]. *August 15th, 1852*); H-B and L, no. 130

Gift of Edith Malvina K. Wetmore. 1945.7

Constantin Guys was the artist whom Charles Baudelaire described as the "painter of modern life."[1] He wrote that Guys "began by being an observer of life, and only later set himself the task of acquiring the means of expressing it. This has resulted in a thrilling originality. . . ."[2] In his introduction to Baudelaire's *Fleurs du mal*, Théophile Gautier wrote of Guys that "he had the particular gift of seizing in a few moments the essence of things."[3]

Guys was born in the Netherlands, where his father was a French naval administrator in an area then under Napoleonic control. He returned to France with his family in 1806. According to an obituary written by Guys's closest friend, the photographer Félix Tournachon (known as "Nadar"), Guys had fought along with the English Romantic poet George Gordon, Lord Byron, in Greece during that country's war of independence, and served in the French cavalry under the Bourbon Restoration.[4] Although Guys had no formal training, he was naturally talented as an artist, and in London in the 1840s, he found work teaching French, and also drawing, to the grandchildren of the English watercolorist Thomas Girtin.

From 1847 until 1860 Guys worked for the *Illustrated London News* (the first of the great pictorial newspapers, founded in 1842), eventually traveling widely in this capacity as one of the earliest journalistic illustrators. Over the years he sent drawings, to be rendered as wood engravings and printed, from France, Turkey, Greece, Egypt, and Spain. He was the newspaper's official correspondent during the Crimean War in 1854–55, witnessing the battles at Inkerman and Balaclava.[5] His compositions are not identified in the periodical, however, but twenty-five of his drawings that were eventually published in the newspaper were shown at the Cleveland Museum of Art in 1978. Karen Smith in her dissertation catalogued drawings for the newspaper and listed seven more, and Pierre Duflo illustrated ninety-three.[6] In the fall of 1857, Guys was employed by *Le monde illustré*, a French paper established in that year on the model of the *Illustrated London News*.

Despite his large volume of reportorial drawings, Guys is still best known today for his images of daily life in the Second Empire, including scenes of figures—especially women—in the street, at cafés, and at the theater, as well as soldiers and horsemen or horse-drawn carriages. Over all, hundreds of

FIGURE 81A | Artist unknown, *Old Soldiers of the Empire*, from the *Illustrated London News*, 20 August 1863. New Haven, Yale Center for British Art.

drawings by Guys still exist. In her dissertation, Karen Smith catalogued 308 drawings; in an appendix, she listed another 312 in the collection of the Musée Carnavalet, Paris, and she also made clear that her work was by no means a complete catalogue raisonné.[7]

The subject of Yale's drawing is an example of the kind of "soft news" occasion that—in addition to wars and other violent or catastrophic events, as well as cultural news or the doings of celebrities—was depicted in the early illustrated newspapers. The drawing shows veterans of the Napoleonic Wars placing wreaths on the iron grill protecting the column honoring Napoleon Bonaparte (Emperor Napoleon I) in the Place Vendôme, Paris. The ceremony was held twice each year, on the anniversaries of Napoleon's birth and death, 15 August and 5 May.[8] This practice began during the so-called July Monarchy (1830–1848), after King Louis Philippe had had a statue of Napoleon I restored atop the Vendôme column in 1833.[9] During the Second Empire (1852–1870)—the reign of Napoleon III, nephew of Napoleon I—the statue was replaced again, in 1863; throughout these years the wreath-laying ceremony reinforced in the public mind the idea of the continuity of rule and the association of the second empire with the glories of the first.

Yale's drawing came to the United States in 1931 as part of a group of twenty-seven that had belonged to a descendant of Herbert Ingram, founder of the *Illustrated London News*. Three creases in the drawing's vertical dimension indicate that it had been folded to a quarter of its size and was presumably sent by post from Paris to London.[10] The drawing is on English paper watermarked with the date 1855. Since Guys had returned to Paris from the Crimea after mid-August 1855, spent several months in London, returned again to Paris in March 1856, and spent July and August 1856 in Spain, there is a good possibility that the drawing was made on 5 May 1856, showing the old soldiers placing wreaths at the base of the Napoleonic column on the anniversary of Napoleon's death.[11] It is also not impossible that the drawing was done somewhat later, even years later, if Guys had acquired a large amount of paper with the 1855 watermark and continued to use it for several years. This drawing, however, was never reproduced in the periodical. An image of the ritual, by an unidentified artist, appeared in the *Illustrated London News* on 20 August 1863 (fig. A), portraying a group of soldiers who look considerably better organized than Guys's somewhat ragtag contingent.[12]

Although celebrated by Baudelaire and admired by Delacroix, Nadar, and Manet, Guys, reclusive all his life, was increasingly isolated toward its end. After being hit by a carriage during the festivities of 14 July 1885, he spent his last seven years in a nursing home, virtually forgotten.

SB

1 "Le Peintre de la Vie Moderne," first published in *Le figaro*, 26 and 28 November and 3 December 1863; Baudelaire 1961, 1152–1192; Baudelaire 1964, 1–40.

2 Baudelaire 1964, 15; Baudelaire 1961, 1165–1166: "Il a commencé par contempler la vie, et ne s'est ingénié que tard à apprendre les moyens d'exprimer la vie. Il en est résulté une originalité saisissante."

3   Baudelaire [1868?], 54: "il avait le don particulier de prendre en quelques minutes le signalement des choses."

4   Duflo 1988, 35–37; originally published in *Le figaro*, 15 March 1892.

5   See Cleveland 1978; Smith 1984, Chapter 5 and pp. 228–280; Duflo 1988, 125–336.

6   See Cleveland 1978; Smith 1984; Duflo 1988. In the only published catalogue of prints after Guys, *IFF après 1800* 10:79–83, only fourteen compositions are listed.

7   Paris 2002–03; Smith 1984 catalogued the drawings in Paris: Bibliothèque Nationale, Musée Carnavalet, Musée du Louvre, and Musée du Petit Palais; London: British Museum, Victoria and Albert Museum; Oxford: Ashmolean Museum; and New York: Cooper-Hewitt Museum, Metropolitan Museum of Art. Besides those two catalogues, as well as Cleveland 1978 and Duflo 1988, drawings by Guys are illustrated in Geffroy 1920; Konody 1930; D'Eugny and Coursaget 1945; Hall 1945; Roger-Marx 1954; Streiff 1957; and Rome 1980; Paris 1895 and New York 1931 have text only.

8   An image of the ritual, in May, after a drawing by Godefroy Durand, was published in *Le monde illustré* of 8 May 1869. See H-B and L and Paris 2002b, 217 (there erroneously identified as taking place in August).

9   Paris 2002b, 218–219.

10 A drawing belonging to Smith College, inscribed as having been made in the Croatian camp, Balaklava, on 19 July 1855, and which was published in the *Illustrated London News* on 8 September, was part of this same group of drawings exhibited at the Kraushaar Galleries in October of that year (New York 1931). In the file for the Smith College drawing, a letter from the scholar Bruno Streiff, dated 31 August 1856, states that a lot of twenty-seven drawings was sold in 1931 by Captain Bruce W. Ingram to Colnaghi's, from where Kraushaar Galleries bought them; Carol Pesner of Kraushaar Galleries kindly verified that this group of twenty-seven drawings did come from Colnaghi's. The Smith drawing, which has folds similar to those of Yale's drawing, bears the number 2253 in its upper right corner. Inv. no. 1952.2, pen and brown ink and blue, gray, and black colored washes over graphite, 33.6 × 50.5 cm; Duflo 1988, 322. I am grateful to Aprile Gallant and Michael Goodison for their help in making the drawing and the file available to me.

Two other drawings by Guys from this group came to the Yale University Art Gallery along with *Old Soldiers of the Empire*; inv. no. 1945.8, *Reception of Emperor Napoleon III at the Hospital "Hôtel Dieu,"* H-B and L, no. 129; inv. no. 1945.6, *A State Ball, presumably with Napoleon III*, H-B and L, no. 131.

11 Duflo 1988 is the best source for the chronology of Guys's movements. See also Jamar-Rolin 1956.

12 *Illustrated London News*, 20 August 1863, 208, 15 × 23.6 cm. The wood engraving was accompanied by the text: "THE EMPEROR'S FETE AT PARIS. Our Engraving represents an incident in the fête of the 15th inst.—the procession of old soldiers of the First Empire 'les vieux de la vieille garde'—to the Column Vendôme, where they each year replace the crowns of immortelles upon the rails surrounding the base."

82 Edgar Degas
Paris 1834–1917 Paris

Portrait of Giulia Bellelli,
ca. 1858–59

Graphite on pinkish-beige paper, 28.5 × 23.4 cm (11¼ × 9⁹⁄₁₆ in.)

WATERMARK: entwined "M" and "S," cut at edge of sheet

INSCRIPTIONS: verso, in pencil, upper left: *Juni 73*; lower left: *Mlle (?) Bellely*; lower center: *8851*; lower right: *14*

PROVENANCE: Atelier Degas, L. 657 (stamp on recto, lower right); Succession Ed. Degas, L. 658 bis (stamp on verso, lower right); Galerie Kornfeld, Bern, by 1971; C. G. Boerner, Düsseldorf

REFERENCES: YUAG Bulletin 34.1 (1972): 46; Boston 1974, no. 61; Cooper 1978; New Haven 2003, no. 1

Stephen Carlton Clark, B.A. 1903, Fund. 1971.56.2

The sitter in this charming portrait of a young girl in profile has previously been identified as the artist's sister Marguerite,[1] but it is more likely to be the artist's cousin Giulia Bellelli. Degas's grandfather had gone to Italy, and his seven children were born there. Degas's father later went to France and married a French woman, but his siblings remained in Italy. Degas's aunt Laura married Gennaro Bellelli, and their daughters Giovanna and Giulia were born in 1848 and 1851.[2]

Degas's sister Marguerite was born in 1842, and several drawings by the young Edgar have been identified as portraits of her. The one in the Detroit Institute of Arts is thought to have been made around 1853/54, when Degas was just beginning as an artist, and Marguerite would have been eleven or twelve, an age that conforms with the look of the sitter (fig. A).[3] Another portrait, dated 1854 and showing Marguerite at the time of her first communion, is in the Clark Art Institute in Williamstown, Massachusetts. It was by comparison with this drawing that Theodore Reff suggested the Detroit portrait was made slightly earlier.[4] The sitter in Yale's drawing, on the other hand, is a child distinctly younger than the one shown in the Detroit and Clark portraits. Reff wrote that the Detroit drawing "is among the first works produced by the young artist after he had given up his legal studies the year before and committed himself entirely to the study of art."[5] If Yale's drawing did show Marguerite, it would have to have been made at least two or three years before this time, when Degas was sixteen or seventeen at most, yet the drawing manifests a technique that is more assured than that of the Detroit and Clark portraits. Simply on the grounds of the artist's development, Yale's drawing must be later, rather than earlier, than the drawings of the eleven- or twelve-year-old Marguerite.

Several further bits of evidence support the identification of the sitter as Giulia Bellelli. The first is the two-word inscription on the verso: the first word is difficult to decipher—although it is possible that it is "Mlle," since there is an underline under the last letters—and the second word is definitely the name "Belley." The inscription is not in Degas's hand—he would probably have spelled the Italian name correctly—but its decisive quality seems to indicate that the writer was knowledgeable. Second are the characteristics of the sitter herself: the torso is that of a girl perhaps six to eight years old, with the waist much higher than that of Marguerite in the Detroit and Clark drawings, and the chest still flat. The face is rounder than Marguerite's, with a more turned-up nose. The sitter's features and the length of her hair are characteristic of Giulia, as seen in numerous drawings that the twenty-four-year-old Degas made of his young cousin—including a portrait of her at the piano (present location unknown), a sketch in a notebook in the Bibliothèque Nationale (fig. B), or the *Portrait of Giulia Bellelli* now in the Louvre[6]—done when Degas lived with his aunt's family in Florence, from August 1858 to March 1859. Giulia, born on 13 July 1851, would have been seven years old during this period. Finally, the paper used for this drawing is identical to that of two drawings now in Bremen, which must have been made in Italy, as they are studies of figures in Michelangelo's *Last Judgment*.[7]

FIGURE 82A | Edgar Degas, *Portrait of Marguerite Degas*, 1853/54. Detroit Institute of Arts.

On 27 November 1858, Degas wrote to Gustave Moreau, "I have two little cousins, good enough to eat. The older one is really a little beauty. The little one [Giulia] has spirit like a devil and goodness like a little angel. I draw them with their black dresses and little white pinafores, which suit them ravishingly."[8] The numerous drawn portrait studies of the family, individually or in groups, eventually culminated in Degas's first masterpiece, the painted *Portrait of the Bellelli Family* now in the Musée d'Orsay.[9] The pinafore with a loose cap sleeve in Yale's drawing is similar to those that Giovanna and Giulia are wearing in the final painting, as well as in numerous preparatory drawings or sketches.[10]

A large number of drawings Degas made in the 1850s and early 1860s have a background of diagonal parallel lines like the ones in Yale's portrait, reminiscent of fifteenth-century works in silverpoint or pen and ink.

These lines are seen as early as the *Portrait of Thérèse in Confirmation Dress* of 1854 (in the Clark), and as late as some of the studies for *Semiramis Building Babylon*, early in the 1860s.[11] Particularly close in technique to Yale's drawing are two other profile portraits of family members, his sister Thérèse and his brother René, as well as a three-quarters view of Thérèse.[12] Such lines are also seen, for example, in the *Study after Raphael* made in Rome, and the *Portrait of Laura Bellelli* made in Florence,[13] so it is clear that Degas employed this technique in both France and Italy, and—although not necessarily in every drawing—over a period of seven or eight years.

According to Jean Boggs, the profile was the view Degas always preferred for Giulia,[14] and although Giulia's final pose in *The Bellelli Family* was a *profil perdu* rather than the strict profile, the latter is seen in many of the prep-

FIGURE 82B | Edgar Degas, *Portrait of Giulia and Giovanna Bellelli*, from Degas's "Notebook 12," 1858/59. Paris, Bibliothèque Nationale de France.

aratory sketches for the painting. When Degas was preparing another portrait, of Giovanna and Giulia only, which he painted around 1865–66, he began by sketching Giulia in profile to the left, although in the final painting she faces right.[15]

The stamp on the verso, "Succession Ed. Degas," indicates that this drawing was not sold in the auctions in 1918 that followed shortly after Degas's death, but was kept in the family. It is not listed in the sale catalogue of the collection of Edgar's youngest brother René in 1927 or that of Jeanne Fèvre, Marguerite's daughter, in 1934, so its whereabouts until it appeared at Galerie Kornfeld in Bern in 1971 are unknown.

SB

1 Cooper 1978; and see New Haven 2003, no. 1.
2 See Boggs 1955; Raimondi 1958, 288 for Bellelli-Degas genealogy, and passim; Copenhagen 1983; Rome 1984–85, 162–200.
3 Inv. no. 65.293, graphite, 31.1 × 19.7 cm; see most recently, Baas and Sojka 2003; also Boggs 1962, no. 7; Reff 1974, no. 1.
4 Inv. no. 71.46, graphite, 32.2 × 23.5 cm. Boggs 1962, no. 6; Williamstown 1987, no. 1. I am grateful to Richard Kendall for discussing this and other Degas drawings, including Yale's portrait, with me.
5 Reff 1974, 27.
6 See Copenhagen 1983, no. 5; Paris, Bibliothèque Nationale, inv. no. Dc 327 d, no. 18, 14.5 × 9.8 cm; see Reff 1976, Notebook 12, p. 52, also Copenhagen 1983, no. 8; Paris, Louvre, inv. no. RF 11689, black chalk, gray wash, and essence heightened with white on cream-colored paper, 23.4 × 19.6 cm; see Copenhagen 1983, no. 26, and Paris–Ottawa–New York 1988–89, no. 21.
7 Bremen, Kunsthalle, inv. no. 69/259, *Studies after Michelangelo's Last Judgment* (recto and verso), on pink paper, 284 × 235 cm; and inv. no. 62/205, *Two Seated Women, Studies of Figures in Michelangelo's Last Judgment*, on pink paper, 288 × 231 cm; see Rome 1984–85, nos. 12, 13.
8 "J'ai deux petites cousines à manger. L'aînée est réellement une petite beauté; la petite a de l'esprit comme un démon et de la bonté comme un petit ange. Je les fais avec leurs robes noires et des petits tabliers blancs qui leur vont à ravir." Reff 1969, 283.
9 Inv. no. RF2210. Lemoisne 1946–48, no. 79; Copenhagen 1983, no. 1; Rome 1984–85, no. 54; Paris–Ottawa–New York 1988–89, no. 20.
10 For instance, see Lemoisne 1946–48, nos. 63–65, 69; Copenhagen 1983, passim; Rome 1984–85, nos. 55, 57, 59, 60; Paris–Ottawa–New York 1988–89, nos. 21, 24, 25. Reff 1976, 73, under Notebook 12, no. 7, lists eleven other studies for the family portrait in the notebooks.
11 For instance Paris, Louvre, inv. no. RF15515, graphite, 30.4 × 22.6 cm; see Paris–Ottawa–New York 1988–89, no. 34.
12 Cambridge, Fitzwilliam, graphite on pink paper, 28.5 × 23.6 cm; see Manchester–Cambridge 1987, no. 8; Philadelphia Museum of Art, inv. no. 1986.26.13, graphite, 3.5 × 23.7 cm; see Allentown 1977, 46–47, and Atlanta 1984, 46–47; Paris, Prat collection, 28.4 × 23.4 cm, graphite on pink paper; see most recently Los Angeles et al. 2004–05, no. 81. The drawing of Thérèse in the Prat collection is also on paper identical to that of Yale's drawing, and the paper of the one in Cambridge is probably the same, too, although no watermark is visible.
13 Baltimore, private collection, black chalk with stumping, 30.3 × 23.8 cm; see Baltimore–Birmingham–Tacoma 2005–06, no. 39; Paris, Louvre, inv. no. RF11688, graphite and green pastel, 26.1 × 20.4 cm; see Paris–Ottawa–New York 1988–89, no. 23.
14 In Copenhagen 1983, 16.
15 Sketches: Lemoisne 1946–48, no. 139; Boggs 1955, figs. 15–17; Copenhagen 1983, Appendix B–D. Painting: Lemoisne 1946–48, 126; Boggs 1955, fig. 12; Copenhagen 1983, Appendix A; Paris–Ottawa–New York 1988–89, no. 65.

83 Honoré Daumier

Marseilles 1808–1879 Valmondois

The Imaginary Invalid, ca. 1860–63

Pen and black and gray ink and gray wash over black chalk, 32.5 × 35 cm (12 11/16 × 13 3/4 in.) sheet; 24.4 × 29.4 cm (9 9/16 × 11 9/16 in.) visible in illustration and mat opening

WATERMARK: partial mark (cut at margin), "HP" in a shield, above "[H]allines," for which see Boston 1984, 260, no. 9

INSCRIPTIONS: recto, lower left, in pen and brown ink: *h. D.*

PROVENANCE: Alexandre Dumas, Paris (sale, Paris, Hôtel Drouot, "Collection de M. D." 16 February 1882, lot 21, as *Le malade entre deux médecins*); Binder, Paris; César M. de Hauke and Co., New York, 1933; Edith Malvina K. Wetmore

REFERENCES: Paris 1878, no. 197; Alexandre 1888, 376; Klossowski 1923, no. 68 D; Buffalo 1935, no. 99; San Francisco 1947, no. 58; Maison 1960, no. 97; Larkin 1966, 192, 193, fig. 89; *YUAG Bulletin* 31.3 (1967–68): 29 and 56; H-B and L, no. 91; Palm Beach 1974, no. 17; Goldstein 1976, 233–234, fig. 6.7; Passeron 1981, 206; *Handbook*, 210; Maison 1996, D-485; Ottawa–Paris–Washington 1999–2000, no. 207

Bequest of Edith Malvina K. Wetmore. 1966.80.6

Honoré Daumier is best known for his nearly four thousand lithographs of political subjects and scenes of daily life, published beginning in the 1820s and continuing throughout most of his life.[1] Some three hundred paintings by him are also known, and more than eight hundred drawings were listed in the catalogue raisonné published in 1967.[2] His lithographs, of course, were the result of drawings he made directly on the stones, and it was with these in mind—more than the drawings on paper—that Charles Baudelaire wrote of Daumier, "He drew because he had to—it was his ineluctable vocation."[3] The majority of Daumier's drawings on paper, in fact, were done during two periods when he was not able to make lithographs for the satirical periodical *Charivari*: after the Revolution of 1848, and between 1860 and 1863.[4] Less generally known is Daumier's sculpture, modeled in clay or wax, the most important of which is a group of small caricatural pieces, and all of which is prized for the same qualities evident throughout the artist's work: his sureness of touch and unerring characterization.[5]

Although Daumier seldom made drawings to illustrate specific literary texts, he loved the theater. When Arsène Houssaye, director of the Comédie-Française from 1849 to 1859, asked him who had been his master in painting, Daumier replied, "Molière."[6] Daumier made more paintings on theatrical subjects than any other group, and among his images of the theater, the plays of Molière, especially *The Imaginary Invalid*, were the ones most frequently treated.[7] Daumier saw *The Imaginary Invalid* at the Comédie-Française in the second half of the 1850s.[8] Yale's drawing is one of five now known that are related to this play.[9] Few of Daumier's drawings can be dated with certainty, but the scholarly consensus is that the ones relating to *The Imaginary Invalid* were probably made during the 1860s. The most famous among them is the watercolor and gouache drawing thought to have been lost during World War II, but which is now in Saint Petersburg (fig. A).[10] That Yale's drawing is related to the Saint Petersburg one, and probably preceded it, seems to be indicated by a small sketch faintly visible at the upper edge (hidden by the mat in the exhibition), upside down in relation to the principal drawing (fig. B), showing the head of the invalid leaning sharply backward so that it is in steep foreshortening, while one doctor looms over him.

Because Yale's drawing is the only one showing the hypochondriac Argan in the company of two doctors, Maison doubted that it was connected with the Molière play. As pointed out by Larkin as well as Haverkamp-Begemann and Logan, however, in Act II, Scene VI, two doctors, Diafoirus and his rather dimwitted son Thomas, flank the invalid, each holding one of Argan's wrists:

ARGAN: I beg you, sir, give me an idea how I am doing.

DIAFOIRUS *(taking his pulse)*: All right, Thomas, take the other arm of the gentleman, to see whether you can form a proper judgment of his pulse. *Quid dicis?*

THOMAS: *Dico*, that the pulse of this gentleman is the pulse of a man who is not at all well.

DIAFOIRUS: Good.

FIGURE 83A | Honoré Daumier, *The Imaginary Invalid*, 1857(?). Saint Petersburg, State Hermitage Museum.

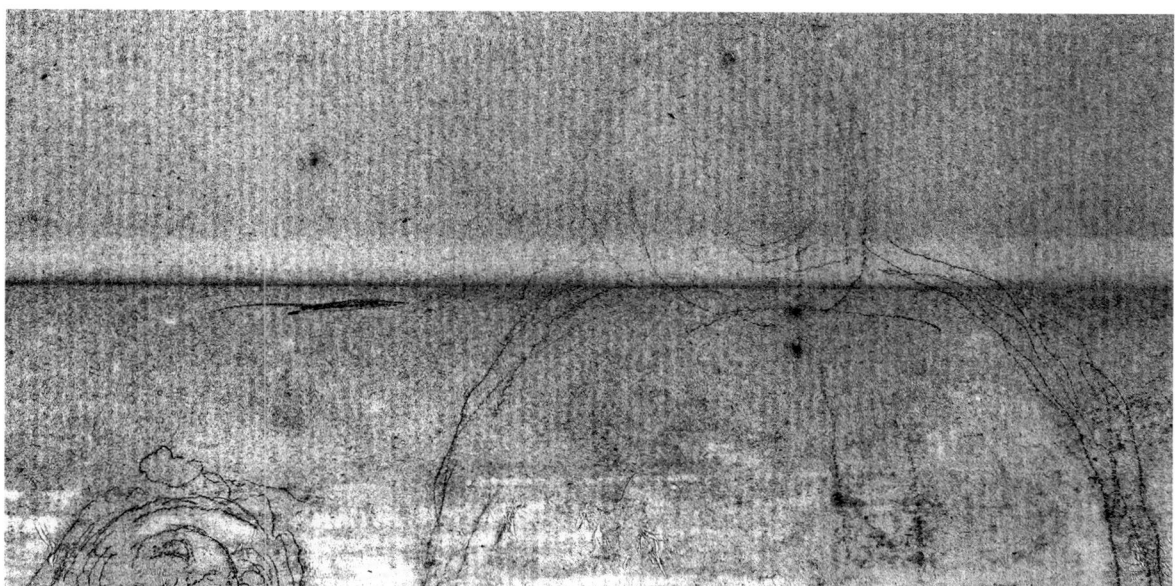

FIGURE 83B | Honoré Daumier, sketch in margin for a version of *The Imaginary Invalid*, detail of cat. no. 83.

THOMAS: That it is *hardiscum*, not to say hard.

DIAFOIRUS: Very good.

THOMAS: Throbbing.

DIAFOIRUS: *Bene*.

THOMAS: Even a little uneven.

DIAFOIRUS: *Optime*.

THOMAS: Which marks an imbalance in the splenetic parenchyma, that is to say the spleen.

DIAFOIRUS: Very good.

ARGAN: No—Monsieur Purgon says it is the liver that is ill.

DIAFOIRUS: Ah! yes. If one talks of the parenchyma one is talking about both the liver and the spleen because of the strong connection between them by means of the *vas breve*, the *pylore* and often the cholodic passages. Undoubtedly he has ordered you to eat roasted food.

ARGAN: No, only boiled.

DIAFOIRUS: Ah! yes. Roasted, boiled, same thing.[11]

Molière's play mocked not only the hypochondria of the "imaginary invalid," but also the pretensions of the doctors, with their use of Latin and elaborate medical terminology to cover their ignorance. With this image, Daumier also directed his irony at all three figures, perhaps somewhat more at the doctors. These two, dressed in robes and pointed hats derived from the *commedia dell'arte*, lean in, almost threateningly, over the patient. The one at the left, presumably Thomas, has a studiously grave expression, while Diafoirus at right seems to be leering at the patient, his intensity emphasized by Daumier's highly charged and expressive lines. The invalid, lying rigidly in his bed, part of his face in darkness because of the dramatic lighting from below, looks out at the viewer in a state of highest anxiety.

SB

1 Delteil, vols. 20–29, is the standard catalogue for the lithographs. In addition, Rümann 1914 or Bouvy 1933 catalogued close to one thousand wood engravings after Daumier's designs. See also Noack and Noack 2005.

2 Maison 1996; see also Frankfurt–New York 1992–93.

3 In "Some French Caricaturists," Baudelaire 1964, 171; Baudelaire 1961, 999: "il dessina, parce qu'il avait besoin de dessiner, vocation inéluctable."

4 Frankfurt–New York 1992–93, x.

5 See Cambridge 1969; Martin Sonnabend in Frankfurt–New York 1992–93, 28–39; Edouard Papet in Ottawa–Paris–Washington 1999–2000, 46–59, 84–161.

6 Houssaye 1971, 2:284.

7 See Passeron 1981, 197–210; Ottawa–Paris–Washington 1999–2000, 352–361.

8 Saint Petersburg 1996, 128.

9 The others are: present whereabouts unknown, Maison 1996, no. D-475; Saint Petersburg, State Hermitage Museum, inv. no. 131-17959, Maison 1996, D-476, Saint Petersburg 1996, no. 45; London, Courtauld Institute of Art Gallery, Maison 1996, D-486, Ottawa–Paris–Washington 1999–2000, no. 206; private collection, Ottawa–Paris–Washington 1999–2000, no. 208; not in Maison 1996.

10 Saint Petersburg, State Hermitage Museum, inv. no. 131-17959, charcoal, pen, and brown ink, watercolor, and gouache, 29.3 × 24.9 cm; Maison 1996, D-476, Saint Petersburg 1996, no. 45.

11 "ARGAN: Je vous prie, Monsieur, de me dire un peu comment je suis. Diafoirus *lui tâte le pouls*: Allons, Thomas, prenez l'autre bras de Monsieur, pour voir si vous saurez porter un bon jugement de son pouls. *Quid dicis?* THOMAS: *Dico*, que le pouls de Monsieur est le pouls d'un homme qui ne se porte point bien. DIAFOIRUS: Bon. THOMAS: Qu'il est duriuscule, pour ne pas dire dur. DIAFOIRUS: Fort bien. THOMAS: Repoussant. DIAFOIRUS: *Bene*. THOMAS: Et même un peu capricant. DIAFOIRUS: *Optime*. THOMAS: Ce qui marque une intempérie dans le *parenchyme splénique*, c'est-à-dire la rate. DIAFOIRUS: Fort bien. ARGAN: Non; Monsieur Purgon dit que c'est mon foie qui est malade. DIAFOIRUS: Eh! oui; qui dit *parenchyme*, dit l'un et l'autre, à cause de l'étroite sympathie qu'ils ont ensemble, par le moyen du *vas breve*, du *pylore*, et souvent des *méats cholidoques*. Il vous ordonne sans doute de manger force rôti? ARGAN: Non—rien que du bouilli. DIAFOIRUS: Eh! oui; rôti, bouilli, même chose. . . . " Molière 1965, 2: 875–876.

84 Johan Barthold Jongkind
Latrop 1819–1891 La Côte-Saint-André

Notre Dame of Paris Seen from the Quai de la Tournelle, 6 June 1863

Watercolor, 34.7 × 52.6 cm (13$^{11}/_{16}$ × 20$^{11}/_{16}$ in.)

INSCRIPTIONS: recto, lower left, in pen and brown ink, in the artist's hand: *Jongkind*; lower right, in black chalk, in the artist's hand: *Paris 6 Juin 1863*

PROVENANCE: William T. Aldrich, Boston: Mr. and Mrs. Robert Hamlin; private collection, USA; Brame and Lorenceau, Paris; Ruth and Bruce Dayton

REFERENCES: Northampton–Williamstown 1976–77, no. 20; *YUAG Bulletin* (2004): 159

Gift of Ruth and Bruce Dayton, B.A. 1940. 2003.19.1

Although Johan Barthold Jongkind spent most of his working life in France and wanted to be thought of as a French artist, his art was grounded in the tradition of his native Holland. Of his nearly nine hundred known paintings, over four thousand watercolors and drawings, and some twenty etchings, the overwhelming majority are landscapes or marine views, Dutch subjects *par excellence*.[1] Jongkind studied with Andreas Schelfhout, a landscape painter and watercolorist in The Hague, beginning in 1837.[2] In 1846 he received a royal stipend that enabled him to go to Paris, where he entered the studio of Eugène Isabey. Jongkind began drawing and painting views of Paris, choosing unexpected vantage points, as in *Notre Dame of Paris Seen from the Quai de la Tournelle*. When he included a major monument in his work, it was never central to the composition, but always simply part of the city, a backdrop to daily life.

By 1855 a lack of funds necessitated Jongkind's return to Holland, but he was desperately unhappy there, and in 1860 a group of friends in Paris organized a sale of paintings—by Camille Corot, Eugène Isabey, Théodore Rousseau (see cat. no. 78), Charles Daubigny, Henri Harpignies, and others—the proceeds of which enabled Jongkind to return to Paris once more. France was his home for the rest of his life.

Jongkind's paintings had been shown in several Salons in Paris beginning in 1848 and including the one in 1855, which was part of the Paris Exposition Universelle that year; Jongkind dismayed his Dutch compatriots by showing his work in the section devoted to French artists. In 1863, three of his paintings were in the historic first Salon des Refusés, along with Édouard Manet's *Déjeuner sur l'herbe* and works by, among others, Camille Pissarro, Henri Fantin-Latour, and James McNeill Whistler.[3] Although today it is perhaps more difficult to understand why Jongkind's work (as opposed to that of some of the other painters) was deemed unacceptable, Jongkind was one of the earliest artists to paint in a loose, sketchy manner—a manner, in fact, that caused him to be described as the "father of Impressionism." Claude Monet had met Jongkind in 1862, and in a newspaper interview many years later he said that it was to Jongkind that he owed the "definitive education" of his eye.[4] In a letter to Gustave Geffroy of 1920, Monet wrote, "One must not forget that . . . [Boudin] had received lessons from a master, Jongkind, whose oeuvre, especially in the watercolors, is the origin along with Corot of what has been called Impressionism."[5] Two years earlier, Étienne Moreau-Nélaton had already implied Jongkind's connection with Impressionism when he wrote, "It is with his watercolor brush that he seizes directly the impression of nature."[6]

A letter from Jongkind himself is evidence that he made his watercolors outdoors, on site. In 1856 he wrote to his friend, the painter Eugène Smits, "I have another painting finished, a view near Rotterdam, and then another in process, and very far along. I made them from nature, that is to say I made watercolors after which I made my paintings."[7] Jongkind's watercolors were always highly prized, not just for the freshness resulting from their having been made *en plein air* but also for the artist's mastery of the medium. The painter Paul Signac admired Jongkind so much that he wrote a book about him—the only artist about whom he did this—ranking Jongkind with two watercolorists acknowledged as supreme practitioners of the genre, Joseph Mallord William Turner and Paul Cézanne. Signac's praise was unqualified: " . . . in 1863," he wrote, "begins the most beautiful series of watercolors that exists in the world."[8] What Signac admired is seen in this watercolor—the quick and free underdrawing; the areas of white paper left untouched, creating an open expanse of sky, highlights on the water, and a feeling of light airiness throughout; and the differentiation of planes and textures by at least seven or eight different blues and greens, varying in intensity.

Following his usual practice, as mentioned in his letter to Smits, Jongkind made a painting, dated 1863, based on this watercolor of 6 June. The scale of the two works is the same, although the proportions are somewhat different; the painting has essentially the same width as the watercolor, but Jongkind has added height to the area of sky.[9] Jongkind evidently had a definite idea of what would be included in the composition, but in working on the watercolor he ran out of space at the right edge of the sheet, so he used some open space in the sky for a more detailed sketch of the buildings on the Quai de l'Hôtel de Ville, on the opposite bank of the Seine; in the oil painting, these buildings are in place at the right edge of the canvas. Jongkind made numerous other drawings and paintings from this same vantage point, or one very close to it, beginning at least as early as 1848, and continuing until 1864, when he made two more dated paintings; these seem to have been his last depicting this view.[10]

SB

1. Stein et al. 2003 lists 890 paintings. Sylvie Brame, François Lorenceau, and Janine Sinizergues are in the process of compiling a catalogue of the drawings and watercolors; as of late 2005 they knew of more than four thousand. Delteil 1:n.p. is still the standard reference for the etchings.
2. Several recent works on Jongkind include extensive chronological accounts of his life: Stein et al. 2003, 22–53; The Hague–Cologne–Paris 2003–04, 217–224; and Auffret 2004, passim. See also Poitout 1999, 11–15.
3. These were *Ruins of the Château at Rosemont, Nièvre* (Paris, Musée d'Orsay), *Skaters in Holland* (Germany, private collection), and *Canal in Holland, Sunset* (location unknown); see Stein et al. 2003, nos. 249, 288, and unrecorded.
4. Quoted in Auffret 2004, 129; Stein et al. 2003, 33.
5. Letter, 8 May 1920: "Il ne faut pas oublier que . . . [Boudin] avait reçu les leçons d'un maitre, Jongkind, dont l'oeuvre, surtout dans ses aquarelles, est à l'origine ainsi qu'avec Corot de ce que l'on a appelé l'Impressionnisme." Wildenstein 1974–91, 4:405.
6. "C'est avec son pinceau d'aquarelliste qu'il saisit directement l'impression de la nature." Moreau-Nélaton 1918, 48.
7. Letter, 22 November 1856: "j'en ai un autre tableau terminé une vue près de Rotterdam et puis une autre entrain et très avancé. je les ai fait après nature bien attendu [entendu.] j ai fait des aquarelles [sic] après les quelles j ai fait mes tableaux"; transcribed from Hefting 1969, 46, no. 41; also quoted in Auffret 2004, 102. Hefting dated this letter to 9 November 1856, but Auffret 2004, 103, n. 70, presented persuasive evidence that it was written on 22 November.
8. Signac 1927, 130: " . . . dès 1863 . . . commence la plus belle série d'aquarelles qui soit au monde."
9. Paris, private collection, 42 × 56 cm; see Stein et al. 2003, no. 293.
10. A drawing, dated 26 September 1848, is Hefting 1975, no. 53, also illustrated in Auffret 2004, 62–63 (private collection); another drawing, of about 1864, is in Auffret 2004, 144 (private collection); Paris 1996, no. 36 (private collection) is yet another. The paintings of 1864 are Stein et al. 2003, nos. 330 (Oxford, Ashmolean Museum) and 331 (Paris, private collection). The paintings—no. 91 in that book, from 1852 (Paris, Petit-Palais, Musée des Beaux-Arts de la Ville de Paris), and nos. 123 and 124, from 1854 (both private collection)—show minor variations in the point of view. Jongkind also made at least one drawing and two paintings of the Seine and the eastern end of Notre Dame from a closer vantage point, the Quai de Montebello, in 1849; the drawing is Hefting 1975, no. 54, also illustrated in The Hague–Cologne–Paris 2003–04, no. 41 (Paris, Musée d'Orsay); the paintings are Stein et al. 2003, nos. 65 (Great Britain, private collection) and 66 (Santa Barbara Museum of Art). See Götz Czymmek's discussion of Jongkind's repetition of motifs in The Hague–Cologne–Paris 2003–04, 165–179.

Watermarks

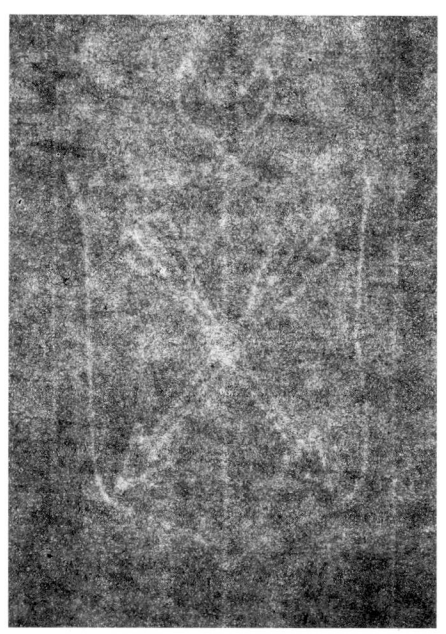

W 12

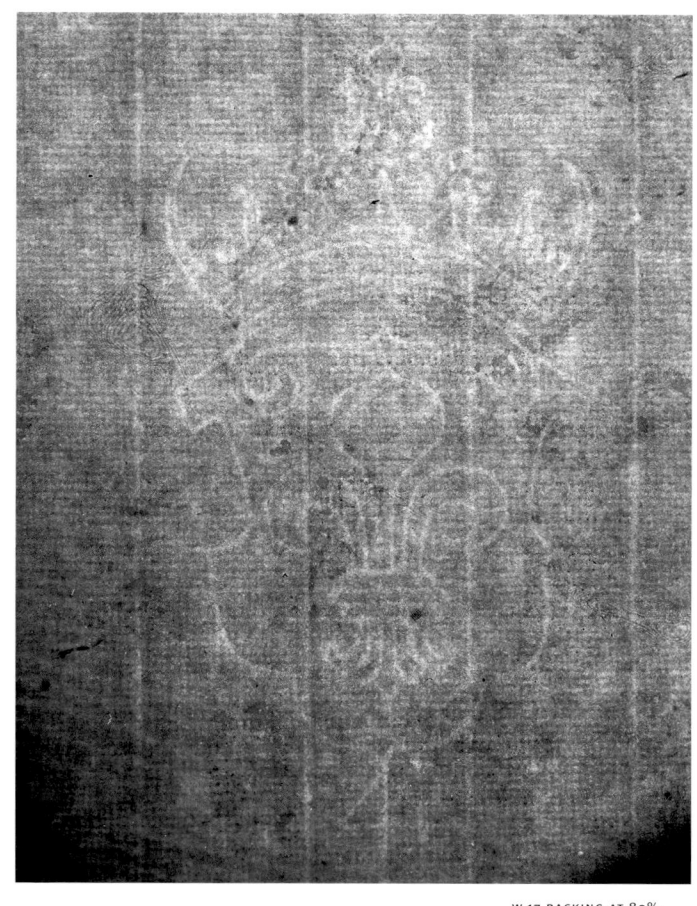

W 17 BACKING AT 80%

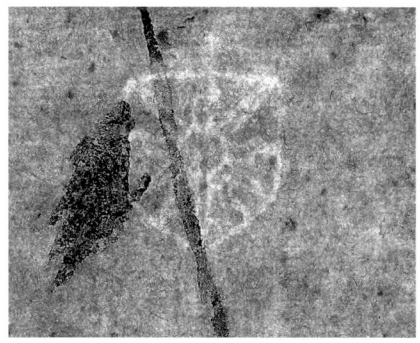

W 24

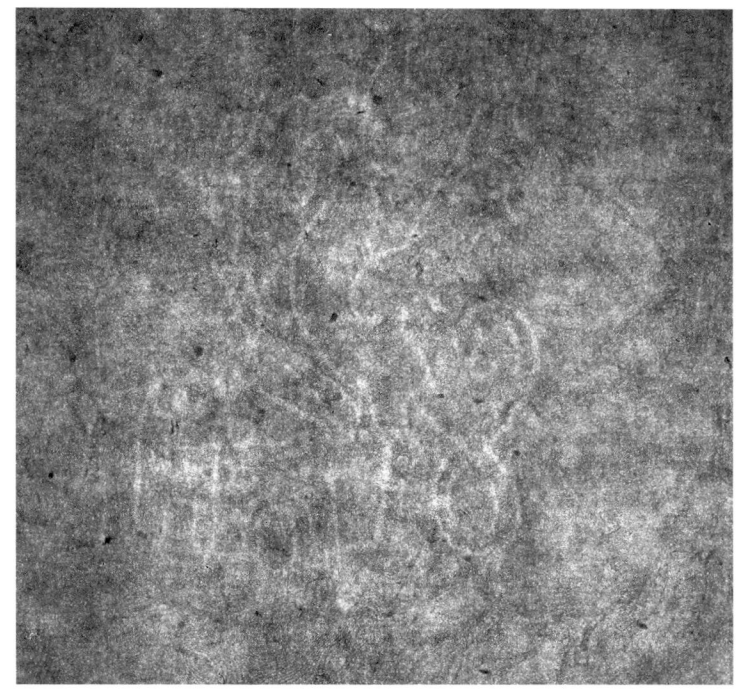

W 26A

W 26B

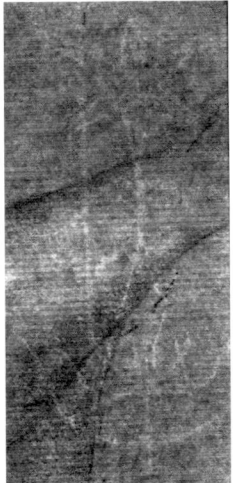

W 28

W 29

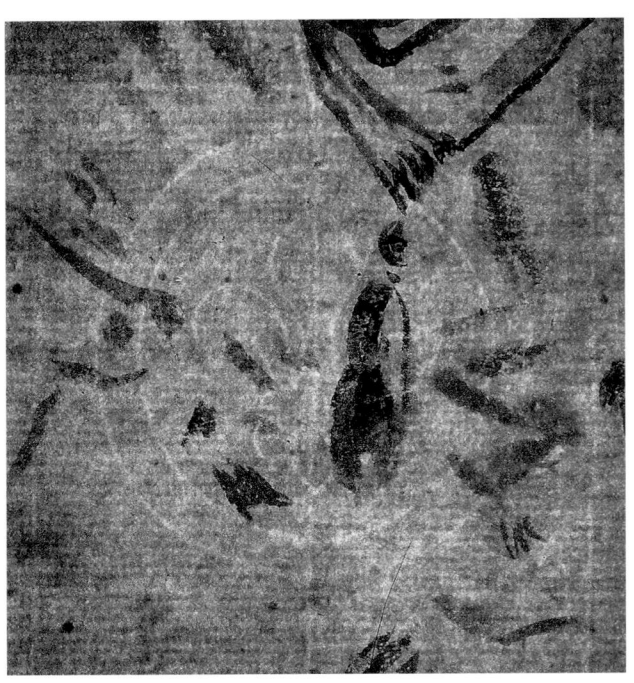

W 29 BACKING

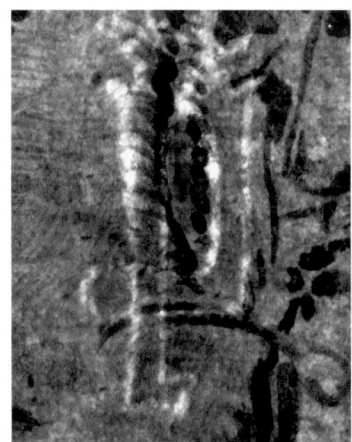

W 30

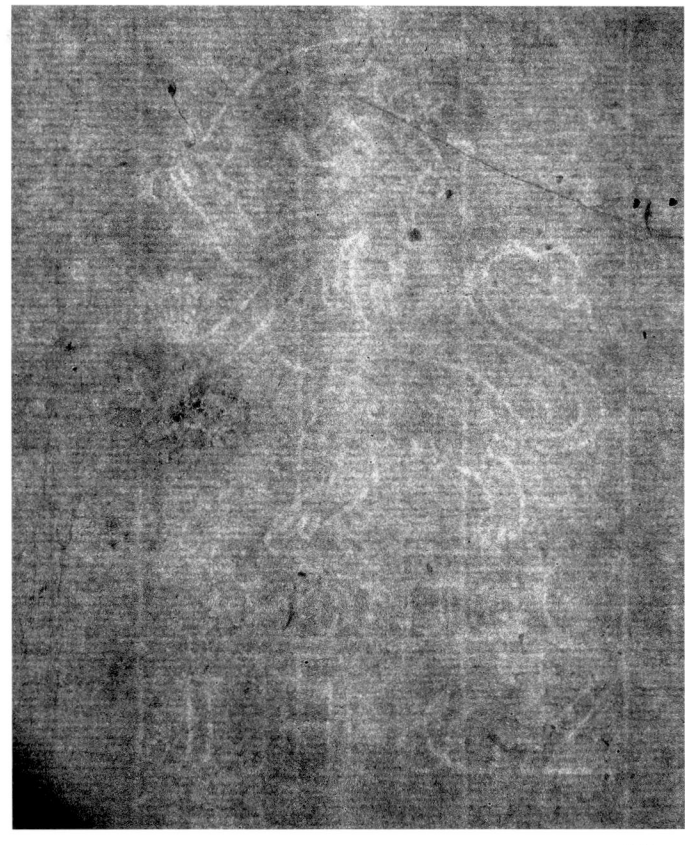

W 33 AT 80%

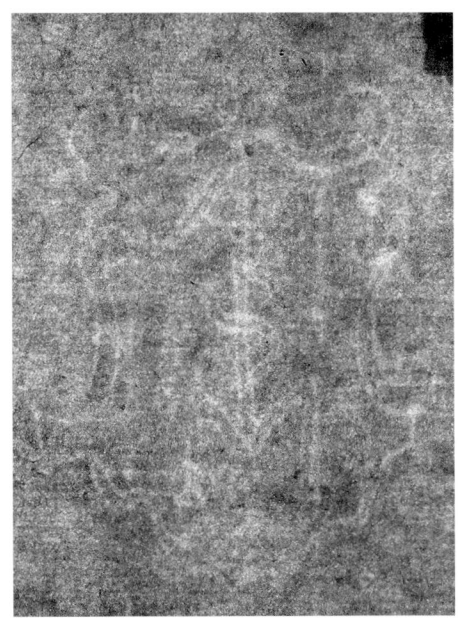

W 34

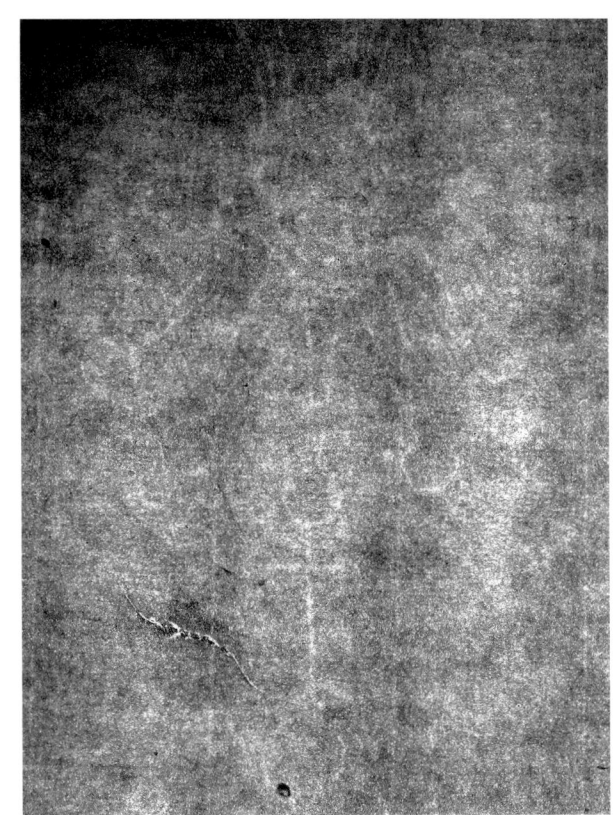

W 44A

W 47

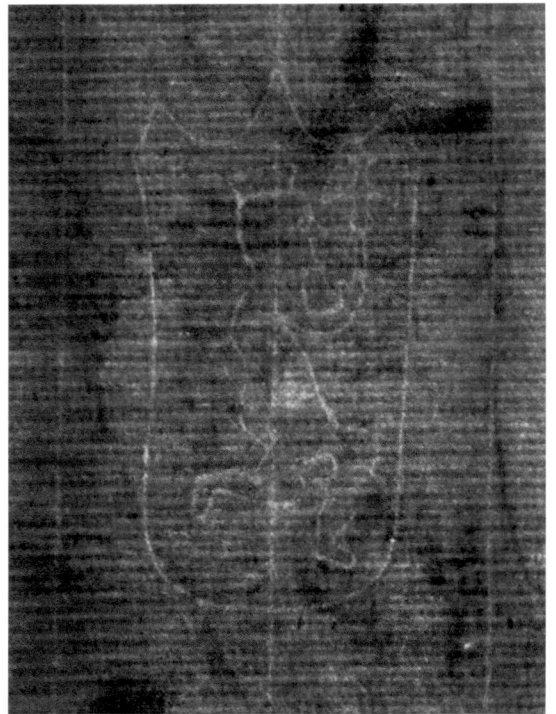

W 48

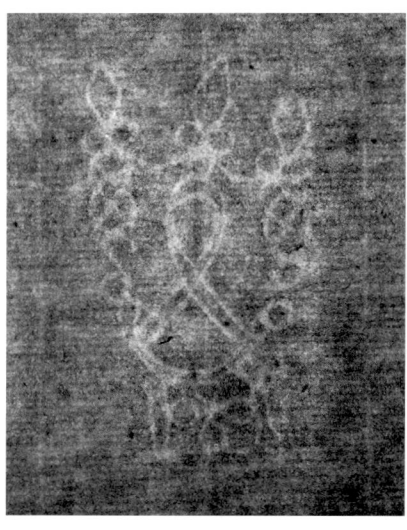

W 50

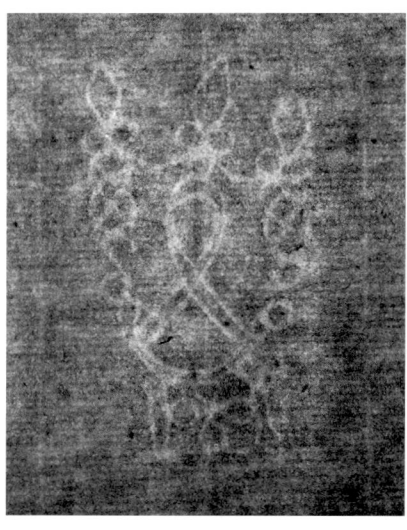

W 53

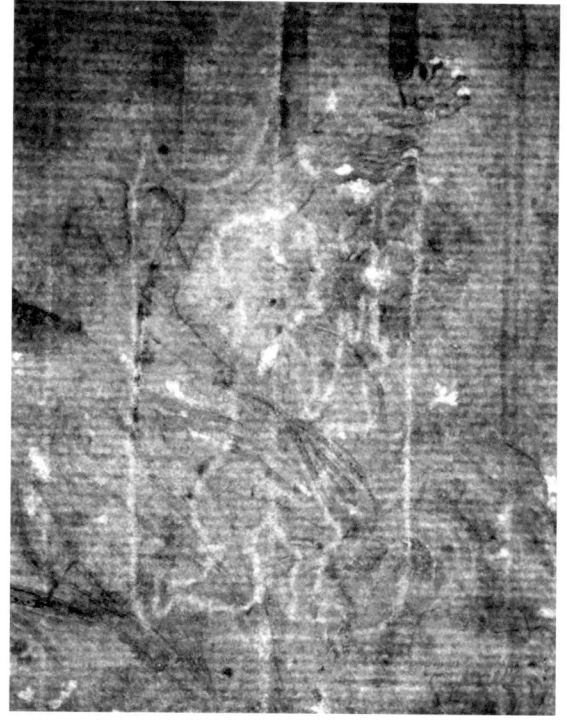

W 54

W 66

W 67

WATERMARKS 251

W 71 COUNTERMARK AT 115%

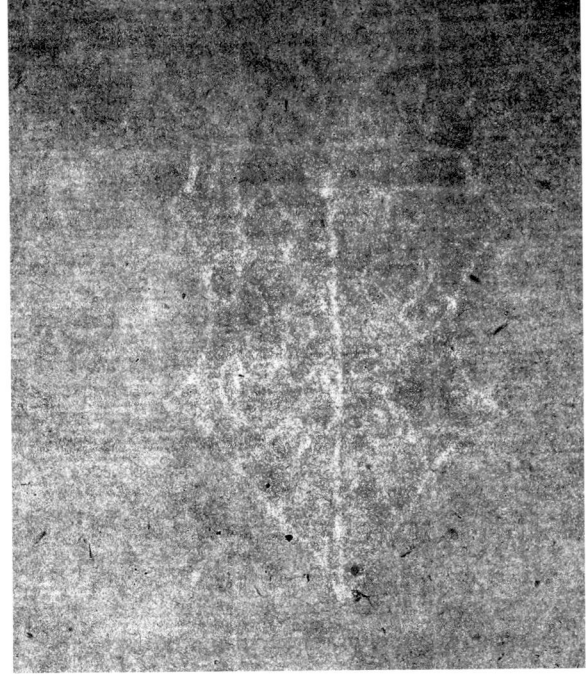

W 71

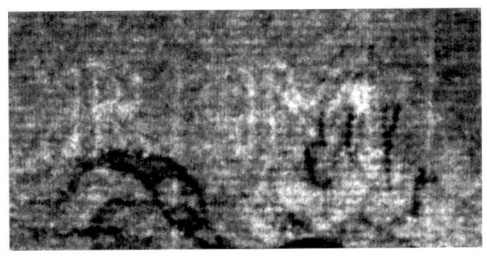

W 72

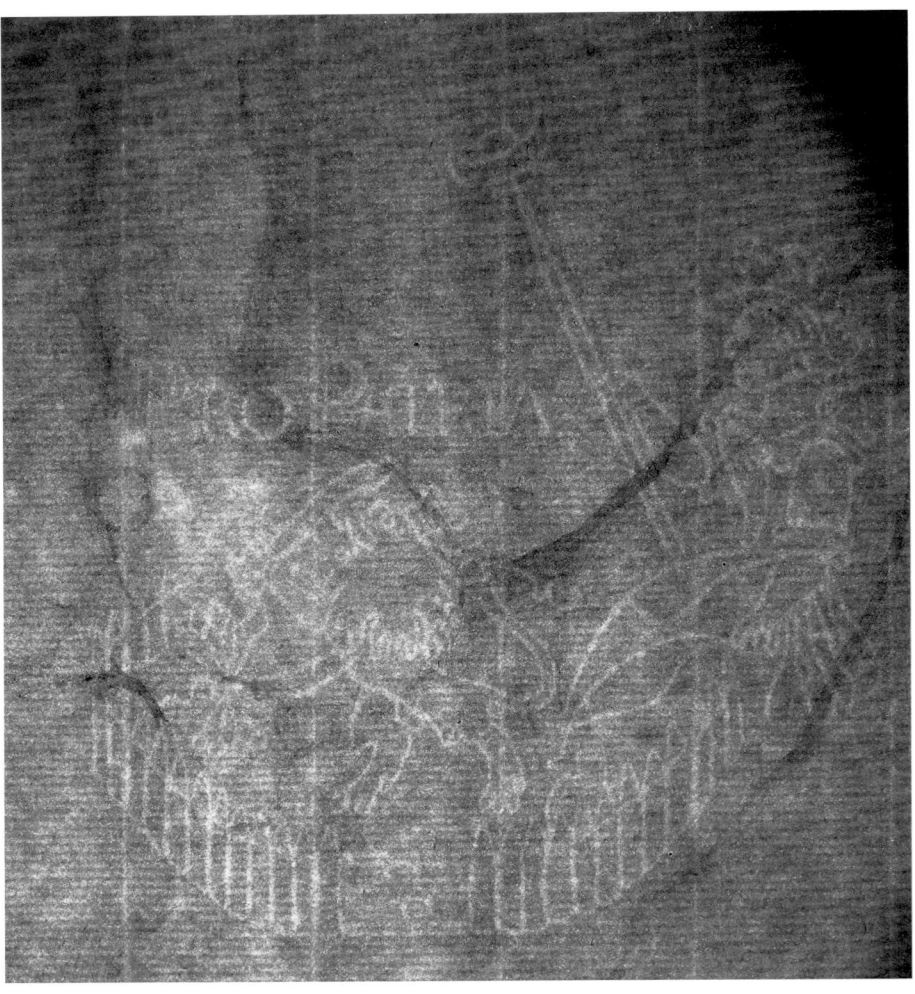

W 73

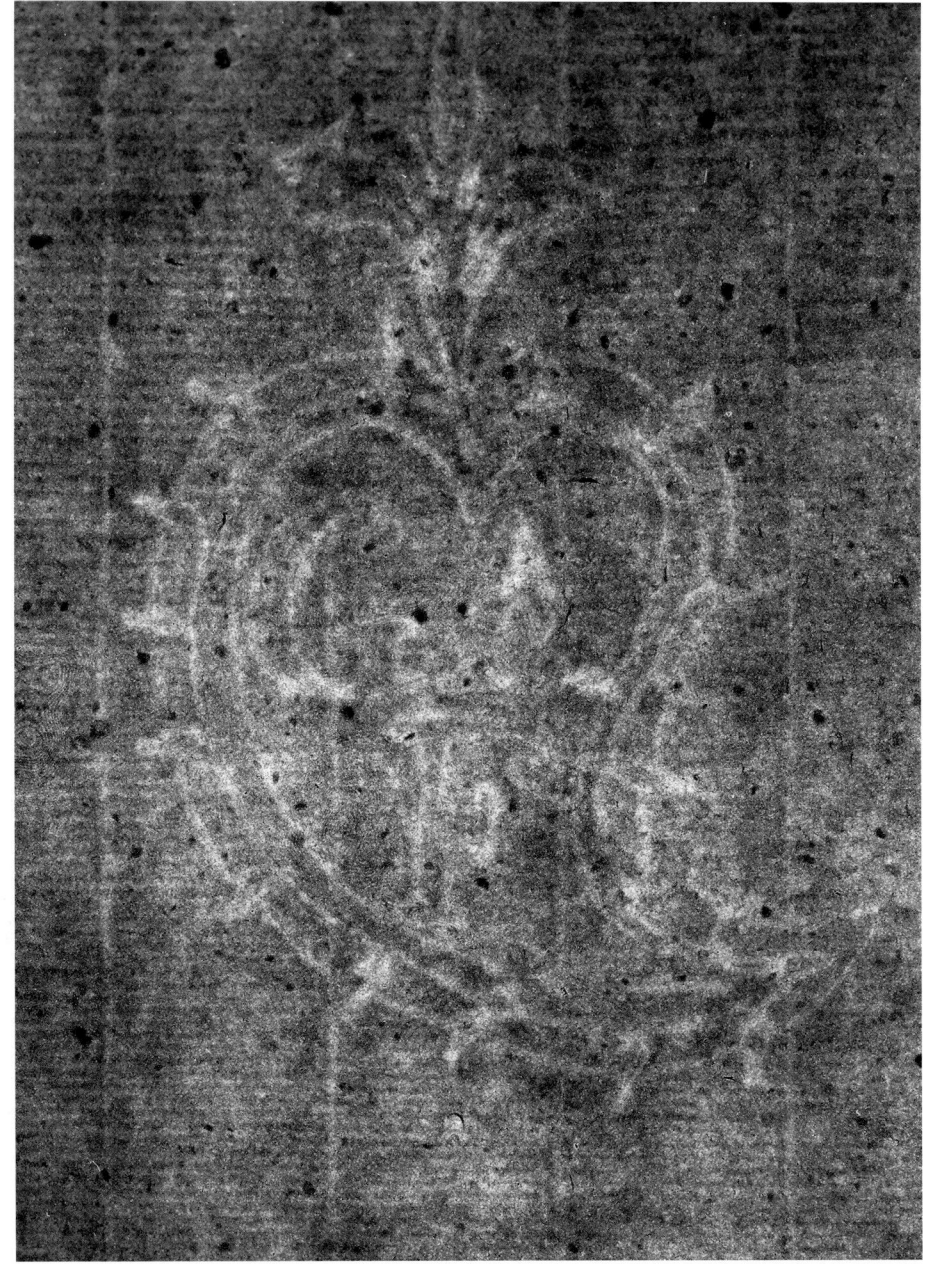

W 74

W 80

WATERMARKS

W 81 AT 90%

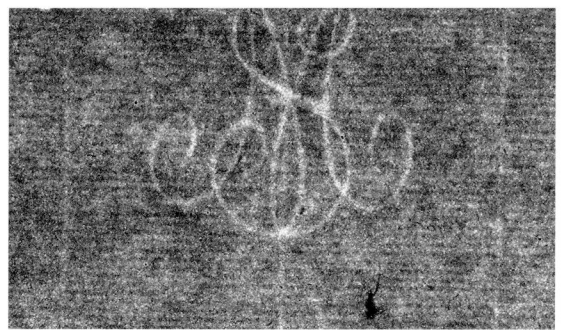

W 82

W 83 AT 85%

Bibliography

KEY TO ABBREVIATIONS

AB	*The Art Bulletin*
B.	Bartsch 1803–21
Briquet	Briquet 1923
Churchill	Churchill 1967
Delteil	Delteil 1906–30
Grove Dictionary	Grove 1996
H-B and L	Haverkamp-Begemann and Logan 1970
Handbook	*Handbook* 1992
Heawood	Heawood 1950
Hollstein DF	Hollstein 1949–
Hollstein G	Hollstein 1954–
IFF après 1800	Laran et al. 1930–
IFF XVIIe siècle	Weigert 1939–
IFF XVIIIe siècle	Roux 1930–
L.	Lugt 1921–56
MD	*Master Drawings*
New Hollstein DF	New Hollstein 1993–
New Hollstein G	New Hollstein 1996–
Piccard	Piccard 1961–
RD	Robert-Dumesnil 1835–71
Thieme-Becker	Thieme and Becker 1907–50
TIB	*Illustrated Bartsch* 1971–
Van Mander (Miedema)	Van Mander 1994–99
Vasari (Milanesi)	Vasari 1889
YUAG	Yale University Art Gallery
YUAG Bulletin	*Bulletin of the Yale University Art Gallery*

BOOKS, ARTICLES AND DISSERTATIONS

Abromson 1978
Morton Abromson. "Clement VIII's Patronage of the Brothers Alberti." *AB* 60 (1978): 531–547.

Acidini Luchinat 1994
Cristina Acidini Luchinat. "Il 'Giudizio Universale' nella cupola e altre pitture." In *La cattedrale di Santa Maria del Fiore a Firenze*. Vol. 2. Florence, 1994: 303–323.

Acidini Luchinat 1998
Cristina Acidini Luchinat. "Vasari's Last Paintings: The Cupola of Florence Cathedral." In *Vasari's Florence: Artists and Literati at the Medicean Court*. Ed. Philip Jacks. Cambridge, 1998: 238–252.

Acidini Luchinat 1999
Cristina Acidini Luchinat. *Taddeo e Federico Zuccari: Fratelli pittori del cinquecento*. 2 vols. Milan and Rome, 1999.

Adhémar 1954
Jean Adhémar. "La rue Montorgeuil et la formation d'un groupe d'imagiers parisiens au XVIe siècle." *Le vieux papier* 21 (April 1954): 25–34.

Agosti 1996
Barbara Agosti. *Collezionismo e archeologia cristiana nel seicento: Frederico Borromeo e il medioevo artistico tra Roma e Milano*. Milan, 1996.

Aikema and Brown 2000
Bernard Aikema and Beverly Louise Brown, eds. *Renaissance Venice and the North: Crosscurrents in the Time of Bellini, Dürer, and Titian*. New York, 2000.

Albricci 1982
Gioconda Albricci. "Luca Penni e i suoi incisori." *Rassegna di studi e di notizie* 10 (1982): 69–166.

Alexandre 1888
Arsène Alexandre. *Honoré Daumier, l'homme et l'oeuvre*. Paris, 1888.

Ames-Lewis 2000
Francis Ames-Lewis. *Drawing in Early Renaissance Italy*. Rev. ed. New Haven and London, 2000.

Ananoff 1961–70
Alexandre Ananoff. *L'oeuvre dessiné de Jean-Honoré Fragonard (1732–1806)*. 4 vols. Paris, 1961–70.

Ananoff 1966
Alexandre Ananoff. *L'oeuvre dessiné de François Boucher (1703–1770)*. 2 vols. Paris, 1966.

Anderson 1988
Jaynie Anderson. "Venetian Art Reinterpreted." *Art History* 11 (1988): 565–568.

Angelini 1998
Alessandro Angelini. *Gian Lorenzo Bernini e i Chigi tra Roma e Siena*. Siena, 1998.

Angulo and Péréz-Sánchez 1975
Diego Angulo and Alfonso E. Pérez-Sánchez. *A Corpus of Spanish Drawings: Spanish Drawings, 1400–1600*. London, 1975.

Ariosto 1772–73
Lodovico Ariosto. *Orlando Furioso*. 4 vols. Venice, 1772–73.

Ariosto 1973
Ludovico Ariosto. *Orlando Furioso*. Trans. Barbara Reynolds. London, 1973.

Ariosto 1998
Ludovico Ariosto. *Orlando Furioso*. Translated, with an introduction by Guido Waldman. Oxford, 1998.

Armenini 1977
Giovanni Battista Armenini. *On the True Precepts of the Art of Painting*. Ed. and trans. Edward J. Olszewski. New York, 1977.

Aronberg Lavin 1956
Marilyn Aronberg Lavin. "Color Study in Barocci's Drawings." *Burlington Magazine* 98 (1956): 435–439.

Arvengas 1965
Jeanne Arvengas. *Raymond Lafage, dessinateur*. Paris, 1965.

Auffret 2004
François Auffret. *Johan Barthold Jongkind, 1819–1891, héritier, contemporain, et précurseur: Biographie illustré*. Paris, 2004.

Baas and Sojka 2003
Valerie Baas and Nancy Sojka. "The Restoration of Edgar Degas's Portrait of Marguerite." *Bulletin of the Detroit Institute of Arts* 77 (2003): 58–59.

Bagni 1992
Prisco Bagni. *Gandolfi: Affreschi, dipinti, bozzetti, disegni*. Bologna, 1992.

Bailey 1992
Colin B. Bailey. "J.-H. Fragonard e H. Robert a Roma." Review of Rome 1990–91. *Burlington Magazine* 134 (1992): 599–600.

Baker 2003
Christopher Baker. "Art Comes with Practice: A Sixteenth-Century Album of Prints and Drawings from the Aldrich Collection." *Apollo* 157 (2003): 35–39.

Baldass 1918
Ludwig von Baldass. "Notizen über hollandische Zeichner des XVI. Jahrhunderts, III: Jan Swart van Groningen." *Mitteilungen der Gesellschaft für vervielfaltigende Kunst*. Supplement to *Graphischen Kunste* 41 (1918): 11–21.

Baldass 1944
Ludwig von Baldass. "Die Entwicklung des Bernart van Orley." *Jahrbuch der Kunsthistorischen Sammlungen in Wien* 12 (1944): 141–191.

Bambach 1999
Carmen C. Bambach. *Drawing and Painting in the Italian Renaissance Workshop*. Cambridge, 1999.

Barocchi 1965
Paolo Barocchi. "Itinerario di Giovambattista Naldini." *Arte antica e moderna* 31/32 (1965): 244–288.

Bartsch 1803–21
Adam von Bartsch. *Le peintre graveur*. 21 vols. Vienna, 1803–21.

Barzman 2000
Karin-Edis Barzman. *The Florentine Academy and the Early Modern State: The Discipline of Disegno*. Cambridge and New York, 2000.

Bauch 1938
Kurt Bauch. "Beiträge zum Werk der Vorläufer Rembrandts, V. Gerrit Pietersz Swelinck, der Lehrer Lastmans." *Oud Holland* 55 (1938): 254–265.

Baudelaire [1868?]
Charles Baudelaire. *Les fleurs du mal, par Charles Baudelaire, précédés par une notice par Théophile Gautier*. Paris, [1868?].

Baudelaire 1961
Charles Baudelaire. *Oeuvres complètes*. Ed. Y.-G. Le Dantec. Paris, 1961.

Baudelaire 1964
Charles Baudelaire. *The Painter of Modern Life and Other Essays*. Ed. and trans. Jonathan Mayne. London, 1964.

Bazzotti 1996
Ugo Bazzotti. "La Clemenza di Alessandro: Una precisazione iconografica per la camera di Attilio Regolo a Palazzo Te." *Quaderni di Palazzo Te* 4 (1996): 92–93.

Bean and Turčić 1986
Jacob Bean, with the assistance of Lawrence Turčić. *15th–18th Century French Drawings in the Metropolitan Museum of Art*. New York, 1986.

Beauvais 2000
Lydia Beauvais. *Charles Le Brun, 1619–1690*. 2 vols. Musée du Louvre, Cabinet des dessins, Inventaire général des gravures, École française. Paris, 2000.

Beets 1914
Nicolaas Beets. "Zestiende-eeuwsche Kunstenaars, I: Jan Swart." *Oud Holland* 32 (1914): 1–28.

Beets 1915
Nicolaas Beets. *De houtsneden in Vorsterman's Bijbel van 1528: Afbeeldingen der prenten van Jan Swart, Lucas van Leyden, e.a., met een inleiding en een kritische lijst*. Amsterdam, 1915.

Béguin 1975
Sylvie Béguin. "Un tableau de Luca Penni." *Revue du Louvre* 5/6 (1975): 359–366.

Béguin 1982
Sylvie Béguin. "Contribution à l'étude des rapports des artistes émiliens et bellifontains." In *Le arte a Bologna e in Emilia dal XVI al XVII secolo, atti del XXIV Congresso Internazionale di Storia dell'Arte*. Bologna, 1982: 51–60.

Béguin 1987
Sylvie Béguin. "Luca Penni peintre: Nouvelles attributions." In *"Il se rendit en Italie": Études offertes à André Chastel*. Rome and Paris, 1987: 243–257.

Béguin 1991
Sylvie Béguin. "À propos de Luca Penni." In *Disegno: Actes du colloque du Musée des Beaux-Arts de Rennes*. Rennes, 1991: 9–17.

Béguin, Guillaume, and Roy 1985
Sylvie Béguin, Jean Guillaume, and Alain Roy. *La galerie d'Ulysse à Fontainebleau*. Paris, 1985.

Béguin et al. 1972
Sylvie Béguin et al. "La galerie François I au Château de Fontainebleau." *Revue de l'art* numéro spécial 16/17 (1972): 3–174.

Bellesi 1998
Sandro Bellesi. "Interventi decorative in Palazzo Pitti tra fine cinquecento e primo seicento." *Paragone* 583 (1998): 49–68.

Bellori 1672
Giovanni Pietro Bellori. *Le vite de' pittori, scultori, et architetti moderni*. Rome, 1672.

Belluzzi 1998
Amadeo Belluzzi. *Palazzo Te a Mantova*. Modena, 1998.

Benesch 1928
Otto Benesch. *Die Zeichnungen der niederländischen Schulen des XV. und XVI. Jahrhunderts*. Vienna, 1928.

Benesch 1954–57
Otto Benesch. *The Drawings of Rembrandt: A Critical and Chronological Catalogue*. 6 vols. London, 1954–57.

Benesch 1979
Otto Benesch. *From an Art Historian's Workshop*. Lucerne, 1979.

Berenson 1938
Bernard Berenson. *The Drawings of the Florentine Painters*. Amplified edition. 3 vols. Chicago, 1938.

Bergeret de Grancourt 1895
Pierre Jacques Onésyme Bergeret de Grancourt. *Bergeret et Fragonard: Journal inédit d'un voyage en Italie, 1773–1774*. Introduction by M. A. Tornézy. Paris, 1895.

Bertin 2001
Eric Bertin. "Premier état du supplément au catalogue Naef des portraits dessinés par Ingres." *Bulletin du Musée Ingres* 73 (2001): 27–31.

Bertolotti 1886
Antonino Bertolotti. *Artisti francesi in Roma nei secoli XV, XVI, e XVII*. Mantua, 1886.

Biesboer 1978–79
Pieter Biesboer. Review of Keyes 1975. *Simiolus* 10 (1978–79): 207–210.

Bjurström and Magnusson 1998
Per Bjurström and Börje Magnusson. *Italian Drawings: Umbria, Rome, Naples*. Stockholm, 1998.

Blanc 1870
Charles Blanc. *Ingres, sa vie et ses ouvrages*. Paris, 1870.

Blumenthal 1980
Arthur Blumenthal. *Theatre Art of the Medici*. Hanover, N.H., 1980.

Blunt 1945
Anthony Blunt. *The French Drawings in the Collection of His Majesty the King at Windsor Castle*. Oxford and London, 1945.

Bober 1985
Jonathan Bober. "A 'Flagellation of Christ' by Giulio Cesare Procaccini: Program and Pictorial Style in Borromean Milan." *Arte Lombarda* n.s. 63–65 (1985): 55–80.

Boccaccio 1473
Boccaccio. *Buch von den hochgeruemten frauen*. Ulm, 1473.

Boccaccio 1541
Boccaccio. *Ein schöne Cronica oder Hystori Buch . . .* Augsburg, 1541.

Boccaccio 1924
Boccaccio. *Des Giovanni Boccaccio Buch: Von den berühmten Frawen*. Ed. S. Hoepfl. Facsimile ed. of Boccaccio 1473. Munich, 1924.

Bock and Rosenberg 1930
Elfried Bock and Jakob Rosenberg. *Staatliche Museen zu Berlin: Die niederländischen Meister*. 2 vols. Berlin, 1930.

Bodmer 1984
Karl Bodmer. *Karl Bodmer's America*. Introduction by William H. Goetzmann, annotations by David C. Hunt and Marsha V. Gallagher. Omaha and Lincoln, Neb., 1984.

Bodnár 2005
Szilvia Bodnár. "Some New Drawings by Johann Kellerthaler in Oxford and Munich." *MD* 43 (2005): 186–192.

Boggs 1955
Jean Sutherland Boggs. "Edgar Degas and the Bellellis." *AB* 37 (1955): 127–136.

Boggs 1962
Jean Sutherland Boggs. *Portraits by Degas*. Berkeley, Calif., and Los Angeles, 1962.

Bol 1989
Laurens J. Bol. *Adriaen Pietersz. Van de Venne, Painter and Draughtsman*. Doornspijk, 1989.

Boon 1978
K. G. Boon. *Netherlandish Drawings of the Fifteenth and Sixteenth Centuries*. The Hague, 1978.

Boon 1992
K. G. Boon. *The Netherlandish and German Drawings of the XVth and XVIth Centuries of the Frits Lugt Collection*. 3 vols. Paris, 1992.

Boorsch 1996
Suzanne Boorsch. "Lorenzo Tiepolo's St. Charles Borromeo Venerating the Crucifix." *Print Quarterly* 13 (1996): 401–410.

Bora 2003
Giulio Bora. "Daniele Crespi a Garegnano." In *La certosa di Garegnano in Milano*. Ed. Carlo Capponi. Milan, 2003: 91–101.

Börsch-Supan 1963
Helmut Börsch-Supan. "Joseph Vivien als Hofmaler der Wittelsbacher." *Münchner Jahrbuch der Bildenden Kunst*, ser. 3, vol. 14 (1963): 129–212.

Boubli 1999
Lizzie Boubli. "The State of Scholarship of Sixteenth- and Seventeenth-Century Spanish Drawings." *MD* 37 (1999): 349–364.

Bouvy 1933
Eugène Bouvy. *Daumier, l'oeuvre gravé du maître*. 2 vols. Paris, 1933.

Bowron 1979
Edgar Peters Bowron. *The Paintings of Benedetto Luti (1666–1724)*. Ph.D. diss., Institute of Fine Arts, New York University, 1979.

Bredius 1902
Abraham Bredius. "Pieter Jansz. Quast." *Oud Holland* 20 (1902): 65–82.

Bredius 1915–22
Abraham Bredius. *Künstler-Inventare: Urkunden zur Geschichte der holländischen Kunst des XVIten, XVIIten, und XVIIIten Jahrhunderts*. 8 vols. The Hague, 1915–22.

Brejon de Lavergnée 1979
Arnauld Brejon de Lavergnée. "À propos de Jean Jouvenet." *Bulletin des amis du Musée de Rennes* 3 (1979): 79–95.

Brejon de Lavergnée 1987
Barbara Brejon de Lavergnée. *Dessins de Simon Vouet, 1590–1649*. Musée du Louvre, Cabinet des dessins, Inventaire général des dessins, École française. Paris, 1987.

Briganti 1982
Giuliano Briganti. *Pietro da Cortona, o, della pittura barocca*. Florence, 1982.

Briquet 1923
Charles-Moïse Briquet. *Les filigranes*. 2d ed. 4 vols. Leipzig, 1923.

Brooks 1999
Julian Brooks. *The Drawings of Andrea Boscoli (c. 1560–1608)*. D. Phil. thesis, Worchester College, University of Oxford, 1999.

Brooks 2000
Julian Brooks. "Andrea Boscoli's 'Loves of Gerusalemme Liberata.'" *MD* 38 (2000): 448–459.

Bruckle 1993
Irene Bruckle. "Blue-Colored Paper in Drawings." *Drawing* 15, no. 4 (1993): 73–77.

Bruyn 1960
J. Bruyn. "Twee St.-Antonius-panelen en andere Werken van Aertgen van Leyden." *Nederlands kunsthistorisch jaarboek* 11 (1960): 36–119.

Buonocore et al. 1996
Marco Buonocore et al. *Camillo Massimo, collezionista di antichità*. Rome, 1996.

Busiri Vici 1980
Andrea Busiri Vici. "Un dimenticato pittore del tardo seicento: Girolamo Troppa." *L'urbe* 43 (1980): 22–28.

Byam Shaw 1962
James Byam Shaw. *The Drawings of Domenico Tiepolo*. London, 1962.

Byam Shaw 1976
James Byam Shaw. *Drawings by Old Masters at Christ Church, Oxford*. 2 vols. Oxford, 1976.

Cailleux 1959
Jean Cailleux. "Four Studies of Soldiers by Watteau: An Essay on the Chronology of Military Subjects." In *L'art du dix-huitième siècle: Notes and Studies on Pictures and Drawings of the Eighteenth-Century*. Supplement to *Burlington Magazine* 101 (1959): unpaginated.

Cantelli 1983
Giuseppe Cantelli. *Repertorio della pittura fiorentina del seicento*. Fiesole, 1983.

Caracciolo 2001
Maria Theresa Caracciolo. "Pour le maître des albums Egmont et ses sources." In *Francesco Salviati et la bella maniera: Actes des colloques de Rome et de Paris*. Rome, 2001: 667–689.

Cardi 1913
Giovanni Battista Cardi. *Vita di Lodovico Cardi Cigoli*. San Miniato, 1913.

Cartari 1976
Vincenzo Cartari. *Le imagini de i dei degli antichi, Venice, 1571*. Facsimile reprint. New York, 1976.

Causa 2000
Stefano Causa. *Battista Caracciolo, l'opera completa*. Naples, 2000.

Causa Picone 1993
Marina Causa Picone. "Giunte a Battistello: Appunti per una storia critica di Battistello disegnatore." *Paragone* 44 (1993): 24–87.

Cavicchioli 2000
Sonia Cavicchioli. "Le incisione del Maestro del Dado fra rimandi raffaelleschi e archeologici: Fortuna e problemi di attribuzione." *Fontes* 3 (2000): 189–204.

Cavicchioli 2002
Sonia Cavicchioli. *The Tale of Cupid and Psyche*. New York, 2002.

Cayeux and Boulot 1989
Jean de Cayeux, with C. Boulot. *Hubert Robert*. Paris, 1989.

Cazort Taylor 1976
Mary Cazort Taylor. "The Pen and Wash Drawings of the Brothers Gandolfi." *MD* 2 (1976): 159–165.

Chappe d'Auteroche 2004
Chappe d'Auteroche. *Voyage en Sibérie fait par ordre du roi en 1761*. Introduction and critical apparatus by Michel Mervaud. 2 vols. Oxford, 2004.

Chappell 1974
Miles L. Chappell. "Cigoli's 'Resurrection' for the Pitti Palace." *Burlington Magazine* 116 (1974): 469–475.

Chappell 1990
Miles L. Chappell. "Drawing in Seventeenth Century Florence." *Drawing* 12, no. 3 (1990): 469–474.

Chappell 2005
Miles L. Chappell. "Reform and Continuity in Later Florentine Drawing." *MD* 43 (2005): 339–348.

Chennevières-Pointel 1847–62
Philippe de Chennevières-Pointel. *Recherches sur la vie et les ouvrages de quelques peintres provinciaux de l'ancienne France*. 4 vols. Paris, 1847–62.

Chiarini 1999
Marco Chiarini. "Il Tasso e la pittura fiorentina del seicento." In *Torquato Tasso e la cultura Estense*. Ed. G. Venturi. Vol. 2. Florence, 1999: 731–735.

Choné 1999
Paulette Choné. "Gillot le Songeur." In Langres 1999: 34–43.

Christoffel 1940
Ulrich Christoffel. *Klassizismus in Frankreich um 1800*. Munich, 1940.

Churchill 1967
William Algernon Churchill. *Watermarks in Paper in Holland, England, France, etc. in the XVII and XVIII Centuries and Their Interconnection*. Amsterdam, 1967.

Ciardi 1974
Roberto Paolo Ciardi, ed. *Scritti sulle arti*. 2 vols. Florence, 1974.

Clark and Bowron 1985
Anthony M. Clark. *Pompeo Batoni*. Ed. Edgar Peters Bowron. New York, 1985.

Clayton 1995
Martin Clayton. *Poussin: Works on Paper*. London, 1995.

Cocke 1968
Richard Cocke. "Mola's Designs for the Stanza dell'Aria at Valmontone." *Burlington Magazine* 111 (1968): 558–565.

Cocke 1991
Richard Cocke. "The Drawings of Michele and Giovanni Battista Pace." *MD* 29 (1991): 347–384.

Cohn 1968
Marjorie B. Cohn. "Profile Portrait of Guillaume Guillon Lethière by J. A. D. Ingres." In *Fogg Art Museum Acquisitions 1966–67*. Cambridge, Mass., 1968: 54–59.

Cohn 1969
Marjorie B. Cohn. "The Original Format of Ingres Portrait Drawings." *Colloque Ingres.* Special number of *Bulletin du Musée Ingres* (1969): 15–27.

Coleman 1988
Robert Randolf Coleman. *Bernardino Lanino and the Laninian Current in Sixteenth-Century Piedmontese-Lombard Painting.* Ph.D. diss., University of Chicago, 1988.

Connors 1996
Joseph Connors. "Borromini in Oppenord's Sketchbooks." In *Ars naturam adiuvans: Festschrift für Matthias Winner zum 11 März 1996.* Mainz am Rhein, 1996: 598–612.

Contini 1989
Roberto Contini. "Densità del Curradi disegnatore." *Paragone* 40 (1989): 99–102.

Cooper 1976
Helen Cooper. "Cincinnatus Called into the Service of the State," 1976, unpublished manuscript, curatorial files, Department of Prints, Drawings, and Photographs, YUAG.

Cooper 1978
Helen Cooper. "An Early Drawing by Degas." *YUAG Bulletin* 37 (1978): 10–13.

Corneille 1998
Pierre Corneille. *La conquête de la toison d'or.* Ed. Marie-France Wagner. Paris, 1998.

Costamagna, Härb, and Prosperi Valenti Rodinò 2005
Philippe Costamagna, Florian Härb, and Simonetta Prosperi Valenti Rodinò, eds. *Disegno, giudizio e bella maniera: Studi sul disegno italiano in onore di Catherine Monbeig Goguel.* Milan, 2005.

Courboin 1900–1901
François Courboin. *Catalogue sommaire des gravures et lithographies composant la reserve des estampes, Bibliothèque Nationale de France.* Paris, 1900–1901.

Cox-Rearick 1964
Janet Cox-Rearick. *The Drawings of Pontormo.* 2 vols. Cambridge, 1964.

Crelly 1962
William R. Crelly. *The Paintings of Simon Vouet.* New Haven and London, 1962.

Crosato 1962
Luciana Crosato. *Gli affreschi nell villa venete del cinquecento.* Treviso, 1962.

Cuzin 1988
Jean-Pierre Cuzin. *Jean-Honoré Fragonard, Life and Work: Complete Catalogue of the Oil Paintings.* English ed. New York, 1988.

Dacier, Hérold, and Vuaflart 1921–29
Émile Dacier, Jacques Hérold, and Albert Vuaflart. *Jean de Jullienne et les graveurs de Watteau au XVIIIe siècle.* 3 vols. Paris, 1921–29.

Dacos 1987
Nicole Dacos. "Peeter de Kempeneer/Pedro Campana as a Draughtsman." *MD* 25 (1987): 359–389.

Dacos 1990
Nicole Dacos. "Le maître des albums Egmont: Dirck Hendricksz. Centen." *Oud Holland* 104 (1990): 49–68.

Dania 1995
Luigi Dania. "Alessandro Maggiori, critico e collezionista." In *Disegni marchigiani dal cinquecento al settecento: Atti del convegno "Il disegno antico nelle Marche e dalle Marche."* Ed. Mario di Giampaolo and Giulio Angelucci. Florence, 1995: 7–18.

Davidson 1987
Jane P. Davidson. *The Witch in Northern European Art.* Freren, 1987.

Dee 1982
Elaine Evans Dee. "Oppenord." In *Macmillan Encyclopedia of Architects.* Vol. 3. Ed. Adolf K. Placzek. London, 1982: 324–327.

Dee 1990
Elaine Evans Dee. "Ornament Thoughts: Gilles-Marie Oppenord." *MD* 28 (1990): 332–337.

De Grazia 1991
Diane De Grazia. *Bertoia, Mirola, and the Farnese Court.* Bologna, 1991.

Delaborde 1870
Henri Delaborde. *Ingres, sa vie, ses travaux, sa doctrine.* Paris, 1870.

Delen 1938
A. J. J. Delen. *Catalogue des dessins anciens du Cabinet des Estampes de la ville d'Anvers, Musée Plantin-Moretus, Écoles flamande et hollandaise.* 2 vols. Brussels, 1938.

Delteil 1906–30
Loys Delteil. *Le peintre-graveur illustré (XIX et XXe siècles).* 31 vols. Paris, 1906–30.

de Marly 1987
Diana de Marly. *Costume and Civilization: Louis XIV and Versailles.* New York, 1987.

Denis 1999
Isabelle Denis. "Henri Lerambert et l'histoire d'Artémise: Des dessins d'Antoine Caron aux tapisseries." In *La tapisserie au XVIIe siècle et les collections européennes: Actes du colloque international de Chambord, 18 et 19 octobre 1996.* Paris, 1999: 33–50.

De Tolnay 1943
Charles De Tolnay. *History and Technique of Old Master Drawings.* New York, 1943.

D'Eugny and Coursaget 1945
Anne d'Eugny, with René Coursaget. *Au temps de Baudelaire, Guys, et Nadar.* Paris, 1945.

Dézallier d'Argenville 1745
Antoine-Joseph Dézallier d'Argenville. *Abrégé de la vie des plus fameux peintres . . .* 3 vols. Paris, 1745.

Dézallier d'Argenville 1762
Antoine-Joseph Dézallier d'Argenville. *Abrégé de la vie des plus fameux peintres . . .* 2nd. rev. ed. 4 vols. Paris, 1762.

Diderot 1957
Denis Diderot. *Salons (1759–81).* Ed. Jean Adhémar and Jean Seznec. 4 vols. Oxford, 1957.

Dimier 1900
Louis Dimier. *Le Primatice: Peintre, sculpteur et architecte des rois de France.* Paris, 1900.

Dittrich 1997
Christian Dittrich. *Van Eyck, Bruegel, Rembrandt: Niederländische Zeichnungen des 15. bis 17. Jahrhunderts aus dem Kupferstich-Kabinett Dresden.* Eurasburg, 1997.

Dodgson 1910
Campbell Dodgson. "Zu den Holzschnitten Jan Swarts." *Mitteilungen der Gesellschaft für vervielfältigende Kunst.* Supplement to *Graphischen Künste* 33 (1910): 33–35.

Draper 1943
Benjamin Poff Draper. "American Indians—Barbizon Style." *Antiques* 44 (1943): 108–110.

Duflo 1988
Pierre Duflo. *Constantin Guys, fou de dessin, grand reporter, 1802–1892.* Paris, 1988.

Dunn 1988
Marilyn R. Dunn. "Nuns as Art Patrons: The Decoration of S. Marta al Collegio Romano." *AB* 70 (1988): 451–477.

Duparc 1980
Frederik J. Duparc. "Een teruggevonden schilderij van N. Berchem en J. B. Weenix." *Oud Holland* 94 (1980): 37–43.

Duplessis 1857
Georges Duplessis. *Mémoires et journal de J.-G. Wille, graveur du roi*. 2 vols. Paris, 1857.

Dupuy-Vachey 2003
Marie-Anne Dupuy-Vachey. *Fragonard et le Roland Furieux*. Paris, 2003.

Durand 1983
Jean-Pierre Durand. *Bronzes de la Renaissance*. Geneva, 1983.

Dürer 1971
Albrecht Dürer: Diary of His Journey to the Netherlands, 1520–1521. Introduction by J.-A. Goris and G. Marlier. Trans. Philip Troutman. Greenwich, Conn., 1971.

Egmont 1920–23
John Perceval, First Earl of Egmont. *Manuscripts of the Earl of Egmont, Diary of Viscount Percival afterwards First Earl of Egmont*. 3 vols. London, 1920–23.

Einem 1976
H. von Einem. "Zur Deutung des Heuwagentriptychons von Hieronymus Bosch." *Castrum Peregrini* 121/122 (1976): 11–30.

Eisler 1958
Colin T. Eisler. "The Egmont Albums: A New Collection of Drawings for Yale." *Yale University Library Gazette* 32, no. 3 (1958): 84–92.

Eisler 1963
Colin T. Eisler. "A New Drawing by Jacques de Bellange at Yale." *MD* 1 (1963): 32–38.

Eisler 1975
Colin T. Eisler. *The Seeing Hand: A Treasury of Great Master Drawings*. New York, 1975.

Eisler 1989
Colin T. Eisler. *The Genius of Jacopo Bellini*. New York, 1989.

Eitner 1972
Lorenz E. A. Eitner. *Géricault's "Raft of the Medusa."* London, 1972.

Eitner 1983
Lorenz E. A. Eitner. *Géricault: His Life and Work*. London, 1983.

Elen 1989
Albert J. Elen. *Missing Old Master Drawings from the Franz Koenigs Collection*. The Hague, 1989.

Elen 1995
Albert J. Elen. *Italian Late-Medieval and Renaissance Drawing Books from Giovannino de' Grassi to Palma Giovane: A Codicological Approach*. Ph.D. thesis, Rijksuniversiteit te Leiden, 1995.

***El Escorial* 1987**
El Escorial: Eighth Wonder of the World. Madrid, 1987.

Ellesmere 1898
Charles Francis Granville Egerton, Lord Ellesmere. *Catalogue of the Bridgewater and Ellesmere Collections of Pictures and Statuary...* London, 1898.

Emiliani 1985
Andrea Emiliani. *Federico Barocci: Urbino, 1535–1612*. Bologna, 1985.

***Encyclopédie* 1782–1832**
Encyclopédie méthodique. Vols. 46–48: *Beaux-arts*. Paris and Liège, 1782–1832.

Falconieri 1835
Carlo Falconieri. *Memoria intorno alla vita ed alle opere di Bartolomeo Pinelli*. Naples, 1835.

Faranda 1986
Franco Faranda. *Ludovico Cardi detto il Cigoli*. Rome, 1986.

Farmer 1981
John David Farmer. *Bernard van Orley of Brussels*. Ph.D. diss., Princeton University, 1981.

Fehl 1979
Philip P. Fehl. "Farewell to Jokes: The Last 'Capricci' of Giovanni Domenico Tiepolo and the Tradition of Irony in Venetian Painting." *Critical Inquiry* 5 (1979): 761–791.

Feinberg 1991
Larry J. Feinberg. "Florentine Draftsmanship under the First Medici Grand Dukes." In Oberlin–Brunswick–Hanover 1991: 8–36.

Fenaille 1903–23
Maurice Fenaille. *État général des tapisseries de la Manufacture des Gobelins depuis son origine jusqu'à nos jours, 1600–1900*. 5 vols. Paris, 1903–23.

Ferrari 1992
Daniela Ferrari, ed. *Giulio Romano, repertorio di fonti documentarie*. Rome, 1992.

Filedt Kok 1990
Jan Piet Filedt Kok. "Jacques de Gheyn II: Engraver, Designer, and Publisher, I." *Print Quarterly* 7 (1990): 248–281.

Filedt Kok 1993
Jan Piet Filedt Kok. "Hendrick Goltzius: Engraver, Designer, and Publisher, 1582–1600." In *Goltzius Studies: Hendrick Goltzius, 1558–1617*. Nederlands kunsthistorisch jaarboek, vols. 42–43. Zwolle, 1993: 159–218.

Filedt Kok 1994
Jan Piet Filedt Kok. "Jan Harmensz. Muller as Printmaker, I." *Print Quarterly* 11 (1994): 223–264.

Filedt Kok 1995
Jan Piet Filedt Kok. "Jan Harmensz. Muller as Printmaker, III: Catalogue." *Print Quarterly* 12 (1995): 3–29.

Filedt Kok, Hinterding, and van der Waals 1994
Jan Piet Filedt Kok, Erik Hinterding, and Jan van der Waals. "Jan Harmensz. Muller as Printmaker, II." *Print Quarterly* 11 (1994): 351–378.

Fiocco 1925–26
Giuseppe Fiocco. "Lorenzo Tiepolo." *Bollettino d'arte* 5 (1925–26): 17–22.

Fourest 1980
Henry Pierre Fourest. *Delftware: Faience Production at Delft*. Trans. Katherine Watson. New York, 1980.

Frangi 1996
Francesco Frangi. "Milan circa 1620: L'accademia di Federico Borromeo e gli esordi di Daniele Crespi." *Nuovi studi* 1 (1996): 125–149.

Freedberg 1993
Sydney J. Freedberg. *Painting in Italy, 1500–1600*. New Haven and London, 1993.

Frey 1982
Karl and Herman-Walther Frey. *Giorgio Vasari, der literarische Nachlass*. 3 vols. Munich, 1930. Reprint, Hildesheim and New York, 1982.

Friedländer, Bock, and Rosenberg 1921–30
Max J. Friedländer, Elfried Bock, and Jakob Rosenberg. *Die Zeichnungen alter Meister im Kupferstichkabinett im Auftrage des Generaldirektors*. 2 vols. Berlin, 1921–30.

Friedländer 1922
Max J. Friedländer. *Die niederländischen Romanisten*. Leipzig, 1922.

Friedländer 1967
Max J. Friedländer, with comments and notes by Nicole Veronee-Verhaegan. *Early Netherlandish Paintings*. Trans. Heinz Norden. 14 vols. New York, 1967.

Fry 1907
Roger Fry. "Claude." *Burlington Magazine* 103 (1907): 267–275.

Fuhring 1989
Peter Fuhring. *Design into Art: Drawings for Architecture and Ornament, the Lodewijk Houthakker Collection*. 2 vols. London, 1989.

Fusconi 1996
Giulia Fusconi. "Un taccuino di disegni di Raymond Lafage." In Buonocore et al. 1996: 45–65.

Galactéros-DeBoissier 1991
Lucie Galactéros-DeBoissier. *Thomas Blanchet (1614–1689)*. Paris, 1991.

Gallenkamp 1960
George Van Derveer Gallenkamp. "Rigaud's Portrait Group at Ottawa: A Key to the Artist's Personal Life." *Journal of the Warburg and Courtauld Institutes* 23 (1960): 225–238.

Gealt 1986
Adelheid Gealt. *Domenico Tiepolo: The Punchinello Drawings*. New York, 1986.

Geffroy 1920
Gustave Geffroy. *Constantin Guys, l'historien du Second Empire*. Paris, 1920.

Geissler 1988
Heinrich Geissler. "Rudolfinische Filiationen in der Zeichenkunst um 1600." In *Prag um 1600: Beiträge zur Kunst und Kultur am Hofe Rudolfs II*. Freren, 1988: 76–78.

Gere and Pouncey 1983
John A. Gere and Philip Pouncey. *Italian Drawings in the Department of Prints and Drawings in the British Museum*. Vol. 5, *Artists Working in Rome c. 1550 to c. 1640*. 2 vols. London, 1983.

Germann-Bauer 1996
Peter Germann-Bauer. "Nachträge zum Werk des Coburber Malers Hermann Weyer." *Jahrbuch der Coburger Landesstiftung* 41 (1996): 429–444.

Gerszi 1992
Teréz Gerszi. "The Draughtsmanship of Lodewijk Toeput." *MD* 30 (1992): 367–395.

Gerszi 1999
Teréz Gerszi. "Recent Contributions to Lodewijk Toeput's Oeuvre of Drawings." In *Ex Fumo Lucem: Baroque Studies in Honor of Klára Glass*. Budapest, 1999: 89–96.

Gheyn 1971
Jacob de Gheyn. *Wapenhandelinghe van roers, musquetten, ende spiessen . . .* The Hague, 1607. Reprint, with a commentary by J. B. Kist, New York, 1971.

Gheyn 1999
Jacob de Gheyn. *The Exercise of Armes*. Ed. with introduction and captions by J. B. Kist. Mineola, N.Y., 1999.

Gibson 1981
Walter S. Gibson. "Artists and 'Rederijkers' in the Age of Bruegel." *AB* 63 (1981): 426–446.

Gibson 1992
Walter S. Gibson. "Speaking Deeds: Some Proverb Drawings by Pieter Bruegel and His Contemporaries." *Drawing* 14, no. 4 (1992): 73–77.

Gibson 2000
Walter S. Gibson. *Pleasant Places: The Rustic Landscape from Bruegel to Ruisdael*. Berkeley, Calif., 2000.

Gilbert 1952
Creighton Gilbert. "On Subject and Not-Subject in Italian Renaissance Pictures." *AB* 34 (1952): 202–216.

Goldner and Hendrix 1992
George R. Goldner and Lee Hendrix. *European Drawings: Catalogue of the [J. Paul Getty Museum] Collections*. Vol. 2. Malibu, Calif., 1992.

Goldstein 1967
Carl Goldstein. "Louis XIV and Jason." *AB* 49 (1967): 327–329.

Goldstein 1976
Nathan Goldstein. *Figure Drawing: The Structure, Anatomy, and Expressive Design of Human Form*. Englewood Cliffs, N.J., 1976.

Goncourt 1875
Edmond de Goncourt. *Catalogue raisonné de l'oeuvre peint, dessiné, et gravé d'Antoine Watteau*. Paris, 1875.

Goncourt 1881
Edmond de Goncourt. *La maison d'un artiste*. Paris, 1881.

Goncourt and Goncourt 1981
Edmond de Goncourt and Jules de Goncourt. *French XVII Century Painters*. Trans. with an introduction by Robin Ironside. 2d ed. London, 1981.

González de Zárate 1992–96
Jesús María González de Zárate. *Real colección de estampas de San Lorenzo de El Escorial*. 10 vols. Madrid, 1992–96.

Gordley 1988
Barbara Pike Gordley. *The Drawings of Beccafumi*. Ph.D. diss., Princeton University, 1988.

Graf 1986
Dieter Graf. *Die Handzeichnungen von Giacinto Calandrucci*. Düsseldorf, 1986.

Grasselli 2001
Margaret Morgan Grasselli. Review of Rosenberg and Prat 1996. *MD* (39) 2001: 310–334.

Gregori 1973
Mina Gregori. *Affreschi della certosa di Garegnano*. Modena, 1973.

Griffiths and Hartley 1997
Anthony Griffiths and Craig Hartley. *Jacques Bellange, c. 1575–1616: Printmaker of Lorraine*. London, 1997.

Grodecki 1987
Catherine Grodecki. "Luca Penni et le milieu parisien, à propos de son inventaire après décès." In *"Il se rendit en Italie": Études offertes à André Chastel*. Rome and Paris, 1987: 259–269.

Grodecki, Perrot, and Taralon 1978
Louis Grodecki, Françoise Perrot, and Jean Taralon. *Les vitraux de Paris, de la région parisienne, de la Picardie, et du Nord-Pas-de-Calais*. Corpus Vitrearum Medii Aevi: France, Recensement des vitraux anciens de la France, vol 1. Paris, 1978.

Grove 1996
Jane Turner, ed. *The Dictionary of Art*. 34 vols. London, 1996.

Guasti 1857
Carlo Guasti. *La cupola di Santa Maria del Fiore*. Florence, 1857.

Guiffrey 1920
Jules Guiffrey. *Les dessins de l'histoire des rois de France, par Nicolas Houël*. Paris, 1920.

Günther 1913
Robert Theodore Günther. *Pausilypon, the Imperial Villa near Naples*. Oxford, 1913.

Hall 1945
Constantin Guys, Flushing 1805: Paris 1892. Introduction by Clifford Hall. Ed. Lillian Browse. London, 1945.

Hall 1979
Marcia B. Hall. *Renovation and Counter-Reformation: Vasari and Duke Cosimo in Sta. Maria Novella and Sta. Croce, 1565–1577*. Oxford, 1979.

Hammond and Austin 1987
John H. Hammond and Jill Austin. *The Camera Lucida in Art and Science*. Bristol, 1987.

Handbook **1992**
Handbook of the Collections: Yale University Art Gallery. New Haven, 1992.

Harris 1977
Ann Sutherland Harris. *Andrea Sacchi*. Oxford, 1977.

Harris 1985–86
Ann Sutherland Harris. Review of Bloomington–Pittsburgh–Oberlin 1983. *MD* 23/24 (1985–86): 94–100.

Harris 1992
Ann Sutherland Harris. Review of Lugano–Rome 1989–90. *MD* 30 (1992): 216–223.

Hartt 1958
Frederick Hartt. *Giulio Romano*. 2 vols. New Haven, 1958.

Harvard 2003
Harvard University Art Museums. *Annual Report 2001–2002*. Cambridge, Mass., 2003.

Haverkamp-Begemann 1969
Egbert Haverkamp-Begemann. "Frans Pourbus the Elder as Draughtsman." In *Miscellanea I. Q. van Regteren Altena*. Amsterdam, 1969: 65–66.

Haverkamp-Begemann and Logan 1970
Egbert Haverkamp-Begemann and Anne-Marie S. Logan. *European Drawings and Watercolors in the Yale University Art Gallery, 1500–1900*. 2 vols. New Haven and London, 1970.

Heawood 1950
Edward Heawood. *Watermarks, Mainly of the 17th and 18th Centuries*. Hilversum, 1950.

Hédou 1879
Jules Hédou. *Jean Le Prince et son oeuvre*. Paris, 1879.

Hefting 1969
Victorine Hefting. *Jongkind d'après sa correspondence*. Utrecht, 1969.

Hefting 1975
Victorine Hefting. *Jongkind: Sa vie, son oeuvre, son époque*. Paris, 1975.

Heikamp 1967
Detlef Heikamp. "Federico Zuccari a Firenze 1575–1579, I: La cupola del Duomo." *Paragone* 207 (1967): 44–68.

Helbig 1943
Jean Helbig. *De Glasschilderkunst in België: Repertorium en Documenten*. Antwerp, 1943.

Held 1931
Julius S. Held. *Dürers Wirkung auf die niederländische Kunst seiner Zeit*. The Hague, 1931.

Held 1967
Julius S. Held. "Tekeningen van Jacob Jordaens." *Kunstchronik* 20 (1967): 94–110.

Held 1972
Julius S. Held. Review of H-B and L. *MD* 10 (1972): 41–45.

Hellyer 1982
Mary-Elizabeth Hellyer. *Recherches sur Jean-Baptiste le Prince (1734–1781)*. Thesis, Sorbonne, 1982.

Herbert 1966
Robert L. Herbert. "Millet Reconsidered." *Museum Studies* 1 (1966): 28–111.

Hind 1938–48
Arthur M. Hind. *Early Italian Engraving*. 7 vols. London, 1938–48.

Hockney 2001
David Hockney. *Secret Knowledge: Rediscovering the Lost Secrets of the Old Masters*. New York, 2001.

Hodgson 1910
F. C. Hodgson. *Venice in the Thirteenth and Fourteenth Centuries*. London, 1910.

Hollstein 1949–
Friedrich Wilhelm Hollstein. *Dutch and Flemish Etchings, Engravings, and Woodcuts, ca. 1450–1700*. Amsterdam, 1949–.

Hollstein 1954–
Friedrich Wilhelm Hollstein. *German Engravings, Etchings, and Woodcuts, ca. 1400–1700*. Amsterdam, 1954–.

Homer 1951
Homer. *Iliad*. Trans. Richmond Lattimore. Chicago, 1951.

Hoop Scheffer 1974
Dieuwke de Hoop Scheffer. "Een serie bedelaars door Pieter Quast." *Bulletin van het Rijksmuseum* 22 (1974): 166–172.

Houbraken 1718–21
Arnold Houbraken. *De groote schouburgh der nederlantsche konstschilders en schilderessen*. 3 vols. Amsterdam, 1718–21.

Houbraken 1976
Arnold Houbraken. *De groote schouburgh der nederlantsche konstschilders en schilderessen*. 's-Gravenhage, 1753. Facsimile reprint, Amsterdam, 1976.

Houssaye 1971
Arsène Houssaye. *Les confessions: Souvenirs d'un demi-siècle, 1830–1880*. 6 vols. Paris, 1885–91. Reprint, Geneva, 1971.

Hulst 1968
Roger-Adolf d'Hulst. "Over enkele tekeningen van Maarten de Vos." In *Miscellanea Jozef Duverger: Bijdragen tot de kunstgeschiedenis der Nederlanden*. Ghent, 1968: 505–518.

Hulst 1974
Roger-Adolf d'Hulst. *Jordaens Drawings*. 4 vols. Brussels, 1974.

Hulst 1980
Roger-Adolf d'Hulst. "Jordaens Drawings: Supplement I." *MD* 18 (1980): 360–370.

Hulst 1982
Roger-Adolf d'Hulst. *Jacob Jordaens*. London, 1982.

Hulst 1990
Roger-Adolf d'Hulst. "Jordaens Drawings: Supplement II." *MD* 28 (1990): 142–172.

Husband 1998
Timothy Husband. "The Dissemination of Design in Small-Scale Glass Production: The Case of the Medieval Housebook." *Gesta* 37 (1998): 178–185.

Hüsken 1996
W. N. M. Hüsken. "The Fool as Social Critic: The Case of the Dutch Rhetoricians' Drama." In *Fools and Folly*. Ed. Clifford Davidson. Kalamazoo, Mich., 1996: 112–145.

***Illustrated Bartsch* 1971–**
Walter L. Strauss, ed. *The Illustrated Bartsch*. New York, 1971–.

Ingamells 1997
John Ingamells. *Dictionary of British and Irish Travellers in Italy, 1701–1800*. New Haven and London, 1997.

Ivins 1953
William M. Ivins, Jr. *Prints and Visual Communication*. Cambridge, Mass., 1953.

Jaffé 1966
Michael Jaffé. "Jordaens Drawings at Antwerp and Rotterdam." *Burlington Magazine* 108 (1966): 625–630.

Jaffé 1994
Michael Jaffé. *The Devonshire Collection of Italian Drawings*. 4 vols. London, 1994.

Jaffé 1997
David Jaffé. *Summary Catalogue of European Paintings in the J. Paul Getty Museum*. Los Angeles, 1997.

Jamar-Rolin 1956
Luce Jamar-Rolin. "La vie de Guys et la chronologie de son oeuvre." *Gazette des beaux-arts*, ser. 6, vol. 48 (1956): 69–112.

James et al. 1997
Carlo James et al. *Old Master Prints and Drawings: A Guide to Preservation and Conservation*. Trans. and ed. Marjorie B. Cohn. Amsterdam, 1997.

Jean-Richard 1978
Pierrette Jean-Richard. *L'oeuvre gravé de François Boucher dans la collection Edmond de Rothschild*. Musée du Louvre, Cabinet des dessins, Inventaire général des gravures, École française, vol. 1. Paris, 1978.

Joachim and McCullagh 1979
Harold Joachim and Suzanne Folds McCullagh. *Italian Drawings in the Art Institute of Chicago*. Chicago and London, 1979.

Joachim 1980
Harold Joachim. *Italian Drawings of the 18th and 19th Centuries and Spanish Drawings of the 17th through 19th Centuries*. Chicago, 1980.

Jobert 1997
Barthélémy Jobert. *Delacroix*. Paris, 1997.

Johnson 1978
Lee Johnson. "La collection Charles Cournault." *Bulletin de la Société de l'Histoire de l'Art Français*. (1978): 249–262.

Johnson 1981–89
Lee Johnson. *The Paintings of Eugène Delacroix: A Critical Catalogue*. 5 vols. Oxford, 1981–89.

Jong 1998
Jan de Jong. "Il pittore a le volte è puro poeta: Cupid and Psyche in Italian Renaissance Painting." In *Aspects of Apuleius' Golden Ass*. Vol. 2. Groningen, 1998: 189–215.

Judson 1969
J. Richard Judson. "Martin de Vos' Representations of 'Jonah Cast over the Side.'" In *Miscellanea I. Q. van Regteren Altena*. Amsterdam, 1969: 82–87.

Judson 1973
J. Richard Judson. *The Drawings of Jacob de Gheyn II*. New York, 1973.

Jullienne 1726–28
Jean de Jullienne. *Figures de différents caractères, de paysage, et études dessinés d'après nature par Jean-Antoine Watteau*. Paris, 1726–28.

Junquera de Vega 1963
P. Junquera de Vega. "El Obrador de Bordado de San Lorenzo de El Escorial." In *El Escorial*. Madrid, 1963: 551–582.

Katritzky 1987
M. A. Katritzky. "Lodewyk Toeput: Some Pictures Related to the 'Commedia dell'arte.'" *Renaissance Studies* 1 (1987): 71–125.

Kaufmann 1988
Thomas DaCosta Kaufmann. *The School of Prague: Painting at the Court of Rudolf II*. Chicago and London, 1988.

Kemp 1990
Martin Kemp. *The Science of Art: Optical Themes in Western Art from Brunelleschi to Seurat*. New Haven and London, 1990.

Keyes 1975
George S. Keyes. *Cornelis Vroom: Marine and Landscape Artist*. Alphen ann den Rijn, 1975.

Keyes 1982
George S. Keyes. "Hendrick and Cornelis Vroom: Addenda." *MD* 20 (1982): 115–124.

Keyes 1984
George S. Keyes. *Esaias van den Velde, 1587–1630*. Doornspijk, 1984.

Keyser 1939–40
Paul de Keyser. "Rhetoricale toelichting bij het hooi en den hooiwagen." *Gentsche Bijdragen tot de kunstgeschiedenis* 6 (1939–40): 127–138.

Kitson 1961
Michael Kitson. "The Place of Drawings in the Art of Claude Lorrain." In *Studies in Western Art: Acts of the XXth International Congress of the History of Art*. Vol. 3. New York, 1961: 96–112.

Kitson 1978
Michael Kitson. *Claude Lorrain: 'Liber veritatis.'* London, 1978.

Klossowski 1923
Erich Klossowski. *Honoré Daumier*. 3d ed. Munich, 1923.

Knowles 1831
John Knowles, ed. *The Life and Writings of Henry Fuseli*. 3 vols. London, 1831.

Knox 1983
George Knox. "Domenico Tiepolo's Punchinello Drawings: Satire, or Labor of Love?" In *Satire in the 18th Century*. Ed. J. D. Browning. New York and London, 1983: 124–146.

Knox 1984
George Knox. "The Punchinello Drawings of Giambattista Tiepolo." In *Interpretazioni veneziane: Studi di storia dell'arte in onore di Michelangelo Muraro*. Ed. David Rosand. Venice, 1984: 439–446.

Konody 1930
P. G. Konody. *The Painter of Victorian Life*. Ed. C. Geoffrey Holme. London, 1930.

Koschatzky, Oberhuber, and Knab 1971
Walter Koschatzky, Konrad Oberhuber, and Eckhart Knab. *Italian Drawings in the Albertina*. Greenwich, Conn., 1971.

Kräftner, Stockhammer, and Körner 2004
Johann Kräftner, Andrea Stockhammer, and Stefan Körner. *Liechtenstein Museum Wien: Die Sammlungen*. Munich, 2004.

Laborde 1877
Léon de Laborde. *Les comptes des bâtiments du roi (1528–1571)*. 2 vols. Paris, 1877. Reprint, Nogent-le-Roi, 1999.

Lafage 1689
Recueil des meilleurs desseins de Raimond La Fage gravé par cinq des plus habiles graveurs, et mis en lumière par les soins de Vander-Bruggen. Paris, 1689.

Lamers 1995
Petra Lamers. *Il viaggio nel sud dell'Abbé de Saint-Non.* Naples, 1995.

Landau 1991
David Landau. "Beccafumi." Review of Siena 1990. *Print Quarterly* 8 (1991): 450–451.

Landau and Parshall 1994
David Landau and Peter Parshall. *The Renaissance Print, 1470–1550.* New Haven and London, 1994.

Landau 1983
Ellen G. Landau. "A 'Fairytale Circumstance': The Influence of Stage Design on the Work of François Boucher." *Bulletin of the Cleveland Museum of Art* 70 (1983): 360–378.

Lankrink 1945
"P. H. Lankrink's Collection." *Burlington Magazine* 86 (1945): 29–35.

Lapauze 1903
Henry Lapauze. *Les portraits dessinés de J.-A.-D. Ingres.* 2 vols. Paris, 1903.

Lapauze 1911
Henry Lapauze. *Ingres, sa vie et son oeuvre.* Paris, 1911.

Laran et al.
Jean Laran et al. *Inventaire du fonds français après 1800.* 15 vols. Paris, 1930–.

Larcher Crosato 1985
Luciana Larcher Crosato. "Di 'Quattro Stagioni' del Pozzoserrato e la grafica fiamminga." *Münchner Jahrbuch der bildenden Kunst* 36 (1985): 119–130.

Larcher Crosato 1988
Luciana Larcher Crosato. "I piaceri della villa nel Pozzoserrato." In Mason Rinaldi and Luciani 1988: 71–78.

Larkin 1966
Oliver W. Larkin. *Daumier, Man of His Time.* New York, Toronto, and London, 1966.

Launay 1991
Elisabeth Launay. *Les frères Goncourt: Collectionneurs de dessins.* Paris, 1991.

Lavin 1990
Irving Lavin. "Bernini and the Art of Social Satire." In *Modern Art and Popular Culture: Readings in High and Low.* Ed. Kirk Varnedoe and Adam Gopnik. New York, 1990: 19–50.

Lebeer and Grauls 1938
Louis Lebeer and Jan Grauls. "Het hooi en de hooiwagen in de beeldende kunsten." *Gentsche Bijdragen tot de kunstgeschiedenis* 5 (1938): 141–177.

Lecchini Giovannoni 1991
Simona Lecchini Giovannoni. *Alessandro Allori.* Turin, 1991.

Le Comte 1699–1700
Florent Le Comte. *Cabinet des singularitez d'architecture, peinture, sculpture, et graveure.* 3 vols. Paris, 1699–1700.

Le Comte 1972
Florent Le Comte. *Cabinet des singularitez d'architecture, peinture, sculpture, et graveure.* Paris, 1699–1700. Reprint, Geneva, 1972.

Leja 2004
Jan L. Leja. *Ferdinand Bol and Rembrandt: Authorship and Iconography in Drawings of Biblical Subjects, c. 1636–c. 1650.* 2 vols. Ph.D. diss., New York University, 2004.

Lemoisne 1946–48
Paul André Lemoisne. *Degas et son oeuvre.* 4 vols. Paris, 1946–48.

Leone di Castris 2001
Pierluigi Leone di Castris. *Polidoro da Caravaggio: L'opera completa.* Naples, 2001.

Lieure 1924–29
Jacques Lieure. *Jacques Callot.* 8 vols. Paris, 1924–29.

Lincoln 2000
Evelyn Lincoln. *The Invention of the Italian Renaissance Printmaker.* New Haven and London, 2000.

Lingo 1998
Stuart P. Lingo. *The Capuchins and the Art of History: Retrospection and Reform in the Arts of Late Renaissance Italy.* Ph.D. diss., Harvard University, 1998.

Lorizzo 2003
Loredana Lorizzo. "Documenti inediti sul mercato dell'arte: I testamenti e l'inventario della bottega del genovese Pellegrino Peri 'rivenditore di quadri' a Roma nel seconda metà del seicento." In *Decorazione e collezionismo a Roma nel seicento.* Ed. Silvia Danesi Squarzina. Rome, 2003: 159–174.

Lugt 1921–56
Frits Lugt. *Les marques de collections de dessins et d'estampes.* 2 vols. Amsterdam, 1921. Supplement, The Hague, 1956.

Lugt 1952
Frits Lugt. "Rembrandt: Follower and Innovator." *Art News* 51, no. 6 (1952): 38–40.

Lugt 1968
Frits Lugt. *Inventaire général des dessins des écoles du Nord, maîtres des anciens Pays-Bas.* Paris, 1968.

Mahon 1947
Denis Mahon. *Studies in Seicento Art and Theory.* London, 1947.

Mahon and Turner 1989
Denis Mahon and Nicholas Turner. *The Drawings of Guercino in the Collection of Her Majesty the Queen at Windsor Castle.* Cambridge, 1989.

Maison 1960
K. E. Maison. *Daumier Drawings.* New York and London, 1960.

Maison 1996
K. E. Maison. *Honoré Daumier: Catalogue Raisonné of the Paintings, Watercolours, and Drawings.* 2 vols. London, 1968. Reprint, San Francisco, 1996.

Malgouyres 2000
Philippe Malgouyres. *Peintures françaises du XVIIe siècle: La collection du Musée des Beaux-Arts de Rouen.* Paris and Rouen, 2000.

Manzitti 1972
Camillo Manzitti. *Valerio Castello.* Genoa, 1972.

Manzitti 2004
Camillo Manzitti. *Valerio Castello.* Turin, 2004.

Marciari 2000
John Marciari. *Girolamo Muziano and Art in Rome, circa 1550–1600.* Ph.D. diss., Yale University, 2000.

Mariette 1851–60
Pierre-Jean Mariette. *Abecedario de P. J. Mariette et autres notes inédites de cet amateur sur les arts et les artistes.* Ed. Ph. de Chennevières and A. de Montaiglon. 6 vols. Paris, 1851–60.

Marijnissen 1987
Roger H. Marijnissen, assisted by Peter Ruyffelaere. *Hieronymus Bosch: The Complete Works*. Trans. Ted Alkins et al. Antwerp, 1987.

Mariuz 1971
Adriano Mariuz. *Giandomenico Tiepolo*. Venice, 1971.

Mariuz 1986
Adriano Mariuz. "I disegni di Pulcinella di Giandomenico Tiepolo." *Arte Veneta* 60 (1986): 265–273.

Mason 2000
Stefania Mason. "Low Life and Landscape: 'Minor pictura' in Late Sixteenth-Century Venice." In Aikema and Brown 2000: 558–613.

Mason Rinaldi and Luciani 1988
Stefania Mason Rinaldi and Domenico Luciani, eds. *Toeput a Treviso: Ludovico Pozzoserrato, Lodewijk Toeput, pittore neerlandese nella civiltà veneta del tardo cinquecento*. Asolo, 1988.

Matheson 2001
Susan Matheson. *Art for Yale: A History of the Yale University Art Gallery*. New Haven, 2001.

Matteoli 1980
Anna Matteoli. *Ludovico Cardi-Cigoli, pittore e architetto*. Pisa, 1980.

Mayer 1931–32
H. Mayer. "H. E. Weyer." *Öffentliche Kunstsammlung Basel Jahresberichte* 28/29 (1931–32): 96–119.

McCullagh 1991
Suzanne Folds McCullagh. "Serendipity in a Solander Box: A Recently Discovered Pastel and Chalk Drawing by Federico Barocci." *The Art Institute of Chicago Museum Studies* 17 (1991): 52–65.

McCullagh and Giles 1997
Suzanne Folds McCullagh and Laura Giles. *Italian Drawings before 1600 in the Art Institute of Chicago*. Chicago, 1997.

McGrath 1998
Thomas McGrath. "Federico Barocci and the History of 'Pastelli' in Italy." *Apollo* 148 (1998): 3–9.

McKim-Smith 1980
Gridley McKim-Smith. "The Problem of Velazquez's Drawings." *MD* 18 (1980): 3–24.

Meijer 1988
Bert Meijer. "A proposito della vanità della ricchezza e di Ludovico Pozzoserrato." In Mason Rinaldi and Luciani 1988, 109–124.

Menegazzi 1957
Luigi Menegazzi. "Ludovico Pozzoserrato." *Saggi e memorie di storia dell'arte* 1 (1957): 165–224.

Menegazzi 1961
Luigi Menegazzi. "Giunte a Ludovico Pozzoserrato." *Arte veneta* 15 (1961): 119–126.

Menegazzi 1988
Luigi Menegazzi. "Grafica del Pozzoserrato." In Mason Rinaldi and Luciani 1988: 65–70.

Mérot 1996
Alain Mérot, ed. *Les conférences de l'Académie Royale de Peinture et de Sculpture au XVIIe siècle*. Paris, 1996.

Mieder and Sobieski 1999
Wolfgang Mieder and Janet Sobieski. *Proverb Iconography: An International Bibliography*. New York, 1999.

Miller 2002
Michael Miller. "Two Drawings by Perino del Vaga for Castel Sant'Angelo." In *Festschrift für Konrad Oberhuber*. Milan, 2002: 98–105.

Mireur 1911–12
Hippolyte Mireur. *Dictionnaire des ventes d'art faites en France et à l'étranger pendant les XVIIIième et XIXième siècles*. 7 vols. Paris, 1911–12.

Moir 1970
Alfred Moir. "Some Caracciolo Drawings in Stockholm." *AB* 52 (1970): 184–187.

Molière 1965
Jean-Baptiste Poquelin de Molière. *Oeuvres complètes*. 2 vols. Paris, 1965.

Monbeig Goguel 1972
Catherine Monbeig Goguel. *Vasari et son temps*. Musée du Louvre, Inventaire général des dessins italiens, vol. 1: Maîtres toscans nés après 1500, morts avant 1600. Paris, 1972.

Monbeig Goguel 1976
Catherine Monbeig Goguel. "À propos d'un dessin retrouvé: Vasari et Zuccaro à la coupole du Dôme de Florence." In *Vasari storiografo e artista*. Arezzo and Florence, 1976: 85–89.

Mongan 1965
Agnes Mongan. "Three Views of a Drummer by Antoine Watteau." In *Fogg Art Museum Acquisitions 1964*. Cambridge, Mass., 1965: 42–48.

Mongan, Hofer, and Seznec 1945
Elizabeth Mongan, Philip Hofer, and Jean Seznec. *Fragonard Drawings for Ariosto*. New York, 1945.

Monnier 1972
Geneviève Monnier. *Pastels: XVIIème et XVIIIème siècles*. Musée du Louvre, Cabinet des dessins, Inventaire des collections publiques françaises, vol. 18. Paris, 1972.

Montagu 1968
Jennifer Montagu. "The Painted Enigma and French Seventeenth-Century Art." *Journal of the Warburg and Courtauld Institutes* 31 (1968): 307–335.

Montagu 1994
Jennifer Montagu. *The Expression of the Passions: The Origin and Influence of Charles Le Brun's "Conférence sur l'expression générale et particulière."* New Haven, 1994.

Montague Massengale 1979
Jean Montague Massengale. "Hubert Robert Drawings and Water-Colors at the National Gallery of Art." *Burlington Magazine* 121 (1979): 64–68.

Montalto 1955
Lina Montalto. "Gli affreschi del Palazzo Pamphilj in Valmontone." *Commentari* 6 (1955): 267–285.

Montanari 1997
Tommaso Montanari. "Gian Lorenzo Bernini e Sforza Pallavicino." *Prospettiva* 87/88 (1997): 42–68.

Montanari 1998
Tommaso Montanari. "Bernini e Cristina di Svezia: Alle origini della Storiografia Berniniana." In Angelini 1998: 344–345.

Montias 1987
John Michael Montias. "Vermeer's Clients and Patrons." *AB* 69 (1987): 68–76.

Morassi 1941
Antonio Morassi. "Domenico Tiepolo." *Emporium* 95 (1941), 265–282.

Moreau-Nélaton 1916
Étienne Moreau-Nélaton. *Delacroix raconté par lui-même*. 2 vols. Paris, 1916.

Moreau-Nélaton 1918
Étienne Moreau-Nélaton. *Jongkind raconté par lui-même*. Paris, 1918.

Moreau-Nélaton 1921
Étienne Moreau-Nélaton. *Millet raconté par lui-même*. 3 vols. Paris, 1921.

Morrall 2001
Andrew Morrall. *Jörg Breu the Elder: Art, Culture, and Belief in Reformation Augsburg*. Aldershot, 2001.

Mortari 1982
Luisa Mortari. *Francesco Salviati*. Rome, 1982.

Mulcahy 1994
Rosemarie Mulcahy. *The Decoration of the Royal Basilica of El Escorial*. Cambridge, 1994.

Munhall 1962
Edgar Munhall. "Claude Gillot's 'Feast of Pan.'" *YUAG Bulletin* 27 (1962): 22–35.

Naef 1958
Hans Naef. "Ingres' Portraits of the Marcotte Family." *AB* 40 (1958): 336–344.

Naef 1977–80
Hans Naef. *Die Bildniszeichnungen von J.-A.-D. Ingres*. 5 vols. Bern, 1977–80.

Nagel 1997
Alexander Nagel. "Gifts for Michelangelo and Vittoria Colonna." *AB* 79 (1997): 647–668.

Nagel 2000
Alexander Nagel. *Michelangelo and the Reform of Art*. Cambridge, 2000.

Nagler 1835–52
G. K. Nagler, ed. *Neues allgemeines Künstlerlexicon; oder, Nachrichten von dem Leben und den Werken der Maler, Bildhauer, Baumeister, Kupferstecher, etc*. 22 vols. Munich, 1835–52.

Neils and Oakley 2003
Jenifer Neils and John H. Oakley. *Coming of Age in Ancient Greece*. New Haven and London, 2003.

Neilson 1973
Nancy Ward Neilson. "Some Drawings by Daniele Crespi." *Burlington Magazine* 115 (1973): 382–385.

Neilson 1996
Nancy Ward Neilson. *Daniele Crespi*. Soncino, 1996.

Nelson 1998
Kristi Nelson. *Jacob Jordaens: Design for Tapestry*. Turnhout, 1998.

Newcome 1975
Mary Newcome. "The Drawings of Valerio Castello." *MD* 13 (1975): 26–40.

Newcome Schleier 1981
Mary Newcome Schleier. "More Drawings by Valerio Castello." In *Per A. E. Popham*. Parma, 1981: 187–189.

New Hollstein 1993–
Friedrich W. Hollstein. *The New Dutch and Flemish Etchings, Engravings, and Woodcuts, ca. 1450–1700*. Rotterdam, 1993–.

New Hollstein 1996–
Friedrich W. Hollstein. *The New German Engravings, Etchings, and Woodcuts, ca. 1400–1700*. Rotterdam, 1996–.

Niederstein 1931
Albrecht Niederstein. "Das graphische Werk des Bartholomäus Spranger." *Repertorium für Kunstwissenschaft* 52 (1931): 1–33.

Noack and Noack 2005
Lillian and Dieter Noack. *The New Daumier Register©: The Digital Catalogue Raisonné on Daumier's Complete Lithographic Work*. Accessible online at http://www.daumier.org/.

North Carolina Museum of Art 1998
North Carolina Museum of Art. *Handbook of the Collections*. Raleigh, N.C., 1998.

Nova 1992
Alessandro Nova. "Salviati, Vasari, and the Reuse of Drawings in their Working Practice." *MD* 30 (1992): 83–108.

Oberhuber 1958
Konrad Oberhuber. *Die stilistische Entwicklung im Werk des Bartholomäus Sprangers*. Ph.D. diss., Universität Wien, 1958.

Oberhuber 1967
Konrad Oberhuber. *Zwischen Renaissance und Barock: Das Zeitalter von Bruegel und Bellange*. Vienna, 1967.

Oberhuber 2000
Konrad Oberhuber. "Visual Teaching of Love: Farnesina and Palazzo Te." *Fontes* 3 (2000): 173–180.

Olsen 1962
Harald Olsen. *Federico Barocci*. Copenhagen, 1962.

Olson 1980
Roberta J. M. Olson. "Bartolomeo Pinelli: An Underestimated Ottocento Master." *Drawing* 2, no. 4 (1980): 73–78.

Olszewski 1981
Edward J. Olszewski. *The Draftsman's Eye: Late Italian Renaissance Schools and Styles*. Cleveland, 1981.

O'Neill 1984a
Mary O'Neill. "Hyacinthe Rigaud's Drawings for his Engravers." *Burlington Magazine* 126 (1984): 674–683.

O'Neill 1984b
Mary O'Neill. "Three Drawings in American Collections after Portraits by Rigaud." *MD* 22 (1984): 186–194.

Orenstein 1996
Nadine M. Orenstein. *Hendrick Hondius and the Business of Prints in Seventeenth-Century Holland*. Rotterdam, 1996.

Orlandi 1704
Pellegrino Antonio Orlandi. *Abecedario pittorico nel quale compendiosamente sono descritte le patrie, i maestri, ed i tempi . . .* Bologna, 1704.

Orlandi 1719
Pellegrino Antonio Orlandi. *L'abecedario pittorico: Dall'autore ristampato corretto et accresciuto di molti professori e di altre notizie spettani alla pittura . . .* Bologna, 1719.

Padovani 2000
S. Padovani. "Il quartiere dei cardinali e principi forestieri: L'arte e la storia." In *Palazzo Pitti*. Ed. Marco Chiarini. Florence, 2000: 45–53.

Parma 2000
Elena Parma. "La 'Favola di Amore e Psiche' interpretata da Perino del Vaga nel Palazzo di Andrea Doria a Genova e in Castel Sant'Angelo a Roma." *Fontes* 3 (2000): 205–223.

Parma Armani 1986
Elena Parma Armani. *Perin del Vaga: L'anello mancante*. Genoa, 1986.

Passeron 1981
Roger Passeron. *Daumier*. New York, 1981.

Pedrocco 1988
Filippo Pedrocco. *Giandomenico Tiepolo a Zianigo*. Villorba, 1988.

Percy and Cazort 2004
Ann Percy and Mimi Cazort. *Italian Master Drawings at the Philadelphia Museum of Art*. Philadelphia, 2004.

Perreau 2004
Stéphan Perreau. *Hyacinthe Rigaud, 1659–1743: Le peintre des rois*. Montpellier, 2004.

Piccard 1961–
Gerhard Piccard. *Die Wasserzeichenkartei Piccard im Hauptstaatsarchiv Stuttgart*. Stuttgart, 1961–.

Pilliod 2001
Elizabeth Pilliod. *Pontormo Bronzino Allori: A Genealogy of Florentine Art*. New Haven and London, 2001.

Pillsbury 1976
Edmund Pillsbury. "Barocci at Bologna and Florence." *MD* 14 (1976): 56–64.

Plomp 1999
Michiel C. Plomp. "Leonaert Bramer (1596–1674) als ontwerper van decoratie op Delfts aardewerk." *Oud Holland* 113 (1999): 197–216.

Plomp 2003
Michiel C. Plomp. "Bernaert van Orley." In "Recent Acquisitions, A Selection: 2002–2003." *Metropolitan Museum of Art Bulletin* 61, no. 2 (fall 2003): 18.

Poitout 1999
Louis Adolphe Poitout. *Johan Barthold Jongkind, 1819–1891, vu par un ami de la famille Fesser: Manuscrit de Louis Adolphe Poitout, 1857–1913, fin de rédaction dans les années 1905–1910*. Paris, 1999.

Poley 1938
Heinz-Joachim Poley. *Claude Gillot, Leben und Werk (1673–1722): Ein Beitrag zur französischen Kunstgeschichte des XVIII Jahrhunderts*. Würzberg-Aumühle, 1938.

Pomponi 1996
Massimo Pomponi. "Schedatura dei disegni del taccuino." In Buonocore et al. 1996: 73–87.

Pope-Hennessy 1948
John Pope-Hennessy. *The Drawings of Domenichino in the Collection of His Majesty the King at Windsor Castle*. New York, 1948.

Popham 1932
A. E. Popham. *Catalogue of Drawings by Dutch and Flemish Artists Preserved in the Department of Prints and Drawings in the British Museum*. Vol. 5, *Dutch and Flemish Drawings of the XV and XVI Centuries*. London, 1932.

Popham 1968
A. E. Popham. "A Drawing by Vincenzo Caccianemici?" *MD* 6 (1968): 246–248.

Populus 1930
Bernard Populus. *Claude Gillot (1673–1722): Catalogue de l'oeuvre gravé*. Paris, 1930.

Portalis 1880
Roger Portalis. "La Collection Walferdin et ses Fragonard." *Gazette des beaux-arts*, ser. 2, vol. 21 (1880): 297–322.

Portalis and Béraldi 1880–82
Roger Portalis and Henri Béraldi. *Les graveurs du dix-huitième siècle*. 3 vols. Paris, 1880–82. Facsimile ed., Paris, 2001.

Poussou, Mézin, and Perret-Gentil 2004
Jean-Pierre Poussou, Anne Mézin, and Yves Perret-Gentil, eds. *L'influence française en Russie au XVIIIe siècle*. Paris, 2004.

Powell 1951
Nicholas Powell. *The Drawings of Henry Fuseli*. London, 1951.

Preiss 1975
Pavel Preiss. "Franz Karl Palko als Zeichner." *Bulletin du Musée Hongrois des Beaux-Arts* 45 (1975): 63–108.

Preiss 1996
Pavel Preiss. *Rakouská kresba 18. století: Vybraná díla z ceskych a moravsk´ch sbírek*. Prague, 1996.

Preiss 1999
Pavel Preiss. *František Karel Palko: Život a dílo malíře sklonku středoevropského baroka a jeho bratra Františka Antonína Palka*. Prague, 1999.

Preiss 2005
Pavel Preiss. "'Remotiora Prope': An Unpublished Galileo Drawing by Franz Karel Palko: A Few Remarks." *YUAG Bulletin* (2005): 115–119.

Prijateli 1980
Kruno Prijateli. "Una nuova 'Sacra Conversazione' di Bernardino Licinio." *Arte veneta* 34 (1980): 151–153.

Procacci 1954
Ugo Procacci. "Una 'Vita' inedita del Muziano." *Arte veneta* 8 (1954): 242–264.

Prohaska 1978
Wolfgang Prohaska. "Beiträge zu Battistello Caracciolo." *Jahrbuch der Kunsthistorisches Sammlung Wien* 74 (1978): 153–269.

Prybram-Gladona 1969
Charlotte von Prybram-Gladona. *Unbekannte Zeichnungen alter Meister aus europäischem Privatbesitz*. Munich, 1969.

Puyvelde 1942
Leo van Puyvelde. *The Flemish Drawings in the Collection of His Majesty the King at Windsor Castle*. London and New York, 1942.

Raimondi 1966
Ezio Raimondi. *Anatomie secentesche*. Pisa, 1966.

Raimondi 1958
Riccardo Raimondi. *Degas e la sua famiglia in Napoli, 1793–1917*. Naples, 1958.

Rand 1914
Benjamin Rand. *Berkeley and Percival: The Correspondence of George Berkeley, afterwards Bishop of Cloyne, and Sir John Percival, afterwards Earl of Egmont*. Cambridge, 1914.

Ratouis de Limay 1946
Paul Ratouis de Limay. *Le pastel en France au XVIIIe siècle*. Paris, 1946.

Raux 1995
Sophie Raux. *Catalogue des dessins français du XVIIIième siècle de Claude Gillot à Hubert Robert*. Lille, 1995.

Ravelli 1988
Lanfranco Ravelli. *Un fregio di Polidoro a Palazzo Baldassini*. Bergamo, 1988.

Rearick 1967
William R. Rearick. "A Drawing by Bernardino Licinio." *MD* 5 (1967): 382–383.

Rearick 2001
William R. Rearick. *Il disegno veneziano del cinquecento*. Milan, 2001.

Reff 1969
Theodore Reff. "More Unpublished Letters by Degas." *AB* 51 (1969): 281–289.

Reff 1974
Theodore Reff. "Works by Degas in the Detroit Institute of Arts." *Bulletin of the Detroit Institute of Arts* 53, no. 1 (1974): 1–44.

Reff 1976
Theodore Reff. *The Notebooks of Edgar Degas: A Catalogue of the Thirty-eight Notebooks in the Bibliothèque Nationale and Other Collections*. 2 vols. Oxford, 1976.

Reff 1981
Theodore Reff. *Modern Art in Paris, 1855–1900: Two-Hundred Catalogues of the Major Exhibitions Reproduced in Facsimile in Forty-Seven Volumes.* 47 vols. New York and London, 1981.

Regteren Altena 1939
I. Q. van Regteren Altena. "Aertgen van Leyden." *Oud Holland* 56 (1939): 17–25, 74–87, 129–138, 245–254.

Regteren Altena 1983
I. Q. van Regteren Altena. *Jacques de Gheyn, Three Generations.* 3 vols. The Hague, Boston, and London, 1983.

Reinold 1981
Lucinda Kate Reinold. *The Representation of the Beggar as Rogue in Dutch Seventeenth-Century Art.* Ph.D. diss., University of California, Berkeley, 1981.

Reinsch 1967
Adelheid Reinsch. *Die Zeichnungen des Marten de Vos: Stilistische und ikonographische Untersuchungen.* Diss., Eberhard-Karls-Universität, Tübingen, 1967.

Reznicek 1956
E. K. J. Reznicek. "Jan Harmensz. Muller als tekenaar." *Nederlands kunsthistorisch jaarboek* 7 (1956): 65–120.

Reznicek 1980
E. K. J. Reznicek. "Jan Harmensz. Muller as Draughtsman: Addenda." *MD* 18 (1980): 115–133.

Reznicek 1993
E. K. J. Reznicek. "Drawings by Hendrick Goltzius, Thirty Years Later." *MD* 31 (1993): 215–278.

Ridolfi 1648
Claudio Ridolfi. *Meraviglie dell'arte.* 2 vols. Venice, 1648.

Robaut 1885
Alfred Robaut. *L'oeuvre complet de Eugène Delacroix: Peintures, dessins, gravures, lithographies.* Paris, 1885.

Robbin 1990
C. R. Robbin. *Ottavio Leoni and Early Roman Baroque Portraiture.* Ph.D. diss., University of California, Santa Barbara, 1990.

Robels 1983
Hella Robels. *Niederländische Zeichnungen vom 15. bis 19. Jarhhundert im Wallraf-Richartz-Museum, Köln.* Cologne, 1983.

Robert-Dumesnil 1835–71
A.-P.-F. Robert-Dumesnil. *Le peintre-graveur français, ou catalogue raisonné des estampes gravées par les peintres et les dessinateurs de l'école française.* 11 vols. Paris, 1835–71.

Roberts 1986
Jane Roberts. *Master Drawings in the Royal Collection: From Leonardo da Vinci to the Present Day.* London, 1986.

Roethlisberger 1961
Marcel Roethlisberger. *Claude Lorrain: The Paintings.* 2 vols. New Haven, 1961.

Roethlisberger 1962
Marcel Roethlisberger. *Claude Lorrain: The Wildenstein Album.* Paris, 1962.

Roethlisberger 1968
Marcel Roethlisberger. *Claude Lorrain: The Drawings.* Berkeley, Calif., and Los Angeles, 1968.

Roethlisberger 1971
Marcel Roethlisberger. *The Claude Lorrain Album in the Norton Simon Inc. Museum of Art.* Los Angeles, 1971.

Roethlisberger 1985–86
Marcel Roethlisberger. "The Drawing Collection of Prince Livio Odescalchi." *MD* 23/24 (1985–86): 5–30.

Roger-Marx 1954
Claude Roger-Marx. *Constantin Guys, 1802–1892.* Paris, 1954.

Roman 1919
Jean Roman. *Le livre de raison du peintre Hyacinthe Rigaud.* Paris, 1919.

Rosand 2002
David Rosand. *Drawing Acts.* Cambridge, 2002.

Rosenberg 1928
Jacob Rosenberg. "Cornelis Hendricksz. Vroom." *Jahrbuch der preuszischen Kunstsammlungen* 49 (1928): 102–110.

Rosenberg 1966a
Pierre Rosenberg. *Inventaire des collections publiques françaises.* Vol. 14, *Tableaux français du XVIIe siècle et italiens des XVIIe et XVIIIe siècles.* Paris, 1966.

Rosenberg 1966b
Pierre Rosenberg, "Jouvenet à Rouen." *Burlington Magazine* 108 (1966): 443–444.

Rosenberg 1971
Pierre Rosenberg. Review of H-B and L. *Revue de l'art* 14 (1971): 112–113.

Rosenberg 1979
Pierre Rosenberg. "Dieu as a Draughtsman." *MD* 17 (1979): 161–169.

Rosenberg 1985
Pierre Rosenberg. "A Drawing by Pierre Monier." *Burlington Magazine* 127 (1985): 786–791.

Rosenberg 1989
Pierre Rosenberg. *Tout l'oeuvre peint de Fragonard.* Paris, 1989.

Rosenberg 2000
Pierre Rosenberg. *From Drawing to Painting: Poussin, Watteau, Fragonard, David, and Ingres.* A. W. Mellon Lectures in the Fine Arts, 1996. Princeton, 2000.

Rosenberg and Brejon de Lavergnée 1986
Pierre Rosenberg, with the collaboration of Barbara Brejon de Lavergnée. *Panopticon italiano: Un diario di viaggio ritrovato, 1759–1761.* Rome, 1986.

Rosenberg and Prat 1996
Pierre Rosenberg and Louis-Antoine Prat. *Antoine Watteau, 1684–1721: Catalogue raisonné des dessins.* 3 vols. Milan, 1996.

Rosenberg et al. 1977
Pierre Rosenberg et al. *Pittura francese nelle collezioni pubbliche fiorentine.* Florence, 1977.

Rosenthal 1980
Donald A. Rosenthal. "Géricault's Expenses for the 'Raft of the Medusa.'" *AB* 62 (1980): 638–640.

Roux 1930–
Marcel Roux. *Inventaire du fonds français, graveurs du XVIIIe siècle.* 15 vols. Paris, 1930–.

Rowlands 1993
John Rowlands. *Drawings by German Artists and Artists from German-Speaking Regions of Europe in the Department of Prints and Drawings in the British Museum.* 2 vols. London, 1993.

Royalton Kisch 1982
Martin Royalton Kisch. "New Works by Valerio Castello." *MD* 20 (1982): 132–135.

Ruby 1990
Louisa Wood Ruby. "Sebastiaen Vrancx as Illustrator of Virgil's Aeneid." *MD* 28 (1990): 54–73.

Rudolph 1977
Stella Rudolph. "Un episodio del barocco romano a Ferrara e alcune considerazioni sul cavalier Girolamo Troppa." *Musei ferraresi bollettino annuale* 7 (1977): 27–36.

Rudolph 1986
Stella Rudolph. "Il progetto di Carlo Maratti per la Galleria Falconieri e altri quesiti sulle decorazione private." *Labyrinthos* 9 (1986): 112–137.

Rümann 1914
Arthur Rümann. *Honoré Daumier: Sein Holzschnittwerk*. Munich, 1914.

Sacchetti 1989
Lucia Sacchetti. "Francesco Curradi, il Carmelo e i temi profani." *Antichità viva* 28, no. 4 (1989): 25–31.

Salazar 1955
Abdon M. Salazar. "El Bosco y Ambrosio de Morales." *Archivo español de arte* 28 (1955): 117–138.

Sanminiatelli 1967
Donato Sanminiatelli. *Domenico Beccafumi*. Milan, 1967.

Saslow 1996
James Saslow. *The Medici Wedding of 1589: Florentine Festival as Theatrum Mundi*. New Haven, 1996.

Savelsberg 1989
Wolfgang Savelsberg. "Ein Reisealtar von Jan Swart van Groningen aus dem Jahr 1562." *Niederdeutsche Beiträge zur Kunstgeschichte* 28 (1989): 77–88.

Schade 1969
Werner Schade. *Dresdener Zeichnungen, 1550–1610*. Dresden, 1969.

Schaefer 1982
Scott Schaefer. "The Studiolo of Francesco I de' Medici: A Checklist of the Known Drawings." *MD* 20 (1982): 125–130.

Schatborn 1974
Peter Schatborn. "Figuurstudies van Nicolaes Berchem." *Bulletin van het Rijksmuseum* 22 (1974): 3–16.

Schiff 1959
Gert Schiff. *Johann Heinrich Füssli und Michelangelo*. Schweizerisches Institut für Kunstwissenschaft, Kleine Schriften, vol. 2. Zurich, 1959.

Schiff 1973
Gert Schiff. *Johann Heinrich Füssli, 1741–1825*. 2 vols. Oeuvrekatalog schweizer Künstler, vol. 1. Zurich, 1973.

Schleier 1990
Erich Schleier. "Disegni di Girolamo Troppa nella collezione tedesche e altrove." *Antichità viva* 29, no. 6 (1990): 23–34.

Schleier 1993
Erich Schleier. "Aggiunte a Girolamo Troppa pittore e disegnatore." *Antichità viva* 32, no. 5 (1993): 16–23.

Schnapper 1967
Antoine Schnapper. "'Les compositions' of Jean Jouvenet." *MD* 5 (1967): 135–143.

Schnapper 1974
Antoine Schnapper. *Jean Jouvenet, 1644–1717, et la peinture d'histoire à Paris*. Paris, 1974.

Schöller 1992
Bernadette Schöller. *Kölner Druckgraphik der Gegenreformation*. Cologne, 1992.

Schulman 1997–99
Michel Schulman. *Théodore Rousseau: 1812–1867*. 2 vols. Paris, 1997–99.

Schulze Altcappenberg 1987
Hein-Th. Schulze Altcappenberg. *"Le Voltaire de l'art," Johann Georg Wille (1715–1808) und seine Schule in Paris*. Münster, 1987.

Schurr 1969
Gérald Schurr. "Continental Dispatch, Théodore Rousseau and His Friends." *Connoisseur* 170 (January 1969): 34.

Scorza 1995–96
Rick Scorza. "Vasari and Gender: A New Drawing for the Sala di Cosimo I." *YUAG Bulletin* (1995–96): 64–74.

Sensier 1872
Alfred Sensier. *Souvenirs sur T. Rousseau*. Paris, 1872.

Sérullaz 1963
Maurice Sérullaz. *Les peintures murales de Delacroix*. Paris, 1963.

Sérullaz et al. 1984
Maurice Sérullaz et al. *Dessins d'Eugène Delacroix, 1798–1863*. 2 vols. Musée du Louvre, Cabinet des dessins, Inventaire general des dessins, École française. Paris, 1984.

Seznec 1945
Jean Seznec. "Fragonard interprète de l'Arioste: La lettre et l'esprit." *Bulletin des études françaises* 28 (November–December 1945): 27–38.

Sievers, Muehlig, and Rich 2000
Ann Sievers, Linda Muehlig, and Nancy Rich. *Master Drawings from the Smith College Museum of Art*. New York, 2000.

Signac 1927
Paul Signac. *Jongkind*. Paris, 1927.

Siqüenza 1963
José de Siqüenza. *La fundacíon del Monasterio de El Escorial*. Madrid, 1963.

Smith 1910
De Cost Smith. "Jean-François Millet's Drawings of American Indians." *Century Illustrated Monthly Magazine* 80, no. 2 (1910): 78–84.

Smith 1978
Graham Smith. "A Drawing by Federico Zuccaro for the 'Last Judgment' in Florence Cathedral." *University of Michigan Museum of Art Bulletin* 1 (1978): 26–41.

Smith 1984
Karen Woodbridge Smith. *Constantin Guys: A Chronological and Stylistic Analysis of His Work*. Ph.D. diss., Case Western Reserve University, 1984.

Soullié 1900
Louis Soullié. *Peintres, aquarelles, pastels, dessins de Jean-François Millet*. Les grands peintres aux ventes publiques, vol. 2. Paris, 1900.

Spear 1967
Richard E. Spear. "The Early Drawings of Domenichino at Windsor Castle and Some Drawings by the Carracci." *AB* 49 (1967): 52–57.

Spear 1982
Richard E. Spear. *Domenichino*. 2 vols. New Haven and London, 1982.

Spear 2002
Richard E. Spear. "Primi dipinti e disegni del Domenichino." In *Una gloriosa gara nelle pagine di Francesco Arcangeli: L'oratorio di San Colombano*. Ed. Jedranka Bentini. Bologna, 2002: 159–167.

Spike 1980
John T. Spike. "New York: Domenico Tiepolo's Punchinello Drawings at the Frick Collection." *Burlington Magazine* 122 (1980): 281–286.

Spinosa 2003
Nicola Spinosa. *Ribera, l'opera completa.* Naples, 2003.

Sproti 1996
Alfredo Sproti. "Caratterische tecniche del taccuino e osservazioni sul restauro (con un' appendice di M. P. Tella Mongini)." In Buonocore et al. 1996: 67–71.

Stampfle 1991
Felice Stampfle. *Netherlandish Drawings of the Fifteenth and Sixteenth Centuries and Flemish Drawings of the Seventeenth and Eighteenth Centuries in the Pierpont Morgan Library.* New York and Princeton, 1991.

Stange 1957
Alfred Stange. *Deutsche Malerei der Gotik.* Munich and Berlin, 1957.

Stanton-Hirst 1982
B. A. Stanton-Hirst. "Pieter Quast and the Theatre." *Oud Holland* 96 (1982): 213–237.

Starcky 1985
Emmanuel Starcky. "Un dessin d'Herman Weyer (1596–ap. 1621)." *Revue du Louvre* 35 (1985): 21–24.

Starcky 1988
Emmanuel Starcky. *Inventaire général des dessins des écoles du Nord: Supplement aux inventaires publiés par Frits Lugt et Louis Demonts.* Paris, 1988.

Stechow 1947
Wolfgang Stechow. "Esajas van de Velde and the Beginnings of Dutch Landscape Painting." *Nederlands kunsthistorisch jaarboek* 1 (1947): 83–94.

Stechow 1966
Wolfgang Stechow. *Dutch Landscape Painting of the Seventeenth Century.* London, 1966.

Stefes 1997
Annemarie Stefes. "Eleven History Drawings by Nicolaes Berchem." *MD* 35 (1997): 367–379.

Steffen 2000
Uwe Steffen. "Die Jona-Geschichte: Darstellungen aus achtzehn Jahrhunderten." *Das Münster* 53 (2000): 2–16.

Stein 1997
Perrin Stein. Review of Raux 1995. *MD* 35 (1997): 73–77.

Stein et al. 2003
Adolphe Stein et al. *Jongkind, catalogue critique de l'oeuvre.* Vol. 1, *Peintures.* Paris, 2003.

Stoughton 1973
Michael William Stoughton. *The Paintings of Giovanni Battista Caracciolo.* Ph.D. diss., University of Michigan, 1973.

Strech 1996
Annette Strech. *Druckgraphik nach Bartholomäus Spranger (1546–1611).* Master's diss., Freien Universität, Berlin, 1996.

Streiff 1957
Bruno Streiff. *Dessins de Constantin Guys.* Lausanne, 1957.

Sullivan 1991
Margaret Sullivan. "Bruegel's Proverbs: Art and Audience in the Northern Renaissance." *AB* 73 (1991): 431–466.

Sullivan 2002
Margaret Sullivan. "The Witches of Dürer and Hans Baldung Grien." *Renaissance Quarterly* 53 (2002): 332–401.

Sumowski 1967
Werner Sumowski. "Eine fruhe Federzeichnung von Goaert Flinck." *Pantheon* 25 (1967): 336–340.

Sumowski 1979–92
Werner Sumowski. *Drawings of the Rembrandt School.* Ed. and trans. Walter L. Strauss. 10 vols. New York, 1979–92.

Sumowski 1983–94
Werner Sumowski. *Gemälde der Rembrandt-Schüler.* 6 vols. Landau, 1983–94.

Ternois 1961
Daniel Ternois. *Jacques Callot: Catalogue de son oeuvre dessiné.* Paris, 1961.

Ternois 1962
Daniel Ternois. *L'art de Jacques Callot.* Paris, 1962.

Ternois 1993
Daniel Ternois. "Dessins de Jacques Callot: Quelques attributions récentes et leurs enseignements." In *Jacques Callot (1592–1635): Actes du colloque.* Paris, 1993: 359–398.

Ternois 1999a
Daniel Ternois. *Jacques Callot: Catalogue de son oeuvre dessiné, supplément, 1962–1998.* Paris, 1999.

Ternois 1999b
Daniel Ternois. *Lettres d'Ingres à Marcotte d'Argenteuil.* Nogent-le-Roi, 1999.

Ternois 2001
Daniel Ternois. *Lettres d'Ingres à Marcotte d'Argenteuil: Dictionnaire.* Nogent-le-Roi, 2001.

Thiem 1977
Christel Thiem. *Florentiner Zeichner des Frühbarock.* Munich, 1977.

Thiem 1993
Christel Thiem. "Lorenzo Tiepolos Position innerhalb der Künstlerfamilie Tiepolo." *Pantheon* 51 (1993): 138–150.

Thiem 1994
Christel Thiem. "Lorenzo Tiepolo as a Draftsman." *MD* 32 (1994): 315–350.

Thieme and Becker 1907–50
Ulrich Thieme and Felix Becker, eds. *Allgemeines Lexikon der bildenden Künstler von der Antike bis zur Gegenwart.* 37 vols. Leipzig, 1907–50.

Thuillier 1992
Jacques Thuillier, ed. *L'art en Lorraine au temps de Jacques Callot.* Paris, 1992.

Thuillier 2000
Jacques Thuillier. *Sébastien Bourdon, 1616–1671.* Paris, 2000.

Thuillier and Foucart 1970
Jacques Thuillier and Jacques Foucart. *Rubens' Life of Marie de' Medici.* Trans. Robert Erich Wolf. New York, 1970.

Tietze et al. 1933
Hans Tietze et al. *Die Zeichnungen der deutschen Schulen bis zum Beginn des Klassizismus. Beschreibender Katalog der Handzeichnungen in der Graphischen Sammlung Albertina,* vols. 4–5. Vienna, 1933.

Tinterow, Hale, and Bertin 2000
Gary Tinterow, Charlotte Hale, and Eric Bertin. "'Portraits by Ingres: Image of an Epoch': Reflections, Technical Observations, Addenda, and Corrigenda." *Metropolitan Museum Journal* 35 (2000): 193–219.

Tomory 1972
Peter Tomory. *The Life and Art of Henry Fuseli.* London, 1972.

Torriti 1990
Piero Torriti. *La Pinacoteca Nazionale di Siena.* Genoa, 1990.

Torriti 1998
Piero Torriti. *Beccafumi.* Milan, 1998.

Tümpel 1974
Astrid Tümpel. "Claes Cornelisz. Moeyaert." *Oud Holland* 88 (1974): 1–163 and 245–290.

Turner 1999
Nicholas Turner. *Italian Drawings in the Department of Prints and Drawings in the British Museum.* Vol. 6, *Roman Baroque Drawings, c. 1620 to c. 1700.* London, 1999.

Turner 2000
Nicholas Turner. *Federico Barocci.* Paris, 2000.

Turner et al. 1997
Nicholas Turner et al. *European Drawings: Catalogue of the [J. Paul Getty Museum] Collections.* Vol. 3. Los Angeles, 1997.

Tuyll van Serooskerken 2000
Carel van Tuyll van Serooskerken. *The Italian Drawings of the Fifteenth and Sixteenth Centuries in the Teyler Museum.* Haarlem, Ghent, and Doornspijk, 2000.

Valogne 1955
Catherine Valogne, ed. "Fragonard, mon grand-père." *Les lettres françaises,* no. 556 (17 February 1955): 1 and 9.

Vandenbroeck 1984
P. Vandenbroeck. "Nieuw material voor de studie van het Hooiwagen-motief." *Jaarboek van het Koninklijk Museum voor schone Kunsten Antwerpen* (1984): 39–65.

Vandenbroeck 1987
Paul Vandenbroeck. "Jheronimus Bosch' 'Hooiwagen': Enkele bijkomende gegevens." *Jaarboek van het Koninklijk Museum voor schone Kunsten Antwerpen* (1987): 107–142.

van der Sman 1997
Gert Jan van der Sman. "Vlaamse tekeningen van de 16de–18de eeuw." *Delineavit et sculpsit* 18 (1997): 7–10.

van der Sman 1999
Gert Jan van der Sman. "Observations on the Master of the Egmont Albums." In *Fiamminghi a Roma, 1508–1608: Proceedings of the Symposium Held at Museum Catharijneconvent, Utrecht.* Ed. Sabine Eiche, Gert Jan van der Sman, and Jeanne van Waadenoijen, trans. Maureen Brown Fant and Alison Stoesser. Florence, 1999: 45–65.

van Mander 1994–99
Karel van Mander. *The Lives of the Illustrious Netherlandish and German Painters, from the First Edition of the Schilder-Boeck (1603–1604).* Ed. Hessel Miedema, with an introduction and translation. 6 vols. Doornspijk, 1994–99.

van Thiel 1987
Pieter J. J. van Thiel. "Gerrit Pietersz.: Addenda en corrigenda." *Nederlands kunsthistorisch jaarboek* 38 (1987): 355–368.

van Treek 2000
P. van Treek. "On the Artistic Technique of Glass Painting in the Age of Dürer and Holbein." In Los Angeles–St. Louis 2000: 57–75.

Vasari 1889
Giorgio Vasari. *Le vite de' più eccelenti pittori scultori ed architettori.* 9 vols. Ed. Gaetano Milanesi. Florence, 1889.

Velde 1975
Carl van de Velde. *Frans Floris (1519/20): Leven en Werken.* Brussels, 1975.

Velde 1979–80
Carl van de Velde. "Nieuwe gegevens en inzichten over het werk van Frans Pourbus de Oudere." *Gentse bijdragen tot de kunstgeschiedenis* 25 (1979–80): 124–157.

Velde 1994
Carl van de Velde. "Frans Pourbus the Elder and the Diffusion of the Style of Frans Floris in the Southern Netherlands." In *Die Malerei Antwerpens, Gattungen, Meister, Wirkungen: Studien zur flämischen Kunst des 16. und 17. Jahrhunderts, Internationales Kolloquium Wien 1993.* Ed. Christiane Stukenbrock. Cologne, 1994: 11–17.

Veldman 1974
Ilja M. Veldman. "Maarten van Heemskerck and Hadrianus Junius: The Relationship Between a Painter and a Humanist." *Simiolus* 7 (1974): 35–54.

Veldman 1977
Ilja M. Veldman. *Maarten van Heemskerck and Dutch Humanism in the Sixteenth Century.* Maarssen, 1977.

Veldman 1980
Ilja M. Veldman. "Seasons, Planets and Temperaments in the Work of Maarten van Heemskerck: Cosmo-Astrological Allegory in Sixteenth-Century Netherlandish Prints." *Simiolus* 11 (1980): 149–176.

Verheyen 1977
Egon Verheyen. *The Palazzo del Té in Mantua.* Baltimore and London, 1977.

Vertova 1975
Luisa Vertova. "Bernardino Licinio." In *I pittori bergamaschi dal XIII al XIX secolo: Il cinquecento.* Vol. 1. Bergamo, 1975: 373–464.

Viale 1969
Vittorio Viale. *Gaudenzio Ferrari.* Turin, 1969.

Viale Ferrero 1957
Mercedes Viale Ferrero. "I disegni scenografici della raccolta Fatio." *Critica d'arte* 23 (1957): 370–395.

Vignau-Wilberg 1988
Thea Vignau-Wilberg. "Künstlerische Beziehungen zwischen Prag und München zur Zeit Rudolfs II." In *Prag um 1600: Beiträge zur Kunst und Kultur am Hofe Rudolfs II.* Freren, 1988: 302–305.

Voss 1920
Hermann Voss. *Die Malerei der Spätrenaissance in Rom und Florenz.* Berlin, 1920.

Wakefield 1979
D. F. Wakefield. "Fragonard's Drawings for Ariosto's 'Orlando Furioso.'" *Connoisseur* 200 (February 1979): 131–134.

Walch 1971
Nicole Walch. *Die Radierungen des Jacques Bellange.* Munich, 1971.

Walsh 1985
John Walsh. "Rembrandt's 'Christ in the Storm on the Sea of Galilee' Re-examined." *Fenway Court* 19 (1985): 7–19.

Ward 1982
Roger B. Ward. *Baccio Bandinelli as a Draughtsman.* Ph.D. thesis, Courtauld Institute, 1982.

Ward 1993
Roger Ward. "New Drawings by Bandinelli and Cellini." *MD* 31 (1993): 395–399.

Wayment 1979
H. G. Wayment. "The Great Windows of King's College Chapel and the Meaning of the Word 'Vidimus.'" *Proceedings of the Cambridge Antiquarian Society* 69 (1979): 365–376.

Weigert 1939–
Roger Armand Weigert. *Inventaire du fonds français, graveurs du XVIIe siècle.* 17 vols. Paris, 1939–.

Weinglass 1982
David H. Weinglass, ed. *The Collected Letters of Henry Fuseli.* London, 1982.

Welcker 1950
A. Welcker. "Goltzius, niet Spranger." *Oud Holland* 65 (1950): 119–120.

Wescher 1928
Paul Wescher. "Hollandische Zeichner zur Zeit des Lucas van Leiden." *Oud Holland* 45 (1928): 245–254.

Weschler 2000
Lawrence Weschler. "The Looking Glass." *New Yorker* 75, no. 44 (31 January 2000): 65–75.

Whiteley 1998
J. J. L. Whiteley. *Claude Lorrain: Drawings from the Collections of the British Museum and Ashmolean Museum.* London, 1998.

Whitman 1963
Nathan T. Whitman. *The Drawings of Raymond Lafage.* The Hague, 1963.

Wichmann 1923
Heinrich Wichmann. *Leonaert Bramer, sein Leben, und seine Kunst: Ein Beitrag zur Geschichte der Holländischen Malerei zur Zeit Rembrandts.* Leipzig, 1923.

Wilde 1953
Johannes Wilde. *Italian Drawings in the Department of Prints and Drawings in the British Museum.* Vol. 2, *Michelangelo and His Studio.* 2 vols. London, 1953.

Wildenstein 1956
Georges Wildenstein. *Ingres.* 2d ed. London, 1956.

Wildenstein 1974–91
Daniel Wildenstein. *Claude Monet: Biographie et catalogue raisonné.* 5 vols. Lausanne and Paris, 1974–91.

Wille 1857
J. G. Wille. *Mémoires et journal . . .* Ed. G. Duplessis. Paris, 1857.

Wilson-Chevalier 1996
Kathleen Wilson-Chevalier. "Sebastian Brant, the Key to Understanding Luca Penni's Justice and the Seven Deadly Sins." *AB* 78 (1996): 236–263.

Wine 1994
Humphrey Wine. *Claude: The Poetic Landscape.* London, 1994.

Wisdom n.d.
John Minor Wisdom, Jr. "On the Chronology of Théodore Rousseau's Drawings," n.d. [1968?], unpublished manuscript, curatorial files, Department of Prints, Drawings, and Photographs, YUAG.

Witcombe 1981
Christopher Witcombe. *Giovanni and Cherubino Alberti.* Ph.D. diss., Bryn Mawr College, 1981.

Wolf 1942
Alice Wolf. *The Edward B. Greene Collection of Engraved Portraits and Portrait Drawings at Yale University.* New Haven, 1942.

Wolk-Simon 1989
Linda Wolk-Simon. Review of Parma Armani 1986. *AB* 71 (1989): 515–523.

Wolk-Simon 2002
Linda Wolk-Simon. "Two Early Fresco Cycles by Perino del Vaga." *Apollo* 155 (2002): 11–21.

Wolk-Simon 2003
Linda Wolk-Simon. Review of Mantua 2001. *MD* 41 (2003): 44–58.

Wollaston 1807
W. H. Wollaston. "Description of the Camera Lucida." *Journal of Natural Philosophy, Chemistry, and the Arts* 17 (1807): 1–5.

Wood 1990
Jeremy Wood. "Padre Resta's Flemish Drawings: Van Diepenbeeck, Van Thulden, Rubens, and the School of Fontainebleau." *MD* 28 (1990): 3–53.

Wood 1992
Jeremy Wood. Review of 's-Hertogenbosch–Strasbourg 1991. *Burlington Magazine* 134 (1992): 327–330.

Wood 2000
Jeremy Wood. "Rubens as Thief: His Use of Past Art and Some Adaptations from Primaticcio." In *Concept, Design, and Execution in Flemish Painting, 1550–1700.* Turnhout, 2000: 153–170.

Wygant 1994
Amy Wygant. "Pierre Corneille's Medea-Machine." *Romantic Review* 85 (1994): 537–553.

Zarco Cuevas 1931
Julián Zarco Cuevas. *Pintores españoles en San Lorenzo el Real de El Escorial (1566–1613).* Madrid, 1931.

Zerner 1969
Henri Zerner. *The School of Fontainebleau: Etchings and Engravings.* New York, 1969.

Zerner 1996
Henri Zerner. *L'art de la Renaissance en France: L'invention du classicisme.* Paris, 1996.

Zika 2002
Charles Zika. "Images of Circe and Discourses of Witchcraft, 1480–1580." *Zeitenblicke* 1 (2002). Accessible online at http://www.zeitenblicke.historicum.net/2002/01/zika/zika.html.

Zweite 1980
Armin Zweite. *Marten de Vos als Maler.* Berlin, 1980.

EXHIBITION AND SALE CATALOGUES

Allentown 1977
French Masterpieces of the 19th Century from the Henry P. McIlhenny Collection. Allentown Art Museum. Allentown, Pa., 1977.

Amherst 1990
Northern Travelers to Sixteenth-Century Italy: Drawings from New England Collections. Amherst, Mass.: Mead Art Museum. Amherst, Mass., 1990.

Amsterdam 1986
W. Th. Kloeck, W. Halsema-Kubes, and R. J. Baarsen. *Kunst voor de beeldenstorm: Noordnederlandse kunst, 1525–1580.* 2 vols. Amsterdam: Rijksmuseum. Amsterdam, 1986.

Amsterdam–Boston–Philadelphia 1987–88
Peter C. Sutton et al. *Masters of 17th-Century Dutch Landscape Painting.* Amsterdam: Rijksmuseum; Boston: Museum of Fine Arts; and Philadelphia Museum of Art. Boston, 1987.

Amsterdam et al. 1991–92
William W. Robinson. *Seventeenth-Century Dutch Drawings: A Selection from the Maida and George Abrams Collection.* Amsterdam: Rijksmuseum; Vienna: Albertina; New York: Pierpont Morgan Library; and Cambridge, Mass.: Fogg Art Museum. Lynn, Mass., 1991.

Amsterdam 1993–94
Dawn of the Golden Age: Northern Netherlandish Art, 1580–1620. Amsterdam: Rijksmuseum. Amsterdam and Zwolle, 1993.

Amsterdam 1996a
Peter van der Coelen. *Patriarchs, Angels, and Prophets: The Old Testament in Netherlandish Printmaking from Lucas van Leyden to Rembrandt.* Amsterdam: Rembrandthuis. Amsterdam, 1996.

Amsterdam 1996b
Christiaan Schuckman, Martin Royalton-Kisch, and Erik Hinterding. *Rembrandt and Van Vliet: A Collaboration on Copper.* Amsterdam: Rembrandthuis. Amsterdam, 1996.

Amsterdam–Paris 2003
Robert Jan te Rijdt. *De Watteau à Ingres: Dessins français du XVIIIe siècle du Rijksmuseum Amsterdam.* Amsterdam: Rijksmuseum; and Paris: Institut Néerlandais. Amsterdam and Paris, 2003.

Amsterdam–New York–Toledo 2003–04
Hendrick Goltzius (1558–1617): Drawings, Prints, and Paintings. Amsterdam: Rijksmuseum; New York: Metropolitan Museum of Art; and Toledo, Ohio: Toledo Museum of Art. Zwolle, 2003.

Antwerp–Rotterdam 1966–67
Roger-Adolf d'Hulst. *Tekeningen van Jacob Jordaens, 1593–1678.* Antwerp: Rubenshuis; and Rotterdam: Museum Boymans van Beuningen. Antwerp, 1966.

Antwerp 1993
Roger-Adolf d'Hulst et al. *Jacob Jordaens (1593–1678).* 2 vols. Antwerp: Koninklijk Museum voor Schone Kunsten. Brussels, 1993.

Athens 2002
The Golden Age of Dutch Painting from the Collection of the Dordrechts Museum. Ed. Angela Tamvaki and Sander Paarlberg. Athens: National Gallery and Alexandros Soutkos Museum. Athens, 2002.

Atlanta 1984
The Henry P. McIlhenny Collection: Nineteenth Century French and English Masterpieces. Atlanta: High Museum of Art. Atlanta, 1984.

Avignon 1992
Esther Moench et al., eds. *Catherine de Sienne.* Avignon: Palais des Papes. Avignon, 1992.

Baltimore–Worcester–Pittsburgh 1992
Roberta J. M. Olson. *Ottocento: Romanticism and Revolution in 19th-Century Italian Painting.* Baltimore: Walters Art Gallery; Worcester, Mass.: Worcester Art Museum; and Pittsburgh: Frick Art Museum. New York and Florence, 1992.

Baltimore–Birmingham–Tacoma 2005–06
William R. Johnston et al. *The Essence of Line: French Drawings from Ingres to Degas.* Baltimore: Baltimore Museum of Art and Walters Art Gallery; Birmingham, Ala.: Birmingham Museum of Art; and Tacoma, Wash.: Tacoma Art Museum. University Park, Pa., 2005.

Berlin 1973
Staatliche Museen Preussischer Kulturbesitz. *Vom späten Mittelalter bis zu Jacques Louis David.* Berlin: Staatliche Museen Preussischer Kulturbesitz. Berlin, 1973.

Berlin 1985
Helmut Börsch-Supan. *Watteau, 1684–1721: Führer zur Austellung im Schloß Charlottenburg.* Berlin: Schloß Charlottenburg. Berlin, 1985.

Bloomington–Stanford 1979
Adelheid M. Gealt and Marcia E. Vetrocq. *Domenico Tiepolo's Punchinello Drawings.* Bloomington: Indiana University Art Museum; and Stanford, Calif.: Stanford University Museum of Art. Bloomington, Ind., 1979.

Bloomington–Pittsburgh–Oberlin 1983
Italian Portrait Drawings, 1400–1800, from North American Collections. Bloomington: Indiana University Art Museum; Pittsburgh: Gallery of Art, University of Pittsburgh; and Oberlin, Ohio: Allen Memorial Art Museum. Bloomington, Ind., 1983.

Boston 1974
Barbara Stern Shapiro. *Edgar Degas: The Reluctant Impressionist.* Boston: Museum of Fine Arts. Boston, 1974.

Boston–St. Louis 1980–81
Clifford S. Ackley. *Printmaking in the Age of Rembrandt.* Boston: Museum of Fine Arts; and St. Louis Art Museum. Boston, 1981.

Boston 1984
Sue Welsh Reed and Barbara Stern Shapiro. *Edgar Degas: The Painter as Printmaker.* Boston: Museum of Fine Arts. Boston, 1984.

Boston 1989
Sue Welsh Reed and Richard Wallace. *Italian Etchers of the Renaissance and Baroque.* Boston: Museum of Fine Arts. Boston, 1989.

Boston–Toledo 1993
Peter Sutton, ed. *The Age of Rubens.* Boston: Museum of Fine Arts; and Toledo, Ohio: Toledo Museum of Art. Boston and Ghent, 1993.

Brunswick et al. 198–86
David P. Becker. *Old Master Drawings at Bowdoin College.* Brunswick, Maine: Bowdoin College Museum of Art; Williamstown, Mass.: Sterling and Francine Clark Art Institute; Lawrence, Kans.: Helen Foresman Spencer Museum of Art; and Toronto: Art Gallery of Ontario. Brunswick, Maine, 1985.

Brussels 1983
Roger-Adolf d'Hulst et al. *Dessins du XVe au XVIIIe siècle dans les collections privées de Belgique.* Brussels: Société Générale de Banque. Brussels, 1983.

Brussels 1994
Dirk Coigneau et al. *Uyt Ionsten Versaemt: Het landjuweel van 1561 te Antwerpen.* Brussels: Koninklijke Bibliotheek Albert I. Brussels, 1994.

Brussels–Rome 1995
Fiamminghi a Roma 1508–1608: Artistes des Pays-Bas et de la principauté de Liège à Rome de la Renaissance. Brussels: Société des Expositions du Palais des Beaux-Arts de Bruxelles; and Rome: Palazzo delle Esposizioni. Brussels and Ghent, 1995.

Buffalo 1935
Master Drawings, Selected from the Museums and Private Collections of America. Buffalo: Albright Art Gallery. Buffalo, 1934.

Cambridge 1940
Master Drawings Lent by Philip Hofer, Class of 1921. Cambridge, Mass.: Fogg Art Museum. Cambridge, Mass., 1940.

Cambridge 1967a
Ingres Centennial Exhibition, 1867–1967: Drawings, Watercolors, and Oil Sketches from American Collections. Cambridge, Mass.: Fogg Art Museum. Greenwich, Conn., 1967.

Cambridge 1967b
Paintings, Drawings, and Sculpture from the Yale University Art Gallery. Cambridge, Mass.: Fogg Art Museum. Cambridge, Mass., 1967.

Cambridge 1969
Jeanne L. Wasserman, assisted by Joan M. Lukach and Arthur Beale. *Daumier Sculpture: A Critical and Comparative Study.* Cambridge, Mass.: Fogg Art Museum. Greenwich, Conn., 1969.

Cambridge 1970
Tiepolo: A Bicentenary Exhibition, 1770–1970. Cambridge, Mass.: Fogg Art Museum. Cambridge, Mass., 1970.

Cambridge–Montreal 1988
Frederik J. Duparc. *Landscape in Perspective: Drawings by Rembrandt and His Contemporaries*. Cambridge, Mass.: Arthur M. Sackler Museum; and Montreal Museum of Fine Arts. Montreal, 1988.

Cambridge–Ottawa–Cleveland 1991
David M. Stone. *Guercino, Master Draftsman, Works from North American Collections*. Cambridge, Mass.: Arthur M. Sackler Museum; Ottawa: National Gallery of Canada; and Cleveland Museum of Art. Cambridge and Bologna, 1991.

Cambridge–New York 1996–97
Bernard Aikema. *Tiepolo and His Circle: Drawings in American Collections*. Cambridge, Mass.: Harvard University Art Museums; and New York: Pierpont Morgan Library. Cambridge, Mass., and New York, 1996.

Cambridge et al. 1998–2000
Alvin L. Clark, Jr., ed. *Mastery and Elegance: Two Centuries of French Drawings from the Collection of Jeffrey E. Horvitz*. Cambridge, Mass.: Harvard University Art Museums; Toronto: Art Gallery of Ontario; Paris: Musée Jacquemart-André; Edinburgh: National Gallery of Scotland; New York: National Academy Museum and School of Fine Arts; and Los Angeles County Museum. Cambridge, Mass., 1998.

Cento 2002
Donatella Biagi Maino, ed. *Gaetano e Ubaldo Gandolfi: Opere scelte*. Cento: Auditorium di San Lorenzo. Turin, 2002.

Chicago 1938
Paintings, Drawings, and Prints by the Two Tiepolos: Giambattista and Giandomenico. Art Institute of Chicago. Chicago, 1938.

Chicago–Detroit 2002
The Medici, Michelangelo, and the Art of Late Renaissance Florence. Art Institute of Chicago; and Detroit Institute of Arts. New Haven and Detroit, 2002.

Cleveland 1978
Karen W. Smith. *Constantin Guys, Crimean War Drawings 1854–1856*. Cleveland Museum of Art. Cleveland, 1978.

Cleveland–New Haven 1978
Edmund P. Pillsbury and Louise S. Richards. *The Graphic Art of Federico Barocci: Selected Drawings and Prints*. Cleveland Museum of Art; and New Haven: YUAG. New Haven, 1978.

Cleveland–Cambridge–Ottawa 1989–90
Hilliard T. Goldfarb. *From Fontainebleau to the Louvre: French Drawing from the Seventeenth Century*. Cleveland Museum of Art; Cambridge, Mass.: Fogg Art Museum; and Ottawa: National Gallery of Canada. Cleveland, 1989.

Copenhagen 1983
Hanne Finsen. *Degas og familien Bellelli, Degas et la famille Bellelli*. Copenhagen: Ordrupgaard. Copenhagen, 1983.

Delft 1994
Jane ten Brink Goldsmith et al. *Leonaert Bramer, 1596–1674: Ingenious Painter and Draughtsman in Rome and Delft*. Delft: Stedelijk Museum Het Prinsenhof. Zwolle and Delft, 1994.

Des Moines–Boston–New York 1975–76
Amy N. Worthen and Sue Welsh Reed. *The Etchings of Jacques Bellange*. Des Moines, Iowa: Des Moines Art Center; Boston: Museum of Fine Arts; and New York: Metropolitan Museum of Art. Des Moines, Iowa, 1975.

Detroit–Chicago 1981–82
The Golden Age of Naples: Art and Civilization under the Bourbons, 1734–1805. Detroit Institute of Arts; and Art Institute of Chicago. Detroit and Chicago, 1981.

Dijon–London 2004–05
Françoise Joulie. *Boucher et les peintres du nord*. Dijon: Musée Magnin; and London: The Wallace Collection. Paris, 2004.

Dordrecht 1977–78
Aelbert Cuyp en zijn familie, schilders te Dordrecht: Gerrit Gerritsz. Cuyp, Jacob Gerritsz. Cuyp, Benjamin Gerritsz. Cuyp, Aelbert Cuyp. Dordrecht: Dordrechts Museum. Dordrecht, 1977.

Dordrecht–Cologne 1998–99
Peter Schoon et al. *Arent de Gelder (1645–1727): Rembrandts Meisterschüler und Nachfolger*. Dordrecht: Dordrechts Museum; and Cologne: Wallraf-Richartz-Museum. Ghent, 1998.

Dordrecht 2002
Sander Paarlberg, ed. *Jacob Gerritsz. Cuyp (1594–1652)*. Dordrecht: Dordrechts Museum. Dordrecht, 2002.

Dresden 1986
Barock in Dresden: Kunst und Kunstsammlungen unter der Regierung des Kurfürsten Friedrich August I. von Sachsen und Königs August II. von Polen, genannt August der Starke, 1694–1733 und des Kurfürsten Friedrich August II. von Sachsen und Königs August III. von Polen, 1733–1763. Dresden: Staatliche Kunstsammlungen. Leipzig, 1986.

Edinburgh 1998
Aidan Weston-Lewis, ed. *Effigies and Ecstasies: Roman Baroque Sculpture and Design in the Age of Bernini*. Edinburgh: National Gallery of Scotland. Edinburgh, 1998.

Essen–Vienna 1988
Prag um 1600: Kunst und Kultur am Hofe Kaiser Rudolfs II. 2 vols. Essen: Kulturstiftung Ruhr Villa Hügel; and Vienna: Kunsthistorisches Museum. Freren, 1988.

Florence–Paris 1980–81
Karel Boon. *L'époque de Lucas de Leyde et Pierre Bruegel: Dessins des anciens Pays-Bas, collection Frits Lugt, Institut Néerlandais, Paris*. Florence: Istituto Universitario Olandese di Storia dell'Arte; and Paris: Institut Néerlandais. Paris, 1981.

Florence–Rome 1983–84
Bert W. Meijer and Carel van Tuyll. *Disegni italiani del Teylers Museum, Haarlem, provenienti dalle collezioni di Cristina di Svezia e dei principi Odescalchi*. Florence: Istituto Universitario Olandese di Storia dell'Arte; and Rome: Istituto Nazionale per la Grafica. Florence, 1983.

Florence 1985
S. Lecchini Giovannoni and M. Collareta, eds. *Disegni di Santi di Tito (1536–1603)*. Florence: Galleria degli Uffizi. Florence, 1985.

Florence 1989
Mary Newcome Schleier. *Disegni genovesi dal XVI al XVIII secolo*. Florence: Galleria degli Uffizi. Florence, 1989.

Florence 1992
Miles Chappell, ed. *Disegni di Lodovico Cigoli (1559–1613)*. Florence: Galleria degli Uffizi. Florence, 1992.

Frankfurt–New York 1992–93
Colta Ives, Margret Stuffmann, and Martin Sonnabend. *Daumier Drawings*. Frankfurt: Städelsche Kunstinstitut und Städtische Galerie; and New York: Metropolitan Museum of Art. New York, 1992.

Genoa 1990
Piero Donati. *Domenico Fiasella*. Genoa: Palazzo Reale. Genoa, 1990.

The Hague 1994–95
Amy Walsh, Edwin Buijsen, and Ben Broos. *Paulus Potter: Paintings, Drawings, and Etchings*. The Hague: Mauritshuis. The Hague and Zwolle, 1994.

The Hague–Cologne–Paris 2003–04
Jongkind, 1819–1891. The Hague: Gemeentemuseum; Cologne: Wallraf-Richartz-Museum, Fondation Corboud; and Paris: Musée d'Orsay. Paris, 2004.

Hamburg–London 1974–75
Gert Schiff. *Henry Fuseli, 1741–1825*. Trans. Sarah Twohig. Hamburg: Kunsthalle; and London: Tate Gallery. London, 1975.

Hamburg 1994–95
Eckhard Schaar. *Rembrandt und sein Jahrhundert: Niederländische Zeichnungen in der Hamburger Kunsthalle*. Hamburg: Kunsthalle. Hamburg and Heidelberg, 1994.

Hartford–San Francisco–Dijon 1976–77
Edgar Munhall. *Jean-Baptiste Greuze, 1725–1805*. Hartford, Conn.: Wadsworth Atheneum; San Francisco: California Palace of the Legion of Honor; and Dijon: Musée des Beaux-Arts. Hartford, Conn., 1976.

Kingston 1966
The Renaissance. Kingston: Queens University. Kingston, 1966.

Krefeld–Oranienburg–Apeldoorn 1999–2000
Horst Lademacher, ed. *Onder den Oranje boom: Niederländische Kunst und Kultur im 17. und 18. Jahrhundert an deutschen Fürstenhöfen*. Krefeld: Kaiser Wilhelm Museum; Oranienburg: Schloss Oranienburg; and Apeldoorn: Stichting Palais Het Loo. Munich, 1999.

Langres 1999
Paulette Choné et al. *Claude Gillot (1673–1722): Comédies, sabbats, et autres sujets bizarres*. Langres: Musée de Langres. Paris, 1999.

Lille 2002–03
Lumière et ténèbres: art et civilisation du baroque en Bohême. Lille: Palais des Beaux-Arts. Paris, 2002.

L'isle-Adam–Grasse 2001–02
Fragonard et le voyage en Italie, 1773–1774: Les Bergeret, une famille de mécènes. L'isle-Adam: Musée d'Art et d'Histoire Louis Senlecq; and Grasse: Musée Fragonard. Paris and L'isle-Adam, 2001.

Lisle sur Tarn 1990
Raymond Lafage, 1656–1684: Dessins et Gravures. Lisle sur Tarn: Musée Raymond Lafage. Lisle sur Tarn, 1990.

London 1914–15
III National Loan Exhibition. London: Grosvenor Gallery. London, 1914.

London 1960
H. M. Calmann: Dealer in Old Master Drawings. Sale cat., London, 1960.

London 1972
Sotheby's, London. *Catalogue of the Ellesmere Collection, Part II: Drawings by Giulio Romano and Other Sixteenth-Century Masters Collected by Sir Thomas Lawrence*. Sale cat., London, 5 December 1972.

London 1974
P. and D. Colnaghi. *Exhibition of Old Master Drawings*. Sale cat., London, 1974.

London 1975
Howard Burns, with Lynda Fairbairn and Bruce Boucher. *Andrea Palladio, 1508–1580: The Portico and the Farmyard*. London: Arts Council of Great Britain. London, 1975.

London 1976
Robert L. Herbert. *Jean-François Millet*. London: Hayward Gallery. London, 1976.

London et al. 1977–78
Viviane Huchard. *The Finest Drawings from the Museums of Angers*. London: Heim Gallery; Liverpool: Walker Art Gallery; Dublin: National Gallery of Ireland; and Birmingham: City Museum and Art Gallery. London, 1978.

London 1978
Fragonard Drawings for Orlando Furioso. London: Thos. Agnew and Sons. London, 1978.

London–Cambridge 1979
Charles McCorquodale. *Painting in Florence, 1600–1700*. London: Royal Academy of Arts; and Cambridge: Fitzwilliam Museum. London, 1979.

London–Washington 1982–83
Clovis Whitfield and Jane Martineau, eds. *Painting in Naples, 1606–1705: From Caravaggio to Giordano*. London: Royal Academy; Washington, D.C.: National Gallery of Art. London, 1982.

London 1983–84
The Genius of Venice, 1500–1600. London: Royal Academy of Arts. New York, 1983.

London 1986
Nicholas Turner. *Florentine Drawings of the Sixteenth Century*. London: British Museum. Cambridge and New York, 1986.

London 1994
Antony Griffiths and Frances Carey. *German Printmaking in the Age of Goethe*. London: British Museum. London, 1994.

London 1999
J. L. Baroni/Colnaghi. *Old Masters and 19th Century Drawings*. Sale cat., London, 1999.

London–Washington–New York 1999–2000
Portraits by Ingres: Image of an Epoch. London: National Gallery; Washington, D.C.: National Gallery of Art; and New York: Metropolitan Museum of Art. New York, 1999.

London–Minneapolis–New York 2003–04
Patrick Noon. *Crossing the Channel: British and French Painting in the Age of Romanticism*. London: Tate Britain; Minneapolis Institute of Arts; and New York: Metropolitan Museum of Art. London and New York, 2003.

Los Angeles 1961
French Masters, Rococo to Romanticism. Los Angeles: UCLA Art Galleries. Los Angeles, 1961.

Los Angeles 1976
Ebria Feinblatt. *Old Master Drawings from American Collections*. Los Angeles County Museum of Art. Los Angeles, 1976.

Los Angeles–New York–Paris 1994–95
The French Renaissance in Prints from the Bibliothèque Nationale de France. Los Angeles: Grunwald Center for the Arts; New York: Metropolitan Museum of Art; and Paris: Bibliothèque Nationale de France. Los Angeles, 1994.

Los Angeles–St. Louis 2000
Barbara Butts and Lee Hendrix. *Painting on Light: Drawings and Stained Glass in the Age of Dürer and Holbein*. Los Angeles: J. Paul Getty Museum; and St. Louis Art Museum. Los Angeles, 2000.

Los Angeles et al. 2004–05
Pierre Rosenberg. *Passion for Drawing: Poussin to Cézanne, Works from the Prat Collection*. Los Angeles County Museum of Art; Toledo, Ohio: Toledo Museum of Art; Naples, Fla.: Naples

Museum of Art; and Philadelphia Museum of Art. Alexandria, Va., 2004.

Lugano–Rome 1989–90
Pier Francesco Mola, 1612–1666. Lugano: Museo Cantonale d'Arte; and Rome: Musei Capitolini. Milan, 1989.

Madrid 1999
Lorenzo Tiepolo. Madrid: Museo Nacional del Prado. Madrid, 1999.

Madrid 2003–04
Patrick Lenaghan. *Imágenes del Quijote: Modelos de representación en las ediciones de los siglos XVII a XIX*. Madrid: Museo Nacional del Prado and Calcografía Nacional. Madrid, 2003.

Manchester–Cambridge 1987
Richard Thomson. *The Private Degas*. Manchester: Whitworth Art Gallery; and Cambridge: Fitzwilliam Museum. London, 1987.

Mantua 1989
Giulio Romano. Mantua: Palazzo Te and Palazzo Ducale. Milan, 1989.

Mantua–Vienna 1999
Konrad Oberhuber, ed. *Roma e lo stile classico di Raffaello: 1515–1527*. Mantua: Palazzo Te; and Vienna: Graphische Sammlung Albertina. Milan, 1999.

Mantua 2001
Perino del Vaga: Tra Raffaello e Michelangelo. Mantua: Palazzo Te. Milan, 2001.

Meaux 2000
Dominique Brême. *Hyacinthe Rigaud, dessinateur*. Meaux: Musée Bossuet. Milan, 2000.

Metz 1988
Jean-Baptiste Le Prince. Metz: Musée d'Art et Histoire. Metz, 1988.

Middletown–New Haven 1988
Elise K. Kenney. *Gian Domenico Tiepolo and the Flight into Egypt*. Middletown, Conn.: Davison Art Center; and New Haven: YUAG. Middletown, Conn., 1988.

Milwaukee–New York 1989–90
E. James Mundy. *Renaissance into Baroque: Italian Master Drawings by the Zuccari, 1550–1600*. Milwaukee Art Museum; and New York: National Academy of Design. Milwaukee and Cambridge, 1989.

Milwaukee 1992
Frima Fox Hofrichter. *Leonaert Bramer, 1596–1674: A Painter of the Night*. Milwaukee: Patrick and Beatrice Haggerty Museum of Art, Marquette University. Milwaukee, 1992.

Minneapolis–New York 1962
The Nineteenth Century: One Hundred Twenty-Five Master Drawings. Minneapolis: University of Minnesota Gallery; and New York: Solomon R. Guggenheim Museum. Minneapolis, 1962.

Minneapolis 1993
Images of a Queen's Power: The Artemisia Tapestries. Minneapolis Institute of Arts. Minneapolis, 1993.

Montpellier 1988
Collection de dessins et de tableaux anciens. Sale cat., Montpellier, 6 May 1988.

Munich 1989–90
Holm Bevers. *Niederländische Zeichnungen des 16. Jahrhunderts in der Staatlichen Graphischen Sammlung München*. Munich: Staatlichen Graphischen Sammlung. Munich, 1989.

Munich 1994
Tilman Falk. *Die deutschen Zeichnungen des 15. Jahrhunderts*. Munich: Staatliche Graphische Sammlung. Munich, 1994.

Munich 1996
Corot, Courbet, und die Maler von Barbizon: Les amis de la nature. Munich: Haus der Kunst. Munich, 1996.

Nagasaki 1993–94
Masters of Dordrecht: 17th, 18th, and 19th-Century Paintings from the Collection of the Dordrechts Museum. Nagasaki: Palace Huis ten Bosch. Nagasaki, 1993.

Nancy 1992
Jacques Callot, 1592–1635. Nancy: Musée Historique Lorrain. Paris, 1992.

Naples 1991
Ferdinando Bologna, ed. *Battistello Caracciolo e il primo naturalismo a Napoli*. Naples: Castel Sant'Angelo and Certosa di S. Martino. Naples, 1991.

Newark 1960
Old Master Drawings. Newark, N.J.: Newark Museum. Newark, N.J., 1960.

New Haven 1974
Edmund Pillsbury and Jean Caldwell. *Sixteenth-Century Italian Drawings*. New Haven: YUAG. New Haven, 1974.

New Haven 1975
Peter Sutton and Otto Naumann. *Dutch Religious Art of the Seventeenth Century*. New Haven: YUAG. New Haven, 1975.

New Haven 1984
French Drawings: Acquisitions, 1970–1984. New Haven: YUAG. New Haven, 1984.

New Haven 1986
Patricia A. Emison. *The Art of Teaching: Sixteenth-Century Allegorical Prints and Drawings*. New Haven: YUAG. New Haven, 1986.

New Haven 1987
Alvin L. Clark, Jr. *From Mannerism to Classicism: Printmaking in France, 1600–1660*. New Haven: YUAG. New Haven, 1987.

New Haven 1991a
Alvin L. Clark, Jr. *Vision and Continuity: Italian Drawings from the Permanent Collection*. New Haven: YUAG. New Haven, 1991.

New Haven 1991b
Elisabeth Hodermarsky. *The Preparatory Process: Art in the Making*. New Haven: YUAG. New Haven, 1991.

New Haven 1992
Beyond Rembrandt: Dutch Drawings at Yale, 1500–1700. New Haven: YUAG. New Haven, 1992.

New Haven 1994
Maia W. Gahtan and Philip J. Jacks. *Vasari's Florence: Artists and Literati at the Medicean Court*. New Haven: YUAG. New Haven, 1994.

New Haven 2003
Jennifer Gross, ed. *Edgar Degas, Defining the Modernist Edge*. New Haven: YUAG. New Haven, 2003.

New York 1931
C. W. Kraushaar Art Galleries. *Exhibition of Modern French Paintings, Water Colors and Drawings, including an Important Group of Drawings and Watercolors by Constantin Guys*. Sale cat., New York, 1931.

New York 1944
Eugène Delacroix, 1798–1863: Loan Exhibition in Aid of the Quaker Emergency Service. New York: Wildenstein Galleries. New York, 1944.

New York 1975
Drawings from the Collection of Mr. and Mrs. Eugene V. Thaw. New York: Pierpont Morgan Library. New York, 1975.

New York 1976
European Drawings from the Fitzwilliam. New York: Pierpont Morgan Library. Washington, D.C., 1976.

New York–Paris 1977–78
Rembrandt and His Century: Dutch Drawings of the Seventeenth Century, from the Collection of Frits Lugt, Institut Néerlandais, Paris. New York: Pierpont Morgan Library; and Paris: Institut Néerlandais. New York, 1978.

New York 1980
Denys Sutton. *François Boucher*. New York: Wildenstein Galleries. New York, 1980.

New York 1985
Mia Weiner. *Exhibition of Old Master Drawings*. Sale cat., New York, 1985.

New York–San Diego–Houston 1985–86
Philippe Grunchec. *Master Drawings by Géricault*. New York: Pierpont Morgan Library; San Diego: Museum of Art; and Houston Museum of Fine Arts. Washington, D.C., 1985.

New York–Detroit–Paris 1986
Alastair Laing et al. *François Boucher, 1703–1770*. New York: Metropolitan Museum of Art; Detroit: The Detroit Institute of Arts; and Paris: Grand Palais. New York, 1986.

New York 1987
J. A. Gere. *Raphael and His Circle*. New York: Pierpont Morgan Library. New York, 1987.

New York 1988
Egbert Haverkamp-Begemann, with Carolyn Logan. *Creative Copies: Interpretative Drawings from Michelangelo to Picasso*. New York: The Drawing Center. London, 1988.

New York 1991
Eugène Delacroix (1798–1863): Paintings, Drawings, and Prints from North American Collections. New York: Metropolitan Museum of Art. New York, 1991.

New York 1991–92
Mary L. Myers. *French Architectural and Ornament Drawings of the Eighteenth Century*. New York: Metropolitan Museum of Art. New York, 1991.

New York 1994
William M. Griswold and Linda Wolk-Simon. *Sixteenth-Century Italian Drawings in New York Collections*. New York: Metropolitan Museum of Art. New York, 1994.

New York 1995
Timothy B. Husband. *The Luminous Image: Painted Glass Roundels in the Lowlands, 1480–1560*. New York: Metropolitan Museum of Art. New York, 1995.

New York 1998
Master Drawings from the Hermitage and Pushkin Museums. New York: Pierpont Morgan Library. New York, 1998.

New York 1999a
Janet Cox-Rearick, ed. *Giulio Romano: Master Designer*. New York: Bertha and Karl Leubsdorf Art Gallery, Hunter College. New York, 1999.

New York 1999b
W. M. Brady and Co. *Old Master Drawings*. Sale cat., New York, 1999.

New York–Ottawa 1999–2000
Alan Wintermute. *Watteau and His World: French Drawing from 1700 to 1750*. New York: Frick Collection; and Ottawa: National Gallery of Canada. London and New York, 1999.

New York 2002a
Hugh Brigstocke. *Procaccini in America*. Ed. Nicholas H. J. Hall. New York: Hall and Knight. New York, 2002.

New York 2002b
Thomas P. Campbell. *Tapestry in the Renaissance: Art and Magnificence*. New York: Metropolitan Museum of Art. New York, 2002.

New York–Los Angeles 2002
Greuze the Draftsman. New York: Frick Collection; and Los Angeles: The J. Paul Getty Museum. London and New York, 2002.

New York 2003
Carmen C. Bambach, ed. *Leonardo da Vinci, Master Draftsman*. New York: Metropolitan Museum of Art. New York, 2003.

New York–Fort Worth 2003
Alastair Laing. *The Drawings of François Boucher*. New York: Frick Collection; and Fort Worth: Kimbell Art Museum. New York, 2003.

New York 2004
David Tunick, Inc. *Jean-Honoré Fragonard (1732–1806): Drawings for Ariosto's Orlando Furioso*. Sale cat., New York, 2004.

New York–London 2004
Jean-Luc Baroni, Ltd. *Master Drawings and Oil Sketches*. Sale cat., New York and London, 2004.

New York–Princeton 2005
Emmanuel Schwartz. *The Legacy of Homer: Four Centuries of Art from the École Nationale Supérieure des Beaux-Arts, Paris*. New York: Dahesh Museum of Art; and Princeton University Art Museum. New Haven and New York, 2005.

New York–London 2005–06
Perrin Stein, with Martin Royalton-Kisch. *French Drawings from the British Museum: Clouet to Seurat*. New York: Metropolitan Museum of Art; and London: British Museum. London and New York, 2005.

Northampton–Williamstown 1976–77
Charles C. Cunningham, with Susan D. Peters and Kathleen Zimmerer. *Jongkind and the Pre-Impressionists: Painters of the École Saint-Siméon*. Northampton, Mass.: Smith College Museum of Art; and Williamstown, Mass.: Sterling and Francine Clark Art Institute. Williamstown, Mass., 1977.

Notre Dame 1972
Eighteenth Century France: A Study of Its Art and Civilization. Notre Dame, Ind.: Art Gallery, University of Notre Dame. Notre Dame, Ind., 1972.

Nottingham–London 1983
Francis Ames-Lewis and Joanne Wright, eds. *Drawing in the Italian Renaissance Workshop*. Nottingham: University Art Gallery; and London: Victoria and Albert Museum. London, 1983.

Oberlin–Brunswick–Hanover 1991
Larry J. Feinberg. *From Studio to Studiolo: Florentine Draftsmanship under the First Medici Grand Dukes*. Oberlin, Ohio: Allen Memorial Art Museum; Brunswick, Maine: Bowdoin College Museum of Art; and Hanover, N.H.: Hood Museum of Art. Oberlin, Ohio, and Seattle, 1991.

Omaha–Little Rock–Sarasota 1997–98
Zirka Filipczak. *Hot Dry Men, Cold Wet Women: The Theory of Humors in Western European Art, 1575–1700*. Omaha: Joslyn Art Museum; Little Rock: Arkansas Art Center; and Sarasota, Fla.: John and Mable Ringling Museum of Art. New York, 1997.

Ottawa 1968–69
Michael Jaffé. *Jacob Jordaens, 1593–1678*. Ottawa: National Gallery of Canada. Ottawa, 1968.

Ottawa 1976
Mary Cazort Taylor. *European Drawings from Canadian Collections, 1500–1900*. Ottawa: National Gallery of Canada. Ottawa, 1976.

Ottawa–Little Rock 1993
Mimi Cazort. *Bella Pittura: The Art of the Gandolfi*. Ottawa: National Gallery of Canada; and Little Rock: Arkansas Art Center. Ottawa, 1993.

Ottawa–Paris–Washington 1999–2000
Daumier, 1808–1879. Ottawa: National Gallery of Canada; Paris: Grand Palais; and Washington, D.C.: Phillips Collection. Ottawa, 1999.

Palermo 1995–96
Vincenzo Abbate, ed. *Maestri del disegno nelle collezioni di Palazzo Abatellis*. Palermo: Palazzo Abatellis. Palermo, 1995.

Palm Beach 1974
Master Drawings and Watercolors from the Yale University Art Gallery. Palm Beach, Fla.: Society of the Four Arts. Palm Beach, Fla., 1974.

Paris 1878
Exposition des peintures et dessins de H. Daumier. Paris: Galeries Durand-Ruel. Paris, 1878.

Paris 1879
Catalogue descriptif des dessins de maîtres anciens exposés à l'École des Beaux-Arts. Paris: École des Beaux-Arts. Paris, 1879.

Paris 1895
Exposition posthume des visions de C. Guys. Paris: Galerie Georges Petit. Paris, 1895. Reprinted in facsimile in Reff 1981: vol. 46, no. 4.

Paris 1944
L'aquarelle romantique et contemporaine. Paris: Galerie Charpentier. Paris, 1944.

Paris 1951
Jean Cailleux. *De Watteau à Prud'hon*. Paris: Galerie Cailleux. Paris, 1951.

Paris 1963
Maurice Sérullaz. *Mémorial de l'exposition Eugène Delacroix*. Paris: Musée du Louvre. Paris, 1963.

Paris 1967
Le cabinet d'un grand amateur, P.-J. Mariette, 1694–1774: Dessins du XVe siècle au XVIIIe siècle. Paris: Musée du Louvre. Paris, 1967.

Paris et al. 1968
Dessins de paysagistes hollandais du XVIIe siècle, de la collection particulière conservée à l'Institut Néerlandais de Paris. Paris: Institut Néerlandais; Brussels: Bibliothèque Albert Ier; Rotterdam: Musée Boymans van Beuningen; and Bern: Musée des Beaux-Arts. Brussels, 1968.

Paris 1972–73
L'école de Fontainebleau. Paris: Grand Palais. Paris, 1972.

Paris–Florence 1980–81
Karel G. Boon. *L'époque de Lucas de Leyde et Pierre Bruegel*. Paris: Institut Néerlandais; and Florence: Istituto Universitario Olandese di Storia dell'Arte. Paris, 1980.

Paris 1981
Le baroque en Bohême. Paris: Grand Palais. Paris, 1981.

Paris 1982a
Dessins baroques florentins du musée du Louvre. Paris: Musée du Louvre. Paris, 1982.

Paris 1982b
Hal Opperman. *J.-B. Oudry, 1686–1755*. Paris: Grand Palais. Paris, 1982.

Paris 1983
Galerie Cailleux. *Rome 1760–1770: Fragonard, Hubert Robert et leurs amis*. Sale cat., Paris, 1983.

Paris 1983–84
Raphael et l'art français. Paris: Grand Palais. Paris, 1983.

Paris 1984–85
Diderot et l'art de Boucher à David. Paris: Hôtel de la Monnaie. Paris, 1984.

Paris 1985a
Le héraut du dix-septième siècle: Dessins et gravures de Jacques de Gheyn II et III de la Fondation Custodia, collection Frits Lugt. Paris: Institut Néerlandais. Paris, 1985.

Paris 1985b
Mary Newcome-Schleier. *Le dessin à Gênes du XVIe au XVIIIe siècle*. Paris: Musée du Louvre. Paris, 1985.

Paris–Hamburg 1985–86
Emmanuelle Brugerolles et al. *Renaissance et maniérisme dans les écoles du Nord*. Paris: École Nationale Supérieure des Beaux-Arts; and Hamburg: Kunsthalle. Paris, 1985.

Paris–New York 1987–88
Pierre Rosenberg. *Fragonard*. Paris: Grand Palais; and New York: Metropolitan Museum of Art. New York, 1988.

Paris–Ottawa–New York 1988–89
Jean Sutherland Boggs. *Degas*. Paris: Grand Palais; Ottawa: National Gallery of Canada; and New York: Metropolitan Museum of Art. New York and Ottawa, 1988.

Paris 1991
Dessins espagnols: Maîtres des XVIe et XVIIe siècles. Paris: Musée du Louvre. Paris, 1991.

Paris 1992–93
Fragonard et le dessin français au XVIIIe siècle dans les collections du Petit Palais. Paris: Petit Palais. Paris, 1992.

Paris 1993
Dessins français du XVIIe siècle, dans les collections publiques françaises. Paris: Musée du Louvre. Paris, 1993.

Paris 1995
Eugène Delacroix à l'Assemblée Nationale: Peintures murales, esquisses, dessins. Paris: Assemblée Nationale. Paris, 1995.

Paris 1996
Jongkind: 1819–1891. Paris: Galerie Brame and Lorenceau; and Le Vieux Poët Laval: Centre International d'Art et d'Animation Raymond du Puy. Paris, 1996.

Paris 2001a
Dessins romantiques français, provenant de collections privées parisiennes. Paris: Musée de la Vie Romantique. Paris, 2001.

Paris 2001b
Ingres et Marcotte: Lettres, documents, dessins et gravures. Paris: Institut Néerlandais. Paris, 2001.

Paris–Geneva–New York 2001
Emmanuelle Brugerolles and David Guillet. *Poussin, Claude and Their World: Seventeenth-Century French Drawings from the École des Beaux-Arts, Paris*. Paris: École Nationale Supérieure des Beaux-Arts; Geneva: Musée d'Art et d'Histoire; and New York: Frick Collection. Paris and New York, 2001.

Paris 2002a
Frédéric Dassas et al. *L'invention du sentiment: Aux sources du Romantisme*. Paris: Musée de la Musique. Paris, 2002.

Paris 2002b
La place Vendôme: Art, pouvoir, et fortune. Paris: 9, place Vendôme. Paris, 2002.

Paris 2002–03
Constantin Guys, 1802–1892: Fleurs du mal. Paris: Musée de la Vie Romantique. Paris, 2002.

Paris 2003–04
Françoise Joulie and Jean-François Méjanès. *François Boucher: Hier et aujourd'hui.* Paris: Musée du Louvre. Paris, 2003.

Paris–Sydney–Ottawa 2003–06
Emmanuelle Brugerolles. *François Boucher et l'art rocaille dans les collections de l'École des Beaux-Arts.* Paris: École Nationale Supérieure des Beaux-Arts; Sydney: Art Gallery of New South Wales; and Ottawa: National Gallery of Canada. Paris, 2003.

Paris 2004–05
Primatice: Maître de Fontainebleau. Paris: Musée du Louvre. Paris, 2004.

Pfäffikon–Geneva 1978
Art vénitien en Suisse et au Liechtenstein. Pfäffikon: Seedam-Kulturzentrum; and Geneva: Musée d'Art et d'Histoire. Milan, 1978.

Philadelphia 1985
Leslie A. Morris and Ridie E. W. Ghezzi. *Carried Away by Indians: Indian Captivity Narratives and the Evolution of a Stereotype.* Philadelphia: Rosenbach Museum and Library. Philadelphia, 1985.

Philadelphia–Houston 1985
Kimerly Rorschach. *Eighteenth-Century French Book Illustration: Drawings by Fragonard and Gravelot from the Rosenbach Museum and Library.* Philadelphia: Rosenbach Museum and Library; and Houston: Museum of Fine Arts. Philadelphia, 1985.

Philadelphia–Pittsburgh–New York 1986–87
Kimerly Rorschach. *Drawings by Jean-Baptiste Le Prince for the Voyage en Sibérie.* Philadelphia: Rosenbach Museum and Library; Pittsburgh: Frick Art Museum; and New York: Frick Collection. Philadelphia, 1986.

Philadelphia–Houston 2000
Edgar Peters Bowron and Joseph J. Rishel, eds. *Art in Rome in the Eighteenth Century.* Philadelphia Museum of Art; and Houston: Museum of Fine Arts. Philadelphia and London, 2000.

Poughkeepsie 1970
Dutch Mannerism, Apogee and Epilogue. Poughkeepsie, N.Y.: Vassar College Art Gallery. Poughkeepsie, N.Y., 1970.

Poughkeepsie 1976
Curtis O. Baer. *Seventeenth Century Dutch Landscape Drawings and Selected Prints from American Collections.* Poughkeepsie, N.Y.: Vassar College Art Gallery. Poughkeepsie, N.Y., 1976.

Princeton–Cleveland–Los Angeles 1981–82
Drawings by Gianlorenzo Bernini from the Museum der Bildenden Künste, Leipzig. Princeton University Art Museum; Cleveland Museum of Art; and Los Angeles County Museum of Art. Princeton, 1981.

Princeton–Washington–Pittsburgh 1982–83
Thomas DaCosta Kaufmann. *Drawings from the Holy Roman Empire, 1540–1680: A Selection from North American Collections.* Princeton University Art Museum; Washington, D.C.: National Gallery of Art; and Pittsburgh: Museum of Art, Carnegie Institute. Princeton, 1982.

Providence 1968
Visions and Revisions. Providence: Rhode Island School of Design, Museum of Art. Providence, R.I., 1968.

Providence 1975
Mary Crawford Volk, ed. *Rubenism.* Providence, R.I.: Bell Gallery, List Art Building, Brown University. Providence, R.I., 1975.

Regina–Montreal 1970
Walter Vitzthum. *A Selection of Italian Drawings from North American Collections.* Regina: Mackenzie Norman Art Gallery; and Montreal: Museum of Fine Arts. Regina, 1970.

Rennes 2001
Jacques Thuillier. *Jacques de Bellange.* Rennes: Musée des Beaux-Arts. Rennes, 2001.

Rome 1978
Galleria W. Apolloni. *Dai manieristi ai neoclassici.* Sale cat., Rome, 1978.

Rome 1980
Constantin Guys, il pittore della vita moderna. Rome: Palazzo Braschi. Rome, 1980.

Rome 1981
F. M. Alberti Gaudioso et al. *Gli affreschi di Paolo III a Castel Sant'Angelo.* 2 vols. Rome: Castel Sant'Angelo. Rome, 1981.

Rome 1982–83
L'immagine di San Francesco nella Controriforma. Rome: Calcografia. Rome, 1982.

Rome 1983–84
Kristina Herrmann-Fiore. *Disegni degli Alberti: Il volume 2503 del Gabinetto Nazionale delle Stampe.* Rome: Gabinetto Nazionale delle Stampe. Rome, 1983.

Rome 1984–85
Degas e l'Italia. Rome: Villa Medici. Rome, 1984.

Rome 1990–91
J. H. Fragonard e H. Robert a Roma. Rome: Villa Medici. Rome, 1990.

Rome–Brussels 1995
Fiamminghi a Roma, 1508–1608: Artistes des Pays-Bas et de la principauté de Liège à Rome de la Renaissance. Rome: Palazzo delle Esposizione; and Brussels: Palais des Beaux-Arts. Brussels, 1995.

Rome 1996–97
Domenichino (1581–1641). Rome: Palazzo Venezia. Milan, 1996.

Rome–Paris 1998
Francesco Salviati (1510–1563), o la bella maniera. Rome: Villa Medici; and Paris: Musée du Louvre. Milan and Paris, 1998.

Rotterdam–Washington 1985–86
Jacques de Gheyn II, 1565–1629: Drawings. Rotterdam: Museum Boymans van Beuningen; and Washington, D.C.: National Gallery of Art. Rotterdam, 1986.

Rouen 1966
Antoine Schnapper. *Jean Jouvenet.* Rouen: Musée des Beaux-Arts. Rouen, 1966.

Rouen 2004–05
Jean-Baptiste Le Prince (Metz, 1734–Saint-Denis du Port, 1781): Le Voyage en Russie, Collections de la ville de Rouen. Cabinet des dessins, Cahier no. 8. Rouen: Musée des Beaux-Arts. Rouen, 2004.

Rutgers 1983
Frima Fox Hofrichter. *Haarlem: The Seventeenth Century.* Rutgers, N.J.: Jane Voorhees Zimmerli Art Museum. New Brunswick, N.J., 1983.

Salzburg 1989
Pavel Preiss. *Franz Karl Palko (1724–1767): Ölskizzen, Zeichnungen, und Druckgraphik.* Salzburg: Barockmuseum. Salzburg, 1989.

San Francisco 1947
19th Century French Drawings. San Francisco: California Palace of the Legion of Honor. San Francisco, 1947.

San Francisco 1989
Lorenz E. A. Eitner and Steven A. Nash. *Gericault, 1791–1824.* San Francisco: California Palace of the Legion of Honor. San Francisco, 1989.

Sarasota 1980–81
William H. Wilson. *Dutch Seventeenth Century Portraiture: The Golden Age*. Sarasota, Fla.: John and Mable Ringling Museum of Art. Sarasota, Fla., 1980.

's-Hertogenbosch–Strasbourg 1991
Alain Roy. *Theodoor van Thulden: Een Zuidnederlandse barokschilder/Un peintre baroque du cercle de Rubens*. 's-Hertogenbosch: Noordbrabants Museum; and Strasbourg: Musée des Beaux-Arts. Zwolle, 1991.

Siena 1990
Domenico Beccafumi e il suo tempo. Siena: Pinacoteca Nazionale. Milan, 1990.

Siena 2000
Alessandro VII Chigi (1599–1667): Il papa senese di Roma moderna. Siena: Palazzo Pubblico and Palazzo Chigi Zondadari. Siena, 2000.

Saint Petersburg 1996
Tatiana Ilatovskaya. *Master Drawings Rediscovered: Treasures from Prewar German Collections*. Saint Petersburg: State Hermitage Museum. Moscow, 1996.

Stuttgart 1979–80
Heinrich Geissler. *Zeichnung in Deutschland: Deutsche Zeichner 1540–1640*. 2 vols. Stuttgart: Staatsgalerie. Stuttgart, 1979–80.

Toronto et al. 1972
Pierre Rosenberg. *French Master Drawings of the 17th and 18th Centuries in North American Collections*. Toronto: Art Gallery of Ontario; Ottawa: National Gallery of Canada; San Francisco: California Palace of the Legion of Honor; and New York Cultural Center, in collaboration with Fairleigh-Dickinson University. London, 1972.

Toulouse 1962
Les dessins de Raymond La Fage. Toulouse: Musée Paul Dupuy. Toulouse, 1962.

Turin 1982
Giovanni Romano, ed. *Gaudenzio Ferrari e la sua scuola: I cartoni cinquecenteschi dell'Accademia Albertina*. Turin: Accademia Albertina. Turin, 1982.

Udine–Bloomington 1996–97
Adelheid M. Gealt and George Knox. *Domenico Tiepolo: Master Draftsman*. Udine: Castello di Udine; and Bloomington: Indiana University Art Museum. Bloomington, Ind., 1996.

Venice Mestre 1997–98
Giandomenico Romanelli and Filippo Pedrocco, eds. *Lorenzo Tiepolo e il suo tempo*. Venice Mestre: Villa Cerese. Milan, 1997.

Vercelli 1985
Paola Astrua and Giovanni Romano, eds. *Bernardino Lanino*. Vercelli: Museo Borgogna. Milan, 1985.

Vienna 1989
Fürstenhöfe der Renaissance: Giulio Romano und die klassische Tradition. Vienna: Albertina. Vienna, 1989.

Washington 1945
A Loan Exhibition of 52 Drawings for Ariosto's "Orlando furioso" by Fragonard. Washington, D.C.: Phillips Memorial Gallery. Washington, D.C., 1945.

Washington–Chicago 1973–74
Regina Shoolman Slatkin. *François Boucher in North American Collections: 100 Drawings*. Washington, D.C.: National Gallery of Art; and Art Institute of Chicago. Washington, D.C., 1973.

Washington 1975
H. Diane Russell. *Jacques Callot: Prints and Related Drawings*. Washington, D.C.: National Gallery of Art. Washington, D.C., 1975.

Washington–Denver–Fort Worth 1977
Franklin W. Robinson. *Seventeenth Century Dutch Drawings from American Collections*. Washington, D.C.: National Gallery of Art; Denver Art Museum; and Fort Worth: Kimbell Art Museum. Washington, D.C, 1977.

Washington 1978–79
Victor Carlson. *Hubert Robert: Drawings and Watercolors*. Washington, D.C.: National Gallery of Art. Washington, D.C., 1978.

Washington–Cambridge 1978–79
Eunice Williams. *Drawings by Fragonard in North American Collections*. Washington, D.C.: National Gallery of Art; Cambridge, Mass.: Fogg Art Museum; and New York: Frick Collection. Washington, D.C., 1978.

Washington–Paris 1982–83
H. Diane Russell. *Claude Lorrain, 1600–1682*. Washington, D.C.: National Gallery of Art; and Paris: Grand Palais. Washington, D.C., 1982.

Washington–Boston 1983
Ellen S. Jacobowitz and Stephanie Loeb Stepanek. *The Prints of Lucas van Leyden and His Contemporaries*. Washington, D.C.: National Gallery of Art; and Boston: Museum of Fine Arts. Washington, D.C., 1983.

Washington et al. 1984
Robert Randolf Coleman. *Renaissance Drawings from the Ambrosiana*. Washington, D.C.: National Gallery of Art; South Bend, Ind.: Snite Museum of Art; Los Angeles County Museum of Art; Cleveland Museum of Art; and Fort Worth: Kimbell Art Museum. Notre Dame, Ind., 1984.

Washington–Paris 1984–85
Margaret Morgan Grasselli and Pierre Rosenberg, with Nicole Parmantier. *Watteau, 1684–1721*. Washington, D.C.: National Gallery of Art, and Paris: Grand Palais. Washington, D.C., 1984.

Washington–New York 1986–87
The Age of Bruegel: Netherlandish Drawings in the Sixteenth Century. Washington, D.C.: National Gallery of Art; and New York: Pierpont Morgan Library. Washington, D.C., Cambridge, and New York, 1986.

Washington et al. 1996–98
Paul Joannides. *Michelangelo and His Influence: Drawings from Windsor Castle*. Washington, D.C.: National Gallery of Art; Fort Worth: Kimbell Art Museum; Art Institute of Chicago; Cambridge: Fitzwilliam Museum; and London: The Queen's Gallery. Washington, D.C., and London, 1996.

Washington 2003–04
Margaret Morgan Grasselli et al. *Colorful Impressions: The Printmaking Revolution in Eighteenth-Century France*. Washington, D.C.: National Gallery of Art. Washington, D.C., 2003.

Wellesley–Cleveland 1993–94
Anne-Marie Logan. *Flemish Drawings in the Age of Rubens*. Wellesley, Mass.: Davis Museum and Cultural Center; and Cleveland Museum of Art. Wellesley, Mass., 1993.

Williamstown 1980
David Martocci. *The Male Nude*. Williamstown, Mass.: Sterling and Francine Clark Art Institute. Williamstown, Mass., 1980.

Williamstown 1987
Rafael Fernandez and Alexandra R. Murphy. *Degas in the Clark Collection*. Williamstown, Mass.: Sterling and Francine Clark Art Institute. Williamstown, Mass., 1987.

Zurich 1973
50 Jahre Kunsthandelsverband der Schweiz. Zurich: Kunsthaus. Zurich, 1973.

Index

Page references to artworks reproduced in the text are given in *italics*. Each artist in the exhibition has been given a catalogue number. This number is in boldface at the end of the entry for the artist. Dates of birth/death or activity are given only for artists.

Aachen, Hans von (1552–1615), 106n.9, 111, 114–115
Abate, Sabatino, Jr., 83
Abbey, Edwin Austin, Memorial Collection, 6
Aesop, 93, 120
Agucchi, Giovanni Battista, 117
Alberti, Cherubino (1553–1615), 26, *109*, 109–110, *248*, **cat. no. 28**
Alden, Bradford R. and Mrs., 4
Aldrich, William T., 245
Algarotti, Francesco, 202
Allan, Eva, 16
Allori, Alessandro (1535–1607), *17–18*, 81
Altschul, Frank, 7
Amsterdam, Museum het Rembrandthuis
   Lastman, 157, 159n.2
Amsterdam, Rijksmuseum
   Boucher, 191
   J. Cuyp, 137n.7
   Jordaens, 163nn.8–9
   J. de Momper the Younger, 92
   Rembrandt, 159n.2
   Victors, 159n.2
   Vouet, 139n.5
André, John (1750–1780), 3
Andreossy, Antoine-François, 196
Angers, Musée des Beaux-Arts
   Monier, 169n.4
Ann Arbor, University of Michigan Museum of Art
   F. Zuccaro, 85n.8

anonymous artist
   Circe, 54
   A Lion, 23, *38–39*, **cat. no. 1**
   Old Soldiers of the Empire, *237*
   Portrait of Cardinal Sforza Pallavicino (after Bernini), 170, *170*
   Scenes from the Lives of Saint Catherine and Saint Roch, 47
   Three Scenes from the Life of John the Baptist, *76–77*, **cat. no. 16**
   Three Scenes from the Life of Saint Nicholas of Myra, 77, *77*
   Virgin and Child with Saint John the Baptist, 3, 4, *5*
Antwerp, Koninklijke Museum voor Schone Kunsten
   Jordaens, 163n.1
Antwerp, Plantin-Moretus House
   de Vos, 91n.6
Antwerp, Rubenshuis
   Jordaens, 163n.10
Apuleius, 66–67, 68n.7
aquatint, use of, 204, 212
Arezzo, Pinacoteca Comunale
   Cigoli, 101–102, *103*
Arezzo, Santa Maria della Pieve
   Barocci, 87
Argentieri, Claudio, 132
Ariosto, 54n.7, 212, 214
Armenini, Giovanni Battista, 42, 45n.8, 59
Artemisia, History of (tapestry series), 77
Artois, Count of, 175n.3
Audran, Jean (1667–1756), 189n.1
Aufsess, Hans Freiherr von und zu, 221
Austin, Tex., Blanton Museum of Art, vii
Azzolini, Decio, 152
Azzolini, Marchese Pompeo, 152

Baderou, Henri, 162
Balducci, Giovanni (ca. 1560–after 1632), 82n.9

Bale, Charles Sackville, 40
Bandinelli, Baccio (1488–1560), 10, 24, 25, *40–41*, **cat. no. 2**
Barbieri, Giovanni Francesco. *See* Guercino
Barendsz., Dirck (1534–1592), 89
Barocci, Federico (1535–1612), 27, 86–88, *86–88*, 133n.6, 160, **cat. no. 20**
Barré, Nicolas, 178n.8
Barroso, Miguel (1538–1590), 96
Barry, James (1741–1806), 224
Barye, Antoine-Louis (1796–1875), 7
Basel, Kunstmuseum, Kupferstichkabinett
   Spranger, 113n.7
Bassano, Jacopo (ca. 1510–1592), 27, 92
Bateson, William, 223
Batoni, Pompeo (1708–1787), 193–195, *193–195*, **cat. no. 64**
Battistello, Il. *See* Caracciolo, Giovanni Battista
Baudelaire, Charles, 236, 237, 242
Bayonne, Musée Bonnat
   Géricault, 224n.3
   Ingres, 226
Beccafumi, Domenico (1484–1551), 24, 32n.33, 63–65, *64–65*, **cat. no. 11**
Beer, M. de, 223
Bellange, Jacques (active 1602–1616), 8, 26, 28, *122–123*, 122–124, 145, *249*, **cat. no. 34**
Bellelli, Gennaro, 239
Bellelli, Giovanna, 239–241
Bellelli, Giulia, 239–241
Bellelli, Laura, 239–240
Bellini, Giovanni (1531/36–1516), 55
Bellini, Jacopo (ca. 1400–1470/71), 39, *39*
Bellori, Giovanni Pietro, 86–87, 167

281

Bensoussan, Nicole, 16
Berain, Jean (1640–1711), 16, 182
Berchem, Nicolaes (1620–1683), *155*, 155–156, **cat. no. 49**
Bergeret, Pierre-Jacques, 212
Bergeret, Pierre-Jacques-Onésyme, 212, 215n.3
Berkeley, George, 10
Berlin, Kunstbibliothek
   Jouvenet, 175, *177*
Berlin, Kupferstichkabinett
   Batoni, 195n.9
   Boscoli, 107, *108*
   Breu the Elder, 52
   Master of 1527, 48
   Oppenord, 182
   van Orley, 46, 47n.9
   Schmutzer, 210
Berlin, Schloss Charlottenberg
   Jordaens, 163n.1
Berlin, Staatliche Museen
   de Vos [destroyed], 89, *90*
Bernini, Gian Lorenzo (1598–1680), 17, 140, 170–172, *171*, 182, **cat. no. 55**
Bertoia, Jacopo (1544–ca. 1573), 161
Bibiena, Antonio Galli (1700–1774), 196
Bloemaert, Abraham (1566–1651), 8–9, 33n.62, 98, 120, 136
Blunt, Anthony, 111
Blyenberch, Abraham van (fl. 1617–1622), 142
Boccaccio, 53, 68n.3
Bodmer, Karl (1809–1893), 233–234, *235*
Boethius, 54n.5
Bol, Ferdinand (1616–1680), 2, 13, 24, *157*, 157–159, *250*, **cat. no. 50**
Bol, Hans (1534–1593), 94
Bologna, Accademia degli Incamminati, 116, 140
Bonaparte, Napoleon, Emperor of France, 237
Bonington, Richard Parkes (1802–1828), 228
Bonnemer, François (1638–1689), 178
Boorsch, Suzanne, 15
Bordon, Paris (1500–1571), 55

Borghini, Vincenzo, 83–84
Borromini, Francesco (1599–1667), 182
Bosch, Hieronymus (1450–1516), 78, 82
Boscoli, Andrea (1560–1608), 28, 102, 107–108, *107–108*, **cat. no. 27**
Boston, Abrams Collection
   Vroom the Younger, 151n.8
Boston, Horvitz Collection
   Rigaud, 181n.3
   Robert, *199*
   Schmutzer, circle of, 211, *211*
Boston, Museum of Fine Arts
   Ingres, 226
Boucher, François (1703–1770), 13, 27, *190*, 190–192, *192*, 203, 212, **cat. no. 63**
Boudin, Eugène (1824–1898), 246
Boullogne, Bon de (1649–1717), 175
Boullogne, Louis de (1654–1733), 175
Bourdon, Sébastien (1616–1671), 167, 169
Boyvin, René (ca. 1525–ca. 1625), 60
Brame, Hector, 184
Bramer, Leonaert (1596–1674), 29, *146*, 146–147, **cat. no. 45**
Braunschweig, Herzog Anton Ulrich-Museum
   Moeyaert, *156*
   Weyer, 126n.3
Bremen, Kunsthalle
   Degas, 240
   Victors, 159n.2
Breschi, Pier Giulio, 132
Breu, Jörg, the Elder (1475/80–1537), *52–53*, 52–54, **cat. no. 7**
Broeck, Crispin van den (1523–1589/91), 16
Bronzino, Agnolo (1503–1572), 81, 102
Brouwer, Adriaen (1605/06–1638), 148
Brown, John Nicholas, 212
Bruegel, Pieter (1525/30–1569), 80n.4, 92–93
Brueghel, Jan, the Elder (1568–1625), 8, *8*

Bruggen, Jean van der, 173
Brühl, Heinrich Graf von, 196
Brunsterin, Dorathea, 115
Brunswick, Maine, Bowdoin College Museum of Art
   Bramer, 147
   Master of 1527, 48
Brussels, Bibliothèque Royale de Belgique
   van Diepenbeeck, 144
   Hogenberg, 78, *80*
   A. Wierix II (after de Vos), 90
Brussels, Musées Royaux d'Art et Histoire
   van Orley, 46, 47n.9
Brussels, Musées Royaux des Beaux-Arts de Belgique
   Jordaens, 163n.1
   Muller, 100n.4
   van Orley, 47
Bruyère, Jean de la, 178n.8
Bryas, Marquise de, 187
Budapest, Szépművészeti Múzeum
   de Gelder, 159n.2
   Millet, 235n.5
Buonaccorsi, Perino. *See* Perino del Vaga
Burke, James, 13
Burton Constable, Chichester-Constable Collection
   Licinio, 55
Buytewech, Willem (1591/92–1624), 127
Byron, George Gordon, Lord, 236

Caccianemici, Vincenzo (d. 1542), 161n.6
Cades, Giuseppe (1750–1799), 221
Calando, E., 196
Caldara, Polidoro. *See* Polidoro da Caravaggio
Caldwell, John, 16
Callot, Jacques (1592–1635), 13, 128–129, *128–129*, 145, 149, 220, **cat. no. 37**
Calvaert, Denys (ca. 1540–1619), 116
Cambiaso, Luca (1527–1585), 6
Cambridge, Fitzwilliam Museum
   Degas, 241n.12
   Giulio Romano, 59n.8
   J. de Momper, 94n.4

Perino del Vaga, 68
Toeput, 93, *94*
Cambridge, St. John's College
   Rigaud, 181, *181*
Cambridge, Mass., Harvard University Art Museums
   Gillot, 184, *186*
   Ingres, 226
   van Orley, 46–47
   Perino del Vaga, 68n.10
   Watteau, 188, *188*
   F. Zuccaro, 85n.7
camera lucida, 226–227
Campbell, D. D., 86
Campi, Bernadino (1522–1595), 31n.14
Caracciolo, Giovanni Battista (1578–1635), 24, 130–*131*, **cat. no. 38**
Caravaggio, Michelangelo Merisi, called (1573–1610), 117, 130, 134, 146, 152
Cardi, Giovanni Battista, 101
Cardi, Ludovico. *See* Cigoli, Il
Cariani, Giovanni (ca. 1485–after 1547), 55
caricatures, 26–27, 140–141
Caron, Antoine (1521–1599), 77
Carpeaux, Jean-Baptiste (1827–1875), 13, *14*
Carracci, Annibale (1560–1609), 116–117, 140, 173
Carracci family, 116, 134, 140, 152, 208
Carriera, Rosalba (1675–1757), 28, 178, 202
Cartari, Vincenzo, 111
cartoons, 24–25, 31n.10, 69–70, 96–97
Castello, Valerio (1624–1659), 24, *160*, 160–161, **cat. no. 51**
Castiglione, Giovanni Benedetto (1609–1664), 164
Catherine II, the Great, of Russia, 204
Caulery, Louis de (fl. 1594–1620), 94n.4
Centen, Dirck Hendricksz. (1542/43–1618), 105
Cerano, Giovanni Battista Crespi, il (ca. 1575–1632), 134
Cervantes, Miguel de, 212

282 INDEX

Cézanne, Paul (1839–1906), 230, 246
Chantilly, Musée Condé
    Watteau, 188
Chapel Hill, Ackland Art Museum
    Naldini, 82n.10
Chappe d'Auteroche, Jean, 204
Chardin, Jean-Siméon (1699–1779), 212
Charivari, 243
Charles V, Holy Roman Emperor, 46, 60
Charpentier, Anne-Catherine Louise, 203
Charpentier, Jean-Baptiste Jude, 203
Chase, Edith, 40
Chase family, 10, 40
Chase, Mrs. Rodney, 40
Châtelet, Claude-Louis (1753–1794), 200
Chatsworth, Devonshire Collection
    Bandinelli, 40
    Barocci, 88n.12
    Beccafumi, 65nn.9–10
Cheramy, P.-A., 228
Cherbourg, Musée Thomas Henry
    Millet, 235n.5
Chicago, Art Institute
    Bandinelli, 40n.3
    Callot, 129nn.3, 6
    Géricault, 224nn.2–3
    Pinelli, 222
    Rigaud, 181nn.3, 13
Chigi, Agostino, 66
Christian II, Elector of Saxony, 115
Christina, Queen of Sweden, 152, 162
Cigoli, Ludovico Cardi, il (1559–1613), 24, 101–103, *101–103*, **cat. no. 25**
Claas, Peter, 98
Claesz, Pieter (ca. 1597–1660), 155
Clapp, Frederick M., Fund, 12, 25–27, 42–43, 66, 132, 208
Clark, Alvin L., Jr., 16
Clark, Stephen Carlton, Fund, 239
Claude Lorrain (1604/05–1682), 12, 14, 27, 150, 152–154, *153*, 191, *250*, **cat. no. 48**
Clemens, August, 178

Clerck, Hendrick de (1570?–1630), 8
Cochin, Charles Nicolas (1715–1790), 184
Codex Vallardi, 39
Colbert, Edouard, 182
Collaert, Adriaen (ca. 1560–1618), 91, 92, 94
Collaert, Hans II (1566–1628), 89
Cologne, Wallraf-Richartz-Museum
    Kellerthaler, 115n.3
Conantré, Baronne de, 187
Congnet, Gillis (ca. 1538–1599), 100n.8
Constable, John (1776–1837), 228
Cooper, James Fenimore, 233–234
Copenhagen, Staatens Museum fur Kunst
    Castello, 161n.5
    Troppa, 165
Corenzio, Belisario (1558–1646), 130
Corneille, Jean-Baptiste (1649–1695), 3–4, 169
Corneille, Pierre, 167
Cornelisz. van Haarlem, Cornelis (1562–1638), 98, 120
Corot, Camille (1796–1875), 245–246
Correggio (1494–1534), 3, 4, 87, 111, 173, 193
Cort, Cornelis (1533–1578), 29, 111
Cotte, Robert de (1656–1735), 178
Cousin, Jean, the Younger (ca. 1522–ca. 1594), 62n.6
Coxcie, Michiel (1499–1592), 67
Coypel, Antoine (1661–1772), 175
Coypel, Noel-Nicolas (1628–1707), 4
Crabeth, Adriaen Pietersz. (d. 1553), 78
Crabeth, Wouter (ca. 1594–1644), 146
Cracow, National Museum, Czartoryski Collection
    Bandinelli, 40n.3
Crespi, Daniele (1597/99–1630), 24, 134–135, *134–135*, **cat. no. 40**
Crozat, Pierre, 173, 182

Curradi, Francesco (1570–1661), 132–133, *132–133*, **cat. no. 39**
Curtius Rufus, Quintus, 57–58
Cuyp, Aelbert (1620–1691), 136
Cuyp, Benjamin Gerritsz. (1612–1652), 136
Cuyp, Gerrit Gerritsz. (ca. 1565–1644), 136
Cuyp, Jacob Gerritsz. (1594–1652), 27, 136–137, *136–137*, **cat. no. 41**

Dandini, Cesare (1596–1657), 132
Dante Alighieri, 83, 216
Darmstadt, Hessisches Landesmuseum
    Bernini, 172n.5
    F. Bol, 159n.8
    J. Cuyp, 137
    Rigaud, 181n.13
Daubigny, Charles (1817–1878), 245
Daumier, Honoré (1808–1879), 7, 242–243, 242–244, 254, **cat. no. 83**
Davent, Léon (fl. 1540–1556), 60, 61, 62, 78
David, Jacques-Louis (1748–1825), 222, 224, 225
Day, Richard, 109
Dayton, Ruth and Bruce, vii, 12, 245
Decker, Cornelis Gerritsz. (d. 1678), 191
Decourcelle, Pierre, 198
Degas, Edgar (1834–1917), 28, 31n.2, 239–241, *239–241*, 254, **cat. no. 82**
Degas, Marguerite, 239–241
Degas, René, 240–241
Degas, Thérèse, 240
Delacre, Maurice, 182
Delacroix, Eugène (1798–1863), 13, 31n.2, *231*, 231–232, 237, **cat. no. 79**
della Bella, Stefano (1610–1664), 129
della Rovere, Giovanni Battista (ca. 1575–ca. 1630), 160
Denon, Dominique-Vivant (1747–1825), 200
Dente, Marco (d. 1527), 40

Derby, Sarah Alden, 31n.11
de' Rossi, Francesco. *See* Salviati, Francesco
Desprez, Louis-Jean (1743–1804), 200
Detroit Institute of Arts
    Degas, 239–240, *240*
Dézallier d'Argenville, Antoine-Joseph, 175, 181
Diderot, Denis, 207
Didot, Pierre, 212
Diepenbeeck, Abraham van (1596–1675), 16, 142, 144–145, 145n.11
Dieu, Antoine (1662–1727), 4
Dijon, Musée des Beaux-Arts
    Géricault, 224nn.2, 5
Dilworth, Mr. and Mrs. J. Richardson, 32n.16
Dine, Jim (b. 1935), 220n.5
Dix, George, 12
Diziani, Gaspare (1689–1787), 164
Dolci, Carlo (1616–1687), 132
Domenichino (1581–1641), 24, 26, 116–117, *116–117*, 140, **cat. no. 31**
Donnadieu, Alcide, 173
Doria, Andrea, 60, 66
Dossi, Dosso (ca. 1486–1542), 54n.7
drawing-books. *See* model-books
Dresden, Grünes Gewölbe
    Kellerthaler, 115
Dresden, Kupferstich-Kabinett
    Lievens, 159n.2
Duke, L. G., 223
Dumas, Alexandre, 242
Durand, Godefroy (1832–ca. 1920), 238n.8
Dürer, Albrecht (1471–1528), 47, 96, 105
Düsseldorf, Kunstmuseum
    Calandrucci, 166n.3
    Mola, 166n.8
Dyck, Anthony van (1599–1641), 162, 178

Eeckhout, Gerbrand van den (1621–1674), 10–11, 157, 159n.2
Egmont Collection (John Percival, 1st Earl of Egmont), 7–10, *11*,

Egmont Collection *(continued)* 15, 26–27, 33n.62, 50–*51*, *55*, *76*, *78*, 89, 92, 104, 118, 122, 136, 138, 146, 148, 150, 155, 170
Elizabeth, Empress of Russia, 203–204
Ellesmere, Francis Egerton, 1st Earl of, 57
Elsheimer, Adam (1578–1610), 150
Empoli, Jacopo da (ca. 1554–1640), 16
Erasmus, Desiderius, 75, 78
Escuriaz, Diego López. *See* López de Escuriaz, Diego
Este, Alfonso IV d', 140
Este, Duke Francesco I, d', 140
Este, Ippolito d', 215n.11
Este, Leonello d', 39n.4

Fantin-Latour, Henri (1836–1904), 246
Farnese, Duke Alessandro, 67, 111
Farnese, Duke Mario, 146
Fatio, Edmond, 182
Feilchenfeldt, Marianne (Mrs. Walter), 228
Feist, Herbert, 142
Fénélon, François, 222
Ferrara, San Vito
  Licinio, 55
Ferrari, Gaudenzio (1475/80–1546), 69–70
Fèvre, Jeanne, 241
Fiasella, Domenico (1589–1669), 161
Field, Richard S., 14
Fiorentino, Rosso. *See* Rosso Fiorentino
Flinck, Govaert (1615–1660), 3, *3*
Florence, Accademia del Disegno, 81, 132
Florence, Duomo
  Vasari, 83, 84
  F. Zuccaro, 3, 31n.12, *83*, 83–84, *85*
Florence, Galleria degli Uffizi
  Barocci, *87*, 87–88
  Beccafumi, 65nn.6, 9
  G. Gandolfi, 208n.5
  Naldini, 81, 82n.11
  Perino del Vaga, *44*
  Salviati, 72n.1
  Vivien, 178
  F. Zuccaro, 85n.7

Florence, Palazzo Pitti
  Batoni, 194, *195*
  Boscoli, 102
  Cigoli, 101, *103*
Florence, Palazzo Vecchio
  Allori, 17, *18*
  Naldini, 81–82
  Vasari, 81
Florence, Santa Croce
  Naldini, 81–82
  Vasari, 81
Florence, Santa Maria Novella
  Naldini, 81
  Vasari, 81, 102
Florence, Santissima Annunziata
  Bronzino, 102
  Pontormo, 82nn.5, 8
Floris, Frans (1519/20–1570), 16, 78
Fontainebleau, Château de, Gallery of Francis I
  Penni, 60
  Primaticcio, 60–61
  Rosso, 60
Fontainebleau, Château de, Gallery of Ulysses
  van Diepenbeeck, 145
  Primaticcio, 142
  van Thulden, 142, 144
Fontainebleau, School of, 60–61, 77, 122, 142
Fosburgh, James W. and Mary C., Fund, 12, 27, 152
Fragonard, Jean-Honoré (1732–1806), 30, 198–199, 211, 212–214, *213*, *252*, **cat. no. 72**
Fragonard, Rosalie, 212
Fragonard, Théophile, 212
Franchoys, Lucas, the Younger (1616–1681), 33n.62
Francken, Frans (1542–1616), 105
Frankfurt, Städelsches Kunstinstitut und Städtische Galerie
  Rigaud, 181n.3
Frederick Henry, Prince of Orange, 146, 151, 162
Friquet, Jacques-Claude (1648–1716), 169n.16
Fruytiers, Philip (1610–1666), 33n.62
Fuseli, Henry (1741–1825), 7, 215–217, *215–217*, 221, *252*, **cat. no. 73**

Füssli, Johann Caspar (1706–1782), 215

Galilei, Galileo, 197
Galle, Cornelis, I (1576–1650), 91
Galle, Philips (1537–1612), 74, 89, 159n.4
Gandini, Giorgio (1489–1538), 31n.7
Gandolfi, Gaetano (1734–1802), 208
Gandolfi, Ubaldo (1728–1781), 14, 208, *209*, **cat. no. 70**
Gaskin, John, 111
Gaulli, Giovanni Battista (1639–1709), 164, 165, 170
Gautier, Théophile, 236
Gavarni, Paul (1804–1866), 7
Geffroy, Gustave, 246
Gelder, Aert de (1645–1727), 159n.2
Gellée, Claude. *See* Claude Lorrain
Genoa, Palazzo Doria
  Perino del Vaga, 66–67, 68n.7
Genoa, San Francesco d'Albaro
  Fiasella, 161
Gentile da Fabriano (ca. 1385–1427), 39
Gentry, J. C., 132
Géricault, Théodore (1791–1824), 13, 223–224, *223–224*, **cat. no. 76**
Gheyn, Jacques de, I (1537/38–1591), 118
Gheyn, Jacques de, II (1565–1629), 26, 29, 33n.62, 118–119, *118–119*, **cat. no. 32**
Gheyn, Jacques de, III (1596–1641), 118
Ghisi, Giorgio (1520–1582), 60
Giani, Felice (1758–1823), 221
Gillet, Nicolas (1712–1791), 203
Gillot, Claude (1673–1722), 13, 29, 184–186, *185–186*, **cat. no. 61**
Giorgione (1477–before 1510), 55
Girardon, François (1628–1715), 178
Girtin, Thomas (1775–1802), 236
Giulio Romano (1492/99–1546), 2, 17, 24, *57–58*, 57–59, 60, 62n.6, 66, 70n.4, 74, 167, 173, **cat. no. 9**

Goddard, Stephen, 16
Goltzius, Hendrick (1558–1617), 17, 29, 89, 98, 111, 118, 150
Goncourt, Edmond and Jules de, 184, 190
Gonzaga, Federico, 66
Goupy, Adolphe le, 178
Goyen, Jan van (1596–1666), 150, 155
Grassi, Luigi, 201
Graves, John T. *See* Egmont Collection
Grebber, Pieter de (ca. 1600–1652/54), 155
Greene, Edward B., 6, 178, 180
Gregory XIII, Pope, 76
Grenoble, Musée des Beaux-Arts
  Licinio, 56
Greuze, Jean-Baptiste (1725–1805), 27, 206–207, *206–207*, 211, **cat. no. 69**
Griggs, Maitland F., Fund, 12, 57, 63, 71, 86, 101, 160
Grimm, Friedrich Melchior, Baron von, 207
Groningen, Jan Swart van. *See* Swart van Groningen, Jan
Guercino (Giovanni Battista Barbieri), called (1591–1666), 27, 140–*141*, **cat. no. 43**
Guérin, Pierre (1774–1833), 224
Guggenheim, Michelangelo, 218
Guiraud, Lucien, 190
Guys, Constantin (1802–1892), 7, 29, *236*, 236–238, *254*, **cat. no. 81**

Haarlem, Teyler Museum
  Boscoli, 107, *108*
Hadley, Margaret E., 16
The Hague, Mauritshuis
  Berchem, 155
  Jordaens, 163n.9
Hamburg, Kunsthalle
  Berchem, 156
  F. Bol, 158–159
Hamlin, Mr. and Mrs. Robert, 245
Hanna, Leonard C., Jr., Fund, 12, 83, 231
Harpignies, Henri (1819–1916), 245
Haverkamp-Begemann, Egbert, 2, 13, 15

Heemskerck, Maarten van (1498–1574), 28, 73–75, *73–75*, 89, 98, 111, 158, **cat. no. 15**
Heer, Gerrit de (active 1634–1652), 149
Heintz, Joseph, the Elder (1564–1609), 111
Henry II, King of France, 77
Henry IV, King of France, 76
Herbert, Prof. and Mrs. Robert L., 10
Heyen, Kasteel, 107
Hoe, Robert. *See* Egmont Collection
Hofer, Philip, 218
Hogenberg, Frans (ca. 1540–ca. 1590), 78, *80*
Homer, 53, 142, 144, 222
Hondius, Hendrick, I (1573–1650), 149
Hoogstraten, Samuel van (1627–1678), 159n.2
Houbraken, Arnold (1660–1719), 136, 155
Houel, Nicholas, 77
Houssaye, Arsène, 243
Houthakker, Bernard, 203
Howes, Mrs. Osborne, 218
Huquier, Gabriel (1695–1772), 182
Huygens, Constantijn, I, 151

Icard, Madame, 198
Illustrated London News, 236–237, *237*, 238n.10
Impressionism, 27, 246
India, Bernardino (1528–1590), 31n.7
Ingouf, Pierre-Charles (1746–1800), 211
Ingram, Bruce, 236, 238n.10
Ingres, Jean-Auguste-Dominique (1780–1867), 7, 29, 225–226, *225–227*, **cat. no. 77**
Isabey, Eugène (1767–1855), 245

Jersey, Edward Villiers, 1st Earl of, 180–181, *180–181*
Jode, Pieter de, I (1570–1634), 89, 108, 111, *113*
John Maurice, Prince of Nassau, 146
Johns, Jasper (b. 1930), 220n.5

Joly, Jules-Jean-Baptiste de (1788–1865), 231
Jonghe, Adrian de, 75
Jongkind, Johan Barthold (1819–1891), vii, 12, 27, *245*, 245–246, **cat. no. 84**
Jordaens, Jacob (1593–1657), 24, 162–163, *162–163*, **cat. no. 52**
Joseph Clemens, Elector-Archbishop of Cologne, 178
Jouvenet, Jean (1644–1717), 3, 25, 169, 175, *176–177*, **cat. no. 57**
Julius II, Pope, 66
Junius, Hadrianus, 75

Kansas City, William Rockhill Nelson Gallery of Art
 Rigaud, 181
Karlsruhe, Kunsthalle, Kupferstichkabinett
 Spranger, 113n.9
Karr Schmidt, Suzanne, 16
Kassel, Gemäldegalerie
 Jordaens, 163nn.1, 7
Katz, Daniel, 120
Kaye, Frederick Benjamin, 4
Kellerthaler, Johann, II (1560/62–1611), *114*, 114–115, *249*, **cat. no. 30**
Kempeneer, Peter de (ca. 1503–ca. 1580), 45
Komor, Mathias, 206
Koninck, Philips (1619–1688), 158
Köster, Geheimrat A., 190

Laer, Pieter van (1599–1642?), 156
Lafage, Raymond (1656–1684), 12, 29, 173–174, *173–174*, **cat. no. 56**
La Fontaine, Jean de, 212
La Fosse, Charles de (1636–1716), 169
Lagrenée, Jean-Jacques (1739–1821), 203
Lagrenée, Louis (1725–1805), 203
Lalouette, Jacques, 77n.6
landscapes, depiction of, 27, 92, 94, 126, 127, 150–152, 191
Lanfranco, Giovanni (1582–1647), 164

Langres, Musée d'Art et d'Histoire
 Gillot, 184
Lanier, Nicholas, 71
Lanino, Bernardino (ca. 1512–1581), 25, 69, 69–70, **cat. no. 13**
Lankrink, Prosper Henry (1628–1692), 9
Lastman, Pieter (1583–1633), 10, 120, 157
La Tour, Maurice-Quentin de (1704–1788), 28
La Vergne, Louis-Élisabeth de, 212
Lawrence, Thomas (1769–1830), 57
Le Brun, Charles (1619–1690), 3, 29, 138, 167, 169, 175, 211
LeComte, Florent, 178
Legentile, Alexandre, 225
Lehman, Robert, 6, 46, 201
Le Lorrain, Louis-Joseph (1715–1759), 203
Lely, Peter (1618–1680), 57, 71
Le monde illustré, 236
Le Moyne, François (1688–1737), 190
Le Nain, Louis (ca. 1600–1648), 142
Le Nain, Mathieu (ca. 1607–1677), 142
Lenartz., Jacob (fl. 1550–1600), 120
Leonardo da Vinci (1452–1519), 23, 24, 25, 27, 69, 70, 71, 87, 140
Leoni, Ottavio (1578–1630), 6, 7, 32n.21
Leo X, Pope, 66
Le Prince, François Simon, 203
Le Prince, Jean-Baptiste (1734–1781), 203–204, *203–205*, 212, **cat. no. 68**
Le Prince, Jean Robert, 203
Lerambert, Henri (d. 1609), 77
Lethière, Alexandre, 226
Lethière, Guillaume Guillon (1760–1832), 226, 228
Leyden, Aertgen van (1498–1564), 48
Licinio, Bernardino (ca. 1489–ca. 1565), 26, 55–56, *55–56*, **cat. no. 8**

Lievens, Jan (1607–1674), 157
Ligozzi, Jacopo (1547–1627), 100n.8
Lille, Musée des Beaux-Arts
 Bandinelli, workshop of, 40
 Gillot, 184, *186*
Lionne, Hugues de, 170
Liotard, Jean-Étienne (1702–1789), 28
Litta-Visconti-Arese, Count Giulio, 101
Logan, Anne-Marie, 3, 13, 15, 142
Lommelin, Adriaen (ca. 1637–ca. 1677), 33n.62
London, British Museum
 Breu the Elder, 52
 Claude, 152
 Giulio Romano, 59n.8
 Guys, 238n.7
 Lafage, 174, *174*
 Naldini, 81, 82n.12
 Perino del Vaga, 68n.9
 Pourbus the Elder, 78
 Salviati, 71, 72, 72n.1
 Solis, 97
 Troppa, 166, *166*
 F. Zuccaro, 31n.6, 84
London, Courtauld Institute of Art Gallery
 Daumier, 244n.9
London, National Gallery
 Lanino, 70n.5
 Poussin, 160n.7
London, Victoria and Albert Museum
 Guys, 238n.7
 Vroom the Younger, 151n.8
López de Escuriaz, Diego (active ca. 1587–1597), 25, *96*, 96–97, **cat. no. 23**
Lorrain, Claude. *See* Claude Lorrain
Los Angeles, J. Paul Getty Museum
 Bandinelli, 40n.4
 Giulio Romano, 59n.8, 62n.6
 Perino del Vaga, 68
 Polidoro da Caravaggio, 45
Louis, Dauphin of France, 178
Louis Philippe, King of France, 237
Louis XIII, King of France, 138
Louis XIV, King of France, 138, 175, 182

Louis XV, King of France, 182, 190
Lowenhaupt, Warren H., 4
Luti, Benedetto (1666–1724), 17, 20

Madrid, Museo del Prado
  Bosch, 80n.12
  G. Gandolfi, 208n.5
Maggiori, Alessandro, 132
Malzeville, Charles Cournault
  Collection, 224n.2
Mander, Karel van (1548–1606), 50
Manet, Édouard (1823–1883), 7, 31n.2
Mantegna, Andrea (ca. 1430–1506), 147
Mantua, Palazzo Te
  Giulio Romano, 57, 58, 66
Maratti, Carlo (1625–1713), 164
Marciari, John, 15, 16
Marcolini, Francesco, 113n.10
Marcotte family, 225–226
  Marcotte, Charles, 225–226
  Marcotte, Marie, 225–226
Margaret of Austria, 46
Margaret of Valois, Queen of France, 68
Maria Anna Christine Victoria, Dauphiness of France, 178
Maria Theresa, Holy Roman Empress, 210
Mariette, Pierre-Jean, 181, 186, 197
Martens, Jan, 127
Mary of Hungary, Regent of the Netherlands, 46
Massys, Quinten, the Younger (ca. 1543–1589), 106
Master D (fl. ca. 1585–1600), 97n.8
Master of 1527 (active ca. 1527), 15, 48–49, *48–49*, **cat. no. 5**
Master of the Apostles' Miracles (fl. ca. 1525–1550), 48
Master of the Die (fl. 1530–1560), 67, *68*
Master of the Egmont Albums (fl. late 16th century), *104–105*, 104–106, *247*, *248*, **cat. no. 26**
Master of the Little Dots (fl. 1800–1825), 227n.12
Master of the Raleigh *Ascension* and *Pentecost* (fl. 1500–1550), 47
Matham, Jacob (1571–1631), 13, *13*, 32n.28

Maurice, Count of Nassau, 118, 119n.7
Maximilian II, Holy Roman Emperor, 111
Maximilian II Emanuel, Elector of Bavaria, 178
Medici family, 81, 100n.8, 102, 128, 129, 129n.6, 132, 178
  Medici, Cardinal Carlo de', 133
  Medici, Catherine de', Queen of France, 76–77
  Medici, Cosimo I de', Grand Duke of Tuscany, 83
  Medici, Cosimo II de', Grand Duke of Tuscany, 129n.1
  Medici, Cosimo III de', Grand Duke of Tuscany, 178
  Medici, Ferdinando de', Grand Duke of Tuscany, 101
  Medici, Marie de', Queen of France, 167
Meeks, Everett V., Fund, 12, 27, 29–30, 48, 52, 57, 60, 66, 69, 73, 83, 96, 98, 107, 109, 114, 116, 120, 125, 127, 128, 130, 134, 157, 162, 164, 167, 173, 182, 184, 187, 190, 193, 196, 198, 203, 206, 210, 212, 221, 228, 233
Mellon, Paul, 223
Mellon, Paul, Fund, 27, 190
Merchersky, Prince, 206
Mercier, Philip (1689/91–1760), 197n.4
Mey, Raphael de (fl. 16th century), 106n.7
Michelangelo (1475–1564), 3, 10, 40, 63, 71, 74, 86, 109–110, 173, 215–216
Mignon, Jean (fl. 1535–1555), 60
Milan, Ambrosiana
  Crespi, 135nn.4–5
  Salviati, 71
Milan, Certosa di Garegnano
  Crespi, 135n.4
Milan, San Nazzaro Maggiore
  Lanino, 69
Milan, Santa Maria della Passione
  Ferrari, 69
Milan, Sant'Angelo
  della Rovere, 160

Millet, Jean-François (1814–1875), 6, 10, 13, 29, *233–234*, 233–235, *253*, **cat. no. 80**
model-books, 21, 23, 25–26, 38–39, 55, 71
Moeller, Martin, 125
Moeyaert, Claes Cornelisz. (1591–1655), 155–157
Mola, Pier Francesco (1612–1666), 140, 164, 165, 166
Molière, Jean-Baptiste, 243–244
Molyn, Pieter (1595–1661), 167
Momper, Bartholomeus de (1535–after 1597), 78
Momper, Joos de, the Younger (1564–1635), 92–93, 94
Moncalvo, Guglielmo Caccia, il (1568–1625), 134
Monet, Claude (1840–1926), 246
Monier, Pierre (1641–1703), 25, 167, *168*, 169, *251*, **cat. no. 54**
Montauban, Musée Ingres
  Ingres, 226
Montorgueil, Rue, prints, 77
Montreal, Canadian Centre for Architecture
  Oppenord, 182n.6
Morales, Ambrosio de (1513–1596), 78
Moreau, Gustave (1826–1898), 240
Moreau, Jean-Michel, called Moreau le Jeune (1791–1814), 203
Moreau-Nélaton, Étienne, 246
Morgan, Mrs. John Hill, 6
Morrison, Captain A., 206
Moscow, Pushkin Museum
  Poussin, 169n.7
  Rembrandt, 159n.2
  Victors, 159n.2
Mosnier, Jean (1600–1656), 167
Mosnier, Pierre. *See* Monier, Pierre
Muller, Harmen Jansz. (ca. 1540–1617), 74, 76, 98
Muller, Jan Harmensz. (1571–1628), 26, 28, *98–99*, 98–100, 111, *113*, *247*, **cat. no. 24**
Munich, Bayerische Staatsgemäldesammlungen
  Vivien, 178

Munich, Staatliche Graphische Sammlung
  van den Eeckhout, 159n.2
  Kellerthaler, 115n.3
Musi, Agostino dei, called Agostino Veneziano (ca. 1490–after 1536), 40, 67, 68n.7
Muziano, Girolamo (1532–1592), 33n.63, 88n.3

Nadar, Félix Tournachon, called (1820–1910), 236–237
Naldini, Giovanni Battista (1535–1591), 26, *81*, 81–82, 132, **cat. no. 18**
Naples, San Girolamo dei Genovesi
  Caracciolo, 130
Naples, Santa Teresa agli Studi
  Caracciolo, 130
Napoleon III, Emperor of France, 237
Nassau-Siegen, Jan van, 118
Natoire, Charles Joseph (1700–1777), 198
Naumann, Otto, 16
New Haven, Conn., Yale Center for British Art, 6, 224
Old Soldiers of the Empire (anonymous artist), *237*
New York, Cooper-Hewitt Museum
  Guys, 238n.7
New York, Metropolitan Museum of Art
  Bandinelli, 40n.3
  G. Gandolfi, 208n.5
  Guys, 238n.7
  de Jode (after Spranger), *113*
  Le Prince, 204
  Master of 1527, 49n.5
  J. Muller, *113*
  Oppenord, 182
  van Orley, 46, 47
  de Passe I (after de Vos), 90, 91
  Perino del Vaga, 68n.10
  Schmutzer, 210, 211, *211*
  Toeput, 95n.9
  Vouet, 139n.5
  A. II and H. Wierix (after de Vos), 90, 91
  F. Zuccaro, 85n.7

New York, Pierpont Morgan
    Library
  Beccafumi, 63
  Bernini, 172
  Breu the Elder, 52
  Callot, 128, 129n.6
  Crespi, 135n.4
  van Heemskerck, 74, 75
  L. Tiepolo, 201, 202n.8
New York, Taubman Collection
  L. Tiepolo, 201
Noort, Adam van (1562–1641), 162
Noort, Catharine van, 162
Norblin de La Gourdaine, Jean-
    Pierre (1745–1830), 187–188
Norblin de La Gourdaine, Martin,
    187
Northampton, Mass., Smith
    College, Museum of Art
  Guys, 238n.10
  Spranger, 111
Northumberland, Alnwick Castle
  Licinio, 56
Nuremberg, Germanisches
    Nationalmuseum
  Petzelt, 115
Nuremberg Chronicle, 53

Odescalchi, Prince Livio, 152
Olry-Roederer, Louis, 212
Oppenord, Gilles-Marie (1672–
    1742), 16, 182, *183*, **cat. no. 60**
optical devices, use of, 226–227
Orlandi, Pellegrino Antonio, 173
Orléans, Duke of, 182
Orléans, Musée des Beaux-Arts
  López, 96
Orley, Bernard van (1488–1541),
    6, 25, *46*, 46–47, **cat. no. 4**
Ostade, Adriaen van (1610–1685),
    148
Ottawa, National Gallery of
    Canada
  Jordaens, 163n.1
  Pinelli, 222n.8
  Rembrandt, 159n.2
Oudry, Jean-Baptiste (1686–1755),
    191, 191–192
Ovid, 60, 108, 175
Owen, Richard, 218, 220
Oxford, Ashmolean Museum
  Fuseli, 217
  Guys, 238n.7
  Jongkind, 246n.10
  Master of 1527, 15, 48
  Master of the Apostles' Miracles,
    48
  Perino del Vaga, 68n.10
Oxford, Christ Church Picture
    Gallery
  Castello, 161n.6

Pace, Giovanni Battista (active
    ca. 1650–ca. 1664), 165–166
Palagi, Pelagio (1775/77–1860), 221
Palermo, Museo Nazionale
  F. Zuccaro, 85n.10
Palko, Anton (d. 1754), 196
Palko, Franz Anton (1717–1766),
    196
Palko, Franz Karl (1724–1767), 28,
    196, 196–197, **cat. no. 65**
Pallavicino, Sforza, 17, *170*
Palma Vecchio (1479/80–1528), 55
Panini, Giovanni Paolo (1691–
    1765), 198
paper, availability of, 21, 38, 117
parchment, use of, 38, 149
Paris, Académie Royale de Pein-
    ture et de Sculpture, 27, 138,
    187
Paris, Assemblée Nationale. *See*
    Paris, Palais Bourbon
Paris, Bibliothèque Nationale de
    France
  Apocalypse (Montorgueil prints),
    77
  Davent, 61, 62
  Degas, 240, *241*, 241n.6
  Guys, 238n.7
  *Three Scenes from the Life of
    Nicholas of Myra* (anonymous
    artist), 77, 77
  Triumphs (prints), 77
Paris, Church of Saint-Sulpice
  Delacroix, 231
Paris, École Nationale Supérieure
    des Beaux-Arts
  Bandinelli, 40n.4
  Monier, 167
  Oppenord, 182
  van Orley, 46, 47
  L. Tiepolo, 201, 202n.8
  Vouet, 139, *139*
Paris, Hôtel de Ville
  Delacroix, 231
Paris, Institut Néerlandais, Lugt
    Collection
  J. Cuyp, 137
  van Orley, 46, 47n.9
  F. Pourbus, 80n.2
  Vroom the Younger, *151*
  Watteau, 188, *189*
Paris, Musée Carnavalet
  Guys, 237, 238n.7
  Jongkind, 246n.10
Paris, Musée d'Orsay
  Degas, 240, 241n.9
  Jongkind, 246nn.3, 10
Paris, Musée du Louvre
  Bandinelli, 40n.3
  Beccafumi, 65nn.6, 9
  Bellange, 124n.2
  Bellini, 39, *39*
  Boucher, 191, *192*
  Caracciolo, 130
  A. Carracci, 117
  Castello, 161
  Claude, 154n.6
  Curradi, 133n.2
  Decker, 191
  Degas, 240, 241nn.11, 13
  Géricault, 224
  Greuze, 206, *207*
  Guys, 238n.7
  Jordaens, 163nn.1, 7
  Le Brun, 169n.10
  Le Prince, 204, 205nn.3, 7
  López de Escuriaz, 97n.8
  Master D, 97n.8
  Master of 1527, 48
  Master of the Egmont Albums,
    106n.7
  Palko, 197n.2
  Polidoro da Caravaggio, 45nn.5, 12
  Quast, 149
  Rigaud, 180, 181n.3
  Story of Ananias, 48
  Swart, 50
  Titian, 134
  Vivien, 178n.4
  Vouet, 139, *139*
  Watteau, 188
  F. Zuccaro, 85n.10
Paris, Musée du Louvre, Galerie
    d'Apollon
  Delacroix, 231

Paris, Musée du Petit Palais
  Guys, 238n.7
  Jongkind, 246n.10
Paris, Palais Bourbon
  Delacroix, 231–232
Paris, Palais du Luxembourg
  Delacroix, 231
Paris, Prat Collection
  Degas, 241n.12
Parizeau, Philippe-Louis (1740–
    1801), 6, *6*
Parmigianino (1503–1540), 111,
    122, 161
Paroy, Jean-Philippe-Guy le
    Gentil, Count of (1750–1824),
    215n.9
Passe, Crispijn de, I (ca. 1565–
    1637), 89, *90*, 91, 106
Passe, Crispijn de, II (ca. 1597–
    ca. 1670), 89
pastels, use of, 27–28, 87, 178
Paul III, Pope, 66–67
Pavia, Certosa de Pavia
  Crespi, 134–135, *135*
Penni, Gianfrancesco (ca. 1496–
    after 1528), 60
Penni, Luca (1505–1556/57), 28,
    30, 60–62, *61*, 78, **cat. no. 10**
Perino del Vaga (1501–1547), 14,
    24, 42, 43–44, *44*, 60, 66–67,
    66–68, *247*, **cat. no. 12**
Persyn, Reinier van (ca. 1614–
    1688), 136
Peter III, Emperor of Russia, 204
Petrarch, 53, 77
Petzelt, Hans (1551–1633), 115
Philadelphia, Museum of Art
  Degas, 241n.12
  Guercino, 140
Philadelphia, Rosenbach Library
  Le Prince, 204
Philip II, King of Spain, 96
Philostratus, 175n.2
Piccini, Nicolò, 212
Pietersz., Gerrit (1566–before
    1612), 29, 120–*121*, 249, **cat.
    no. 33**
Pillsbury, Edmund P. (Ted), vii, 13,
    16, 38, 81, 140
Pinelli, Bartolomeo (1781–1835),
    14, 221–222, *221*–222, **cat.
    no. 75**
Pippi, Giulio. *See* Giulio Romano

Pisa, San Francesco
  Vanni, 160
Pissaro, Camille (1831–1903), 246
Pius V, Pope, 111
plein air, 27, 152, 228, 245–246
Plutarch, 53, 111
Poelenburch, Cornelis van (1594/95–1667), 146
Poggi, Christine, 16
Polidoro da Caravaggio (ca. 1499–ca. 1543), 24–26, *42–43*, 42–45, 60, **cat. no. 3**
Pompadour, Madame de, 190
Pontormo, Jacopo (1494–1556), 81, 82nn.5, 8
Poorter, Willem de (1608–after 1648), 159n.2
Pordenone (1483?–1539), 56n.1
Post, Pieter Jansz. (1608–1669), 150
Potter, Paulus (1625–1654), 149
Pourbus, Frans, the Elder (1545/5–1581), 78–80, *79*, *247*, **cat. no. 17**
Pourbus, Pieter (1523/24–1584), 78
Poussin, Nicolas (1594–1665), 167, 169n.7, 175, 231
Pozzoserrato, Ludovico. *See* Toeput, Lodewijk
Prague, Church of Saint Nicholas
  Palko, 197
Prague, Narodni Gallery
  Schmutzer, 210
Prat, Louis-Antoine, 188
Primaticcio, Francesco (1504–1570), 30, 60, 61, 62n.5, 142, 173
Princeton, University Art Museum
  Barocci, 88n.2
  Guercino, 140n.4
Procaccini, Giulio Cesare (1574–1625), 134, 161
Providence, Rhode Island School of Design
  Toeput, 93

Quast, Pieter Jansz. (1605/06–1647), 27, *148*, 148–149, **cat. no. 46**

Raffaellino da Reggio (ca. 1550–1578), 96

Raleigh, North Carolina Museum of Art
  Jordaens, 162, *163*
  Lievens, 159n.2
  Master of *Ascension* and *Pentecost*, 47
Raphael (1483–1520), 2, 26, 61–62, 66, 117, 167
  school of, 24, 42, 60, 61, 66, 87
Ravenet, Simon-François, the Elder (1706/21–1774), 188
Regensburg, Städtischen Kunstsammlungen
  Schwender, 115n.7
Rembrandt van Rijn (1606–1669), 91, 120, 127, 146, 148, 157, *158*
  school of, 3, *3*, 157
Rémond, Jean Charles Joseph (1795–1895), 228
Renard, Jean-Augustin (1744–1807), 200
Reni, Guido (1575–1642), 32n.21
Rewald, John, 231
Ribera, Jusepe de (1591–1652), 197
Ridolfi, Carlo, 91n.1
Rigaud, Hyacinthe (1659–1743), 6, 180–181, *180–181*, **cat. no. 59**
Robert, Hubert (1733–1808), 27, *198–199*, 198–200, 212, *251*, **cat. no. 66**
Robert, Léopold (1794–1835), 225
Robusti, Jacopo. *See* Tintoretto
Rochefort, Pierre de, 184
Roederer, Louis, 212
Rome, Bibliotheca Hertziana
  Polidoro da Caravaggio, 45n.5
Rome, Castel Sant'Angelo
  Perino del Vaga, 44, 45n.8, 66–68
Rome, Istituto Nazionale per la Grafica
  C. Alberti, 110
  F. Zuccaro, 85n.7
Rome, Museo del Palazzo Venezia
  Pinelli, 222n.7
Rome, Oratory of San Giovanni Decollato
  Salviati, 72
Rome, Palazzo Baldassini
  Perino del Vaga, 43
  Polidoro da Caravaggio, 43, *44*
Rome, Palazzo Corsini
  Batoni, 193, *194*

Rome, Palazzo della Cancelleria
  Salviati, 72n.2
Rome, Palazzo Sacchetti
  Salviati, 72
Rome, San Pietro in Vincoli
  Domenichino, 116, *117*
Rome, Sant'Agata
  Troppa, 166
Rome, Santa Marta
  Troppa, 166, 166n.7
Rome, Sant'Andrea al Quirinale
  Portrait of Cardinal Sforza Pallavicino (anonymous artist), 170
Rome, Santissima Trinità dei Monti
  Naldini, 82
Rome, Vatican City, Vatican Museums
  Belvedere Cleopatra (Sleeping Ariadne), 60, 167
Rome, Vatican City, Vatican Palace
  Michelangelo, 40, 71
  Perino del Vaga, 66
Rome, Villa Farnesina
  Raphael, 66
Romney, George (1734–1802), 31n.16
Rosenbach, A. S. W., 212
Rosenfeld, Daniel, 16
Rossi, Francesco de'. *See* Salviati, Francesco
Rosso Fiorentino (1494–1540), 60, 61, 103n.7
Rouart, Henri, 233
Roubiliac, Louis François, 107
Rouen, Musée des Beaux-Arts
  Jouvenet, 175, *177*
Rousseau, Pierre-Étienne-Théodore (1812–1867), 27, *228–229*, 228–230, **cat. no. 78**
Rubens, Peter Paul (1577–1640), 142, 145, 155
Rublé, Baronne de, 187
Rudolf II, Holy Roman Emperor, 111
Ruisdael, Jacob van (1628/29–1682), 151

Sabatelli, Luigi (1772–1850), 221
Sacchi, Andrea (1599–1661), 170
Sadeler, Aegidius (1555–1609), 89, 114
Sadeler, Jan I (1550–1600), 89

Sadeler, Jan II (ca. 1588–1665), 89
Sadeler, Raphael I (1560/61–1628/32), 89
Sadeler, Raphael II (1584–1627/32), 89
Saenredam, Pieter Jansz. (1597–1665), 150
Saint-Non, Abbé de (1727–1791), 199, 212
Saint Petersburg, State Hermitage Museum
  Daumier, 243, *243*, 244n.9
  Salviati, 72
Salon des Refusés (1863), 31n.2, 245
Salviati, Francesco (1510–1563), 6, 71–72, *71–72*, **cat. no. 14**
Sandby, Paul (1725–1809), 78
San Francisco, California Palace of the Legion of Honor
  Rigaud, 181
Sangallo, Bastiano (Aristotile) da (1481–1551), 216
Santa Barbara, Museum of Art
  Jongkind, 246n.10
Santi di Tito (1536–1602), 101, 107
Sarasota, Fla., John and Mable Ringling Museum, vii
Sarto, Andrea del (1486–1530), 26, 81
Saulier, Guillaume, 77n.6
Scaglia, Desiderio, 146
Scenes from the Lives of Saint Catherine and Saint Roch (anonymous artist), 47
Schelfhout, Andreas (1787–1870), 245
Schiavonetti, Luigi (1765–1810), 216, 217
Schmutzer, Jakob Matthias (1733–1811), 210–211, *211*
  circle of, 29, 33n.58, 210–211, *210–211*, *252*, **cat. no. 71**
Schwender, Jacob (fl. ca. 1600), 115n.7
Schwerin, Staatliches Museum
  Oudry, 191, *191*
Scorel, Jan van (1495–1562), 73
Seligman, Jacques, 225
Shestack, Alan, 13, 16

Siena, Duomo
  Beccafumi, 63, *65*
Siena, Pinacoteca
  Beccafumi, 65n.4
Siena, San Francesco
  Zucchi, 16
Signac, Paul (1863–1935), 246
Simon, Norton, 152
Sireul, Jean-Claude-Gaspard de, 190–191
Sitwell, Sacheverell, 217n.2
Slodtz, René-Michel (1705–1764), 198
Smits, Eugène (1826–1912), 246
Snellinck, Jan the Elder (1544/49–1638), 80n.2
Solis, Virgil (1514–1562), 97, *97*
Solms, Amalia van, 162
Speeckaert, Hans (ca. 1540–1577), 106n.9
Spenser, Edmund, 217
Spranger, Bartholomaeus (1546–1611), 26, 29, 98, 100, 111–113, *112*, 120, *248*, **cat. no. 29**
Stella, Jacques (1596–1657), 33n.62
Stirling, Lt.-Col. William, 73
Stirling-Maxwell, Sir William, 73
Stockholm, Nationalmuseum
  Bandinelli, 40n.3
  Caracciolo, 130
  Crespi, 135n.5
  Polidoro da Caravaggio, 45
  Rembrandt, 159n.2
Stoddard, Enoch Vine, Fund, 12, 111
Stoning of Saint Stephen, The (anonymous artist), 19, 22
Strada, Jacopo, 45n.8
Stuttgart, Staatsgalerie, Graphische Sammlung
  Breu the Elder, 52
Subleyras, Pierre (1699–1749), 19
Sutherland, Duke of, 57
Sutton, Peter, 16
Swart van Groningen, Jan (ca. 1500–at least 1562), *50–51*, **cat. no. 6**
Sweelinck, Gerrit. *See* Pietersz., Gerrit
Sweelinck, Jan Pietersz., 120
Sylvester, Peter, 9, 155, 156n.1
  tapestry, designs for, 17, 24–25, 77, 162, 191

Tassi, Agostino (ca. 1579–1644), 152
Tasso, Torquato, 108, 212
Temkin, Ann, 16
Tempesta, Antonio (1555–1630), 16, 106
Thacher, John S., 7, 215
Thulden, Theodoor van (1606–1669), 14, 15–16, *142–144*, 142–145, *249*, **cat. no. 44**
Tibaldi, Pellegrino (1527–1596), 96
Tiepolo, Giovanni Battista (Giambattista) (1696–1770), 6, 7, 196, 201, 202n.4, 218
Tiepolo, Giovanni Domenico (1727–1804), 6, 12, 30, 201, *218–219*, 218–220, *253*, **cat. no. 74**
Tiepolo, Lorenzo Baldissera (1736–1776), 6, *201*, 201–202, *251*, **cat. no. 67**
Tintoretto, Jacopo Robusti, called (ca. 1518–1594), 89, 91n.1, 92
Titian (1488/90–1576), 26, 55, 134
Tito, Santi di. *See* Santi di Tito
Tivoli, Villa d'Este, 199, 200n.2
Tocqué, Louis (1696–1772), 203
Toeput, Lodewijk (ca. 1550–1604/05), 27, 28, 92, 92–95, *94*, **cat. no. 22**
Trometta, Nicolò (ca. 1540–ca. 1610), 96
Troppa, Girolamo (1630–1710), 24, 164–166, *164–166*, *250*, **cat. no. 53**
Turin, Accademia Albertina
  Lanino, 70
Turin, Biblioteca Reale
  Lanino, 70n.5
Turin, Galleria Sabauda
  Batoni, 195n.6
Turner, Joseph Mallard William (1775–1851), 246

Udney, Robert, 107
Ussieux, Louis d', 212

Valenciennes, Musée des Beaux-Arts
  Jordaens, 163n.1
Valgrisi, Vincenzo, 113n.10
Vanderbilt, Mrs. Cornelius, 6

Vanni, Francesco (1563–1610), 160
Vasari, Giorgio (1511–1574), 40, 58, 60, 81, 83–84, 87, 102
Velazquez, Diego (1599–1660), 97n.11
Velde, Esaias van de (1587–1630), 27, 32n.18, 127, *127*, 150, **cat. no. 36**
Velde, Hans van de (1552–1609), 127
Velde, Jan van de, I (ca. 1568–1623), 127
Velde, Jan van de, II (ca. 1593–1641), 127
Velde, Jan van de, III (1620–1662), 127
Veneziano, Agostino. *See* Musi, Agostino dei
Venice, Ca' Rezzonico
  D. Tiepolo, 220n.1
Venice, Cini Foundation
  G. Gandolfi, 208n.5
Venice, Santa Maria Gloriosa dei Frari
  Licinio, 55, *56*
Venne, Adriaen van de (1528–1662), 148
Ventimiglia, San Francesco
  Fiasella, 161
Veronese, Paolo (1528–1588), 196
Vico, Enea (1523–1567), 72n.4
Victors, Jan (1619–after 1676), 159n.2
Vienna, Albertina
  Bellange, 124nn.2, 9
  Cornelisz. van Haarlem, 100n.4
  van Diepenbeeck, 144
  van Hoogstraten, 159n.2
  Mola, 166n.8
  Perino del Vaga, 68n.9
  F. Pourbus, 80nn.2, 8
  Schmutzer, 210
  F. Zuccaro, 31n.6, 85n.8
Vienna, Kunsthistorisches Museum
  Jordaens, 163n.1
  Spranger, 113n.10
Vienna, Liechtenstein Museum
  Batoni, 194, *195*
Viennot, Charles (fl. ca. 1700), 180, *181*
Vigoureux, Charles le, 77n.7

Villamena, Francesco (1564–1624), 160
Villot, Frédéric, 232
Virgil, 17, 222
Virgin and Child with Saint John the Baptist (anonymous artist), 3, *4*, *5*
Visscher, Claes Jansz. (ca. 1550–ca. 1612), 127, 149
Visscher, Cornelius (1629–1658), 6
Vivien, Joseph (1657–1734), 6, 28–29, 31n.13, 178, *179*, **cat. no. 58**
Vleughels, Nicolas (1668–1737), 191
Vliet, Jan van (ca. 1605–ca. 1668), 158
Voltaire, 204
Vorsterman, Willem (ca. 1500–1550), 50
Vos, Maarten de (1532–1603), 28, *89*, 89–91, 94, 111, **cat. no. 21**
Vouet, Simon (1590–1649), 24, 138–139, *138–139*, **cat. no. 42**
Vrancx, Sebastian (1573–1647), 17, *19*, 92
Vries, Adriaen de (ca. 1545–1626), 98, 111
Vroom, Cornelis, the Younger (ca. 1591–1661), 27, 150–151, *150–151*, *250*, **cat. no. 47**
Vroom, Hendrick Cornelisz. (1563–1640), 150

Walferdin, Hippolyte, 212
Wals, Goffredo (ca. 1605–ca. 1638), 152
Warsaw, National Museum
  Lastman, 157, 159n.2
  Toeput, 95n.14
Washington, D.C., National Gallery of Art
  Beccafumi, 65n.5
  Polidoro da Caravaggio, 43, *44*
  Toeput, *93*, 94
watermarks, 37, 247–254
Watteau, Jean-Antoine (1684–1721), 27, 184, 187–189, *187–189*, 191, **cat. no. 62**
Webb, Electra Havemeyer, 7
Webb, J. Watson, 7

Weenix, Jan Baptist (1621–1660/61), 155, 156
Weir, John Ferguson (1841–1926), 3, 4
Weir, Julian Alden (1852–1919), 4
Weir, Robert Walter (1803–1889), 3, 175
Wenz, Walter von, 107
Wetmore, Edith Malvina K., 7, 225, 236, 242
Weyer, Gabriel (1576–1632), 125
Weyer, Hermann (1596–after 1621 [1672?]), 27, 29, 125–126, *125–126*, **cat. no. 35**
Whistler, James McNeill (1834–1903), 246
Wichtendahl, Oskar, 125
Wick, Mrs. Paul, and children, 12, 218
Wierix, Anton, II (1555/59–1604), 89, *90, 91*
Wierix, Hieronymus (1553?–1619), 89, *90, 91*
Wildenstein, Georges, 152
Wille, Johann-Georg (1715–1808), 206, 210
William Louis of Nassau, 119n.7
Williams, Lyle, 16
Williamstown, Mass., Clark Art Institute
 Degas, 239–240
Wils, Jan (ca. 1600–1666), 155
Winckelmann, Johann Joachim, 215
Windsor, Royal Library
 Bernini, 172
 Domenichino, 116, *117*
 Guercino, 140
 J. Muller, 98, *99*
 Poussin, 169nn.6–7
Witte, Mme de, 187
Wolf, Vanessa, 16
Wollaston, William Hyde, 226–227
Woodburn, Samuel, 57
Worms, Kunsthaus Heylshof
 Jouvenet, 175, *177*

Zaltieri, Bolognino (active 16th century), 113n.10
Zampieri, Domenico. *See* Domenichino

Zuccaro, Federico (1540/42–1609), 3, 14, 26, 31n.12, *83*, 83–85, *85*, 96, 111, **cat. no. 19**
Zucchi, Jacopo (ca. 1541–1596), 16, *17*
Zurich, Kunsthaus
 Fuseli, *217*

Artists in the Catalogue

Note: numerals refer to catalogue numbers.

Anonymous French(?), 16
Anonymous Italian, 1
Cherubino Alberti, 28
Baccio Bandinelli, 2
Federico Barocci, 20
Pompeo Batoni, 64
Domenico Beccafumi, 11
Jacques Bellange, 34
Nicolaes Berchem, 49
Gian Lorenzo Bernini, 55
Ferdinand Bol (Attributed), 50
Andrea Boscoli, 27
François Boucher, 63
Leonaert Bramer, 45
Jörg Breu the Elder, 7
Jacques Callot, 37
Giovanni Battista Caracciolo, 38
Valerio Castello, 51
Ludovico Cardi, il Cigoli, 25
Claude Lorrain, 48
Daniele Crespi, 40
Francesco Curradi, 39
Jacob Gerritsz. Cuyp, 41
Honoré Daumier, 83
Edgar Degas, 82
Eugène Delacroix, 79
Domenichino, 31
Jean-Honoré Fragonard, 72
Henry Fuseli, 73
Ubaldo Gandolfi, 70
Théodore Géricault, 76
Jacques de Gheyn II, 32
Claude Gillot, 61
Giulio Romano, 9
Jean-Baptiste Greuze, 69
Guercino, 43
Constantin Guys, 81
Maarten van Heemskerck, 15
Jean-Auguste-Dominique Ingres, 77
Johan Barthold Jongkind, 84
Jacob Jordaens, 52
Jean Jouvenet, 57
Johann Kellerthaler II (Attributed), 30
Raymond Lafage, 56
Bernardino Lanino, 13
Jean-Baptiste Le Prince, 68
Bernardino Licinio, 8
Diego López de Escuriaz, 23
The Master of 1527, 5
The Master of the Egmont Albums, 26
Jean-François Millet, 80
Pierre Monier, 54
Jan Harmensz. Muller, 24
Giovanni Battista Naldini, 18
Gilles-Marie Oppenord, 60
Bernard van Orley, 4
Franz Karl Palko, 65
Luca Penni, 10
Perino del Vaga, 12
Gerrit Pietersz. (Attributed), 33
Bartolomeo Pinelli, 75
Polidoro da Caravaggio, 3
Frans Pourbus the Elder, 17
Pieter Jansz. Quast, 46
Hyacinthe Rigaud, 59
Hubert Robert, 66
Pierre-Étienne-Théodore Rousseau, 78
Francesco Salviati, 14
Jakob Matthias Schmutzer (Circle of), 71
Bartholomaeus Spranger, 29
Jan Swart van Groningen, 6
Theodoor van Thulden, 44
Giovanni Domenico Tiepolo, 74
Lorenzo Baldissera Tiepolo, 67
Lodewijk Toeput, 22
Girolamo Troppa, 53
Esaias van de Velde, 36
Joseph Vivien, 58
Maarten de Vos, 21
Simon Vouet, 42
Cornelis Vroom the Younger, 47
Jean-Antoine Watteau, 62
Hermann Weyer, 35
Federico Zuccaro, 19

Photography Credits

Photographs have been provided by the owners or custodians of the works reproduced, except for the following. Every effort has been made to credit the photographers and the sources; if there are errors or omissions, please contact Yale University Press so that corrections can be made in any subsequent edition.

Alinari/Art Resource, New York: figs. 20A, 31A, 76A

Nicolo Orsi Battaglini/Art Resource, New York: fig. 19A

Bildarchiv Preussischer Kulturbesitz/Art Resource, New York: fig. 27A

W. M. Brady and Co., New York: fig. 75A

Cameraphoto/Art Resource, New York: fig. 8A

Christie's Images, London: fig. 61B

Didier Aaron Inc., New York: fig. 68B

eikonos/Ghigo Roli, Rome: fig. 12A

Foto Lensini Siena: fig. 11A

Istituto Centrale per il Catalogo e la Documentazione, Rome: fig. 64B

Courtesy of the National Gallery of Art, London: fig. 50A

Réunion des Musées Nationaux/Art Resource, New York: figs. 1A, 63B

The Royal Collection © Her Majesty Queen Elizabeth II: figs. 24A, 24B, 24C, 24D, 31B

By permission of the Master and Fellows of St. John's College, Cambridge: fig. 59A

Scala/Art Resource, New York: figs. 64C, 69A

Michel Schulman: figs. 78A, 78B